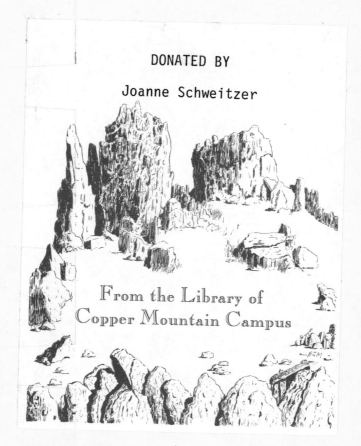

To Mine
Father Mine
Happy Fathers Day
June 1980
Love,
Barbara

Books by Bruce Catton

THE WAR LORDS OF WASHINGTON

MR. LINCOLN'S ARMY

GLORY ROAD

A STILLNESS AT APPOMATTOX

THIS HALLOWED GROUND

AMERICA GOES TO WAR

GRANT MOVES SOUTH

GRANT TAKES COMMAND

The Centennial History of the Civil War

THE COMING FURY

TERRIBLE SWIFT SWORD

NEVER CALL RETREAT

In the Library of American Biography

U. S. GRANT AND THE AMERICAN MILITARY TRADITION

For Young People

BANNERS AT SHENANDOAH

With William Catton

TWO ROADS TO SUMTER

GRANT TAKES COMMAND

General Ulysses S. Grant at Cold Harbor in 1864

Grant
Takes Command

by BRUCE CATTON

With maps by SAMUEL H. BRYANT

LITTLE, BROWN AND COMPANY · BOSTON · TORONTO

The frontispiece is reproduced by courtesy of The United States
Military Academy Archives.

Published simultaneously in Canada
by Little, Brown & Company (Canada) Limited

PRINTED IN THE UNITED STATES OF AMERICA

For David

Foreword

AFTER the capture of Vicksburg on July 3, 1863, Grant's army starts a period of occupation, absorbing its conquest of the Mississippi valley. In the east, the Army of the Potomac rests after its great victory at Gettysburg. In central Tennessee, the Federal Army of the Cumberland is moving to drive Confederate forces back into Georgia. The Federal government in Washington, sensing a turning point in the war, starts to cast about for the best path to final victory. As the authorities begin this task, they realize that their most successful soldier is the one they know least about.

Contents

List of Maps

GRANT TAKES COMMAND

Political Innocent

OFFICIALLY, John A. Rawlins went to Washington to carry dispatches telling how Vicksburg had been won. To be sure, the great victory spoke for itself so plainly that the written tale did not make much difference; but if the victory was clear the man who had won it was not. In this summer of 1863, Washington was more interested in Ulysses S. Grant than in any other man alive, but it knew very little about him. Except for a few people like Major General Henry W. Halleck, the General-in-Chief, and the industrious Illinois Congressman Elihu Washburne, hardly anyone had so much as set eyes on him. It was time to get him into better focus, and if Grant could not be present in person it would be worthwhile to talk to his right-hand man.

Rawlins got a warm reception. He reached Washington on July 30, went first to the War Department to talk with Halleck and with Halleck's assistant adjutant general, Colonel J. C. Kelton, and he wrote happily to Grant: "It is worth a trip here to see how delighted they are over your success. There is nothing left undone by them to make me feel that I am here properly." They were impatient, said Rawlins, only because Grant had not yet told them which of his subordinates he wanted to have promoted; the implication being that any favors Grant asked for would be done. Rawlins also reported that Halleck heartily endorsed, "as being proper as well as wise," the surrender terms by which Grant's 31,000 Confederate prisoners had been released on parole — a matter on which Halleck earlier had been somewhat critical.[1] After this pleasant meeting Rawlins went to the White House to see the President and the cabinet. To President Lincoln Rawlins presented the following letter:

SIR: the bearer of this, Lieut. Col. John A. Rawlins, is the assistant adjutant-general of the Army of the Tennessee. Colonel Rawlins has been con-

nected with this army and with me in every engagement from the battle
of Belmont to the surrender of Vicksburg. Colonel Rawlins goes to Washington now by my order as bearer of the reports of the campaign just
ended, and rolls and paroles of prisoners captured. I would be pleased if
you could give Colonel Rawlins an interview, and I know in asking this
you will feel relieved when I tell you he has not a favor to ask for himself
or any other living being. Even in my position it is a great luxury to meet
a gentleman who has no ax to grind, and I can appreciate that it is infinitely more so in yours.

I have the honor to be, very respectfully, your obedient servant,

U. S. GRANT [2]

President and cabinet members were favorably impressed. By this
time they had met a great many officers from the staffs of commanding generals, but they had not yet seen anyone quite like Rawlins. He
was pale, the pallor made more striking by his burning eyes and his
luxuriant dark beard; a profane ascetic Puritan whom the War Department's special observer of westerners, Charles A. Dana, character-
ized as "a very industrious, conscientious man who never loses a moment and never gives himself any indulgence except swearing and
scolding." (Grant once told a friend that he kept Rawlins on his staff
"to do my swearing for me.") Secretary of the Navy Gideon Welles,
who tended to be suspicious of all army officers, confessed that he was
"much pleased with him, his frank, intelligent and interesting description of men and of army operations." Mr. Welles went on to say that
he liked Rawlins's "unpretending and unassuming manners" and said
that "the unpolished and unrefined deportment of this earnest and sincere patriot and soldier pleased me more than that of almost any other
officer whom I have ever met." Welles confessed that Rawlins "was
never at West Point and has had few educational advantages," but he
said that Rawlins was a sincere friend of General Grant, "who I think
sent him here for a purpose." [3]

Welles was right. In his march toward victory on the Mississippi
Grant had put a heavy foot straight through one of Abraham Lincoln's most delicate political deals: the maneuver by which the President, in the summer of 1862, had given Major General John A. Mc-
Clernand of Illinois what amounted to a promise of top command in
the Vicksburg campaign. During the winter, with Halleck's support,
Grant had steadily cut McClernand down to size, making him a corps
commander in Grant's army rather than an independent commander

of an army of his own; then, a few weeks before Vicksburg fell, Grant removed the man altogether, sending him back to Illinois and going on to victory without him. McClernand was full of energy, ambition and old-fashioned temper, and he had been demanding justice ever since; he was also uttering veiled threats to tell some tales that would do Grant no good. Near the end of June he had written to Secretary of War Edwin M. Stanton asking for "an investigation of Gen. Grant's and my conduct as officers from the battle of Belmont to the assault of the 22nd," and not long afterward he wrote to President Lincoln demanding an investigation of Grant's conduct and his own from start to finish, saying that this "would bring to light many things, both military and personal, which are unwritten or unheeded." [4]

McClernand obviously was threatening to restate the old charge that General Grant now and then drank more than his situation required. But McClernand had to be obtuse as well as vengeful to suppose that at this late date the authorities would waste any time on this accusation. It had been said too often, and it meant too little, and anyway a review would simply confirm what everybody already knew — that Grant was the most successful of all Federal generals, a man who had captured two Confederate armies *en bloc*. It was most unlikely that Grant's position could be shaken by anything McClernand might say about occasional deviations from strict sobriety. Still, a little fence-mending could do no harm. Grant after all had crushed a presidential favorite and upset a presidential program, and it might be just as well to make sure that the President understood what Grant had done and why he had done it. As Welles suspected, Rawlins had been sent for a purpose. It may be that General Grant was not the utter political innocent he is sometimes thought to have been.

Army command in the Civil War was no job for a political innocent, and the McClernand case illustrates the fact. McClernand was a dedicated War Democrat, and now and then the army needed such men no matter how badly they lacked military capacity; in this war a general's ability to win and keep the support of friendly civilians in his rear might actually outweigh his failure to deal with the armed foes in his front. Lincoln had given McClernand a special assignment, not because he supposed that he was an especially competent soldier but because McClernand's political influence in the West would bring the army recruits and political support which it had to have if the Mississippi valley was to be won. McClernand had done precisely what President Lincoln hoped he would do. It is possible that Grant, who discarded the general after this particular and priceless contribution had been made, had likewise carried out the President's wishes.

Anyway, Rawlins was on hand to explain everything, and Welles thought he did it very well. He gave evidence about McClernand, said Welles, proving that he was "an impracticable and unfit man — that he has not been subordinate and intelligent but has been an embarrassment, and instead of assisting has really been an obstruction to army movements and operations." Welles admitted that Rawlins's statements showed prejudice, but he felt that Rawlins did prove that "there can hardly be a doubt McClernand is at fault, and Rawlins has been sent here by Grant to satisfy the President of the fact. In this I think he has succeeded." [5]

Grant objected to McClernand for two reasons. The first was that McClernand just was not a competent general. This became obvious on May 22, when the army made a dismally unsuccessful assault on the Vicksburg lines because McClernand insisted that his corps could break through if the rest of the army supported it properly — an argument that collapsed in blood and dust when the assault was made and failed. What was even worse, however, as Grant saw it, was that it was impossible to get along with McClernand under any circumstances. When he was not arguing with Grant McClernand was arguing with the other corps commanders, William T. Sherman and James B. McPherson, and after the May 22 disaster it was clear that there would be no harmony in the Army of the Tennessee as long as McClernand stayed there. Grant placed a high value on harmony, by this time Lincoln placed a high value on Grant . . . and so McClernand was kept on the shelf, and to give the affair special point Sherman and McPherson were promoted; already major generals of volunteers, they were now made brigadier generals in the regular army. Rawlins was made brigadier general of volunteers, McClernand's corps had already been taken over by Major General E. O. C. Ord, and there was no more backbiting in Grant's army.

And that was what mattered to General Grant. An army commander had enormous powers, by the book, but this meant little unless there was a good understanding with the generals who had to carry out the commander's orders. No matter what the book said, in this war the man who gave the orders finally ruled by consent of the governed: a point painfully impressed on Major General Ambrose E. Burnside when he tried to use the Army of the Potomac after the disastrous battle of Fredericksburg.[6] Grant's attitude came out clearly while Rawlins was in Washington, when Secretary Stanton proposed that Grant be brought east and given command of the Army of the Potomac.

This was an assignment Grant did not want, and the big reason he did not want it was the notorious fact that the Army of the Potomac's officer corps was hopelessly divided into cliques, jealous and full of suspicion, quick to resent any implication that an "outsider" might someday be brought in to take charge. Dana and Halleck sounded Grant on the matter, learned how he felt, and managed to talk Mr. Stanton out of his plan. On August 5 Grant wrote to Dana, confessing that "it would cause me more sadness than satisfaction to be ordered to the Command of the Army of the Potomac." He went on to explain:

Here I know the officers and men and what each Gen. is capable of as a separate Commander. There I would have all to learn. Here I know the geography of the Country, and its resources. There it would be a new study. Besides more or less dissatisfaction would necessarily be produced by importing a General to command an Army already well supplied with those who have grown up, and been promoted, with it. . . . I feel very grateful for your timely intercession in saving me from going to the Army of the Potomac. Whilst I would disobey no order I should beg very hard to be excused before accepting that command.

A little later he wrote in the same vein to Congressman Washburne:

Had it not been for Gen. Halleck and Dana I think it altogether likely I would have been ordered to the Potomac. My going could do no possible good. They have there able officers who have been brought up with that Army, and to import a Commander to place over them certainly could produce no good. Whilst I would not possitively disobey an order I would have objected most vehemently to taking that Command, or any other except the one I have. I can do more with this Army than it would be possible for me to do with any other without time to make the same acquaintance with others I have with this. I know that the soldiers of the Army of the Ten. can be relied on to the fullest extent. I believe I know the exact capacity of every General in my Command to command troops, and just where to place them to get from them their best services. This is a matter of no small importance.

[7]

Grant was not the only one who saw the danger. Late in July the powerful antislavery leader from Massachusetts, Senator Henry Wilson, got wind of the proposed appointment and sent a stiff protest to Washburne, saying he hoped Grant would have nothing to do with the job. "I fear," wrote Senator Wilson, "if he should take the Potomac army that he would be ruined by a set of men in and out of that army. I am confident his great success has excited envy, and that if an opportunity should offer he would be sacrificed."

Senator Wilson spoke as an unrelenting abolitionist who believed that the "set of men" who dominated the Army of the Potomac wanted to fight the Rebels without fighting slavery. The abolitionists suspected that although they as radical Republicans were running the war the nation's principal army somehow was under the control of soft-war Democrats; and what was interesting just now was that Wilson was hurrying to Grant's support although Grant had never been either a Republican or an abolitionist. Wilson told Washburne that he had been talking with Dana, who assured him that Grant "is in favor of destroying the cause of this civil war — of overthrowing slavery — and that his army is deeply imbued with the same feeling. I am glad to hear from so good a judge such an account of Grant and his noble army." [7]

Washburne got confirmation on this point from Grant himself. When he wrote to the Congressman about his unwillingness to command the Army of the Potomac Grant explained his position in detail:

The people of the North need not quarrel over the institution of Slavery. What Vice President Stephens acknowledges the Corner Stone of the Confederacy is already knocked out. Slavery is already dead and cannot be ressurrected. It would take a standing army to maintain slavery in the South if we were to make peace today, guaranteeing to the South all their former Constitutional privileges. I never was an Abolitionist, not even what could be called anti-slavery, but I try to judge fairly and honestly and it became patent to my mind early in the rebellion that the North & South could never live at peace with each other except as one Nation, and that without slavery. As anxious as I am to see peace reestablished I would not therefore be willing to see any settlement until this question is forever settled. [8]

He may not have known that he was doing it — probably did not, for he acted by instinct in such matters, and to explain why he did what he did was usually beyond him — but in the summer following Pemberton's surrender Grant moved through the political maze with a good deal of skill. He laid the McClernand affair to rest; he dodged the threat of a transfer to that graveyard for the hopes of ambitious generals, the Eastern army; and he quietly asserted his dedication to the principle of an antislavery war, which the abolitionists could ponder over at their leisure. At the same time he was emerging as a hero of the Northern Democrats, whose principal organ in the east, the New York *World*, found room to quote extensively from a speech made in St. Louis by Major General Frank Blair, commander of a division in Sherman's army corps. Blair was vigorously rebutting McClernand's attempt to take credit for the Vicksburg campaign, and he declared that "when any ambitious or vainglorious chieftain comes back and attempts to claim for himself great deeds which have immortalized and ought to immortalize General Grant, the whole army of Grant will repel the idea and we will proclaim everywhere that the leading spirit, the great chief and leader of the expedition, was General Grant."

The *World* printed this with approval, ignoring the fact that Blair's real target was the eminent War Democrat McClernand and implying that the speech really showed that the victory at Vicksburg was not a Republican achievement at all. What Blair said, the *World* argued, proved that neither Halleck nor Stanton deserved any credit for what had been done; the victory was all Grant's.[9]

The victory was his, and so was the responsibility. No matter how he played the political caroms, Grant's real job was to find out what his army ought to do next and then to go and do it. He felt at first that his men were worn out and needed to spend a good deal of time resting and refitting; but it was widely known that troops kept their health better on the march than they did in camp, it seemed likely that Vicksburg's steamy summer heat would induce a ruinous sick list, and anyway to lie idle was not appealing; and Dana notified Secretary Stanton that Grant "has no idea of going into summer quarters" and wanted to strike another blow. What Grant needed, said Dana, was "to be informed whether the Government wishes him to follow his own judgment or to co-operate in some particular scheme of operations." Grant waited for word from Halleck, confessed privately that "I have but little idea what is to be done with our western forces," and studied the situation to see what chances were open.[10]

[9]

There were certain possibilities: accompanied, as usual, by various problems.

East of Vicksburg Sherman with 50,000 men had driven Confederate Joseph E. Johnston, who had 31,000, away from the city of Jackson, where Johnston had come to rest when his efforts to raise the siege of Vicksburg failed. Neither Grant, Sherman nor Halleck himself felt that Johnston really needed to be pursued; the weather was fearfully hot, the roads were bad, and it seemed that if Johnston would just get out of Mississippi and go wherever he chose in Alabama that would be good enough. Sherman, who believed that a summer campaign in this climate was impossible anyway, predicted, blithely that Johnston's 31,000 would quickly "perish by heat, thirst and disappointment," and he brought his own troops back to Vicksburg, summing up the Jackson operation with the exultant report: "The inhabitants are subjugated. They cry aloud for mercy. The land is devastated for 30 miles around." The devastation was real enough — Sherman's men were becoming expert at that sort of thing — and Grant suspected that Johnston's army was so demoralized that it would lose half of its numbers before a new campaign began. He also believed that Pemberton's paroled force was evaporating and that even if the men were finally exchanged very few of them would ever fight for the Confederacy again. These estimates were somewhat too optimistic, but one fact was clear: Mississippi was wide open, and Union troops here could do about as they pleased.[11]

Grant suspected that much the same was true of the area beyond the big river. This vast stretch of land, the trans-Mississippi Confederacy, running from the Missouri line to the Rio Grande, its western border dissolving somewhere in the dusty Indian country, was commanded by the distinguished, mysteriously ineffective strategist, General Edmund Kirby Smith. Smith was cruelly handicapped because he was almost totally cut off from the rest of the Confederate world, he had been unable to reduce the Federal pressure on Vicksburg even with the life of the Confederacy at stake, and Grant had such a low opinion of his force that he told Halleck that Smith had to use half of his army to keep the other half from deserting.[12] That this might be another bit of overoptimism mattered little; the trans-Mississippi offered the Federals no strategically important targets, and it called for campaigning only to protect the flanks of Federal forces in Missouri and east of the Mississippi.

Federals in Missouri were under Major General John M. Schofield, a harried young officer who had to keep the peace between furiously discordant Union factions in St. Louis while he checked Confederate raiding parties elsewhere in the state and kept Kirby Smith from sending an invading force up from Arkansas. Not long after Vicksburg fell, Grant assured Schofield that "I will have troops available for anything that will go to put down the rebellion," and a few days later, Halleck having suggested a general mopping-up along the river, Grant sent Schofield five thousand men to help keep Arkansas secure. He also sent two thousand more to do garrison duty in and around Memphis, sent one brigade into the Yazoo delta and another downstream to Natchez, and ordered the Ninth Corps returned to General Burnside, who was preparing to move on Knoxville from the Ohio River. Burnside had been getting impatient, and Lincoln assuaged him with a wire remarking that "Grant is a copious worker and fighter, but a very meagre writer or telegrapher. No doubt he has changed his purpose in regard to the Ninth Corps for some sufficient reason but has forgotten to notify us of it." [13]

Grant got the corps off at the end of July and Burnside's soldiers went north, their experience broadened by hard service under Sherman. They had learned that generals in the West behaved differently than generals behaved in the East: Sherman usually rode the lines wearing an old blue coat that was rusted and weathered to a dingy bottle-green, accompanied by two unimpressive aides, and the men reflected that in the Army of the Potomac the generals went forth with more glitter and dash.[14] In any case, the Ninth Corps departed, and although his force had been diminished Grant still had three army corps ready for service.

With both flanks secure and the rear properly attended to, Grant looked downstream toward Louisiana, held along the river — from the Mississippi line down through New Orleans to the Gulf — by Major General Nathaniel P. Banks, an excellent man in whom the Union cause found both an asset and a problem.

Banks was another officer who once had been slated to take charge of the campaign against Vicksburg. When he reached New Orleans at the end of 1862, replacing the egregious General Benjamin Butler, Banks carried papers instructing him to move up the river from the south and authorizing him to assume command of Grant and Grant's troops as soon as the two armies made contact; which would have been a very good trick if Banks had been able to do it. He was former Speaker of the House of Representatives and former Governor of Massachusetts, and he had been commissioned just as McClernand had been, for reasons of high politics. He happily lacked McClernand's contentious readiness to take offense, and he had a personal integrity that made him a good man to deal with the mess which Butler's regime had left in New Orleans, but his military skills were limited. In the summer of 1862 he had commanded Federal troops in the Shenandoah, and Stonewall Jackson's famous valley campaign had been conducted largely at Banks's expense; and the task of fighting his way up the Mississippi and taking over Grant's army proved to be beyond him. Grant went ahead and took Vicksburg without him, while Banks, after floundering about in western Louisiana, laid siege to Pemberton's southern stronghold, Port Hudson. This place held out until Vicksburg fell and then immediately surrendered, and by that time the notion that Banks ought to be Grant's superior officer had been forgotten by everyone, including Banks himself.

Banks adjusted himself to the situation without difficulty, and now he and Grant were anxious to cooperate. In sending congratulations to Banks after Port Hudson surrendered, Grant reflected his own uncertainty about future moves by writing: "So far as anything I know of being expected from my forces, I can spare you an army corps of as good troops as tread American soil. No better are found on any other." In the middle of July Banks sent to Grant a suggestion that had long echoes. The Federal power, he said, ought to move at once to capture Mobile, Alabama.

The suggestion made sense. Mobile was the last important Confederate seaport on the Gulf Coast east of Texas, to close it would greatly tighten the blockade, and a Federal army based there could move northeast toward the rear of the Confederate armies in Tennessee and Virginia. Sherman had suggested such a campaign on July 12, just as the Jackson operation was coming to a close, and on July 18 Banks strongly urged Grant to make the move, saying the capture would be almost as important as the opening of the Mississippi itself: "Mobile is the last stronghold in the west and southwest. No pains should be spared to effect its reduction." [15]

Grant also saw the possibilities, and he mentioned them in a dispatch to Halleck, written apparently before he got Banks's letter. He pointed out that Mobile was properly in Banks's department, said that an overland approach from his own position was inadvisable because "the country through which an army would have to pass is poor and water scarce," and remarked that the expedition probably should originate in New Orleans. Either Sherman or McPherson, he said, would be a good commander for this operation; both were highly competent, "and with such men commanding corps or armies there will never be any jealousies or lack of hearty cooperation." He added that "I have not studied this matter, however, it being out of my department." By odd chance, on the same day Banks and Grant independently proposed this offensive, President Jefferson Davis warned Joe Johnston that the next Federal move was likely to be an attack on Mobile from New Orleans.[16]

Halleck's enthusiasm was no more than lukewarm, and he told Grant that any move of this kind must be preceded by a comprehensive cleanup of the whole Grant-Banks-Schofield area. With Johnston rendered harmless, Arkansas thoroughly pacified and western Louisiana made secure, Halleck said, "there will be a large available force to operate either on Mobile or Texas." He pointed out that the navy was not able to give much help at this time; its ironclads would be available only after the current attack on Fort Sumter succeeded — a thin hope, because the Federals had been attacking Charleston ever since spring, with very little success and no good prospect of any. Grant gave more thought to the project, concluded that the navy's ironclads were not essential, and on August 1 sent a new message to Halleck: "Mobile can be taken from the Gulf Department, with only one or two gunboats to protect the debarkation. With your leave, I would like to visit New Orleans, particularly if the movement against Mobile is organized."

Two unrelated events, tied together only by chance, make up the background for this dispatch. On July 30, Halleck wrote a cryptic telegram instructing Grant to send an army corps to General Banks, and on August 1 Grant and Banks, who did not yet know that this order had been written, sat down together in Vicksburg to confer about the Mobile offensive. Banks was in a hurry — he got in that morning and he started back the same evening — and from the tenor of a message he sent to Halleck just before leaving Vicksburg it seems clear that he and Grant went over the Mobile operation in some detail. It also appears that Grant's mind was still making itself up. Banks was fully committed, aroused enough to make a flying trip up the river, and Sherman was taking it for granted now that he and his troops would be marching from Mobile into Georgia before the autumn was out; but Grant's own involvement was still a bit tentative, and his August 1 message is not quite the utterance of a man who has really put his back into a chosen program.[17]

It makes little difference, because Grant soon learned that Washington had other ideas. Halleck told him there was no objection to his visiting New Orleans, but indicated that the Mobile operation probably would have to wait. On August 6 he sent Grant this message: "Please send a special messenger to Major General Banks with the following telegram, and also give him all necessary assistance for its execution: 'Major General Banks, New Orleans: there are important reasons why our flag should be restored in some part of Texas with the least possible delay. Do this by land, at Galveston, at Indianola or at any other point you may deem preferable. If by sea, Admiral Farragut will co-operate. There are reasons why the movement should be as prompt as possible.' " Three days later President Lincoln sent Grant a few explanatory sentences: "I see by a despatch of yours that you incline quite strongly toward an expedition against Mobile. That would appear tempting to me also were it not that, in view of recent events in Mexico, I am greatly impressed with the importance of re-establishing the national authority in western Texas as soon as possible. I am not making an order, however; that I leave, for the present at least, to the General-in-Chief." [18]

Recent events in Mexico involved the occupation of Mexico City by a French army sent there by Emperor Napoleon III, a volatile monarch who was suspected of a willingness to aid the Confederacy, and who was taking advantage of the American Civil War in order to fracture the Monroe Doctrine. His French troops were preparing to install the Austrian Archduke Maximilian as Emperor of Mexico, and although Washington obviously was not going to stand for this it could not do much about it while the war was going on; the best it could think of, as a warning to all concerned, was to establish a Federal army somewhere near the Mexican border — near enough so that neither Maximilian nor his French supporters could help seeing it whenever they looked northward. So Washington had suddenly lost interest in Mobile and had begun to think about Texas. This was probably inevitable, but it meant that the Confederacy's dire weakness in the Deep South was not going to be exploited just now.

When he looked back on it, long after the war, Grant saw the summer of 1863 as a time of unendurable frustration caused entirely by General Halleck's eccentric notions of strategy. "The possession of the trans-Mississippi by the Union forces seemed to possess more importance in his mind than almost any campaign east of the Mississippi," he wrote. Consequently "I was obliged to settle down and see myself put again on the defensive as I had been a year before in west Tennessee." Grant went on to say that Halleck not only rejected his plan for an attack on Mobile but refused even to give him permission to go to New Orleans to talk about it with General Banks; the net result of everything being, as Grant put it, "the depletion of an army which had won a succession of great victories."

This is a strong indictment, and when he framed it — in his *Memoirs*, which he wrote twenty years after the war ended — Grant was influenced by a temporary lapse of memory and by a powerful hatred which by that time he had developed for General Halleck.

During the war Grant liked Halleck and considered him a true friend, but sometime after Appomattox he examined certain War Department files and discovered that instead of being a friend, Halleck, at a certain crucial period, had tried to cut Grant's throat. After the battle of Fort Donelson Grant went under a cloud, and narrowly escaped losing his command and being driven out of the army. At the time he believed that Halleck was shielding him, but when he got at the files he learned that Halleck was actually the author of his troubles. The files showed that Halleck had borne false witness to General McClellan, then the general-in-chief, telling him that Grant's army was totally demoralized, that Grant had left his post without permission and made no reports, and — most damaging of all, and entirely without foundation — that "a rumor has just reached me that since the taking of Fort Donelson General Grant has resumed his former bad habits." [19]

Toward his enemies on the field of battle Grant was properly famous for his magnanimity, but in purely personal matters he now and then was singularly unforgiving. He did not enter many names in his little black book, but a man who did get into it usually stayed there. This was especially so in the case of Halleck, and when time for reminiscence came Grant could not seem to recall anything good about him. The backward glance was warped by the knowledge that Halleck had been a false friend, and this threw the tragic might-have-beens into strong relief. The summer of 1863 looked worse in retrospect than at close range. It was of course true that Washington made a huge mistake when it struck at Texas rather than at Mobile, but this was not entirely Halleck's doing and Grant was not especially disturbed at the time; nor did he then protest at the way his army was depleted. Looking back, he simply blamed everything on Halleck, and he somehow got the idea that Halleck had meanly refused to let him go to New Orleans, although Halleck had specifically given permission. Altogether, Halleck paid a stiff price for his double-dealing in the post-Donelson period.[20]

For Grant and his army, this summer was simply the interim between two great victories. Grant was kept busy with routine chores, and on August 11 he outlined some of these in a message to Halleck: "I have no doubt movements here seem slow since the fall of Vicksburg, but this could not possibly be helped." Engineer officers were laying out a new line of defensive works around Vicksburg so that the city could be held with no more than five thousand men, and these works now were being built — slowly, because the heat was oppressive, "and I do not want the white men to do any work that can possibly be avoided during the hot months." Grant was trying to recruit Negro troops, spurred by a message from President Lincoln, who hoped that at least 100,000 colored soldiers could be raised in the Mississippi valley and who had sent the Adjutant General of the Army, Lorenzo Thomas, to speed the work along. Grant hoped that Vicksburg could be garrisoned largely by these new troops, and he remarked: "The Negro troops are easier to preserve discipline among than are white troops, and I doubt not will prove equally good for garrison duty. All that have been tried have fought bravely."

Lincoln hoped that the mere existence of 100,000 Negro troops would cause the Confederacy to collapse, and it was true that to put the Negro into Federal uniform struck Mississippians as terrifying and unnatural. Anyone capable of rational thought on race relations, however, might have reflected that the ex-slave as a soldier under discipline was much less to be feared than the ex-slave roaming the plantation country on his own hook, armed and under no discipline at all, full of hot resentment and for the first time in his life able to give his resentment unrestrained expression. During this month of August, bands of former slaves were flitting across the lower Delta country, and a number of planters had been killed by them in the area around Deer Creek.

Grant reported that this "probably was but a case of retribution," since "some of the citizens in that country have attempted to intimidate the Negroes by whipping and (in a few instances) by shooting them." The onetime slave knew nothing about legalities, and that he had at last discovered the cruel effectiveness of the law of the fang and the talon was just the planters' hard luck; especially so, in that Grant would not send out troops to restore the former chattels to obedience, holding that citizens who felt unsafe could come inside the Federal lines for protection. Men who did this must, in Sherman's contemptuous phrase, simply "leave their property to revert to a state of nature for the use of alligators and Negroes." To a delegation of men who came in to protest the lawless acts of the slaves they used to own, Sherman said bluntly that the planters had brought the whole trouble on themselves "by rebelling against the only earthly power that insured them the rightful possession of such property." [21]

If the colored man took much of the commanding general's time and attention, the cotton which the colored man had been raising — the cotton which was the reason for his slavery in the first place — took a good deal more. Cotton traders swarmed around the army like blowflies, drawn by corruption, creating more of it. Grant flatly opposed any trade whatever "until the rebellion in this part of the country is entirely crushed out," and he protested that the mere fact that the trade was being carried on robbed his army of at least a third of its strength. This was a moderate estimate. The contraband goods that went south in return for cotton were chiefly what kept the Confederacy's western armies alive, and long afterward a careful student concluded that this trade caused the war to last a full year longer than it should have lasted. Considering the number of lives lost in the war's final year, this trade was as ruinously costly as any ever carried on by Americans. . . . But Grant was helpless; borne down, not only by the vast power of human greed, but by a force even mightier and more mysterious — the invisible weight of continental economics, which compelled the North and the South to be one nation even as they tried to destroy each other. The South had to have Northern help and the North had to give that help, and so the Civil War was made unfathomably complicated; and Grant found that Washington simultaneously commended and nullified his efforts to suppress the cotton traders. [22]

Nullification was approaching just now in the person of William P.

Mellen, Supervising Special Agent for the Treasury Department at Cincinnati, sent to Vicksburg by Secretary of the Treasury Salmon P. Chase to explain to Grant that it was neither just nor feasible to be as rigorous about cotton as Grant was trying to be.

All cotton traders in this war had to have Treasury Department permits, which were worth many times their weight in gold; but Grant had ruled that even these men might not deal for cotton south of Helena, Arkansas — the idea being that this cotton was mostly held by Secessionists and that to buy it was inevitably to help the Confederacy. Chase believed that all would be well if the traders were allowed to buy what they could where they could, bonding themselves not to make any deal that would give aid and comfort to the enemy, and Special Agent Mellen had long since made it clear that it was no part of his business "to investigate the *morals* of transactions connected with any lot of cotton previous to its shipment from any post where our official duties are exercised." [23] Mellen was not being callous: he was simply pointing out that loyalist cotton looked exactly like secessionist cotton, and that no bale could carry a pedigree. But he was also making it evident that to try to catch illicit traders with this bonding system would be about like trying to snare a tornado with a butterfly net, and Grant had no illusions about what was going to happen next.

Neither did his staff. Grant's officers knew all anyone needed to know about the evils of the cotton trade, and what they knew brought a campfire outburst one evening this summer from Major T. S. Bowers, one of the most dedicated and appealing of Grant's aides. A former Illinois newspaperman, Bowers had come into the army as a private in the 48th Illinois, had been assigned to headquarters as a clerk, won Grant's liking, and before long was made a commissioned officer and a member of the official family. He was known as Joe Bowers — there was a popular song beginning "My name is Joe Bowers" — and he was that rarity, a staff officer who was highly popular with the enlisted men, who had learned that if a soldier wanted a favor at headquarters the person to see was Major Bowers. Anyway, this evening, after denouncing the system under which the army did all the work while the traders got rich, Bowers announced angrily: "I think I'll resign and go into cotton." Then he reached into his pocket, drew out one penny which was all that remained of his last pay, and added ruefully: "At least I would if I had the money." Grant

chuckled, and tossed him half a dollar, remarking: "Here, Joe, take this for a stake." Bowers took the coin, and a day or so later he went to a jeweler and had Grant's words engraved on it. He kept it with him all the rest of his life, and when he was killed in a railroad accident not long after the war it was still in his pocket, inscribed with the words he liked to remember . . . *Here, Joe, take this for a stake.*[24]

The war was still to be won, and victory lay far away, beyond the darkness, but already Grant was thinking about rebuilding the broken Union. Lincoln was trying to work out a step-by-step reconstruction program, and in July Halleck asked Grant to submit his ideas about the creation of civil governments in the occupied areas. Grant already saw this as central to the cotton trade problem, suspecting that trade and self-government must revive together. He had told Secretary Chase that "the people in the Mississippi Valley are now nearly subjugated," and he suggested that if the traders could be suppressed a few months longer "the work of subjugation will be so complete that trade can be opened freely with the states of Arkansas, Louisiana and Mississippi." The people of these states, he said, were beginning to see how much they needed the protection of Federal laws and institutions: "they have experienced the misfortune of being without them, and are now in a most happy condition to appreciate the blessings."[25]

It went beyond cotton, of course. If, as Grant was beginning to hope, Southerners were losing faith in the Confederacy it was time to nourish a restoration of their regard for the Union, and this could not be done by force. He had used the word "subjugation" but this did not actually represent his thinking; he was famous as "Unconditional Surrender Grant" but he did not think that the army must keep on hammering until the last Southerner had come to an abject and enforced submission. Sooner or later the Southerner must *want* to return, and he could not be made to want this.

Here Grant disagreed with his favorite lieutenant, Sherman, who held that to restore civil government now "would be simply ridiculous." Halleck had asked Sherman the same question he had put to Grant, and Sherman replied with characteristic vigor. For years to come, he said, it would be unwise to revive state governments along the river, "or to institute in this quarter any civil government in which the local people have much to say." He enlarged on this: "They had a government, and so mild and paternal that they gradually forgot they had any at all, save what they themselves controlled; they asserted absolute right to seize public moneys, forts, arms and even to shut up the natural avenues of travel and commerce. They chose war. . . . We accepted the issue, and now they begin to realize that war is a two-edged sword."

Sherman sent a copy of this letter to Grant, and as things worked out Grant did not have time to comment in detail. He did send Halleck a note, however, which showed that he was thinking in terms of reconciliation rather than subjugation:

I have just read General Sherman's private letter to you, but do not fully coincide with the general as to the policy that should be adopted toward these people. While I believe with him that every effort should be made to fill up our thinned ranks, and be prepared to meet and destroy their armies wherever found, I think we should do it with terms held out that by accepting they could receive the protection of our laws. There is certainly a very fine feeling existing in the state of Louisiana and in most parts of this state toward the Union. I enclose you copies of resolutions sent me by citizens of both Louisiana and Mississippi showing something of this feeling.[26]

The fine feeling was partly real. Near the end of August the people of Memphis gave Grant two banquets. Grant did not like these affairs, and at the first one — August 25, a dinner offered by the board of trade — he refused to say a word, and when a toast was offered to him he had a staff officer reply: "General Grant believes that he has no more than done his duty, for which no honor is due." Next night there was a more relaxed dinner, given by the mayor and the city council, and Chaplain John Eaton of the 27th Ohio, who was watching closely, noted approvingly that Grant turned his wine glass down and drank nothing. Grant seems to have been the only one who behaved so: the mayor managed to upset a plate of soup in the lap of Lorenzo Thomas, who was long and lean and full of bureaucratic dignity, and a bit later the mayor somehow uncorked a bottle of champagne so clumsily that Thomas's bald head was liberally sprayed: after which the mayor fled in disorder, the offended adjutant general offering to beat him. Inevitably, and despite minor disturbances, there were speeches. As before, Grant refused to make one, and when a toast was offered to him he again had a staff officer respond with a few prepared sentences expressing the commanding general's pleasure at "the first public exhibition in Memphis of loyalty to the government which I represent in the Department of the Tennessee." The little statement continued: "The stability of this Government and the unity of this nation depend solely on the cordial support and the earnest loyalty of the people. . . . I am profoundly gratified at this public recognition, in the city of Memphis, of the power and authority of the Government of the United States." [27]

From Memphis Grant went back to Vicksburg; and there, at the end of August, he took a steamer for New Orleans, bound south on a trip whose real meaning he almost certainly could not have explained. He wanted to talk strategy with Banks, to be sure, although the strategy he and Banks had been devising had been canceled; he wanted to see what remained of the Mobile project (the answer: nothing whatever remained of it) and it may be that he wanted to get out of Vicksburg and away from the vexing problems of army administration. It is also quite likely that New Orleans simply pulled him. Eighteen years earlier an American expeditionary force had sailed from this city for Texas and Mexico, taking with it Brevet Second Lieutenant U. S. Grant, who left his youth behind him here and entered on the career of a professional soldier. That earlier departure from New Orleans had taught him and molded him and given him a new understanding of his own country and an abiding love for the country south of the Rio Grande, and it may be that Grant now was doing no more than trying to touch base with something that had happened to him when the world was young. Anyway, he went on down the great river that he had made free, and this trip was a dividing line. The interim after Vicksburg ended here. After this, he would follow a new path.

CHAPTER TWO

The Road to Chattanooga

O N September 4 the New Orleans *Era* took note of a big party
that had been held the evening before. "By far the grandest
affair of the kind that ever took place in New Orleans," wrote
an enthusiastic reporter, "was the levee of General Grant at the residence of General Banks last evening. For hours streams of people
poured through the spacious parlors. Grant received the 'storming
party' with as much coolness and calmness as he conducted those
which assaulted the stout walls of Vicksburg" — and altogether it was
a big evening, and everybody who was anybody turned out to see the
new hero of the United States Army.[1]

Grant reached New Orleans on September 2, after a stop at
Natchez to see how his troops there were getting along, and he
checked in at the St. Charles Hotel. There was an impromptu reception at the St. Charles that night, with hundreds of citizens and soldiers coming in to have a look, and toward the shank of the evening
the convocation rendered a serenade and demanded a speech. Once
more, Grant refused to talk. A staff officer, making himself heard
eventually, explained that "General Grant never speaks in public,"
but he thanked the people in Grant's name for the serenade and
offered the General's congratulations on the fact that the Mississippi
River now was open from Cairo to the Gulf.

Next morning General Banks called to take Grant for a ride. Grant
had already thought of this, he had a hired carriage with "two spank-
ing bays" waiting, and he and Banks set out on a tour of the city,
Grant holding the reins for the first time since he had left Galena,
more than two years earlier. Nothing in the world pleased Grant quite
as much as driving a good team at a fast clip, and he and Banks drove
out of the downtown area, set off on the smooth shell roads of the

suburbs, and went cracking along at a pace that left everyone behind. They got back to the hotel after a time, and when the team was sent back to the livery stable the owner shook his head and muttered that "General Grant must be a terrible driver; these horses steam like a locomotive." (The liveryman just had not met General Grant before, give Grant good horses and he liked to go fast.) That evening, of course, there was the big levee at General Banks's house; and next morning there was a grand review of the troops at the suburb of Carrollton, a few miles up the river from New Orleans.[2]

The review was one more gaudy affair, and if Grant had supposed he would have a little time to himself on this trip he was mistaken. Two army corps were drawn up in line — Ord's Thirteenth Corps, from Grant's own army, and Banks's Nineteenth Corps, commanded by a West Point classmate of Grant, Major General William B. Franklin, who was one of the slightly indecipherable characters of the Civil War. Franklin had been a protégé of General George B. McClellan, and Grant always thought well of him, but his record in the Army of the Potomac had been undistinguished, and he had been sent to Louisiana on the theory that he would do less harm here than in Virginia; now he was going to command the first wave of the expedition to Texas. Franklin had his troops massed beside the Thirteenth Corps, and when it came time for the generals to ride past the waiting infantry Grant once more indulged his fondness for a rapid pace.

He was riding a large, imperfectly broken charger provided by General Banks, who boasted that his horses were the fastest in the army and said that Grant had "the fleetest and best." This horse liked to gallop and Grant liked to have him gallop, and as the officers rode along the lines — troops cheering, colors dipping in regiment after regiment — Banks and the other officers had trouble keeping up with him. "In truth," a staff officer wrote, "they did not keep up . . . the brilliant cavalcade of generals and staff officers were left behind by the hero of Vicksburg, stringing along behind like the tail of a kite." The hard ride ended at last, and Grant and the others halted in a shadow of a big oak tree and waited for the formal march-past of the troops. When Ord's men went by, "moving along with that easy, careless, accurate swing which bespeaks the old Western campaigner," Grant was deeply stirred. He did not ordinarily care for military pageantry, but a staff man who watched him now felt that his emotion was understandable: "Terrible is an army with banners — if those banners are torn by the shot and shell of a score of battles. . . . It was not surprising that the usually calm and collected Grant lifted his hat with reverence and deep feeling as the grand old colors, surrounded by his old Shiloh and Vicksburg companions-in-arms, passed before him." [3]

After the review was over, Grant and Banks and other officers — including Adjutant General Thomas, who seems to have found that his assignment to organize colored regiments required his presence in New Orleans this week — adjourned to the establishment of one Mays, for what a participant described as "a handsome *déjeuner* — music, wine, choruses, etc." Afterward the officers got their horses to return to town, and Grant's superb horsemanship was unexpectedly tried beyond its capacity.

On all ordinary affairs, in battle or out of it, Grant weighed the odds unemotionally, but a horse that was lightning fast and half-wild always presented a challenge that he could not resist. Confederate General James Longstreet once said that at West Point Grant was known as "the most daring horseman in the Academy," and Federal General Rufus Ingalls recalled that when an unruly horse was added to the string at the Academy stables Grant always got the task of subduing it. One of Grant's classmates remembered warning Grant not to ride an especially fractious animal named York, saying, "That horse will kill you some day" — to which Grant casually replied, "Well, I can't die but once." In Mexico City in 1847, after the fighting had stopped, a young Mexican officer with whom Grant had become friendly had the same attitude, and begged to be allowed to ride a fiery horse belonging to one of Grant's messmates. Grant doubted that the boy was enough of a horseman but he understood exactly how he felt, sympathized with him, and arranged for the ride. His misgivings proved tragically justified, for the horse threw the young Mexican from the saddle at full gallop, and the boy struck his head against a tree and died. No horse ever threw Grant from the saddle: Banks noted that "General Grant's seat is secure — but not at all elegant"; but any man who made a habit of riding powerful horses not yet broken to man's control was bound to understand that someday the law of averages was likely to overtake him. The trouble today was that the horse galloped into an accident in which neither security nor elegance could be of the least use. [4]

As before, the pace was fast, and Grant's big horse (as one witness remembered it) "grew quite unmanageable and flew like the wind," leaving less expert horsemen clattering desperately along far in the rear. Trouble came at a place where the highway ran beside a railroad track, when a locomotive suddenly came round a curve and sounded a piercing whistle. Grant's horse shied away, lost its footing on the smooth roadway and came down with a crash . . . knocking Grant unconscious, pinning him to the ground, and inflicting crippling injury to his left side and leg. Grant was carried into an inn, Banks hastily got doctors to the scene, and the doctors found that although no bones had been broken Grant would have to stay in bed for days, possibly for weeks. The festivities were over.[5]

Grant suffered a good deal of pain — he wrote later that his leg was badly swollen, knee to thigh, with swelling extending all along the side of his body, and he said the pain "was almost beyond endurance" — but he eventually managed to make himself fairly comfortable, and a friend who called on him a day or so later found him propped up with pillows, chatting with callers and reading "that drollest of books, Phoenixiana."[6] Luncheon Host Mays sent flowers. Grant smoked meditatively and talked of this and that with his visitors, telling one caller that although he at first opposed the enlistment of Negro soldiers he now favored it highly and thought that a bright young officer could do much worse than take a commission in a Negro regiment. He may or may not have learned at this time that the first stage of the Texas expedition had ended in flat failure. Franklin took 4,000 men off to Sabine Pass, on the Texas-Louisiana border, intending to batter his way in as the opening step of what Banks hoped would be an occupation of Houston and Galveston, which "would have given us ultimately the possession of the state." The Confederates had a six-gun fort at Sabine Pass, manned by fewer than fifty men; but two of the four light-draft gunboats that escorted Franklin's force were disabled when the firing started, Franklin concluded that the odds were against him, remarked that the navy had not done its part, and sailed back to New Orleans, bringing his contingent into the mouth of the Mississippi before Grant was able to get out of bed. Banks dutifully notified Washington that Grant had been hurt, and back in Vicksburg Rawlins heard of the accident but learned nothing definite about it.[7] Grant was on the mend, he was laid up when his presence was not especially needed anywhere, and that was that. Except . . .

. . . except that this was U. S. Grant, about whom army gossip spun unending tales.

If he ran a cotton trader out of town, found one of his outposts overrun by guerrillas, missed a chance in battle or offended a politically important general — if Grant did any of these things people would immediately say: Grant was drunk. To a limited extent it was so now. Rawlins heard rumors, remembered them, and reminded the General of them much later. Banks wrote to Mrs. Banks, in pious horror: "I am frightened when I think that he is a drunkard. His accident was caused by this, which was too manifest to all who saw him." And Franklin, who had a deft and malicious hand with gossip, assured a friend that the accident was a lifesaver because "Grant had commenced a frolic which would have ruined his body and reputation in a week." [8]

This may or may not mean as much as it seems to mean. Franklin's complaint takes care of itself. A man who in two days builds up a bender that is going to destroy him has to work at it, and Grant simply had not had time. He had been in New Orleans just forty-eight hours, he had been on public display all of the time, the rank and file of two army corps had spent the morning looking at him, and if he had been off on a drunk of such cosmic proportions the thing inevitably would have become notorious — not just a matter of thirdhand rumor, but something certified and attested to. (Of all of the sprees charged to Grant, this one — if spree it was — was by far the most public. It could hardly have had more witnesses.) Banks said the accident was due to drink; and yet this was not the sort of accident that befalls a drunkard swaying helplessly in the saddle. Grant was not thrown; he had the kind of fall that is always a real and present danger for the horseman who likes to try a dangerous horse to the utmost. The remarkable thing about the whole affair, indeed, is not that it caused so much talk but that it caused so little.

Among those who were present that day was Major General Cadwallader C. Washburn, brother of Grant's political sponsor, Congressman Elihu Washburne (the brothers spelled the family name differently), and Washburn liked to give the Congressman intimate details about Grant, not shrinking on occasion from setting down the sharpest criticism. On September 5, writing to his brother, General

Washburn contented himself by saying casually that "after the review was over and Grant was returning to the city, his horse fell with him and injured him severely." [9] There was a big review, then there was a relaxing lunch, Grant relaxed along with everybody else, Grant's horse fell, Grant was hurt . . . and after a time Grant went on back to Vicksburg.

He went back a little less than two weeks after the accident, reaching Vicksburg just twenty-four hours after Rawlins had finished a letter to James H. Wilson saying that "I have a rumor" that Grant had been hurt. Rawlins added: "I have no other knowledge than that which rumor has put afloat." Grant's steamer docked on September 16, and Grant was carried ashore and put to bed in his headquarters on the first floor of the home of a wealthy businessman named William Lum, a fine twenty-six-room mansion on a hill with spacious grounds, back of South Washington Street, into which the general had moved immediately after Vicksburg surrendered.[10]

The Lum house was a good place for an injured man to recuperate, but what helped Grant most was undoubtedly the fact that shortly after he got there his wife Julia reached Vicksburg, bringing their youngest son, Jesse, a bouncy five years old, going on six. To have his wife and one or more of his children with him was always the best medicine Grant could have, and it was so now.

Julia came from St. Louis, where she had gone — about the time Grant went to New Orleans — to place the older Grant children in school. These youngsters were Fred, who was thirteen; Ulysses, Jr., generally known as Buck, who was eleven; and their eight-year-old sister Ellen, whom everybody called Nelly. They were to live in the home of Julia's cousin, Grant's onetime real estate partner, Harry Boggs; Harry and his wife Louisa were probably the Grants' closest friends, and because the children felt perfectly at home with them it was possible for Julia to spend a good deal of time at headquarters.

Rawlins was always glad to have her at headquarters, because he was convinced that accidents like the regrettable one at New Orleans never happened when Julia was with the general. Yet Rawlins at this moment was preoccupied. He was falling in love — deeply, everlastingly in love — and for once he was not worrying much about General Grant. Instead he was worrying about John A. Rawlins. He had always had a niggling doubt: the eerie shadow that is cast across the vision of what a man wants to be by his inner fear of what he may actually become. Being in love had compelled him to take this doubt out and reexamine it.

Rawlins had just become engaged to Miss Mary Emma Hurlbut, a native of Danbury, Connecticut, who had come down to visit the Lum family before the war began, and had stayed with the Lums all through secession and the siege. Rawlins met her after Grant moved into Vicksburg, found that she had been a good Union girl all the way through, and — as a decorous newspaper put it — "offered himself and was accepted." The sky opened, a lost vision became real: but Rawlins had mistaken self-doubt for self-knowledge, and he was always uneasy.

His father was James D. Rawlins, by all accounts a carefree, somewhat improvident Illinois farmer and charcoal burner, who wandered west in California gold rush days, wandered back sometime later without any gold, and in general let things slide so that at eighteen John Rawlins had to take care of a mother, a sister and six brothers. Rawlins lifted himself by his own bootstraps, with vast self-denial and hard work, he blamed his troubles largely on his father's fondness for strong drink — and then, characteristically, came to suspect that he himself had the same weakness. As far as anyone knows, John Rawlins was a lifelong teetotaler; but he carried this shadow, so that what worried him most, far down inside, was perhaps less the fear that Grant would someday give way to drink than the fear that he himself might do so. When he denounced whiskey — as he did, constantly: Wilson remembered how Rawlins used to say that "he would rather see a friend of his take a glass of poison than a glass of whiskey" — Rawlins was denouncing a personal enemy.[11]

The fear that lay beneath the attitude comes out clearly in a letter he sent to Miss Hurlbut after they became engaged. He mentioned the fear, "which came so near ending forever our talk of an engagement," and he went on to bare his soul: "I tell you, my dearest Emma, unless the blighting shadow of intemperance had hung like a pall over one's pathway all his life, and prevented the consummation of his fondest hope, and made him from its continuous presence fear to ask himself the question, 'Am I to die a drunkard?' — he can only poorly appreciate my feeling on the subject." [12]

Rawlins had been married before, in the 1850's, to Miss Emily Smith of Goshen, New York. She had borne him three children — James, now seven, the eldest, and two daughters, Jennie and Emily —

and in 1861 she had died of tuberculosis, leaving Rawlins with another fear: the fear that he himself one day must die of the same disease. But she also left him something gentler: a remembered love so enduring that it somehow became part of his love for Mary Emma Hurlbut, as Rawlins told Miss Hurlbut with a clumsy, rather touching frankness. In mid-October he wrote to her thus: "There is a still, sweet whisper in my heart, coming from the 'echoless shores' from the one who has gone on before us, Emma, commendatory of her whom I have chosen to be the mother of my children and saying that they should be brought together that they may be brought to love her and one another." [13] So John Rawlins was haunted, sometimes by pleasant spirits, sometimes by dreadful ones, and if now and then he was a hard man for Grant to get along with he was equally difficult for himself.

Grant was on the mend. Three days after his return he told Halleck that he was "still confined to my bed, lying flat on my back," but he felt that his recovery was sure, he thought he could handle routine tasks, and he hoped that before long "I may be able to take the field at any time I may be called on to do so." Two days later he wrote to Banks: "I am still confined on my back as much as when I left New Orleans, but hope for a permanent cure in the course of time," and on September 25 he reported that although he was quite weak he was able to get out of bed and hobble about on crutches. He was glad that he no longer had to dictate all of his letters and orders, and on September 28 he was able to send Secretary Chase a disquisition on the cotton trade problem. He would abide by the Treasury Department's regulations — a point on which he had no choice — but "should I find that any system adopted works badly I will write you fully on the subject." He did not think any satisfactory system could be devised, because "there is too much corruption in the country for it," but he added philosophically: "Our country, I believe, is not peculiar in this respect. The same spirit has been shown in all countries, in all ages, during the war." [14]

Grant's partial recovery came none too soon, for during the final week in September the war took an unexpected turn that would speedily give him a new assignment and a new burden. Far off to the northeast, General William S. Rosecrans and his Army of the Cumberland fell into serious trouble.

Grant first learned that something was wrong on September 22, when General Stephen A. Hurlbut, commanding Grant's rear echelon at Memphis, forwarded a slightly mystifying dispatch from Halleck saying that "all the troops that can possibly be spared in west Tennessee and on the Mississippi river should be sent without delay to assist General Rosecrans on the Tennessee river." Grant had no idea what was going on — the last he heard, Rosecrans had been moving southeast from central Tennessee in a smartly handled campaign to drive Confederate General Braxton Bragg out of Chattanooga — but the order was peremptory and he acted promptly. One of McPherson's divisions, commanded by General John E. Smith, had previously been sent to Helena, Arkansas, to help in the pacification of that state; Grant now sent a staff officer to Smith with a message canceling the earlier order and directing Smith to take his division to Memphis instead. He also notified Sherman, who had the four divisions of his Fifteenth Corps in camp on the Big Black River, fifteen miles from Vicksburg, to start one division for Vicksburg immediately and to report in person at headquarters. Sherman got General Peter Osterhaus's division moving that evening, and called on Grant the next morning. By now a little more light was available — an earlier message from Halleck, sent on September 13 but badly delayed in transit, which read: "It is quite possible that Bragg and Johnston will move through northern Alabama to the Tennessee to turn General Rosecrans's right and cut off his communication. All of General Grant's available forces should be sent to Memphis, thence to Corinth and Tuscumbia, to co-operate with Rosecrans, should the Rebels attempt that movement." [15]

Rosecrans was a general to remember. He had a big red face framed in a hard black beard, he was by turns jovial and blustery, his soldiers admired him enormously — they called him "Old Rosey," which was the sort of nickname fighting men gave only to a general they liked — and he had everything except that final ten percent that lifts a man into greatness. At the end of 1862 his army had fought Bragg's army in the fearful battle of Stone's River, where each lost nearly a third of its numbers and was so badly mangled that six months passed before it could make another move. All through Grant's Vicksburg campaign Rosecrans kept his army in camp, harassing Washington with demands for more men, horses, equipment and sympathy, and he had not felt ready to advance until after Vicksburg had fallen. Then he moved with great skill, maneuvering Bragg out of middle Tennessee and compelling him to evacuate Chattanooga and withdraw into northern Georgia. Rosecrans crossed the Tennessee River, occupying Chattanooga on September 9 and driving on in headlong pursuit, fondly imagining that the Confederates were in panicky retreat.

Unfortunately the Confederates were not in the least panicked. Bragg pulled his army together around Lafayette, Georgia, while Rosecrans continued to think of it as making a disorganized flight and spurred his men on to chase the disordered fragments. Richmond, understanding that permanent loss of Chattanooga was simply inadmissible, scraped together reinforcements for Bragg from the Deep South and even went to the length of detaching Longstreet's corps from Lee's army and sending it west. By September 12 Rosecrans realized that Bragg was about to make a counterstroke. He hastily ordered his scattered army to regroup behind Chickamauga Creek, fifteen miles south of Chattanooga, got just time enough to do this when Bragg's first offensive combinations failed, and sent Washington urgent telegrams which revealed that he was badly worried. His concern was infectious — the more so when the War Department began to hear about Longstreet's move — and it was in the light of this knowledge that Halleck ordered Grant to send troops to Tennessee.

The situation was both complex and ominous. Disaster obviously was approaching, and the men who saw it coming and tried to head it off were beset by a nightmarish slowness, so that everything they did came a little too late. By the time Halleck's messages reached Grant the remedy Sherman's troops were supposed to apply was already out of date. Longstreet joined Bragg, and the reinforced Confederate army struck Rosecrans with tremendous force on September 19 and 20 in the battle of Chickamauga — a dreadful, paralyzing engagement which duplicated the story of Stone's River, putting nearly a third of each army out of action. Rosecrans's army was broken and driven off, and it escaped actual destruction only because of a fabulous last-ditch defense directed by General George H. Thomas, who kept the defeat from becoming a total rout. By September 22 the badly beaten Army of the Cumberland was back in Chattanooga, hemmed in by triumphant Confederates and beginning to wonder whether it was ever going to get out alive.

Grant was in the dark about all of this. Washington had a direct wire to Chattanooga and knew from hour to hour what was happening there, but it usually took a week and often it took longer than that to get a message to Grant. On September 23, when Grant told Sherman to follow the divisions of Osterhaus and John Smith to Memphis with the divisions of Generals Morgan Smith and Hugh Ewing, the defeat his men were supposed to avert had already taken place. To make things worse, Sherman and his four divisions had to go east along the line of the Memphis & Charleston Railroad, repairing the road as they went, using it as their supply line. Since this railroad had already been two-thirds wrecked by warring armies, and ran across territory where Confederate cavalry and guerrillas could get at it whenever they chose, this was certain to make for slow progress. By the time Sherman got to Chattanooga, whatever was going to happen to Rosecrans would probably have happened beyond recall.[16]

The situation at Chattanooga was not static. If Bragg could not get in Rosecrans could not get out; indeed, he could not even stay where he was much longer, because his supply problem was bad and it grew worse day after day. Rosecrans could not wait for Sherman; and so, on September 23 — while Grant was hastily rounding up steamboats and Sherman was getting his troops ready to embark on them — President Lincoln had an evening meeting with General Halleck and Secretary Stanton and arranged to send help from the Army of the Potomac. Two corps were detached from that army, the army's former commander, General Joe Hooker, was put in charge of them, and while Sherman's force moved up the Mississippi Hooker's got on a fleet of special trains and sped overland to central Tennessee. Hooker had 20,000 men — Oliver Otis Howard's Eleventh Corps and Henry Slocum's Twelfth Corps — and by early October these men began to detrain at the town of Stevenson on the Tennessee River, with rail connections running back to the great supply base at Nashville. An advance guard was posted northeast of Stevenson, at Bridgeport.

In an air line Hooker was hardly thirty miles from Chattanooga, but armed Confederates held the ground between, the only available road looped interminably roundabout through the mountains to the north, and although Hooker could exchange messages with Rosecrans he was not immediately able to do much for him. Rosecrans had to devise some means by which he and Hooker, moving in coordination from opposite ends of the line, could raise the siege; and this, as Washington soon concluded, was beyond him. The general ordinarily was full of drive, with good strategic sense and the ability to make and execute sound plans, but in the month that followed Chickamauga he was oddly ineffective. Newspaperman Henry Villard, who talked

with Rosecrans at this time, found him "nervous, vindictive, irreso-
lute, with little courage and self-reliance left," and concluded that he
showed "the demoralizing effect of the lost battle." Dana, posted at
Chattanooga as confidential observer for Secretary Stanton, was
equally critical, sending Stanton reports whose tone ranged from mere
gloom to outright despair: "The general organization of this army is
ineffective and its discipline defective . . . wagons are eight days
making the journey from Stevenson to Chattanooga . . . it does not
seem possible to hold out here another week without a new avenue of
supplies . . . the practical incapacity of the general commanding is
astonishing, and it often seems difficult to believe him of sound mind."
After a while, enough was enough.[17]

Trying to get in closer touch with Washington, Grant late in September sent Colonel Wilson up to Cairo, to sit at the end of the telegraph line and make sure that messages for Grant got to Vicksburg
rapidly. Ordinarily, when a telegram for Grant reached Cairo it was
given to a messenger to take downriver by steamer. Usually the messenger (apparently figuring that the war was going to go on a long
time and that two or three days one way or the other mattered little)
made a leisurely trip out of it. Wilson fixed it so that telegrams got
through in five or six days instead of the week or ten days that had
been standard. This was just as well, because on October 3 he got this
message: "It is the wish of the Secretary of War that as soon as General Grant is able to take the field he will come to Cairo and report by
telegraph."

Grant received this on October 9 or 10, set off for Cairo on the
same day, accompanied by his staff, and on October 16 notified Halleck of his arrival. Back came a crisp message: Grant must go at once
to the Galt House in Louisville, Kentucky, where an officer of the
War Department would have orders and instructions. Grant was to
take with him his staff and the whole headquarters apparatus.[18]

Grant left Cairo promptly the next day, accompanied by Julia and
Jess, taking the train and going by way of Indianapolis, where he was
delayed by news that a special train had just arrived bearing the War
Department official whom Grant was to meet at Louisville. This func-
tionary boarded Grant's car now and proved to be a man with whom
Grant had exchanged many letters and telegrams but whom he had
never actually met: Secretary of War Stanton, terrifying Old Man
Mars in the flesh, impressive despite the fact that he was wheezing

[33]

with chronic asthma and coming down with a cold on top of it; impressive even though he mistook Grant's bearded medical director, Dr. E. D. Kittoe, for Grant, pumping his hand vigorously and announcing that he recognized him from his pictures.[19] This having been cleared up, Stanton sat down with Grant and told him what Washington had in mind.

The government, said Stanton, was setting up a new Military Division of the Mississippi, comprising the existing Departments of the Ohio, the Cumberland and the Tennessee, and Grant was being put in charge of it; in effect, he now would command everything from the Alleghenies to the Mississippi, except for Louisiana. Stanton carried two versions of the War Department order that would formalize all of this, and he handed them to Grant telling him to take his choice. They were identical, except that one left subordinate command arrangements as they were and the other specified that General Rosecrans was relieved of his command and replaced by General Thomas. Grant unhesitatingly chose the one that put Thomas in Rosecrans's place, Stanton accepted his choice, and late on an evening that was raw with rain, which did Stanton's bronchial tubes no good at all, the train got into Louisville.[20]

General and Secretary spent a day in Louisville, comparing notes on this and that, and late in the day Grant found that they had just about talked themselves out so he called for a horse and took a ride. A correspondent for the New York *Herald* said that although Grant needed a crutch and a cane when he walked he could ride well enough once he had been helped into the saddle, and wrote stoutly that "even in his feeble condition it would require a strong effort on the part of a horse to unseat him." People crowded about the Galt House just to get a look at this general, and the *Herald* man reported that most of them were surprised to find that Grant was so small. "I thought he was a large man," one bystander observed. "He would be considered a small chance of a fighter if he lived in Kentucky."[21]

When Grant got back from his ride he found Secretary Stanton in a state of high excitement. Stanton had just got a more than commonly pessimistic dispatch from Dana saying that Rosecrans was about to order a retreat. As it happened, this was not accurate; Old Rosey had indeed made a Job's listing of his woes that day, saying amid much else that "Our future is not bright," but he was by no means prepared to run away. However, Stanton had to go by what his observer told him, and he fluttered vigorously at Grant; who had the War Department announcement of the new military arrangement and the change in command telegraphed at once to Chattanooga and sent Thomas an additional wire: "Hold Chattanooga at all hazards. I will be there as soon as possible. Please inform me how long your present supplies will last, and the prospect for keeping them up." Back from Thomas came a straightforward, unemotional reply:

"Two hundred and four thousand four hundred and sixty-two rations in store-houses; ninety thousand to arrive tomorrow, and all the trains were loaded which had arrived at Bridgeport up to the 16th — probably 300 wagons. I will hold the town till we starve." [22]

The only part of this telegram that the general public ever paid the least attention to was the final sentence, which was taken as a splendid cry of defiance. Taken as a whole, however, Thomas's report was sobering. In substance he was saying that he had five days' rations on hand, with about two days' rations expected soon. Beyond that, there was a full wagon train at Bridgeport, and at that time a loaded wagon train at Bridgeport needed eight days to get to Chattanooga. The picture was not at all good, and Thomas's promise to "hold the town till we starve" was just a grim reminder that starvation was only a few days away.

It was obviously necessary for Grant to get to the front as quickly as possible; obvious, too, that Chattanooga just now was no place for the commanding general's wife and small son. Fortunately, Julia had relatives in Louisville, a Mr. and Mrs. Page, her aunt and uncle; she went to board with them until such time as she could rejoin the general. Secretary Stanton went back to Washington, and Grant took the train south to Stevenson, Alabama, where the Nashville & Chattanooga Railroad intersected the line of the Memphis & Charleston. Nearly two hundred miles to the west Sherman's men were toiling slowly along this road; and ten miles northeast of Stevenson, at Bridgeport, the line was sharply broken, the bridge by which the railroad crossed the Tennessee at this place having been destroyed. (Even if the bridge still existed, the Confederates controlled the railroad from the Tennessee crossing to Chattanooga.) At Stevenson General Howard, who commanded Federal troops around Bridgeport, came aboard Grant's car to pay his respects.

Howard must have been a man after Rawlins's heart. He was widely known as "the Christian general," a pious and dedicated abstainer from alcohol, given to all manner of good works; slightly priggish, and yet a good soldier for all that. He had lost an arm in the fighting on the Virginia peninsula in 1862, he commanded a corps that had acquired a bad name at Chancellorsville and Gettysburg, and now he and his soldiers were in Tennessee to see whether they might do better here than they had done in the east. Howard was mildly surprised when he saw Grant; he had expected someone rough and burly and he found a slight, pale little man, "not larger than McClellan," with a quiet way of talking and an engaging smile. Stevenson was the town where Joe Hooker had his headquarters, and while Howard talked with Grant a swanky officer from Hooker's staff came in with a message: General Hooker would be happy to entertain General Grant at his headquarters, and would provide transportation. Grant's reply — made "with some emphasis," as Howard remembered it — was: "If General Hooker wishes to see me he will find me on this train." Hooker's man went away, Howard reflected that "Grant never left the necessity for gaining a proper ascendancy over subordinate generals, where it was likely to be questioned, to a second interview," and before long Hooker himself showed up, all military courtesy, quite unabashed. He had just been trying it on for size.[23]

Grant had another caller that evening — Rosecrans, soberly making his way north, a general without an army. He had turned the controls over to Thomas as soon as Grant's telegram arrived, and he left Chattanooga quietly before the army knew he had been replaced, drafting a moving farewell message to be read to the troops after his departure. The adjutant who wrote this out for him followed army style all the way, and when he gave the document to Rosecrans it closed with the words ". . . farewell, and may God bless you. By command of General Rosecrans." Rosecrans had a strong religious faith, and he promptly handed the paper back, explaining that even though he was a major general he could not command God to bless anyone; he could only ask it, earnestly and hopefully. The offending "by command of" was removed.

Rosecrans and Grant disliked each other, and the meeting in Grant's car must have been hard for both of them, but they greeted one another cordially and things went smoothly enough. Rosecrans explained how matters stood at Chattanooga, told what plans had been made to improve conditions, said goodbye, and went his lonely way. Grant felt that Rosecrans's plans were good, but his real estimate of the man crops out in the remark he added when he wrote his *Memoirs:* "My only wonder was that he had not carried them out." [24]

Grant went on that night to Bridgeport and stayed with Howard in a plain wall tent pitched in what Howard considered a muddy, desolate and altogether cheerless region. Howard saw a humorous glint in Grant's eye when they came into the tent; the first thing visible was a flask of whiskey hanging by the tent pole. Howard hastily explained that the flask was not his; it had been left there by some other officer, and as for Howard himself, "I never drink." Grant replied, "Neither do I," and Howard, describing it years later, said that "his answer was not in sport." During the evening Howard got an insight into Grant's attitude toward "the selfishly ambitious." Apparently trying to put Hooker's performance in a better light, Howard said that after all it was hard for a man to pass (as Hooker had done) from a higher command to a lower one, and Grant responded: "I don't think so, Howard; a major general is entitled to an army division and no more. Why, I believe I should be flying in the face of Providence to seek a command higher than that entrusted to me." [25]

The next morning, October 22, Grant was up at sunrise to make the long ride to Chattanooga. Howard saw Rawlins lift him into the saddle "as if he had been a child," and when the general and a small escort set off Howard felt that Grant was still lame and suffering and that the trip that lay ahead would have been an ordeal for a man in robust health.

. . . A chaplain who was in the army at this time wrote that profanity was one of the worst evils of army life, "almost all the soldiers being not only addicted to it but practicing it in the worst form I have ever heard." Of all the people who swore, the chaplain said, the army's teamsters were by far the worst: "Their blasphemy is sometimes awful. I have heard wicked men among the soldiers, shocked by the profanity of the teamsters, declare that they would never swear again." [26] It seems likely that the chaplain had been listening to men who had to take loaded wagons over the road from Bridgeport to Chattanooga. Of all the villainous roads of war, this one seems to have been best calculated to provoke powerful language.

The length of this route was variously estimated at anything between sixty and seventy-five miles. From Bridgeport a tolerably easy stretch led north around a big curve in the Tennessee River to the hamlet of Jasper. (Easy, that is, by comparison with the rest of the road; but Rosecrans had warned Hooker a few days earlier that "it will be necessary to make extraordinary efforts" to make this part passable.) From Jasper the road went northeast for twenty miles or more, up the valley of the Sequatchie River, and a long spell of heavy rains had turned the whole valley into a quagmire, making most of the fords unusable and leaving the road belly-deep in mud. Finally the road turned to the right, east by south, getting out of the river valley to cross the rocky mass of Walden's Ridge; and here it was nothing better than a trail that had been improvised by putting logs against projecting ledges. Wagons now were lightened in every way imagi-nable — even the brine was drained from barrels of salt pork — and about half of the priceless cargoes of forage and rations were often thrown away so that the other half could get through. A wagon would go jolting up the mountainside, half pulled and half carried; there might be sixteen mules in harness, one man with a whip assigned to each mule, while as many foot soldiers as could find room shoved the wagon box from behind or wrestled with the muddy spokes of the wheels.

Rawlins called "the valley the muddiest and the mountain road the roughest and steepest of ascent and descent ever crossed by army wagons and mules," and his loathing for the whole infernal highway finds expression in his assertion that "one riding over it, if he did not see with his own eyes they did get over, would not believe it possible for him to do so." At one time five hundred teams were hung up be-tween the mountain and the river, unable to move in any direction. The mountain region was unutterably barren, offering no food for men or animals; Rawlins said the only people they saw were refugee Unionist families, half-clothed women carrying small children, "ex-posed to the beatings of the storm, wet and shivering with cold. I have seen much of human misery consequent on this war, but never before in so distressing a form as this." [27]

Grant's party, traveling light, needed two full days to make the trip. Once Grant's horse slipped in the mud and fell, hurting Grant's injured leg afresh, there were pelting rains and cold mountain winds . . . and at last, on the night of October 23, the little group got to Chattanooga and checked in at George Thomas's headquarters, where the reception seems to have been somewhat chilly.

Thomas, of course, was a special case. He was massive, majestic, self-contained, and people who tried to describe him usually began by

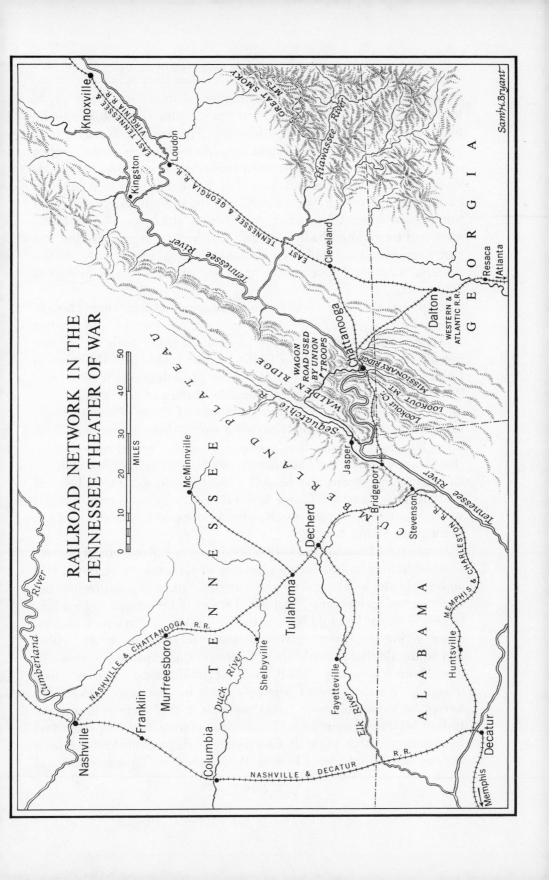

RAILROAD NETWORK IN THE TENNESSEE THEATER OF WAR

MILES
0 10 20 30 40 50

Sam'H.Bryant

CUMBERLAND PLATEAU

TENNESSEE

ALABAMA

GEORGIA

Knoxville

Loudon

Kingston

EAST TENNESSEE & VIRGINIA R.R.

EAST TENNESSEE & GEORGIA R.R.

GREAT SMOKY MTS.

Hiawassee River

Tennessee River

Cleveland

Chattanooga

WALDEN RIDGE

WAGON ROAD USED BY UNION TROOPS

MISSIONARY RIDGE

LOOKOUT MT.

Lookout Ct.

Dalton

Resaca

Atlanta

WESTERN & ATLANTIC R.R.

Sequatchie R.

Jasper

Bridgeport

Stevenson

Tennessee River

McMinnville

Decherd

Tullahoma

Shelbyville

Duck River

Fayetteville

Elk River

MEMPHIS & CHARLESTON R.R.

Huntsville

Decatur

Memphis

NASHVILLE & CHATTANOOGA R.R.

Murfreesboro

Franklin

Columbia

Nashville

NASHVILLE & DECATUR R.R.

Cumberland River

comparing him to George Washington; without intending to he looked as if he had just come from the sculptor. His soldiers found him warmly human, and called him Pap Thomas, which they would not have done if they had found him bloodless or awesome, but to outsiders he was remote. A newspaperman said that just to look at his deep eyes, heavy brows and firm chin "made one feel as if he were gazing into the mouth of a cannon; and the cannon said nothing." A subordinate once complained to Thomas that the War Department had treated him badly, and said that he "could not help but feel that a serious wrong had been done him": to which Thomas replied soberly, "Colonel, I have taken a great deal of pains to educate myself not to feel."

It appears that there was a coolness between Grant and Thomas, dating back as men believed to the early summer of 1862, when Thomas had been put in charge of Grant's army while Grant was given a meaningless title a bit farther up the ladder; and this evening Colonel Wilson of Grant's staff came into headquarters to find Thomas sitting ponderously on one side of the fireplace while Grant sat on the other side, rain-soaked, a puddle of water under his chair, his uniform steaming, nobody saying a word. Wilson, who was brash enough to meet any situation, spoke to Thomas about this, explaining that Grant was wet, tired and hungry, and ought to have dry clothing and something to eat; and he said Thomas came to and set his staff bustling about so that Grant was taken care of properly. Wilson wrote that neither Grant nor Rawlins ever quite forgot the coldness of their reception.

It may have been so; and yet General Joseph J. Reynolds, Thomas's chief of staff, who had been a classmate of Grant at West Point, told author Hamlin Garland after the war that "there was no feeling between Grant and Thomas" and said Thomas did not mean to be inhospitable. Thomas had told Reynolds: "Tell Grant to have no hesitancy about giving me orders. I will be ready to obey his every wish." Reynolds said that the only thing Grant ever had against Thomas was that Thomas was slow: "And," said Reynolds, using a quaint colloquialism, "it's the God of Mighty's truth he *was* slow." When he looked back Joe Reynolds could not believe that there was any bad feeling between Grant and Thomas. They were both big men, said Reynolds, and that night at Chattanooga "there couldn't have been any discourtesy." Colonel Horace Porter, then on Thomas's staff and later on Grant's, remembered that Grant was given dinner as soon as he arrived, adding that after dinner someone on Thomas's staff pointed out that Grant might like a change of clothing. Thomas at once offered dry clothing and a bedroom, but Grant refused to change and contented himself with pulling his chair close to the fire.[28]

However this may have been, Grant spent the night there, and either then or the next morning the two generals put in motion the operations that freed Thomas's army from the strangling effect of the road up the Sequatchie Valley and across Walden's Ridge.

CHAPTER THREE

I Have Never Felt Such Restlessness Before

O N THE morning of October 24 Charles A. Dana at Chattanooga notified Secretary Stanton that "Grant arrived last night, wet, dirty and well." He added that the General had just gone out with Thomas to examine what looked like a weak spot in the encircling Confederate lines. Grant, who had renewed pain in his freshly injured leg, and who said that the trip from Bridgeport had been made in a continuous rain "over the worst roads it is possible to conceive of," was up early this day, and by ten o'clock he was riding north of the Tennessee to grapple with his most pressing command problem — the matter of finding some way to break the siege before the army became too weak to fight.[1]

He had the right men with him on this ride: Thomas, who had already endorsed a plan to break the siege, and the chief engineer officer of the Army of the Cumberland, Brigadier General William Farrar Smith, who had devised the plan and was prepared to execute it. Smith was universally known as "Baldy" — not, as a friend said, because he was notably bald, but just because there were so many Smiths in the army that each one needed a distinguishing nickname — and he had had his ups and downs; had commanded a corps in the Army of the Potomac, ranking as major general, had lost command and rank when he fell into disfavor after Fredericksburg, and now he might be on his way back up. He could be brilliant one month and torpid the next. Luckily he was in his brilliant phase just now, and today he wanted to explain geography to General Grant.

Geography was all-important. Chattanooga was locked in by the mountains. Looking south, the army in Chattanooga saw on its left the long diagonal of Missionary Ridge, three hundred feet high, touching the river east of town and then going south by west for seven miles. The crest of this ridge was held by armed Confederates who had had a month to dig in, and there was no opening here no matter how long the commanding general might stare. When the army in Chattanooga looked to its right it saw something worse: the upper end of Lookout Mountain, a massive reef that came up one hundred miles out of Alabama, its axis pointing a little east of north, touching the river a few miles west of the city. Lookout Mountain rose one thousand feet above city and river, its upper third a vertical palisade of sheer rock, with a long slope of farm and forest country sliding down from the base of the palisade to the river and the open country below. This slope, like Missionary Ridge, was heavily populated by Bragg's soldiers, and between the mountain and the ridge the Federals were imprisoned. They could see their enemies, flickering campfires by night, emplaced guns and entrenched infantry by day, but the sight gave no comfort; from Fredericksburg through Gettysburg to Vicksburg the soldiers in this war had learned that to fight uphill against a properly prepared army was very bad going.

Lookout Mountain mattered most, because it controlled the routes the Federals had to use to get in or out of Chattanooga.

In ordinary times there were four of these routes. There was the railroad, coming south of the river at Bridgeport and snaking through a pass in Raccoon Mountain to come around the end of Lookout into Chattanooga. There was a highway, good enough as American country roads went in those days, running near the railroad and accompanying it around the foot of the slope at Lookout's northern end. There was also the river, usable by steamboats at most stages of the water, and the river skirted the northern tip of Lookout Mountain. Railroad, highway and river were all blocked now, because the Confederate soldiers on the Lookout Mountain slope could lay fire on all three. For a fourth route there was a road that hugged the northern bank of the Tennessee, coming east from Bridgeport, and this one was blocked also because a good part of it lay within easy range of Confederate riflemen on the northern slope of Raccoon Mountain — a north-south ridge, much lower than Lookout, west of it, running more or less parallel to it, separated from it by the valley of Lookout Creek.

Four routes, then, all of them closed. The fifth was the one Grant had taken from Bridgeport, four times as long and ten times as difficult as the others. A small party could always get through by this road, up the Sequatchie and over Walden's Ridge, but supply trains that had to use it could not give the Army of the Cumberland the volume of rations and forage it had to have, the chief trouble being that they could not carry the things the army needed plus the hay and grain their own teams needed to eat. (Half-starved, their teams grew weaker and weaker while the roads grew worse, and so the loads that could be carried kept growing smaller.) Grant later told Halleck that the incredible number of 10,000 animals had perished on this road; the troops were on half rations, and it was perfectly clear that when winter came the road could hardly be used at all. Unless a better route could be opened soon the army was going to die, and so on this morning of October 24 Grant was out to see what Thomas and Baldy Smith had learned about geography and about Confederate troop dispositions.[2]

They had learned a good deal, all of it encouraging.

Flowing west at Chattanooga, the Tennessee River abruptly turns south as soon as it is past the city, and it keeps on flowing south for two or three miles until it touches that northern toe of Lookout Mountain. Then it swings around in a sharp hairpin turn and goes back north again, enclosing a long finger of land known as Moccasin Point, the river's hairpin turn bearing the name of Moccasin Bend. Having gone north until it is several miles above the latitude of Chattanooga, the Tennessee goes northwest, west and southwest, making its way around the northern end of Raccoon Mountain. All of these facts, of course, were visible to anyone who examined a map or climbed a hill and looked about him, but Thomas and Smith wanted Grant to reflect on certain other facts they had uncovered.

Across the base of Moccasin Point, hidden from Confederate view by woods and hills, there was an insignificant little road that left the river opposite Chattanooga and reached the river again at a nowhere of a place called Brown's Ferry, little more than a mile from the city by this road but a good nine miles by water, and comfortably out of range of the Confederate guns on Lookout Mountain. The two generals led Grant to Brown's Ferry and showed him where opportunity beckoned.

On the opposite side of the river was the mouth of a valley that cut west across Raccoon Mountain, and after four or five miles this valley touched the river again at Kelley's Ferry — which could easily be reached by road or by steamboat from Bridgeport. The opportunity, as Smith pointed out, was simply this: if the Federals unexpectedly put a pontoon bridge across the river at Brown's Ferry and seized the road through the valley across Raccoon Mountain they would have a direct route to Chattanooga from Bridgeport and the blockade would be ended.

To do this, of course, it would be necessary to drive the Confederates away from Raccoon Mountain, but this might be easy because Bragg's army held this area weakly. Bragg's left was commanded by Longstreet, who was as good a defensive tactician as the Confederacy had, but Longstreet had posted most of his army corps on the eastern and northern slopes of Lookout Mountain, detailing only one brigade to hold the valley of Lookout Creek and the northern part of Raccoon Mountain. At the break in the hills just opposite Brown's Ferry there appeared to be no more than a company of infantry, and the soldiers north of there were mostly scattered detachments of riflemen arrayed so that they could keep the Federals from using the road on the north bank of the Tennessee.

The Confederates here, in short, could be had, and Baldy Smith knew how to take them. He outlined his plan: stealthily, and by dead of night, float a brigade of troops in pontoon boats down the river from Chattanooga, gambling everything on the belief that they could slip around Moccasin Bend before the Confederates caught on, and have these men go ashore opposite Brown's Ferry and seize the eastern end of the valley that cut across the mountain to Kelley's Ferry. Meanwhile, march another brigade across Moccasin Point by the road the generals themselves had just used, and while the brigade that had floated downstream was making the Raccoon Mountain beachhead secure let this brigade, using the flat boats that had brought the first brigade downstream, build a pontoon bridge and as soon as it was done go over the river and lend a hand with the job of driving all hostile parties away from the Kelley's Ferry road. (This second brigade would have brought artillery, and guns would be in place on the northern bank to cover the first landing party as soon as it appeared.)

All of this, said Smith, could be started in darkness and completed by a short time after daylight. The Confederates were not present on Raccoon Mountain in enough strength to prevent it; and although they had an abundance of troops around on the northern and eastern sides of Lookout Mountain the especial virtue of this Brown's Ferry route was that once the pontoon bridge was in place the Federals in Chattanooga would actually be closer to the scene of action than the

Confederates on Lookout; if there should be a pitched battle along this part of Raccoon Mountain the Union troops would have all of the advantages. Furthermore, there was one more ace to be played.

Over in the Bridgeport-Stevenson area there was General Joe Hooker, who had two army corps that were not now being used. They were made up of four divisions, sadly understrength, and one of these divisions was stationed along the railroad that went north to Nashville, but even so Hooker had a sizable body of soldiers at his disposal. Let him, accordingly, be ordered to cross the Tennessee at Bridgeport and march toward Chattanooga along the line of the railroad and its accompanying highway. This would bring him out at a place called Wauhatchie, on the eastern slope of Raccoon Mountain approximately four miles south of Brown's Ferry. Hooker could easily occupy the country between Wauhatchie and the Tennessee River, and once he did this the Confederates on Lookout Mountain could not interfere with the traffic between Bridgeport and Brown's Ferry without fighting against odds under most unfavorable conditions.[3]

Thus General Smith's plan: simple, brilliant, promising a quick solution for the army's worst single problem. General Thomas had already approved it, and preliminary activities were even now under way; all that these generals wanted was final approval from General Grant — that, and the assurance that the project had top priority and would get overriding directives in case of need. The approval and the assurance were quickly given, Thomas and Smith hurried off to get the operation into high gear, and Grant rode to his newly opened headquarters to see what other matters needed his attention.

As he rode he realized that the hard physical effort of active campaigning was good for him. The ride from Bridgeport, to be sure, had been torture, and he wrote to Julia that the long trip in the rain had covered "the worst roads I ever saw," but somehow his crippled leg had become healed. Three days after reaching Chattanooga he told Julia: "The very hard ride over here and necessary exercise since to gain a full knowledge of location, instead of making my injury worse has almost entirely cured me. I now walk without the use of a crutch or cane, and mount my horse from the ground without difficulty." He added that "this is one of the wildest places you ever saw," and the hardships endured by the few civilians who remained in Chattanooga impressed him deeply: "People about Vicksburg have not seen war yet, or at least not the suffering brought on by war."

Back at headquarters there were various items awaiting his attention, the most serious being a telegram from General Halleck:

"From advices received last night it is pretty certain that Ewell's corps, from 20,000 to 25,000 men, has left Lee's army and gone to Tennessee, probably by way of Abington. (In other words, it would enter Tennessee from the east.) As Burnside will be obliged to move all his forces up the valley, you must guard against Bragg's entrance into East Tennessee, above Chattanooga." [4]

It turned out later that this report was entirely wrong, because Lee was not sending anybody to Tennessee; but Grant had to take it at face value and consider the damage a mobile force of 25,000 Confederates might accomplish in this part of the country.

East Tennessee was never-never land; a mountain-locked valley whose inhabitants owned few slaves and were mostly Unionist in sentiment, so important in Abraham Lincoln's eyes that he believed the Confederacy must perish "like an animal with a thorn in its vitals" if Federal troops once established themselves there. Through two years of war Lincoln had tried without success to get some general to see things as he did. The way to east Tennessee was long and hard, the problem of getting an army there and sustaining it while it carried out a thorn's function struck the generals as insoluble, and except for George Thomas (who had not been in a position to do anything about it) the responsible officers in this part of the country had never warmed up to the President's idea. But during the past summer something had been done. While Rosecrans maneuvered Bragg out of the central part of the state, in the campaign that began so brilliantly and ended so disastrously, Burnside took an army from Ohio into central Kentucky, found a way south across the Cumberland plateau, and shortly before the battle of Chickamauga established himself in and around Knoxville.

He did not establish himself very solidly, because the supply problem was just as bad as all the other generals had supposed it would be, and Burnside's army — Army of the Ohio, officially — was small. It contained no more than 25,000 men, of whom fewer than 17,000 were infantry, and it was attempting to hold a stretch of Tennessee extending two hundred miles from west to east. Burnside's problem was complicated because the high command seemed to look on his force as a sort of reinforcement for Rosecrans rather than as an army with a mission of its own, and in the dark days just before and after Chickamauga both Rosecrans and Halleck repeatedly called on Burnside to hurry down the Tennessee River and help out at Chattanooga.

This Burnside was not able to do. He had troops spread out all the way from Kingston, on the west, to the Watauga River on the east, he had to hold Knoxville and Cumberland Gap, he had outposts here, there and elsewhere, it was impossible for him to assemble everybody and march to Chattanooga in the time available, and to abandon the east Tennesseeans to Confederate authority just after the presence of a Union army had encouraged them to throw off all restraint and declare their loyalty to Washington seemed to Burnside to be a terrible idea. (It impressed the east Tennesseeans the same way.) Burnside could do no more than hold on where he was, and if a Confederate army entered the state from Virginia he would be in serious trouble.[5]

Grant worried less about Burnside, however, than about the way this Confederate move might upset Federal arrangements all across the state. Burnside would have to concentrate as far up the valley as possible, to guard his tenuous line back to Kentucky, and Grant saw that these invading Confederates might slip past Burnside and come to the town of Cleveland, twenty-five miles east of Chattanooga. Here they would strike a railroad that gave direct connection with Atlanta, so their line of supply would be secure; and from Cleveland they could go north of the Tennessee River and drive northwest above Walden's Ridge toward Nashville itself, getting into the vulnerable rear of the Army of the Cumberland and forcing that army into a difficult retreat. With such a possibility in view it was necessary to make a countermove at once.

The only force that could make such a move was Sherman's, toiling eastward along the line of the Memphis & Charleston, repairing and protecting the railroad as it came, making a snail's progress. Sherman was at Corinth, Mississippi, and Grant immediately got off a message to him:

Drop everything east of Bear Creek [roughly, east of the Mississippi-Alabama line] and move with your entire force toward Stevenson until you receive further orders. The enemy are evidently moving a large force toward Cleveland and may break through our lines and move on Nashville, in which event your troops are the only forces at command that could beat them there. With your forces here before the enemy cross the Tennessee, we could turn their position so as to force them back and save the possibility of a move northward this winter.[6]

There were details for Grant to arrange. Since Sherman could no longer use the railroad the commissary at St. Louis must send supplies to him by steamer, up the Tennessee River to the town of Eastport; 250,000 rations must be shipped at once, with 500,000 more within the week. Work on the defensive lines at Chattanooga was rushed in the hope that some of Thomas's troops could be sent back nearer to the base, thus reducing the volume of supplies that had to be carried to Chattanooga, and the rear echelon was ordered to hurry up construction of a railroad spur from Bridgeport to Jasper. Grant told Halleck about the Thomas-Smith plan for opening a new route to Bridgeport. "If successful, and I think it will be," he said, "the question of supplies will be fully settled."

Grant also sent a message to Burnside, asking if he knew anything about the approach of part of Lee's army, and explaining that if this threat materialized Burnside could not expect much immediate help from Chattanooga: "Thomas' command is in bad condition to move, for want of animals of sufficient strength to move his artillery, and for want of subsistence." To Halleck, Grant wrote that Sherman probably would come up before the Confederates reached Cleveland; if so, there would be ample force to protect the rear, and Thomas could then move eastward and attack the rear of Bragg's right. For the rest:

"I will endeavor to study up my position well and post the troops to the best of my judgment, to meet all contingencies. I will also endeavor to get the troops in a state of readiness for a forward movement at the earliest possible day." [7]

It was the forward movement that mattered most. Grant had come to Chattanooga not merely to save the Army of the Cumberland from destruction but to drive Bragg away and open the heart of the southland to a Federal invasion, and everything he did was keyed to the idea that the army must soon take the offensive. However, first things had to come first, and the immediate task was to open the Brown's Ferry route. Until this was done any talk of an offensive was out of the question.

Grant approved the Brown's Ferry plan around noon on October

24, and things began to happen at once. Smith ordered Colonel Timothy Stanley of the 18th Ohio to put his regiment and details from other regiments to work preparing the fifty pontoon boats that would be needed. Forty of these unwieldy craft were available; Colonel Stanley's men would have to build ten more, they would also have to make at least a hundred and fifty oars, and they would have to hurry because the lot must be in use long before daylight on October 27. Each boat had to have a crew, four privates and a corporal, and these crews had to be chosen and told what to do. Meanwhile, Brigadier General William B. Hazen learned that his brigade would furnish the landing party that would do the fighting — twenty-five men in each of the fifty scows, the whole flotilla organized in four divisions, with an officer in command of each division.

While this work went forward, Smith took Hazen and his principal officers over to Brown's Ferry by road, so that they could see how the land lay and understand what was expected of them. Altogether, some 1,250 of Hazen's men would go down the river. The rest of the brigade (perhaps 750 men, including cooks, clerks and other extra-duty men) would fall in with the brigade of General John B. Turchin, and when the boats left Chattanooga Turchin would lead the infantry over to Brown's Ferry by road, taking specialized bits of lumber along to built the pontoon bridge as soon as Hazen's men disembarked. Smith saw to it that certain men in each boat carried axes, so that when they got ashore on the Confederate side of the river they could cut down trees to build defense works and abatis. He also selected places on the north bank of the river where range-light bonfires might be lit at the proper moment, for the guidance of the contingent on the river.

Meanwhile, General Thomas undertook to provide a little insurance. Hooker was under orders to leave one division on the railroad from Stevenson to Nashville and to start out with the other three, on the morning of October 27, for Wauhatchie; and this meant that the country behind him, between his marching force and Bridgeport, would be empty, exposed to forays by Confederate cavalry or infantry. To guard against this Thomas ordered General Gordon Granger, who commanded the Fourth Corps, to send two brigades down the river by the Walden's Ridge route, coming out at a spot called Rankin's Ferry, halfway between Kelley's Ferry and Bridgeport, to cover Hooker's rear and meet any emergencies that might arise. Granger's men started off at two in the morning of October 25, marching in a pouring rain and finding the road over the ridge and down the Sequatchie Valley just as bad as everybody said it was. It took them three days to make the trip and in the end they were not especially needed, but Thomas believed in leaving nothing to chance.[8]

There was a good deal to do but somehow it all got done — Colonel Stanley's men finished the last of the oars just in time — and somewhere around one o'clock on the morning of October 27, Hazen's brigade was aroused and marched down to the waterfront at Chattanooga. Orders were to keep very quiet: they had nine miles to go, along nearly seven of those miles the south shore of the river would be lined with Confederate pickets, there were enough Confederate guns in position to blow everybody out of the water if the pickets saw what was happening, and the men in the boats carried nothing but rifles, axes and ammunition — things that might rattle, bayonets, tin cups and the like, were all left behind.

There had been a bright moon, which was bad, but by three o'clock in the morning the moon went down, which was good, and a wispy fog lay on the dark river, which was even better. And at three o'clock, right on schedule, the men went clumping aboard the heavy oblong scows, the permanent pontoon bridge at Chattanooga was opened to let the boats through, General Hazen got into the fourth boat in line, and General Thomas, who had come down to see that the expedition got under way promptly, sent a courier galloping over to Brown's Ferry to say that the boats were on the move.

The men were nervous, and at first they tried to relieve the tension by making jokes. As they embarked, somebody called out: "No falling out for water!" and as they passed the bridge a rear-rank irrepressible looked at the queer vessels all about him and wisecracked: "This reminds me of a picture I saw of George Washington crossing the Alps." There was a general laugh, followed by a savage order from an officer: "Shut up, you damned fools — do you think this is a regatta?" Quiet was restored — broken once, and no harm done, when an officer was struck by an overhanging branch on the north bank and went splashing into the water, to be fished out by the next craft in line — and the fleet drifted on down the river toward Moccasin Bend, the oarsmen dipping their oars just enough to maintain steerage way.

Confederate picket fires were visible, and now and then some lonely picket could be heard singing to keep himself awake. One Federal noticed a quaint picture: by a little bonfire on the Confederate side two pickets sat astride a log, facing each other, their rifles propped up beside them, and one picket was teaching the other how to whistle a little tune. The Federal all his life remembered these two boys, lips carefully puckered up, whistling away, while fifty scows full of soldiers drifted by unheard. At another place two pickets thought they saw something, looked intently at the dark water for a time, and at last told each other that the moving shapes they saw were nothing but floating driftwood.

On around Moccasin Bend they went, the armed slope of Lookout Mountain looming on the left like a darker shadow, patches of friendly mist still lying on the surface of the river. They were going north, now, sliding up the western side of Moccasin Point, and in the leading boat was Lieutenant Colonel James C. Foy of the 23rd Kentucky, whose job it was to take the first contingent ashore and drive all hostile parties away from the landing place. The night was almost gone now, the expedition was still undiscovered — and at last the range lights touched off by Smith's details on the north bank were visible.

Then, out of the darkness, came a sharp call from General Hazen, breaking the long silence: "Pull in, Colonel Foy, pull in!" On the heels of this came an order from the right bank: "Pull across the river — head for the ridge — dig in" . . . and in all the boats the oarsmen began to splash and tug with their oars, the Confederates suddenly came awake and began to fire their muskets, while off in the hills drums rolled and bugles were sounded. Colonel Foy's boat grounded and he and his squad went running across the shallows and up the sand, men from other boats following as fast as they could. As they made their way toward the higher ground, inland, some of the men noticed that the empty boats were going away, across the river, they thought they were being deserted, and one nervous soldier cried out: "What does that mean?" A comrade barked a blunt answer: "That means fight and be damned to you!"

Clearing the Confederates away from the landing place was easy, but there were stronger bodies back in the hills and firing became heavier as Hazen's details took possession of the mouth of the valley. The parties that reached the hilltops found things confusing: there was a half-light of early dawn up there, but the valley and the river were still deep in shadow and mist, it was hard to tell where anybody was, and the trees and the dead air in the low places trapped the noise and made the firing sound heavier than it was. Then Turchin's men began to come across, landing a little farther downstream and flanking the few defenders who were present — and at last the Confederates went streaming southward toward Lookout Mountain, the Federals had possession of the landing places and the hills and the open end of the valley, the firing stopped, and as full daylight came and the last of the mist shredded away General Hazen went tramping along his lines, exultantly telling his men: "We've knocked the cover off the cracker box." Loss had been insignificant — only six men killed, with enough wounded and missing to raise the total casualty list to thirty-eight — the Confederates were gone, and everybody could relax. Now if Joe Hooker brought his troops across Raccoon Mountain on schedule, the whole operation would be a success.[9]

Hooker got his men on the road that morning at about the time Turchin's brigade was crossing the river, and he put Howard and the two Eleventh Corps divisions in the lead. Howard's men came east along the railroad, went through Wauhatchie, brushed a few Confederate skirmishers out of the way, swung left down Lookout Valley, and by five in the evening were in camp a mile south of Brown's Ferry, in comfortable reach of Hazen's force. Following Howard was General John W. Geary, with a small division from the Twelfth Corps. The commander of the Twelfth Corps, Slocum, had remained in the rear with the division that was guarding the Nashville Railroad; personal relations between him and Hooker were so bad that no battlefield was big enough for the two of them, and when Hooker went to the front Slocum had to stay in the rear. Geary put his men in position at Wauhatchie, and when the sun came up October 28 every single detail of Smith's plan had worked according to schedule, and Thomas had more than 20,000 men south of the Tennessee and west of the Lookout Mountain promontory, precisely where he needed them. Unless Bragg pushed these men out of the way at once the blockade of the Army of the Cumberland was at an end.

Bragg tried, that night, but the push was not very vigorous. He wanted Longstreet to attack Geary in force, but Longstreet seemed unable to get more than a couple of brigades into action. He probably underestimated the strength of the opposition; he knew that he would be facing men of the Eleventh and Twelfth Corps, he said contemptuously that "these troops have more notoriety for their want of steadiness under fire than for anything else," so he may have made the attack with his left hand. Anyway, his plan was to destroy Geary's force with one quick blow and then go on down and overpower the Federal troops at Brown's Ferry, and he launched his assault sometime after midnight. His men struck Geary's lines, made a temporary lodgment on high ground, and then were driven away when Howard advanced a fresh division and sent it uphill on a wild bayonet charge in the dark. By daylight the Federal position was restored, Longstreet's troops were all back where they started from, and Howard's soldiers (who had been taking the blame for the Chancellorsville defeat for many weary months) suddenly found that they were shock troops, heroes, and Joe Hooker's pet lambs.

. . . Howard's medical director reported himself puzzled. There had been sharp fighting in the darkness at close range, and this medical director had 109 wounded Federals to care for. All of these men, he said, had become casualties during Howard's bayonet charge, and it was clear that they had been in hand-to-hand fighting because a number of them had obviously been laid low by clubbed muskets; but of actual bayonet wounds there were none at all— "I looked for them, but neither saw nor heard of any. There was none." Not for the first time, it was demonstrated that although generals often talked big about bayonet work the Civil War soldier very rarely used this weapon. . . .

So now Brown's Ferry was safe. Hooker's divisions had lost 416 men — one of them, shot dead at his gun, was General Geary's son, Lieutenant E. R. Geary, a Pennsylvania artillerist — but the Confederates had lost more, and the Federal position was too strong to be shaken. On the evening of October 28 Grant sent a telegram to Halleck:

General Thomas' plan for securing the river and south side road hence to Bridgeport has proven eminently successful. The question of supplies may now be regarded as settled. If the Rebels give us one week more time I think all danger of losing territory now held by us will have passed away, and preparations may commence for offensive operations.[10]

It remained to put the steamboats to work. Of these there were two, although they still had to be taken on faith because one was at Chattanooga, upstream from the powerful Confederate batteries on Lookout Mountain, and the other one, at Bridgeport, was still under construction. Grant told Thomas to get the Chattanooga boat down to Bridgeport at once, letting it run past the Confederate batteries at night, Vicksburg style, and if necessary tear down a house or two to provide fuel for its wood-burning furnaces; and before daylight on October 30 this vessel made the trip, getting downstream a little shot-worn but whole. The boat that took shape at Bridgeport was strictly a creation of the Army Quartermaster Corps, and looked it; it resembled a New England woodshed on a scow, with an unmistakably rural gabled roof above the hurricane deck, and canvas walls to the cabins — but it would float, it would carry a modest cargo, and it had just enough power to go up to Kelley's Ferry. It went up on October 29, unloaded rations for a waiting wagon train, and steamed back to Bridgeport for another load.

At about this time some of Hazen's soldiers, in camp on the high ground overlooking Brown's Ferry, heard a good deal of cheering down at the mouth of the valley where the road that crossed Raccoon Mountain went out to the pontoon bridge. It sounded like the kind of noise soldiers made when a popular general appeared, it seemed likely that Grant would come over to inspect things, and if he did these soldiers wanted to see him, because so far he was only a name; and so they sent an emissary down to see what was going on. This man reached the landing, found soldiers standing about, and asked the nearest one: "Has Grant come?"

"Grant be damned," said this soldier, without heat. "A boatload of rations has come." [11]

As far as the soldiers were concerned the new supply route was "the cracker line" because it brought boxes of the basic army ration, hardtack; and Grant got most of the credit for opening it simply because it happened a few days after his arrival. In his messages to the War Department, Grant was scrupulous to give the credit to Thomas and Smith, making it clear that the plan had been "set on foot before my arrival"; but he had automatically become a miracle worker when he captured Vicksburg and by now any good thing that happened in his jurisdiction was certain to be ascribed to him. Besides, a new atmosphere had unquestionably come in with him. General Howard spoke of it, later this fall, in a letter to Senator Wilson: "This department was completely 'out of joint' when we first arrived. A *most complete & perfect want* of system prevailed, from Louisville to Chattanooga. I can now feel the difference . . . I cannot be too thankful for the policy that placed these three Depts. under Grant." Long after the war, a veteran assured Hamlin Garland: "You have no conception of the change in the army when Grant came. He opened up the cracker line and got a steamer through. We began to see things move. We felt that everything came from a plan. He came into the army quietly, no splendor, no airs, no staff. He used to go about alone. He began the campaign the moment he reached the field." [12]

This was all very well, and after a long period in which he never seemed to get much recognition for what he had done Grant may have found it pleasant to get a little too much: and yet, even though opening this cracker line was one of the decisive events of the whole Chattanooga campaign — it meant, in effect, that Bragg had gone over from the offensive to the defensive, although Bragg did not yet realize it — Grant still had problems. The road and the river now put him in touch with railhead at Bridgeport, but the railroad itself was inadequate; it was in bad shape, so that wrecks were common, it had been poorly operated, and two days after the close of the Brown's Ferry operation Grant was telegraphing to J. B. Anderson, the new superintendent of military railroads at Nashville, that he must send down thirty freight cars of rations every day. If he could send more that would be fine, but thirty was the absolute minimum and thirty must come at all costs; and when he wrote his report on the whole Chattanooga campaign Grant confessed that the capacity of the railroad and the steamboats was by no means sufficient to meet all of the needs of the army, though "actual suffering was prevented." [13]

Another problem was that the army's whole transportation system — that is to say, the huge array of horses and mules that pulled wagons, guns and ambulances, without which the army could not travel — had been ruined by the blockade, and the damage could not be set right immediately. Montgomery C. Meigs, Quartermaster General of the army, had come out to Tennessee to do what he could to improve matters, and on October 25 he sent a gloomy report back to the War Department: "The animals with this army will now nearly all need three months rest to become serviceable. They should be returned to Louisville for this purpose. Hard work, exposure, short grain and no long fodder have almost destroyed them." The thinking around Grant's headquarters comes out in a letter Rawlins sent on November 2 to General McPherson, at Vicksburg: "Owing to the difficulties of getting forward supplies and the poverty of the animals, a forward movement from here, before spring, is exceedingly problematical." On the same day Grant had to tell Halleck that although the enemy was collecting some sort of force at Cleveland it was impossible for the Federals to move up and disperse this force because of a lack of provisions and forage. It was quite true, as he pointed out, that steamboats now were running regularly between Kelley's Ferry and Bridgeport, "thus nearly settling the subsistence and forage questions," but all that had really been settled was that the army was not going to starve. To restore the army's mobility would be another matter altogether.[14]

The railroad problem got first attention. What Grant really needed was a double-track line between Nashville and Stevenson, where the Nashville & Chattanooga Railroad joined the Memphis & Charleston, the line that ran east to Bridgeport, and just to keep this single-track road in operation was about all anyone could manage. But seventy miles west of Stevenson, at Decatur on the Tennessee River, the Nashville & Decatur road came south from Nashville to intersect the Memphis & Charleston, and if this road could be put into service Grant would just about have the equivalent of a double-track system. Getting the Nashville & Decatur back into operation might be hard; the road was about one-hundred miles long, the southern half had been more or less wrecked by Confederate cavalry and guerrillas — eighteen bridges, for instance, had been totally destroyed — and there was a woeful shortage of rolling stock and rails. It seemed easier, however, to do this than to double-track the Nashville & Chattanooga, and Grant got at it.

He picked a first-rate man for the job: Brigadier General Grenville Dodge, who commanded an infantry division under General Hurlbut, in western Tennessee, and who was under orders to join Sherman in the cross-country march to Chattanooga. Grant ordered Dodge and his men to forget about Sherman for the time being and to take possession of the Nashville & Decatur, rebuilding bridges, relaying track, and keeping evilly disposed Confederates from interfering. Slightly unhappy, because he had been looking forward to combat service, but game enough, Dodge planted his men along the dilapidated railroad and got to work, while Grant stirred things up to make the job easier. He ordered his railroad superintendent, Anderson, at Nashville, to place contracts with northern manufacturers for bents and stringers for the bridge builders, reminded him that the government had half-a-dozen prefabricated bridges in a warehouse at Louisville, and told him to get them down to Dodge at once, warning him sharply that "it is of vast importance that the road from Nashville to Decatur be opened as soon as possible." To McPherson, in Vicksburg, went orders to round up all of the locomotives and freight cars in his area and ship them north, keeping only two locomotives and ten cars for his own use, and all over western Tennessee and Kentucky gangs went to work tearing up branch lines to provide rails and ties.[15]

Making these arrangements, Grant was thinking about Burnside's army as well as the army at Chattanooga. Burnside's supply problem was desperate, and early in November Grant sent Joe Bowers to Nashville to arrange for light-draft steamers to carry one million rations far up the Cumberland, to the mouth of the Big South Fork River in south-central Kentucky. Here Burnside's wagons could pick up the cargoes and take them down to Knoxville by a bad hundred-mile road over the mountains. This route was a makeshift at best. If the water level in the Cumberland fell the steamers could not get through; if they did, the wagon road was subject to raids by Confederate cavalry, and in any case the road would be impassable in winter. Sooner or later Burnside's supplies would have to go to him by way of Chattanooga, and on November 4 Burnside notified Grant that if the Federals did not soon occupy the railroad that ran from Chattanooga to Knoxville, via Cleveland, the army in East Tennessee would suffer greatly.

This would be done eventually but it could not be done now, and Grant told Burnside that if he had any steamboats at Knoxville he must sheath pilot houses and engine rooms in heavy oak planking and send them down the river to Chattanooga, braving whatever Confederate rifle fire they might encounter along the way. But Burnside had no steamboats, and although one was being built it would not be ready for several weeks.[16]

It was at least beginning to be clear that the 25,000 men Lee was reported to be sending into East Tennessee were not coming. They never had been coming, because Lee simply did not have 25,000 men to spare; the best the Confederacy had been able to do was assemble some 6,000 men in the southwestern tip of Virginia under General Samuel Jones, chiefly to guard against a thrust by Burnside (or by detached Federal troops in West Virginia) at the important salt works and lead mines in that area. Jones's troops, by their mere presence off Burnside's flank, did exert a certain amount of pressure, and they undoubtedly would take advantage of any opening that might develop, but nothing like a Confederate advance into east Tennessee was contemplated.

Yet even as this threat evaporated a new one appeared. On November 4, acting on a suggestion from President Davis, Bragg ordered Longstreet to take two divisions of infantry and some cavalry, leave the lines around Chattanooga, and move up the railroad toward Knoxville, with the injunction: "Your object should be to drive Burnside out of East Tennessee first, or better, to capture or destroy him." Bragg knew that Sherman was on the way to join Grant, and he seems to have hoped that Longstreet could dispose of Burnside and then get back in time to help Bragg meet any attack Grant's reinforced army might make. (At the very least, Longstreet's move might compel Grant to detach troops to help Burnside.) Longstreet, who had lost all confidence in Bragg, knew that the 12,000 infantry he would be taking were an utterly inadequate force, and he wrote bitterly that it was this army's sad fate "to wait until all good opportunities had passed and then in desperation to seize upon the least favorable one." [17] With hindsight, it is easy to see that when he sent Longstreet away Bragg made a ruinous blunder; but in the first week in November, 1863, the move looked extremely ominous to the Federal authorities, in Chattanooga and in Washington, partly because the size of Longstreet's force was grossly overestimated. Grant found himself obliged to meet a new crisis.

Grant talked it over with Thomas and on November 7 gave him written instructions, saying that "it becomes an imperative duty for your forces to draw the attention of the enemy from Burnside to your own front." The way to do this was to move to the left, up the Tennessee, and strike southeast toward the town of Dalton, Georgia, some thirty-five miles from Chattanooga. At Dalton the Western & Atlantic Railroad, on which Bragg depended for his supplies, met a branch line that ran up to Cleveland, where it joined the east-west trunk line that connected Chattanooga with Knoxville and the east. If the Federals broke this line between Dalton and Cleveland Longstreet would be cut off entirely and Bragg would be in grave danger of losing his own supply line, and one or both would obviously have to retreat. So

Thomas was ordered to attack and carry the northern end of Missionary Ridge, so that his troops could get out of Chattanooga, and then march toward the railroad.

Grant of course knew that the army was almost immobilized by the loss of so many of its teams and the weakness of the animals that survived, but this was an emergency and extraordinary measures must be taken. To move his artillery, Thomas was to take horses and mules from his ambulances and wagons, and if necessary he could dismount his officers and use their horses as well; there would be no supply train, and the men must carry four days' rations in their haversacks. Grant's order closed as it began on a note of extreme urgency: "Immediate preparations should be made to carry these orders into execution. The movement should not be made one moment later than tomorrow morning." Grant told Halleck and Burnside what was afoot, assuring the latter that this move "must have the effect to draw the enemy back from your western flank." [18]

These were confident words, but Grant was almost immediately obliged to eat them. On the morning of November 8 he had to tell Halleck that "General Thomas cannot make the movement telegraphed yesterday for several days yet," and that evening he gave Burnside the same news in darker form: Thomas could not attack Missionary Ridge and march out of Chattanooga until Sherman's men came up, which meant a delay of at least a week, probably longer. Grant hoped that Hooker could clear the Confederates off of the west side of Lookout Mountain and then move up Lookout Valley in such a way as to compel Bragg to recall Longstreet, but at best this was a thin hope. All Grant could promise was that a real attack would be made after Sherman arrived. [19]

Soldiers as grimly tenacious as Grant and Thomas would not lightly admit that what had to be done could not be done, but the army at this time literally could not move. To all intents and purposes it had no transportation system whatever; it was stalled as hopelessly as a motorcar whose gas tank is empty. The infantry, to be sure, could walk, but Grant confessed that it could go only as far "as the men can carry rations to keep them and bring them back." The artillery could not go at all. Using every expedient to provide teams, Thomas could move only one out of every six of the imposing array of cannon at his command. Nearly a fortnight after this, the army was still paralyzed, and Grant had to tell Halleck: "I have never felt such restlessness be-

fore as I have at the fixed and immovable condition of the Army of
the Cumberland." After the war Grant apparently came to feel that
Thomas might have pushed things just a bit harder, but no such feeling appears in anything he said or wrote at the time. There was nothing to do but urge Sherman to hurry, prepare for his coming, and try
at long range to keep Burnside's spirit firm.[20]

Not in all the war did Grant live through a more tantalizing situation. By sending away Longstreet and two divisions of infantry,
Bragg had prepared the way for his own defeat; Grant knew it, knew
that a hard blow well delivered must drive the Confederate army back
into Georgia — and found himself utterly unable to strike. From
Moccasin Bend to the end of Missionary Ridge, the Confederate army
was in plain sight, its campfires making a crescent against the sky night
after night, its picket lines so close that Northern and Southern boys
fraternized daily in a most unwarlike manner; but Grant and Thomas
and all of their men might as well have been north of the Ohio River
for anything they could do about it.

Grant may have been frustrated, but he was not discouraged. His
state of mind comes out in a letter he sent to Julia on November 14,
explaining that he was extremely busy but that things were going
well: "At present I am confronting a large force here. The enemy are
at work on the Mobile & Ohio Railroad towards Corinth; on the Mississippi Central towards Holly Springs; moving a force up east of me
towards Knoxville, thus threatening Memphis, Corinth, East Tennessee & Chattanooga; and the responsibility of guarding all, to a great
extent, devolved upon me. With all this I loose no sleep, except I do
not get to bed before 12 or 1 o'clock at night, and find no occation to
swear or fret. I am very hopeful and fully believe, if not failed by any
officer in immediate command, that all will show the Union forces in a
more favorable position twenty days hence than they have been in
since the beginning of the rebellion."

He added, somewhat apologetically — as if he ought not to bother
Julia with details about his job — "I did not intend writing to you
thus when I commenced but we are on the point of important events
and I have been receiving, and answering, important dispatches bearing
on the subject, and whilst I write long after 12 o'clock other dispatches
are being disciphered which I have to answer. Since Vicksburg fell this
has become really the vital point of the rebellion and requires all the
care and watchfulness that can be bestowed upon it." He had begun

to realize that the spotlight was on him, and a few days earlier he had written Julia to say: "I see the papers teem with all sorts of rumors of the reason for recent changes. This time I do not see myself abused. I do not know whether this is a good omen or not. I have been so accustomed to seeing at least a portion of the press against me that I rather feel lost when not attacked from some quarter. The best of feeling seems to prevail with the Army here since the change. Thomas has the confidence of all the troops of Rosecrans' late command." [21]

To the general on the spot, thus, things looked good. Yet Washington was alarmed. Halleck believed that Burnside was likely to retreat, abandoning East Tennessee and running back to Kentucky as best he could, and Grant got repeated telegrams from Halleck urging him to stiffen the spine of the isolated man at Knoxville. Actually, Burnside needed little encouragement; he had plenty of stamina, and he was considerably helped by the fact that Longstreet's movements were sluggish and clumsy. Grant was not nearly as worried as Halleck was, and he reassured Burnside on November 17 with an encouraging telegram: "You are doing exactly what appears to me to be right. I want the enemy's progress retarded at every point, all it can be, only giving up each place when it becomes evident that it cannot longer be held without endangering your force to capture." In another message, urging Burnside to fight against any odds if a showdown came, Grant expressed his own credo as a fighting man:

"I can hardly conceive the necessity of retreating from East Tennessee. If I did so at all, it would be after losing most of my army." [22]

Meanwhile, they would wait for Sherman.

CHAPTER FOUR

The Miracle on Missionary Ridge

G ENERAL SHERMAN reached Bridgeport after dark on November 13. He spent most of the next day arranging campsites for his infantry and parking places for his wagon trains — his 17,000 men were stretched out along the roads two or three days' march to the rear, and he wanted to concentrate the whole force before he brought it the rest of the way — and at the end of the day he took the steamboat up the river to Kelley's Ferry, got a horse there, and rode on into Chattanooga to see General Grant.

Grant, Thomas and a few other officers were waiting for him, in a room at headquarters, and General Howard noticed that when Sherman "came bounding in after his usual buoyant manner" Grant greeted him warmly, with an affectionate good humor the others did not often see in him. As Howard reproduced the two generals' conversation it was friendly but somewhat ponderous.

Grant began by giving Sherman a cigar and motioning him toward a rocking chair, saying: "Take the chair of *honor*, Sherman."

"The chair of honor? Oh no — that belongs to you, General."

"Never mind that. I always give precedence to age."

"Well, if you put it on that ground I must accept" — and Sherman, as the older man, sat in the rocker and took a light for his cigar. The two men had different ways of smoking, said a man who saw a good deal of both of them. Grant liked to lean back, taking his ease, smoking meditatively, enjoying it; Sherman got at it with energy, "as if it were a duty to be finished in the shortest imaginable time," destroying his cigar as rapidly as possible.

With sparks and ashes flying, then, Sherman told how his four divisions had marched some two hundred miles in a fortnight, and explained that they had had plenty to eat. From Sherman's telegrams and letters Grant had already learned that when Sherman's men

[63]

crossed the Tennessee at Eastport and started eastward, getting into the Elk River valley well north of the Tennessee, they found that although the road was bad it was practically awash with milk and honey: with the foragers' equivalent of milk and honey, meaning beef and pork and corn and poultry, and plenty of hay for the animals. Sherman, who began his military career by refusing to let his soldiers do any foraging at all and was now at the point where he encouraged them to do as much as possible, reported tolerantly: "I never saw such greedy rascals," and after digesting his reports Grant notified Halleck that by putting a couple of light-draft gunboats in the Tennessee above Muscle Shoals the Federals could get for themselves huge quantities of food and forage that now went south to feed Confederate soldiers. If they did this, he believed, so much could be collected at Chattanooga "as to make this a secure base of operations for months."

Before long the meeting at headquarters got down to a serious discussion of how General Bragg was to be dealt with, and Howard suddenly realized that he had never attended a strategy conference like this one: matters were not handled so informally in the Army of the Potomac. Grant and Thomas and Sherman simply talked things out, putting a whole campaign in review — Sherman bubbling with ideas, as always, Thomas full of solid facts about the roads and mountains and rivers where they would have to fight, Grant listening to both men and now and then putting in an observation of his own. Howard, who was not especially fanciful, felt that it was almost like being in a courtroom: Thomas was the learned judge, Sherman the brilliant advocate, and Grant was the jury whose verdict would settle everything.[1]

On the day after this the generals crossed the Tennessee and rode a few miles upstream, eastward of Chattanooga, to examine the area where Bragg's right flank could be assailed. Bragg had had Missionary Ridge all to himself for nearly two months, but up here where the northern tip of the ridge came down toward the river he did not seem to be very strong, and Grant's plan for the battle hardened as the generals studied the scene with their field glasses from the north side of the Tennessee.

If Sherman marched over from Bridgeport he could go north of the river at Brown's Ferry and continue upstream opposite Chattanooga behind a range of hills that would shield him from Confederate view; and he could come out at water's edge a short distance east of where the generals were now. Here Baldy Smith would have a fleet of pontoon boats — with a diligence Grant admired greatly, Smith had taken over an abandoned sawmill, cut stacks of boards, and built a large number of these useful craft — and in these boats Sherman's men could cross the river and smite Bragg's flank before Bragg realized what was afoot. To distract Bragg's attention, Sherman could detach a brigade or so to move up Lookout Valley, over beyond the Confederates' left, as if to make an assault on that flank. Sherman could also lend Thomas horses and mules so that Thomas could move his artillery and ammunition wagons, and Thomas could attack the lower part of Missionary Ridge while Sherman was attacking it near the river. If things were done properly Bragg's army should be roundly defeated.[2]

Working all of this out took the entire day, and Sherman stayed over night in Chattanooga. Next day was November 16, and Sherman went back to Bridgeport to get his part of the job organized; and on this day, too, John Rawlins wrote a sad letter to Emma Hurlbut: ". . . matters have changed, and the necessity of my presence here made almost absolute, by the free use of intoxicating liquors at Headquarters, which last night's developments showed me had reached to the General commanding. I am the only one here (his wife not being with him) who can stay it in that direction and prevent evil consequences resulting from it. I had hoped, but it appears vainly, that his New Orleans experience would prevent him ever again indulging with this his worst enemy."

Even more doleful, attaining misty heights of melancholy eloquence, was a letter Rawlins on the same day wrote to Grant himself.

"I appeal to you, in the name of everything a friend, an honest man and a lover of his country holds dear," he wrote, "to immediately desist from further tasting of liquors of any kind no matter by whom asked or under what circumstances." If Grant did not desist, said Rawlins, "the bitterest imprecations of an outraged and deceived people" would descend on him, because "in all humanity or heaven there is no voice of palliation or excuse" for a general who got drunk at a time like this. Rawlins pointed out that not since Washington crossed the Delaware "with his bare-footed patriots to the attack of Trenton" had so much responsibility rested on any American as now rested on Grant. He asserted that "two more nights like the last will find you prostrated on a sick bed unfit for duty," and he urged him "for the sake of my bleeding country and your own honor" to abstain from drink hereafter.[3]

Altogether, a moving indictment; resting, as it happens, upon nothing at all. Dedicated Rawlins had his facts wrong. It is rarely possible to prove a negative in a case of this kind; but here it can be shown that the lapse Rawlins was lamenting so emotionally had not taken place. The episode is worth examining briefly simply because it throws a strange new light on the dreary old triangle of Grant, Rawlins and whiskey.

What had happened was this. On November 13 Grant got a visitor; a civilian from Pennsylvania, one William W. Smith, a cousin of Grant's wife Julia, and a man with whom Grant had been intimate since the old days in Missouri. At Grant's invitation Smith had come down to Chattanooga in the amiable hope that he might be able to see a battle. Smith sent his baggage on ahead. It contained, among other things, a little gift which Grant's mother, Hannah Grant, had asked him to take to her son — a bottle of Kentucky wine, which Smith picked up when he stopped to visit Hannah Grant in Covington on his way south. It also contained, for the use of other ranks, several bottles of whiskey, carefully hidden beneath bottles of pickles and ketchup and boxes of cigars. Smith had dinner that night at Grant's table: plain fare, roast beef and boiled potatoes and bread and butter, with Grant carving like any good family man. After dinner Smith played euchre with friends on the staff, and for a time Grant stood behind his chair, making comments on his cards and the way he played them after the age-old manner of onlookers at card games. Amongst those present was a Colonel Clark Lagow, who had been one of Grant's aides from the early part of the war but who seems to have outlived his usefulness; two weeks earlier Dana wrote to Stanton recommending that he be mustered out, saying that Grant was willing to get rid of him. Lagow was a carefree type, and similar types clustered about him, and in his diary that night Smith wrote that "Lagow's friends are pretty lively larks."

They got livelier, next evening. This was November 14, and Grant (who during the day had received his mother's gift of wine) was busy this evening at the conference with Sherman and Thomas; and Smith wrote that "the headquarters are very quiet, as much so as a private house." But Lagow and his friends, with some of Smith's whiskey, found a room somewhere and had what Smith considered "quite a disgraceful party," going on with it far into the night — going on with it, in fact, until four in the morning, when an angry Grant came in and broke the party up, saying a word or two to Lagow. Whatever he said, it raised blisters. Next day Lagow, "greatly mortified at his conduct," refused to show his face around the mess, and a day or so afterward he resigned and headquarters saw him no more.

On November 15, the morning after the unfortunate Lagow's party, Grant got another visitor — a highly placed one, this time, Major General David Hunter, who had been sent west by Secretary Stanton to inspect Grant's command. As a War Department emissary Hunter got the full treatment; on the morning he arrived he moved into Grant's bedroom, and he was Grant's roommate for the three weeks of his stay. Smith reported that Hunter — twenty years Grant's senior, not a close friend, and a somewhat dour type — was "a great Puritan," and said the man complained that there was a lot of card playing in the army; to which Grant replied that he thought this was about as innocent an amusement as the men could have. Anyway, in mid-December Hunter sent Stanton a letter describing his visit, saying that he had been with Grant constantly, day and night, and had had a good chance to judge him. He assured Stanton that Grant was conscientious and hard-working, and most temperate to boot — "he only took two drinks during the three weeks I was with him." [4]

The record is clear; Grant had been as abstemious as any man needs to be during all of the time covered by Rawlins's letters. Rawlins himself apparently learned this, because he never gave Grant the letter he had written, thereby wasting much overwrought prose. He simply tucked the letter away in his files, scribbling on it the notation: "This letter was written hastily with a view to handing it to the one to whom it is addressed, but on reflection, it was not given to him, but I talked to him on the subject to which it relates which had the desired effect."

Rawlins "talked to him," and he could hardly have done so without learning the truth. And at this point the episode begins to look most odd. As a lawyer, and as an army chief of staff, Rawlins knew all about the enduring quality of a documentary record; and so why did he carefully file that unsent letter where future historians were bound to see it, and where it would spread an enduring stain on the reputation of the man to whom Rawlins was so devoted?

. . . on Tuesday, November 17, Sherman's troops began to move east from Bridgeport, and that night Grant notified Burnside that Sherman had sent one division far enough south in Lookout Valley to threaten Bragg's left, which might or might not force Bragg to recall Longstreet. (It did not: the Federals went to a good deal of trouble to suggest that the southern passes in Lookout Mountain were going to be forced, but they do not seem to have had much practical effect on anybody.) The rest of Sherman's people would march in the morning, and "there will be no halt until a severe battle is fought or the railroads cut supplying the enemy." The presentation of alternatives indicates that Grant's plan was highly flexible, so that whether it led to a big fight or an elaborate maneuver would depend largely on circumstances — on what Sherman found when he got past the northern end of Missionary Ridge, and on how Bragg responded to his appearance there. Similarly, Thomas was to mass his own men so that they could cooperate with Sherman or strike a blow of their own, as headquarters might direct: Hooker's troops were to hold Lookout Valley, and perhaps they would be ordered to drive the Confederates off of the mountain's northern slope. On Thursday, November 19, Secretary Stanton telegraphed to President Lincoln (who had gone to Gettysburg to make a speech) that Grant had things moving at Chattanooga and that "a battle or falling back of the enemy by Saturday, at furthest, is inevitable." [5]

Others were not quite that positive. On the day Stanton sent his wire to the President, General Thomas wrote an informal letter to General Rosecrans, with whom he had always been on friendly terms, explaining that matters at Chattanooga were still difficult but that better days might be ahead.

"I was in hopes," wrote Thomas, "after opening the road to Bridgeport on this side of the river that we would have some little relief, but I do not see that our labors have been diminished, for we have been compelled to build and corduroy the entire road from here to Kelley's Ferry. However, we have quite a good road now and have accumulated something like fifteen days rations ahead. We also have in position twelve heavy guns, with sufficient ammunition to fight two battles. Our horses however are entirely exhausted and the RR has entirely given out. If, however, we can hold out for a month longer, our position will be entirely secure." [6]

No general on either side hit harder or with better effect in the battle of Chattanooga than did Thomas; yet the quality in him that led people to consider him deliberate about getting into action in the first place — the quality that caused Joe Reynolds to confess, "It's the God of Mighty's truth he *was* slow" — becomes visible in this letter. Less than a week before the opening of the battle, with plans all made and preliminary movements under way for the great attack that broke the whole Confederate position in the west and put the Confederacy eternally on the defensive, Thomas was privately calculating that the Federal position would be safe enough if "we can hold out for a month longer." There was never anything slow about Thomas once the fighting began, but he did like to have everything all ready, down to the last belt buckle, before the action started.

Another skeptic was Sherman, who discovered that getting over to the jumping-off place above Chattanooga was going to take much longer than he had supposed. It began to rain and it kept on raining for two days, turning the roads to fathomless mud and reducing the march to a crawl. Sherman organized his march so that each division was followed by its cumbersome wagon train — a natural decision, in view of the notorious shortage of supplies at Chattanooga, but fatal to swift movement. Finally, the heavy rains caused a rise in the Tennessee River, the swollen waters carried much driftwood downstream, the driftwood battered at the pontoon bridge at Brown's Ferry, and before Sherman had all of his men across there the bridge was swept away. On each of three successive days Grant had to notify Thomas that the attack would have to be postponed. In the end, instead of being in position to open the battle on Saturday, Sherman could do no better than get the head of his long column into position north of the Tennessee late on Monday, November 23.

This disturbed Thomas, who felt that with all of this delay Bragg was bound to discover what the Federals were going to do. On Sunday, accordingly, Thomas urged Grant to revert to the original plan and have Hooker attack Lookout Mountain — on the sound theory that Bragg could strengthen his right to meet Sherman only by weakening his left. To be sure, Hooker by now commanded a decidedly mixed aggregation. Howard's two divisions had been moved over to Chattanooga to cooperate with Sherman, and of his original force Hooker retained only General John W. Geary's division, of Slocum's Twelfth Corps. He also had with him, more or less by accident, two of Thomas's brigades, the division of General Charles Cruft, of Granger's Fourth Corps, which had been sent downstream sometime earlier to help open the cracker line; and temporarily there was General Peter J. Osterhaus's division of Sherman's army, marooned on the south side of the river when the Brown's Ferry bridge collapsed. These were small divisions, totaling perhaps 10,000 combat soldiers altogether, and none of the three divisions had ever gone into action with either of the others, but if Bragg had taken troops away from Lookout Mountain this force should be strong enough to do the job.

Grant agreed, moved partly by a suspicion that Bragg might be preparing to retreat. On November 20 Bragg had sent a cryptic note to Grant under flag of truce: "As there may still be some non-combatants in Chattanooga, I deem it proper to notify you that prudence would dictate their early withdrawal." This was the kind of note a general sent across the lines when he was about to bombard and assault an occupied town, and Grant had no notion that Bragg planned to do anything of the kind; he showed the note to cousin-in-law William Smith, grinned, and said that he had not answered it "but will when Sherman gets up." Still, the note might be a ruse to cover a withdrawal; and two days later, when a Confederate deserter came into camp and said that Bragg's army was beginning to retreat, Grant concluded that it was time to act. . . . The deserter was wrong, although he thought he was telling the truth; misguided to the end, Bragg had detached one more infantry division and sent it to east Tennessee to help Longstreet. After the war someone suggested to Grant that Bragg could have done this only in the belief that his position on Missionary Ridge was invulnerable. Grant thought a moment and then said: "Well, it *was* invulnerable."

So orders were revised. On Monday, November 23, Thomas was told to drive in Bragg's skirmish line, on the rolling ground in front of Missionary Ridge; if Bragg had really begun to leave, Grant said that he was "not willing that he should get his army off in good order," and in any case a brisk demonstration would show whether he was leaving or holding his ground. At the same time Grant sent new orders to Hooker and Osterhaus, over on the far side of Lookout. If by the morning of November 24 Osterhaus was still unable to cross the river he was to place himself under Hooker's orders; whereupon Hooker was to take everybody he had and assault Lookout Mountain, as the original plan had contemplated. By this time Sherman would be ready to make his own attack, and Bragg would be assailed at both ends of his long line; and Thomas would be massed in front of his center, ready for anything.[7]

So it fell to George Thomas, after all, to open (and, finally, to win) the battle of Chattanooga; and if his note to Rosecrans had revealed the quality that made men think him slow, what he did now showed why men forgot all about the slowness once the action began.

What he was supposed to do was pure routine: advance just enough men to make the opponent show his hand. What he actually did was move up everybody he had, in a massive advance of unlimited potentialities. Not for Thomas was the business of tapping the enemies' lines lightly. If he hit at all, he hit with a sledgehammer; and on November 23 he put the better part of two army corps in line and sent them rolling forward in a movement that had a strange, unintentionally spectacular aspect — which somehow set the tone for the entire battle.

For Chattanooga, from first to last, was the most completely theatrical battle of the entire war. This seems odd, considering the fact that Grant and Thomas were two of the least flamboyant soldiers who ever wore the United States army's uniform, but that is how it was. The battle was almost unendurably dramatic, giving rise to innumerable legends, and it stirred Grant himself, so that a week later he wrote to Congressman Washburne: "The specticle was grand beyond anything that has been, or is likely to be, on this Contenent. It is the first battle field I have ever seen where a plan could be followed and from one place the whole field be within one view." [8] As usual, Grant was careless about his spelling; but the fearful pageantry of this battle got under his skin, just because he could see it all at once. Civil War battles mostly were like modern battles: that is, the ordinary soldier could see nothing whatever except what happened within a few dozen yards of him, and he never really knew what was going on anywhere outside of his immediate vicinity. At Chattanooga, almost everybody could see almost everything. The soldier not only knew what was happening to him: he could see what his comrades were doing five miles away, he was a participant and a spectator at the same time, and in some indefinable way what he saw had a profound effect on what he did. This battle was a spectacular, in the modern sense, and nobody quite knew what to make of it.

Thomas's lines, in front of Chattanooga, were perhaps two miles away from the foot of Missionary Ridge. Between the ridge and the town lay open country, mostly a rolling plain, and halfway across there was a chain of low hills, of which the highest was called Orchard Knob. On Orchard Knob and the modest elevations that tailed away from it, Bragg had a skirmish line, and it was this skirmish line that Thomas proposed to dislodge. To do it he put three divisions in line of battle, with a fourth massed where it could go in and help if anybody needed help. The Federals spent half an hour ostentatiously dressing their ranks, and from the top of Missionary Ridge the Confederates looked down, saw it all, and concluded that the Yankees were going to hold a review. Then Thomas sent his men forward, and the flood tide swept up over Orchard Knob and the little ridges around it, and the mile-wide line of advance, its front all sparkling with the fire of the skirmishers, flooded the plain and the higher ground and drove Bragg's outpost line back to the rifle pits at the foot of Missionary Ridge. Thomas's men dug in on Orchard Knob and on both sides of it, and when sundown came the first day's fight was over.

Considered strictly as a fight, it had been small. Thomas lost fewer than two hundred men, Confederate losses were no greater, and nothing very much had been done — except that the Federals knew Bragg was not retreating, Thomas had taken a position from which he could make a real fight whenever necessary, the Federal lines in Chattanooga were less cramped than they had been, and Bragg had been forced to reflect on the insecurity of his own battle line. A correspondent for the Richmond *Dispatch*, watching this affair from on top of the ridge, wrote that night that "General Grant has made an important move . . . likely to exert an important influence on military operations in this quarter," and predicted that Bragg would be obliged to weaken his force on Lookout Mountain in order to strengthen his right.

The prediction was correct. That night Bragg took one of the two divisions that had been posted on Lookout Mountain and moved it far around to the upper end of Missionary Ridge, to strengthen the position which seemed to be menaced by Thomas's advance. That night, also, Sherman got three divisions in place north of the Tennessee, just across from the upper end of Missionary Ridge; and as far as anyone at Federal headquarters could see, Bragg could be hit hard on both flanks the next morning.[9]

So much for November 23: a curtain raiser, setting the stage, setting also the tone, giving the defenders on Missionary Ridge a long look at an army that began to seem irresistible. Next morning came in with a cold drizzle, and from Orchard Knob anyone who looked to the north saw the Tennessee River full of crowded pontoon boats as Sherman's men made their crossing. This operation took time, and by noon the people at headquarters were wondering why more of a fight was not developing there; and then, from far to the right, down on the western slope of Lookout Mountain, there came an immense crash of musketry and artillery fire, and no matter what Sherman was doing Joe Hooker was going into action.[10]

With his own division and a brigade of Cruft's, Geary started out from Wauhatchie, moved a mile or more to the south, crossed Lookout Creek, turned back to the north, and formed on the western slope of Lookout Mountain, his right flank touching the base of the high palisade and his left flank reaching all the way down to the creek. Then he started forward, moving toward the Tennessee River, pivoting on his advancing right, sweeping the slope; and as he did so Cruft and Osterhaus, down in the valley, attacked the Confederate line that had been drawn behind the lower part of Lookout Creek; and Thomas's guns over on Moccasin Point opened a heavy bombardment. Taken in front and in flank, the Confederate line was compelled to give ground, and foot by foot the Federals cleared the western slope of the big mountain and swung around to attack the northern slope.

Here the going became harder. The ground was steep, cluttered with boulders and cut up by irregular little gullies, there was a dense fog so that men fought blindly, and to maintain a coherent battle line while advancing along the side of a steep hill was difficult; and at the foot of the northern end of the high palisade there was a little open plateau where the Confederates had an entrenched position, and in this place they put up a stout resistance. The noise of the firing seemed to be intensified as the sound waves echoed off the vertical rock walls that towered over this strange battlefield, and to Thomas's men down in the great open place between Lookout Mountain and Missionary Ridge it seemed that a titanic struggle must be taking place. Not being in action themselves, these men watched intently from afar. They could see nothing but battle smoke drifting up from a mountainside that was still hidden by the fog.

Then, unexpectedly, came one of the improbable, dramatic moments of this battle of Chattanooga. The Confederate defense line on Lookout now extended from south to north, facing west, it was badly outnumbered, and by midafternoon it began to give way — and at that moment the fog suddenly drifted away, the sun came out, and the whole scene was visible. The men of the Army of the Cumberland could see everything, the Confederates were in full retreat, and around the curving slope came rank after rank of Hooker's men, flags flying, rifle barrels shining in the sunlight, victory achieved in plain view of everybody — and Thomas's soldiers jumped up and yelled and tossed their caps in the air, regimental bands spontaneously began to play from one end of the line to the other, the artillery fired wild salutes aimed haphazardly at Missionary Ridge, and the noise of the fighting was drowned in the noise of a general jubilee. Then, just as if a stage manager knew when to close a brilliant scene, the clouds hid the sun again, the drifting fog came back, the Lookout Mountain battle lines vanished from sight; and Grant, who had been over on the left of Thomas's line, came riding back toward the center, as leisurely and unemotional (thought Julia's cousin) as a farmer going out to inspect his acres. He dismounted, got down on one knee, rested his order book on the other knee, and scribbled messages to make sure Hooker got any reinforcements he might need. Then darkness came, and as the mist vanished once more Hooker's campfires could be seen, snaking up and down the long slope, with snapping spits of light out in front where pickets and skirmishers kept up an intermittent fire. Grant's staff stayed up late to enjoy the sight, and Grant remarked that all of the Confederate troops would be gone from Lookout by morning.[11]

During the whole fight the Confederates had had troops on the flat summit of Lookout, above the high palisade, but they had been ineffective because they could not depress their guns enough to hit the Federals on the slope; and during the night they left the mountaintop and joined the other displaced defenders of Bragg's left in a march up the length of Missionary Ridge. Hooker, who had his own eye for drama, sent patrols up a winding road on the eastern side of the mountain before daylight, and at dawn a party from the 8th Kentucky reached the topmost, outward-jutting crag of rock on the summit. There the men waited, and when the sun came out they unfurled the biggest flag they had and waved it in the morning air, and everybody on the plain saw it and let off a new outburst of cheers and band music. An emotional officer on the plain confessed that "the pealing of all the bands was as if all the harps of Heaven were filling the dome with triumphant music," and after this promising beginning he added that "it

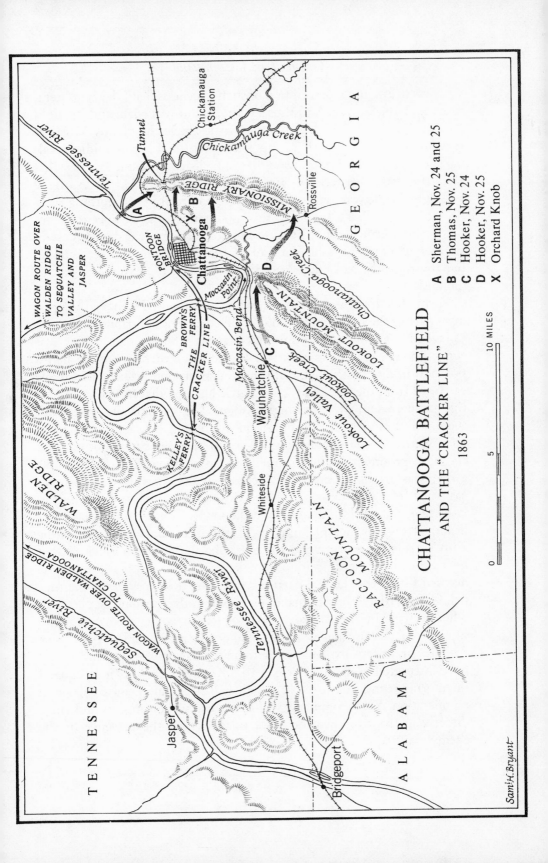

CHATTANOOGA BATTLEFIELD
AND THE "CRACKER LINE"
1863

A Sherman, Nov. 24 and 25
B Thomas, Nov. 25
C Hooker, Nov. 24
D Hooker, Nov. 25
X Orchard Knob

0   5   10 MILES

Sam'l H. Bryant

is useless to attempt a description of such a scene as that"; leaving literature much the poorer. And thus a great legend was born, and the fight
on Lookout Mountain became "the battle above the clouds," thence-
forward and forever, with its impossible picture of heroic soldiers scaling sheer precipices under heavy fire. The legend became so great that
after the war it irritated General Grant, who called it "one of the
romances of the war" and said that there had really been nothing worthy of being called a battle on this mountain: "It is all poetry." This
was going a little too far, because Hooker's troops had done a certain
amount of fighting along with all of their climbing and scrambling,
but the romance had taken enduring form and there was no way to
diminish it.[12]

Meanwhile there was Sherman, who was supposed to have the principal part in the battle and who on November 24 contributed nothing
to legend but something to misunderstanding. Sherman's advance was
across the river early in the day, by noon or thereabouts he had a
pontoon bridge finished, and during the afternoon he began to move
eastward from the river and sent a battle line up what he supposed was
the northern end of Missionary Ridge. The ground was steep but
there was strangely little opposition — nothing but a little rifle fire
from scattered Confederate patrols — and Sherman's men got up onto
the high ground without trouble. Ahead of them, less than a mile
away, was a bulging eminence beneath which the railroad that ran
eastward from Chattanooga ducked through a tunnel, and this height,
known as Tunnel Hill, looked like the key to Bragg's whole position;
headquarters' advance planning had written Tunnel Hill down as the
army's principal objective in the entire battle. Sherman believed that
he was in an excellent position to make an assault, and that evening he
notified Grant that he had carried Missionary Ridge as far as the tunnel. Grant ordered him to make the attack in the morning, saying that
Thomas would either strike Bragg's center or come up in Sherman's
support as circumstances might make advisable. Grant then gave
Thomas his orders, explaining Sherman's situation and concluding: "I
have instructed General Sherman to advance as soon as it is light in
the morning, and your attack, which will be simultaneous, will be in
co-operation. Your command will either carry the rifle-pits and ridge
directly in front of them or move to the left as the presence of the
enemy may require." [13]

It was an excellent plan and it probably would have worked, except that Sherman was not where he thought he was.

Grant, Thomas, Sherman and Baldy Smith had gone over their maps carefully and had studied the ground as well as they could on that excursion north of the Tennessee River, and in some inexplicable way they had made a profound mistake. The high ground that Sherman occupied on the afternoon of November 24 was not the northern end of Missionary Ridge at all; it was simply a detached hill, completely separated from Missionary Ridge by a deep valley with steep sides. Far from having reached a good place from which to assault Tunnel Hill, Sherman had reached the worst spot imaginable. In effect, he would have to fight a battle just to get to the place from which he could mount his main attack. Bragg had finally seen what was coming, and had sent a division led by his best combat soldier, General Pat Cleburne, over to hold Tunnel Hill and the knobby ground north and east of it. Cleburne got there about an hour before Sherman's skirmishers came on the scene, and he worked energetically all that night to dig in and get ready; and the Confederate division that had lost Lookout Mountain was started over to help him early on the morning of November 25.

The truth began to be visible at Federal headquarters somewhere around seven in the morning, when Sherman's attack failed to develop. Dana had sent a wire to Stanton saying that there was no firing at the front, and expressing the belief that Bragg had gone off in retreat, but a couple of hours later he sent a second wire correcting himself; Bragg was still there, "and has been moving troops all morning toward the front of Sherman's position." What Dana saw was the mass of Confederate General Carter L. Stevenson's division — the men Hooker's brigades had driven off of Lookout — threading its way along the top of Missionary Ridge from Bragg's extreme left to Cleburne's position. The division came under Federal artillery fire as it moved, and the last of it did not reach Cleburne until nine-thirty.[14]

By this time Sherman's men had begun to advance. They moved slowly. Getting down from their own ground into that unanticipated valley was bad enough, because there were Confederates on the far side shooting at them, but going up the opposite side was much worse, because Cleburne's artillery and infantry could send a vicious fire slicing all along this slope. One Confederate remembered that when a

Union advance was driven back "it looked like a lot of the boys had been sliding down the hillside, for when a line of the enemy would be repulsed they would start down hill and soon the whole line would be rolling down like a ball, it was so steep a hillside just there." The advance took so long that in Cleburne's opinion the real battle did not begin until around eleven o'clock. By that time Sherman managed to push one brigade almost up to the main defensive works on Tunnel Hill, and off to the southwest — in the flat country where the railroad line ran eastward toward the mouth of the tunnel — some of Sherman's infantry seized a farmhouse and outbuildings and found a good spot for sharpshooters. A Confederate counterattack drove these men away, Federal reinforcements regained the position, there was another hard counterblow that drove them away again, and toward noon Grant told Thomas he had better send Sherman some help. General Absalom Baird's division went marching up, cross-lots, and Baird discovered that Sherman did not need any more men — he already had all he could put into action: what was stopping him was the strength of the Confederate position, and the fury with which Cleburne's men were defending it — and so Baird's division went marching back, having had a three-hour hike for nothing.[15]

As soon as he learned that Sherman was going to be late, Grant postponed Thomas's attack and sent word to Joe Hooker to march south along the eastern foot of Lookout Mountain. After four or five miles Hooker could turn left and hit the southern end of Missionary Ridge at Rossville Gap, which would put him on Bragg's left flank in position to drive northward along the ridge, crumpling the Confederate line as he came. Then, even if Sherman's assault remained hung up, Thomas could strike his own blow at the center.

Thomas's part had always been thought of as supplementary, simply because to storm the main line on Missionary Ridge seemed impossible unless most of the Confederate army was kept busy elsewhere. At the foot of the ridge there were rifle pits, halfway up there were a few uncompleted works, and all the crest was lined with infantry and artillery. An attacking column would be under artillery fire for nearly a mile before it even reached the rifle pits, and the slope beyond the pits was so steep that one of Thomas's generals told his officers to leave their horses behind. During the night a Confederate staff officer rode the length of the crest and noticed that the line was pretty thin; there was only one rank, and the men were spaced farther apart than was usually considered advisable. He told General William J. Hardee, one of Bragg's corps commanders, and Hardee agreed with him — the line *was* thin, but the natural strength of the position was so great that the Yankees probably would not attack at all.[16]

They would not . . . except that Chattanooga was a battle in which nothing was quite as it seemed. Maybe the field was under a spell. There had been dazzling moonlight, night after night, all week; then, last night, there was a total eclipse, the moon went dark and the earth went shadowy-gray, and the thousands of campfires on the sides and crest of the ridge and on the broad plain below glowed like dying embers on a lunar landscape. Many of the soldiers were wakeful, and they agreed that this was a powerful omen meaning bad luck for somebody. Nobody was quite sure which side was going to get the bad luck.

At the very least, plans would go wrong. The plan that involved Hooker gave way almost at once. Hooker had to cross Chattanooga Creek, which was more of an obstacle than the word "creek" implied, the bridge he was to use had been destroyed, and for several hours he had to wait while a new bridge was built, and while he waited Thomas waited and Sherman got nowhere, and Grant's whole battle plan was stalled. And at last — two o'clock, perhaps, or near it — Grant concluded that Thomas must attack no matter what was happening elsewhere.

So Thomas got new orders — to "carry the rifle pits at the foot of Missionary Ridge, and when carried to reform his lines on the rifle pits with a view to carrying the ridge."

Grant was giving himself two chances, based on the belief that the Confederates were not strong enough to repulse two offensives at the same time, and it did not matter which chance worked. Grant believed that Bragg had weakened his center to defend his right, and if this was true Thomas ought to be able to break through. On the other hand, when Thomas attacked, Bragg might recall troops from his right, and if he did this Sherman could take Tunnel Hill. General Thomas J. Wood, who commanded one of Gordon Granger's two divisions (Phil Sheridan had the other one) said that Grant told him that the army "ought to do something" to help Sherman, adding: "I think if you and Sheridan were to advance your divisions and carry the rifle pits at the base of the ridge it would so threaten Bragg's center that he would draw enough troops from the right to secure his center and insure the success of General Sherman's attack." Wood replied that he would be glad to try it, and said he believed the rifle pits could be taken. After this, he said, Grant talked to Thomas, Thomas talked to Granger, and at last Granger came over with the orders: Wood and Sheridan were to charge, take the rifle pits at the foot of the ridge, and await further orders. The advance would begin on signal from the artillery on Orchard Knob — six guns, fired at regular intervals . . . While preparations were being made, Grant went down behind the hill with General Hunter, Dr. Kittoe and William Smith and sat on a log by a fire to have some lunch Smith had just brought from the headquarters cooks. After lunch they had a quiet smoke, and finally Grant went back up the hill to see what was happening.[17]

So far, nothing at all had happened. It took time for orders to filter all the way down to the front line, an hour had passed since Grant told Thomas to make the assault, the afternoon was wearing away, and Grant was beginning to show signs of impatience — when, at last, the signal guns went off. There had been so much sporadic artillery fire all afternoon that the soldiers had trouble recognizing the six spaced reports, but in one way or another they got the word, and around half-past three the officers on Orchard Knob heard a swelling roar of cheers coming up from the plain. For a few moments they could see nothing, because most of Thomas's line was invisible from the hilltop; then the soldiers appeared, rank upon blue rank, forming up to face Missionary Ridge, flags in the wind, sunlight coming down from beyond Lookout Mountain to slant along the endless rows of bright muskets, and the final scene had opened.

Thomas was sending in four infantry divisions, 20,000 men or more, more men than Pickett had used at Gettysburg, and the charge was something to see. As the men marched forward, out in the open, a waiting Confederate wrote of "this grand military spectacle," Grant remembered it as "the grand panorama," and the mass of infantry swung forward, more than a mile from flank to flank, three double-ranked lines deep. Sheridan rode in front of his division, and he said afterward that he looked back just as the men broke into a run; the line suddenly became a crowd, all glittering with bayonets, and Sheridan was stirred by "the terrible sight" and hoped it would have a moving effect on the defenders who had to look at it. The advancing host brushed the Confederate skirmishers out of the way and kept moving on, and the long crest of the ridge ahead and above broke out with clouds of dirty white smoke slashed with flame as Bragg's artillery went into action. A thinner haze came up along the rifle pits below as the Federals got into musket range, and now the open ground in front was all speckled and streaked with the bodies of men who had been hit. The charging mass came nearer and nearer, and here and there defenders broke from the trenches and ran back to the ridge; then the whole immense weight of the charging infantry swept into the pits and swamped them, the Confederates there either surrendered or ran for it, and Grant's order to take the line at the foot of the ridge had been carried out in full.[18]

And now Chattanooga produced its second immortal legend, fit to go with the tale about the battle above the clouds. Just here, according to the legend, this became the soldiers' battle, the victory that got away from the generals and was won by the spontaneous valor of soldiers who led themselves; and hypercritical Dana watching from Orchard Knob said that what happened next was "as awful as a visible interposition of God." For instead of carefully re-forming their ranks and awaiting further word from headquarters, the men of the Army of the Cumberland stayed in the pits just long enough to get their breath and then moved on to storm Missionary Ridge itself. They came out of the trenches in knots and clusters, with ragged regimental lines trailing after the moving flags and a great to-do of officers waving swords and yelling, and then they went up the five hundred foot slope and broke General Bragg's line once and for all and made his army retreat all the way back into Georgia.

The legend is that they did this on their own hook, fired up by the feeling that Grant considered them second-class troops and needed to be shown a thing or two. In unromantic fact they made the attack for the most ancient and universal of military reasons — because their officers told them to. To be sure, the rifle pits made an unprotected target for the Confederate gunners, and as veterans these Federals could see that they would be safer climbing the ridge, where there was a good deal of dead ground, than they were here in the open. But the famous picture of four infantry divisions taking matters into their own hands and making a charge nobody had called for belongs with the picture of Hooker's men scaling a vertical wall of rock under heavy fire; it makes a good legend but nothing more. The storming of Missionary Ridge came under orders.[19]

The division on the left of the assault wave belonged to General

Baird, who was in John Palmer's Fourteenth Corps, and Baird reported that the staff officer who brought him Thomas's order to advance told him that taking the rifle pits was just the first step in a general assault on the mountain, "so that I would be following his wishes were I to push on to the summit." Baird instructed his brigadiers accordingly, and most of his colonels simply reported that "we were ordered" to storm the crest and let it go at that. Next in line were Granger's two Fourth Corps divisions, Wood's and Sheridan's, and on the extreme right was Palmer's other division, led by General Richard W. Johnson. Johnson said he had been ordered to advance with the left of his division touching the right of Sheridan's, and he was to conform to Sheridan's movements. If Sheridan went up the slope, Johnson would go with him.

The legend seems to have been born with Granger and Wood. Granger felt that he was ordered merely to "make a demonstration" and he said that once the rifle pits were taken, "my orders had now been fully and successfully carried out." Wood agreed: "We had been instructed to carry the line of intrenchments at the base of the ridge and there halt." Granger said the men went up the slope without orders, "animated with one spirit and with heroic courage," and Wood wrote that "the vast mass pressed forward in the race of glory, each man anxious to be first on the summit." Actually, these remarks prove nothing except that corps and division commanders do not always know what is going on in the combat zone. Wood had two of his brigades in front, and the commander of one of them, General August Willich, said that he understood all along that they were to storm the crest; not until after the battle did he learn that they were supposed to stop when they had taken the rifle pits. The other brigadier was Hazen, who had taken his men on that float trip down the river to open the Brown's Ferry route. Hazen said his orders were to halt once the pits had been occupied, but the artillery fire from above was so severe that "the only way to avoid destruction was to go on up . . . the necessity was apparent to every soldier of the command." So, after giving his men five minutes to get their breath, he ordered them to go on up the slope. The third brigadier in Woods's division, General Samuel Beatty, behaved as Hazen did, sending his men forward simply because he saw they could not stop in the rifle pits.[20]

That leaves Sheridan. When his men swept into the rifle pits, Sheridan suddenly realized that his orders were vague and that he did not know whether he was to stop here or go on. He sent an aide galloping back to Orchard Knob to find out, and during the aide's absence some of Sheridan's regiments went beyond the pits to find more sheltered ground at the base of the ridge and on the slope; whereupon Sheridan got the idea that the only solution was to keep going forward. When the aide returned, with Granger's order to halt, Sheridan cried: "There the boys are, and they seem to be getting along; stop them if you can; I can't stop them until they get to the top." Then Sheridan rode along the line, waving his hat in one hand and his sword in the other, calling at the top of his voice: "Forward, boys, forward! We can go to the top!" He came to a dirt road that went snaking its way up toward the crest, started his horse up the road, and yelled: "Come on, boys, give 'em hell! We will carry the line!" [21] So Sheridan's men went forward, and the officers back on Orchard Knob realized that all four divisions were going straight on up Missionary Ridge.

The advance across the plain had been orderly, a broad mass of soldiers trotting ahead in trim military formation, closing ranks automatically as the Confederate gunners took their toll. The charge up the ridge was complete disorder. The men went up in groups, one regiment here and another there, the flag always at the front, and there was nothing resembling a regular battle line — on a slope so steep and broken, there could not be a formal line. A number of little roads like the one Sheridan found led up to the crest, and many of the regiments followed these. Others threaded their way up shallow ravines that furrowed the slope, taking advantage of the protection the hollow ground offered. In one way or another, most of the little columns found a good deal of shelter; actually, their heaviest losses came earlier, down on the open ground, and although it took a brave man to make this ascent the going was not quite as bad as it looked.

The general lack of order seems to have worried Grant a little, just at first. Quartermaster General Montgomery Meigs was standing beside him, and as the long climb began he said Grant told him this was not quite what he had ordered. As Meigs remembered it, Grant said that "he meant to form the lines and then prepare and launch columns of assault, but as the men, carried away by their enthusiasm, had gone so far, he would not order them back." Granger's chief of staff said that Grant asked Thomas who had ordered this charge, and when Thomas replied that he had not Grant muttered that somebody would catch it if the charge failed; after which he clamped his jaw on his cigar and watched in silence. It became clear, at last, that this incredible attack was going to succeed, whereupon Cousin Smith got his horse and rode hastily back to headquarters: he wanted to follow the generals to the crest, once the crest had been won, and thought it would be advisable to refill his pocket flask, because he would have to ride across an open mile all littered with wounded men and as a civilian who was not used to looking at such people he felt that he ought to fortify himself. On top of the ridge Confederate Hardee saw the tide coming in and sent word over to Cleburne to bring all the men he could spare to the center because the Yankees were pressing hard — Grant's notion that an attack here would weaken the Confederate line in front of Sherman was not too far off, after all. Cleburne took two brigades and came down the ridge, but before he could get to the center the Confederate line had been hopelessly broken and he could do no more than draw a line across the ridge, facing south, to keep the Federals from driving north to destroy his own command.[22]

Astoundingly, and against the odds, the charge was a swinging success. Grant had given himself two chances and one of them had worked; the impregnable line had collapsed when Pap Thomas swung his hammer and the Confederates had lost the battle, the mountain barrier to the Deep South and all chance of recovering Tennessee. Scribbling his story of the fight, General Meigs summed it up with breathless enthusiasm: "Invasion of Tennessee and Kentucky indefinitely postponed. The slave aristocracy broken down. The grandest stroke yet struck for our country . . . It is unexampled — another laurel leaf is added to Grant's crown." Both victors and defeated were amazed by what had been done, and it is clear that even though the assault had not been the spontaneous, grass-roots explosion that it soon became in legend, something remarkable had happened when the officers told the men to go up the steep mountainside. Dana assured Secretary Stanton that "the storming of the ridge by our troops was one of the greatest miracles in military history," and the soldiers themselves felt the same way. On the crest of the captured ridge, Union soldiers yelled and straddled the captured cannon, "completely and frantically drunk with excitement," hardly able to believe that they had done what they had done. Long afterward, one of them wrote: "The plain unvarnished facts of the storming of Mission Ridge are more like romance to me now than any I have ever read in Dumas,

Scott or Cooper." Dana expressed the simple truth when he said that "No man who climbs the ascent by any of the roads that wind along its front can believe that men were moved up its broken and crumbling face unless it was his fortune to witness the deed."

That evening a worker for the Christian Commission, visiting a field hospital, asked a wounded Federal where he had been hurt. "Almost up," replied the soldier. The Commission man explained that he meant "in what part are you injured?" The soldier, still gripped by the transcendent excitement of the charge, insisted: "Almost up to the top." Then the civilian drew back the wounded man's blanket and saw a frightful, shattering wound. The soldier glanced at it and said: "Yes, that's what did it. I was almost up. But for that I would have reached the top." He looked up at the civilian, repeated faintly, "Almost up," and died.[23]

CHAPTER FIVE

The Enemy Have Not Got Army Enough

BRAXTON BRAGG never quite understood what happened on Missionary Ridge. When the beaten fragments of half of his army went spilling down the far slope in the smoky twilight of November 25, the Confederate commander could do no more than try to save as much as possible from the wreckage. His actual battle losses in killed and wounded had been comparatively light — 2,500 men, or thereabouts, in three days of fighting — but more than 4,000 Confederates had been taken prisoner, the Federals had captured three dozen pieces of artillery, and a huge amount of stores had to be abandoned when the advance base at Chickamauga Station was given up. Only a stout defense by Cleburne, who held the area around Tunnel Hill all night and then fought a series of stubborn rear-guard actions while the rest of the army stumbled southeast to Dalton, Georgia, kept the disaster from being total. When he wrote his report of the battle Bragg found himself unable to account for the defeat.

Apparently the brief halt made by Thomas's men at the rifle pits at the foot of the ridge had persuaded Bragg that the whole assault had been repulsed, and he said that he was riding along the crest, congratulating everybody on the success of the defense, when he discovered that his line on top of the ridge had been broken, infantry running away, guns abandoned, everything in confusion. "A panic which I had never before witnessed seemed to have seized upon officers and men," he wrote, "and each seemed to be struggling for his personal safety, regardless of his duty or his character." He felt that there was no good excuse for this collapse: "The position was one which ought to have been held by a line of skirmishers against any assault column," and the Federals who reached the crest were so exhausted by their hard climb that "the slightest effort would have destroyed them." But that effort had not been made. Instead, the men had run away, and Bragg could think of only one explanation: "They had for two days confronted the enemy, marshalling his immense forces in plain view, and exhibiting to their sight such a superiority in numbers as may have intimidated weak-minded and untried soldiers." Yet this explanation did not quite satisfy him, because his men were neither weak nor untried; on the contrary they were veterans "who had never before failed in any duty assigned them, however difficult and hazardous," and when the Federal advance began "not a doubt crossed my mind." Unable to explain it, Bragg took the only course open to him and sent in his resignation, which the authorities at Richmond promptly accepted.[1]

A correspondent for the Richmond *Dispatch* told his readers that Chattanooga had been "the most ignominious defeat of the whole war," and said that "for the first time during our struggle for national independence our defeat is chargeable to the troops themselves and not to the blunders or incompetency of their leaders." One of the soldiers wrote to a girl friend that he was "very much mortified" by what had happened, because the troops "ignominiously left a field which could have been theirs had they but nerved their hearts to take it." He admitted that the Yankees had attacked "in the most gallant style," but said the Confederate position was so strong "it would have been but child's play" to hold it. He could only add: "Instead of this, they fled panic-stricken before the enemy." [2]

The panic was real enough, but it did not last long. Grant made a quick pursuit, following his defeated foe with vigor, and the next day at Chickamauga Station there was an odd reversal of the traditional Civil War picture — hungry Federals were rejoicing in the abundance of foodstuffs seized in a captured Confederate base, and they lugged sides of bacon and sacks of cornmeal as they continued their march.[3] But at Taylor's Ridge a little distance short of Dalton, Hooker met a bruising repulse when he tried to sweep Cleburne's tough division out of the way, and Grant called a halt. He explained this in his report of the battle:

"Had it not been for the imperative necessity of relieving Burnside, I would have pursued the broken and demoralized retreating enemy as long as supplies could have been found in the country. But my advices were that Burnside's supplies would only last until the 3rd of December. It was already getting late to afford the necessary relief. I determined therefore to pursue no farther." Less formally, he described the situation in a letter to his Illinois friend, Russell Jones:

"An army never was whipped as badly as Bragg was. So far as any opposition the enemy could make, I could have marched to Atlanta or any other place in the Confederacy. But I was obliged to rescue Burnside. Again, I had not rations to take nor the means of taking them, and this mountain country will not support an army. Altogether I feel well satisfied, and the army feel that they have accomplished great things. Well they may."

In a letter to Julia, Grant allowed himself a brief moment of exultation. He told her that the fighting was over, and went on to say: "I went with the advance, in pursuit over twenty miles. Every mudhole for that distance showed evidence of the utter rout and demoralization of the enemy. Wagons and caissons would be found stuck in the mud and abandoned in the haste of the enemy to get away. Small arms were found everywhere strewn. We have now forty-two pieces of artillery taken from the enemy and over six thousand stand of small arms, and no doubt many more will be found. The number of prisoners taken is about seven thousand." [4]

Substantial though the victory was, the importance of rescuing Burnside was impressed upon Grant in the messages he got from Washington. During the height of the action on November 25 Grant received a telegram from President Lincoln: "YOUR DISPATCHES AS TO FIGHTING ON MONDAY AND TUESDAY ARE HERE. WELL DONE. MANY THANKS TO ALL. REMEMBER BURNSIDE." A short time later Halleck sent a similar dispatch: "I CONGRATULATE YOU ON THE SUCCESS THUS FAR OF YOUR PLANS. I FEAR GENERAL BURNSIDE IS HARD PRESSED AND THAT ANY FURTHER DELAY MAY PROVE FATAL. I KNOW THAT YOU WILL DO ALL IN YOUR POWER TO RELIEVE HIM." [5]

Before the fighting stopped on the evening of November 25, Grant notified Thomas that he must send Gordon Granger and 20,000 men to Knoxville as soon as such an expedition could be organized. Shortly after that he ordered Sherman to advance along the railroad as far as the Hiawasse River, a short distance north of the railroad junction town of Cleveland; here Sherman could act as flank guard for Granger, who was to follow the Tennessee River, and could prevent any further dispatch of troops from Bragg's army at Dalton. But it seemed to Grant that Granger was slow in getting started, and on November

29 he informed Halleck that he had ordered Sherman to assume command of Granger's corps in addition to his own force and to take everybody to Knoxville as quickly as possible. He did this, he said, "knowing Sherman's promptness and ability," and he believed that if Burnside could hold out just a little longer he would be relieved and Longstreet would be driven away.

To Sherman, Grant used language blunter than he had used in his telegram to Halleck: "Granger is on his way to Burnside's relief, but I have lost all faith in his energy and capacity to manage an expedition of the importance of this one." Dana told Stanton that "Grant is very angry with Granger for misconduct in the Chattanooga battle," and Dana believed that this was because of the excitable way Granger had behaved on Orchard Knob during the hour or so just before the final assault.[6] It seems probable, however, that Grant's real complaint was something that happened that night, after Bragg's line had been broken.

Sheridan that evening led his men down the far side of Missionary Ridge and then swung to his left, trying to get over to the railroad at or below Chickamauga Station. Plowing his way through the debris of Bragg's beaten army in the autumn moonlight, Sheridan found that Cleburne and the men who had defended the Confederate right so stoutly had not yet retreated; if the Federals could seize Chickamauga Station and the railroad that night Cleburne would be cut off, and the one part of this Confederate army that had not been routed could be destroyed. It would take more than Sheridan's single division to do this, however, and toward midnight Sheridan galloped back to Missionary Ridge to get help.

Grant and Thomas had returned to Chattanooga, Granger was the ranking officer present, and Granger had gone to bed. Sheridan roused him, but the man refused to budge; Sheridan quoted him as "saying he thought we had done well enough." Sheridan insisted, Granger at last told him to keep moving and promised to support him if he met real opposition, and Sheridan returned to his division. Sometime after midnight he got within half a mile of Chickamauga Station, at which point, even though he had not yet run into Cleburne's troops, he felt that he must halt unless he got reinforcements. To make Granger believe that he had met the kind of opposition Granger had been talking about, Sheridan lined his men up along a deserted creek and ordered them to fire heavy volleys into the empty woodland on the far side.

This weird sham battle in the moon-streaked darkness between midnight and dawn made a fine racket but accomplished nothing, Granger sent no help, and Sheridan had to bivouac where he was. By daylight Cleburne got his men away, and a few hours later Grant came up, heard Sheridan's story, and (according to Sheridan) realized that a bright chance had been missed.

Years later Grant apparently confirmed the story, when he told John Russell Young that the battle of Chattanooga would have wiped out Bragg's army "but for our mistake in not knowing the ground." He went on to explain, in words that can fit nothing except the lost opportunity described by Sheridan:

If I had known the ground as well before the battle as I did after, I think Bragg would have been destroyed. I saw this as soon as the battle was over and was greatly disappointed. Sheridan showed his genius in that battle, and to him I owe the capture of most of the prisoners that were taken. Although commanding a division only, he saw in the crisis of that engagement that it was necessary to advance beyond the point indicated by his orders. He saw what I could not know, on account of my ignorance of the ground, and with the instinct of military genius pushed ahead. If others had followed his example we should have had Bragg's army. The victory satisfied the country, but it might have been more fruitful.[7]

In any case, Bragg did manage to reassemble his army at Dalton, and Sherman's powerful force moved off toward Knoxville, while Grant and Thomas withdrew the rest to Missionary Ridge. In less than a week Burnside was out of danger. Longstreet had applied pressure much less vigorously than had been anticipated — for some reason he had been strangely inert throughout this campaign — and although he had forced Burnside to pull back inside the fortified lines at Knoxville and prepare to stand a siege, Burnside had handled his troops smartly and had suffered little harm. Longstreet finally assaulted the Federal lines on the morning of November 29 and was sharply repulsed; after which, learning that Bragg had been defeated, Longstreet ordered a withdrawal, moving off sixty miles to the northeast. Sherman reached Knoxville on December 4 and found that Burnside's army was safe enough: safe, and actually better fed than Sherman's men were, since Longstreet had never quite shut off Burnside's lines of supply, so that Burnside's troops had not been in real danger of starvation although they had nothing much to live on but cornmeal and bacon. Sherman left Granger and Granger's corps with Burnside to guard against further trouble and brought his own troops back to the vicinity of Chattanooga. The long operation that had begun on October 23, when Grant limped into Thomas's headquarters "wet, dirty and well" had at last come to its end.[8]

When Grant observed that "the result satisfied the country" he put it mildly. In the North there was a chorus of rejoicing, led by the cynical New York *Herald*, which asserted that "Gen. Grant is one of the great soldiers of the age . . . without an equal in the list of generals now alive." The anti-administration New York *World* declared: "General Grant, out of a maze of tactics more wondrous than ever before puzzled the brains of observers afar off, has evolved a victory for our arms the importance of which it is yet impossible to estimate." The victory struck the *World* as especially noteworthy because it was "not coupled with news of a great and terrible slaughter." (This was true enough; Grant's casualties for the three-day fight came to no more than 5,824, probably under ten percent of the total number engaged.) On his return from Knoxville Sherman sent Grant his own word of praise: "We know that it is all nonsense to blame Bragg; it was his army, his men, that broke. Bragg, Hardee or no man could have held his army after our combinations were made." Even Rawlins — heartened perhaps because the end of the campaign meant that he could at last go north to marry his Mary Emma Hurlbut — sent her a jubilant note: "Grant's 'star' is still in the ascendent and will continue to be while it lightens the patriot's path. If there was ever a doubt about the propriety of the removal of General Rosecrans, Grant's great achievements have entirely dispelled it." [9]

Unquestionably the battle had been one of the decisive engagements of the war, and although Sherman was much too lenient in saying that Bragg could not be blamed for losing — Bragg's act in sending three divisions to east Tennessee must rank as one of the principal blunders of the entire conflict — Sherman was correct in his remark that Grant's "combinations" had been extremely effective. Oddly enough, however, in the years since the war the battle of Chattanooga has often been made to look like a victory that Grant won in spite of himself. It has been argued that he sent Thomas against Missionary Ridge under the wholly mistaken impression that Bragg had weakened his center to strengthen his right, and that when the advance was made the soldiers took things into their own hands and made a successful assault that Grant had not meant them to make.

The first thing to note is that these criticisms contradict each other to the point of absurdity. They say, on the one hand, that Grant was entirely wrong in his belief that Bragg had weakened his line on Missionary Ridge; on the other hand, they argue that his soldiers, making an attack he had not dared to order, found that this line was even weaker than the deluded Grant supposed. The upshot, by this argument, is that Thomas's men won a victory by doing something Grant had not ordered, and that Grant would have been entirely wrong if he had ordered it.

It is probably true that Grant and the other officers on Orchard Knob overestimated the extent to which the Confederates sent troops to their extreme right on November 25, and one Northern critic asserted that "not a single Confederate soldier was withdrawn from Thomas's front to Sherman's on this final day of the battle." [10] The fact remains, however, that the Federals did see extensive troop movements on Missionary Ridge that day, all of them seeming to show that heavy reinforcements were going to Cleburne; and if the Federals misinterpreted what they saw they at least came up with the right conclusion — namely, that the Missionary Ridge line had been thinned beyond the point of safety, as Hardee himself confessed the night before. Bragg had seven infantry divisions in this battle, and when the climax came he had only two of them in the place where Thomas struck. [11]

Furthermore, the fact that Thomas attacked Bragg's center did not hinge on this supposed shifting of Confederate troops. It was only the timing of the attack that was affected. Grant's battle plan, as laid out in his orders of the night before, is clear enough: Thomas was to strike the center, including the ridge itself, while Sherman and Hooker assailed the flanks. By the afternoon of November 25 Sherman had run hard aground and Hooker had been delayed, and the troop movements Grant saw from Orchard Knob led him to order Thomas to attack then rather than later; but the hard smash at Missionary Ridge had been in the cards all along, and Grant's only concern when he saw the Army of the Cumberland going on from the rifle pits to storm the crest came from the fact that he had meant for them to pause long enough to organize a more coherent column of assault. He dominated the battlefield from beginning to end, he did just about what he had intended to do before the first shot was fired, and a postwar comment of Sherman's is largely justified: "It was a great victory — the neatest and cleanest battle I was ever in — and Grant deserves the credit of it all." [12]

Characteristically, Grant saw the victory at Chattanooga, not as a finished achievement to be savored at leisure but as the beginning of a new chapter in the grand strategy of the war. He had learned something since the time of Shiloh, when he held his army in camp, let his beaten antagonist get away without pursuit, and waited for his superiors to formulate a new campaign. This battle of Chattanooga had barely ended before Grant's mind was ranging far afield, devising a new way to strike the enemy. On November 29 — the day he told Sherman to take change of the Burnside relief expedition — he described his ideas to Dana, who at his request got off a report to Secretary Stanton.

Grant believed, said Dana, that an immediate advance toward Atlanta was out of the question, since it would be necessary before making such a move to accumulate at least six months' supplies for men and animals in Chattanooga. At the same time, simply to hold Chattanooga while these supplies were being brought forward would take only part of the army, "and instead of holding the remainder in winter quarters he proposes to employ them in an offensive campaign against Mobile and the interior of Alabama."

This return to the Mobile plan marked a new step in Grant's development as a soldier. During the summer he had argued for this move but he had never really pushed it; it was as if he had had to give his mind time to make itself up. Now he saw this plan as the completely logical sequel to victory in Tennessee. He had at last reached the point where he could see that final triumph for the Union depended on crowding a beaten foe without respite, permitting no breathing spell in which the weaker antagonist could regain his balance and repair damages — using the superior power of the North, in short, to apply unrelenting pressure of a sort the Confederacy had not the resources to resist.

Dana set forth Grant's argument for a Mobile campaign in these words:

For this purpose he thinks not more than 35,000 men will be necessary, which number he will draw from the armies of Sherman and Thomas. Embarking at Nashville, as if to return to west Tennessee and Vicksburg, he can land them all at New Orleans and probably at Pascagoula Bay before the enemy get wind of his design. Investing Mobile, he will leave a sufficient force to hold his lines and keep the garrison imprisoned without any unnecessary fighting, while with the mass of his army he operates in the interior against Montgomery, Selma or whatsoever point invites attention. He has asked me to lay this plan before you and to ask for the approbation of the Government. He will himself write to General Halleck on the subject and perhaps also to yourself. I earnestly hope that you will agree to his design, and as soon as may be give your assent to its execution. A winter campaign may be made there with little if any difficulty.[13]

Thinking thus, Grant was considering the Confederacy as a whole, and not just the force that lay in his own front. A hard blow in the Deep South would inevitably affect what Lee did in Virginia, and while Sherman was still on the march toward Knoxville Grant was toying with the idea of doing something at once, before the Mobile plan even got under way, to break Confederate communications between Virginia and the far interior. To Sherman he sent a letter suggesting that once east Tennessee had been cleared of the enemy Sherman start a cavalry expedition southeast, "to strike through into South Carolina to destroy their east and west roads." This would be a raid pure and simple, like the one General Grierson had made in Mississippi in the preceding spring — the raid that had been so helpful in the campaign against Vicksburg. The men would take no transportation, living entirely on the country, damaging the roads as much as possible, burning Confederate supply depots and taking all of the good horses they found. They need not return to Tennessee; if they reached the Federal lines anywhere along the Carolina coast all would be well. Grant did not think more than 1,200 or 1,500 cavalrymen need make the trip, because "they do not go to fight but to avoid fighting if possible."

To command such an expedition, Grant suggested either General George Crook, who then commanded a cavalry division in Thomas's army, or the energetic young officer on his own staff, James Harrison Wilson, for whom Grant had recently obtained a brigadier general's commission. He made it clear that at this point he was simply thinking out loud: "I do not insist upon this expedition, but if you deem it at all practicable, start it." [14]

In the end the expedition was not sent, various developments making it seem inadvisable; but Grant's suggestion shows how his mind was working just then, and in his general concept of the move — "they do not go to fight but to avoid fighting" there is at least a suggestion of the notion that eventually governed Sherman's final march to the sea.

As Dana had said he would do, Grant wrote to Halleck about the Mobile plan. In a letter dated December 7, Grant explained that an extensive campaign from Chattanooga toward Atlanta was out of the question for the present; the land was mountainous, roads were bad in winter, the country would provide little support for an invading army, and the supplies and transportation now available in Chattanooga were woefully inadequate. He would like to hold the line, therefore, with a small force, repairing the railroads so that a proper backlog of food, animals and wagons could be got together. Then — Mobile.

"With the force thus relieved, and what can be gathered from other parts of this military division," he wrote, "I propose, with the concurrence of higher authority, to move by way of New Orleans and Pascagoula on Mobile. I would hope to secure that place or its investment by the last of January. Should the enemy make an obstinate resistance at Mobile I would fortify outside and leave a garrison sufficient to hold the garrison of the town, and with the balance of the army make a campaign into the interior of Alabama and possibly Georgia. The campaign, of course, would be suggested by the movements of the enemy. It seems to me this move would secure the entire states of Alabama and Mississippi and a part of Georgia, or force Lee to abandon Virginia and North Carolina. Without this course the enemy have not got army enough to resist the army I can take." [15]

It was time, in short, to get away from the old idea of the war in the west as something separate and to make it part of an overall design. The kind of campaign Grant was proposing was in fact to be a blow at Lee and at the stability of the Richmond government itself. It rested on the belief that the Federal government had the strength to win the war if it just applied it, so that a blow struck along the Gulf Coast could and should have an immediate and ruinous impact on the Confederacy's war in Virginia. Technically, of course, Grant as western area commander had no concern with what happened in the east, but as a strategist he had to think about it. He had put his finger on the most important single factor in the whole situation: "The enemy have not got army enough." From Chattanooga to Appomattox, this was the chief point in Grant's strategic planning.

Grant was maturing. The old army men often said that Sam Grant was a nice chap but that he was too easygoing and friendly to make a good general; but his orders now reflect a toughness the old army friends had not recognized. Shortly before Burnside was rescued, the excellent Major General Orlando B. Willcox, commanding a segment of Burnside's troops at Cumberland Gap, sent a desperate appeal to Halleck: he was all alone and all beset, and would somebody please tell him "whether I shall run the risk of sacrificing all my cavalry in a demonstration below Clinch river in an attempt to aid Burnside? If so, I am ready." Halleck sent the message to Grant, who was unmoved by the do-or-die dramatics and gave Willcox a stiff answer:

If you had shown half the willingness to sacrifice yourself and command at the start you do in your dispatch you might have rendered Burnside material aid. Now, I judge, you have got so far to the rear you can do nothing for him. Act upon the instructions you have and your own discretion, and if you can do anything to relieve Burnside, do it. It is not expected that you will sacrifice your command but that you will take proper risks.[16]

He was equally caustic when Governor Thomas E. Bramlette of Kentucky wrote that the good people of Paducah were disturbed because Grant had ordered the rails removed from the Paducah railroad in order to repair the Nashville & Chattanooga; this would cause them severe financial loss, and could not the general find the rails somewhere else? Grant remembered the people of Paducah from of old. He had seized the town early in the fall of 1861, as the first step in what quickly became the Federal occupation of Kentucky, he recalled that the town was all bedecked with Confederate flags when he got there, and three days after the breakthrough on Missionary Ridge he sent Governor Bramlette this note:

My experience satisfies me that the citizens of Paducah, almost to a man, are disloyal and entitled to no favors from the government. The President of the road, and no doubt nine-tenths of the Paducah stockholders, are disloyal men. The road never was completed by them, but if I am not mistaken some 8 or 10 miles was built by the government to connect it up with the Ohio and Mobile road. I will, however, suspend taking up the track, except the portion laid by the government, until the matter can be referred to higher authority.[17]

Getting full railroad service into Chattanooga was of first importance, and Grant became impatient with the long delay in making the line serviceable. Early in November he had told J. B. Anderson, the civilian superintendent of construction, to contract with as many outside parties as he could for the construction of prefabricated bridges. Nearly three weeks later Anderson wrote that he had been able to find only one man who would do the work; he named him, and asked Grant if it would be all right to sign a contract with him. Grant immediately replied that a great deal of valuable time had been lost, that he supposed the contractor was a proper person to do the work, "but in the meantime I want trestles built and the road running." A three-week delay in signing the contract impressed him as all wrong, he carried his complaint to General Meigs, and before long he got action: on December 19 Colonel D. C. McCallum, the War Department's hard-driving Superintendent of Military Railroads, was ordered west to take charge. McCallum brought an expert military engineer and a corps of three hundred construction men, Anderson was eventually shelved, and by the first of 1864 all hands were hard at work.

They found things in a bad state. The Nashville & Chattanooga, one officer reported, was "a rickety, stringer-tie, dilapidated affair, never worth much before the rebellion" and badly used up by wartime demands. It did not have nearly enough locomotives or cars, only half of the ones it had could be used, and all in all "the whole line of the road was a vast cemetery of rolling stock." McCallum found the railroad organization "decidedly defective" and said there was "a lack of well-directed energy and seeming want of ability to comprehend the magnitude of the undertaking." McCallum and his men got results, and by January 14 service was open all the way to Chattanooga — at which moment, for the first time since the battle of Chickamauga, the Army of the Cumberland was able to go off half-rations and get the full allowance. Locomotives and cars were brought in from everywhere, and a vast construction job was begun at Nashville; one warehouse more than a quarter of a mile long was built, a "broad shed" measuring 600 by 190 feet was erected, and a third building, almost equally large, was put up for various subsistence stores. Grant insisted that Nashville must by spring contain six months' supplies for the army operating out of Chattanooga; this meant, among other things, that fully 54,000 tons of hay and grain for animals had to be accumulated.[18]

While this was going on, Grant began to realize that when he contemplated Mobile and the road northeast through Alabama he had to begin by looking at east Tennessee. Longstreet and his army were preparing to pass the winter in the general vicinity of the town of Greeneville, and although they were not doing any especial harm to anyone their mere presence there was a problem the Federal commander could not ignore. Grant told Halleck that he himself would shortly move his headquarters to Nashville, and "if there is still a chance of doing anything against Longstreet" he would go to Knoxville to get it done. He wanted the Confederates driven out of the state, he confessed, so that he could have strategic freedom of action; he wanted "to be able to select my own campaign in the spring instead of having the enemy dictate it for me."

The authorities in Washington felt the same way. Dana went to the capital early in December, and on December 21 he wrote to Grant saying that he had discussed Grant's plans with President Lincoln, with Secretary Stanton and with General Halleck. They approved of the Alabama campaign, he said, and Grant would be told to go ahead with it "but for the anxiety which seems to exist regarding East Tennessee. If Longstreet were expelled from that country you could start for Mobile at once."

Dana gave the authorities a suggestion Grant had apparently discussed with him — that the best way to get Longstreet out of Tennessee would be to have General Meade and the Army of the Potomac take the offensive against General Lee. The response, Dana told Grant, was that this might well be so but that "from that army nothing is to be hoped under its present commander." This, he said, led him to advance another idea that had been discussed by Grant and his staff: give either Sherman or Baldy Smith command of the Army of the Potomac. Dana believed that this proposal was well received, but he pointed out that nothing had been settled; Grant must remember that both Stanton and Halleck had grave doubts about Smith, whom they considered contentious, erratic and hard to handle. They would probably promote him, as Grant had asked, but they were not sure that he ought to have Meade's job.

Once again, Grant had reached out beyond his own province, although he had done so informally, indirectly and in a most tentative way. The identity of the commander of the Army of the Potomac was not, strictly speaking, any of his business; yet when he laid out his own strategic plans he found that it was his business, after all; what that army did affected what his own armies could do. To be sure, when the final power to name or remove commanders was given to him, Grant retained Meade. But it was this winter inevitable for him to think about the possibility of change simply because he could not discharge his own responsibilities without thinking about it.

Halleck wrote to Grant on the same day Dana wrote. He was brief enough, and he said nothing about any change in command; but he hinted, ominously enough, that there might have to be a change in plan. The Alabama venture, he said, was approved, provided the whole state of Tennessee was first cleared of the enemy and protected against any possibility of reinvasion. But there was a possible complication: "Circumstances may be such by the time that your spare forces reach Port Hudson or New Orleans as to require their services west of the Mississippi; if so, the latter part of the plan" — the heart of it, that is: the part involving the capture of Mobile and the march to the interior — "would be somewhat varied or its execution delayed." [19]

Whatever might happen west of the Mississippi, the east Tennessee problem obviously came first, and at the end of December Grant did what he always liked to do in such cases — he went to the scene to study things for himself. It did not take him long to see that a speedy offensive against Longstreet looked very different in Knoxville than it looked in Washington, or for that matter in Nashville.

It looked different because when it was examined at close range it was clearly impossible. To begin with, there was a command problem. Burnside fell ill and resigned. He was replaced by General John G. Foster, and Foster could not take the field because his horse fell on him and opened a wound Foster had received in the Mexican War. Growing slightly desperate, Grant told Thomas to get ready to go to Knoxville and take charge, but before this could be done Grant had to admit that the shortage of supplies was a crippling handicap no matter who was running things. (Once the troops got away from the river or the railroad, they could not eat. Lack of animals immobilized the artillery and the wagon trains, and because rations, shoes, blankets and tents were short not more than sixty percent of the infantry could take the road.) Grant had Foster replaced by General John M. Schofield, who had been in command at St. Louis, but this did not help. Schofield was young, active and full of energy, but he had to confess that it would be two months before he could do anything at all. Confederate Longstreet had been able to do no more than keep his own army alive, but just because he was in east Tennessee, Longstreet exercised a veto power.[20]

A subtler and more enduring handicap was imposed by Washington.

What Grant really wanted all along was to prosecute the Alabama plan, and his only reason for wanting Longstreet driven out of Tennessee was to clear the way for the campaign against Mobile and the interior. Now, however, Halleck sharpened his earlier warning: the Alabama idea was all very well, but it was less important than Texas. General Banks was still trying to reestablish the Federal power in that state. Halleck admitted that this campaign "was undertaken less for military reasons than as a matter of state policy," but regardless of that it had been undertaken and it had top priority; the President had decided on it, what the President said was final, and Halleck reminded Grant that "it may have an important influence on your projected operations during the coming winter."

In Arkansas the Federals had a small army under General Frederick Steele, and Halleck told Grant that Steele now was under his command. This represented a new responsibility, however, rather than an asset, because Grant would have to use Steele — reinforced probably by some of Sherman's troops — to help General Banks win a success in Texas. Banks had established garrisons at the mouth of the Rio Grande and on Matagorda Island near Corpus Christi, but by themselves these amounted to little. Banks now was planning to go up the Red River valley in Louisiana and strike at the interior of Texas, and Halleck outlined the problem to Grant in a letter dated January 8:

"Keeping in mind the fact that General Banks' operations in Texas, either on the Gulf Coast or by the Louisiana frontier, must be continued during the winter, it is to be considered whether it will not be better to direct our efforts, for the present, to the entire breaking up of the Rebel forces west of the Mississippi River rather than to divide them by also operating against Mobile and Alabama." Banks was too weak to continue his campaign without Steele, and Steele was too weak to go down from Arkansas without Sherman; consequently, "it is worth considering whether such forces as Sherman can move down the Mississippi river should not co-operate with the forces of Steele and Banks on the west side." [21]

Grant stuck to his guns. Far from looking toward the trans-Mississippi, he was more and more looking toward the east, and on January 19 he wrote to Thomas, insisting that in the next campaign the line for his army to follow ought to be the line between Chattanooga and Mobile, with Atlanta and Montgomery as the important intermediary points. He had said this, he went on, in a letter to Halleck, and he was about to write another letter to Halleck "giving him my views of the cooperation we should have from the eastern armies." He outlined these views for Thomas:

"I shall recommend that no attempt be made toward Richmond by any of the routes heretofore operated on, but that a moving force of 60,000 men be thrown into New Berne or Suffolk (favoring the latter place) and move out, destroying the road as far toward Richmond as possible; then move to Raleigh as rapidly as possible; hold that point, and open communication with New Berne — even Wilmington. From Raleigh the enemy's most inland line would be so threatened as to force them to keep on it a guard that would reduce their armies in the field much below our own." To Halleck, at the same time, Grant wrote asking whether "an abandonment of all previously attempted lines to Richmond is not advisable, and in lieu of these one be taken farther south." To base the major Federal effort in the east at Hampton Roads and then to strike for Raleigh and Wilmington would "virtually force an evacuation of Virginia and indirectly of East Tennessee" and would compel the Confederates to abandon "campaigns of their own choosing, and for which they are prepared," and undertake new lines of operations which the Confederate authorities had "never expected to become necessary." [22]

As long as Washington insisted on dealing first with the far-off Confederate armies in the trans-Mississippi area, of course, all of this was daydreaming. About the time Grant wrote to Thomas and Halleck, Baldy Smith and Wilson wrote to Dana, urging him to persuade Stanton to support Grant's strategy. Smith told Dana that if Grant had to use Steele in Banks's Red River campaign, the operation against

Atlanta would have to be postponed; and "we look on Atlanta as the head of the rebellion now and when we get that we think the war as a war of battles will be over as the force west of the Miss is entirely cut off and can never be reinforced. When the army that covers Atlanta is beaten the Trans Miss force falls without a battle." Wilson said bluntly that "to go west of the river is to travel in the wrong direction" and urged: "Let's crush the head and heart of the rebellion, and the tail can then be ground to dust or allowed to die when the sun goes down." [23]

Grant's thinking on strategy was taking on a dimension neither Smith nor Wilson grasped. He was beginning to suspect that the trans-Mississippi and the war in Virginia were somewhat alike: they were less vital than they seemed to be. He wanted to turn the war upside down. The Confederacy's only chance to win was to make war on a continental basis, and if the Federals seized Atlanta and held the interior of North Carolina the Confederacy could not fight that way. Maybe all of the "forward to Richmond" offensives meant less than they seemed to mean. Richmond would die on the vine, and the spangled dream of a Southern empire would die with it, if the Federal armies got at the heartland. The war was not going to be won in Virginia any more than it was going to be won along the Louisiana-Texas border. It would be won, eventually, somewhere south and west of Richmond, and Grant wanted to get on with it.

There is in all of this a curious reversal of what always seemed to be basic in Grant's military thinking — the idea that the only important objectives were the enemy's armies in the field, and that the way to win the war was to strike them hard and forget about the mere occupation of territory. Grant was thinking now, obviously, about the advantage that would be gained by the seizure of Atlanta and central Georgia, and Smith probably expressed his thought when he said that if this could be done "the war as a war of battles" would be over. To go on from there and think of a more effective move for the Army of the Potomac was wholly logical. Perhaps the war had entered a new phase; perhaps, at last, it was time to think about positional warfare.

However he may have reached this idea, in advancing it Grant of course was stepping even farther out of his own sphere than he had done when he suggested to Dana that maybe a new man ought to command the eastern army. Now, however, he was doing it on request. Halleck had asked him to present his views on grand strategy, and Halleck had done this simply because Grant's sphere was about to broaden enormously. The tip-off comes in an editorial which the New York *Herald* printed on December 9: "It is proposed in Congress to revive the office of Lieutenant General. It is stated that the rank is to be revived that it may be conferred on General Grant, in the hope no doubt that such a high military position will switch him off the Presidential track . . . If the politicians think they are going to beat General Grant, General McClellan or any other general out of the Presidency by any humbug of this sort they will find themselves woefully mistaken." [24]

Like all cynics, James Gordon Bennett, the proprietor of the *Herald,* had seen the truth but was unable to say what it really meant. The industrious Illinois Congressman, Elihu Washburne, had introduced a bill to revive the rank of lieutenant general, and everybody in Washington from Abraham Lincoln down to the dullest member of Congress knew that this bill was going to be passed and that when it did pass the new commission would go to Grant; which meant that before long Grant would outrank every soldier in the army and would be in charge of the whole Federal military effort. This was going to happen, not because designing politicians wanted to keep Grant from running for the presidency, but because he was clearly the best soldier the North had. Halleck was unquestionably acting for the administration when he tried to get a line on Grant's overall planning.

On December 12 Grant sent a letter to Washburne, obviously in response to what Washburne was trying to do:

I feel under many obligations to you for the interest you have taken in my welfare. But recollect that I have been highly honored already by the government and do not ask or feel that I deserve anything more in the shape of honors or promotion. A success over the enemy is what I crave above everything else, and desire to hold such an influence over those under my command as to enable me to use them to the best advantage to secure this end.[25]

CHAPTER SIX

The High Place

JAMES F. RUSLING was a colonel on the Quartermaster General's staff, and he reached Nashville in January just after Grant got back from Knoxville. Rusling was fresh from the Army of the Potomac, where the military life was formal and commanding generals, however they might act, at least looked like generals; and he confessed that his first glimpse of Grant was "a decided disappointment." The man seemed wholly unmilitary, not to say slouchy, and he went stumping about headquarters in an unbuttoned coat and a battered hat, head down, hands in pockets, looking "for all the world like a country storekeeper or a western farmer." Grant at the moment was worn down by hard service. He weighed no more than a hundred and thirty-five pounds and he was weather-beaten both in his person and in his clothing; the return from Knoxville had been a rough trip because Grant came back by way of Cumberland Gap, Big Hill, Richmond and Lexington to see for himself whether travel by these atrocious roads was as hard as the supply services said it was. (He found out that it was: much of the time he and his staff had to wade through deep snow, leading their half-frozen horses, with icicles in the commanding general's beard.) He was not, in short, much to look at just now, and Rusling felt that he was "evidently intent on everything but show."

Before long, however, Colonel Rusling found that in his own way Grant was impressive: "As you caught his eye you found it clear and penetrating, and saw that it could be hard as flint as well as soft as dew," and there seemed to be a look in his face and a set to his jaw that said he could "dare great things, and hold on mightily, and toil terribly" when the proper time came. Grant (Rusling went on) did not have much to say, but "he knew exactly *what* he wanted, and *why*, and when he *wanted* it," and he never had any trouble making himself

[104]

understood. Rusling found that Grant disliked long letters and wordy reports, but noted that he had a telegraph in his office and that he spent much time talking, by wire, with all parts of his big military division, so that "every night he knew precisely where the enemy was, and what he was doing, and what we were able to do and dare." It developed, as well, that Grant knew how to make up his mind. Rusling recalled how a Quartermaster officer went to Grant that winter with a report involving the spending of some millions of dollars on one phase of the approaching campaign. Grant glanced at the report, approved it, and told the officer to go ahead with it. Suspecting that Grant was making a snap judgment the quartermaster pointed out that the action would cost a great deal of money, and asked bluntly whether Grant was sure he was right. Grant's reply was equally blunt.

"No, I am not," he said, "but in war anything is better than indecision. *We must decide*. If I am wrong we shall soon find it out and can do the other thing. But *not to decide* wastes both time and money and may ruin everything." [1]

Rusling of course wrote about all of this long after the war, when it was easy to see that the unassuming man at Nashville headquarters was someone special; but in the winter of 1864 Grant was drawing everybody's attention because if what he was might be hard to decipher what he had done spoke for itself. Chattanooga and Vicksburg added up to something bigger than any Northern general had yet accomplished, and Grant was beginning to see that he might soon be in politics as well as in the army. Sherman saw it coming, and just before the first of the year he wrote to Grant begging him to "preserve a plain military character." What Grant had done, said Sherman, gave him a reputation as a soldier "far above that of any man living," and he warned him that "partisans will maneuver for your influence."

The partisans had already begun. Two weeks earlier the antiadministration New York *World* had expressed studied concern over Grant's health. The *World* had been informed that he was in poor shape and that "his friends are apprehensive for his life"; his death, said the *World* (which saw no reason for identifying Lincoln's generals with Lincoln's administration), "would at this time be the gravest disaster that could befall the Union cause," because his victories not only made him "a terror to the enemy" but put him in a position "to compel the administration to obey him rather than he them." Bennett's New York *Herald* went farther, and called on the plain people of the country to confound the politicians of both parties by making Grant the next President. The *Herald* believed that this could be done easily; it praised Grant's military ability and his extreme modesty, and it made an asset of something that, rationally thought of, might be considered a grave liability — the fact that "his opinions on parties and party questions" were completely unknown. "Let the independent masses of the people," cried the *Herald*, "who have cut themselves loose from the machinery of the corrupt and dismantled political parties of the day, take this Presidential business into their own hands and bring General Grant at once into the field. A few town and country meetings, as in the case of General Jackson, will put the ball in motion; and once fairly in motion it cannot be arrested."

A few days later the *Herald* enlarged upon this idea. The next President must be a military man, it said; the country had had quite enough of a civilian commander in chief, and anyway Lincoln was bound hand and foot by the Republican leaders and shifted his position so often that nobody quite knew where he stood. It was in Grant's favor that "he knows more of tanning than of politics," and the *Herald* felt that precisely because of this he would, as President, be free to pick the best men regardless of politics. Having thus adopted the nation's hoariest political fallacy, the *Herald* added:

General Grant celebrated Independence Day of 1863 by marching into Vicksburg, where he coolly enjoyed his cigar, and on Thanksgiving Day of the same year he coolly gave Bragg a tanning and a thrashing. Perhaps he has something in store for Christmas, and he may give the rebels a call on New Year's Day in Atlanta. On the fourth of March, 1865, he will be in Washington.[2]

James Gordon Bennett, to be sure, was apt to say anything, if only from a restless itch to stir things up; but other men were beginning to feel that Grant was made to order as a presidential candidate — in opposition, of course, to Abraham Lincoln, who would come up for reelection in the fall — and Grant was beginning to hear from them.

Even before the *Herald* started to beat the drum, Grant got a letter from a man named Brown, chairman of the State Central Committee of the Democratic Party in Ohio. Brown pointed out that Ohio had a state Democratic convention coming up early in January, at which "it may be desirable to express the preference of the War Democracy for some Gentleman for the Presidency," and he came quickly to the point: "Your successful military career, your unfaltering devotion to your country in its darkest hours of trial, your indomitable energy in overcoming all obstacles, your consummate skill and dauntless courage on the field of battle, all have combined to call the public mind to you as the man to whom the affairs of this great Nation should be committed at the close of the present incumbent's term of office." Therefore — would not Grant permit Mr. Brown to present his name as a Democratic candidate for the presidency at the next election?[3]

Grant replied on December 17:

Your letter of the 8th inst. asking if you will be at liberty to use my name before that convention of the "War Democracy" as candidate for the office of the Presidency is just received. The question astonishes me. I do not know of anything I have ever done or said which would indicate that I could be a candidate for any office whatever within the gift of the people. I shall continue to do my duty, to the best of my ability, so long as permitted to remain in the army, supporting whatever administration may be in power in their endeavor to suppress the rebellion and maintain National unity, and never desert it because my vote, if I had one, might have been cast for different candidates.

Nothing likely to happen would pain me so much as to see my name used in connection with a political office. I am not a candidate for any office nor for favors from any party. Let us succeed in crushing the rebellion in the shortest possible time, and I will be content with whatever credit may then be given me, feeling assured that a just public will award all that is due.

Although he was flatly refusing to be a candidate, Grant did not want to make any statement on the matter for public consumption, and he warned Brown:

Your letter I take to be private. Mine is also private. I wish to avoid notoriety as far as possible, and above all things desire to be sparred the pain of seeing my name mixed with politics. Do not therefore publish this letter, but wherever and by whatever party you hear my name mentioned in connection with the candidacy for any office say that you know from me direct that I am not "in the field" and cannot allow my name to be used before any convention.

In this refusal to take a public position on the matter Grant was by no means being coy. For all of Bennett's threshing about, the movement to make Grant a presidential nominee had not yet generated any real head of steam, and Grant obviously understood politics well enough to know that the surest way to bring one's candidacy before the public may be to rush into print with denials that such a candidacy exists. Rawlins probably expressed Grant's point of view in a letter he wrote later in the winter to Wilson, who had been transferred to Washington for duty as head of the Bureau of Cavalry. Explaining the refusal to make an open declaration, Rawlins told Wilson: "The nomination for the office has not been tendered him by the people; nor has it by either of the great political parties or any portion thereof, through delegates from the people and duly authorized to do so. To write a letter of declination now would place him much in the position of the old maid who had never had an offer declaring that she 'would not marry'; besides, it would be by many construed into a modest way of getting his name before the country in connection with the office, having as he always has avoided public notice of newspaper talk relating to him. His letter to the Democratic Committee of the State of Ohio he says was written in the strictest confidence and he wishes it still to be so considered." [4]

To Congressman J. N. Morris of Quincy, Illinois, Grant wrote much the sort of letter he had written to Brown. Morris, a determined foe of Lincoln, had tried to sound Grant out about possible political aspirations, and Grant replied as follows:

. . . I am not a politician, never was, and hope never to be, and could not write a political letter. My only desire is to serve the country in her present trials. To do this efficiently it is necessary to have the confidence of the Army and the people. I know no way to better secure this end than by a faithful performance of my duties. So long as I hold my present position I do not believe that I have the right to criticize the policy or orders of those above me, or to give utterance to views of my own except to the authorities at Washington, through the General-in-Chief of the Army. In this respect I know I have proven myself a good soldier.

In your letter you say I have it in my power to be the next President. This is the last thing in the world I desire. I would regard such a consummation as being highly unfortunate for myself, if not for the country. Through Providence I have attained to more than I had ever hoped, and with the position I now hold in the regular Army, if allowed to retain it, will be more than satisfied. I certainly shall never shape a sentiment, or the opening of a thought with the view of being a candidate for office. I scarcely know the inducement that could be held out to me to accept the office, and unhesitatingly say that I infinitely prefer my present position to that of any civil office within the gift of the people. This is a private letter not intended for others to see or read, because I want to avoid being heard from by the public except through acts in the performance of my legitimate duties.[5]

To friends who wrote to him on the subject Grant was equally outspoken. Captain Daniel Ammen of the navy, whom Grant had known since boyhood, was one who asked whether Grant proposed to be a candidate, and Grant replied bluntly: "I have always thought the most slavish life any man could lead was that of a politician. Besides, I do not believe any man can be successful as a soldier whilst he has an anchor ahead for any other advancement. I know of no circumstances likely to arise which could induce me to accept any political office whatever. My only desire will be, as it always has been, to whip out the rebellion in the shortest way possible, and to retain as high a position in the army afterwards as the administration then in power may think me suited for." And to Major General Frank Blair, who had also made inquiry, Grant in February sent these lines:

Your letter of the 16th inst. is but just received. It is on a subject upon which I do not like to write, talk or think. Everybody who knows me knows I have no political aspirations either now or for the future. I hope to remain a soldier as long as I live, to serve faithfully any and every Administration that may be in power, and which may be striving to maintain the integrity of the *whole Union*, as long as I do live.

However far the powers that be may choose to extend my authority I will always endeavor to realize their expectations of me. However much my command may be reduced I will serve with the same fidelity and zeal.

Under no circumstances would I use power for political advancement, nor whilst a soldier take part in politics. If, in the conventions to meet, one candidate should be nominated whos election I would regard as dangerous to the country, I would not hesitate to say so freely however. Further than this I could take no part . . . I hope you will show this letter to no one unless it be the President himself. I hate to see my name associated with politics either as an aspirant for office or as a partizan.[6]

The general's father, irrepressible Jesse Grant, had taken an alert interest in the talk of a presidential candidacy, and he seems to have expressed himself in public on the matter. To him, shortly after he wrote to Frank Blair, Grant sent a curt note:

I am not a candidate for any office. All I want is to be left alone to fight this war out; fight all rebel opposition and restore a happy Union in the shortest possible time. You know, or ought to know, that the public prints are not the proper mediums through which to let a personal feeling pass. I know that I feel that nothing personal to myself could ever induce me to accept a political office. From your letter you seem to have taken an active feeling, to say the least, in this matter, that I would like to talk to you about. I could write, but do not want to do so. Why not come down here and see me?

Another to whom Grant made his attitude clear was roughhewn Rear Admiral David D. Porter, who commanded the navy's squadrons in the Mississippi valley and with whom Grant had developed a good understanding during the Vicksburg campaign. Porter wrote to Assistant Secretary of the Navy Gustavus Fox, in January, describing the situation as he saw it: "Grant could not be kicked into the Presidency, he would not have it at 40,000 per year, he dont like anything but fighting and smoking, and hates politics as the devel does holy water — he dont want even to be a Lieut. General until the war is over. So having no aspirations of a political nature, he should have as big a command as he can manage, and the success of the next year depends on his having all the Mississippi — it is indeed a necessity." [7]

One man who shared in the curiosity about Grant was President Lincoln himself. General Blair and Assistant Secretary Fox may or may not have told him what they knew about Grant's feeling: if they had, the reassurance apparently was not quite good enough, and from long experience with generals who had deep political aspirations — Porter complained that Banks's desire to be President was the real reason for his Red River campaign — the President wanted to know more. He was very well aware that as things then stood, if Grant really wanted anything from the voters he was quite likely to get it: he was about to become general-in-chief, and if he had anything in particular on his mind now was the time to find out. Early in 1864 Lincoln consulted Congressman Washburne.

"About all I know of Grant I have got from you," said Lincoln. "I have never seen him. Who else besides you knows anything about Grant?"

Washburne replied that he himself did not know Grant as well as most people thought he did. The best man to talk to, he suggested, might be the United States Marshal at Chicago, J. Russell Jones, formerly of Galena, an old-time friend who had kept in intimate touch with Grant all through the war. Lincoln accepted Washburne's advice, and off to Jones went a message from the White House: Come to Washington at once, the President wants to see you.[8]

Jones was a man Grant liked and trusted: a good friend, and also a canny investment counselor. After years of grinding poverty, Grant at last was able to save money and put something by for the future. As a major general he had an income of six thousand dollars a year, life in camp cost him no more than a thousand dollars a year even allowing for his one extravagance, the maintenance of a string of good saddle horses, and Julia Grant's living expenses were moderate: as early as the spring of 1862 Grant had written her that his debts would soon be paid and that he could then put aside at least three hundred dollars a month "after supporting both of us." When Julia's cousin William Smith visited Grant at the time of the battle of Chattanooga, Grant told him that he had bought real estate in Missouri, that he had five thousand dollars invested in government bonds, and that he was preparing to buy stock in a Chicago street railway company. A few months after this Grant wrote to Jones in these words:

> I wish to keep what funds I have, collect the interest on the bonds, and retain the gold so collected as a special deposit. I also send herewith $500 more and will continue to send as I can save from my pay. At any time you see any little investment for me with the funds on hand, make it without hesitation. You are also authorized to run me in debt as far as you can borrow on the bonds besides.[9]

Like many another man, Jones in December had watched the New York *Herald*'s attempt to create a presidential boom, and he wrote Grant a friendly note saying that he hoped Grant would pay no attention to the *Herald*'s talk. Grant sent back a plainspoken reply: "I am receiving a great deal of that kind of literature, but it soon finds its way into the waste basket. I already have a pretty big job on my hands, and my only ambition is to see this rebellion suppressed. Nothing could induce me to think of being a presidential candidate, particularly so long as there is a possibility of having Mr. Lincoln re-elected." It happened that this letter landed in Jones's mailbox on the day Jones was leaving Chicago for Washington. He stopped at the post office on his way to the railroad station and read the letter on the train.

In due course Jones got to Washington, and at eight one evening he went to the White House. President Lincoln received him alone in his study, and for a time they talked about the general situation in Chicago; then Jones (sensing, as he said, that the President wanted to talk about Grant) took out the letter from Grant and gave it to Lincoln. Having read it, Lincoln stood up, put his hand on Jones's shoulder, and said: "My son, you will never know how gratifying that is to me. No man knows, when that Presidential grub gets to gnawing at him, just how deep it will get until he has tried it; and I didn't know but what there was one gnawing at Grant." Later, Jones concluded that the incident "established a perfect understanding" between the President and the general.[10]

The only thing that was gnawing at Grant this winter was the urge to get on with the war, and here he was somewhat frustrated. It was becoming clear that the force in east Tennessee could not be expected to take solid offensive action before spring, and with Longstreet where he was a general advance from Chattanooga by Thomas was out of the question. Washington was insisting that Banks's move toward Texas by way of the Red River had first claim on western military resources, and Grant's dream of a combined operation against Mobile and the interior of Alabama was fading out. He clung grimly to his plan to have Sherman strike eastward from Vicksburg to Meridian, Mississippi, and he seems to have hoped that Sherman might be able to go on from there and capture Mobile unaided; but although Sherman moved from Vicksburg on February 3 with 20,000 men and seized Meridian without much opposition his operation was a raid and nothing more. He wrecked the Confederate railroad network in eastern Mississippi, and McPherson reported that the men had destroyed fifty-five miles of track and fifty-three bridges and culverts: in his report on the campaign, Sherman grimly exulted that "Meridian with its depots, store-houses, arsenals, hospitals, offices, hotels and cantonments no longer exists." It remained true, however, that the underlying plan had been frustrated. Sherman had a cavalry corps of 7,000 men under General W. Sooy Smith march down from Memphis to join him in the Meridian area, but Bedford Forrest's Confederates fell upon Smith's force at Okolona, mauled it cruelly, and sent it back to Memphis in disorder, and Sherman finally had to return to Vicksburg.[11] Of the plans Grant had made for the winter's operations, only this part had been carried out, and it had not been worth what it cost. The all-out offensive was going to have to wait until spring.

Meanwhile, Grant kept busy, and in one respect this midwinter period was made pleasant for him. Julia Grant was able to join him at Nashville, late in February, and although Grant spent just about as much time as ever at headquarters, or out inspecting forts and camps, he suddenly became a regular attendant at Sunday services in a little Methodist church that stood near his headquarters. (Rusling piously noted that "his devout example told for righteousness on all our forces in his Military Division.") Except on Sundays, Julia had time on her hands, and she spent a good deal of it visiting the army hospitals — and quickly learned that her husband did not want her to tell him what she saw and heard there. Long after the war she told the novelist, Hamlin Garland, that when she tried to describe her experiences and her conversations with the soldiers Grant told her: "Now my dear I don't want to hear anything at all about that. I don't want you to come to me with any of these tales of hospitals or any of these petitions and messages. I have all I can bear up under outside of my home, and when I come to you I want to see you and the children and talk about other matters. I want to get all the sunshine I can." [12]

As always, the sun shone for Grant when he was with his family, and the extent of the pressure the Tennessee campaign put upon him is indicated by the fact that it was not until February that he felt it possible to have Julia join him. She had been staying with relations in Louisville; Grant wanted her with him whenever that was possible not merely because of his need for her but also because it seemed to be almost impossible for her to get along pleasantly with one of Grant's sisters, so that she was unable to spend much time in the home of Grant's father at Covington. Grant understood this situation, sympathized fully with Julia, and assured her that the difficulties were not of her making, but he could not do anything about it, and the unhappy problem simply had to be accepted as insoluble. Julia Grant summed it up by confessing to author Garland that "it was not particularly pleasant for me at Father Grant's house"; when she could stay at army headquarters the problem did not have to be thought about.[13]

Grant's thirteen-year-old son Fred had been with him through a good part of the Vicksburg campaign and its aftermath, and this winter he had gone to visit in the St. Louis home of Julia's cousin Harry Boggs, who had been Grant's partner in a real estate venture before the war. Late in January, Grant got alarming news: Fred was critically ill, with "typhoid pneumonia," and might not survive. Grant blamed himself for having exposed the boy to the hardships of camp life, and wired Washington for permission to go to St. Louis. Secretary Stanton approved, but specified that on this trip Grant must retain direct command of all of his forces, keeping in communication with his subordinates and with Washington just as if he was staying at Nashville.

Leaving Rawlins at headquarters, Grant got away as quickly as he could, reaching St. Louis on January 26 to learn that the crisis in Fred's illness had passed and that the boy was recovering nicely. He lingered in St. Louis a few days, glad enough to take a small respite from business and to enjoy the company of the Boggs family; and during this visit it was borne in upon him that he was a public figure with the limelight forever on him. With his family and Mrs. Boggs, he went one evening to the theater, sitting in a box at a performance of the drama *Richelieu*, and between the acts the crowd realized that he was present and set up a cry of "Grant! Grant! Get up!" Grant rose and bowed, but the crowd refused to stop shouting until he moved his chair to the front of the box, where everybody could see him. Two nights later there was a banquet at the Lindell Hotel, attended by two hundred people, among them Grant's father-in-law, the venerable Missouri planter Colonel Dent, and the applause was even more spirited. One guest remembered that Grant took the cheering "with great modesty and evident embarrassment," and another said: "His face never changed its unmoved expression. It never lit up with excitement."

The toast of the evening, of course, was to "Our distinguished guest, Major General Grant," and Grant had to get to his feet. He said nothing further than "Gentlemen, in response it will be impossible to do more than thank you"; and then he took out a cigar and made a little project of lighting it — a trick he had learned during his travels across Kentucky, where he had found that a crowd usually would accept this bit of stage business in place of a speech. After the banquet the streets outside the hotel were jammed, bonfires were burning and rockets were being fired, and Grant was obliged to step out on a balcony. He used the cigar routine again, told the crowd "Making speeches is not my business," thanked everyone for coming out to greet him, and was at last allowed to retire.[14]

One of the dignitaries at the speaker's table was General Rosecrans, as jovial and cordial as if he and Grant had never had the least disagreement. Also present was General Schofield, who had not yet departed for east Tennessee, and who sat at Grant's right. Schofield noticed that Grant did not even touch any of the many glasses of wine that were placed by the side of his plate, and at last he remarked upon it. According to Schofield, Grant replied: "I dare not touch it. Sometimes I can drink freely without any unpleasant effect; at others I could not take even a single glass of wine." Recording this remark when he wrote his autobiography, Schofield commented: "A strong man indeed, who could thus know and govern his own weakness!" [15]

There is no reason to doubt that Grant said what Schofield said he had said, but it may be that he was simply giving Schofield the brush-off. At this time he and Schofield hardly knew each other, and it is not recorded that Grant ever said to any of his intimates what he said that night to Schofield. His mother had seen no reason why she should not send him a bottle of wine; General McPherson, who knew him well and wished him well, had not hesitated to offer him a brimming glass of whiskey, on the headquarters boat at Vicksburg; they would hardly have acted so if they had known that Grant considered alcohol an enemy with whom he dared not trifle, and if he really felt that way they almost certainly would have known it. There really is very little support for the theory that one sniff of the cork was enough to send Grant over the moon.

Rawlins meanwhile was fretting from afar. He felt that Grant ought not to be away from headquarters, and even though Julia was accompanying him on this trip to St. Louis Rawlins was afraid of the things the general might do if his chief of staff were not present as a guardian . . . and altogether Rawlins was living up to the character William Smith gave him, shortly after the battle of Chattanooga, when he made this diary entry: "Rawlins acts sometimes ugly. Like General Wilson his sudden elevation has spoiled him." It should be added that Smith went on to pay a grudging tribute: "But he is invaluable to the General and I hope he may always prosper so long as he continues true to him." [16]

Rawlins displayed his feeling at this time in a letter to his Emma, written on January 31 while Grant was still in St. Louis: "I see by the papers he was to have a supper given him at the Lindell last night. I'm sorry it is so, for I had hoped he would go there and return without permitting himself to be paraded before the public, but the fact is — you know the General pretty well — he can't say no, and then there is one other thing which may do to tell the masses: that is, he dislikes these public ovations. He may appear awkward in the midst of them, but he likes them nevertheless. At least I've yet to know of his declining one. You are fully aware of my fears in all this. I need not state them."

Rawlins expected that Grant would be back in Nashville by February 2, but instead of Grant Rawlins that day got a telegram from him: he was in Louisville, and would linger there a day or so longer unless his immediate arrival at Nashville was absolutely necessary. Indignantly, Rawlins wrote to Emma that "I replied that important matters demanded his attention here, to which I received no answer and infer he is on his way . . . Here is his proper place." Grant showed up on February 4, looking well and happy, and Rawlins told Emma: "His non-arrival last night made me nervous, and you will not be surprised to know that it caused me to break over my resolution not to swear. I feared everything was not as it should be with him, but his appearance has agreeably disappointed me and for once I have done him injustice in my thoughts." As it happened, the chief business going on at headquarters just then was literary, Rawlins and Joe Bowers being busily engaged putting together the general's report on the battle of Chattanooga — "which," Rawlins wrote, "I assure you is a very unpleasant and I might say thankless undertaking, for the General is very tenacious of the claim that he writes his own reports and it is necessary for us to follow the text as nearly as possible." Rawlins did recognize, however, that Grant's writing style — simple, direct, unadorned, in marked contrast to his own — was highly effective, and a few weeks later he wrote to Wilson: "General Grant's official report of the Battle of Chattanooga has gone forward. It is full and complete, written in his usual happy narrative style, void of pomposity or parade." [17]

Rawlins was a difficult man to live with this winter. His profound anxiety to protect Grant reduced him now and then to querulous nagging. He was deeply concerned over his own health, because he suffered from a persistent cough which his doctors seemed unable to relieve, and although they assured him that his lungs were not affected he suspected, apparently correctly, that the tuberculosis he had always dreaded was at last laying its ghostly fingers on him. Dana told Wilson that he feared Rawlins's lungs "might be more seriously affected than I had supposed," and when Rawlins saw a photograph of himself that looked "sad and death-like," he confessed to Emma that the picture might be a correct likeness.

In addition, Rawlins was frightened by Grant's approaching elevation to the supreme command. He told Emma that "I grow dizzy in looking from the eminence he has attained, and tremble at the great responsibility about to devolve upon him"; and this fear somehow crossed Rawlins's ingrained Puritanism which at times seems to have made him feel that Grant ought not to have any lighter moments at all. Once this winter Grant and members of his staff went to Louisville, and Grant's medical director, Dr. Kittoe, remembered that when two St. Louis ladies whom Grant had known before the war took seats in the car Grant's party occupied, produced from a luncheon hamper a bottle of wine and offered Grant a drink, Rawlins looked on in acute dismay. Grant refused to accept the wine, but Rawlins "gave vent to his indignation in terms more profanely forcible than elegant, and in so loud a tone that the two objects of his wrath plainly heard what he said and bore evidence of their mortification by their looks." In Louisville the Grant party went to the theater — an activity of which Rawlins never approved — and Rawlins moodily wrote to Emma: "I was supremely disgusted with the use of opera glasses (I am sorry to say even my distinguished chieftain was one of those who used them) on the stage and peeping from behind the curtains; also at the eagerness, or willingness rather, of him we love to say is so modest and unassuming to acknowledge the notice people are taking of him. In one who had less reputation for modesty it would be pardonable." Then Rawlins burst out with a final cry: "Oh greatness, how dost thou lift up in themselves those whom thou favorest. I feel that to go with them is ascending heights too far above the level of my plebian birth; beyond the reach of any influence I can exert for my country's good." [18]

If it is a little hard to understand the wretched part played in all of this by the opera glasses, the reason for Rawlins's uneasiness is clear enough. The spotlight now was on his general and it was going to stay that way, and it might reveal a person very different from the unassuming Sam Grant who had called Rawlins from Galena a little more than two years ago. Grant had come up from far down and he was reaching the high place, where there were no concealing shadows and the steady light was pitiless. He had had to leave the army in humiliation ten years earlier, and now an army twenty times larger than the one that had been too big for him was going to be his to use as he saw fit, with the nation's future depending on the way he used it; and Rawlins was beginning to see that however much Grant might protest he got a deep inner satisfaction from the cheering crowds and the bonfires in the streets. Greatness was lifting him up, as Rawlins said, and it was taking him to a height where Grant would be on his own forever after, beyond the reach of any moralistic supervision by a dedicated chief of staff.

But Grant was not being lifted up *in himself*, as Rawlins feared. He had his own qualms about what lay ahead, but they were based largely on that very modesty of desire which Rawlins believed was about to be smothered. After the war Grant told Washburne that "nothing ever fell over me like a wet blanket so much as my promotion to the lieutenant-generalcy," and he explained why: if he remained a junior major general he might, when the war ended, be given command of the comparatively unimportant Pacific Coast division, with headquarters in San Francisco. (The last time he saw San Francisco he had been flat broke, a man without a future leaving the army under a cloud, and in order to get back east he had had to borrow money from a fellow officer; he seems to have felt that it would be nice to go back to San Francisco permanently with a general's stars on his shoulders.)

Apparently he did not tell Rawlins about that desire, but he did let him know that he did not especially want promotion, and Rawlins explained Grant's position that winter in a letter to Washburne — a letter, incidentally, whose labored prose helps one see why Grant insisted on writing his own reports. Rawlins's letter includes these lines:

I see by the papers the Bill creating a Lieutenant General is still undisposed of. So far as General Grant may be regarded in connection with it, I can only say that if the conferring of the distinguished honor upon him would be the taking him out of the field, or with a view to the superseding of General Halleck he would not desire it, for he feels that if he can be of service to the government in any place it is in command of an army in the field & there is where he would remain if made a Lieut General, besides he has great confidence in and friendship for the General in Chief & would without respect to rank be willing at all times to receive orders through him.

The advocacy of the New York *Herald* and other papers of the General for the Presidency gives him little concern, he is unambitious of the honor, and will voluntarily put himself in no position nor permit himself to be placed in one if he can prevent that will in the slightest manner embarrass the friends of the government in their present grand effort to enforce its rightful authority and restore the Union of the states; of his views on this matter I suppose he has fully acquainted you.[19]

In the course of the years Grant came to feel that the high offices that he attained came more or less as rewards from the American people for faithful service, and although this pleased him it left him feeling that he owed somebody something. He once explained this in words Rawlins would have approved if he had been alive to hear them, because they show that Sam Grant still survived after years on the high place. In the spring of 1876, when Grant was nearing the close of his second term as President, a friend visiting him in the White House mentioned the chance that Grant might be given a third term. Grant replied that he personally would much prefer to return to private life, and then he said a strange thing: "If it would be possible in any way for me to make a sacrifice for the American people, I would like to repay them by some sacrifice for the great honors they have conferred on me. I have never been able to make a sacrifice for them. I have tried several times, but every sacrifice I have attempted has turned out to be an additional reward." The historian John Lothrop Motley, who had many conversations with Grant during and after the White House years, told Oliver Wendell Holmes: "I cannot get over the impression he made on me. I have got something like it from women some times, hardly ever from men — that of entire loss of self-hood in a great aim which made all the common influences which stir up other people as nothing to him." [20]

However much Grant may have disliked the idea of superseding Halleck, the plain fact was that deep dissatisfaction with Halleck was one of the primary reasons why most Congressmen were willing to pass the bill creating the office of lieutenant general, knowing that if they did Grant would certainly be appointed. The well-informed newspaper correspondent Noah Brooks said that "the most outspoken and malignant Copperhead in Congress" was not denounced by the radical all-out-war members as bitterly as they denounced the general-in-chief, and Brooks believed they voted for the bill largely because they thought the war would not be prosecuted vigorously until Halleck was replaced. (Most of them voted for it, that is: as prominent a radical as Thaddeus Stevens of Pennsylvania spoke against it.) Halleck had brought this on himself, not so much by incapacity as by his faulty conception of his powers and duties as commanding general of the army. This winter Halleck wrote frankly to Sherman: "I am simply a military adviser of the Secretary of War and the President, and must obey and carry out what they decide upon, whether I concur in their decisions or not. As a good soldier I obey the orders of my superiors. If I disagree with them in opinion I say so, but when they decide it is my duty faithfully to carry out their decision." [21]

He had not begun that way. Lincoln told Secretary John Hay that when Halleck was first brought to Washington he intended to be a strong man. Hay remembered the President saying: "When McClellan seemed incompetent to the work of handling an army and we sent for Halleck to take command, he stipulated that it should be with full power and responsibility of commander-in-chief. He ran it on that basis till Pope's defeat; but ever since that event he has shrunk from responsibility whenever it was possible." Correspondent Brooks once told Lincoln that people disliked Halleck because they thought him too timid, and he said the President "looked grave, almost severe" and replied that he was Halleck's friend because nobody else was.[22]

Although the bill at last passed Congress with many votes to spare, it did not go through automatically. Stevens opposed it, remarking that "Saints are not canonized until after death," implying that the high grade ought not to be awarded until after the war had been safely won. Garfield, who had recently resigned as brigadier general in order to serve in Congress, took the same line, arguing that if this promotion was a reward of merit it ought to be made after all the returns were in; it would be mortifying, he said, to make a man lieutenant general now and then be obliged to shelve him a few months later, and anyway if the President wanted a new commanding general he had ample power to remove the man who now held that office and put any major general of his choice in his place. But although the bill hung fire for weeks, so that every member who felt like it could speak his mind, there was never any real doubt that it would pass; and the underlying reason seems to have been a general feeling that the turning of the tide had at last begun and that victory would come sooner than anyone had expected if this hard new man from the west were given full power to push matters. Washburne said repeatedly that he did not believe the war would be ended until Grant was given supreme command, and he shouted: "I can't wait. I want this now.

Grant must fight out this war, and he will never leave the field!" [23]

Grant of course knew about the progress of the bill, but he seems not to have realized how great a change it would make in his life. He still looked upon himself as responsible for the war in the west, and assumed that he would remain in the west no matter what happened about his promotion. In the middle of February he told Julia that except for a brief visit "to the front" — that is, to east Tennessee — he expected to remain in Nashville until the opening of the spring campaign, sometime in April; consequently she could spend a month or six weeks with him there, and he hoped she would make the visit as quickly as she could. A few days later he remarked that they had better make the most of this chance to be together, because active fighting would begin in April, "after which there is no assurance when we will meet again." Then he went on to suggest that if the promotion came through it might be possible for them to meet a little more often:

"The passage of the Lieut. Gen. bill, if it does pass, may effect a change however in this respect. With such a change it might be necessary for me to pass from West to East occationally, where of course we would meet. I do not want you to repeat what I say on this subject."

Before February had ended the bill had gone through Congress and had been signed by the President, and it was not long before Grant discovered that he was not going to see a great deal more of the west. On March 3 he got a wire from Halleck:

"The Secretary of War directs that you report in person to the War Department as early as practicable, considering the condition of your command. If necessary you will keep up telegraphic communication with your command while en route to Washington." This was speedily followed by another telegram from Halleck: "The Secretary of War directs me to say to you that your commission as lieutenant-general is signed and will be delivered to you on your arrival at the War Department. I sincerely congratulate you on this recognition of your distinguished and meritorious services." [24]

When he offered his friendly congratulations Halleck undoubtedly was sincere. He wrote to his friend Francis Lieber to say that "Genl Grant is my personal friend and I heartily rejoice at his promotion," and he went on to explain the legal issues involved in creation of the new rank, in words that fully answered Garfield's objection:

The act of April 4th, 1862, authorized the President to assign to commands officers of different rank but of the same grade. Under this I was assigned to the command as Genl-in-Chief, although there were other Major Genls of prior date. But since then the higher grade of Lt Genl has been created & filled, and as soon as Genl Grant receives his commission & enters upon the duties of *that grade* he must *ex necessitate*, perform the duties & incur the responsibilities of Genl in Chf. The President cannot appoint me or anyone else of the grade of Major Genl to that office for the reason that it is not "the same grade" as that of Lieut. Genl. It is true that the law creating the grade of Lieut Genl does not *require* the President to assign that officer to the general command of the army, but, without the authority of law, the President cannot require a senior officer to obey a junior, and the law applies only to officers of the *same grade*. I look upon the matter solely as a question of law in which individual feelings or preferences cannot enter. Undoubtedly it will be said that I throw up my office in dudgeon, because Genl Grant has been promoted over my head. There is no possible ground for such an accusation . . . The honor was fully due to him, and with the honor he must take the responsibilities which belong to his office. No one else can legally perform its duties or assume its responsibilities.[25]

The point here was that by creating a new higher rank and giving it to General Grant the administration was pointedly serving notice on every officer in the army that Grant was going to be the boss to the end of the war. As lieutenant general, raised above everyone else by formal act of Congress, he would have a prestige and an authority much greater than anything he would get simply by a presidential appointment. As long as the government used him at all it would have to use him in the top spot; this act was to all intents and purposes irrevocable, and it put an end to all political scheming by ambitious generals anxious to get into the supreme command. In effect the government was staking everything on the bet that Grant was going to win the war.

That this would place an enormous pressure on him — much was being given to him, and much would certainly be expected of him — seems not to have bothered Grant. As he closed up his office at Nashville and prepared to go to Washington he expressed a different sort of concern in a letter to the soldier he trusted most, General Sherman. Just before he left for the east he sent Sherman this letter, marked "private":

DEAR SHERMAN: The bill reviving the grade of lieutenant-general in the army has become a law, and my name has been sent to the Senate for the place. I now receive orders to report to Washington immediately in person, which indicates either a confirmation or a likelihood of confirmation.

I start in the morning to comply with the order, but I shall say very distinctly on my arrival there that I accept no appointment which will require me to make that city my headquarters. This, however, is not what I started out to write about.

Whilst I have been eminently successful in this war in at least gaining the confidence of the public, no one feels more than me how much of this success is due to the energy, skill, and the harmonious putting forth of that energy and skill, of those who it has been my good fortune to have occupying a subordinate position under me.

There are many officers to whom these remarks are applicable to a greater or less degree, proportionate to their ability as soldiers, but what I want is to express my thanks to you and McPherson as the men to whom, above all others, I feel indebted for whatever I have had of success. How far your advice and suggestions have been of assistance, you know. How far your execution of whatever has been given you to do entitled you to the reward I am receiving, you cannot know as well as me. I feel all the gratitude this letter would express, giving it the most flattering construction.

The word *"you"* I use in the plural, intending it for McPherson also. I should write to him, and will some day, but starting in the morning I do not know that I will find time just now.

Your friend,
U. S. GRANT [26]

CHAPTER SEVEN

Continue to Be Yourself

G RANT never could make an entrance, and he came to Washington like an unsung job-hunter from the far places. The White House had designated proper persons to meet the train and escort him to his hotel, but somehow the arrangements fell through and Grant was met by nobody. He arrived late in the afternoon of March 8, accompanied by his son Fred (going on fourteen, and nicely recovered from his St. Louis illness), and Grant got to Willard's Hotel unattended, travel-stained and rumpled, a plain linen duster hiding most of his uniform. A bored registration clerk looked at him, saw nobody in particular, and said that there might be a room on the top floor. Grant said this would be all right, and signed the register, and the clerk swung the book around, to write down a room number after the name, and saw the entry: "U. S. Grant and son, Galena, Ill." The clerk suddenly came alive, remembered that there was a fine reservation on the second floor — bridal suite, or some such, apparently — and came bustling out from behind the desk to carry the general's bag upstairs personally. Grant and his son freshened up, and then came down to the dining room for dinner.

For a few minutes all was quiet. But Fred Grant remembered all his life how the people at the nearby tables looked, looked again, and began to whisper excitedly to one another. There was a general buzz of "There's Grant!" and presently some officious citizen stood up, hammered on a table with his knife until he had everyone's attention, and called out that he had the honor to announce that Lieutenant General Grant was present in the dining room. People scrambled to their feet, there was a rhythmic shout of "Grant! Grant! Grant!" and someone called for three cheers, which were promptly given. Grant stood up, fumbled with his napkin, bowed impersonally to all points of the compass, and then sat down and tried to go on with his dinner.

He did not get much to eat, because too many people were swarming about him, and before long the General and the boy left the dining room and went up to their living quarters.[1]

Not long after this a political person came to Grant's door — former Secretary of War Simon Cameron, as Fred remembered it; Congressman James K. Moorhead of Pennsylvania, by reporter Brooks's account — and he bustled Grant off to the White House. There was a presidential reception this evening, it had been reported that Grant might make an appearance, and although the March night was wet and raw an oversized crowd was present. Either at the hotel or at the White House door, Grant was joined by two members of his staff who had accompanied him from Nashville. One of them of course was Rawlins, pleased because Grant had behaved modestly on the long trip east, but deeply worried by the fear that his own ill health might make it impossible for him to serve as chief of staff to the general of the armies. The other was Lieutenant Colonel Cyrus B. Comstock, a competent engineer officer, West Point trained, who was becoming one of the most influential members of Grant's official family. On arrival at Washington these two had gone direct to the War Department to see Halleck; not finding him there they had gone to his home, but he had not been there either and they gravitated back to Grant just in time to go with him on his visit to the White House.[2]

When Grant came inside the White House the crowd parted like the Red Sea waves, leaving an open lane for him, everybody telling his neighbor that this really was General Grant; and at the far end of the lane there was Abraham Lincoln, all lanky six feet four of him, wearing (as a sympathetic friend confessed) a collar one size too large and a necktie "rather broad and awkwardly tied." Lincoln stepped forward, his hand outstretched, a smile on his face, and Grant walked toward him; a White House secretary considered it "a long walk for a bashful man, the eyes of the world upon him," and when the walk ended and the two men shook hands President Lincoln's three-year search for a general had ended. The President pumped Grant's hand vigorously, saying "Why, here is General Grant! Well, this is a great pleasure, I assure you!" The handshaking over, the two stood together for a moment, Lincoln beaming down in vast good humor (he was the taller of the two men by a good eight inches) and Grant looking up at him, his right hand grasping the lapel of his uniform coat. Then the President beckoned to Secretary of State William H. Seward, who took Grant off to present him to Mrs. Lincoln; and a few minutes later Seward led him into the East Room, where most of the crowd was waiting.

When Grant came in enthusiasm boiled over, and people began to cheer and press forward, and Grant had to stand up on a sofa, partly so that he could shake the hands that were thrust at him and partly to avoid being trampled underfoot. Gideon Welles, Secretary of the Navy, looked on uneasily, considering the scene "rowdy and unseemly," and Brooks said of the cheering crowd that "it was the only real mob I ever saw in the White House." Incredibly enough, Grant had to stand on the sofa for the better part of an hour, and Brooks wrote: "For once at least the President of the United States was not the chief figure in the picture. The little, scared-looking man who stood on a crimson-covered sofa was the idol of the hour." At last Seward and some of the others managed to extricate Grant and take him to the Blue Room, where President Lincoln and Secretary Stanton were waiting. The President now explained that Grant must return to the White House the next day for a special ceremony — the formal presentation of his commission as lieutenant general.

When he presented the commission, said Lincoln, he would make a very short speech — not more than four sentences, altogether — and he wanted Grant to make a brief reply. So that Grant would know what was coming, the President gave him a copy of the remarks he proposed to make, and as Presidential Secretary John Nicolay recalled it Lincoln went on to say:

There are two points that I would like to have you make in your answer, first, to say something which shall prevent or obviate any jealousy of you from any of the other generals in the service, and second, something which shall put you on as good terms as possible with the Army of the Potomac. Now, consider whether this may not be said to make it of some advantage; and if you see any objection whatever to doing it, be under no restraint whatever in expressing that objection to the Secretary of War, who will talk further with you about it.[3]

The White House understood the uses of publicity just as well in 1864 as it does today, and the presentation ceremony of course was strictly an attention-getting device; as Lincoln frankly told Grant, what was said by the President and the General would be said "for an object," and to make the affair more newsworthy the President convened the entire cabinet. It was about one in the afternoon when Grant came in, accompanied by Fred and the two staff officers, and while the cabinet members looked curiously at this soldier of whom they had heard so much President Lincoln and General Grant took their positions, standing face to face, and Lincoln read his little statement:

General Grant: The nation's appreciation of what you have done, and its reliance upon you for what remains to do, in the existing great struggle, are now presented with this commission, constituting you Lieutenant General in the Army of the United States. With this high honor devolves upon you also a corresponding responsibility. As the country herein trusts you, so, under God, it will sustain you. I scarcely need to add that with what I here speak for the nation goes my own hearty personal concurrence.

Now it was Grant's turn. He had written his reply out with pencil the night before, on his return to the hotel from the White House, with Fred looking on, and he had the original draft in one hand. He seemed most ill at ease when he began to read it, and the first few words came out blurred and hardly audible: one of the listeners thought that Grant simply had not taken enough air in his lungs, tried to get through the whole thing in one rush, and found it impossible. After this shaky start Grant paused, gripped the paper more firmly, top and bottom, with both hands, took a deep breath, and went on in a loud clear voice. What he had to say was brief enough:

Mr. President: I accept this commission with gratitude for the high honor conferred. With the aid of the noble armies that have fought on so many fields for our common country, it will be my earnest endeavor not to disappoint your expectations. I feel the full weight of the responsibilities now devolving on me and know that if they are met it will be due to those armies, and above all to the favor of that Providence which leads both Nations and men.

Secretary Nicolay considered this speech "brief and to the point" but remarked that the General had entirely ignored the two requests Lincoln had made regarding the content of the speech.[4]

Before and after the White House formalities Grant found time to inspect the defenses of Washington, and, apparently, to discuss his new assignment with the President and with Secretary Stanton.

Twenty-four hours in Washington were enough to show how the capital could overwhelm an incautious general with social engagements, and Grant wanted to get away. Rawlins felt the same, and wrote to Emma: "I am doing all I can to get him away from here." He added darkly: "Tonight he dines with Mr. Seward, Secretary of State. I shall accompany him, though it is not my pleasure to do so. You know where I am wine is not drunk by those with whom I have any influence. Were it otherwise I should consult my pleasure." [5]

The dinner at Secretary Seward's house apparently went off to Rawlins's full satisfaction, and the next day, March 10, Grant got down to business. He went to the headquarters of the Army of the Potomac at Brandy Station to talk with that army's commander, Major General George Gordon Meade.

Between them, this army and its commander seemed to offer the general-in-chief his most pressing immediate problems. Grant had been given his job because the administration wanted a more forceful and energetic prosecution of the war, and he supposed that Charles A. Dana had summed up the general feeling about Meade and his army when he wrote Grant, late in December, that White House and War Department felt that "from that army nothing is to be hoped under its present commander." [6] Grant had assumed, from this and from pressure applied at his own headquarters, that his first step toward a successful summer campaign would be to find a new man for Meade's place, and Meade suspected that Grant felt that way. On the day Grant reached Washington, Meade wrote to his wife to warn her: "As he is to be commander in chief and responsible for the doings of the Army of the Potomac he may desire to have his man in command, particularly as I understand he is indoctrinated with the notion of the superiority of western armies and that the failure of the Army of the Potomac to accomplish anything is due to their commanders." Yet if Grant had once felt that way he did not feel that way now, and when Meade opened their conversation by saying that he would uncomplainingly step down and serve in a subordinate capacity if Grant wanted some western officer such as Sherman to command the Army of the Potomac, Grant told him he had no intention whatever of making a change. When he wrote his *Memoirs*, Grant confessed that "this incident gave me even a more favorable opinion of Meade than did his great victory at Gettysburg the July before." [7]

One reason for Grant's changed attitude may have been the simple fact that he and Meade hit it off on sight. Grant had known Meade very slightly in the Mexican War, and he had the casual knowledge of the man that was common to fellow officers in the old army, but he was to all intents and purposes meeting him now for the first time, and he liked what he saw. He told John Russell Young, after the war, "I had a great fondness for him," and a few days after the meeting Meade assured Mrs. Meade: "I was much pleased with Grant, and most agreeably disappointed in his evidence of mind and character. You may rest assured he is not an ordinary man." [8] In short, the two men sensed that they could work together, and although nothing remotely like the affectionate bond between Grant and Sherman ever developed here there was warmth and mutual respect.

In addition, Grant quickly learned that he had been grossly misinformed about the administration's attitude. Neither Lincoln nor Stanton especially wanted to remove Meade, and although they were ready to remove him if Grant requested it they did not blame Meade for the fact that the Army of the Potomac had done less than they thought it should have done. Meade after all ran his army within limits laid down by Halleck, who displayed little initiative himself and did not encourage it in his subordinates, and the President and Secretary of War probably realized that Meade would do more if his immediate superior insisted that he do more. Meade himself felt a few weeks after Grant's appointment that he could be a more effective commander now. He told his wife that his own fame would probably suffer, because he would be overshadowed by Grant, but this seemed only fair after all and Meade went on to make his point: "He is so much more active than his predecessor, and agrees so with me in his views, I cannot but be rejoiced at his arrival, because I believe success to be the more probable from the above facts. My position before, with inadequate means, no power myself to increase them, and no effort made by others to do so, placed me in a false position, causing me to be held responsible when in fact I could do nothing." [9]

Beyond all of this, Grant found that an unseemly scramble for Meade's job was going on, and the fact that officers close to him were responsible for part of it did not help much. Joe Hooker, the chronic malcontent, was doing what he could to get Meade out and himself in, although he must have been an undefiled optimist if he really believed the administration would ever go along with such a scheme. He had been complaining to Secretary Stanton that the newspapers were unfair in their accounts of the storming of Lookout Mountain, and he protested that Grant had tried to make Hooker's part in this fight inconspicuous, "Grant's object being to give the eclat to his old army." Hooker considered this partly due to Baldy Smith, on whom Grant had relied so much at Chattanooga: "he has an ascendancy over Grant, who is simple-minded." [10] Hooker's campaign to be sure was getting nowhere, but Smith himself was a most active candidate — his principal sponsor being, of all people, General James H. Wilson. From his office in the Cavalry Bureau, Wilson had played politics vigorously to get Grant made lieutenant general and to get Rawlins confirmed as his chief of staff, and he had plenty of energy left to work for Smith as well. On February 10 he had sent Smith a report on his activities:

A few days ago, Major Halpine, A.A.G. — you may know him — he runs the semi-official newspaper department, that is to say creates public opinion in favor of what the government wishes — called upon me. I discussed the matter of the general campaign with him and urged most strenuously that the best possible way to assist General Grant was to say what he could in favor of a new commander to the Army of the Potomac and the necessity of its cooperation with the armies in the West. He assured me he would strike at once, would write to Greeley and Bryant and get them interested if possible and by the means thus indicated bring such a clatter about Mr. Lincoln's ears as would compel him to do something.

Wilson enlisted Dana's aid, and a week after sending this letter he wrote again to Smith to say: "Mr. Dana and I have had a long talk, and conclude first that Meade is not full nor nearly equal to the occasion — he is weak, timid and almost puerile." Unfortunately, said Wilson, the authorities if left to themselves would not remove Meade: Halleck was "cold, selfish and timid" and the only hope was in Grant. Once Grant became general-in-chief he could advance or remove men as he saw fit: "I am assured that President and Secretary will gladly leave the machine into the hands of General Grant." A few days after this Wilson assured Smith: "I am quite certain the General can and will put you right before the country and at the same time secure to the Army of the Potomac a commander of intelligence, equal to its control, capable of carrying it wherever he wishes." [11]

Wilson was promising more than he could deliver, and the situation contained elements beyond the grasp of a cocksure junior. Grant spent less than twenty-four hours at Meade's headquarters, but that was time enough for him to see that this particular command situation had best be left alone. The administration was not pressing for a change, Meade himself was a perfectly good man, and anyway Grant was now dealing with that most sensitive and touchy of military organisms, the Army of the Potomac. The very fact that he had been made lieutenant general (by, as it were, a special act of Congress) implied a criticism of everything that army had been and had done. This was sharpened by the fact that this was election year and that this army's creator, General George B. McClellan, was going to run against President Lincoln; which meant that the army itself was almost certain to become a political issue. The army's natural response to all of this was to close ranks against the outsider, and in his brief visit Grant found officers who frankly told him that he was going to find war in the east much tougher than war in the west: "You have not faced Bobby Lee yet."

Meade's chief of staff at this time was the highly capable regular army officer, General Andrew A. Humphreys, and because the day of Grant's arrival was rainy and Meade was suffering from a bad cold Humphreys went to the railroad station to meet Grant and escort him to headquarters. Humphreys seems to have been prepared in advance to dislike this newcomer, but that night he wrote to his wife that he had been "agreeably disappointed in Genl. Grant's appearance," saying that "he is good looking, with an intellectual face and head which at the same time expresses a good deal of determination." Humphreys felt that Grant was almost too quiet, and owned that "a reserved, cautious manner on his part necessarily gave rise to the same on mine," as a result of which "I have had but little intercourse or interchange of ideas with him." However, Grant was cordial to the old friends he met at headquarters, and with Meade he was "cordial and demonstrative."

Under the surface — not very far under it, probably — Humphreys thought he "perceived a something (aspiring chiefly from his own manner) that indicated that it was the visit of a rival commander to a rival army, or at least the meeting of the commanders and officers of rival armies"; a little of which may have been due to the fact that Baldy Smith, whose ambitions were no secret, came down to Brandy Station with Grant. However, Smith did not stay to dinner, and all in all things were not as difficult as Grant had thought they might be. He confessed afterward that "I was afraid of the spirit that pervaded that army" and feared that "some of the generals might treat me as they had treated Pope," and he was glad to see that this distrust was not warranted.[12] But it was obviously no time to bring in a westerner as rough along the edges as Sherman or as unpopular both with the administration and with the army as Smith, and on March 11, when Grant went back to Washington, Colonel Comstock made a diary entry indicating that Meade's position was secure.

"Grant, who at Chattanooga thought Baldy Smith should have it, now says no change," wrote Comstock. "The programme is, Halleck here as office man and military adviser, Sherman to take Grant's place, McPherson Sherman's, Grant in the field." [13]

That summed it up, and Grant and Rawlins left for Nashville that evening, leaving Comstock in Washington to await their return. In order to make his departure, Grant firmly and bluntly turned down a White House dinner invitation from President Lincoln, explaining "Really, Mr. President, I have had enough of this show business"; and on the day after this the War Department issued orders formalizing the change in command, taking pains to let General Halleck down gently. The orders stated that Halleck, "at his own request," had been relieved from command of the armies of the United States, that Grant was succeeding him, and that Halleck was assigned to duty in Washington as chief of staff, "under the direction of the Secretary of War and the Lieutenant-General commanding." Sherman became head of Grant's old Military Division of the Mississippi, thus becoming what modern military usage would call an army group commander; McPherson took command of the Department and Army of the Tennessee, and headquarters of the general-in-chief would be wherever the general-in-chief happened to be. (He would be with the Army of the Potomac, although the War Department order did not say so.) There was a final sop for any bruised feelings Halleck might have: "In relievin Major General Halleck from duty. as General-in-Chief, the President desires to express his approbation and thanks for the able and zealous manner in which the arduous and responsible duties of that position have been performed." [14]

The chief point here was that Grant had had his way on the matter that had worried him most: he would not have to stay in Washington. He had told intimates that he would not take this new job if it meant burying himself in the capital, and he had originally planned to establish himself at Chattanooga and go with Thomas's army on a drive toward Atlanta. If he had come to see that it would be better for him to travel with the Army of the Potomac this implied no distrust of Meade: rather it seems to have reflected a justified feeling that only the massive authority of the general-in-chief, exercised on the spot, could properly protect this army both from its own internal divisions and jealousies and from the interference Washington would inevitably exert unless someone prevented it. When he left for the west he told the President that he would be back in nine days. That would be time enough, with Sherman's help, for him to get western affairs in order, close out the old headquarters at Nashville, and come east with the slate clean.

Sherman himself was coming up from Mississippi to meet Grant at Nashville. He was full of enthusiasm, and like Rawlins he was also worried about what the lofty new position would do to Grant. He wrote to him while he was en route, replying to the letter Grant had sent him, and thanking him for it. Then he went on:

You are now Washington's legitimate successor, and occupy a position of almost dangerous elevation; but if you can continue, as heretofore, to be yourself — simple, honest and unpretending — you will enjoy through life the respect and love of friends and the homage of millions of human beings that will award you a large share, in securing to them and their descendants a government of law and stability.

When Sherman was enthusiastic he went all out, and now he poured forth his admiration and affection in extravagant terms:

I believe you are as brave, patriotic and just as the great prototype, Washington; as unselfish, kind-hearted and honest as a man should be, but the chief characteristic is the simple faith in success you have always manifested, which I can liken to nothing else than the faith a Christian has in a Savior. This faith gave you victory at Shiloh and Vicksburg. Also, when you have completed your last preparations you go into battle without hesitation, as at Chattanooga, no doubts, no reserves; and I tell you it was this that made us act with confidence. I knew wherever I was that you thought of me, and if I got in a tight place you would come if alive. My only points of doubt were in your knowledge of grand strategy, and of books of science and history, but I confess your common sense seems to have supplied all these.

Then Sherman went on to offer his word of advice, the tone of it perfectly expressing that western outlook which the Army of the Potomac officers resented:

Don't stay in Washington. Halleck is better qualified than you to stand the buffets of intrigue and policy. Come West; take to yourself the whole Mississippi Valley. Let us make it dead sure, and I tell you the Atlantic slopes and Pacific shores will follow its destiny as sure as the limbs of a tree live or die with the main trunk. We have done much, but much still remains. Time and time's influences are with us; we could almost afford to sit still and let these influences work. Even in the seceded States your word would go further than a President's proclamation or an act of Congress. For God's sake and your country's sake come out of Washington. I foretold to General Halleck before he left Corinth the inevitable result, and I now exhort you to come out West. Here lies the seat of the coming empire, and from the West, when our task is done, we will make short work of Charleston and Richmond and the impoverished coast of the Atlantic.[15]

When he spoke of Grant's unshakable self-confidence Sherman put his finger on one of Grant's most important characteristics as a soldier. Just at this time Grant got a new man on his staff, a former newspaperman named Adam Badeau, who had been wounded in the foot at Port Hudson, still went about on crutches, and came in as a sort of military secretary under some idea that he would eventually write a military history; and one of the first things Badeau learned was that Grant firmly believed in his own ability to meet all of his obligations. Badeau reflected that at this moment almost everything depended on Grant, and he asked him point-blank if he really and always hoped to succeed.

"He answered in simple terms," wrote Badeau, "that he was perfectly certain of success; that he felt now as he had felt at Donelson, and Vicksburg, and Chattanooga, when the dangers, though less in extent, were equally alarming. He had no fear of not doing all that he was put in his place to do. He did not know, he said, how long it might be before he accomplished his task, nor what interruptions or obstacles might intervene, but of its eventual accomplishment no shadow of a doubt ever seemed to cross his mind. This confidence never deserted him. There was no moment, however dark or distressing, when he was not more than hopeful."

In all of this there was no dedicated belief in his star or in his destiny, and a generation accustomed to Napoleonic postures by generals concluded that Grant was almost pathologically retiring and self-effacing, and described him at times as if he were no more than a Uriah Heep in shoulder straps. General Schofield was one who knew better, and he told Hamlin Garland after the war: "Grant was very far from being a modest man, as the word modest is generally understood. His just self-esteem was as far above modesty as it was above flattery . . . He knew his own merits as well as anybody, and he knew his own imperfections. When his attention was called to a mistake he had committed he would see and admit it with a smile, which expressed the exact opposite of that feeling which most men are apt to show under like circumstances . . . His absolute confidence in his own judgment upon any subject which he had mastered added to his accurate estimate of his own ability." [16]

Not everybody recognized this trait, and in an odd way the man who suffered because it went unrecognized was John Rawlins. Rawlins's name was before the Senate, which was considering confirmation of his recent promotion to brigadier general and which found itself mildly puzzled. Rawlins was Grant's chief of staff, but Halleck had been named chief of staff of the army when Grant became general-in-chief, and it was a little hard for the Senators to see why there had to be two chiefs of staff; and anyway, generals' commissions usually went only to line officers and Rawlins's service had been strictly on the staff. To get Rawlins confirmed it was necessary to apply the heat, and Grant applied it in a letter to Senator Henry Wilson of Massachusetts, the committee chairman immediately concerned. Rawlins, said Grant, had "most richly earned" his promotion, and "he comes the nearest to being indispensable to me of any officer in the service." If Rawlins failed of confirmation, both the service and Grant personally would suffer; furthermore, the rejection would indicate that a capable officer injured himself by serving in the staff instead of in the line, and "I shall feel that by keeping with me a valuable officer, because he made himself valuable, I have worked him an injury." [17]

That probably would have done it, because the Senate just now was inclined to give Grant anything he wanted; but Grant's former staff member and Rawlins's good friend, General Wilson, had time to spare and political wires to pull this spring, and he undertook to rally support for Rawlins's confirmation. To every Senator and Congressman he could reach, Wilson argued that Grant needed Rawlins to keep him on the rails and that he would be successful "as long as Rawlins stood by him as guide, philosopher and friend." In his autobiography, reciting his efforts along this line, Wilson said that the whole question of Grant's promotion and Rawlins's confirmation "was decided on the probabilities that, as Grant had been successful with the support of those nearest him, he would continue to be successful as long as they continued to stand by him." Thus Wilson industriously strengthened the legend that Grant would have become a drunkard if someone had not been looking out for him; and Rawlins, understanding what was going on, innocently wrote to Emma that he was confident of confirmation because of "the wholesome influence I am supposed to exercise for his good, which is not unknown personally to several gentlemen of great influence in Washington."

For John Rawlins it was a tragic spring. Ahead of Grant lay dangerous heights, steep and dizzying, evoking in Rawlins the darkest of worries. Despite the intimate knowledge possessed by several gentlemen of great influence, confirmation hung fire for weeks, and Rawlins bleakly confessed that if the Senate voted him down "I go out of the service . . . to strike hands with poverty and wrestle with existence." His own failing health depressed him; he had been taking large doses of medicine, and he told Emma that "the quantity of opium has affected my whole system inasmuch as to produce a sensation of numbness and drowsiness." Worst of all, although Grant was as cordial as ever in personal relationships, a gap was developing between the lieutenant general and his chief of staff, and Rawlins no longer had quite the influence he used to have.[18]

Washington being what it was and is, Grant soon became aware of what was being said concerning Rawlins's indispensability, whether or not he knew that Wilson had been saying it; and although he probably would not have held a lasting resentment about the gossip regarding his supposed taste for alcohol — he must have been case-hardened to that, by now — Wilson had also created the impression that Rawlins supplied Grant with brains as well as conscience. Long afterward, Wilson flatly told the newspaperman, Sylvanus Cadwallader, that "Rawlins was at least one-half of Grant," and this spring the campaign to get Rawlins confirmed was strongly tinged with that point of view, so that Rawlins was beginning to look like an unseen master of strategy without whom Grant would have been helpless. This touched that quality of self-esteem which General Schofield described. Two decades later, when Grant wrote his *Memoirs*, it was noticed that although he spoke now and then of "my chief of staff," he hardly ever mentioned Rawlins by name. General Sherman wrote to an army friend saying that this was not surprising: "Some of Rawlins' flatterers gave out the impression that he, Rawlins, had made Grant, and had written most of his orders and dispatches at Donelson, Shiloh and Vicksburg — Grant disliked to be patronized — and although he always was most grateful for all friendly service he hated to be considered an 'accident.' " [19]

Although he was ready enough to bristle at any suggestion that he went about in someone else's leading strings, Grant retained that odd quality of unintentionally vanishing from view in any crowd. An incident that took place now, on his trip back to Nashville, was perfectly characteristic. Grant was breaking the journey at Cincinnati, and his father Jesse, knowing when Grant's train was arriving, sent a carriage and driver to the railroad station. After a while, Jesse saw Grant coming up to the house on foot, carpetbag in hand, featureless coat over his uniform; the driver, it developed, had gone to the station but had been unable to find him.[20]

At Nashville Grant talked with the man he most wanted to see, Sherman, and with a few others especially trusted — McPherson, Grenville Dodge, John A. Logan, Rawlins, and the hardheaded young general who had won Grant's heart at Chattanooga, Phil Sheridan. With these men for a few days Grant had a conference in which casual informality was blended with attention to business; Grant could relax here, with these men, even while attending to important affairs, as he never could relax at headquarters in the east. As a matter of protocol he took his officers to the State House to call on Governor Andrew Johnson. Looking back afterward, Dodge remembered that "we were a hard-looking crowd" in service uniforms that showed much wear, and he said that a quizzical look in the governor's eye indicated that Andy Johnson had taken note of this fact. Grant came to the rescue by telling the governor that he had not given his men time to change to dress uniforms, and Dodge reflected that "Grant knew we had no others" than the stained clothes they were wearing.

After they got away from the State House the generals went to the theater to see *Hamlet*, even Rawlins apparently being of the party; and Sherman, who liked going to the theater above all other pleasures, felt that the unskillful actors were murdering the play, and said so repeatedly, out loud, until Dodge managed to quiet him by pointing out that the audience was full of soldiers and that if their attention were drawn to Grant's party they would probably create a scene. When the play at last reached the graveyard sequence, and Hamlet picked up Yorick's skull to soliloquize over it, some soldier in the audience, who had seen enough skulls and open graves for a dozen dramatists, sang out: "Say, pard, what is it — Yank, or Reb?" In the uproar that followed Grant's party left the theater, and then they went all over Nashville looking for a restaurant where they could buy some oysters. They found one at last, sat around a table talking brightly over bowls of stew, and dawdled so much that the proprietress (recognizing neither her customers nor the fact that they constituted enough top brass to suspend any military regulation) ejected them, somewhat wrathfully, with the remark that General Grant's curfew regulations compelled her to close at midnight.

. . . Next day at headquarters the generals assembled in Grant's office to hear about Grant's trip to Washington. Sherman prodded him with questions, and Dodge remembered that Grant confessed that the Army of the Potomac was "the finest army he had ever seen, far superior to any of ours in equipment, supplies and transportation."

"After discussing the Army of the Potomac, and having nothing but praise for it," said Dodge, Grant went on to say that "he would make his headquarters with that army and leave Sherman in command of the armies in the West, also informing us that he proposed to take several of us East with him. Sherman protested strongly against this, and it was finally compromised by his taking Sheridan and leaving the rest of us with Sherman. During the two or three days we were with Grant he outlined in a general way his plan of campaign — that every army should move against the enemy, so that Lee and Johnson could not detach any of their command to reinforce the others. He said, 'I will try to keep Lee from sending any force to Johnston,' but he said to Sherman, 'If he does, I will send you two men where he sends one.' He also informed us of the necessity of closing the war with this campaign." [21]

While he was in Washington, Grant told the generals, he had grappled with one of the most vexing problems of army administration — the fact that the various army staff departments, quartermaster, commissary, ordnance and so on, were by tradition and established practice out from under the control of army commanders. These agencies considered themselves independent, and they were quite likely to ignore orders from a field commander unless the orders were confirmed by their own chiefs in Washington. Grant insisted that the general-in-chief must have control, and when a certain commissary officer refused to carry out one of his orders Grant told him (as Dodge recalled it) that "while he could not force him to obey the order he could relieve him and put in his place one of the line officers, who would obey all the orders." The matter finally went to President Lincoln, and Grant said the President told him that although he could not legally give him command of the staff departments, "there is no one but myself that can interfere with your orders, and you can rest assured that I will not." [22]

It appeared that the White House would support Grant all the way. Somewhat similar to this anecdote is a tale Rawlins told to William Conant Church, editor of the *Army and Navy Journal*. As Church remembered it, Grant a little later this spring ran afoul of Secretary Stanton, who complained that Grant was withdrawing too many men from the Washington fortifications and demanded an explanation.

"I think I rank you in this matter, Mr. Secretary," said Grant.

"We shall have to see Mr. Lincoln about that," Stanton replied.

So off to the White House they went, secretary of war and general-in-chief, where the secretary explained the point at issue. To him President Lincoln replied:

"You and I, Mr. Stanton, have been trying to boss this job, and we have not succeeded very well with it. We have sent across the mountains for Mr. Grant, as Mrs. Grant calls him, to relieve us, and I think we had better leave him alone to do as he pleases." [23]

In one way or another, Grant wound up his affairs in Tennessee. When he started back east he had Sherman accompany him as far as Cincinnati, and the two men spent a day there going over Grant's plans for the coming campaign. Then Grant went on to Washington; and Sherman, who had begged him "to be yourself — simple, honest and unpretending," worried for fear that Grant would be too confiding and would tell the politicians too much about his military program. To his brother, Senator John Sherman, General Sherman wrote his own distrust of the civilians: "He ought not to trust even Mr. Lincoln, and as to a member of Congress I hope Grant will make it a death penalty for one to go south of the Potomac." [24]

Grant reached Washington on March 23, accompanied by Julia, who was half sick with an infection in her eyes, and by six-year-old son Jess, the other children staying in St. Louis with Harry and Louisa Boggs. Julia and Jess established themselves in a Washington boarding house and Grant went to the town of Culpeper, a few miles down the Orange & Alexandria Railroad line from Brandy Station, where Meade had his headquarters. Meade met him at the railroad station and rode with him to the house Grant's staff had taken over for Grant's use, and next day Grant sent a little report to Julia:

I arrived here yesterday well but as on my former trip brought wet and bad weather. I have not been out of the house today and from appearances shall not be able to go out for several days. At present however I shall find enough to be indoors. From indications I would judge the best of feelings animate all the troops here toward the changes that have been made.

Then Grant dropped the army to talk about what really interested him most at the moment — the well-being of his wife and the behavior of their small son. He went on: "I hope you have entirely recovered. It is poor enjoyment confined to bed in Washington. There is one thing I learned in Washington just on leaving that wants attending to. You know breakfast lasts from early in the morning until about noon, and dinner from that time until night. Jess runs about the house loose and seeing the guests at meals thinks each time it is a new meal and that he must necessarily eat. In this way he eats five or six times each day and dips largely into desserts. If not looked after he will make himself sick."

Not much time passed before Grant and Meade learned something about the publicity buildup that inevitably attends a new man in high position. The headquarters house at Culpeper had been taken for Grant on Meade's recommendation. On his first visit east Grant had asked Meade's advice, saying he wanted to be near Meade's position and away from Washington, and Meade had said that the only possible choices were Culpeper and Warrenton, with Culpeper preferred because it was nearer to army headquarters. So Grant had taken this house in Culpeper: and now the newspapers hailed the choice as Grant's own and symbol of a new deal — this energetic new general-in-chief had posted himself six miles nearer the enemy than the commander of the Army of the Potomac![25]

CHAPTER EIGHT

Campaign Plans and Politics

WHEN he opened headquarters at Culpeper, Grant had at his command, in all of the armies, approximately 662,000 men, present for duty. No other American soldier had ever commanded so many, but the number was not as large as it looks. It included service troops, detailed men and the assortment of militarily displaced persons inevitable in any army; of actual effectives, combat soldiers on duty and ready to go, there were probably 533,000, of whom more than 40,000 were stationed in the nine Northern and Western departments where armed Confederates never came. Of the 490,000 that remained, thousands were guarding supply lines and advanced bases, or were garrisoning cities and forts in occupied regions, so that they could hardly be counted on for battlefield service. (For an example, typical of all, there is the case of General George Thomas. He had 102,000 soldiers in his Department of the Cumberland, but he could take no more than 60,000 of them into the army group with which Sherman was going to invade Georgia.) As the last week in March began, Grant faced the task of planning, organizing and directing things in such a way that the maximum number of these soldiers could be put simultaneously into action. By the time schedule he set for himself he had just six weeks to do it.[1]

The most important thing, of course, was to cut down on manpower wastage, and when Grant started looking for waste his eye fell immediately on the expedition which General Banks was taking up the Red River toward Texas. This expedition was a strategic absurdity, leading 40,000 veteran soldiers directly away from the scene of effective action, but it had been formally blessed by the War Department, the Department of State and the White House itself and there was no way to cancel it. It might be possible to keep the venture within bounds, however, and while he was still in Nashville, on March 15,

Grant tried to define these bounds in an urgent telegram to Banks. As a first step on his progress toward Texas, abundant cotton and the destruction of Confederate power beyond the Missisisppi, Banks was moving heavily toward Shreveport, in the northwest corner of Louisiana, and in his column there were 10,000 men under General A. J. Smith, belonging to Sherman and loaned to Banks by Sherman for thirty days. Grant warned Banks that he had better move fast, because Smith's men had to go back on time even if that meant calling off the entire Red River expedition. If Banks took Shreveport, Grant continued, he was to forget about any further advance, garrison the place, trust the navy to defend the line of the river, and get everybody but the Shreveport garrison back to New Orleans for the long-talked-of thrust at Mobile. One of the first things Grant did after he got to Culpeper was to order Halleck to repeat these instructions in a new telegram. Banks was to be told that after he took Shreveport he could strengthen his Mobile column with at least 8,000 men from Steele in Arkansas and Rosecrans in Missouri, with still more coming from Sherman if necessary. Whatever happened, he was to start thinking about Mobile.[2]

Much wastage also was involved in protecting the border states. This guard duty was essential, but the men who performed it were putting no pressure on the Confederacy, and Grant believed they could guard their areas just as well by advancing as by standing still; if they advanced, the Confederates would have to assemble troops to meet them or lay their own territory open to invasion. A case in point was the command of General Franz Sigel, who had 26,000 men along the upper Potomac, the lower Shenandoah and the mountain passes to the west, guarding the line of the Baltimore & Ohio Railroad, the Pennsylvania border and loyalist West Virginia. Before March ended, Grant had instructed Sigel to form a column near the mountain town of Beverly and have it advance toward the Virginia & Tennessee Railroad at the extreme western tip of Virginia. A few days later he amplified this by telling Sigel to take the men who held the lower part of the Shenandoah Valley and prepare to move them toward Staunton and Lexington. He explained to President Lincoln that by making these moves Sigel could protect the country entrusted to him just as well as he could do if he remained motionless; furthermore, by advancing he would give General Lee something new to worry about, which would make Meade's task easier. Lincoln caught the point at once, and endorsed it.

"Oh yes, I see that!" he said. "As we say out West, if a man can't skin he must hold a leg while somebody else does." [3]

Lincoln's reply tickled Grant, and he used the expression in his own correspondence. (Like many another man who hears and adopts an apt locution, he forgot to give credit to the author.) Perhaps the fact that Lincoln understood him so easily, and found just the homely frontier expression for his thought, symbolized the unique relationship that quickly developed between the President and his general-in-chief. It was quite unlike anything any other general had with Abraham Lincoln; the President trusted Grant as he had trusted none of his predecessors, trusted him so completely that he did not even ask him how he intended to use the immense power that had been given him. The first thing Grant did on his return from Nashville was to go to the White House, where for the first time he and Lincoln talked with no third party present; and Grant seems to have felt that he had better be somewhat reticent, because both Stanton and Halleck had warned him not to tell the President his plans — the President found it almost impossible to keep a secret. But this interview had hardly begun when Lincoln gave Grant the same warning. People were always asking him, he said, what was going to happen next, "and there was always a temptation to leak," so he did not want to know what Grant was going to do. Naturally, after this, Grant kept his own counsel, and he wrote that the President told him that "all he wanted or ever had wanted was someone who would take the responsibility and act, and call on him for all the assistance needed, pledging himself to use all the power of the government in rendering such assistance."

A few days after this interview Grant gave an account of the conversation to the newest member of his staff, Horace Porter, recently promoted to lieutenant colonel and appointed one of Grant's aides.

President Lincoln, said Grant (as Porter wrote it down afterward), "told me that he did not pretend to know anything about the handling of troops, and it was with the greatest reluctance that he ever interfered with the movements of army commanders; but he had common sense enough to know that celerity was absolutely necessary; that while armies were sitting down waiting for opportunities to turn up which might, perhaps, be more favorable from a strictly military point of view, the government was spending millions of dollars every day; that there was a limit to the sinews of war, and a time might be reached when the spirits and resources of the people would become exhausted. He had always contended that these considerations should be taken into account, as well as purely military considerations, and that he adopted the plan of issuing his 'executive orders' principally for the purpose of hurrying the movements of commanding generals; but that he believed I knew the value of minutes, and that he was not going to interfere with my operations."

Somewhat diffidently, Lincoln told Grant of a campaign plan of his own, "which he wanted me to hear and then do as I pleased about." Lincoln brought out a map of Virginia, marked to show all the positions the Union and Confederate armies had occupied thus far, and pointed to two streams which empty into the Potomac: might not an army land between the mouths of those streams and then advance safely with the two rivers protecting its flanks? Grant did not describe this proposal to Porter, telling him only that the President made a suggestion which was quite impracticable "and it was not again referred to in our conversations." In his *Memoirs*, Grant said simply: "I listened respectfully but did not suggest that the same streams would protect Lee's flanks while he was shutting us up." [4]

Despite minor reservations, Grant began his career as general-in-chief by establishing an uncommonly warm working relationship with the President. But he had not been in Washington more than forty-eight hours before he was reminded that there was one aspect of his job that went beyond the range of a chat between himself and Mr. Lincoln. It was up to General Grant to deal with those generals whose connections put them in a class apart. This came to his attention first in the case of General Sigel, who was not extremely important but who did help bring the problem to attention.

It developed that General Sigel felt that the 20th and 21st regiments of Pennsylvania cavalry properly belonged to his forces and that they were being detained somewhere back in their home state; so Sigel sent a telegram to Congressman K. V. Whaley of West Virginia, asking him to find out whether these regiments had been ordered forward and, if they had not, to see to it that such orders were issued. Grant got a copy of this wire and telegraphed the gist of it to Halleck, adding a suggestion which Halleck passed on to Sigel verbatim: "I know no reason why these two regiments should not be ordered to the Department of West Virginia, but it is time General Sigel should learn to carry on his official correspondence through proper channels and not through members of Congress. Please call his attention to the fact that improper official correspondence will not be tolerated in the future."

Halleck told Grant that this kind of thing was extremely common. So many officers were writing to Congressmen, members of the Cabinet and other influential civilians asking for help in connection with applications for transfer, leave of absence, promotion and the like that the War Department and the office of the chief of staff were fairly swamped. Grant immediately had the adjutant general issue a new order, warning all officers that papers on army matters from now on must circulate only through army channels; that is, through military men, not through politicians. No applications or correspondence made in violation of this order would get any consideration, and officers who sent in such documents would either be court-martialed for disobedience or recommended to the President for dismissal from the service.[5]

That was helpful; but the case was a symptom of an incurable malady. No general in the Civil War could exercise high command very long without encountering officers who believed, sometimes correctly, that they were entitled to live by rules of their own; officers who had so much political influence that they were beyond the reach of an adjutant general's order. That there should be generals with powerful political connections was inevitable, given a civil war in a nation addicted to the wholehearted practice of democracy; if there ever was a war that met the textbook definition and was simply an extension of politics — ward and county and state-house politics, politics at the most intensely lived-in levels — it was this one, and nobody but professional soldiers was especially shocked thereby. A President who trusted his commanding general so much that he did not even want to know what his military plans were was also trusting him to understand about this matter of military-political influence. Grant was supposed to see that in many cases the political general had to be used because it would cost too much to discard him. The lieutenant general commanding was not expected to come running to the White House every time he found such a person in his path.

Sigel himself, to be sure, was a military cipher, and it did not really make much difference whether in the future he did or did not send his letters through the proper channels; the fact to digest here was that

Sigel was where he was because he was politically important and for no other reason. So was Banks, inexpertly prosecuting an ill-conceived campaign in a manner which, as Grant was about to learn, was entirely beyond anybody's control. McClernand had been another of the same sort. It had been possible to plow around him and at last to get rid of him because Washington had quietly hinted that this was desirable, and because Grant had managed to handle the business in a way that did not compel the President himself to intervene. Now there was another officer, politically the most untouchable of the lot, whom Grant was about to meet for the first time: Major General Benjamin F. Butler, commanding the Department of Virginia and North Carolina, with headquarters at Fort Monroe.

General Butler could be all things to all men, but he was very careful about his timing. Four years earlier he had been a famous Massachusetts doughface, a Northern politician with Southern sympathies, and at the Democratic convention in Charleston in 1860 he had done his utmost to get Jefferson Davis nominated for the presidency of the United States. When Davis finally attained a different presidency and went to war with the United States Butler became the most ardent of Northern war Democrats, and because Abraham Lincoln greatly needed Democratic support Butler was made a general; and although his military contribution was modest he devised for the Northern cause a canny legalism which made the Negro slave contraband of war and so made it possible for men to set the slave free without becoming abolitionists. The Southern people hated Butler as they hated no other Yankee — partly because he had hanged a Louisiana patriot without due process of law, partly because he had wickedly derided the sanctity of Southern womanhood, and partly, no doubt, because he was a remarkably easy man for anybody to hate — and in the spring of 1864, with a presidential election coming up, no Northern politician could forget that Butler was an all-out war man with a strong Democratic following and the most intimate ties with the Republican radicals. He was rarely accused of having principles that went much deeper than self-interest required, and it was easy to imagine him trying to take Lincoln's place in the White House. If the unpredictable fortunes of war and politics went wrong, it was not hard to imagine him succeeding.

So it was that on April 1 a steamer from Washington docked at Old Point Comfort and General Grant came ashore to confer with General Butler. Grant appears to have approached this meeting in a matter-of-fact spirit; Butler's past was no great concern of his, the man was there and there was no point in wishing that he might be somebody else, and it was time to have a talk with him. Butler and Grant had never worked together, and Grant knew nothing about him from personal experience. Halleck had undoubtedly warned him, because Halleck had strong feelings in the matter. Not long after this, speaking his mind about political generals as a class, Halleck wrathfully wrote to Sherman: "It seems but little better than murder to give important commands to such men as Banks, Butler, McClernand, Sigel and Lew Wallace, and yet it seems impossible to prevent it." As a man given to the commonsense approach, Grant would have retained only the words ". . . impossible to prevent it." Adam Badeau unquestionably summed up Grant's attitude when he wrote that although Butler "was not a professional soldier, and his military career had not been brilliant," it was nevertheless true that "his energy was great, his ability undoubted, and his political influence such that the government was unwilling to disturb him. Grant therefore did not insist on his removal." [6]

Grant's first impression of Butler was favorable and even Rawlins — who had a hawk's eye for men or events that might do harm to the lieutenant general — was similarly impressed; not long after this, Rawlins wrote jubilantly to Emma that "in Sherman, Meade and Butler, General Grant has three generals, all in important commands, whom he can trust," adding: "They are all three loyal to their country, friends of the General, and consequently with no ambitions to be gratified that look not to the success of our arms in obedience to and in accordance with his orders and plans." Colonel Comstock, to be sure, after watching Butler at the first meeting, confided to his diary that "Butler is sharp, shrewd, able . . . over-bearing. A bad man to have against you"; but Grant was inclined to be optimistic: "Before giving him any order as to the part he was to play in the approaching campaign, I invited his views. They were very much such as I intended to direct, and as I did direct, in writing, before leaving." [7]

On the wall of the room where the generals met there was a large map, and when the conference opened Butler went to this map and traced on it the movements which he believed Grant would want him to make. The newspaperman Albert D. Richardson, who was not with Grant on this trip but who was well informed about things that happened at Grant's headquarters, wrote that the move Butler lined out on the map was just about the move Grant actually was planning, and said that "Grant returned to Washington with a good deal of respect for Butler's clear-headedness and capacity." [8]

Grant's general design for the war in the east was by this time fairly simple: he would aim Meade's army at Lee and Butler's army at Richmond. If Lee's army could be destroyed in the field, well and good; if not, he hoped that Meade and Butler could eventually join hands south of the James River, and when at last he wrote his report on the 1864 campaign he used these words: "My first object being to break the military power of the rebellion and capture the enemy's important strongholds made me desirous that General Butler should succeed in his movement against Richmond, as that would tend more than anything else, unless it were the capture of Lee's army, to accomplish this desired result." On the day after his conference with Butler, Grant wrote out Butler's orders in some detail. Since his entire Virginia campaign was built around the ideas expressed in this document it is worth examining:

In the spring campaign, which it is desirable shall commence at as early a day as practicable, it is proposed to have co-operative action of all the armies in the field, as far as the object can be accomplished. It will not be possible to unite our armies into two or three large ones, to act as so many units, owing to the absolute necessity of holding on to the territory already taken from the enemy; but, generally speaking, concentration can be practically effected by armies moving to the interior of the enemy's country from the territory they have to guard. By such movement they interpose themselves between the enemy and the country to be guarded, thereby reducing the number necessary to guard important points, and at least occupy the attention of part of the enemy's force, if no greater object is gained. Lee's army and Richmond being the greater objects toward which our attention must be directed in the next campaign, it is desirable to unite all the force against them.

The necessity for covering Washington with the Army of the Potomac and of covering your department with your army makes it impossible to unite these forces at the beginning of any move. I propose, therefore, what comes nearest this of anything that seems practicable. The Army of the Potomac will act from its present base, Lee's army being the objective point. You will collect all the forces from your command that can be spared from garrison duty — I should say not less than 20,000 effective men — to operate on the South Side of the James river, Richmond being your objective point. To the force you already have will be added about 10,000 men from South Carolina, under Major General Gillmore, who will command them in person. Maj. Gen. W. F. Smith is ordered to report to you to command the troops sent into the field from your own department.

Grant's plans were drawn up to serve several purposes. General Quincy A. Gillmore and a small army had spent the better part of a year amid the sand dunes and lagoons just below the entrance to Charleston Harbor, trying without any success to capture that storied city. Gillmore and his soldiers were not now being used for anything important; to bring them north and add them to Butler's force would reduce the manpower waste that annoyed Grant so much and would in effect put 10,000 new troops into action. In addition, by naming Gillmore and Baldy Smith as Butler's principal subordinates, Grant believed he would be giving Butler precisely the kind of help Butler needed most — professionally competent juniors who could handle troops in the field while Butler himself provided the energy and the leadership to drive for Grant's chosen goal. Finally, this appeared to offer an excellent spot for Smith, whom Grant still considered one of the best men in the army.

The orders Grant wrote for Butler went on to say that when his expedition moved its first task was to take City Point, a hamlet on the south side of the James River at the mouth of the Appomattox, a few miles below the important railroad center of Petersburg. Butler was to entrench himself there, concentrate his field troops as fast as possible, and prepare for further action.

"The fact that has already been stated," Grant wrote, "that is, that Richmond is to be your objective point and that there is to be co-operation between your force and the Army of the Potomac, must be your guide. This indicates the necessity of your holding close to the south bank of the James as you advance. Then, should the enemy be forced into his intrenchments in Richmond, the Army of the Potomac would follow, and by means of transports the two armies would become a unit." [9]

From now on, as far as Butler's operation went, it was simply a matter of expediting arrangements already made, orders to Gillmore and Smith to join this column having been issued before Grant went down from Washington. Butler himself was a good expediter, and once the orders had been written Grant could go north and get on with other tasks. Besides Rawlins and Comstock, Grant was accompanied on this trip to Old Point Comfort by Julia Grant, by two women friends of hers, and by Congressman Washburne, and Butler undertook to be the gracious host and arranged sight-seeing trips to Hampton and elsewhere in the neighborhood. No time was lost because of this, inasmuch as a violent storm swept lower Chesapeake Bay just then and made an immediate return to Washington impossible, but Rawlins fumed that this junketing was most irregular and grumbled in a letter to Emma: "We may be here for two days yet. This much for having one's wife with him. If Mrs. Grant had remained in Washington we would not have mixed with this trip any curiosity or pleasure not strictly in the line of duty . . . When a man's wife is with him he can't help bending a little to the desire of pleasing her." The Rawlins who complained because Grant had Julia with him here was the same Rawlins who had complained so bitterly because Grant did not have Julia with him at Chattanooga, because "if she is with him all will be well." All seems to have been well at Old Point Comfort, and Grant returned to Culpeper with this part of the approaching campaign well in hand.[10]

Although Baldy Smith was to have command of an army corps under Butler, and was expected (by Grant, at least, if not by Butler himself) to be the guiding genius for the whole operation, it was nevertheless true that Smith was not quite getting what he wanted. His attempt to replace Meade as head of the Army of the Potomac had long since dropped out of sight — if indeed it had ever been taken seriously by anyone but Smith and Wilson — and now his cherished plan for an attack that would swing far south of Richmond, going from the Hampton Roads area down into the Carolina interior, was likewise disappearing. Smith did not give up easily, but a fortnight before Grant saw Butler it was clear that Grant was cooling off on Smith's plan, and Smith was complaining that "Meade's statements and Halleck's wisdom rather befogged him," so that "with ample means to make his important movement wherever he pleased . . . he has determined to take the line of operations on which he found the Army of the Potomac and work on that." Smith was of course neither the first nor the last general to protest that higher authority was being obtuse, but since an important part of the 1864 campaign would hinge on his inability to adjust his own ideas to those of his superiors his complaints here are worth a moment's study. To his friend Wilson, in

mid-March, Smith set forth what he called "my three simple propositions":

There is no hope of forcing Lee into a battle until he wishes to fight,
and there is nothing in the question that should make him willing to fight
and run a great risk before he gets to Richmond.

If we can then avoid the siege of Richmond and put ourselves on his
line when we are near our base and he must come out and fight us on our
own ground or starve and disband, it is certainly our business to do it.

I hold that the vicinity of Weldon [a railroad junction town on the
Roanoke River, some seventy-five miles south of Richmond] is such a
place, and that we can get there by secrecy and celerity and wait there to
see what is then to turn up . . . If in all this you see anything which
would seem to be important enough to press upon the General, go in and
strike from the shoulder.[11]

In view of the fact that Lee proved most eager to "fight and run a
great risk" long before he got to Richmond, and of the added fact that
a siege of Richmond was what Lee most wanted to avoid, it is clear
that Smith's appraisal of the strategic situation differed from Lee's appraisal as much as it differed from Grant's. He persisted in advocating
his plan so hard that Rawlins grew mistrustful, and in a letter to
Emma written a little more than a week after the return from Hampton Roads Rawlins set forth his own thoughts:

You see, I have no doubt, much in the newspapers as to the plan of
coming campaigns. For these of course we care little, but you know my
opinion of General William F. Smith, who has altogether a different plan
from that of the General, and feels very badly that Grant don't fall into
his views. General Wilson falls in with General Smith, and I believe from
his talk he thinks General Grant has adopted it. Fortunately, however,
neither of these soldiers (and able soldiers they are too) know what the
General's plans are. He has not communicated his plans to either of them.
Of one thing the country can be assured, the General does not mean to
scatter his army and have it whipped in detail. No such calamity as this
will happen to us, I am certain. If I have ever been of signal service to
General Grant it has been in my constant, firm advocacy of massing large
forces against a small one, in other words, of always having the advantage
of numbers in our side. Such is the General's notion of battles.

Rawlins went on to say that Smith had recently written to Wilson a
letter "in which all the selfishness of his nature is evinced"; Wilson

gave it to Rawlins to read, and Rawlins in turn showed it to Grant, to show Grant "just what sort of man he has to deal with in General Smith." With the opening of the campaign less than a month away here was a powerful hint that one of Grant's principal lieutenants was likely to be a very hard man to work with. Since Smith was teamed up with Butler, who himself was one of the most difficult men to work with in all American military history, this was an ominous sign if anyone cared to notice it.[12]

Immediately after his return to Culpeper, Grant got off another letter to Sigel, repeating his earlier instructions, stressing the point that the thrust at the Virginia and Tennessee Railroad was to be made in harmony with the movements of the other armies, and specifying that this expedition might have to return, after accomplishing its task, by way of the Shenandoah Valley. Consequently, "you should collect any available force you may have at a convenient point from which to march on Staunton to meet them," bearing in mind that it probably would be necessary to take along a supply train large enough to feed Sigel's own column and also "to feed those you go to meet." A day or so later, Grant pointed out that if the Confederates tried to take the offensive against any part of Sigel's line, that would be all to the good: "Your forces would be accomplishing at home the greatest advantage expected of them by moving south, if the enemy do attack you in force — that is, they would divide him."

To Sherman, at the same time, Grant sent a general summary of his plans.

"It is my design, if the enemy keep quiet and allow me to take the initiative in the spring campaign, to work all parts of the army together and somewhat toward a common center," he wrote. As he saw things early in April, this would involve the following operations:

Banks was to conclude his Red River campaign as quickly as possible, turn over that territory to Steele and the navy, abandon all of Texas except for an outpost on the Rio Grande, reduce the number of troops on the lower Mississippi to the smallest possible total, and in all of these ways to collect at New Orleans at least 25,000 men, to which force Grant would add 5,000 more from Rosecrans's force in Missouri. Banks then was to move against Mobile, and "it will be impossible for him to commence too early."

Butler would have a total of 33,000 men, including the 10,000 Gillmore was bringing up from South Carolina, and with Gillmore and

Smith as his corps commanders he was to move up the south side of the James. As far as the main thrust in Virginia was concerned, "I will stay with the Army of the Potomac, increased by Burnside's corps of not less than 25,000 effective men, and operate directly against Lee's army wherever it may be found." Sigel would move along the lines already laid down: General E. O. C. Ord, who had succeeded Mc-Clernand in front of Vicksburg, would command the column that marched from Beverly, and he would be joined on his way east by cavalry under General George Crook. (In the upshot, Ord did not accompany this force, and it was commanded by Crook.) Grant confessed that he did not expect great results from this West Virginia operation, but "it is the only way I can take troops from there," and he borrowed Lincoln's expression: "If Sigel can't skin himself he can hold a leg whilst someone else skins." Somewhat hopefully, Grant said that he wanted to get everything moving by April 25.[13]

This optimistic time schedule was modified within a few days, and when he gave Meade a breakdown on the campaign, "for your own perusal alone," Grant admitted that Banks probably could not get his command together before May 1. He told Meade what he had told Sherman — that "all the armies are to move together and toward one common center" — and after explaining what the other armies were going to do he got down to the instructions that applied specifically to Meade:

Lee's army will be your objective point. Wherever Lee goes, there you will go also. The only point upon which I am now in doubt is whether it will be better to cross the Rapidan above or below him. Each plan presents great advantages over the other, with corresponding objections. By crossing above, Lee is cut off from all chance of ignoring Richmond and going north on a raid; but if we take this route all we do must be done while the rations we start with hold out; we separate from Butler, so that he cannot be directed how to co-operate. By the other route, Brandy Station can be used as a base of supplies until another is secured on the York or James river. These advantages and objections I will talk over with you more fully than I can write them.

Grant went on to say that Burnside's corps would reinforce Meade. At the beginning, Burnside would defend the railroad supply line, so that Meade could collect all of his strength around Brandy Station without worrying about his rear. Meade meanwhile must cut the army's baggage as sharply as possible; two wagons for a five-hundred-man regiment would be the limit, with one wagon each for brigade and division headquarters and perhaps two for corps headquarters. Finally:

Should by Lee's right flank be our route, you will want to make arrangements for having supplies of all sorts promptly forwarded to White House on the Pamunkey. Your estimates for this contingency should be made at once. If not wanted there, there is every probability they will be wanted on the James river or elsewhere.[14]

The question whether he should move by Lee's right or by Lee's left was the biggest single point Grant had to decide on this spring, and fourteen years later he said that he seriously considered going by Lee's left, moving from the Rapidan all the way to Lynchburg, hoping to get behind Lee and invest Richmond and, in effect, to repeat the maneuver that had succeeded so well at Vicksburg.

"I thought of massing the Army of the Potomac in movable columns, giving the men twelve days' rations, and throwing myself between Lee and his communications," he said. "If I had made this movement successfully — if I had been as fortunate as I was when I threw my army between Pemberton and Joe Johnston — the war would have been over a year sooner. I am not sure that it was not the best thing to have done; it certainly was the plan I should have preferred. If I had failed, however, it would have been very serious for the country, and I did not dare take the risk."

Grant's instinct was calling for a Virginia campaign quite unlike the one he finally made: a war of quick movement and sharp maneuvering, carried out as if such words as "attrition" and "hammering" had never been invented. Clearly enough, he finally came to see that the plan was a little too risky. This was, after all, an election year, and risks had to be held down because failure now could have a prohibitive price. In addition, there was the point that had haunted Grant ever since his promotion — the lingering doubt whether he could do with this army and its officers what he had done with armies and officers in the west. He went on to explain:

What deterred me was the fact that I was new to the army, did not have it in hand and did not know what I could do with the generals or men. If it had been six months later, when I had the army in hand, and knew what a splendid army it was and what the officers and men were capable of doing, and if I could have had Sherman and Sheridan to assist in the movement, I would not have hesitated for a moment.[15]

If Grant at this time had doubts about the Army of the Potomac, that army had its own doubts about him. His mere presence seemed to imply a criticism of what the army had done in other campaigns, and the veterans who must soon cross the Rapidan at his bidding wanted to be shown. Typical was the comment written by Colonel Charles S. Wainwright, chief of artillery for the Fifth Corps, who mused: "It is hard for those who knew him when formerly in the army to believe that he is a great man; then he was only distinguished for the mediocrity of his mind, his great good nature and his insatiable love of whiskey . . . From what I heard at corps headquarters this evening [March 24] there was no enthusiasm shown by the men on the arrival of their new commander." A few days later, having had a close-up glimpse of the new general-in-chief, Colonel Wainwright confessed that "he is not so hard-looking a man as his photographs make him out to be," but he complained that at a review "Grant rode along the line in a slouchy unobservant way, with his coat unbuttoned and setting anything but an example of military bearing to the troops. There was no enthusiasm." [16]

The eagerness with which newspapers and magazines worked to build up the new lieutenant general irritated the army, especially the officer corps. The *Army and Navy Journal* exulted that Grant's arrival would "restore to that army the primacy which it long held but was finally compelled to yield to the grand Army of the West, to which the nation is indebted for the only victories of the war that have been fruitful in great practical results"; and this made unpleasant reading for an army that had the victories of Antietam and Gettysburg on its record. The case was not helped when the *Journal* went on to say that "no General arose capable of bringing victory out of the Army of the Potomac," and held that successes won in the west "covered up for the time the humiliation of our failures in Virginia."

Even more irritating were the stories that blossomed out in the daily press. It was reported that Grant would have no reviews, because these wasted the soldiers' time in vain display, that he had given orders to stop the balls and horse races that were held now and then at the different headquarters, and that he was firmly opposed to the luxury in which so many officers lived. (This last undoubtedly grew from a seed planted by Secretary Stanton back in the winter of 1862. Observing that during the inactive winter months some Army of the Potomac officers were having quite a pleasant war, Stanton announced sternly that "while men are striving nobly in the west the champagne and oysters on the Potomac must be stopped." There was a good touch of Rawlins in Secretary Stanton.) It was also printed that Grant lived strictly on soldiers' rations, chiefly pork and beans, and that when he took the train between Washington and Culpeper he invited enlisted men to ride in his car.

Meade wrote angrily that "all these are humbugs, and known to the writers to be without foundation," but his anger was assuaged when he found that Grant had not planted the stories, heartily disapproved of them, and refused to take them seriously. To his wife Meade wrote that Grant "laughs at the statement in the papers of his remarks about balls, etc., and says he will be happy to attend any innocent amusement we may get up, he including among these horse races, of which he is very fond." [17]

As a matter of fact, Meade's subordinates were more disturbed than Meade himself. The good impression Grant and Meade made on each other at the first meeting stood up during the difficult weeks that followed: difficult, not only because of the newspaper stories, but also because the unusual command setup was bound to create friction, with the general-in-chief sitting almost at the elbow of the major general commanding the country's principal army. Meade's chief of staff, General Humphreys, held that there were in effect "two officers commanding the same army," which, he said, "naturally caused some vagueness and uncertainty as to the exact sphere of each." But Meade himself made few complaints and he wound up by testifying that the arrangement worked out very well. Before Grant had done more than establish himself at Culpeper, Meade wrote that "he seems not at all disposed to interfere with my army in details," and noted that Grant "at once adopts all my suggestions."

At about this time Horace Greeley appeared in Washington, urging that Meade be replaced — a flareback, possibly, from the precious scheme devised by General Wilson, although Grant did not know it — and Grant told Meade that "if he saw Greeley he would tell him that when he wanted the advice of a political editor in selecting generals he would call on him." Meade assured Mrs. Meade that Grant seemed both honest and fair, disposed to give Meade full credit for anything Meade did, and said that he "seems desirous of making his stay here only the means of strengthening and increasing my forces." When Grant reviewed General John Sedgwick's Sixth Corps he was highly impressed and seemed to be "quite astonished at our system and organization," and Meade stoutly insisted: "My relations with Grant continue friendly and confidential, and I see no disposition on his part to take advantage of his position." [18]

As a matter of fact, Grant was prepared to go a good deal farther than any of his officers realized in establishing complete harmony in the Army of the Potomac. This army had been beset by politics from the beginning, but Grant understood what many of the army's officers could never understand — that the political fetters were partly self-imposed, so that to set the army free of politics required something of the men in uniform as well as of the men in the Republican party. Grant tried to explain what he wanted in a conversation years later with John Russell Young.

"When I took command of the army I had a dream that I tried to realize — to reunite and recreate the whole army," he said. "I talked it over with Sherman. Sherman and I knew so many fine, brave officers. We knew them in West Point and the army. We had the sympathy of former comradeship. Neither Sherman nor I had been in any way concerned in Eastern troubles, and we knew that there were no better soldiers in the army than some of those who were under a cloud with Mr. Stanton. Then I wanted to make the war as national as possible, to bring in all parties. I was anxious especially to conciliate and recognize the Democratic element. The country belonged as well to the Democrats as to us, and I did not believe in a Republican war. I felt that we needed every musket and every sword to put down the Rebellion.

"So when I came East I came prepared and anxious to assign McClellan, Buell and others to command. I had confidence in their ability and loyalty, confidence which, notwithstanding our difference in politics, has never faltered. But I was disappointed."

There is no record that any formal overtures were made at this time to McClellan, by Grant or by any spokesman for him; although Postmaster General Montgomery Blair, whether with or without any authorization from anyone except himself, was writing earnestly to McClellan's friend Samuel Barlow, urging that McClellan ask or accept reinstatement in the army and forget about the presidential race of

1864. But definite moves were made in Buell's direction. At one time both Sherman and Thomas were prepared to give him command of the Fourteenth Corps, and Grant himself once suggested that Buell be put in command at Memphis. Some echo of this reached Governor Andrew Johnson, who detested Buell with all the fervor of a feuding Tennessee loyalist, and Johnson sent a hot wire to President Lincoln: "I TRUST IN GOD THAT GENERAL BUELL WILL NOT BE SENT TO TENNESSEE. WE HAVE BEEN CURSED WITH HIM HERE ONCE, AND DO NOT DESIRE ITS REPETITION." Buell would have none of it, and Grant told Young that "the generals were not in a humor to be conciliated."

It struck Grant, looking back, that when an officer was crippled by politics it was usually the officer's own fault: "What interfered with our officers more than anything else was allowing themselves a political bias." It was the bias itself that was bad, and whether it was Republican or Democratic made little difference. From his long wartime experience Grant drew the moral: "The generals who insisted upon writing emancipation proclamations and creating new theories of state governments and invading Canada all came to grief as surely as those who believed that the main object of the war was to protect Rebel property and keep the Negroes at work on the plantations while their masters were off in the Rebellion." [19]

CHAPTER NINE

The Fault Is Not With You

AFTER his visit to Butler, Grant had hardly more than a month to get ready for the 1864 campaign, but he found time to review the different units of the Army of the Potomac in the camps around Culpeper and Brandy Station. The reviews were not social occasions, as in the old days, for Grant was not interested in parades. He preferred to ride down the lines, looking intently at the soldiers in the ranks, as if he wanted to see the faces of the men who were going to fight for him; he was trying to size up this army and it seemed more important for him to see the soldiers than for the soldiers to see him. Grant liked what he saw, his natural optimism rose, and as the time of preparation came near a close he wrote to Halleck: "The Army of the Potomac is in splendid condition and evidently feel like whipping somebody; I feel much better with this command than I did before seeing it. There seems to be the very best feeling existing." [1]

For their part the soldiers were respectful but not enthusiastic. Their curiosity was as great as his, but they had seen generals come and they had seen them go, and although they were impressed they did not make a big noise about it. A Wisconsin veteran summed up the general response by saying, after an inspection: "He looks as if he meant it." One of Meade's staff officers agreed, remarking that "Grant wears an expression as if he had determined to drive his head through a brick wall and was about to do it." As a matter of fact, the Army of the Potomac slipped into much the attitude Grant's own westerners had had. A veteran of the Vicksburg campaign said that Grant "was a man in whom the men had confidence, but they did not love him"; and he added that Grant never got the spontaneous cheers that always followed men like Logan and McPherson. The eastern army reached this point easily. The men had expended most of their enthusiasm long ago. In the early days they had had McClellan, and they had been almost ritually drilled to have and to express a high admiration for him; when he made an inspection, staff officers used to ride ahead to tell the troops that he was coming and to warn them that they were expected to give him a warm reception. With McClellan's departure, and with much experience of hard campaigning and hard fighting added since his day, the army had grown more taciturn. Some of the divisions had refused to cheer Meade after Gettysburg — not, as one soldier explained, because the men had anything against Meade, but simply because they did not feel like cheering for generals anymore. A fair expression of the common attitude is found in a letter written this spring by an officer in the Second Corps: "There is no enthusiasm in the army for Gen. Grant; and on the other hand there is no prejudice against him. We are prepared to throw up our hats for him when he shows himself the great soldier here in Virginia against Lee and the best troops of the Rebels." [2]

What Grant really was would appear when the battles came. Meanwhile, although everyone in and out of the army was trying to appraise him all anyone could be sure of was that he was the last chance. He himself had told his intimates at Nashville that the coming campaign had to be the last one, and implicit in his promotion had been the belief that he was the man who would win the war; implicit, also, was the notion that he would win it quickly, and this built up added pressure. Men looked for more than they could see; wanting to see greatness, and seeing instead the very essence of the ordinary, they felt that there must be unfathomable depths here, a quality no one could understand because nobody could see it. Even Sherman once cried out: "To me he is a mystery, and I believe he is a mystery to himself." An officer who served with him in the west agreed: "There is no great character in history . . . whose sources of power have seemed so difficult to discover as General Grant's." A woman who saw something of him in Washington wrote that although he was the most democratic of men he seemed to keep everyone at arm's length, and said that "he walked through a crowd as though solitary." Lieutenant Morris Schaff of Meade's staff saw "a fascinating mystery in his greatness," and said that at headquarters Grant somehow was "the center of a pervasive quiet." [3]

The mystery perhaps came because Grant did not look the part. Incurably, he remained the man who could walk into a room without being noticed; there must be more here than met the eye, because what met the eye usually seemed to be nothing at all. Men who talked with him felt that there was an air of reserve about him; yet this was largely because Grant found it hard to relax with strangers. General Jacob Cox felt this reserve when he met Grant in east Tennessee, but he concluded that Grant simply had no knack for small talk except when he was with men he knew well. Grant would smoke, listen, look pleasant and say nothing — and yet with people he knew he enjoyed light conversation and was very much at his ease. Sherman agreed that "Grant is really social and likes to see people and hear them talk of old times and old things." Sherman warned that on duty Grant did not like to hear much talk: "The best way to deal with Grant is 'on paper,' giving dates, facts and figures." A man who visited Grant at Chattanooga believed that Grant's success was due mostly "to his fine common sense and the faculty he possesses in a wonderful degree of making himself understood." A mail clerk at Grant's headquarters said that an officer warned him when he came to work: "All you have to do to get along with the general is to take straight orders and go straight at them. He will tell you what to do but not how or where or why to do it. He will turn his back and expect it to be done. Look him straight in the eye and don't say 'Sir' too much." This same clerk told Hamlin Garland after the war that he never knew Grant to hesitate about anything, and never saw him flurried or excited: "He was a man who always knew just exactly what he wanted to do." [4]

Some men looked at Grant and to their dismay saw in him no trace of breeding or gentility. They felt that the nation's principal general ought to have these qualities, but Grant evidently did not; like the President who had appointed him, he was just an outlander. The distinguished Richard Henry Dana, Jr., expressed it after he met Grant in Willard's Hotel one day late in April. Dana concluded sadly that the man was no gentleman; he "had no gait, no station, no manner"; he was smoking a cigar, he had "rather the look of a man who did, or once did, take a little too much to drink," and altogether he seemed to be an "ordinary, scrubby looking man with a slightly seedy look, as if he was out of office on half pay." A week or so later Dana visited the White House, saw Lincoln, found him no better, and wrote to his father: "Such a shapeless mass of writhing ugliness as slouched about in the President's chair you never saw or imagined." In a letter to his wife, Dana admitted that it was hard to keep from feeling an interest in the President — "a sympathy and a kind of pity" — and it seemed clear that Lincoln had "qualities of great value"; yet Dana could not avoid the belief that "his weak points may wreck him, or wreck something." [5]

The war had got into the wrong hands. There was no help for it, and Back Bay and Beacon Street were suffering along with tidewater Virginia. The country was finding its leaders, to say nothing of its stoutest followers, among the men who had no ancestors as Massachusetts and Virginia understood such matters; the salient fact of the war this spring was that Lincoln and Grant had at last gone into partnership, and a well-bred observer was bound to shudder at the thought.

Grant himself seems to have understood that the army would judge him by what he did rather than by what he looked like; and here, as the man in Chattanooga had said, he had no trouble making himself understood. One day not long before the opening of the campaign Brigadier General Rufus Ingalls, chief quartermaster of the Army of the Potomac, needed to confer with him. In this army a meeting with the commanding general was always a formal occasion, with everybody turned out just so, and Ingalls put on his best uniform and boots of a dazzling polish and rode over in a covered wagon drawn by four dapple-gray horses which had been groomed as carefully as if the fate of the nation depended on it. Four orderlies, all in their best and riding horses equally well cared-for, rode in attendance, and altogether it was as showy and impressive as anything one would care to see.

On a road near Culpeper, Ingalls saw Grant riding toward him, coming back from a review. Ingalls had his driver pull to a halt; Grant saw him, and rode over beside the wagon to shake hands — after all, he and Ingalls had been classmates at West Point. Ingalls remarked that he had business to talk about, and Grant said: "Very well — we can talk it over here as well as any place." Grant dismounted, and Ingalls got down from his comfortable seat, and the two men started walking up and down the road together, Ingalls explaining what he had on his mind, Grant nodding his head, now and then asking a question.

The road was extremely muddy. There was a slow drizzle. There was a good deal of traffic, and every time a horse or wagon went by the generals were spattered. They kept on walking back and forth for an hour, and at last Grant said: "That's all — goodbye, General." Grant mounted and rode away, Ingalls got in his wagon and went back to the Army of the Potomac, and the meeting was over; and

Ingalls was muddy and bedraggled, the shine on his boots all gone. He was heard to mutter that this was the last time he would dress up to call on any general, and when he saw Meade Ingalls said: "I tell you, Meade, Grant means business." And the orderlies wagged their heads and remarked that the general-in-chief did not care much about spit and polish.[6]

This of course was a trait that pleased the enlisted men. What pleased them even more was the relentless way Grant reached out to take soldiers from the bombproof Washington garrison and add them to the fighting force. The Washington forts were manned by regiments of heavy artillery, men who had been trained to act both as gunners and as infantry, and these men had been enjoying a pleasant war, doing no fighting and no marching and living in comfortable barracks instead of in pup tents. Grant extracted thousands of them from their happy assignments, turned them into line infantry, and brought them down to Culpeper and Brandy Station to join the Army of the Potomac. Colonel Theodore Lyman of Meade's staff noted that the army considered this a wonderful joke; the soldiers liked to stand by the roadside when one of these Washington regiments came to camp and sing out derisively: "How are you, Heavy Artillery?"[7]

To get soldiers, Grant reached a good deal farther than the Washington garrison. At the end of March he told Halleck: "I think it advisable that governors of states and commanders of all Northern departments be notified to forward to the field all recruits, new organizations and all the old troops it is possible to spare from their departments, with all possible dispatch. They can strip their departments to the lowest number of men necessary for the duty to be performed." Halleck passed the word along, a sample of the orders he sent out being the one that went on April 8 to General S. P. Heintzelman at Columbus, Ohio. Heintzelman was told to "get every available man into the field as early as possible" and to reduce the number of troops in his department to the lowest possible total. This sort of thing delighted Rawlins, who described the results in a letter to Emma: "From New York City alone we get 3,000 men, or thereabouts, that have been for months virtually dead to the service. In all the Northern states there are many troops, kept mainly that some of our major generals might have commands in Peace Departments commensurate with their rank. These are all being gathered up and brought to the front."

Not all of the behind-the-lines generals liked this, of course, and some of them — most notably, General Rosecrans in St. Louis — made vigorous objection. Rosecrans commanded a border state beset by guerrilla wars and now and then threatened by actual invasion, he believed that Confederate sympathizers in Missouri were making dangerous plots, he insisted that he needed every soldier he could get . . . and he dragged his feet stubbornly, delaying the dispatch of troops he had been ordered to send to Sherman and protesting bitterly. On May 1 he got from Grant a telegram that was about as sharp as anything Grant ever wrote:

Have you sent any troops from your department at any time in obedience to orders from me? The troops which you are detaining, without authority and in violation of orders, are a part of the garrison for keeping open the Mississippi. With the troops belonging to your department proper, with other commanders interposing between you and all organized forces of the enemy, I do not understand your threat of disaster as a consequence of permitting veterans to return to where they belong, unless it means that you must do as you please or be held in no way responsible. You can bring troops from places where you have more than is necessary to hold your depots safely.

Rosecrans replied that he faced dreadful dangers, outlined them (unfortunately they impressed Grant not at all), and closed by saying: "If you think it safe after my statement of these facts to risk sending off these troops without bringing some disciplined infantry to take their place, your orders will be obeyed." The troops moved, at last, and Colonel Comstock made a tart note in his diary: "The Gen. ordered him to spare 5,000 troops — instead he seizes two regiments of Sherman and cries that disaster will follow if they are taken away. His telegram is a model for quick — insolent — disobedience of orders. If Grant had the power he would be mustered out of service." [8]

Grant had told Sigel that "in the spring campaign it is desirable to bring into the field all the troops possible"; and although the official figures at this time showed that the Army of the Potomac was very large indeed the official figures were highly deceptive. The April returns, for instance, showed that the Army of the Potomac contained 97,273 men, present for duty equipped, including 13,287 cavalry. But late in April Meade confessed to two callers — former General Garfield and Governor William Dennison of Ohio — that he could put only 60,000 men into action. Of his cavalry, he said, only 7,000 could be used. These callers, being politicians, immediately leaked the news, and Meade received a rebuke from Secretary Stanton. Meade had to confess that Garfield and Dennison had quoted him correctly, and he said that he had simply been referring to the fact that all armies necessarily contained large numbers of men whose duties made them noncombatants.[9]

Along with getting more men to the front there went the task of perfecting the organization of the men who were already there. After consulting with Sherman and Thomas, Grant made a mild shake-up in the western forces. General Gordon Granger, who had impressed Grant so poorly at Chattanooga, was relieved of his command of Thomas's Fourth Corps, being replaced by General Oliver Otis Howard. The old Eleventh and Twelfth Corps, badly understrength, were combined into a new Twentieth Corps, command of which went to Joe Hooker; and because Slocum, the old commander of the Twelfth Corps, still found himself unable to get along with Hooker, Slocum was relieved and sent to command the garrison at Vicksburg. In the east, Meade performed the reorganization, ordering it before Grant came down, although because it went into effect soon after Grant's arrival most of the army assumed it was Grant's doing. Meade broke up the old First Corps and Third Corps, which had been brutally mauled at Gettysburg and had never been brought up to strength afterward. The survivors from those corps were assigned to other units, and the Army of the Potomac now contained but three corps — Second Corps under Winfield Scott Hancock, Fifth Corps under G. K. Warren, and John Sedgwick's Sixth Corps. The old units had been under proper corps size; also, Meade simply did not have five competent corps commanders. The two generals displaced, George Sykes and John Newton, were quietly given more modest tasks in the west.

As the coming weeks would show, Meade's army actually did not contain as many as three men really suited for corps command. The editor of the *Army and Navy Journal* warned when Grant was promoted that he must "strike at the tap root of one of the prime evils that have afflicted the Army of the Potomac — we mean incapacity in certain of the commanders of the corps." The evil went down to division and brigade level, in many cases, and the *Journal* hoped that Grant would "put to rest forever all that spirit of jealousy, rivalry and ambition on the part of those in subordinate commands that has been the bane of the Army of the Potomac." The problem was notorious. Slocum said that being sent west was the best thing that ever happened to him, because "I passed away from the field of controversy and faction to the field of hearty co-operation"; and a Sixth Corps officer boasted that the generals in his corps were "without a trace of that dilatory or critical spirit to which no small share of the mishaps of the Army of the Potomac must be attributed." [10]

There was not much that anyone could do about this; it was fairly easy to see that some generals were being tried beyond their strength, but it was not at all easy to see where good replacements could be found. Partly for this reason, and perhaps even more because he was trying to leave Meade alone in the conduct of the army, Grant did not try to make any changes, except that he did insist on bringing in a new man to command the army's cavalry. This man, of course, was Phil Sheridan, who was none too pleased at leaving the western army, where he felt at home, and being put into the Army of the Potomac, about which he had reservations. Sheridan found that most of the cavalry's strength and time was wasted on picket and outpost duty, and he insisted on bringing the separate parts together so that the cavalry could move and fight as a corps. He was a short-tempered man and so was Meade, they had different ideas about the way cavalry ought to be used, and in the weeks to come the two men would strike sparks from each other; yet in the main the new command would work out well. Sheridan had three divisions. Two remained under their old leaders, Generals A. T. A. Torbert and David McM. Gregg. The third was given to the man who had gone from Grant's staff to the Cavalry Bureau in Washington, James H. Wilson.

With so much going on at headquarters, Grant was rarely able to go to Washington to see Julia, and in the middle of April he sent her a letter of explanation: "In the first place I do not like being seen so much about Washington. In the second it is not altogether safe. I cannot move without it being known all over the country, and to the enemy who are hovering within a few miles of the railroad all the time. I do not know that the enemy's attack on the road last Friday was with the view of catching me, but it was well timed." Meanwhile, he was living well enough at Culpeper — "plain and well, surrounded with mud."

On April 27 Grant passed a small milestone, and he wrote to his wife about it: "This is my forty-second birthday. Getting old, am I not? — I received a very short letter from you this evening scratched off in a very great hurry as if you had something much more pleasing if not more important to do than write to me. I'll excuse you though. It's only gratifying a little desire to appear angry that I am indulging in. Your letter enclosed three horseshoes from Mrs. McDowell which I will wear — in my pocket — for the purpose named, i.e., *to keep off witches*. I am still very well. Don't know exactly the day when I will start or whether Lee will come here before I am ready to move. Would not tell you if I did know . . . Kisses for yourself and Jess." [11]

The work of tightening up on military administration kept Grant busy, but in the end he and the Union cause would stand or fall on his ability to devise and execute a basic strategic plan. So far the Federal government had never really had a plan. It had an intense desire to win the war and it had a number of good armies, but it had never been able to make the armies work together. One was forever lying in camp while another went out to fight, the Confederacy often was able to take men from an inactive front to reinforce some other front, and Grant remarked, in his final report, that up to 1864 the separate Union armies had been like a balky team, with no two horses pulling at the same time.

Above everything else Grant had to correct this. He had to put everyone to work and make certain that they worked in harmony, and he who could not skin must at least hold a leg. The key to everything was the point Grant had made in his midwinter dispatch to Halleck — that "the enemy have not got army enough" to resist the pressure that would be exerted if all the major Union armies moved in proper coordination. The government had the strength to win if it applied it properly. It was up to Grant to apply it.

One of his first acts when he got to Washington was to ask Halleck for a map that had been prepared at headquarters, with long red lines showing the areas held by the Union at the end of each year of the war — the important line, of course, being the one that showed the territory under Union control at the beginning of 1864. Stabbing out from this line, a blue pencil had drawn the lines of advance contemplated for all the Union armies in the coming campaign. Grant immediately had Colonel Comstock send a copy of this off to Sherman.

By the time Sherman got it some of the blue lines were out of date.

They still included Baldy Smith's idea for an advance from New Berne to Raleigh, North Carolina, and they had another one projecting an advance from Sabine Pass, on the Gulf Coast, up to Shreveport and on to the Indian Territory; Smith's idea had been discarded, the Sabine Pass operation had been superseded by Banks's operation on the Red River, and the all-important move toward Richmond would not begin from York River, as this map said it would. But the big offensives were all there. There would be a drive on Richmond, going on to Lynchburg and the southwest if all went well; there would be another drive from Chattanooga down to Atlanta, and a third one coming up to Atlanta from Mobile by way of Selma and Montgomery; and, strikingly enough — because it was the first definite projection of what eventually became the famous March to the Sea — there was a blue line running down from Atlanta by way of Milledgeville to Savannah. All of these offensives were to begin at the same time, and it would be seen whether the Confederacy had army enough.

Sherman took fire when he saw it, and he was jubilant, almost incoherent, when he wrote to Comstock: "That map to me contains more information than a volume of printed matter . . . From that map I *see all*, and glad am I that there are now minds at Washington to devise, and for my part if we can keep our councils I believe I have the men and ability to march square up to the position assigned to me and to hold it . . . Concurrent action is the thing. It would be wise that the Genl through you or some educated officer should give me timely notice of all contemplated movements with all details that can be foreseen. I now know the result arrived at. I know my base, and have a pretty good idea of my lines of operation. No time shall be lost in putting my forces in mobile condition so that all I ask is notice of time, that all the Grand Theatres of war shall thus be simultaneously active. We saw the beauty of time in the Battle of Chattanooga, and there is no reason why the same harmony of action should not pervade a continent." [12]

When Sherman exalted "the beauty of time," he of course was talking about what anyone else would have called the importance of timing. A grand forward movement that would have all the great armies rolling ahead at the same moment, each one by its advance helping the progress of the others, could be irresistible. Lincoln had thought of it, to be sure, away back in the winter of 1862, and he had impulsively ordered everybody to go on the offensive on Washington's Birthday.

His order was ignored, nobody moved a muscle, and the whole project was widely derided as a sample of the President's bumbling ignorance; but the idea had been perfectly sensible, made futile because there had been no general able to see its importance and put it into effect. Now it would be done, and the war would go into a new chapter.

In Virginia Grant's aim was simple: to pin Lee down and make him fight the kind of war he could not win . . . the simplicity of this concept being tarnished only by the difficulty of finding some way to make it operative.

The first element here was the Army of the Potomac. It was to press Lee so closely that he would never have the time or the room to lash out with one of those deadly counterstrokes that had ruined so many "forward to Richmond" movements. The next element was Butler's army, which was to move up the south side of the James River as far as it could go. The final element was the determination that no matter what Lee did when Meade advanced — whether he fought or retreated — Meade's and Butler's armies would before long be brought together on the south bank of the James, dooming Lee to a hopeless defensive and threatening to destroy him outright by seizing Richmond.

As the April weeks passed, the plan took clear shape. Grant had already given Meade and Butler their orders. Now he began to put more and more emphasis on the river that came down from Richmond to the sea, and on April 18 he sent Butler an explanation: "With the forces here I shall fight Lee between here and Richmond, if he will stand. Should Lee, however, fall back into Richmond, I will follow up and make a junction with your army on the James river." To Halleck, on April 29, he repeated the same warning: "Should Lee fall back within his fortifications at Richmond, either before or after giving battle, I will form a junction with Butler and the two forces will draw supplies from the James river." The matter of supplies was important, because the army had a cumbersome train; Ingalls reported that when the army moved it would take 3,500 wagons, 29,000 horses and 20,000 mules. Grant had stationed Burnside with the freshly recruited Ninth Corps along the Orange & Alexandria Railroad to guard Meade's supply line, but that was only temporary: "When we get once established on the James river there will be no further necessity of occupying the road south of Bull Run." [13]

In all of this there may have been too little concern about how Lee might respond when the Army of the Potomac advanced. Grant was so intent on the part his own army was to play that he ignored the fact that Lee might have plans of his own; and it seems faintly odd to find Grant wondering whether Lee would stand and fight at all. But Grant was simply applying a necessary corrective. In the past the Federal army had spent altogether too much time worrying about how Lee was going to behave. It had wondered, "What is Lee going to do?" so obsessively that as soon as he began to do it a kind of paralysis developed; one unhappy result being the calamity that descended on General Hooker at Chancellorsville. Each Federal offensive had been based upon a strangely defensive frame of mind, a symbol of which was the insistence with which Army of the Potomac officers had kept reminding Grant, "You have not yet met Bobby Lee." The first victory of all had to be won in the commanding general's mind; Grant's whole program rested on the belief that no matter what happened he could force the Army of Northern Virginia to keep step with the Army of the Potomac.

As a matter of fact, it ought to be said that if Lee had elected, when the campaign began, to spar and fall back and look for an opening as Meade advanced he would have been following a perfectly rational strategy. This was the way Joe Johnston acted when Sherman moved, and it took Sherman as long to reach the Atlanta fortifications as it took Grant and Meade to reach those in front of Richmond. In any case, the point is that Grant's immediate, primary objective was the James. If he had to fight to get there, well and good; once he was there he could operate where Lee was most vulnerable, because this objective led to two others, so closely linked that they were inseparable — Lee's army, and Richmond itself. To win one was almost certainly to win both, and when both were gone the Confederacy must die.

. . . It would work this way, probably, if every Federal army did its part. Not only must there be continued pressure on Lee's army; there must be similar pressure on every other Confederate army, the most important one being Johnston's. To get the point properly grasped, Grant on April 19 sent Sherman what Sherman had asked for — an "educated officer" to explain what was being planned in Virginia and to make certain that Sherman understood how that would affect his own operations. Out to Nashville went Colonel Comstock, and he gave to Sherman a letter from Grant reading as follows:

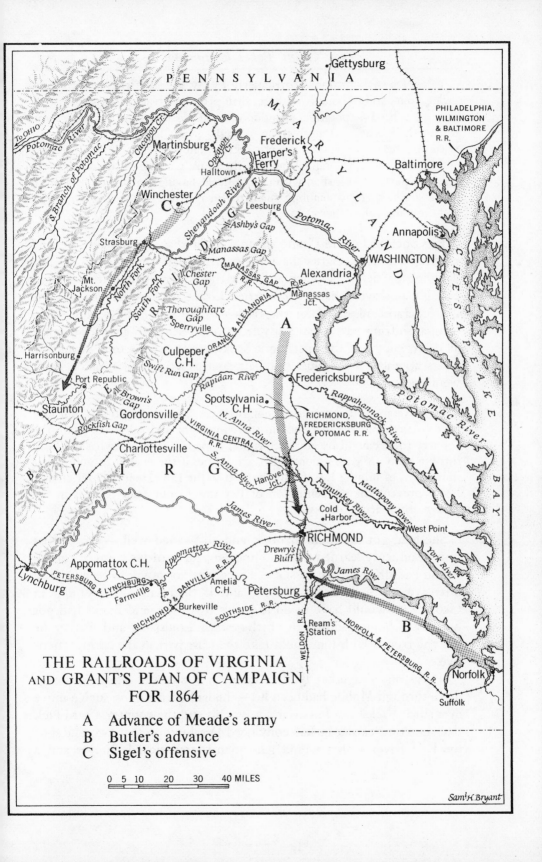

THE RAILROADS OF VIRGINIA
AND GRANT'S PLAN OF CAMPAIGN
FOR 1864

A   Advance of Meade's army
B   Butler's advance
C   Sigel's offensive

0 5 10   20   30   40 MILES

Sam.¹ H. Bryant

What I now want more particularly to say is that if the two main attacks, yours and the one from here, shall promise great success, the enemy may, in a fit of desperation, abandon one part of their line of defense and throw their whole strength upon a single army, believing that a defeat with one victory to sustain them is better than a defeat all along the line; and hoping too at the same time that the army meeting with no resistance will rest perfectly satisfied with their laurels, having penetrated to a given point south, thereby enabling them to throw their force first upon one and then upon the other.

For once in his life Grant wrote a letter that needs a slow second reading, his usual clarity having been dimmed when pronouns and dangling participles momentarily got the better of him. It is obvious enough, however, that what worried Grant was the danger that the Confederates might repeat the trick used so successfully at Chickamauga, shifting part of an army from one theater to another to meet an emergency and then getting it back before anyone took advantage of its absence. That must not happen this year, and Grant's letter went on:

With the majority of military commanders they might do this. But you have had too much experience in traveling light and subsisting upon the country to be caught by any such ruse. I hope my experience has not been thrown away. My directions, then, would be, if the enemy in your front show signs of joining Lee, follow him up to the full extent of your ability. I will prevent the concentration of Lee upon your front if it is in the power of this army to do it.[14]

Sherman got the point at once, and all seemed well — except that Grant suddenly learned that an important piece of his western combination had dropped out of sight. There was not going to be a Federal offensive northeast from Mobile, and if Sherman did anything in Georgia he would have to do it on his own. General Banks had got hopelessly bogged down in northwestern Louisiana, and neither he nor the troops with him could take the least part in the spring offensive.

It was not altogether Banks's fault. In a way the whole idea of a drive through Mobile had been his — he had been urging such a move ever since Vicksburg fell — and it was his and the country's hard luck that sometime earlier he had convinced Washington that a conquest of the Red River valley would gain many strategic advantages and a great deal of cotton. Washington had thought about this during the winter, had thought also about the need to establish Federal control over Texas, had issued binding orders . . . and late in March Banks set out to capture Shreveport, a Red River port far up in the northwest corner of Louisiana. He was under firm orders from Grant to get back in time to attack Mobile by the beginning of May, when the big offensives would begin, and the outlook at the start was fairly good. Banks had upwards of 20,000 men of his own and the 10,000 under General A. J. Smith borrowed from Sherman; Steele was coming down across Arkansas to join him with 15,000 more. Admiral Porter was steaming up the Red River with a dozen gunboats and a fleet of transports and supply vessels, and if all went well the thing might perhaps be done.

Nothing went well. Steele ran into swarms of aggressive Confederate cavalry, found his supply problem insoluble, and never did make connections. Banks's advance struck a Confederate army led by General Richard Taylor at a place called Sabine Crossroads, thirty or forty miles short of Shreveport, and on April 8 was roundly defeated. Smith's men next day routed a Confederate force at Pleasant Hill, but Porter found the water in the Red River falling so fast that he could not go any farther upstream no matter what the army did, and the army and navy together went sagging unhappily back to Alexandria. There, at the beginning of the last week in April, Banks got a message from Grant telling him that he must send Smith and his 10,000 men back to Sherman at once no matter what it cost him.

By now Grant had made up his mind to cancel the whole Red River operation, but even that could not be done quickly. The river was so low that Porter could not get his fleet past the Alexandria shallows on its way downstream to the Mississippi; Porter sent a frantic telegram to Sherman saying that if Smith left Banks would follow him and the whole fleet would be lost; and Grant at last agreed that Smith must stay until the gunboats got out of trouble, specifying that at the earliest moment Banks must bring everyone back to New Orleans. To Halleck Grant sent an indignant message: "General Banks, by his failure, has absorbed 10,000 veteran troops that should now be with General Sherman and 30,000 of his own that would have been moving toward Mobile, and this without accomplishing any good result." He also requested that Banks be relieved of his command — getting in reply a wire from Halleck saying that the President did not see his way clear to relieve Banks just now.[15] Grant had to accept the fact that the authority of the general-in-chief did after all have limits.

In the end the fleet was saved and Banks's army got back to New Orleans, badly shopworn but still in one piece. A Wisconsin colonel in the command managed to increase the depth of water on the Alexandria rapids by building a set of wing dams that narrowed and deepened the stream just long enough to enable the gunboats to escape, and by the middle of May the whole operation had come to an end. It had been a flat failure, made endurable only because the fleet had been saved: and Grant at last got Banks under control by creating a new military division west of the Mississippi, giving top command of it to Major General E. R. S. Canby, whose instructions in substance were: Clean up the mess. Banks retained his command but he was under Canby now, confined largely to administrative duties in Louisiana, and no more was heard about an offensive west of the big river.[16]

Nor was anything more heard about an offensive from Mobile up into Alabama and Georgia, because by this time it was too late. When Sherman moved down toward Atlanta he would have to move without Smith's 10,000 veterans — Porter had said this was the only contingent in Banks's army that had not been demoralized by the Red River adventure — and Joe Johnston would get some 15,000 reinforcements who should have been kept busy in southern Alabama. Grant's western plan had not quite been crippled, but it had been placed under a severe handicap.

Even more important, probably, was that Grant got a new insight into the way in which political requirements could affect the operations of the general-in-chief.

Late in April Rawlins told Emma that Grant had asked to have Banks relieved but that it remained to be seen whether his request would be granted, and Rawlins explained: "Thus far everything he has desired has been accorded to him. General Banks, however, stands very high with the Government and is I have no doubt a statesman of a high order of talents, but certainly has shown himself a miserable failure in the command of troops, if we are to judge by his success or failure." And on May 3 Halleck sent Grant an informal letter explaining the ins and outs of the case:

General Banks is a personal friend of the President and has strong political supporters in and out of Congress. There will undoubtedly be a very strong opposition to his being removed or superseded, and I think the President will hesitate to act unless he has a definite request from you to do so, as a military necessity, you designating his successor or superior in command . . . To do an act which will give offense to a large number of his political friends the President will require some evidence in a positive form to show the military necessity of that act. In other words, he must have something in a definite shape to fall back upon as his justification. You will perceive that the press in New Orleans and in the Eastern States are already beginning to open in General Banks' favor. The administration would be immediately attacked for his removal. Do not understand me as advocating his retention in command. On the contrary, I expressed to the President months ago my own opinion of General Banks' want of military capacity.[17]

This was putting it on the line. If Grant wanted to dismiss a politically important general he would have to take all of the responsibility and he would have to take it publicly. He would have to do it at the opening of a presidential campaign in which for the first time a democracy would try the desperate experiment of holding a national election while it fought for survival in a civil war. He would have to balance military needs against political intangibles, knowing that a defeat at the polls could be even more costly than a defeat on the battlefield. And, finally, by the time he got Halleck's letter it was too late. The armies were going to start moving that very night. Neither Banks nor anyone else could possibly reassemble the Red River army into a force that could attack Johnston's rear in time to make Sherman's progress toward Atlanta any easier. The beauty of time that Sherman talked about had already been marred, but nothing could be done about it. Grant wasted no energy complaining. He simply went ahead with what was left.

The handicap politics placed on Grant was no worse than the handicap his predecessors had borne. The difference was that Grant saw why he had to carry it and saw, too, that whether he liked it or not he must work uncomplainingly within the limits it laid down. Out of this there was developing an asset the Union cause had never yet enjoyed — unshakable understanding and trust between the President and the general-in-chief. We have two little glimpses into each man's mind that show how this was beginning to bear fruit.

The first is provided in the reminiscences of William O. Stoddard, who was a member of the White House secretariat that spring.

Stoddard had been ill when Grant reached Washington, and he returned to duty not long before the opening of the spring campaign. It was a Sunday, both Nicolay and Hay were absent, and Stoddard found Lincoln stretched out on a sofa, his hands clasped behind his head, "looking as if he did not care two cents for the past, present or future." Lincoln sat up, shook hands, had Stoddard take a chair, asked about the state of his health and seemed disposed to chat. Inevitably, Stoddard's first question was: What sort of man is Grant? Lincoln replied that Grant was "the quietest little fellow you ever saw," and remarked that several times Grant had been in the room for a minute or so before the President even knew he was there; Lincoln added: "The only evidence you have that he's in any place is that he makes things git! Wherever he is, things move."

Then Stoddard wanted to know about Grant's capacity as a general. Lincoln abruptly sat up and pointed a long forefinger at his secretary. As Stoddard remembered it afterward, the President said: "Stoddard, Grant is the first general I've had! He's a general!" Stoddard asked what he meant by this, and Lincoln explained:

"I'll tell you what I mean. You know how it's been with all the rest. As soon as I put a man in command of the army he'd come to me with a plan of campaign and about as much as say, 'Now, I don't believe I can do it, but if you say so I'll try it on,' and so put the responsibility of success or failure on me. They all wanted me to be the general. It isn't so with Grant. He hasn't told me what his plans are. I don't know, and I don't want to know. I'm glad to find a man who can go ahead without me."

Stoddard was willing to be encouraged, but he reverted to the old question: how would Grant stand up when he confronted Lee? At this point, said Stoddard, the President's face "put on his story-telling expression," and he made a reply that had nothing to do with Lee but that did show just how the President felt about Grant:

"You see, when any of the rest set out on a campaign they'd look over matters and pick out some one thing they were short of and that they knew I couldn't hope to give them and then tell me they couldn't win unless they had it; and it was most generally cavalry."

Lincoln began to laugh silently, and Stoddard suddenly realized that "his lying there so contentedly on the sofa this Sunday afternoon was due to the fact that the army had been lifted from his shoulders by someone competent to carry it on." In Stoddard's version, Lincoln went on:

"When Grant took hold I was waiting to see what his pet impossibility would be, and I reckoned it would be cavalry as a matter of course, for we hadn't horses enough to mount even what men we had. There were fifteen thousand or thereabouts up near Harper's Ferry, and no horses to put them on. Well, the other day, just as I expected, Grant sent to me about those very men; but what he wanted to know was whether he should disband them or turn 'em into infantry.

"He doesn't ask me to do impossibilities for him, and he's the first general I've had that didn't." [18]

The other glimpse comes from an exchange of letters between Grant and Lincoln. At the end of April Lincoln wrote to Grant wishing him success. The letter, which resembles no letter Lincoln sent to any other general, is as follows:

Not expecting to see you again before the Spring campaign opens, I wish to express in this my entire satisfaction with what you have done up to this time, so far as I understand it. The particulars of your plans I neither know nor seek to know. You are vigilant and self-reliant; and, pleased with this, I wish not to obtrude any constraints or restraints upon you. While I am very anxious that any great disaster, or the capture of our men in great numbers, shall be avoided, I know these points are less likely to escape your attention than they would be mine. If there is anything wanting which is within my power to give, do not fail to let me know it. And now with a brave army, and a just cause, may God sustain you.

To this Grant made the following reply:

Your very kind letter of yesterday is just received. The confidence you express for the future and satisfaction for the past in my military administration is acknowledged with pride. It shall be my earnest endeavor that you and the country shall not be disappointed. From my first entrance into the volunteer service of the country to the present day, I have never had cause of complaint — have never expressed or implied a complaint against the Administration or the Secretary of War, for throwing any embarrassment in the way of my vigorously prosecuting what appeared to be my duty. And since the promotion which placed me in command of all the armies, and in view of the great responsibility and the importance of success, I have been astonished at the readiness with which everything asked for has been yielded, without even an explanation being asked. Should my success be less than I desire and expect, the least I can say is, the fault is not with you.[19]

No other general had talked to Abraham Lincoln that way. McClellan had complained, Hooker had bragged, Halleck had labeled himself a mere advisor . . . and Grant quietly destroyed his alibi in advance and then put the great armies in motion.

CHAPTER TEN

In the Wilderness

THE wagons began to move during the afternoon of May 3, jolting clumsily along toward the lower crossings of the Rapidan, heading for the haunted clearings at Chancellorsville, where unburied skeletons lay among dead leaves. The wagons were what the army lived by but they were also a crippling drag on its progress so they started before the infantry did, and they raised great clouds of dust which the Confederate lookouts on Clark Mountain saw and wig-wagged about from their high signal stations. Federal cavalry moved ahead of the wagon trains with a great jingling and creaking of metal and oiled leather, while bronzed young men who thought well of themselves lolled at ease in their saddles and looked for enemies who were not there. The Army of the Potomac was beginning its last campaign; the curtain was going up on the terrible final act of the war.

A little after midnight the infantry was roused out of its camps around Culpeper and Brandy Station, and brigade after brigade formed up in the trampled fields and swung into column in the night. Times of departure and order of march had been expertly organized — Meade's staff knew all about the business of getting an army into motion — and in the dark hours before dawn the endless lines went down the roads, bound for the Rapidan and for whatever might lie beyond. Engineer detachments went in front, ready to lay pontoon bridges, with cavalry going along to drive enemies away from the river crossings, and by five o'clock Meade and his escort had joined the march. When full daylight came the sky was clear, with a soft spring breeze and a promise of warmth, and the men tramped past woodlands that were light green with new leaves, wild flowers all in blossom below, white dogwood shining in the morning light. A war correspondent wrote that he had never seen the army move in better order with less straggling, although he noticed that as the sun came out thousands of men tossed their overcoats in the ditches, figuring they would not need them again. One of the soldiers said that as his regiment went over the crest of a hill he could see the whole country-side laced with long dark lines of men — dense, heavy lines that hardly seemed to be moving and looked like fences except that the sun sparkled on polished musket barrels and all the flags were flying.[1]

It was eight o'clock before Grant finally left his headquarters house at Culpeper and came out to join the march. He had written his fare-well letter to Julia two nights earlier, and considering the fact that he was about to begin the most important campaign of his life the letter has a strangely detached tone. It went thus:

The train that takes this letter will be the last going to Washington. This then is the last letter you can receive from me until the Army strikes some new base. The telegraph will be working for a few days however so that you will hear through the papers what the Army is doing.

Before you receive this I will be away from Culpeper and the Army will be in motion. I know the greatest anxiety is now felt in the north for the success of this move, and that the anxiety will increase when it is once known that the Army is in motion. I feel well myself. Do not know that this is any criterion from which to judge results because I have never felt otherwise. I believe it has never been my misfortune to be placed where I lost my presence of mind, unless indeed it has been when thrown in strange company, particularly of ladies. Under such circumstances I know I must appear like a fool . . . Love and kisses for you and Jess.

The night before the army moved Grant stayed up late, going over plans with his staff and then relaxing for a long chat with Rawlins and with Congressman Washburne, who had come down to accompany the general for a few days. When the headquarters party started Grant was riding his big bay horse, Cincinnati, occupying a worn saddle that he had been using ever since Fort Donelson, and he was formally dressed in the full regalia of a lieutenant general — unbut-toned uniform frock coat over a blue waistcoat, pants neatly tucked into knee-length boots, yellow thread gloves on his hands and black felt hat with a golden cord on his head, sash about his waist and a sword at his side. Grant hardly ever wore a sword; Adam Badeau be-lieved that he did so today because "he seemed to consider the occa-sion one of peculiar dignity."

A little past noon Grant crossed the Rapidan at Germanna Ford, and after crossing he dismounted in front of an abandoned farmhouse and sat on the porch to watch Sedgwick's Sixth Corps go by. As he waited for the servants to prepare lunch, he remarked that he was relieved that the army had been able to seize the fords and make the crossing without opposition. He knew that the opposition would develop in the near future; while he was waiting for lunch a courier brought a message from a signal corps station in the rear, which had intercepted and deciphered a dispatch from a Confederate station on Clark Mountain — General Richard Ewell, commanding the left wing corps of Lee's army, was already moving forward, apparently meaning to cut the Federal line of march.[2]

This line of march led straight into a jungle of second-growth timber, a region with few roads and fewer clearings, bad country to fight in and worse country to maneuver in; an area known as the Wilderness, extending twelve or fifteen miles from east to west and ten miles from north to south. Chancellorsville lay on its eastern fringe, and a forsaken little stream known as Mine Run lay near the western fringe; and the Germanna Ford Road, going south through the center of it, came a few miles below the Rapidan to a run-down inn called Wilderness Tavern. Here it struck the principal east-west highway, the Orange Turnpike, that came from Fredericksburg by way of Chancellorsville and went on to Orange Courthouse, where Lee had his headquarters. (If Ewell was advancing he would be coming east along this road.) A few miles south of the turnpike there was another important east-west road, the Orange Plank Road, roughly parallel to the Turnpike, going also from Chancellorsville to Orange Courthouse; and from Wilderness Tavern a highway known as the Brock Road led south across the Plank Road and then swung southeast to Spotsylvania Courthouse, intercepting all of the secondary roads that ran west toward Lee's country. Turnpike, Plank Road and Brock Road — if the Army of the Potomac proposed to go anywhere in the Wilderness it had to have freedom of movement on these three.

At Mine Run, six miles west of Wilderness Tavern, the Confederates had a strong line of entrenchments, and although this played no part in the battle that was about to begin its mere existence had a good deal to do with the movement that was being made.

The Army of the Potomac had seen this line of works before. This happened at the end of November, 1863, when Meade took the army down across the Rapidan, turned west to attack Lee, found the Mine Run works altogether too strong to be carried, and unhappily took his army back to Brandy Station and Culpeper and went into winter quarters. Grant had no more desire to storm the Mine Run line than Meade had had in November, and he was trying to flank Lee out of it and force him to fight in the open country. The Army of the Potomac would hold the area around Wilderness Tavern, planting two corps so as to control the Turnpike and the Plank Road; a third corps, coming around from Chancellorsville by meandering country roads, would swing well to the south and then turn west so as to come in south of the headwaters of Mine Run. If it did this Lee would have to abandon his Mine Run works and either retreat or offer battle without the benefit of a prepared line of entrenchments. In November, Lee had waited quietly at Mine Run for the Federals to attack. If he did so now, he would be flanked.

Fast movement obviously was called for, and this was why Meade had put his army on the road immediately after midnight. Yet the movement must not be too hasty, because if the army marched away from its wagon train Lee might very well send an infantry column slicing in past the Federal rear, destroy the whole train, and compel the Army of the Potomac to go back across the Rapidan. Therefore the movements on May 4 did not go as far as they might have gone. By the middle of the day Hancock's powerful Second Corps, which had crossed the Rapidan half-a-dozen miles below Germanna Ford, by the Ely's Ford Road, went into bivouac around Chancellorsville, waiting for the endless line of wagons to come up and go into park. (These trains as a matter of fact did not finish their crossing of the river until late on the afternoon of May 5.) Warren and the Fifth Corps, leading the army's other column, got to Wilderness Tavern by two in the afternoon and went into camp there, with pickets thrown out to the west along the Turnpike; and Sedgwick's Sixth Corps, following close behind, got across the river and bivouacked beside the Germanna Road, with General James B. Ricketts's division left on the riverbank to guard the crossing. By the middle of the afternoon, in other words, the whole army had halted, although it could easily have gone a good many miles farther; and the halt, as Meade's Chief of Staff, General Humphreys, explained, was made because of the need to keep the army between the wagon train and Lee's infantry.

Grant had a fourth army corps at his disposal, Burnside's Ninth

Corps, which contained eight brigades numbering something like 25,000 men. This corps was not as powerful as it looked, because nearly two-thirds of its men were raw recruits and one of its four divisions, led by General Edward Ferrero, was made up of two brigades of colored troops, which had never fought before and whose fighting qualities were considered uncertain. Burnside's men had been in camp along the line of the Orange & Alexandria Railroad, from Manassas Junction all the way to Rappahannock Station, and Grant had warned Halleck that once he reached the James he would abandon that line of railroad and let the Rebel raiders do as they pleased with it. Now, on the porch of the house at Germanna Ford, learning that at least part of Lee's army was advancing to meet him, Grant made up his mind to abandon the road immediately. Back to Burnside went a courier with orders to start at once and join the Army of the Potomac: "Make forced marches until you reach this place. Start your troops now in the rear the moment they can be got off, and require them to make a night march." [3]

Toward evening, Grant's people put up the headquarters tents in a field near the house where Grant had spent the afternoon. In front of Grant's tent they built a fire out of fence rails — not for warmth, because the evening was mild, but just to make things cheerful. Meade, who had gone on ahead to Wilderness Tavern, rode back after supper, and he and Grant had cigars together in front of the fire, talking over plans for the next day. (It appears that the inveterate smoker Grant had a rather modern sort of lighter, flint and steel with a coil of oiled wick, so that he could light a cigar no matter how hard the wind might be blowing.) Grant's quarters were moderately Spartan: the tent he occupied contained a portable cot, a tin washbasin on an iron tripod, two folding camp chairs and a plain pine table. At some time during this evening a courier came up with telegrams: Sherman, Butler and Crook had all advanced that morning, as ordered. At an early hour Meade went back to his own headquarters, and Grant went to bed.

As on the first day, the emphasis in the plans for the movement on May 5 was on an early start and a moderate advance. The army began to move at five o'clock in the morning, and Hancock had the longest march — a swing south from Chancellorsville and then west, crossing the Brock Road at Todd's Tavern, going over the Po River at Corbin's Bridge, and halting at Shady Grove Church on the Catharpin

Road, eight miles south of Wilderness Tavern in an air line, substantially farther as the wandering roads went. Warren was to make a shorter march, going southwest from Wilderness Tavern and planting the head of his column on the Plank Road at Parker's Store, three miles west of the place where the Plank and Brock roads crossed, four miles or more from Wilderness Tavern. Sedgwick was simply to come up to Wilderness Tavern, throw infantry west on the Turnpike, and await developments. When all of these units had reached their objectives Hancock was to extend his right to make contact with Warren's left, and Warren in turn was to make firm contact with Sedgwick. Meanwhile Burnside's corps was expected to reach Germanna Ford after a grinding all-night march, ready to protect the army's right flank and rear and available to reinforce any part of the line if serious fighting developed.[4]

The big question mark in all of this, of course, was General Lee. Grant and Meade had a good line on Lee's position on May 4, when the Army of the Potomac began to move. Ewell's corps was on the Orange Turnpike, half-a-dozen miles east of Orange Courthouse. A. P. Hill had his corps at the courthouse, placed so that he could move east on the Plank Road. Longstreet, with the third corps, was near Gordonsville, eight or ten miles south and somewhat west of Hill; a little too far back, as things worked out, to get into action as promptly as Lee wished. Longstreet was supposed to have three divisions, but one of them, George Pickett's, was down below the James River, and Longstreet's force at Gordonsville came to about 14,000 men. At this moment the Federals did not know that Pickett was absent, and they assumed that when Lee moved he would have some 75,000 men of all arms. It was clear that Lee knew that the Army of the Potomac was across the Rapidan, but what he proposed to do about it was completely unknown. The only certainty was that he would not remain passive, and Grant did not expect him to. The newspaper correspondent Sylvanus Cadwallader, who often was fairly well informed about Grant's designs, had sent a confidential message to his paper, the New York *Herald*, on May 3, saying that the army was about to cross the Rapidan and warning: "Immediate and obstinate fighting is apprehended."[5]

This expectation was entirely justified. At seven-thirty on the morning of May 5 Grant got a message from Meade at Wilderness Tavern:

The enemy have appeared in force on the Orange Pike, and are now reported forming line of battle in front of Griffin's division, Fifth Corps. I have directed General Warren to attack them at once with his whole force. Until this movement of the enemy is developed, the march of the corps must be suspended. I have, therefore, sent word to Hancock not to advance beyond Todd's Tavern for the present. I think the enemy is trying to delay our movement, and will not give battle, but of this we shall soon see. For the present I will stop here, and have stopped our trains.

Grant waited for the head of Burnside's column to reach the river, and sent Meade this reply:

Your note giving movement of enemy and your dispositions received. Burnside's advance is now crossing the river. I will have Ricketts's division relieved and advanced at once, and urge Burnside's crossing. As soon as I can see Burnside I will go forward. If any opportunity presents itself for pitching into a part of Lee's army, do so without giving time for disposition.

Half an hour later Meade sent word that Warren was getting ready to attack and that part of Sedgwick's corps would move up in support. He added: "I think, still, Lee is making a demonstration to gain time. I shall, if such is the case, punish him. If he is disposed to fight this side of Mine Run at once, he shall be accommodated."

Grant concluded not to wait for Burnside. Leaving a note for that general, telling him to close up as rapidly as possible on Sedgwick, he had his staff mount, and sometime before nine o'clock he rode forward to join Meade in the Wilderness.[6] Meade was posted near Wilderness Tavern, and Grant put his own headquarters not far away, on an open hillock just north of the Turnpike, and got from Meade a quick appraisal of the situation.

Apparently Lee meant to make trouble on the Turnpike. Not long after dawn, Federal pickets on that road had discovered an approaching column of Confederate infantry. The road was held by General Charles Griffin's division of Warren's corps; Griffin had his men throw up a defensive line of breastworks astride of the Turnpike, and he sent a skirmish line forward half a mile or more to develop the enemy's intentions. It was on the basis of this information that Meade suspended the march toward Lee's flank and ordered Warren to attack along the Turnpike. Meade wanted immediate action, and he told

Warren: "If there is to be any fighting this side of Mine Run, let us do it right off."

Immediate action was impossible to get. The army was cumbersome, and on this morning of May 5 it covered a great deal of ground, with poor roads and dense woodland between the separate pieces. Hancock was far away, and the head of his column a couple of miles beyond Todd's Tavern on the Catharpin Road. He halted obediently when Meade's orders reached him, and while Wilson's cavalry division scouted the area in his front Hancock awaited further orders. He was not exactly out of reach, but it would take an hour or two for any courier to reach him with a dispatch from Meade and it would take even longer for him to act in response; obviously it would not be possible to bring Hancock's corps into action until sometime after noon.

Most of Warren's corps was stretched out along three miles of a twisting country road that went off southwest from the Turnpike toward Warren's original objective, Parker's Store on the Plank Road. The corps was slightly embarrassed by the fact that it was the tail of the column rather than the head of it that occupied the Turnpike and that had first touched the enemy. It was even more embarrassed by geography. Three of Warren's four divisions were on this country road, which was narrow and unhandy. Warren's pioneers had worked hard for hours to put the road in shape, building half-a-dozen bridges and cutting down trees so as to give the little lane a minimum width of twenty feet, but the road was still hemmed in by heavy forest growth and it was a bad place for maneuvering. The head of this infantry column — actually, the extreme left of Warren's line, once the corps halted and went into line of battle facing west — was composed of General Samuel Crawford's division, two brigades of Pennsylvania Reserves, veteran troops which had refused to reenlist and which this morning had less than four weeks to serve before their time expired.

The order to halt, sent to Crawford by Warren at 7:30 A.M., reached Crawford at an unfortunate moment. He had just reached an open, slightly elevated position, the Chewning Farm, only a mile short of Parker's Store, and this was an excellent place for the Federals to hold if there was going to be any fighting on the Plank Road, which ran past it a little to the south. Such fighting apparently would develop before long; Wilson had sent a detachment of Federal cavalry to Parker's Store, and when Crawford halted on the Chewning Farm this cavalry was skirmishing with Rebel infantry, which proved to be the advance of A. P. Hill's corps. Now Crawford found himself ordered to send one of his two brigades off to support the division on his right, General James Wadsworth's, which was under orders to go north to the Turnpike and help Griffin. Somewhat taken aback, Crawford asked if he should abandon his position in order to support Wadsworth, and got in reply a message from Warren: "You will move to the right as quickly as possible." One of Warren's staff officers was with Crawford, and he sent back a sharp protest: "It is of vital importance to hold the field where General Crawford is. Our whole line of battle is turned if the enemy get possession of it. There is a gap of half a mile between Wadsworth and Crawford. He cannot hold the line against an attack." This did no good, the Chewning Farm position went by default, and the Fifth Corps was going to make its fight along the Turnpike.[7]

It was not going to make it immediately, however. Between the moment when a commanding general makes up his mind to attack and the moment when his troops actually go into action there is always a time lag; these things can be told about much more quickly than they can be done. This time lag was especially bad in the Wilderness because the roads by which orders moved forward from headquarters were so few and so bad and the country between the roads was so often impassable for a man on horseback. To make matters still worse, it quickly developed that some of the generals did not think they ought to attack at all, and there were time-consuming arguments. As a result Meade, who at seven o'clock had ordered Warren to attack at once, found that six hours went by before the attack took place, and when it did take place it was not at all the smashing hammerblow he had wanted.

Meade's order to attack went to Warren, who sent it off to General Griffin, who in turn passed it along to General Romeyn B. Ayres, who commanded Griffin's advance brigade. Ayres sent a staff officer back to Griffin to say that they ought to wait: it looked as if the Confederates themselves were about to attack, and anyway the Rebel position was very strong. Griffin went to the front himself, talked to Ayres and other officers, apparently was convinced, and sent the staff officer back to tell Warren that the assault ought to be delayed. (After the war the staff officer said that as he remembered it he was sent back twice with this message.) Warren talked to Meade and Grant and apparently got a caustic rebuke from Meade, not to mention a remark by Grant to the effect that the army seemed reluctant to start a fight; and at last Warren rode to the front, and somewhere after one o'clock in the afternoon Griffin's division moved forward. Meanwhile the rest of Warren's corps was still lined up along the blind road to Chewning's Farm, under orders to move and getting ready to move but not yet actually moving. Over on the Plank Road the skirmishing grew heavier, the handful of Federal cavalry had to retreat, and Crawford was unable to do anything about it.[8]

It might have been as well if the attack had been made earlier, because General Lee was not nearly as eager to get into a major battle that day as he seemed to be. On May 4 he had seen a bright opportunity in Grant's advance into Wilderness; he told a staff officer that Grant was losing much of his numerical advantage by going into this region and that he was making the same mistake Joe Hooker had made a year earlier, and at daybreak on May 5 Ewell was under orders to advance on the enemy and "bring him to battle now as soon as possible." But as the morning wore away Lee had second thoughts. Longstreet was far in the rear and could not be up until the next day, and after the skirmishing began Lee sent word to Ewell to regulate his advance by that of Hill, who was going slowly along the Plank Road, Lee himself riding with him. Lee explained that he did not want to bring on a general engagement until Longstreet's force was on hand, and Ewell instructed his generals accordingly; but Lee was in the same boat with Meade and Grant — once the armies came into contact here the fighting itself took charge no matter what a commanding general wanted. Early in the afternoon Griffin's division went swinging forward on both sides of the Turnpike and the battle had begun.[9]

Griffin's battle line struck Ewell's advance brigade just after that brigade had been warned to "fall back slowly, if pressed." The attack caught it off balance, the brigade was splintered and routed, its brigadier was killed, and Griffin's men went shouting forward for three-quarters of a mile through the saplings and underbrush beside the road. Their moment of triumph did not last long. Meade had ordered General Horatio Wright's division of Sedgwick's corps to advance on Griffin's right, and Warren had two of his own divisions trying to come up on the left, but none of these managed to reach the scene and Griffin's men suddenly found themselves isolated. They could see nothing at all. The forest growth was so heavy that they were fighting in a thick twilight, made thicker by powder smoke and by the fact that the dead leaves on the forest floor had caught fire and were adding a heavier smoke. Most of the men could not even see their enemies — one officer remarked that this was a fight of invisibles against invisibles — but they realized that they had no friends either on the right or on the left, and when Ewell sent in reinforcements to make a counterattack the flanks were broken and the whole Federal division had to go scrambling back to its starting point. Griffin rallied his men at last, set them to work improvising breastworks, and with the position stabilized galloped back to headquarters to complain that he was not being supported.[10] Griffin was a hard, leathery type, Old Army to his fingertips, with a hot pride in his division, and he was furious because of this reverse. He found Meade talking to Grant in the clearing, staff officers all about, Grant sitting on a stump smoking; and Griffin came up with his temper out of control, bitterly shouting that Wright and Warren had let him down. Meade had a quick temper, too, and ordinarily it was not safe to storm at him this way, but he remained calm, soothed Griffin with the promise that supporting troops would soon be up, and sent him back to his division. It was Rawlins who got angry. He was not used to an army where division commanders made public complaint against their superiors, and he said loudly that this language was mutinous. Grant seems to have felt the same way, although he showed no anger, and he asked Meade: "Who is this General Gregg? You ought to arrest him." Meade told him, "His name's Griffin, not Gregg, and that's only his way of talking." Then, quaintly, Meade reached forward and buttoned Grant's coat for him, and the tension ended.[11]

The attempt to bring the Fifth Corps into action went wretchedly; and indeed the story of the fighting this day is a study in the failure of division and corps command. Nobody could do anything right. Wadsworth's division left the Chewning Farm road at last and tried to go in on Griffin's left, a mile away, buried in trackless woods. The generals did not seem to know exactly where the battle was. Wadsworth did his best, but to move a division through this forest was hard, everyone lost direction, and after Griffin had retreated this division drifted into action with its battle line somehow facing north instead of west. The left flank brushed Ewell's line — Ewell was getting three divisions into action now — and the Rebels opened a killing fire that broke regiments apart and sent Wadsworth's division back out of action with nothing to show for it but a high casualty list.

Coming up in support was another of Warren's divisions under General John Robinson. It blundered forward just as the Confederates who had beaten Wadsworth were advancing, and it too was driven back in blind retreat. The brigade that Crawford sent over to help was no luckier. It came stumbling up through the undergrowth just in time to be flanked by the charging Confederates, and it was routed with the loss of several hundred men captured and as many more killed or wounded. The rest of Crawford's division went back from Chewning's Farm to a position a little more than a mile southwest of the Wilderness Tavern, and at last a front of sorts was stitched together, everybody working to build breastworks, the burning woods all full of helpless wounded men crying for help. The Fifth Corps, which was supposed to be on the offensive, had gone into action in driblets and now was fighting to stay alive.

Hours overdue, Wright's division of the Sixth Corps, which had had as much trouble getting through the woods as everybody else, came up into line on Griffin's right. It dug in, beat off an attack by two Confederate brigades, and settled down to an afternoon of noisy skirmish-line firing. It never made its weight felt, as far as the offensive was concerned, but at least it helped make sure that the original position would not be lost; and for the rest of the day the troops on the Turnpike stayed where they were, secure enough and maintaining a steady fire but not trying to make any more advances.[12]

So the contest on the Turnpike settled down to a costly but indecisive fight between half-hidden lines of infantry; and the real weight of the battle suddenly developed several miles to the south, along the Plank Road.

Confederate General Hill had been bringing two divisions east on this road all morning. He was not coming fast, because Lee still was not ready to open a full-dress battle, but he was moving and the few hundred Federal cavalry that opposed him offered no particular obstacle; and by midmorning it occurred to Grant and Meade that Hill's advance was dangerous, because if the Confederates seized the crossing of the Plank and Brock roads the Union army would be cut in half, with Hancock isolated off to the south and everybody else engaged along the Turnpike. At hand to meet this threat was a Sixth Corps division commanded by General George W. Getty, drawn up near Wilderness Tavern. Somewhere between nine and ten in the morning Getty was ordered to send one brigade to help General Wright and take the rest of his division — some 6,000 effectives, in all: veterans, ranked with the best men in the army — down to the Plank Road, move west, and drive the Confederates away. Hancock, still waiting for orders in the general vicinity of Todd's Tavern, was instructed to bring his corps back to the Plank Road and help Getty.

Getty got the word first and moved promptly. A tough, competent soldier in his mid-forties, classmate of Sherman and Thomas at West Point, Getty marched his men down to the vital road crossing just in time to see the last of the Federal cavalry screen evaporate. The Confederates were coming down the road, but they were not pressing hard; Getty shook out a skirmish line, drove the leading patrols back, formed two lines of battle across the road, moved forward a few hundred yards and then came to a halt. He was supposed to reach out and touch Warren's left, but when his troops went groping north through the woods they found large numbers of armed Confederates, Warren's left having moved away, and so Getty settled down to wait for Hancock. For two hours there was a lull, although from the rear it sounded like quite a battle; out in front the skirmish lines were firing steadily, but although men were being hit and little streams of wounded were trickling to the rear, nobody was being very aggressive.[13]

Getty was outnumbered. A. P. Hill was putting all of his men into action, and conditions for a Federal offensive along the Plank Road were not ideal. But the Army of the Potomac was under new management now and headquarters was impatient, and by midafternoon Meade sent a staff officer to tell Getty to attack without waiting for Hancock. Luckily, the head of Hancock's column was just coming up, Hancock himself in the lead, and while the two generals examined the situation Hancock's leading troops began to form a line along the length of the Brock Road just south of the Plank Road. The Brock Road was like all the others — narrow, closely hemmed-in by trees — and it was also full of parked artillery, and while the brigades slowly took their places Hancock urged Getty to wait until the Second Corps was ready to go in with him. But Getty was getting messages from Meade telling him to attack without further delay, and finally (three-thirty or four o'clock, or such a matter) Getty ordered his men forward. Hancock managed to bring in two divisions to help —

David Birney's men on the right of Getty's line, and Gershom Mott's on the left, with the promise of more before long — and suddenly the battle flared up to a crescendo.

Never before had the army fought a battle like this one. It was almost impossible to use artillery because the guns could not be moved off the road, and it was impossible for the infantry to see what it was doing because of the infernal saplings and underbrush; yet the firing seemed more intense than ever before, and all along the line of battle high-pitched rattle of musketry was incessant. One dazed Federal wrote that "the steady firing rolled and crackled from end to end of the contending lines as if it would never cease"; another, more matter of fact, said that it sounded like a house falling down, and everybody agreed that they had never heard such a sustained, continuous racket of rifle fire alone. On both sides the men in the front lines lay flat on the ground, or knelt or squatted behind stumps or logs or any little mound of earth they could find, and fired blindly at a wall of billowing smoke that hung close to the ground and kept them from seeing whether they were hitting anything. They were hitting a good deal, as a matter of fact; they were all veterans and they were firing low; bullets came keening in a couple of feet off the ground, and before long the rival battle lines locked themselves into immobility — if a man stood up, whether to advance or simply to run away, he was almost certain to be hit, so everybody stayed where he was, loaded and fired as fast he could, and hoped for the best. It was a bad afternoon for officers. Their uniforms were brighter, what with the gold lace and the swords, and so they were good targets; afterward the medical director of the army reported that more officers were shot here, in proportion to enlisted men, than in any other battle he could remember.[14]

In spite of the blinding, fog-choked wilderness, the Federals on the Plank Road were making progress. As the afternoon wore away the Federal advantage in numbers became dominant. Hancock had most of his corps in action, Getty's division was still fighting valiantly in spite of heavy losses — his Vermont brigade alone seems to have lost 1,000 men this afternoon — and off to the right Wadsworth was bringing his luckless division down to attack Hill's left, which had lost contact with Ewell's force. Wadsworth's men had almost as much trouble finding their position here as they had had earlier when they tried to help Griffin, and they never did make a real attack this day, but by evening Wadsworth had his division up to the skirmish line, his left in contact with Hancock's right, and his mere presence was a weight that hampered Hill's defense. One of Hill's three divisions, that of R. H. Anderson, was still on the road, coming east from Orange Courthouse, and it would be unable to reach the battlefield before morning. By dusk, Hill with two divisions was facing roughly a third of Meade's army; his men gave ground, his line was all disarranged, and only the coming of darkness saved him from outright defeat.

Darkness brought a pause, but in this battle even a lull was not a time of quiet. As the firing died down, the front was alive with the sound of axes and falling trees, as soldiers worked desperately to improvise wooden breastworks. Any movement at all — details going into the forest to collect wounded men, patrols trying to explore the front, displaced soldiers wandering about trying to find their regiments — could set off a new wave of firing, with everybody grabbing his musket and letting off a few rounds until it sounded, in the rear, as if the battle had started up all over again. Here and there it had been possible to put field artillery in position, and when the infantry began firing the guns would join in, flogging the thick woods with shell, stabbing the night with flame, here and there causing an accidental casualty.

Malignant little fires worked through the underbrush and the matted dead leaves all across the front, and along with all of the other sounds of battle there was a steady calling by wounded men who wanted to be rescued before they were burned to death. In front of the 5th Maine a disabled Federal screamed for help when the flames reached him. Two men ran forward to help, and each was shot down, skirmish-line shooting being heavy just now. At last a sergeant who dared not go forward took careful aim with his musket and shot the wounded man to death to put him out of his agony. In front of Wadsworth's division, where lay many dead and wounded of both armies, a dying Confederate kept calling: "My God, why hast Thou forsaken me!" After the war General Humphreys estimated that at least 200 Federals died in the forest fire that night.[15]

The night was streaked with flame, made dreadful by gunfire and the cries of the wounded, and back in the clearing by Wilderness Tavern the man who had willed all of this reflected on what was going to happen next. It seemed to Grant that a decisive victory lay within reach — General Humphreys is said to have believed that one more hour of unattainable daylight would have brought victory that evening — and the priceless hour might come at dawn. Grant told Meade to have Hancock take the offensive at four-thirty in the morning, when the first light came. Meade knew how things were — exhausted men sprawling every which way in the dark, fear and weariness lying on them heavily — and he begged for more time. Grant relented a little, and let him postpone the hour of attack until five.

Grant's instinct to strike quickly was sound. The Federals knew that Longstreet was coming up, and so was Anderson's division of Hill's corps. Not long after the sun rose, Lee would be reinforced by 20,000 good troops right where he most needed them, and it was necessary to hit him before they got there. To strengthen the Federal attack Grant made up his mind to bring in Burnside.

Burnside's corps was not technically part of the Army of the Potomac, so it was under Grant's orders but not under Meade's. Burnside had commanded the Army of the Potomac when Meade was a mere division commander, and the situation between the two men was slightly delicate; at this time it seemed better to have Burnside an independent commander, and so it was Grant who ordered him into action. Burnside's leading division, that of General Thomas G. Stevenson, was to come up to Wilderness Tavern at once, and in the morning it would join Hancock on the Brock Road. The next two divisions, under Generals Orlando Willcox and Robert Potter, must be at Wilderness Tavern at daylight so that they could fill the gap between Hancock and Warren and join in the attack on Lee's right. Everybody who was going to fight in this offensive was temporarily put under Hancock's orders.[16]

Lee understood the situation just as clearly as Grant did, and early in the morning he had Ewell's corps open a heavy fire on their foes along the Turnpike in the hope that this would relieve the expected pressure on Hill. This it did not do. Ewell went into action just as a rolling spatter of firing off to the south showed that Hancock's skirmish lines were pushing forward, and by a little after five o'clock there was a tremendous uproar of rifle fire from end to end of the whole disconnected battle line. Warren's grip on the position along the Turnpike was unshaken. Hancock's main force swung forward, Wadsworth's division at last came into action on Hancock's right, and the Confederate right bent, cracked and began to give way. Colonel

Theodore Lyman of Meade's staff reached Hancock just at this time, at the corner of the Brock and Plank roads, and found Hancock elated.

"We are driving them, sir!" cried Hancock. "Tell General Meade we are driving them most beautifully. Birney has gone in and he is just cleaning them out beautifully!" Lyman noticed that the noise of battle was receding, showing that the Federal lines were advancing, but he had to tell Hancock that the first of Burnside's divisions was only now coming up, to go into action as soon as it could find an opening. Hancock was all hot impatience, and he burst out: "I knew it! Just what I expected! If he could attack *now*, we would smash A. P. Hill all to pieces!" [17]

The first of Burnside's troops, Stevenson's division, did come up before long, and its two brigades were sent west along the Plank Road. Willcox and Potter were following, but they had to be diverted at Wilderness Tavern, and sent into action somewhere on Warren's left and it would be hours before they could make their presence felt. On the Plank Road, in an hour's desperate fighting, Hancock's men advanced more than a mile. The Federals in fact had almost reached Lee's trains, Lee himself was at the front trying to form a firm defensive line, the Union victory that had seemed so near the night before was clearly visible now, just beyond the treetops — and then the whole Federal advance came sluggishly to a halt, the weight of its own numbers too great a load to carry through the tangled second growth that made up the battlefield.

Wadsworth's division — down to 2,000 men this morning, from 5,000 the morning before — had swept the Confederates from its front, but it came in across the Plank Road at an angle, forcing Birney's troops off to the left, breaking up brigade and division formations, leaving thousands of men jammed together so bewilderingly that to attack was temporarily impossible. The entire Federal front was hopelessly confused, with odd gaps in one place and men lined up a dozen ranks deep a hundred yards away, and General Birney was forced to call a halt so that he could get his troops reorganized . . . and just at this moment the van of Longstreet's hurrying columns came up and struck the disordered Federal line with a sharp counterattack.[18]

Abruptly, the grand Federal offensive ceased to be an offensive and all along Hancock's front the men who had been advancing so triumphantly were now struggling to hold their ground. Shortly after the battle opened, Hancock had sent Meade a note saying that his troops were moving west on the Plank Road, taking a good many prisoners — to which Lyman added a note that among the prisoners were some of Longstreet's men. Three-quarters of an hour later Lyman reported that "we about hold our own against Longstreet" but he said that many regiments were tired and shattered and that it would be as well if Burnside's divisions could come into action promptly. Not long after seven o'clock Hancock wrote an even more somber dispatch: "They are pressing us on the road a good deal. If more force were here now I could use it, but I don't know whether I can get it in time or not." Meade replied, encouragingly, that Burnside's two divisions had advanced nearly to Parker's Store and were under orders to attack to their left, adding that "they ought to be engaged now, and will relieve you." Meade, unfortunately, was quite mistaken. Willcox and Potter were nowhere near Parker's Store, having found that to march through the Wilderness was a much more time-killing process than they had imagined, and for some time to come Hancock would be on his own.[19]

What Hancock was really up against — what both sides were up against in the Wilderness, turn and turn about — was the unpleasant fact that any prolonged advance against opposition in this wooded country sooner or later brought crippling disorganization. Troops thus disorganized were largely at the mercy of any compact column of attack whose ranks had not yet been disordered by an hour of blind fighting in the overgrown ravines. Longstreet's men were shock troops, and they had broken good Yankee lines on other fields — Rosecrans's veterans from Chickamauga could have testified on the point — but what was working most in their favor this morning was that they had just come into the Wilderness and were attacking men who had struggled there until they lost their military formation.

In addition, Hancock's own left, which he had thought perfectly secure, turned out to be unprotected. From the moment the morning's fighting began Hancock had known that Longstreet's corps could be expected before long, and the logical assumption was that it would strike the left of the Federal line. To guard against this, Hancock had stationed Barlow's division and practically all of the corps artillery on an open stretch of high ground some distance to the south of the Plank Road. This force he had entrusted to one of his best generals, John Gibbon — whose own brigades had gone into action with Birney and all the rest — and it was Gibbon's job to protect the flank. As the Federals advanced a substantial gap opened between Birney's troops and Gibbon's, but this seemed unimportant, particularly since early reports seemed to show that Longstreet was moving directly on Gibbon's position. These reports, as it happened, were false: one grew out of a noisy cavalry fight, off to the south somewhere, and another came when Gibbon's outposts saw a column of Federal replacement troops coming up from the left and rear — coming up from Chancellorsville, as a matter of fact, sent by the wrong road through some foul-up in planning — and mistook the column for Confederates. For the time being these reports were accepted as correct, and not until Longstreet went into action against Birney did Hancock realize where the Confederate counterattack was actually taking place. He immediately sent word to Gibbon to advance and strike Longstreet in the flank, and if this had happened Birney could probably have resumed the offensive.

It did not happen, and nobody ever quite knew why. Hancock sent the message off to Gibbon, but Gibbon insisted to the end of his life that he never got it; and whether the courier got lost in the underbrush, or whether Gibbon got some sort of message and did not understand it as an order to move forward and attack, was something the army's historians argued about for decades to come. It makes little difference where the fault lay. All that mattered was that the reply to Longstreet's attack was not made, and as a result Longstreet was given a bright opportunity of which he took full advantage.

Longstreet's troops first struck Birney's left more or less head-on, Hill's missing division came up at about the same time, and Birney's disarrayed fighting lines came to a halt while Federal officers tried desperately to get them regrouped. By the middle of the morning Longstreet realized that Birney's left flank was entirely in the air, unsupported, and he took a good part of his command off through the woods, formed line of battle along an unfinished railroad embankment a mile south of the Plank Road, and then drove his men forward in a crunching drive that completely shattered the Union line. Hancock's front had never regained its cohesion, and when Longstreet's men hit the flank everything fell apart. Just when they needed it most the Federals got a respite; Longstreet's flank attack, moving north, got all entangled with Hill's battle line, which faced east, and now it was the Confederates who had to halt and regroup. Longstreet himself was

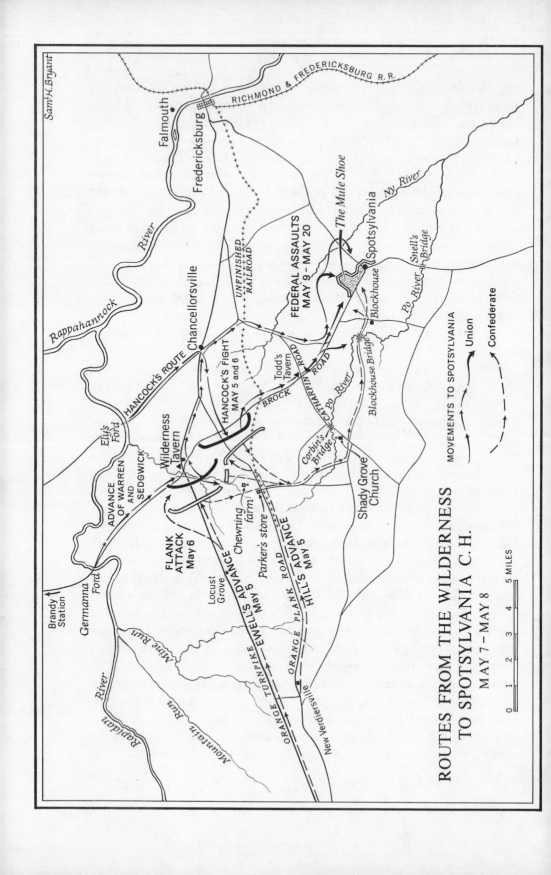

Sam'l H. Bryant

RICHMOND & FREDERICKSBURG R.R.

Falmouth

Fredericksburg

Rappahannock River

Ely's Ford

HANCOCK'S ROUTE

Chancellorsville

UNFINISHED RAILROAD

FEDERAL ASSAULTS
MAY 9 – MAY 20

The Mule Shoe

Spotsylvania

Ny River

Po River

Snell's Bridge

Blockhouse

Blockhouse Bridge

Po River

HANCOCK'S FIGHT
MAY 5 and 6

Todd's Tavern

BROCK

CATHARPIN ROAD

TODD'S ROAD

Corbin's Bridge

Shady Grove Church

Wilderness Tavern

ADVANCE OF WARREN AND SEDGWICK

FLANK ATTACK
May 6

Chewning farm

Parker's store

Locust Grove

EWELL'S ADVANCE May 5

ORANGE PLANK ROAD

HILL'S ADVANCE May 5

ORANGE TURNPIKE

Brandy Station

Germanna Ford

Mine Run

Mountain Run

Rapidan River

New Verdiersville

MOVEMENTS TO SPOTSYLVANIA

Union

Confederate

ROUTES FROM THE WILDERNESS
TO SPOTSYLVANIA C.H.
MAY 7 – MAY 8

0 1 2 3 4 5 MILES

critically wounded, and Hancock had the time he needed to withdraw his forces and put them in position behind the log entrenchments his men had built earlier on the Brock Road. Runaways were rounded up, broken brigades were reorganized, and sometime after noon the front was made secure, the Confederates in line a few hundred yards to the west.

By three in the afternoon there was a general lull: not quiet, because a good many men were continuing to fire, but uneventful as things went in the Wilderness. Grant had not had enough; Willcox and Potter were at last in position, and orders went forward to Hancock and Burnside: at 6 P.M., resume the offensive. The orders never came to anything, because Lee had the same idea and executed it first, and a little after four o'clock the reinvigorated Confederates surged forward in a mighty assault on Hancock's line along the Brock Road. This was a tough one, because if the Rebels got through here the Federals had lost the battle beyond recall, and for a few tense moments the Rebels looked as if they were going to do it. They broke a hole in the line held by Mott's division, and came swarming over the log breastworks that had taken fire and were blazing furiously, so that this was an almost impossible place to fight a battle, and there was a fine to-do all along the narrow lane, with men shouting and officers swacking about with their swords and guns going off in every direction. But Hancock had reserves, chiefly Colonel Sprigg Carroll's brigade of Gibbon's division — the same outfit that had plugged a hole in Meade's line on the evening of the second day's fighting at Gettysburg — and Carroll's men drove the intruders back and restored the flaming line, Carroll himself being wounded and a great many of his men being shot down. By darkness the firing had subsided and the Confederates had drawn back far enough so that there was a no-man's-land between the lines . . . a vast smoldering brush fire dotted with corpses. Burnside's troops had got into the offensive at last, but after the casualty list had been suitably increased their fight died down and along the Plank Road the battle was over.[20]

It was not over farther north, however, and just as the dusk grew thick the extreme right of the Union line fell in with a great crash.

The extreme right belonged to John Sedgwick. He was Meade's senior corps commander, "Uncle John" to his troops, who considered him the best general alive, and Grant and Meade esteemed him as highly as any man in the army; but he had his troubles here in the

Wilderness. Except for Getty's division his troops had never quite pulled their weight, and somehow on May 6 his line north of the Turnpike was imperfectly posted, its right flank unguarded, a wide stretch of empty country extending beyond it all the way to the Rapidan. Ewell's people discovered this opening, and just before night came a Confederate brigade led by John B. Gordon worked its way around and struck Sedgwick's flank hard. Part of Ricketts's division was routed at once, two generals and a good part of one Federal brigade were taken prisoner, and suddenly the woods behind the Union right were full of demoralized infantrymen, the noise of gunfire sounded alarmingly close to headquarters and displaced mounted officers came galloping in with wild tales of disaster.

Meade had gone over to talk to Grant, and Humphreys, left in charge at Army of Potomac headquarters, got the word first. He scraped together such troops as were immediately at hand — the provost guard and men from the reserve artillery mostly — and sent word to Grant and Meade. They came over at once, listened to the tales of disaster and agreed on how the situation could be restored. Neither man showed any especial alarm. Meade said that if there had been a breakthrough, the Pennsylvania Reserves were nearby and could plug the gap, and Grant flatly refused to believe that the trouble could be as bad as first reports said. There had been hard fighting all day, he said, and "Lee hasn't had time to mass his forces in front of Sedgwick." He believed that "we shall soon hear a different story." On one gloomy staff officer who said that Lee would now throw his whole army between the Federals and the Rapidan, Grant turned coldly and said that he was "heartily tired of hearing about what Lee is going to do"; it was time for the Federals to think about what they themselves were going to do, and, having thought, to get on with it.

They got on with it now, a new flank position was adopted and made secure, the Confederate attack (which after all had been made with only part of Ewell's corps) trailed off into sporadic skirmish firing and then into midnight silence, and the scare was over. It had been bad enough while it lasted. Sedgwick had gone forward into a twilight forest full of runaways, riding along the broken lines swinging his sword and crying: "Halt! For God's sake, boys, rally! Don't disgrace yourselves and your General this way!" A Confederate officer came riding up, pointing a revolver at Sedgwick and shouting: "Surrender, you Yankee Son of a Bitch!" Someone shot the Confederate, Sedg-

wick's horse was wounded, he was swept back toward the Union rear
— and at last, with the help of Wright and other officers, he restored
a solid line. For a time headquarters supposed that both Sedgwick and
Wright had been captured; in his diary Colonel Comstock wrote that
Grant and Meade "for a little while were in the greatest anxiety," and
Grant himself told Halleck, next day: "Had there been daylight, the
enemy could have injured us very much in the confusion that prevailed."

Apparently the Confederate attack had not actually been as massive
as first reports indicated. The redoubtable Confederate General Jubal
Early, to whose division the attacking column belonged, said afterward that he was glad darkness stopped the fighting before the Federals saw how badly the Confederates had been disorganized by their
advance through the woods; if there had been more daylight, he believed, the Federals could have punished them severely. To be sure
the soldier immediately responsible for the charge, General Gordon,
disagreed strongly with this for all the rest of his days, arguing that if
the attack had only been made earlier Grant would have been beaten
as disastrously as Hooker had been beaten a year earlier. Gordon may
have been right, but once the fighting stopped Grant wasted no more
time thinking about it. He went to bed, and ten minutes later, bringing him a new report from the stabilized right, Colonel Porter entered
his tent and found him sound asleep.[21]

CHAPTER ELEVEN

If It Takes All Summer

THE morning of May 7 was foggy, and in the smoky wilderness dreadful odors drifted across an uneasy quiet. Meade's people were astir promptly, sending out patrols which learned that the Confederate front had been pulled back for three-quarters of a mile all along the line. They learned nothing more, except that whenever one side began to shoot the other would immediately reply. Colonel Lyman found that each army had got some artillery forward and that meaningless cannonades burst out at the least sigh of movement, but anyone at headquarters who had ears knew this without being told. Everybody was edgy. It was impossible to say what Lee might do next.

Grant was up at dawn, and he knew no more about Lee's intentions or the present position of the armies than anyone else. He did know however, what he himself was going to do, and at six-thirty — about the time when the first patrols began to explore the desolation between the armies — Grant wrote orders for General Meade. As he wrote them, the war quietly began to turn a corner, finding at last a new orientation. The orders are as follows:

Make all preparations during the day for a night march to take position at Spotsylvania Court House with one army corps, at Todds Tavern with another, and another near the intersection of Piney Branch and Spotsylvania road with the road from Alsop's to the Old Court House. If this move is made the trains should be thrown forward in the morning to the Ny river.

I think it would be advisable, in making the change, to leave Hancock where he is until Warren passes him. He could then follow and become the right of the new line. Burnside will move to Piney Branch Church. Sedgwick can move along the pike to Chancellorsville and on to his destination. Burnside will move on the Plank road to the intersection of it with the Orange and Fredericksburg Plank road and then follow Sedgwick.

It is more than probable that the enemy concentrate for a heavy attack on Hancock this afternoon. In case they do we must be prepared to resist them, and follow up any success we may gain with our whole force. Such a result would necessarily modify these instructions.

At the same time, Grant ordered the pontoon bridges at Germanna Ford dismantled and moved east, to Ely's Ford, where they might be used for the evacuation of the Federal wounded, who were most numerous. Doing this, he destroyed his own line of retreat. Retreat was the last thing Grant was willing to think about.[1]

Spotsylvania Courthouse was one of those fated places, like Gettysburg, that drew fire on themselves simply because they were where the important roads met. It lay a dozen miles southeast of Wilderness Tavern — a dozen miles nearer the James River, if anyone cared to measure it that way — and if Grant meant to pass Lee's flank he had to start by going to Spotsylvania. If he got there first he would be closer to Richmond than Lee was, and Lee would have to attack him or retreat; conversely, if Lee got there first Grant must either swing out to the flank once more or fight to win the roads he wanted. The point of course was that if he went to Spotsylvania, or tried to go there, he would have the Army of the Potomac do what it never did before: follow up a setback with a renewal of the offensive.

When he ordered this move Grant had no idea whether he had won or lost the battle of the Wilderness. At noon on May 6 he had sent Halleck a note that "there has been no decisive result, but I think all things are progressing favorably"; and today, May 7, he sent off another report: "At present we can claim no victory over the enemy, neither have they gained a single advantage. The enemy pushed out of his fortifications to prevent their position being turned, and have been sooner or later driven back in every instance. Up to this hour, the enemy have not shown themselves in force within a mile of our lines."

Relaxing after breakfast on the morning of May 7 Grant remarked to his staff that it looked like a drawn battle; but he went on to say that the Federals did after all retain possession of the field and that the Confederates apparently had assumed a defensive position. As a result, he said, he could carry out his intention of moving to the left, and this might force the enemy to come out and make a stand-up fight in the open country where there was not so much underbrush. Once, around breakfast time, a brief cannonade broke out on Warren's front, and for a moment it was supposed that Ewell might be making a new attack, but in a short time word came that Warren had simply been firing to drive back an overbold skirmish line.[2]

Grant may not have been sure who had won the battle but at least he knew that he had been in a fight. Theodore Lyman heard him say that "Joe Johnston would have retreated after two such days," and Badeau said Grant told him that the Wilderness fighting was the worst he had ever seen, worse even than Shiloh. Since Grant admired Johnston above all other Confederate strategists, and always remembered Shiloh as the ultimate in applied violence, the remarks are eloquent; and if Grant had had any doubts there were the casualty figures. In two days of fighting the Army of the Potomac and Burnside's corps between them had lost 2,265 men killed, 10,220 wounded and 2,902 missing, for a total of 15,387. This, to be sure, was lower than the total recorded at the battle of Chancellorsville, fought a year earlier on much the same ground. Hooker's loss at Chancellorsville came to a little more than 17,000, with fewer men killed and more captured than in the Wilderness. The comparison does not mean much, the chief difference between the two fights being that Hooker accepted his battle as a defeat and retreated, while Grant accepted his as an incident and ordered the army to go on with the advance.

Confederate losses of course were not known. In his letter to Halleck Grant said that "the loss of the enemy must exceed ours," but he confessed that "this is only a guess" based upon the fact that the Confederates attacked and were repulsed so often. Grant's estimate of Confederate casualties was almost certainly a good deal too high, although to this day no reliable figures on Confederate losses in this battle have ever been obtained. The general estimate is that Lee's losses were smaller than Grant's but that they were in about the same proportion to the numbers engaged.[3]

Grant had not actually seen much of the battle. Nobody had, for the Wilderness was a battlefield without panoramas. There was no place, as there had been on such fields as Gettysburg and Chattanooga, where a general could establish himself on a commanding elevation and take in a great part of the battlefield in one sweeping glance. Grant rode out to the front with Warren on the morning of May 5, and Badeau said Grant and Meade went out together once or twice on May 6, but they could see no more than anyone else could see and

Grant spent practically all of his time on the little knoll near Wilderness Tavern. Here he sat on a stump or lolled on the ground, incessantly smoking, frequently whittling at a twig, talking with Meade or with his own staff and apparently quite unexcited. Charles Francis Adams, Jr., got a glimpse of him and called him "the coolest man I ever saw," Colonel Lyman said that for the most part Grant looked "sleepy and stern and indifferent," the newspaperman Charles Page saw his general demeanor as "indescribably imperturbable," and Meade's Provost Marshal, General Marsena Patrick, who tended to be grumpy, confided to his diary: "I do not see that Grant does anything but sit quietly about, whittle, smoke and let Genl. Rawlings talk big."

The only sign of strain Grant showed was that he smoked more than usual, using a briarwood pipe when he was not smoking a cigar. Colonel Porter said that Grant put twenty-one cigars in his pockets on the morning of May 6; in the evening, when Hancock came to headquarters, Grant reached to offer him a cigar and found that only one was left. His least easy moments came when he was waiting for Burnside's divisions to get into action, and he told Porter: "The only time I ever feel impatient is when I give an order for an important movement of troops in the presence of the enemy and am waiting for them to reach their destination. Then the minutes seem like hours." Badeau remembered that several times on that afternoon Grant remarked that on the next day he would probably move to his left, to see if he could get between Lee and Richmond.[4]

Grant of course had more things to think about than the fate of Meade's army. He was responsible for all of the Union armies, and about all he learned in the Wilderness was that they had moved forward on schedule. On the afternoon of May 6, however, he did get a wire from Ben Butler, written the afternoon before and sent up from Fort Monroe, giving a few details. Butler had sailed up the James and had landed a division of colored troops at City Point, at the mouth of the Appomattox River, a few miles northeast of the important railroad center of Petersburg. Butler's cavalry was sent up on both sides of the James, one contingent making threatening motions in front of Williamsburg on the Virginia peninsula while a stronger force — 3,000 men led by General A. V. Kautz — swung inland south of the river to strike at the railroads. Butler's principal force, the Tenth Corps and Eighteenth Corps, under Generals Quincy A. Gillmore and Baldy Smith, had gone ashore at Bermuda Hundred, an ancient river landing on the southern shore of the James a few miles upstream from City Point; presumably, the landing having been quite unopposed, this force would immediately move inland to cut communications between Richmond and Petersburg.

The news from Butler was important. Lee's army drew most of its supplies from Richmond, and most of what Richmond got came up from the south by railroads that centered in Petersburg. To take Petersburg, or to break the connection between Richmond and Petersburg, was accordingly to strike a powerful blow at Lee's rear and at the line of supplies that kept his army alive, and so what happened on the south side of the James meant almost as much as what Meade's army did below the Rapidan. As far as Grant could see, all was going well. Butler, at Bermuda Hundred, closed his telegram by proudly stating: "We are landing the troops during the night — a hazardous service in the face of the enemy." [5]

. . . this final sentence gives an unexpected insight into the complicated personality of the most unusual soldier, Major General Benjamin F. Butler.

The last adjective anyone ever thinks of applying to Butler is the word "naïve"; yet in one corner of his being Butler was extremely naïve, and the fact has to be taken into account because it is partly responsible for some of the odd things he did. Butler was devious, worldly wise, an eternal sophisticate whose eye rarely got off of the main chance; and yet, as a soldier, he was among other things a complete romantic. He fancied himself as a general, not merely because conceit and ambition led him so, but also in a way that was unexpectedly dream-smitten. No soldier with any military sophistication whatever, landing troops unopposed with the full support of the United States navy, could conceivably have told Grant (of all people) that this was "a hazardous service in the face of the enemy." Butler said it, because he was playing a part whose audience consisted exclusively of Ben Butler. Out of this innocent trait would grow complications harmful to the Union cause. Precisely because he was a romantic, Butler took himself very seriously as a soldier.

Both Baldy Smith and Grant, each in his own way, seem to have sensed this. Before the campaign got under way, Smith (scenting trouble from afar) tried to get Grant to give Butler a dominant staff officer who would run things for him, but Grant flatly refused. In his belief that Butler desperately needed such a man, Smith was entirely correct; in his sober awareness that Butler simply would not put up with it, and that the idea therefore was quite impractical, Grant was equally correct. Butler had to be accepted for what he was. If Smith and Gillmore could take Butler's grand designs and make battlefield sense of them, all might be well; but the underlying fact was that this operation had been committed to a man who fondly saw his most routine operation as "a hazardous service in the face of the enemy." [6]

On May 7, of course, Grant's immediate concern was the movement of the Army of the Potomac, and when the skirmish line along Hancock's front discovered that the anticipated Confederate attack was not going to take place Meade issued detailed orders to put the host in motion. The great wagon trains at Chancellorsville were to begin to move south in midafternoon, and the corps trains, parked near the front, were to go east to Chancellorsville and then move south after them. After dark, Warren's corps was to leave its trenches and go down the Brock road to Spotsylvania, passing along the rear of Hancock's battle line, which still held the charred breastworks where there had been such murderous fighting the afternoon before. When Warren's corps had passed Hancock was to fall in behind and follow; meanwhile, Sedgwick would go back to Chancellorsville and turn south there, and he was to be followed by Burnside.

These were the orders, carried out as night came down; and in the light shed by these orders the question whether the fearful battle of the Wilderness had been a victory or a defeat suddenly becomes irrelevant. Warren had failed dismally along the Turnpike, Hancock had been knocked back on the Plank Road, Sedgwick had been flanked near the river, thousands of Federal soldiers had been shot, and tactically the Army of the Potomac had had a hard time of it . . . yet after two days the Army of the Potomac was on the roads again, going south, pushing on past the hideous thickets below the Rapidan just as it had meant to do from the start, and the war was going as it had not gone before. Around eight-thirty that evening the headquarters tents were struck and Grant, Meade, their staffs and their escorts cantered off for the Brock Road to accompany Warren's advance.

Lee's people were on the alert. When the Federal wagons moved they raised an immense cloud of dust, the roads being dry and powdery, and this rolling pillar of cloud warned the Confederates that the Yankees were going somewhere. At the same time Ewell's scouts discovered that the Federal right no longer held the Germanna Ford and that the pontoon bridges there had been removed. Clearly enough, Grant was not going to go back across the Rapidan. He might be going to Fredericksburg — to retire across the Rappahannock, to establish a new base on tidewater, or simply to turn south — or he might be going to Spotsylvania Courthouse. One of these things he must be doing, and Lee did not know which it was, but that made little difference because in any case Lee's own move was obvious: he must get to Spotsylvania Courthouse himself as quickly as he could. So Lee issued orders for a night march, just as Meade had done, the most important paragraph being the provision that Longstreet's Corps — now commanded, Longstreet having been wounded, by General R. H. Anderson — should move at 11 P.M. To expedite this movement, engineer troops were put to work cutting a lane through the woods to lead to the east-west roads that ran from behind the Confederate position to the objective point.[7]

The Brock Road was a terrible road that night. A few rods to the west patchy fires flickered across the floor of the Wilderness, sending heavy smoke back across the road, along with the dreadful smell of burned bodies and of other bodies that should have been buried but had not been buried. All along the west side of the road for more than a mile Hancock's men were in position, most of them lying down trying to get a little sleep; the moving column that went south on the east side of the road had to walk carefully to keep from stepping on them, and it raised a choking dust that mixed with the woodsmoke. Here and there ambulances jolted along, their slow progress marked by the screams of the wounded men who rode in them and who suffered agonies when the wheels bumped against ruts, stones or logs. Warren's corps was on the move, the dark road was all congested, and now here came the whole headquarters cavalcade, riding along with staff officers out in front to tell the men to stand aside and let them through. It was too dark for Hancock's men to recognize any individuals, but they knew the headquarters detachment when they saw it — and suddenly the soldiers realized that the generals were riding south. *South:* that meant no retreat, no defeat, maybe the battle had been a victory after all even though it had not exactly felt like one . . . and the men of the Second Corps sprang to their feet and began to cheer, and kept on cheering as long as they had breath for it. For the first time, Grant had won the spontaneous applause of the Army of the Potomac.

Grant's big horse, Cincinnati, pranced and tossed his head with excitement and became hard to control, and as he mastered him Grant told staff officers to tell the men not to cheer: the Rebels would hear and might guess the move that was being made. Grant appreciated the cheers, however, even if he tried to stop them, and years afterward he wrote that when the men saw that the army was moving south "it indicated to them that they had passed through 'the beginning of the end' in the battle just fought." This was putting it a little strong, perhaps, but the enthusiasm was genuine. In Sedgwick's corps, along toward midnight, when the column turned south at Chancellorsville the men realized that the army was treating the battle as a victory, and they cheered while someone set a band playing a camp ditty called "Ain't I glad to get out of the Wilderness." [8]

Grant and his staff got past Hancock's corps and moved on toward Todd's Tavern; and once, late at night, finding the road clogged, with the forest fire smoldering right down to the road's edge, they rode down a lane to the right, a guide having assured them that it would lead them to the place they wanted to reach. Like many another man that evening the guide was all confused, and before long it was clear that the party was going in the wrong direction, and so Colonel Comstock cantered on to see what he could find out. What he found was a solid column of Confederate infantry crossing the lane a few hundred yards ahead, and he came pelting back in a hurry: unless the lieutenant general wanted to become a prisoner of war he had better go back to the Brock Road and find some other way.

Now the party almost came to grief because of one of Grant's odd, lifelong quirks: when he took a wrong road, anywhere, he did not like to turn around and retrace his steps. Even as a boy in Ohio, riding errands for his father, he would make almost any sort of detour to avoid such a thing, and now he wanted to strike off blindly through the woods and make it to Todd's Tavern that way. The staff was finally able to convince him that this, considering the dense undergrowth and the closeness of Confederate infantry, was utterly out of the question, and at last, somewhat put out, Grant rode back to safer territory and waited for another guide to find a better route. Sometime after midnight, he and his party reached the clearing about Todd's Tavern. Finding no better place, Grant stretched out on the ground and went to sleep, with an overcoat for a blanket. In the morning he discovered that he had made his bed right beside a pigpen.

The pig who ordinarily lived there was nowhere to be seen; beyond any question he had been eaten by Sheridan's cavalry.[9]

Grant now learned that things had begun to go wrong with the movement to Spotsylvania Courthouse. There were a good many reasons for this, ranging all the way from poor handling of the Federal cavalry to the fact that the woods were on fire behind Lee's lines near the Plank Road; what they add up to may be simply that when an army tries an all-night march after two days of battle and one day's tense alert on the battlefield, nothing is going to work quite right.

On the night of May 7 the important feature of the landscape was the Po River, an inconsiderable but annoying stream that rose near Parker's Store on the Plank Road, ran southeast for three miles, turned east for five or six miles, swung sharply south two miles west of Spotsylvania, and then drifted off to the east again, south of Spotsylvania. It was just deep enough, and its steep banks were covered with just enough second-growth timber, to make it a real obstacle to the passage of an army, and if Lee meant to go to Spotsylvania he had to cross the Po somewhere. He might do this at one of two places. During its eastward course the river ran a short distance north of Shady Grove Church on the Catharpin Road, the spot originally designated as Hancock's objective on May 5, and at Shady Grove Church the Catharpin Road, coming eastward from Lee's rear, turned northeast, crossing the Po by Corbin's Bridge and coming two miles thereafter to Todd's Tavern; and if the Yankees allowed him to use it this was one route Lee could take. From Shady Grove Church, meanwhile, south of the river, another road ran east on a tolerably direct route toward Spotsylvania, and after four or five miles it crossed the Po by Block House Bridge, two miles west of Spotsylvania. As a matter of fact there was a third crossing, Snell's Bridge, directly south of Spotsylvania, but it offered a badly roundabout route and it did not figure in Lee's planning. To beat the Federals to Spotsylvania Lee had to use either Corbin's Bridge or the Block House Bridge. If the Federals could seize and hold those two bridges they would have Lee sealed off and they could win the race to the courthouse.

During the afternoon of May 7 Sheridan took two cavalry divisions down to Todd's Tavern. One was Torbert's, commanded temporarily by General Wesley Merritt, Torbert having become ill, and the other was Gregg's, and with these two Sheridan drove Stuart's cavalry out of Todd's Tavern. When darkness came the retreating Confederate cavalry apparently had withdrawn to Spotsylvania, and Sheridan put Gregg's and Merritt's people in bivouac along the Brock Road just below the tavern. His plan for May 8 was simple. He would take his two divisions southwest at daybreak, cross Corbin's Bridge, post Gregg at Shady Grove Church to hold the bridgehead, and march Merritt east along the road south of the Po to seize the Block House Bridge. His third division, Wilson's, would move down from the area south of Chancellorsville, enter Spotsylvania from the north and east, drive the Confederate cavalry out of the place, and go on south through the town to seize and hold Snell's Bridge; after which the three divisions, all on the far side of the Po, would fan out, maintain contact with each other, and form a cordon that could delay Lee's advance until after the Federal infantry came up.[10]

Sheridan's plan was sound enough, but it did not allow for the unexpected activity of the Confederate General Anderson, who that night was marching a column of 12,000 infantry along the Shady Grove Church road bound for Block House Bridge. Anderson in fact was moving faster than Lee had contemplated, and this fact had a profound effect on the battles that were soon to be fought for possession of the Spotsylvania road crossings.

Anderson had been ordered to leave the battlefield after dark and march to his right and rear by a temporary road through the Wilderness. Reaching the Shady Grove Church Road he was to give his men a few hours' rest, and at 3:30 A.M. he was to resume his march and go on to the bridge and the courthouse. Anderson got his men out at 11 P.M., but the woods were all on fire and there was no place where he could take his men off the road and give them a chance to sleep; so, like a good soldier, he kept on going along the Shady Grove Church Road, figuring that he could find open country and a proper bivouac area somewhere near Spotsylvania. As a result, his weary soldiers kept tramping along all night, and sometime after sunrise they got across the Block House Bridge, found some fields and broke ranks to get a little rest.

Meade reached Todd's Tavern a little after midnight, to find Merritt's and Gregg's divisions in bivouac. Merritt and Gregg had not yet received Sheridan's orders for the next day and did not know what they were supposed to do. Meade knew no more about Anderson's march than Sheridan did, but the head of Warren's column was coming up, a division of Stuart's cavalry was somewhere on the Brock

Road between Todd's Tavern and Spotsylvania, and it seemed to Meade that this was no time for Federal cavalry to be sleeping; and so he issued his own orders to the cavalry division commanders without waiting to see Sheridan. Gregg was told to move southwest down the Catharpin Road to hold the ground east of Corbin's Bridge, and Merritt was to march down the Brock Road, drive Stuart's cavalry away, and send a brigade west to hold the Block House Bridge; after which he was to send the rest of his division back to his left and rear to guard the trains, which were somewhere off between Fredericksburg and Spotsylvania. Meade's order to Merritt was crisp: "It is of the utmost importance that not the slightest delay occur in your opening the Brock road beyond Spotsylvania Court House, as an infantry corps is now on the way to occupy that place." [11]

It takes time to get two divisions of cavalry out of bivouac and on the road, and when the head of Warren's infantry column passed Todd's Tavern, around three in the morning, the whole road was full of mounted men. Warren had his men close up and halt, noting that the soldiers immediately fell asleep right in the dusty road, and in the course of time the cavalry moved off, Gregg heading for Corbin's Bridge while Merritt's squadrons trotted down the Brock Road toward Spotsylvania. By six o'clock Warren's troops were moving at last, and from over the treetops far ahead of them came a rising sound of rifle fire.

On schedule, Wilson had taken his cavalry division into Spotsylvania Courthouse and by nine o'clock in the morning he reported that he had driven the enemy cavalry clear through the little town; immediately after which he collided with Confederate infantry and had had to retreat, drawing off to the northward. Merritt got into a brisk fight along the Brock Road a mile or two short of the courthouse, made no especial progress, and sent back to Warren for help; and Warren's leading division advanced in line of battle, forced the Confederate cavalry to give ground — and then, on elevated open ground around the Alsop farm, ran into Confederate infantry, assaulted, fell back in some disorder, and began building entrenchments.

The Confederate infantry encountered by Wilson, Merritt and Warren was of course Anderson's, which would have been nowhere near the scene if the woods fires had not kept Anderson from giving his men their scheduled rest at midnight. When Anderson finally made his halt, around 8 A.M., a short distance west of Spotsylvania

Courthouse, his men had hardly so much as found places to lie down when Stuart's couriers came galloping in calling for help. Anderson sent one brigade into the little town to drive off Wilson's cavalry, and started another column northwest along the Brock Road, where it reached the edge of the Alsop clearing just in time to relieve the overmatched Confederate cavalry there.[12]

So the Federals got an unpleasant surprise. Warren sent out his leading division, Robinson's to drive the Confederates away from Alsop's, and when the fighting began Warren assumed that he had only cavalry in his front, sending back word to Meade that "the opposition to us amounts to nothing as yet." He was quickly disillusioned. Robinson went down with a wound that would cost him a leg and end his military career, his leading brigade was sharply checked, and a second brigade, coming up in support, was routed by long-range fire before it could get fairly into action.

There seems to have been a nightmarish touch to this fight, the soldiers on both sides being numb from weariness and lack of sleep. Circumstances favored the Confederates, just a little and just enough; it was a trifle easier for worn-out soldiers to lie down and shoot at an attacking line than it was to form line of battle and charge several hundred yards across open country, and when a Federal assault collapsed the beaten men who tried to run back to safety found they could do no more than shamble along like invalids. One officer, who confessed that he tried to retreat at top speed, found himself stumping along using his sword as a cane, too exhausted to manage anything faster than a walk.

It took the generals a little while to appraise the situation. As late as ten-fifteen Meade, in the rear, said that he did not think Longstreet's people could have reached Spotsylvania Courthouse yet, adding that Lee might have stiffened Stuart's resistance by sending him some mounted infantry; but by noon or a little after Warren had to report that his attack was a flat failure. His men were straggling all over the place, apparently from sheer fatigue, and he told Meade he could not take Spotsylvania with the force he had. Meade ordered Sedgwick to bring his corps into line on Warren's left, and said that he wanted an attack "made with vigor and without delay," but what Meade wanted he could not get on the afternoon of May 8. It was five in the evening before Sedgwick could get his men into position, by this time Ewell's troops had come up to help Anderson's, when the Federal attack was made it involved little more than one of Warren's divisions, and by dusk the offensive had sputtered out in an ineffective fire fight that did nothing except increase the casualty list. By a narrow but decisive margin, the Federals had lost the race for Spotsylvania Courthouse.[13]

Looking back on it long after the war, Grant seems to have felt that Warren did not quite have the touch for sharp offensive operations, and he set forth his criticism thus:

Warren's difficulty was two-fold; when he received an order to do anything, it would at once occur to his mind how all the balance of the army should be engaged so as properly to co-operate with him. His ideas were generally good, but he would forget that the person giving him his orders had thought of others at the same time he had of him. In like manner, when he did get ready to execute an order, after giving most intelligent instructions to divisions commanders, he would go in with one division holding the others in reserve until he could superintend their movements in person also, forgetting that division commanders could execute an order without his presence. His difficulty was constitutional and beyond his control.[14]

These were postwar thoughts. At the moment Grant took Warren at face value, and assumed — probably correctly — that the real trouble this day was that the army was temporarily too weary to make the kind of fight that was needed. Grant's own spirits were high, and toward noon of May 8, just after he had opened headquarters at Piney Branch Church, a couple of miles east of Todd's Tavern, he got off a dispatch to Halleck:

The army commenced moving south at nine P.M. yesterday, and when closed up to the position assigned for the first day's march will stand thus: General Warren's corps at Spotsylvania Court House; Hancock's at Todd's Tavern; Sedgwick's on road from Piney Branch Church to Spotsylvania, and General Burnside at Alrich's. It is not yet demonstrated what the enemy will do, but the best of feeling prevails in this army and I feel at present no apprehension for the result.

Obviously, this was written before Grant learned that the Federal advance was not going to get into Spotsylvania Courthouse immediately. Now as previously, however, Grant was looking beyond the immediate battlefield to the James River, and he was coming more and more to feel that the fight in the Wilderness had been something better than a drawn battle. His dispatch continued:

My efforts will be to form a junction with General Butler as early as possible, and be prepared to meet any enemy interposing. The result of the three days fight at Old Wilderness was decidedly in our favor. The enemy having a strong entrenched position to fall back on when hard pressed, and the extensive train we have to cover, rendered it impossible to inflict the heavy blow on Lee's army I had hoped. My exact route to the James river I have not yet definitely marked out.[15]

Grant's attitude in the 1864 campaign begins to be clear. He does not quite know what his enemy is going to do and he does not care very much; he himself is going to go on to the James, and although he does not know how he is going to get there, or how many battles he may have to fight along the way, his mind is made up. Years later, Horace Porter remembered something Grant had said when the chips were down. On the confused night of May 6, said Porter, when the Federal right had been pulled back under heavy attack, some staff officer told Grant that if the army lost this position all of the trains would be captured. Porter went on:

"The General's lips pressed a little together, and he seemed to me to stand a foot higher than ever before or since as he responded: 'When this army is defeated and when I am driven from this line, it will be when I have so few men left that they will not want any trains.'"[16]

Moving forward with unrelenting determination was all to the good, but it was a new note in the history of the Army of the Potomac and it was apt to be attended by misunderstandings down the chain of command; and one of these boiled over at midday of May 8. Meade put his headquarters near Grant's, at Piney Branch Church, and one of his first acts was to summon General Sheridan and complain that Sheridan's cavalry had got in the way of Warren's infantry in the hours before dawn.

The interview was stormy. Sometime during the evening before, Meade had sent Sheridan word to get his cavalry off the Brock Road so that the infantry could go through. Sheridan somehow never got the order, and now he found himself taking a scolding just when he wanted to complain that Meade had ordered the cavalry about without consulting the cavalry's commander. Clearly enough, the cavalry had failed, each general believed that it was the other general's fault, and for a time the air was full of sparks. The row came to a head at last when Sheridan hotly announced that he himself would not give the cavalry another order — Meade could command it himself, that apparently being what Meade wanted to do. This of course was quite insubordinate, and when Sheridan added that if he were left to himself he could take his troopers out and whip Jeb Stuart, Meade stalked off to see Grant.

Grant listened impassively while Meade told his story, but he came to life when Meade told him what Sheridan had said about whipping Jeb Stuart.

"Did Sheridan say that?" asked Grant. "He usually knows what he is talking about. Let him go ahead and do it." [17]

Meade seems to have taken this with good grace, although he undeniably had a grievance. The commanding general had not supported him, in a bitter argument between Meade and one of Meade's underlings, and by the ordinary standards of military procedure Grant was wrong. But Grant was looking for aggressive action, and if an obstreperous cavalry commander believed that he could beat the Confederate cavalry Grant wanted to see it done. So that afternoon, at Grant's request, Meade gave Sheridan new orders: he was to assemble his cavalry, march south and attack the Confederate cavalry, break Lee's supply line if possible, continue until his own supplies were exhausted, and then get in touch with General Butler and resupply himself, after which he was to return to the Army of the Potomac. Early the next morning Sheridan set out, thirteen miles of mounted men making a wide swing around the rear of the Federal army to go slicing down eastward of Lee, all hands moving at a walk: not really trying to reach any especial destination, just looking for a fight, the division commanders slightly dubious but stiffened by Sheridan's words: "I shall expect nothing but success." [18]

Strictly speaking, Sheridan's move was somewhat eccentric — a chapter out of the book of Jeb Stuart, in 1862, when a dashing cavalry raid was considered a military achievement regardless of whether it actually accomplished anything worth the effort. Grant apparently had two things in mind. For one thing, he wanted the entire army, horse, foot and guns, to be on the offensive; for another, and probably more important, when he ordered Sheridan south he was planning to have the whole army move south at the same time, half of the infantry going down west of Spotsylvania and half of it east, with Dabney's Mills on the North Anna River, fifteen miles to the south, as the objective point. Grant was not yet convinced that Lee meant to make a stand at Spotsylvania, and it is quite likely that he remembered the

Vicksburg campaign, where a long ride by General Benjamin Grierson's cavalry confused the Confederate General Pemberton and left him uncertain where the main offensive was going to strike. As things went, Lee was concentrating his entire army at Spotsylvania and the orders which Grant drafted for the infantry that afternoon of May 8 were never issued, but the record is fairly clear. Grant wanted a continuing advance, and the movement of the cavalry makes good sense when it is considered as a part of a general march to the North Anna.[19]

Next day, May 9, was a day of preparation, during which Grant learned that Lee was in firm possession of Spotsylvania Courthouse so that the projected march forward could not be made without a big fight. Preparations for such a fight were made promptly. During the morning Hancock had been held at Todd's Tavern, lest the Confederates strike at the Federal flank by way of Corbin's Bridge; but in the afternoon, when it became evident that the last of Lee's men had gone past Shady Grove Church along the Block House route to Spotsylvania, Hancock was ordered to leave Todd's Tavern and march southeast along the Brock Road. Coming up on Warren's right late in the day, Hancock formed line of battle half a mile short of the Po River and awaited developments. On Warren's left, Sedgwick's corps was perfecting its position, digging trenches and gun emplacements while the Confederates opposite did the same; and Burnside moved out in a wide arc still farther to the left, under orders to come in toward Spotsylvania Courthouse from the northeast. There was a good deal of scrimmaging along the skirmish lines in front of Warren and Sedgwick, and although an outright battle did not develop there was a hot long-range fire all day long.

This fire cost the Army of the Potomac more than anybody wanted to lose. During the morning, after a conference with Grant, Sedgwick rode forward to an elevation near the center of his position, found that his men were a little nervous because of the fire of Confederate sharpshooters, assured them that there was nothing to worry about because "they couldn't hit an elephant at this distance" — and then himself fell dead with a sharpshooter's bullet in his brain. His staff got an ambulance and took his body to the rear, Grant remarked that to lose Sedgwick was as bad as to lose a whole division of infantry, General Horatio Wright was named to command the Sixth Corps . . . and the best-loved general in the army was gone forever.[20]

During the afternoon Grant got another bulletin from Butler, who reported that he was sending out two divisions to break the Richmond-Petersburg Railroad and who said brightly: "Up to this moment, have exceeded my most sanguine expectations." Butler went on to say that he was entrenching, "for fear of an accident to the Army of the Potomac"; he wanted reinforcements, and he believed that in three days his line would be entirely secure. This was faintly disconcerting, because Butler was supposed to be conducting an offensive, not digging in for a defensive stand, but there was nothing to be done about it at the moment and Grant wired Halleck: "If matters are still favorable with Butler send him all the reinforcements you can. The enemy are now moving from our immediate front, either to interpose between us and Fredericksburg or to get the inside road to Richmond. My movements are terribly embarrassed by our immense wagon train. It could not be avoided, however." [21]

Grant's appraisal of the situation came from a slight misreading of the evidence. There did not seem to be any especial Confederate force on the far side of the Po, in front of Hancock, but there was a steady buildup of strength in front of Warren and Wright, Ewell's corps was taking position on a line running toward the northeast, and when Burnside advanced from the extreme Union left he ran into fairly stiff opposition. This seemed to indicate that Lee was shifting to the east, probably to strike at the Spotsylvania-Fredericksburg road in the Federal rear, and Grant assumed that if Lee was doing this he must be leaving his own flank uncovered. Grant proposed to take advantage of this opening immediately. Hancock was told to send Mott's division off to the left, so as to fill the gap in the Union line between Wright and Burnside, and to take his other three divisions across the Po, swing left, and move toward Spotsylvania Courthouse from the west. Hancock got under way at once, and by nightfall he had all of his troops except Mott's division south of the Po, ready to attack Lee's left and rear. It was impossible to complete the assignment that evening, because Hancock had crossed into the angle that the river made when it turned south near the Block House Bridge; to get at Lee it would be necessary for the Federals to cross the north-south stretch of the river, and although pontoon bridges were laid that night the attack itself could not be made until morning.

It would have been well if the fight could have been made that evening, because at the moment Lee's flank was wide open, just as Grant suspected, but Hancock, whose aggressive instinct was strong enough for anybody, concluded that the thing could not be done in pitch darkness, and nobody questioned his conclusion. The trouble was that by morning the opportunity was gone. Lee had not actually been trying to outflank Grant from the east; he had simply been posting his outnumbered army in what looked like the best position to check Grant's attack, and when Hancock crossed the Po on the evening of May 9 Lee at once took warning. During the night he withdrew Jubal Early and two infantry divisions from the line they had been holding farther east and got them over to the area facing Hancock. They industriously dug themselves in to cover the river crossing, and when daylight came Hancock saw that with the enemy present in strength he could not, with three divisions, force his way across and storm the defensive works.

When he got Hancock's report Grant of course realized that this move was no longer good. He still wanted to find a soft spot, however, and he suspected that if Lee had strongly reinforced his left he must have weakened his line somewhere to the north of town. Accordingly, at midmorning Grant issued new orders. Warren and Wright were to attack the Confederate center that afternoon, Hancock was to bring two of his divisions back and join in the assault, taking general charge of the whole operation, and Burnside was to examine his own front and attack if he saw an opening. Grant got off a note to Halleck: "The enemy hold our front in very strong force and evince a strong disposition to interpose between us and Richmond to the last. I shall take no backward step." He asked Halleck to send any infantry he could find, and called for enough ammunition to give 100,000 men fifty rounds apiece — which apparently represents his estimate of his numbers at the moment.[22]

The soft spot Grant was looking for did not exist. It was quite true that Lee had taken a substantial number of men away from his center, and it was also true that the country around Spotsylvania was more open than the Wilderness, so that it was easier to get a battle line into action. However, there was one immense complication. The era of trench warfare, which had been slowly building up all through the war, had suddenly come to full development, and the hard fact was that by this time a good line of improvised fieldworks could be held securely with a much smaller force than had previously been needed to hold a defensive position.

Lee himself had pioneered in the use of trenches, back in 1862 in front of Richmond, and by now the private soldiers had learned that almost impregnable works could be created in much less time than most generals supposed. Theodore Lyman observed during this campaign that a shallow trench giving fair protection to kneeling riflemen could be thrown up in an hour. The rule, he said, was that in one day a defensive army could build a solid line of rifle pits, in two days it could convert this line into deep trenches with a proper parapet, and in three days it could add an abatis in front and get the artillery into good emplacements — and sometimes, he added, "they put this three days work into the first twenty-four hours." The men who awaited attack in these works had rifled muskets which could inflict killing losses at a distance of at least three hundred yards. (A Civil War rifle could of course kill a man at a much greater distance than that; the point is that at three hundred yards the fire of the entire line could be fully effective.) As a result an old-style frontal assault on a prepared position was extremely difficult. General Humphreys remarked that these fieldworks virtually quadrupled the strength of a defensive line; if there were enough men to occupy the works properly, he said, "there is scarcely any measure by which to gauge the increased strength thereby gained." [23]

The Federal attack on May 10 got under way late in the day. Warren struck first, and was driven back with loss. A bit later Hancock attacked, farther north, and had no better luck. The Confederate position was not shaken, the two Federal corps between them lost something like 3,000 men, and the whole venture was a flat failure. Only on the front of the Sixth Corps was there a success, and here a promising beginning flickered out in a tragic lost opportunity.

Wright's Sixth Corps was ordered to attack farther toward the Union left, facing east, striking at the side of an immense, northward-jutting salient in the Confederate line. This assault was made by twelve regiments which had been given to a brilliant young colonel named Emory Upton, who commanded a Sixth Corps brigade and who believed he knew how a line of trenches should be attacked.

Upton thought that if you were going to storm an entrenched position you had to move fast. To stop and open fire — standard procedure, at that time — was to lose, simply because men standing up in the open got shot much more rapidly than men concealed behind earthworks. Upton told his men to keep going without a halt and without firing a shot, and he organized them in four compact lines, making an assaulting column that was narrow and deep. The first line was to swarm over the Rebel parapet with fixed bayonets, the next two would fan out to right and left to clear the trenches on each side, and the fourth line was to provide reinforcements wherever they were needed. If all of this worked, Upton believed, his men could punch a narrow but deep hole in the Confederate line; if supporting troops then came up to exploit the opening, Lee's position could be broken and the road to Richmond, James River and the unimaginable future would be open and the whole army could use it.

About six o'clock that evening Upton's twelve regiments formed up, broke out of the covering woods that concealed them from their foes, and ran toward the Confederate fieldworks, cheering mightily, the evening sun glinting off of shining points of steel. Amazingly, it worked. The first wave reached the Confederate line without suffering great loss, stabbed down into the trenches with bayonets, fought hand-to-hand for a few moments, and then swamped the defenders and kept running forward. The supporting waves came up and overran the trenches on each side, the final wave surged in with helping hands, and in a few minutes the line had been broken, Upton's men had taken the second line of defense, 1,000 prisoners had been captured, and the impregnable line of earthworks had been shattered. All that Upton's regiments had to do now was hold on to what they had gained while supporting troops came up and exploited their success.

The supporting troops made an abject failure. Mott's division of Hancock's corps had been ordered to advance on Upton's left, and it took off when Upton's men broke into the Confederate position. The division had half a mile to go, up a long rise over open country; it came under artillery fire and before the men went far they wavered, fell into confusion, and then turned and ran back to where they had come from without getting within three hundred yards of the Confederate position. This left Upton's force in a bad spot. The Confederates were counterattacking savagely, from in front and from both flanks, no help was at hand, and night was coming down. Grant realized that Upton could do nothing more, and as darkness came in he ordered everybody back to the starting point. Upton's men withdrew with difficulty, leaving a thousand of their own numbers dead and wounded, and instead of the victory that had been within grasp there had been just another repulse.[24]

The trouble of course lay in the collapse of Mott's division. Two years ago it had been Joe Hooker's, proud of itself and of its commander and justly rated one of the best combat units in the army. Since then it had suffered hard usage under less capable leaders, it contained a number of regiments whose time in service was just about to expire, it had been manhandled and dismally routed by Longstreet's corps in the Wilderness, and by now it had obviously lost its fighting edge. That night, at headquarters, Wright told Meade: "General, I don't *want* Mott's men on my left; they are not a support; I would rather have no troops there!" Mott himself told his men next day that they were "sacrificing the reputation of Hooker's old division," that there was no excuse for their conduct, and that company, regimental and brigade officers must provide better leadership, but this did no good. In a couple of days Hancock asked for authority to transfer Mott's brigades into Birney's division, saying bluntly: "Otherwise the fourth division will soon be of no service under its present commanders, who seem not to control their men." Meade promptly gave him the authority he wanted, and before the week was over Mott's division went out of existence.[25]

Grant's only recorded criticism was that "Upton had gained an important advantage, but a lack in others of the spirit and dash possessed by him lost it to us." Before the campaign began Grant had been empowered to promote officers on the field for special acts of gallantry, so now he made Upton a brigadier general; he also made a note about the tactics Upton had used, and on the afternoon of the next day, May 11, he told Meade to renew the offensive on the following morning.

"Move three divisions of the Second Corps by the rear of the Fifth and Sixth Corps under cover of night so as to join the Ninth Corps in a vigorous assault on the enemy at 4 A.M. tomorrow," he wrote. "I will send one or two staff officers tonight to stay with Burnside and impress him with the importance of a prompt and vigorous attack. Warren and Wright should hold their corps as close to the enemy as possible to take advantage of any diversion caused by this attack, and to push in if the opportunity presents itself. There is but little doubt in my mind but that the assault last evening would have proven entirely successful if it had commenced one hour earlier and had been heartily entered into by Mott's division and the Ninth Corps."

On the morning of May 11, before he wrote this order for Meade, Grant showed that his characteristic optimism still ran strong. Congressman Washburne had to return to Washington, and while they waited at headquarters for the cavalry escort that would take the Congressman back to Belle Plain, the Potomac River steamboat landing, Washburne said that he would be seeing the President and the Secretary of War on his return and asked Grant if he could give them any message about the army's progress. Grant replied that he was making fair progress and that so far the fighting "has been in our favor," but he said that the campaign began to look like a long one and that he did not want to say anything that would arouse false hopes. He reflected briefly, then added: "I will write a letter to Halleck, as I generally communicate through him, giving the general situation, and you can take it with you." So Grant went into his tent, sat down at his table, puffed at a cigar, and wrote out a message that was to become one of his most famous dispatches. It ran as follows:

We have now ended the sixth day of very heavy fighting. The result to this time is much in our favor. But our losses have been heavy, as well as those of the enemy. We have lost to this time eleven general officers killed, wounded and missing, and probably twenty thousand men. I think the loss of the enemy must be greater, we having taken over four thousand prisoners, whilst he has taken from us but few except a few stragglers. I am now sending back to Belle Plain all my wagons for a fresh supply of provisions and ammunition, and purpose to fight it out on this line if it takes all summer.

The arrival of reinforcements here will be very encouraging to the men, and I hope they will be sent as fast as possible, and in as great numbers. My object in having them sent to Belle Plain was to use them as an escort to our supply trains. If it is more convenient to send them out by train to march from the railroad to Belle Plain or Fredericksburg, send them so.

I am satisfied that the enemy are very shaky, and are only kept up to the mark by the greatest exertions on the part of their officers, and by keeping them entrenched in every position they take.

Up to this time there is no indication of any portion of Lee's army being detached for the defense of Richmond.[26]

CHAPTER TWELVE

Beyond the Bloody Angle

I<small>T HAD</small> been raining all afternoon and all evening, and the night was as dark as it was wet. In the woods near the house where General Hancock had his headquarters, signalers groped through drenched pine thickets with lighted candles, hunting for the wires that had been strung the day before to connect corps with army on the new field telegraph system. Sometime after midnight division commanders called their brigadiers into huddled consultation by lantern light and gestured largely regarding the black night off to the south. On the long slope in front of headquarters, 15,000 infantrymen who had tramped over here from their proper bivouac stood in the drizzle, shifting from one foot to the other to keep from getting completely mired, and made such remarks as seemed to be pertinent. They were grouped in one immense, steaming mass, the formation Emory Upton had devised, and as soon as there was light enough Grant would learn whether an army corps could do in the dawn what a brigade had done in the evening.

There was light enough, General Hancock decided, at four-thirty, which is to say that the sky was gray instead of black, and the outlines of things could be seen. For the moment the rain had stopped, but a heavy shallow fog lay on the ground, and as Hancock sat on his horse and watched his men go past him they waded in a thick mist so that only their heads and upper bodies were visible. A staff officer who was with him remembered that the swaying line had a strange, billowing effect, and he heard Hancock say something about an army of turtles creeping over the hills. Hancock was full of optimism, and as he watched the corps go off into the distance he cried confidently: "They will not come back. I know they will not come back." [1]

All Hancock meant was that his men were certain to reach their goal. Yet the words he used, transposed into a different key, might have been spoken in anticipation of doom itself; might indeed have been used by one of Hancock's own division commanders, General Francis Barlow, whose troops formed the front wave of this assaulting column. Barlow felt that there had been no preparation worth mentioning for this assault. He did not know what was in front of him (except that a great many Rebels were off there, somewhere) and the staff officer who had come over from Grant's headquarters to guide him did not seem to know, either. Barlow anticipated the worst, and one of his aides remembered that he did not use the brusque, half-sardonic remark with which he generally called his staff into action: "Make your peace with God and mount, gentlemen; I have a hot place picked out for some of you today." It was not in him to talk that way this morning, and the aide said that as he got the division into motion Barlow's voice "was subdued and tender." [2]

The lack of preparation was not quite as bad as Barlow supposed. On the afternoon before — afternoon of May 11, that is: this attack was being made on the morning of May 12 — Grant's Colonel Comstock and some of Hancock's staff had gone out to study the ground which the attack would have to cover. They had not learned much they did not already know, because the swirling rain made it hard to see and anyway Mott's skirmishers had failed to clear the Rebel pickets out of the way so that the staff officers could study things at close range. The staff officers did discover, however, that an undulating open glade four hundred yards wide, downhill halfway and then up a gentle slope, led due south to the position Grant wanted taken by storm.

This position was a long salient in Lee's line, known to Confederates as "the mule shoe" from the shape of it on the map — a huge bulge, three-quarters of a mile deep and half a mile wide, held chiefly by Ewell's army corps and prepared with good earthworks and artillery emplacements. The tip of such a salient was always considered a weak spot because it was hard for the defenders to concentrate their fire in front of it, and it was the tip that Hancock's men were supposed to strike this morning; and although Barlow's guide may have given him inadequate directions, it was the tip that Barlow actually hit, as accurately as if the engineers had surveyed the whole thing and marked out guide lines.

Hancock's corps was not going in alone. Off to its left — that is, around to the east, slightly out of touch, invisible in the foggy dawn — Burnside was to march forward when Hancock marched, striking the eastern face of the salient while Hancock struck the tip of it. On Hancock's right was the Sixth Corps, with General Wright prepared to go into action on call, and still farther over there was Warren's Fifth Corps, also alerted to stand by for action. If the charge cracked the line the way Upton's charge had done, the effect was not to be lost for lack of supporting troops.

Down the slope went the heavy mass of troops, and as the wispy fog drifted up through the trees some of the men noticed that the birds were beginning to sing. The advance division cheered briefly when it reached the Confederate picket line, and a few shots were fired, but there was no halt; and before long the unwieldy column went over a little belt of shrubs and swampy ground at the foot of the incline, started up the far side, and came at last to a heavy entanglement of sharpened stakes and felled trees, built by industrious Rebels the day before. Here there might have been serious trouble, for the main line of Confederate works lay only two hundred yards beyond, and Barlow's division had to wait while parties with axes ran forward to cut openings in the barrier; but instead of heavy volleys of musketry from the Rebel trenches there came only a scattering of ineffective single shots, and the racking artillery fire that might have wrecked Barlow's division never began. And finally the abatis was broken and torn apart, and the whole army corps began to run and yell, crowding up the rise without formation or order, a heavy disarrayed crowd of troops that swept up to the Confederate earthworks and went on over them like a big wave at high tide.

The defense here had not been completely taken by surprise, but it had not exactly been ready for the blow either. The worst trouble was that two dozen pieces of artillery, posted near the tip of the salient right where they could have made great trouble for the Federals, had been taken away the night before, the Confederate high command having believed that Grant was about to make a flanking movement. Long before daylight the high command discovered its error and sent the guns back, but they got to the salient just too late to be of any use, and the cheering Federals swarmed all over them and captured twenty of them. They also captured two general officers, upward of 3,000 other prisoners, thirty-two stands of colors, and an important half-mile segment in the very center of General Lee's line. Here, by all ordinary standards, was a big breakthrough and decisive victory.

But ordinary standards meant nothing at Spotsylvania. The Federal charge that was so overwhelming was also unmanageable. Support troops had crowded up so closely on the heels of the first wave that organization was lost, and because the officers had gone into action dismounted it was all but impossible for generals to send staff officers about with the necessary orders. Just short of the captured earthworks the Federal soldiers formed an excited, jostling crowd twenty or thirty ranks deep, there was almost an entire division of captured Confederates to be taken back through this crush to the Federal rear, and when Barlow's men went plowing on ahead to exploit the victory they were the spray of a wave that had lost its momentum. The intermittent rain began to come down again harder than ever, and a few hundred yards in advance a new Confederate line of battle came swinging down with a savage counterattack.

If it had not been for the fury of this counterattack Barlow's people could probably have made the kind of deep penetration that would have forced Lee to retreat, but the Confederate second line fought desperately to save the day — Lee himself was at the front, preparing to lead a charge in person until his men restrained him — the Federal advance line had by now lost its cohesion, and after half an hour of hard fighting the defenders forced their assailants back, out of the littered woodland enclosed by the mule-shoe salient, back to the earthworks that had been seized in the first rush. The Federals got into the captured trenches, recovered their lost equilibrium, and opened a killing fire of their own. Immediately behind them and on their right was the rest of Hancock's corps, most of the men lying flat on the ground and firing as fast as they could — at Confederate soldiers, when they could see any, otherwise at the smoky mist that lay beyond the earthworks.

There were wild flurries of hand-to-hand fighting. Here and there the Confederates came all the way up to the line of trenches, and there were places where Federals crouched on one side of a log breastwork while Confederates crouched on the other side, not five feet away. Men shot through the chinks between the logs, or jabbed through them with bayonets, or held their muskets overhead at arm's length, muzzles pointed downward, to shoot blindly over the parapet. Now and then soldiers on either side would clamber on top of the logs, firing at point-blank range until they were killed. There were times when soldiers leaned over the parapet, seized their opponents, and hauled them over bodily, making prisoners of them.

The fighting was worst of all at a place a few hundred yards west of the actual tip of the salient, a place where the trench made a sudden turn, and this spot was known forever after, with excellent reason, as the Bloody Angle. The trenches were knee-deep in mud and rain-water, wounded men drowning there, dead men falling on top of them. For a final touch, the soldiers occasionally had to stop fighting and lift the broken bodies out of the trench so that they themselves could stand there.

Where the fighting was not actually hand-to-hand the opposing troops in most places were not more than a few dozen yards apart, and the men on both sides fired without a letup; and as a matter of fact the fighting in such cases was probably deadlier than it was at the angle itself, because if the battle lines were a little farther apart they were unprotected. One Confederate officer said afterward that "there was one continuous roll of musketry from dawn until midnight," and the storm of bullets splintered the log breastworks, whipped trees and bushes into fragments, killed and wounded men and then cut up their bodies until they were unrecognizable, and made it impossible for the Federals to do anything with the guns they had captured. The guns simply stood there in the mud, no one firing them, no one hauling them away, dead bodies lying across the trails and under the wheels.[3]

Lee kept sending in more troops, and a Federal headquarters staff officer asserted that the Confederates made five separate assaults during the day. Far to the rear, Lee had men building a new entrenchment across the base of the mule shoe, and to save his army he had to hold the disputed ground until this line of works was finished. Building it was an all-day job, so the Confederates up in front had to stay there and slug it out. Hancock's men stayed there too — he had known what he was talking about when he said that these men were not coming back — and the rifle fire rose to a pitch never heard in any battle before. Along the line of the disputed trench there were occasional lulls, as exhausted men tried to catch their breath and nerve themselves for a new effort; then, as often as not, a whole regiment would suddenly stand erect, fire a hasty volley, and duck down immediately afterward to escape the volley that would come in reply. The rain kept on falling, and the battleground was all soft mud in which dead and wounded men sank half out of sight. The wounded men who lay in the mud were in a bad plight, because it was hard for stretcher bearers to work here. Federal doctors said afterward that in ordinary battles most of the wounded were able to walk, or to drag themselves, back to the dressing stations; but at Spotsylvania on May 12 not one-quarter of the wounded could get to the rear without being carried. Meade's medical director wrote that "the amount of shock and depression of vital power was noticed to be comparatively much greater in the wounded of this battle than in any preceding one of the campaign." This was especially true, he said, among the wounded from Hancock's corps, which went into action without breakfast or a morning cup of coffee.[4]

Out of sight, off to the east, Burnside's corps came into action. It advanced a little late and its attack was not well coordinated, nor was it driven home with the vigor that marked Hancock's assault, but when they struck the Rebel line Burnside's men did some hard fighting. The division led by General Robert Potter hit the east face of the salient, where A. P. Hill's corps held the right of Lee's line, and at first everything went well. Potter's soldiers drove the Confederates out of a section of trench, taking prisoners and a couple of field pieces, but the dispossessed Rebels rallied in a second line of works, got reinforcements, and struck back savagely, recapturing the lost guns and forcing the Federals to retreat. Potter's men did not go back far, but dug in facing the works they had first taken and then lost, and by nine in the morning they were in contact with Hancock's corps, so that the Federals had a continuous battle line — a great crescent that curled around the whole mule-shoe complex and extended off to the south, toward the eastern approaches to Spotsylvania Courthouse.

Sometime later, Burnside managed to get the division of General Orlando Willcox into action at the extreme left end of the Union line. Willcox took his men in through a pine thicket, got close to the Confederate trenches, engaged in a hard fire fight, was attacked in the flanks, and had to withdraw. He had delayed his attack in order to arrange a bank of artillery to protect his original position in case the attack failed, and these guns now became very useful. The Confederates made a hard counterattack and were finally repulsed chiefly by the weight of the close-range artillery fire. Willcox entrenched under the protection of these guns, and the position at last was stabilized. Burnside lost something like 1,200 men during the day, with nothing to show for it except the negative achievement of keeping Lee from reinforcing his center from his right.[5]

Hancock got better help from Wright's Corps, which sent a division (with Emory Upton's brigade in front) up to the western face of the northern part of the salient at about six in the morning. These men helped Hancock's soldiers hold on to the ragged position in and near the captured earthworks — it appears that they were the ones engaged at the Bloody Angle — but although they maintained a steady fire they were unable to blast the Confederates out of the way. Once Upton ordered a battery right up to the front, in a move that was as fantastic as it was horrible. The gun crews were under fire all the way, horses were killed in full gallop and were dragged along by the frantic teams, the wheels of the guns ran over dead and wounded men and rammed them deeper into the mud, and although the effect of the guns' fire, when at last they got into battery, was devastating — they were firing canister at foes only a few yards away — the fire did not last long because most of the gunners were quickly shot. The guns stayed there, silent and useless as the ones that had been captured earlier, black and ugly on a desolate, rain-swept landscape, gun carriages and caissons reduced almost to kindling wood by the incessant storm of rifle fire.[6]

Grant was up at dawn, and he sat in a canvas chair by a campfire in front of the headquarters tents, getting progress reports and sending staff officers about with orders. Once Meade came over for a brief conference, returning before long to his own headquarters to order Warren to make an attack along the right of the Union line. The campfire was more smoke than flame, by now, and the gusty wind alternately hid Grant behind clouds of smoke and flipped the cape of his overcoat over his face, so now and then he got up to pace back and forth in the unrelenting rain. The first reports he got showed that things were going well, and when he learned that Hancock had captured almost all of a division of Confederate troops he displayed what was, for him, outright enthusiasm, remarking that this was the kind of news he wanted to get. Not long afterward Meade came back, bringing with him a prisoner — Major General Edward Johnson, commander of the captured division. Johnson had known both Grant and Meade before the war, and Grant gave him a chair by the smoldering fire and chatted with him in friendly fashion before having him escorted to the rear.

If the reports from Hancock and Wright were good those from Burnside and Warren were less satisfactory, because each man seemed to have trouble getting his attack organized. Grant had Colonel Comstock accompany Burnside today, and during the morning he sent Comstock repeated messages urging him to persuade Burnside to be more aggressive. Once or twice Comstock and Burnside had angry words about this, Comstock considering Burnside too slow, Burnside feeling that Comstock was sending Grant reports that were unduly critical.[7]

With Warren, things came close to an actual break. In the middle of the morning Meade sent word to Grant that "Warren seems reluctant to assault," adding: "I have ordered him at all hazards to do so, and if his attack should be repulsed to draw in the right and send his troops as fast as possible to Wright and Hancock." In reply, Grant sent a curt note: "If Warren fails to attack promptly, send Humphreys to command his corps and relieve him." [8]

Grant sent this message reluctantly, and he probably was glad that as the day wore on Meade concluded that this drastic step was not necessary. Grant had been highly impressed with Warren at the start of the campaign, and he told Horace Porter that at one time he had felt that if anything happened to Meade Warren would make a good replacement for him. Now he was revising his opinion, and the revision came hard. His suggestion that Humphreys would do well in corps command was undoubtedly a good one. Humphreys had been a most competent combat commander earlier in the war; he was a highly charged, aggressive leader who actually enjoyed fighting, and Theodore Lyman, who had had to go with him into a number of hot places, once burst out ruefully: "I do like to see a brave man, but when a man goes out for the express purpose of getting shot at he seems to me in the way of a maniac." Assistant Secretary of War Dana said that Humphreys was intolerant of human error and would make the air around headquarters blue when any staff officer fouled things up. Humphreys and Sherman, said Dana, commanded the most "distinguished and brilliant profanity" of any men in the army. General John A. Logan was good, too, he said, but after all he was only a civilian soldier: Humphreys and Sherman were West Pointers.[9]

Warren's men at last got into action, and when they did go in they fought hard, acquiring a painfully impressive casualty list. Yet the assaults by Warren and Burnside, valiantly made, did not change the course of the battle, or cause any slackening of the terrible fighting around the tip of the salient. That night young Captain Oliver Wendell Holmes, Jr., a staff officer at Wright's headquarters, made a grim entry in his diary: "Burnside who attacked on Hancock's left didn't make much. He is a d——d humbug — Warren, who is a ditto, did about the same." He added that Meade should have "slapped in all he could spare on Hancock's front," and went on to say that "I think Warren represented himself harder pressed than he was." [10]

The fact was that by the middle of the morning the battle had become a deadlock. The center of it all was a comparatively small space, some 1,500 yards wide, where Hancock's and Wright's men fought in, over and around the captured trenches, and there was no use in sending them reinforcements because they already had more men in this confined area than they could effectively use. The only chance seemed to be to strike hard at the Confederate lines on each side of them, but when these attacks were made they were a little too far away to be of much help, and besides they struck well-built earthworks manned by veterans who proved once more that in trench warfare the defense had all of the advantages. Yet the battle did not stop. It continued all day, unabated, and the firing around the tip of the salient went on long after nightfall. The complete savagery of this fighting was appalling, so that men believed that losses were much higher than they were — although the exact figures were high enough, in all conscience. Once toward the end of the afternoon Hancock reported that his corps had lost more than 7,000 men, and although this turned out to be more than twice the actual number the mere fact that he made such a report shows how the fight had looked to him. [11]

Grant saw more of the fighting here than he did in the Wilderness because the country was more open. During the afternoon he saddled up and rode out to several points where he could watch the fight for the tip of the salient. Instead of riding Cincinnati today he was on Jeff Davis, a little horse with a quiet disposition and an easy gait, seized by the army on the Davis plantation in Mississippi during the Vicksburg campaign and bought by Grant for his own use from the Quartermaster people, and on Jeff Davis Grant saw what there was to see of this appalling battle that was both a victory and a repulse all at the same time. It seemed to him that on balance things had gone well, and that evening back at headquarters he sent Halleck a wire summing up his impression:

The eighth day of battle closes, leaving between 3,000 and 4,000 prisoners in our hands for the day's work, including two general officers and over 30 pieces of artillery. The enemy are obstinate and seem to have found the last ditch. We have lost no organization, not even that of a company, while we have destroyed and captured one division (Johnson's) one brigade (Doles') and one regiment entire of the enemy.[12]

Grant was telegraphing, of course, on the basis of incomplete information, some of it wrong. General George Doles's brigade, a hard-fighting unit that had tangled with Burnside's men, had not been captured, and Grant's figure for the guns taken was exaggerated. Yet the number of prisoners was undeniably impressive. Counting today's haul, the Army of the Potomac had captured more than 7,000 Confederates since it crossed the Rapidan, and a figure of that size was usually considered a sure sign that the enemy was being outfought. On the evening of May 11 Grant had sent Julia an optimistic message. He was not then entirely certain where she was; she had been staying in New York, at the home of Colonel William S. Hillyer, who had resigned from the army after long service on Grant's staff, she was about to go to St. Louis — had actually gone there, in fact, by May 11 — and Grant sent the message to Hillyer trusting that he would know how to get it to her. The wire Hillyer sent to Mrs. Grant read as follows:

He says "We have ended the sixth day of very hard fighting with a fair prospect of having at least a week more to do. So far the advantages have been on our side and I feel no doubt about the result in the end. We as well as the enemy have lost very heavily. We have taken in battle over four thousand prisoners and I should think killed and wounded at least twenty thousand of the enemy. I never felt better in my life." [13]

Hancock's patrols moved forward early, on the morning of May 13, and sent back exciting news: the Rebels were gone from the salient! For a little while headquarters nursed the wild hope that Lee might be in full retreat, but further investigation showed that he was still there: he had simply abandoned the mule shoe, he held the new line that had been built across its base, his right and left were where they had been the day before, and it would take another fight to move him. There could be no fight today; everybody badly needed a rest, the sullen rain continued to fall, and although Grant had made up his mind to shift his army around to the east and make another try at hitting Lee's right flank he did not want to begin the move before darkness. He devoted himself mostly to headquarters chores, accepted and passed on to Secretary Stanton Meade's recommendations for promotions growing out of the recent fighting, and added a strong word of his own about Meade himself.

"General Meade has more than met my most sanguine expectations," he wrote. "He and Sherman are the fittest officers for large commands I have come in contact with. If their services can be rewarded by promotion to the rank of Maj. Gen. in the regular Army the honor would be worthily bestowed and I would feel personally gratified." Cautiously, and remembering the sectional and professional jealousies that had to be balanced, Grant added: "I would not like to see one of these promotions at this time without seeing both." [14]

Grant wrote this recommendation after a lively meeting with his staff in which a number of his officers strongly urged him to bypass Meade entirely and issue his own orders directly to the corps and divisions of the Army of the Potomac — suggesting, in effect, that he either remove Meade outright or make him a figurehead, exercising the active command of the army himself. They argued that time was lost under the present system, that when Grant's orders filtered downward through Meade's headquarters, force and vigor were lost, and that Meade was so hot-tempered that it was hard for anybody to get along with him. To an extent, this line of argument probably reflected nothing more than the antagonism that inevitably developed between two general staffs that had to operate side by side with their respective fields imperfectly defined. Part of it, however, doubtless came from a growing feeling around Grant's headquarters that something was wrong with the command system in the Army of the Potomac; troop handling at corps and division levels had been woefully inexpert on several occasions, and orders from above had been executed slowly in some cases and feebly in others. Grant quietly told the protesting staff people that he could not possibly assume active command of this army and continue to function as commanding general of all the armies; for him, a westerner, to remove Meade would antagonize this army of easterners, and anyway Meade was doing his job capably and Grant saw no reason to change the existing arrangement.

Grant's argument was unquestionably sound. Yet the dual command arrangement was cumbersome, and this fact was recognized at Meade's headquarters as well as at Grant's. Writing after the war, General Humphreys put it bluntly: "There were two officers commanding the same army. Such a mixed command was not calculated to produce the best results that either singly was capable of bringing about. It naturally caused some vagueness and uncertainty as to the exact sphere of each, and sometimes took away from the positiveness, fullness and earnestness of the consideration of an intended operation or tactical movement that, had there been but one commander, would have had the most earnest attention and corresponding action." Meade's provost marshal, General Patrick, at this time had no use for Grant at all, and he confided to his diary that Meade these days was "cross as a bear, at which I do not much wonder with such a man as Grant over him." No one felt the difficulty of the situation more than Meade himself, but he was philosophical about it, explaining to sympathetic visitors that "gradually, and from the very nature of things, Grant had taken over the control." He pointed out to Mrs. Meade that "Coppee, in his Army Magazine, says, 'The Army of the Potomac, directed by Grant, commanded by Meade and led by Hancock, Sedgwick and Warren,' which is quite a good distinction and about hits the nail on the head." [15]

Men who looked at the captured works that day saw things worse than any the war had yet shown them. A brigadier in Wright's corps said that in the Bloody Angle trench, between traverses in a space measuring no more than fifteen by twelve feet, he counted 150 bodies. A Pennsylvania officer reported that in places the dead men were sprawled eight or ten bodies deep, filling the rifle pits, and a man in the 5th Maine who went to look for a company officer who had been killed said that the man's body had been so dreadfully mangled by rifle fire that "there was not four inches of space about his person that had not been struck by bullets." Confederate testimony was much the same, edged sometimes by awe at the determination of the Federal attacks. A North Carolina man wrote to his mother that "there has never been such fighting I reckon in the history of war," adding that "Old Grant is certainly a very stubborn fighter," and a Louisiana soldier asserted: "We have met a man this time who either does not know when he is whipped, or who cares not if he loses his whole Army, so that he may accomplish an end . . . I have as you know been in a good many hard fights, but never saw anything like the contest of the 12th." [16]

Back in Washington, where nobody had to look at the hideous varieties of death in the mud, there was a rising wave of high enthusiasm. News from the front was fragmentary but what there was of it sounded very good, and on the evening of May 9, when it was learned that Grant had moved south after the fighting in the Wilderness, a crowd of cheering people came up to the portico of the White House, bringing an army band along to give the President a serenade. Lincoln stepped out to receive the cheers, remarking that he supposed this was due to "the good news received today from the army." He was careful to remind his listeners that a great deal remained to be done, but he confessed that he was glad that Grant "has not been jostled in his purposes," and a few days later the *Army and Navy Journal* remarked that the past week had provided "seven days unparalleled in the history of the war." It went on to give a semiprofessional appraisal of what had been done:

> The great battle of the Wilderness was no essential part of Grant's plan. He did not avoid it, but he did not seek it. His plan was to flank the enemy, with or without battle. To such a statement confirmation is added by the speech of the President, who announced that Gen. Grant had not been jostled from his original design. The advance was substantially analogous to that of General Hooker. The battle-ground was the same. The tactics of the enemy were the same. But the results were diverse. And on familiar ground, while our army had yet failed to get into a thorough maneuvering position, the enemy fought three days and then hastily withdrew.

The message Congressman Washburne brought back was made public about the time the War Department announced that Grant had taken thousands of prisoners and had cracked the Rebel line at Spotsylvania, and it seemed that a great victory had been won. Again a crowd surged around the White House in the evening, and Lincoln came out to recite the gist of Grant's message, with its stirring promise to "fight it out along this line if it takes all summer." Correspondent Noah Brooks said that "there was something like delirium in the air; everybody seemed to think that the war was coming to an end right away . . . most people thought that Grant would close the war and enter Richmond before the autumn leaves began to fall."

All of this worried President Lincoln, who knew well enough that what had been done so far represented little more than a promising beginning, and a few weeks later he soberly told Brooks: "To me the most trying thing of all this war is that the people are too sanguine; they expect too much at once. I declare to you, sir, that we are today farther ahead than I thought, one year and a half ago, that we should be . . . As God is my judge, I shall be satisfied if we are over with the fight in Virginia within a year." [17]

Lincoln could understand that excessive enthusiasm now would probably mean an excessive depression of spirits later on — and this with a presidential election campaign about to open — but there was not much that he could do about it. The state governors kept begging the War Department for good news. They were preparing for a new draft, and they were also raising thousands of 100-day troops which, if they would not be of much use on the fighting fronts, would at least free behind-the-lines contingents of veterans for field service, and to get volunteers it seemed necessary to spread hopeful tidings. As far as he could, Secretary Stanton told the governors what they wanted to hear, and Grant's accomplishments began to look larger than life-size. When he first came to Washington Grant had been hailed as the man who was going to win the war quickly, and all across the North people now were beginning to believe that he was actually doing it.

Beyond the seas the London *Times*, which was never consumed with enthusiasm for the Union cause, found the general's record impressive.

"Grant has stamped a new character on the tactics of the Federals," said the *Times*. "No other general would either have advanced upon the Wilderness after the severe battle of the 5th or followed up an almost victorious though retiring enemy after the still harder fighting on the 6th. None but he again would have attacked his adversary so resolutely on the 8th and on the 9th or held his ground so tenaciously in spite of failure. Under his command the Army of the Potomac has achieved in invading Virginia an amount of success never achieved before except in repelling invasion. The Confederate forces were once arrested by McClellan and once by Meade, but that was when they thought to carry the war into Northern Territory. Grant has already done more than this."

Closer home, the Chicago *Tribune* exultantly reported: "The remark is reported of the President's on this campaign which may or may not be authentic but which conveys much truth. 'Any other commander that the Army of the Potomac has had,' he is rumored to have said, 'would have at once withdrawn his army over the Rapidan after that first day's reception.' " [18]

As Grant laid out his next move, on May 13, it began to be evident that no other campaign in the war had been like this one. Battles as grim as any in American history had been fought here, but they brought neither victory nor defeat; brought nothing, indeed, except weariness, pain, death and more fighting. People in Washington might go serenading in the happy belief that the war was being won, but the army knew that the war was simply being fought. Grant's aim was unchanged. He would cripple Lee's army in combat if he could, but no matter what happened he would keep going until he crossed the James River. Then there would be time to see who was winning and who was losing. All that mattered now was the determination to go on with it.

He got on with it with as little delay as might be. On the morning of May 13 he sent Meade a note: "I do not desire a battle brought on with the enemy in their position of yesterday, but want to press as close to them as possible to determine their position and strength. We must get by the right flank of the enemy for the next fight." [19]

On this same day Grant found time to write a letter to Julia: a singular letter, reflecting an optimism that was as much the product of his own determination as of an objective appraisal of the situation. The letter reads:

The ninth day of battle is just closing with victory so far on our side. But the enemy are fighting with great desperation entrenching themselves in every position they take up. We have lost many thousand men killed and wounded and the enemy have no doubt lost more. We have taken about eight thousand prisoners and lost likely three thousand. Among our wounded the great majority are but slightly hurt but most of them will be unfit for service in this battle. I have reinforcements now coming up which will greatly encourage our men and discourage the enemy correspondingly.

I am very well and full of hope. I see from the papers the country is also hopeful.

Remember me to your father and Aunt Fanny. Kisses for yourself and the children. The world has never seen so bloody or so protracted a battle as the one being fought and I hope never will again. The enemy were really whipped yesterday but their situation is desperate beyond anything heretofore known. To lose this battle they lose their cause. As bad as it is they have fought for it with gallantry worthy of a better.

That night the new move began. Warren and his corps, after dark, left their trenches on the Union right, found behind-the-lines roads, and set out on a wide swing past the whole Union rear to reach a new battleground east of Spotsylvania Courthouse, and after this corps moved Wright took his corps to the rear and followed. The idea behind the move was sound. Lee's line east of Spotsylvania did not extend far beyond the place where his men had fought with Burnside's on May 12. A Federal attack mounted south of Burnside's position at dawn on May 14 would have met little resistance and might well have overwhelmed Lee's right flank before reinforcements could come over from the other end of the Confederate line. But the everlasting rain made all the roads ankle-deep in mud and the march of Warren's corps was a failure, not through any fault of Warren but simply because conditions made failure inevitable. Men floundered blindly along in utter darkness and dripping mist, and although Warren posted staff officers and guides along the route, and had had bonfires lighted to show the way, this did not help much. Each segment of the moving column fell farther and farther behind the one in front of it. Men straggled all across the night from sheer weariness and confusion and although the head of the column reached its goal by dawn the rest of the corps was far behind, and to make an attack was out of the question. By breakfast time Grant had to admit as much, and he sent a wire to Halleck:

The very heavy rains of the last 48 hours have made it almost impossible to move trains or artillery. Two corps were moved last night from our right to the left, with orders to attack at 4 A.M., but owing to the difficulties of the roads have not got fully into position. This, with continued bad weather, may prevent offensive operations today.

This gloomy forecast proved correct. Nothing much was done on May 14, except that one of Warren's brigades briskly attacked and routed a Confederate detachment that held a little hill the Federals wanted — an action welcomed by both Grant and Meade as evidence that Warren's offensive spirit was reviving — and on May 15 Grant sent Halleck a report that began just as the last one had begun: "The very heavy rains of the last three days have rendered the roads so impassable that but little will be done until there is a change of weather, unless the enemy should attack, which they have exhibited but little inclination to do for the last week." [20]

Nothing very substantial had been done since the fight at the salient, yet in one week there had been a complete shift in the army's position. When the Federals first tried to fight their way into Spotsylvania Courthouse on May 8 they had been coming down from the northwest. During the following week, amid all the consuming fury of battle, the army had been slowly but steadily swinging around to its left, fighting head-on most of the time but always feeling persistently for Lee's right flank. By May 15, in place of the semicircle it had occupied north of town, the Federal army was drawn up in a more or less straight, north-and-south line due east of Spotsylvania Courthouse. Lee's army still faced it, behind impregnable trenches, but Lee's army no longer lay squarely between the Army of the Potomac and the James River crossings.

Grant had been asking for reinforcements ever since he left the Wilderness, and now he began to get them. Some 6,000 men, mostly heavy artillery regiments extracted from the Washington fortifications, came down at this time, and Halleck reported that he had assembled 1,500 more from the troops that had been guarding the line of the Orange & Alexandria Railroad. By May 13, Halleck said that he had forwarded 10,000 men altogether and that as many more were under orders to go down in the immediate future. Some of the heavy losses in the first ten days of fighting were being made good.

But the accepted story that the Federal government this spring sent down an inexhaustible stream of replacements, so that Grant had "unlimited numbers" at his command to make up for all his losses, is pure myth and nothing more. General Humphreys, who was in a position to know exactly what was being done, wrote after the war that the War Department figures showed that 27,811 men were sent to the Army of the Potomac during the first six weeks of the campaign — May 4 to June 12, from the Rapidan to the James. These figures are grossly misleading, he explained, because they include the "present and absent" totals, as well as all of the men who were on extra duty. In actual fact, said Humphreys, the army got, in this six-weeks' period, about 12,000 effective men as replacements. Furthermore, these would hardly have kept the army up to strength even if there had been no fighting at all.

For the unhappy fact was that thousands of three-year veterans who were the hard core of the combat force were going home. Their enlistments had expired, they had refused to reenlist, and the army was losing them just when it needed them most. It is not possible to get an exact figure for this loss, but it was substantial. On May 11 Meade reminded corps commanders that the time-expired regiments that were being sent back to be mustered out might just as well make their last days useful by escorting wagon trains back to Belle Plain. Humphreys said that the army in this way lost thirty-six regiments of infantry during the first two months of the campaign; which meant that the effective replacements coming into the army did little more than balance the loss of the men who were being mustered out. This drain on the army's strength was felt well before the time the regiments actually started for the rear; for the most obvious, human, understandable reasons, men who knew they were going to leave the service in a few days were not likely to fight all-out when they were asked to attack lines of prepared earthworks. To top it all, during this Wilderness-Spotsylvania period the army sent more than 4,000 sick men back to the Washington hospitals — not battle casualties, just men who had fallen ill.[21]

Altogether, therefore, battle casualties were not actually being replaced at all. During the first six weeks, the army probably received fewer men than it lost even when battlefield losses are left out of consideration.

Grant and Meade still were looking for a soft spot in Lee's line, and two of Meade's best lieutenants — General Humphreys and General Wright — thought they had spotted one. Lee had been extending his right to meet the Federal shift, and these generals suggested that he must thereby have weakened his left; possibly the line he had drawn behind the captured salient on May 12, which was now the extreme left of the Confederate army, was too thinly held? Grant accepted the idea, and on the morning of May 18 Hancock and Wright were ordered to make an attack there. The theory turned out to be wrong. The line was powerful, there were heavy abatis-entanglements all along the front, and there were plenty of Confederates present; the Federal assault quickly failed, with a loss of perhaps 2,000 men; and

Meade wrote to his wife that the Confederate position was so strong that "even Grant thought it useless to knock our heads against a brick wall." There were no more Federal attacks at Spotsylvania, and Meade wrote that "we shall now try to maneuver again, so as to draw the enemy out of his stronghold, and hope to have a fight with him before he can dig himself into an impregnable position." [22]

Such a fight, as it happened, developed in a limited way on May 19. Suspecting that Grant had overshifted toward the south, Lee had Ewell's corps make a thrust past the Federal right flank, aiming for the vulnerable area where the ponderous wagon trains were parked. Luckily for the Federals, the 6,000 heavy artillerists just down from Washington had marched into this area shortly before Ewell's men struck at it, and after piling their overstuffed knapsacks in long, parade-ground rows the heavies swung forward and after a sharp fight compelled the Confederates to retreat. Hancock had sent a division over to help, but it was not needed; coming up behind the line in the place where the new troops had piled their knapsacks, the veterans broke ranks, looted the knapsacks with practiced hands, and then marched blithely away. The heavy artillerists had been initiated, both to combat and to the ways of the Army of the Potomac . . . and there was no more fighting at Spotsylvania Courthouse.

Orders were out for the Army of the Potomac to start moving south, past Lee's right flank, on the night of May 20. As the long march for the James was resumed, men's spirits rose. The endless rains had stopped, the roads were dry and it seemed like spring once more, the country was more cultivated and infinitely less dreary and God-forsaken than anything the men had seen since they crossed the Rapidan, and everybody was glad to be moving. The Army took new heart, and one veteran remembered that it "never returned through all the rest of the great campaign to such a feeling of depression as hung over it through the Wilderness and part of Spotsylvania."

There were minor incidents as the men broke camp. In the artillery brigade of the Fifth Corps, beef cattle had been distributed to the various commands some days earlier, and in one battery the gunners suddenly realized that they had not yet killed and eaten the steer that had been assigned to them. During the week the men had made a sort of pet out of this beast, and when the authorities ordered the animal slaughtered before the army moved the men protested; they had got so they liked this steer's company. The regimental butcher snorted in disgust.

"Gettin' tender-hearted!" he said. "I shouldn't wonder if you fellers would be a-killin' men before night."

When the army finally moved, the last of this luckless beast had been eaten.[23]

CHAPTER THIRTEEN

Roll On, Like a Wave

GENERAL SHERMAN, Secretary Stanton told the governors, had driven the Rebels out of Dalton and was pursuing them far down into Georgia. General Butler was attacking Fort Darling, key to the southern defenses of Richmond, and probably he was even now in the act of capturing it. General Sheridan had broken Lee's communications, whipping Jeb Stuart's cavalry and killing Stuart himself, and after doing this he had joined Butler's forces; Lee was in full retreat, possibly fleeing to Lynchburg, far off in southwestern Virginia a long way from Richmond. Grant, who was advancing, had been heavily reinforced and all of his battle losses would soon be made good.

Thus Secretary Stanton, on May 15, seeking to encourage the patriotic and addressing the governors of Ohio, Indiana, Illinois, Iowa, Wisconsin and Kentucky. The secretary of war was according to his lights an honest man, not wanting to deceive anyone; and yet his message was the sort of thing that should have been chanted by a tribal harper in a raftered hall full of bearded warriors drinking mead out of horn goblets. It had a bardic quality to it, based upon fact but heavily built up with legend; it offered the substance of things hoped for rather than a recital of things actually done. Mr. Stanton undoubtedly described things as he saw them, but Grant by this time saw them differently.

To be sure, Grant was optimistic. On May 16 he told Halleck: ". . . The army is in the best of spirits and feels the greatest confidence in ultimate success. The promptness with which you have forwarded reinforcements will contribute greatly to diminishing our mortality list and ensuring a complete victory. You can assure the President and the Secretary of War that the elements alone have suspended hostilities and that it is in no manner due to weakness or exhaustion on our part." [1] It was also perfectly true that Sherman was driving Joe Johnston south, that Butler's troops had at least seen the frowning earthworks of Fort Darling, and that Sheridan had done most of what Mr. Stanton said he had done. Yet all of these items did not add up to what the Secretary seemed to be thinking about, and when the Army of the Potomac began to move south past Lee's right flank Grant was painfully aware that at close range — seen across the reeking wastelands of Spotsylvania, with the endless ambulance trains carrying broken bodies back to the hospitals — the war did not look quite the way it looked in Washington.

Sheridan's cavalry thrust, for instance, held little real nourishment. Sheridan had struck Lee's supply depot at Beaver Dam Station, on the Virginia Central Railroad, tearing up tracks, wrecking trains, burning a vast store of rations and releasing several hundred Union prisoners taken in the Wilderness; yet although this had alarmed the Confederate government and had brought Lee's army for a time down to short rations it had not compelled that army to flee to Lynchburg or anywhere else, the railroad was quickly repaired, the lost rations were made good, and the blow had been an annoyance rather than a major achievement. Sheridan had done as he had been told, and he had unquestionably whipped Stuart's cavalry — Stuart himself was dead, as evidence of it — but the war was going to go on about as it would have gone if the Federal cavalry had not ridden out at all.

Like Secretary Stanton, Sheridan had got a faulty picture. He fought Stuart at Yellow Tavern on May 11, six miles from Richmond, and then he took his troopers off to the east, broke through the outer line of Confederate works along the Chickahominy, and paused as if he meant to assault the inner lines and go on into the city. He did not really mean to do this, because the inner lines were strong even though they were manned by factory workers and War Department clerks, but Sheridan had been told that Butler's army, south of the James, was only four miles from Richmond, and he wanted to cross the river and join him so that the two forces together could capture the place. But Butler was not where Sheridan thought he was — far from capturing Fort Darling he was stumbling back to safety inside his own lines at Bermuda Hundred, sweating lest he lose his whole army — and Sheridan had to withdraw, swing far around to the southeast, and take refuge at last at Haxall's Landing on the James, below the plateau of Malvern Hill. There he could do no more than collect rations and other supplies, and on May 17 he turned north to ride back to the Army of the Potomac.

On his way back Sheridan sent General George Armstrong Custer's brigade off to destroy Lee's advance base at Hanover Junction, but Custer could do nothing because the place was strongly held by Confederate infantry: and this infantry, ominously enough, was coming up from the James, where it was no longer needed to oppose Butler, to reinforce Lee's battered army. When the cavalry finally got back the best Grant could say was that by drawing off the Confederate cavalry Sheridan had at least made it easier to protect the Union army's wagon trains.[2]

Butler's expedition had been a flat failure. With better leadership it could have won a smashing success, because when Butler put his 30,-000 men ashore at Bermuda Hundred on May 5 the Confederacy had hardly anyone to oppose him. He had three options — to seize Petersburg, the railroad center that supported Richmond, to plant himself solidly on the railroad and highway that led from Petersburg to Richmond, or to move at once on Richmond itself. Either of the first two things he almost certainly could have done without difficulty, and the third option would have had a fine chance of success; and if he had done any of these three things, Sheridan's operations in Lee's rear would have forced Lee to make the kind of retreat Mr. Stanton was dreaming about.

Unfortunately, Butler did none of them. In a situation that demanded bold, swift movement, he edged forward slowly and with extreme caution, making small, tentative advances and then pulling back whenever a detachment of Confederates showed up to make a fight of it. More than a week was simply wasted. Ten days after Butler had landed, the Confederate commander south of the James, General P. G. T. Beauregard, had managed to assemble a force of more than 20,-000 men, which he handled so ably that what Butler might easily have done early in May became quite impossible by the middle of the month.

That Butler turned out to be an incapable field commander was no surprise. The real surprise was that the two professionals who commanded his infantry corps, General Smith and General Gillmore, did so little to make up for his deficiencies. If they had more skill than Butler they had even more caution, and they handled their troops throughout as if they faced superior numbers. Their first act was to build an excellent defensive line across the neck of the Bermuda Hundred peninsula — good insurance against disaster, but this army was supposed to be making a driving offensive — and they never showed a trace of the go-ahead spirit the operation called for. A sample of the attitude that prevailed is given in a dispatch sent on May 11 to Secretary of the Navy Welles by Rear Admiral S. P. Lee, commander of the Federal squadron on the James, who had been talking to the generals. He told Welles: "General Smith thinks that as the Petersburg railroad is cut, the Rebel army must, from want of supplies, retreat, if it does not break up, into North Carolina, and that General Grant may take Richmond without further fighting."

Technically, Smith was right. The railroad from Petersburg to Richmond had been broken, Smith's corps having edged forward far enough to tear up several miles of track. After doing this, however, the Federals retired to their defensive line, leaving their foes plenty of time to make repairs, which they speedily did, and the operation had no effect whatever on Lee's ability to sustain himself. Butler began to see that he was being poorly served, but he could think of nothing better to do than write indignant letters about Gillmore; which put his discontent on record but did nothing to instill the offensive spirit into his subordinates or to dispel Smith's quaint notion that General Lee's army must now retreat or dissolve.

Butler finally got his army on the road in a hesitant advance toward Richmond, but by now Beauregard was ready for him, with nearly equal numbers in good earthworks. A successful Federal assault was out of the question, and on May 16, while Butler and his generals were pondering on this fact, Beauregard struck hard, driving the invaders off in full retreat, inflicting 4,000 casualties, and compelling Butler's men to get back as fast as they could inside the protecting lines across Bermuda Hundred neck. Here they were safe; and so were Petersburg, Richmond and the railroad. Beauregard entrenched a line immediately opposite Butler's, and if he could not force a way in the Federals could not force a way out. Butler was locked up on Bermuda Hundred; sometime later, when he understood just what had happened, Grant wrote that Butler's army was as much out of the strategic picture now "as if it had been in a bottle strongly corked." Since he was able to hold his lines with only part of his force, Beauregard sent nearly 7,000 men north to join Lee, with the promise of more to follow.[3]

It was a long time before Grant understood all about what had happened to Butler, but as he started his army south from Spotsylvania on the night of May 20 he knew very well that Stanton's bright estimate of the situation along the James was completely wrong. Grant could also have taken issue with the assertion that his own battle losses were being made good. In the Wilderness and Spotsylvania together — two and one-half weeks, or thereabouts, since the Rapidan was crossed — he had lost 33,000 men. So far he had received between 6,000 and 7,000 replacements, and the total he would get before he reached the James would be far below the total he had lost. Right now, Lee was actually being reinforced more heavily than Grant. In addition to the men Beauregard sent him, Lee was getting 2,500 more under General John Breckinridge, whose appearance was grim evidence that one more prop had been knocked out from under Grant's campaign plan.[4]

Breckinridge and his men were showing up because General Sigel had been ignominiously beaten in the Shenandoah Valley. Advancing toward Staunton, in the hope that he could join forces with General Crook's column that was coming east from West Virginia, Sigel had been routed by Breckinridge in a battle at New Market on May 15 and had made a disordered twenty-five-mile retreat. Correctly assuming that for the time being Sigel was out of the war, Breckinridge left a good part of his force in the valley to guard against accidents and brought two brigades east to reinforce Lee.

Grant did not learn of this until May 17, when he sent Halleck a message saying that he wanted Sigel to occupy the upper valley and cut off the supplies Lee was getting from that area. Back from Halleck came the reply: "I have sent the substance of your dispatch to General Sigel. Instead of advancing on Staunton he is already in full retreat on Strasburg. If you expect anything from him you will be mistaken. He will do nothing but run. He never did anything else. The Secretary of War proposes to put General Hunter in his place."[5]

So two good ideas had gone wrong, and the march of the Army of the Potomac was hindered rather than helped by what the other armies had done. The army moved forward, regardless, and on the night of May 20 Grant sent Hancock and the Second Corps down the road toward Richmond, east of the line of the Richmond, Fredericksburg & Potomac Railroad, with the other corps following after a slight interval. Hancock's road led past Lee's right, not very far away, and Grant hoped that Lee would move out to attack him; the rest of

the army could come up fast, and if the Confederates gave battle outside of their trenches they would probably be beaten. Lee refused to
rise to the bait, knowing as well as Grant that he stood to lose much
more than he could gain by trying to force the fighting. Instead he
dropped back, seeking at all costs to stay between Grant and Richmond, and he took position behind the North Anna River, covering
the direct road south and also protecting Hanover Junction, where
the Virginia Central Railroad — the line that came east from the
Shenandoah, which Grant had hoped Sigel could cut — reached the
railroad that came down to Richmond from Fredericksburg.

Here Lee awaited Grant's next move. He had checked Grant's new
advance, cutting in ahead of him just as he had done at Spotsylvania
Courthouse . . . but he was twenty-five miles nearer the James
River than he had been, and there was a curious reversal in strategic
roles. Before the campaign opened Grant had told Meade: Wherever
Lee's army goes, there you will go also. Now the rule was upside-
down: Wherever Meade's army went, there Lee would go. For the
first time in the war a Federal army taking the offensive in Virginia
was retaining the initiative.

On May 21 Grant reached Guinea Station. He pitched his headquarters tents on the lawn of a pleasant country estate, and when he
went over to the dwelling house to explain his presence the lady who
lived there told him that this was the place where Stonewall Jackson
had died, two years earlier. Grant replied that he had known Jackson
at West Point and in Mexico, that he considered him a good man and a
good soldier, "and I can understand fully the admiration your people
have for him." The lady described Jackson's last hours, and wept, and
when Grant went back to his tent he posted a guard to make sure that
house and property came to no harm.[6]

The life and death of the departed Jackson did not stay long on
Grant's mind. Instead he was concentrating on the James River.
Something obviously was amiss there and Grant did not know what it
was; before he could do anything about it he had to know what was
happening and what the remaining chances were, and so he presently
got off a wire to Halleck:

"I fear there is some difficulty with the forces at City Point which
prevents their effective use. The fault may be with the commander,
and it may be with his subordinates. General Smith, whilst a very able
officer, is obstinate, and is likely to condemn whatever is not suggested

by himself. Either those forces should be so occupied as to detain a force nearly equal to their own, or the garrison in the entrenchments at City Point should be reduced to a minimum and the remainder ordered here. I wish you would send a competent officer there to inspect and report by telegraph what is being done and what in his judgment it is advisable to do."

Halleck immediately ordered the Quartermaster General, Montgomery C. Meigs, and General J. C. Barnard of the Engineer Corps to go down to the James and examine the situation. He told them that Grant wanted an appraisal "of the enemy's force and defenses, the condition of our army, whether active operations on our part are advisable, or whether it should limit itself to its defensive position, and, if so, what troops can be spared from that department to re-enforce the Army of the Potomac." What Halleck did not put in writing but almost certainly told the generals orally was that Grant chiefly wanted a size-up of Butler's relations with his principal lieutenants.[7]

During the next few days, as he drew the Army of the Potomac up to test Lee's position along the North Anna, Grant gave more thought to the subsidiary offensives. He told Halleck that "The force under Butler is not detaining 10,000 men in Richmond and is not even keeping the roads south of the city cut," and his first impulse was to have Butler leave a small garrison at City Point and bring everybody else up to reinforce Meade. Then, being incorrectly informed that Lee was falling back on Richmond, he concluded that Butler's army ought to stay where it was, prepared to exploit any opening. Learning at last, through solid battlefield evidence, that Lee was standing fast, he reversed himself and ordered Butler to send as many men as possible to the Army of the Potomac, retaining enough to hold the James at least as far as City Point.

He approved of Hunter as a replacement for Sigel, and as Hunter took over Sigel's beaten troops and got ready to move forward Grant told Halleck that Hunter should do what Sigel had failed to do: occupy Staunton and then come east of the Blue Ridge "if he does not meet too much opposition." Shortly afterward, reflecting that once Crook joined him Hunter would have a force of 17,000 men or more, and understanding more clearly the great importance to the Confederacy of the supply line that came east from the upper Shenandoah Valley, Grant expanded these instructions: "If Hunter can possibly get to Charlottesville and Lynchburg he should do so, living on the country. The railroads and canals should be destroyed beyond possibility of repair for weeks." After doing this, he said, Hunter could either withdraw to the valley or force his way farther east and join hands with Meade near Richmond.[8]

Meanwhile, the Army of the Potomac marched down to the North Anna to see what sort of opposition General Lee was going to make. The army moved on a broad front. Hancock's corps came along the Telegraph Road, the main highway from Fredericksburg to Richmond, which lay here a short distance west of the Richmond, Fredericksburg & Potomac Railroad. Four or five miles farther west, Warren and Wright took their soldiers on lesser roads that approached the river at Jericho and Quarles Fords; and between these columns on the right and on the left Burnside moved in the center, heading for a crossing known as Ox Ford.

The weather was good and morale was high. The army was out of the gloomy Wilderness jungles, it had left the Spotsylvania battlefields far behind, it was going through clean country that had not yet been marched over, picked over and fought over, and it was beginning to believe that something big was being accomplished. An officer in the Fifth Corps wrote to tell his wife that although the Wilderness battles had been discouraging he was beginning to see a good pattern: "By continual, persistent, generally unsuccessful assaults, charges, and by skilled maneuvering, Gen. Grant worried out the enemy and forced him to fall back to Spots. C.H., and then by flanking him when too much exhausted and demoralized to fight in an open field he forced him back of the North Anna." An officer in Hancock's corps said that by this time "there was an idea that we were still advancing, that there was a plan that would be carried out successfully. . . . When we reached the North Anna I think the general feeling was that we should roll on, like a wave, up to the very gates of Richmond." [9]

There was a visible touch of this feeling on the evening of May 23, when Hancock's corps came down to the river and found Confederates posted on the north bank covering the approaches to the Chesterfield Bridge. The country here was open, and there was a broad, easy slope leading up to the Confederate position: it was just before sunset, and when General Birney advanced two brigades and lined them up for an assault this minor engagement unexpectedly became the kind of theatrical performance that men remember when they forget weightier things. Hancock and most of the rest of the corps looked on while the two brigades formed up and then charged. Rebel artillery south of the river hammered at them, and Hancock's artillery hammered back, there was a tremendous noise, and fat white smoke clouds from the batteries went drifting up the evening sky — and then the attackers swept over the Confederate position (which, truth to tell, had not been very strong) and took Chesterfield Bridge before the defenders could destroy it; and next morning Hancock's corps crossed the North Anna without further opposition.

At the western end of the Union line there was even less resistance. The Jericho Ford crossing was wholly unopposed, and Warren got his corps over the river and moved forward, beating off an attack made by A. P. Hill's troops, and then digging in; and next morning Wright's corps came across and dug in beside him. In the center Burnside found that the southern bank at Ox Ford was more solidly held; he prepared to attack, discovered that the position was much too firm to be taken by any battle line that had to wade the river under fire, and so he sent one division off to support Hancock and another to help Warren.

By the night of May 24, thus, the Federal center was north of the river, along a front three-quarters of a mile wide, and the right and left wings were both south of the river. These wings were no more than four or five miles apart in an air line, but they were fifteen or twenty miles apart by the only available bridges, fords and plantation roads. To get troops from one wing to the other would be a hard all-day job.

General Lee, in short, had taken a position that was unassailable. Both Hancock and Warren moved men forward on May 25 to tap at his lines and found them formidably entrenched, with extensive slashings of felled timber and spiked saplings all along the front, the flanks perfectly secure. The generals had to report the fact, and Grant had to accept it, that as things now stood the army could do Lee no harm whatever . . . The invulnerability of a well-entrenched position was at last being understood. The enlisted men, it should be remarked, had understood it all along, and now it was beginning to color what they did. The same men who had come to feel themselves part of an irresistible wave rolling on to victory were also perfectly capable of refusing to try to carry enemy earthworks; as one man put it, "When we saw *them* before us, we halted." [10]

Grant spent a day examining his position and concluded that it was time to take to the road again. He made up his mind to move by his left, as he had done after the Wilderness and after Spotsylvania, making a wide swing and trying once more to get between Lee and Richmond. A few miles from Grant's left, the North and South Anna rivers joined to form the Pamunkey, and what Grant proposed now was to withdraw from his present position and march southeast on the far side of the Pamunkey, heading for a place called Hanover Town, where the river could be crossed. As the roads went, Hanover Town was more than thirty miles away, but Sheridan could ride on ahead and seize the crossings and the Pamunkey itself would protect the army from Lee's interference along the way. On the night of May 26 Grant put the army in motion. In a telegram to Halleck he explained the reasoning that led to this move:

> To make a direct attack from either wing would cause a slaughter of our men that even success would not justify. To turn the enemy by his right, between the two Annas, is impossible on account of the swamp on which his right rests. To turn him by his left leaves Little River, New Found River and South Anna River, all of them streams presenting considerable obstacles to the movement of an army, to be crossed. I have determined, therefore, to turn the enemy's right by crossing at or near Hanover Town. This crosses all these streams at once, and leaves us where we can still draw supplies.

A factor in Grant's thinking was his supply train — heavy, slow and vulnerable, a drag on the army's movements ever since the crossing of the Rapidan. To move past Lee's left would give the train an impossibly long, difficult route; on the march from Spotsylvania down to the North Anna Grant had shortened the length of the wagon haul by shifting his base of supplies from Belle Plain, on the lower Potomac, to Port Royal, on the Rappahannock, and now he ordered it shifted again — to White House, on the Pamunkey, fifteen or twenty miles downstream from Hanover Town.

Before he finished his dispatch to Halleck, Grant let his optimism bubble forth:

> Lee's army is really whipped. The prisoners we now take show it, and the action of his army shows it unmistakably. A battle with them outside of intrenchments cannot be had. Our men feel that they have gained the morale over the enemy and attack with confidence. I may be mistaken, but I feel that our success over Lee's army is already insured.[11]

In view of the furious fighting Lee's army would provide for months to come, it seems odd to find Grant voicing such a belief. But he was not the only Federal who felt that way, and on the basis of what men could see at that time there seemed to be some reason for it. Meade just now was writing to his wife, using the same expression Grant used: "We undoubtedly have the morale over them, and will eventually, I think, compel them to go into Richmond; after that, *nous verrons.*" A few days later he assured Mrs. Meade that once the Confederates lost Richmond "I think, from the tone of the Southern press and the talk of the prisoners, that they will be sensible enough to give it up. They are now fighting cautiously but desperately, disputing every inch of ground but confining themselves exclusively to the defensive." Colonel Rufus Dawes of the 6th Wisconsin wrote on May 24: "The enemy has lost vigor in attack. Their men are getting so they will not fight except in rifle pits. My conclusion is that Gen. Hill's corps could be defeated on an open field by half their number of resolute men." Assistant Secretary of War Dana, who was accompanying the army these days to keep Secretary Stanton filled in on everything, spoke of a recent haul of 1,000 Confederate prisoners and declared: "They were more discouraged than any set of prisoners I ever saw before. Lee had deceived them, they said, and they declared that his army would not fight again except behind breast works . . . The Confederates had lost all confidence and were already morally defeated." Even General Warren, a confirmed pessimist, assured his brother: "The Rebs are getting dispirited and out of provisions, and I think would fall back if they had any place to go to. We are growing more and more hopeful." [12]

These men may have been misreading the evidence, but the obvious fact was that Lee's army this spring was not doing what it had always done before. It was not seizing the initiative. After its violent but unsuccessful blows in the Wilderness, it had attacked feebly or not at all; apparently it had accepted the defensive. For the first time the Army of the Potomac could pause, in the immediate presence of the enemy, to prepare for a new advance, without suddenly finding that it had unexpectedly come under attack: for the first time it could safely march past its opponent's flank. On the North Anna the wings of Grant's army had been divided, with Lee between them; by all military logic the Confederate army there had a great opportunity to smash one of the Federal wings and drive the whole army off in retreat. No such attack had been made, or tried; and the obvious deduction seemed to be that Lee's army was no longer the instrument it used to be. It occurred to nobody that the Federal army now was being handled in such a way that Lee never really had an opening for the kind of thrusts that had overwhelmed McClellan, Pope and Hooker.[13]

Whatever the truth may have been, the Army of the Potomac moved on down to Hanover Town without difficulty. The base had been changed, and the long wagon route would no longer be a source of weakness. Also, Grant had attended to an item of military housekeeping: instead of keeping Burnside's corps as an independent unit, answerable to himself alone, he formally incorporated it into the Army of the Potomac, so that Burnside hereafter would get his orders direct from Meade. In addition, Grant made up his mind to see what Baldy Smith could do if he were taken out from under Butler's immediate control, and on May 28 a fleet of transports went up the James to Bermuda Hundred. Smith, with 16,000 men from his own and Gillmore's corps, came aboard, and the fleet sailed down around the Virginia peninsula to come up to White House on the Pamunkey, to help Grant and Meade in the final stage of the drive toward Richmond.

Meigs and Barnard had submitted their report, using a good many words to leave things about as they had been before. Butler, they said, was "a man of rare and great ability," but he lacked battlefield experience and things would really go better if Butler stuck to purely administrative duties and let Smith handle the fighting. Butler, unfortunately, "evidently desires to retain command in the field"; but "if his desires must be gratified" it might be advisable to remove Gillmore, give Smith command of both army corps with good subordinates under him, and leave Butler somewhere up above as a king who reigned but did not rule. The generals felt that "General Butler will probably be guided by Smith, and leave to him the suggestions and practical execution of army movements ordered." This turned out to be one of the most striking miscalculations of the war; the proof would come later, however, and meanwhile Butler contented himself by writing to his wife that Meigs and Barnard had come down as "a sort of smelling committee," and he concluded that "they have gone away satisfied." [14]

The fountainhead of Grant's difficulties with Butler, which were to be numerous, lay in that casual aside ". . . if his desires must be gratified." Butler's desires did have to be gratified, and Grant had known it from the start. According to Adam Badeau, Grant originally came east with his mind made up to remove Butler from his command. At his first meeting with Lincoln and Stanton, however, "he was informed that political considerations of the highest character made it undesirable to displace Butler; the administration needed all its strength and could not afford to provoke the hostility of so important a personage." As he had done before in a somewhat similar case, Grant settled down to make the best of it. Early in the Vicksburg campaign General McClernand had been so insubordinate that both Rawlins and Wilson urged Grant either to relieve him outright or give him such a stern rebuke that McClernand would pull in his horns. Wilson told Badeau, after the war: "The General's answer was prompt and in the following words: 'No, I can't afford to quarrel with a man whom I *have to command*.' These are his exact words . . . Particular stress was laid on the word 'have.' " Now Grant *had* to command Butler.[15]

The full story of Grant's dealings with the strange man he had to command would be told later; meanwhile there was the Army of the Potomac's move down toward the James. The campaign went by steps, a march and a fight, another march and another fight, all of the steps much the same, making a coherent sequence. There was the step across the Rapidan, and then the big fight in the Wilderness; the step down to Spotsylvania, and another big fight; the step to the North Anna, and a standoff; and now there was this long step down to the Pamunkey River, Hanover Town and the crossings, with Richmond and the great tidal river just over the horizon.

The big clock was ticking, at Hanover Town Richmond was only seventeen miles away, and the Army of the Potomac kept moving. The meandering roads led through Hawes' Shop, Pole Green Church, Polly Huntley's Corners, Bethesda Church and other places that wore homely, well used, backcountry names. The land was featureless, with sluggish little rivers looping across flatlands that could turn into swamps when the rains came, and there was Totopotomoy Creek to cross and after it there was the Chickahominy River, where this army had been two years before . . . very close to the Confederate capital, that time, although not at all close to victory . . . By the morning of May 29 the army was across the Pamunkey and it groped its way forward to the headwaters of the Totopotomoy, where the Army of Northern Virginia was waiting for it. Lee had been unable to keep the Federal army from coming down on the far side of the Pamunkey but he had understood what it was trying to do, and he faded back from behind the North Anna so deftly that when the Federals began to move forward toward Richmond his veterans once again were all in line across every path.

As the Army of the Potomac moved along, prodding and skirmishing to see just where the Rebel formations were, it found itself by May 30 arrayed on a long, loosely connected line that faced generally toward the southwest. There were Confederates in front, on every lane and at every crossroads, alert and very quick on the trigger, and on this day and the next there was musketry and artillery fire all along the line: not a regular battle anywhere, but a great deal of heavy shooting, marked here and there by sharp fights that accomplished little for either side but caused a good many casualties. The Federal left, under Warren, was posted at Bethesda Church; Richmond was just ten miles away, but those miles were likely to offer tough going. By May 31 Grant could see there was no opening anywhere on this front. It was time to think about another move by the flank.

Grant did not have much choice, because he was beginning to run out of space. The way from the Rapidan down to Richmond was a huge inverted triangle. There had been plenty of room up above, but now Grant was down at the apex; in addition, he had to do something to protect his road to the rear. His new base at White House lay nearly due east of Richmond, and as the armies now stood Lee was almost as close to it as Grant was. If Grant swung off to his right he would expose White House to capture — a danger given added point by the fact that at noon on May 30 Baldy Smith's troops were starting to disembark there. Before he moved anywhere Grant had to protect his own rear and cover the route Smith must use when he came up to reinforce the Army of the Potomac. Accordingly, on May 31 Sheridan was ordered to go down below the Federal left and take proper protective measures.

None of the roads ran straight, in this country, but the principal route Lee's people would use if they struck at White House picked up the Chickahominy crossings a little north of Richmond and then came east across an uneven dusty plain, about four miles south and slightly east of Warren's position at Bethesda Church. On its way across the plain the road passed a run-down tavern that gave its name to the whole area and to the battle that would be fought there — one of the hard and terrible names of the Civil War, perhaps the most terrible

[257]

one of all: *Cold Harbor*. Sometimes the name was given as Cool Arbor, but either way it baffled the Union soldiers who had to fight here. There was no arbor in sight, and there certainly was no harbor within many miles, and in the hundred-degree heat that prevailed just now it was impossible for them to see why anybody would ever have called it Cold or Cool. The best explanation seems to be that the expression came from England, where it once signified a tavern where people could get overnight accommodations but no hot meals. In any case, Sheridan brought two cavalry divisions down here and on the afternoon of May 31 he moved forward to seize the crossing where the road from Warren's position met the Cold Harbor road.

There was Confederate cavalry here, and a handful of infantry, but Sheridan's men carried repeating carbines and they were more dangerous when they fought on foot than they were when they stayed on their horses. Sheridan dismounted them and sent them on in a charge that forced the Confederates off in retreat and secured the road crossing. The Confederates promptly counterattacked; Lee had just received reinforcements, General Robert Hoke's division of 4,000 men, sent north by Beauregard, and Sheridan's cavalry was hard pressed. Sheridan at last sent back word that unless he could be reinforced he would have to retreat, but Meade ordered him to hold his ground at all hazards, and General Wright's corps was pulled out of the far end of the Union line and was sent down to Cold Harbor on an all-night march.

Sheridan's troopers held their ground, after hard fighting, and on the morning of June 1 Wright's infantry came up and relieved them. The Federal rear now was safe, if Grant meant to maneuver by his left he would have a little room for it, and when Smith's corps came up, midafternoon or a bit later, the Federals had a firm grip on Cold Harbor. Early that evening Wright and Smith attacked, Wright's corps on the left of the east-west road to Richmond, Smith's on the right of it. It was a hard fight — no skirmish-line tussle, this time, but a regular battle — and the two Federal corps between them lost something like 2,200 men. They scored a success, however, driving the Confederates out of their first line, taking several hundred prisoners, and apparently winning a position from which a heavier attack could be made.[16]

On that night of June 1 Grant could see only what was visible across the murky flats in the battlefield twilight; and what he saw, dimly but unmistakably, was opportunity. This position was beyond

Lee's entrenched flank, and the Rebels who held it had been hastily assembled and had had no chance to dig themselves in solidly. The Federals already had two army corps here; if they had one more, at dawn, drawn up on the left of the two that were already in position, they should be able to overwhelm the defense and get the break-through they had been trying to get, without success, ever since the Wilderness. If they did that, Grant would at last have what he wanted most — a fighting ground between Lee and Richmond.

There was everything to gain and the chances looked good, so that evening Hancock was ordered to bring the Second Corps down from the extreme right, marching behind the Union line all night and taking position on Wright's left at daybreak; this would give him a ten-mile march, but Meade estimated that he could be in position, ready to fight, by six in the morning. Wright and Smith were told to be pre-pared to renew the offensive at that hour, Warren was told to move forward on Smith's right when the fighting began, and the army was ready for its great, climactic offensive.

That is . . . the army was believed to be ready. Actually it was not, and the result was a military tragedy. When Grant looked back, long afterward, he confessed that this second assault at Cold Harbor was one of the two attacks he ordered during the war that he wished had not been made. (The other was an attack on the Vicksburg trenches on May 22, 1863.) It is true that a genuine opportunity had been glimpsed on the evening of June 1, and it is perfectly possible that a smashing attack at dawn on June 2 would have succeeded. But the attack was not made on the morning of June 2, or anywhere near there, because this army simply did not have the right kind of reflexes. From the fall of 1861 onward, it had never been quite ready. On the battlefield it was heroic but slow. Realizing all too well that haste makes waste, its generals resolved to waste nothing. The man who had to explain why a movement took longer than had been expected would always get a hearing, heads nodding thoughtfully in sympa-thetic understanding, everybody fully aware that speedy action can hardly be looked for in an emergency. Now the army was twenty-four hours late for the offensive that might have won the war. This was not anybody's fault, in particular. The army was just late.

The night was hot, dark and windless, the soldiers were tired, and when Hancock's corps began its march to the left it lost its way and went down a narrow lane in a dense woods, over its head in a choking cloud of dust — blinded, breathless and finally unable to move at all. Artillery got jammed between trees, infantry brigades piled up on one another, regimental formations were lost, and officers who tried to restore order groped helplessly in a noisy, confusing midnight. After an interminable delay the corps managed to find its way to another road, and at last — six-thirty in the morning, or later — the leading elements of the long column were beginning to reach the goal. Most of the corps, however, was stretched out for miles to the rear, straggling had reduced regiments to fragments, it would take hours to get the corps assembled and formed up, and an attack this morning was entirely out of the question. Grant ordered the offensive postponed until four in the afternoon; but it developed that Smith's corps was not in shape to move forward, Hancock's soldiers were staggering with exhaustion, and a couple of hours after noon Grant sent Meade a note:

"In view of the want of preparation for an attack this evening, and the heat and want of energy among the men from moving during the night last night, I think it advisable to postpone assault until early tomorrow morning. All changes of position already ordered should be completed today and a good night's rest given the men preparatory to an assault at, say, 4:30 in the morning." Meade accordingly notified the corps commanders of the postponement, and ordered: "Corps commanders will employ the interim in making examination of the ground in their fronts and perfecting their arrangements for the assault." [17]

Everyone realized, of course, that it was dangerous to give Lee this extra time to get ready. On the night of June 1 Wright warned that the enemy was reinforcing heavily on his front, Meade remarked that "if we give them any time they will dig in so as to prevent any advance on our part," and Wright reported that if he and Hancock could not attack promptly at dawn "I may lose what I have gained." At noon on June 2 Meade thought that Lee had not yet had time to perfect his defenses, and he told Smith that it was "quite important to dislodge and, if possible, rout him before he can entrench himself." He had Warren shift toward the left, extending a skirmish line to make contact with Smith's troops, and Burnside, who now held the extreme right of the line, was pulled back to what looked like a better defensive position.

During the afternoon these movements by Warren and Burnside

stirred up a fight, and a Confederate force advanced and made a vigorous attack, most of it directed at Burnside. His troops repulsed this
attack, after a hard fight, and Grant did not know about it until it was
all over; according to Badeau, he felt that Warren and Burnside had
missed a good chance, because for once they had a chance to fight
Rebels outside of earthworks, "and his chagrin was extreme when he
learned of the failure to assault in return." Whether from this encounter or from the belief that Lee was being compelled to draw his line
rather thin, the Federal high command believed that some sort of opportunity might be open along the right, and after dark Meade wrote
to Grant about it.

Meade believed that by strengthening his right Lee must be weakening his left. Accordingly, he told Grant, he had ordered Warren and
Burnside to attack "at all hazards" at 4:30 A.M., hoping that they
could swing around to the left and crush the flank of the Confederate
force that was facing Smith. On the other hand, if Lee was strong
opposite Warren and Burnside he must be weak at the other end of
the line, the three-corps attack there ought to prevail, and "we will
swing by the right and move up on Warren's left." This sounded logical, but it was wrong; in the end Warren was unable to attack at all
and Burnside could do no more than go through the motions, and
everything had to stand or fall by what Hancock, Wright and Smith
could do at Cold Harbor.

Meade's thinking may have reflected Grant's. Whether it did or
not, Grant was going to bet the stack on the big offensive on his left.
He was thinking, perhaps, of the way Hancock had broken the line at
Spotsylvania, and of Thomas's amazing assault on the impossible
Rebel position at Missionary Ridge; and he believed that this offensive
could be called off quickly, with no great harm done, if Lee's works
on the rolling ground overlooking the Cold Harbor plain proved genuinely impregnable. His orders stood. Night came down, with a driz-
zling rain that laid the dust, cooled things off, and gave the weary
soldiers one good night of sleep — last night before the long one, for
many of them — and when things began to get light early on the
morning of June 3 the men in the selected assaulting columns formed
up, looked at the wet gray landscape in front of them, and waited for
the word.[18]

Lee had been given just a little too much time. He had brought
reinforcements to his right, and for twenty-four hours his men had

been digging a series of interlocking trenches, with abundant artillery in place, sometimes out in front of the infantry, so that it could lay a killing cross fire on all of the avenues of approach. What might have been done on the morning of June 2 was altogether impossible by the morning of June 3. All Lee's veterans had to do was wait. The men who were about to attack them understood this perfectly well. Horace Porter of Grant's staff went forward to the front just before the battle began and found the Federal soldiers recording their own verdict; each man was writing his name on a slip of paper and pinning the paper to his uniform, so that his body could be identified after it was over.[19]

Four-thirty, with the gray light getting stronger. And after a little time — five minutes, an hour: nobody really knows — the taut silence was suddenly broken by a crashing salvo from the Federal artillery. Officers waved their swords and shouted commands, and then the long blue lines began to move forward.

CHAPTER FOURTEEN

On the Banks of the James

THE Cold Harbor plain looked empty, and the fact that everybody knew that it was not empty made it sinister, like the blank face of a dreadful haunted house. The ground was broken here and there by swamps and little ravines, in front of the Federal lines it rose after a few hundred yards to a low chain of flat hills, and all along this higher ground there was a scar on the earth — a trench of freshly turned dirt, zig-zagging in and out, disappearing in thin mist to right and left. It was marked by regimental flags, limp in the windless wet morning, and there did not seem to be anybody in it. Nobody was in the least deceived; and yet, except for the Rebel skirmishers, who were posted far out in front, the advancing Federals could see hardly any of their enemies. They could not see many friends, either, because there were gaps between the army corps, so that each division would have to fight its own battle. No Federal soldier could see more than a fragment of the field.

The battle lines swung up to the skirmishers, scattered them, and moved on toward that ominous scar along the low ridges. Closer they came, and closer; and suddenly, in front of them and beyond vision to right and left, the length of that ugly trench came alive with Confederate soldiers standing up to strike. An endless sheaf of glittering rifle barrels swung forward, tilting down over the parapet; then there was a blinding sheet of flame, two miles of it, from one horizon to the other, as Lee's infantry opened fire. Hundreds of rifles were going off every second; and the massed Confederate artillery joined in, smashing and tearing the Federal troops with shell and solid shot. There was a fearful clamor, like the noise of the Wilderness and Gettysburg together, all in one, and a tumbling cloud of smoke flattened out across the plain. Survivors remembered that to be out there was like being in the heart of an exploding thundercloud, like trying to fight a battle in the center of a volcano, like something language had no words for: the ultimate storm, more terrible than anything men had seen before.

Along most of the front the charge was stopped before it had properly begun. Wright's corps was pinned down from the start. Some of the troops advanced a short distance and then dropped to the ground, using tin cups and bayonets to scoop out shallow rifle pits; some of them did not move at all. One brigadier reported that he was supposed to guide his movement by the progress of the division to his right; the division failed to stir, and "for some cause the charge was not made." Emory Upton simply reported that "another assault was ordered, but being deemed impracticable along our front was not made." One unit beat through the Rebel skirmishers and got within two hundred and fifty yards of the main line, but had to retreat because Smith's corps, on its right, was unable to move.

Smith's people, for their part, felt that they were hung up because Wright's corps did not advance. Some of Smith's troops made a brave try, and paid for it heavily. The division of General John Martindale moved up a shallow ravine, ran into a furious fire from both flanks that dropped men by platoons, and could do no more than stagger to a halt and dig in. The division on Martindale's right could not move at all; the one on his left made some progress and then found itself isolated, its leading brigade almost obliterated by a terrible cross fire that came from across the ground where Wright's troops were supposed to be fighting. One of Martindale's soldiers said afterward that from first to last he saw nothing of this battle except flame and smoke, in front of him and on both sides; he never once set eyes on a Confederate soldier, and he suspected that the repulse of this part of the attack might not have cost the foe a single casualty. It may not have been quite that bad; still, the attack by Wright's and Smith's corps was broken up in no more than half an hour.[1]

Things began better on Hancock's front, but the only result was that they quickly got worse. That is, more men were killed in this corps than in either of the others, all because they got off to a more promising start.

Hancock sent in two divisions side by side, Barlow on the left and Gibbon on the right, with his third division, Birney's, held in reserve. Barlow's men charged with the spirit that had taken them through the mule shoe at Spotsylvania, and for a dazzling moment it seemed that they might do as well here. They got to the main line, seized a Confederate trench, sent two or three hundred prisoners to the rear and captured three guns. But there was Rebel artillery posted so that it could fire down the length of the captured trench, and the canister at this close range made a butchery in the narrow confining ditch. Barlow sent back for supports, but somehow the orders went awry and the supports did not come. His men had to fall back, and they dug shallow works close to the Confederate line and awaited new orders.

Gibbon could do no better. His men struck a swamp that nobody had known about — Meade's orders for a careful study of the ground to be covered by the charge seem to have gone unheeded — and the line split in half, part of it striking in one place and the rest of it coming up, out of reach, far to the right. Some of the men managed to get to close quarters, but when Gibbon sent back for his reserves a brigadier got confused and moved his regiments pointlessly off to the flank instead of coming straight ahead; and in a short time Gibbon's men had to withdraw. Like Barlow's, they dug in near the enemy line and under a heavy fire waited to see what the high command proposed to do next.[2]

The high command today was Meade. He was handling the battle, as far as anyone could handle something that had gone almost totally out of control. (Next day he told Mrs. Meade: "I had immediate and entire command on the field all day, the Lieutenant General honoring the field with his presence only about one hour in the middle of the day."[3]) At dawn Meade went to Wright's headquarters, as a central command post where he could be in touch with everybody by field telegraph. It was as good a place as any; and yet, inevitably, it was a place in which a commanding general could know only what he was told. Much that Meade was told today was either wrong to begin with or was inevitably misunderstood on arrival, and there was nothing he could do about it because it was impossible for anybody to go out and appraise all of the battle by what he could see with his own eyes.

Meade was told that Hancock had made a penetration, that his men held an advanced position, and that Hancock might soon renew the assault. This sounded most promising, and instructions to other commanders were framed in the light of that promise. An hour later, Hancock reported: "I consider that the assault failed long since"; but the pattern formed earlier was not easily discarded, especially because the generals kept talking about the victory that could be won if all hands did their part. Wright could carry the works in his center if his flanks were supported; Smith was gloomy, but thought he could do something if *his* flanks were supported; Warren and Burnside were "getting the enemy back," and Burnside had carried the first line of enemy works and would go on as soon as he had re-formed his line. It did seem that one concerted push would win the day. Meade told the generals to keep fighting, and at eight forty-five he sent orders to Hancock: "It is of the greatest importance no effort should be spared to succeed. Wright and Smith are both going to try again, and unless you consider it hopeless I would like you to do the same."

Somewhat earlier, Meade summarized the first encouraging reports in a dispatch to Grant, saying: "I should be glad to have your views as to the continuance of these attacks, if unsuccessful." Grant made about the only reply he could make: "The moment it becomes certain that an assault cannot succeed, suspend the offensive, but when one does succeed push it vigorously, and if necessary pile in troops at the successful point wherever they can be taken. I shall go to where you are in the course of an hour." [4]

Actually, by the time Meade got this message the offensive was gone beyond hope of redemption, although there was no way for Meade to know it. Wright and Smith were completely stymied. Warren was not advancing at all; could not, because his corps held three miles of front and was spun out so thin that by noon it was necessary to send Birney's division over so that Warren could be sure of staying where he was. In a hazy sort of way, Burnside was under Warren today, and Warren's hopeful report grew out of his belief that Burnside was making progress. Yet Burnside really was doing little more than make a demonstration to keep the Rebels from removing troops from their left, and his happy belief that he had captured the first line of works on his front simply meant that he had driven in the enemy's skirmishers. The Federals were succeeding nowhere, and had no chance of success; yet the unbroken fire of infantry rifles and field artillery, going on almost unabated hour after hour, made the battle seem fluid, as if something could still be done with it, and the crescent of flame that burned the front and flanks of every Federal division that had tried to go forward blazed on and on without a letup. To a visitor this morning, General Lee confessed that he had no reserves, not one regiment; yet he needed none, his line was invulnerable, all his soldiers had to do was stay in their trenches and shoot Yankees. This they did with unwearying tenacity.

Toward noon, Grant rode forward, not to see Meade immediately but to talk to the corps commanders. He got the picture, finally, and he wrote orders for Meade: "The opinion of corps commanders not being sanguine of success in case an assault is ordered, you may direct a suspension of further advance for the present. Hold our most advanced positions, and strengthen them." [5]

Meade sent out the orders, and the men who had made the fruitless attacks did what they could — in broad daylight, close to the enemy lines — to improvise entrenchments along their new position. There was a good deal of firing all the rest of the day, with sharp clashes between skirmishers here and there, but the battle really was over: an unvarnished repulse, with fearful losses and nothing of any consequence gained. Except perhaps for the bloody December day in front of the sunken road at Fredericksburg, in 1862, Lee's army had never broken up a massive Federal onslaught at so little cost to itself. At Cold Harbor on June 3 the Federals lost rather more than 7,000 men, most of them in the first two hours of fighting. Confederate losses for the day were probably below 1,500.

It was a little while before either Grant or Meade understood just how one-sided the battle had been. That afternoon Grant sent a wire to Halleck describing the situation as he saw it then: "We assaulted at 4:30 o'clock this morning, driving the enemy within his entrenchments at all points but without gaining any decisive advantage. Our troops now occupy a position close to the enemy, some places within 50 yards, and are entrenching. Our loss was not severe, nor do I suppose the enemy have lost heavily." Meade's own picture of the battle is set forth in a letter he sent to Mrs. Meade on June 4: "We had a big battle yesterday, on the field of the old Gaines's Mill battle-ground, with the positions of the contending forces reversed. The battle ended without any decided results, we repulsing all attacks of the enemy and they doing the same; losses estimated about equal on both sides; ours roughly estimated at seven thousand five hundred in all." Rawlins saw things about as Meade did. He told Mrs. Rawlins that there had been a severe but indecisive battle: "Our loss in killed, wounded and missing will reach at least 5,000. That of the enemy cannot be less, for each side attacked in turn the fortified position of the other and was repulsed, the exception being that we carried the rifle pits of their skirmish line, which we still hold."

Commanding generals, to repeat, know what people tell them, and both Meade and Rawlins (and presumably Grant along with them) thought that the day had been one of unsuccessful assaults by both sides. Lee's infantry had in fact struck at Warren, at Burnside and at Wilson's cavalry screen beyond Burnside's flank, and after dark there were jabs at Hancock's front; all of these were simply counterattacks, not nearly as massive as the main Federal assaults, and yet at headquarters one fight looked much like another, and at the moment the battle was hard to interpret.[6]

It has been hard to interpret ever since. It gave final proof that good trenches properly manned cannot be stormed and that an offensive against an entrenched foe is hard to manage, much easier to start than to stop; but beyond these points the battle meant less than it seemed to mean. It neither robbed Grant's army of the initiative, imposed a serious delay on it nor forced it to abandon its original plan. It was dreadfully costly — and yet of the three major engagements fought between the time the army crossed the Rapidan and the time it crossed the James, Cold Harbor took the smallest toll in Federal casualties. The army remained capable of rapid movement, and its morale seemed to be as high as ever, because when all was said and done the soldiers felt that they had made genuine progress in a month of campaigning; one of Birney's men expressed the private soldiers' viewpoint when he wrote proudly that "Grant does not know how to retreat" and said that "confidence is unbounded in him."

The army was on McClellan's old ground these days, and Horace Porter told his wife that McClellan would not like what the soldiers were saying now: "They all say if he had not retreated with them, himself leading the way, but stood and let them fight it out as Grant is doing, they would have been in Richmond two years sooner." Charles Francis Adams, Jr., a captain in the 1st Massachusetts Cavalry, in Gregg's division, wrote that "so far Grant has out-generalled Lee and he has, in spite of his inability to start Lee one inch out of his positions, maneuvered himself close to the gates of Richmond." A regular army man in Warren's corps assured his parents: "Grant has been successful in all his movements during the campaign and his men feel sanguine of success, although it will no doubt take time to do it"; and one of Baldy Smith's soldiers wrote jubilantly: "We have the gray backs in a pretty close corner at present and intend to keep them so. There is no fall back with U. S. Grant." [7]

In addition to these bits of evidence about morale after Cold Harbor there is the case of the 4th Ohio Volunteer Infantry.

This regiment belonged to Colonel Thomas A. Smyth's brigade, in Gibbon's division. It took part in Gibbon's unsuccessful assault near the swamp in that ghastly dawn on June 3, dug in close to the enemy's line after the attack failed, and on the morning of June 5 it got formal notice that its term of service had expired and that it could forthwith march to the rear and get out of the war forever. It would of course have been suicidal for the regiment to start the march in daylight, so the regiment waited for darkness. That night, at about eight o'clock, it left its trench, formed column, and set out for home. Just then the restless Confederates — aroused by this movement, or perhaps by something else — opened a heavy fire of artillery. In the darkness the Rebel gunners could hardly hope to hit anything, but the firing was incessant and it might be the first act of a Rebel counteroffensive, and so the retiring regiment came to a halt, faced about, and swung into line of battle. An officer was sent off to tell Colonel Smyth that this regiment, having had three years of it, did not propose to march out of the war to the sound of the enemy's guns: it would stay in line while the firing lasted, and it would perform any duty the colonel might require. It stayed, and after a time the firing died away, there was no Confederate attack, and the colonel required nothing further; and so the 4th Ohio finally got back into marching column and headed for White House landing and the steamboat that would take it on the first leg of its one-way trip to Ohio. Its military pride was still intact. [8]

Grant wasted no effort now trying to put Cold Harbor into perspective. He wanted to get on with the war, and there was a lot of paper work to do. Yet he indulged himself a little, on June 4, doing what the humblest private soldier might have done — giving way to thoughts of loved ones back home — and before he began to draft the orders that would set the army marching he took time off to write a letter to his daughter Nelly.

Nelly was eight years old, and with her two older brothers she was in St. Louis. She had made some kind of appearance at a big Sanitary Commission Fair a few days earlier; she had also, all unaided, written her father a letter, and she apparently had a high regard for a Shetland pony named Little Rebel, which was a part of the family entourage. And so about twenty-four hours after he had written the order that stopped the battle of Cold Harbor, Grant wrote to his daughter:

My Dear little Nelly:

I received your pretty well written letter more than a week ago. You do not know how happy it made me feel to see how well my little girl not yet nine years old could write. I expect by the end of the year you and Buck [*her brother, Ulysses, Jr., not quite twelve*] will be able to speak German, and then I will have to buy you those nice gold watches I promised. I see in the papers and also from Mama's letters that you have been representing "the old Woman that lived in a Shoe" at the Fair; I know you must have enjoyed it very much. You must send me one of your photographs taken at the Fair.

We have been fighting now for thirty days and have every prospect of still more fighting to do before we get into Richmond. When we do get there I shall go home to see you, Ma, Fred, Buck and Jess. I expect Jess rides Little Rebel every day. I think when I go home I will get a little buggy to work Rebel in so that you and Jess can ride about the country during vacation. Tell Ma to let Fred learn French as soon as she thinks he is able to study it. It will be a great help to him when he goes to West Point. . . . Be a good little girl as you have always been, study your lessons, and you will be contented and happy.[9]

The day after he wrote this letter to Nelly, Grant had to attend to a delicate matter of military protocol involving the relief of the army's wounded men, some of whom had been lying on the battlefield, unattended, for forty-eight hours. On June 5 Hancock asked Meade if some arrangement for the rescue of these men could not be made, and Meade passed the note along to Grant, saying the Confederate sharpshooters made it impossible to bring the wounded back inside the Union lines and suggesting a flag of truce to arrange for a brief armistice. Such a flag, said Meade, would have to go out in Grant's name, because "the enemy do not recognize me as in command whilst you are present." So Grant wrote a letter to Lee, proposing that when no actual fighting was going on either side should feel free to send out unarmed litter-bearers to collect wounded men, and adding: "Any other method equally fair to both parties you may propose for meeting the end desired will be accepted by me." It took time to get a note across the lines. A Federal officer carried a white flag and Grant's letter over to the Confederate outposts at three that afternoon, and it was nearly midnight when the reply came back. The reply did not reach Grant until next morning, June 6.

Lee wrote that Grant's proposal would simply lead to confusion all around, and continued: "I propose, therefore, instead that when either party desires to remove their dead or wounded a flag of truce be sent, as is customary. It will always afford me pleasure to comply with such a request." Grant wrote in response that he would like to send stretcher-bearers out under a white flag between noon and three o'clock that afternoon; he would honor similar flag-of-truce parties sent out by the Confederates. This drew a stiff answer from Lee, who regretted that he had not made himself understood; if either side wanted to bury its dead and collect its wounded it should first ask permission, by flag of truce, in the usual way, and until Lee received "a proposition from you on the subject to which I can accede with propriety, I have directed any parties you may send out under white flags as mentioned in your letter to be turned back."

The wounded men were still lying on the dusty field, under a very hot sun: but apparently the big point was that by ancient military tradition an army that asked for an armistice so that it could bury its dead and collect its wounded was thereby admitting that it had just lost a battle. If such an admission was what Lee wanted he now got it. On the afternoon of June 6, Grant wrote that the plight of the wounded men "compels me to ask a suspension of hostilities for sufficient time to collect them in, say, two hours." Any hours Lee chose, he said, would be acceptable, and if during those two hours Lee wanted to bring in his own wounded men the Federals would not interfere.

This was acceptable. At seven o'clock that evening, Lee replied that he was sorry it had not been possible to set a truce during daylight, but he would designate the period between eight and ten that night for the purpose. At that time, he said, his army would collect any of its own wounded who still remained on the field. Unfortunately, this letter was not delivered at the Federal outposts until after ten P.M., when the time had expired, and Grant did not get it until after eleven. So the Federals sent out no rescue parties that night, and one group of Confederates that came out was captured by Federal skirmishers, who knew nothing about any truce. Next morning, June 7, Grant sent Lee a letter telling him about the delay, promising to return the captured Confederates, and concluding by "regretting that all my efforts for alleviating the sufferings of the wounded men left upon the battlefield have been rendered nugatory." (Rawlins must have written that one: "rendered nugatory" somehow does not sound like Grant.)

This of course had to have a reply, and Lee wrote one on the afternoon of June 7. He was sorry about the mix-up, and he suggested that the hours from six to eight that evening be set aside for parties with white flags; he would tell his army to recognize Unionists who came out under such flags, and would tell his people that they also could go out, flag-laden, to pick up any Confederate wounded they might find. This, to be sure, was exactly the procedure Grant had proposed on the morning of June 6; and that night the stretcher-bearers went out to do what they could. They got a slim harvest, because by now most of the wounded men had either died or had been rescued by comrades who risked life and limb to save them, but all of the formalities had been observed.[10]

While all of this was going on Grant managed to keep Julia posted. She learned nothing of military value, but she did hear from her husband, who seemed quite undaunted. On June 6 he told her: "This is likely to prove a very tedious job I have on hand but I feel very confident of ultimate success. The enemy keeps himself behind strong intrenchments all the time and seems determined to hold on to the last." Holding on to the last might involve some terribly bloody battles, but the general-in-chief was matter-of-fact about it. Next day he had a haircut, and as she had asked him to do he sent his wife a lock of his hair, with a note which read: "Today has been the quietest since leaving Culpeper. There has been no fighting except a little artillery skirmish firing and some skirmishing driving the enemy's pickets south of the Chickahominy at two of the bridges below our main line. War will get to be so common with me if this thing continues much longer that I will not be able to sleep after a while unless there is an occasional gunshot near me during the night."

Immediately after this Grant found himself involved in another matter of protocol. With most unfortunate results, General Meade devoted himself to setting the line that should govern the conduct of newspaper reporters who were attached to army headquarters.

Edward Crapsey was a war correspondent for the Philadelphia *Inquirer*, and shortly before the big fight at Cold Harbor the *Inquirer* printed a story saying that at the close of the battle of the Wilderness Meade had wanted to take the army back to the north side of the

Rapidan. Grant "saved the army and the nation, too," said Crapsey, by overruling Meade and ordering the offensive to continue. Crapsey's dispatch was widely reprinted and when Meade saw it his hot temper went altogether out of control. He called Crapsey to his tent and demanded to know where Crapsey got such a story. Naturally enough, Crapsey refused to reveal his source, saying only that this had been the talk of the camp. Meade retorted that it was "a base and wicked lie" which he would now punish in a way that would make other reporters more careful.

So, on the morning of June 8, the luckless Crapsey was bound, put astride the most disreputable mule that could be found, and, facing to the rear, and wearing a big placard reading "Libeler of the Press," he was paraded all across the camp, escorted by members of General Patrick's provost guard, while the drums beat out the Rogue's March. Meade said that this delighted the army, "for the race of newspaper correspondents is universally despised by the soldiers." Crapsey was taken back to White House, put on a steamer for Washington, and told never to return. Grant was present when Meade made out the order for all of this; he said that he knew Crapsey's family back in Illinois and that it was "a respectable one," but he refused to interfere. Deeply humiliated, Crapsey was drummed out of camp, and sardonic General Patrick chuckled that "it will be a warning to his tribe."

As it happened, Crapsey's story was wrong. Grant assured a correspondent that Meade had never counselled a retreat, adding that the rumor was "entirely idle and without the shadow of a foundation," and he gave a copy of his letter to Meade; and Secretary Stanton sent Meade his assurances that "the lying report . . . was not even for one moment believed by the President or myself." Meade was vindicated: and yet, as anyone who knew anything about newspaper reporters could have told him, he succeeded only in ruining his press relations once and for all. By common consent — and later, according to Sylvanus Cadwallader of the New York *Herald*, by "an expressed understanding" that reached all the way down to the publishers' offices — newspaper dispatches from the Army of the Potomac henceforth left out Meade's name entirely. Everything that was done was done by Grant, the army became "Grant's army" and Meade was the forgotten man.

A day or so afterward there was a slightly similar case, when General Burnside took offense at a story written by William Swinton of the New York *Times*. Grant had had his own troubles with Swinton, to whom he had been introduced at the start of the campaign by Congressman Washburne, who in Grant's quaint phrasing assured him that Swinton "was a gentleman, and was not a newspaper correspondent, but a literary man who proposed to write a history of the war after it was over." On the night after the first day's battle in the Wilderness, Swinton was caught hiding behind a tree, eavesdropping on a conference at Grant's headquarters, and was ejected from the camp. He had returned, attaching himself to Burnside, and now he had written something Burnside did not like; and Burnside hotly demanded that he be given the same treatment Crapsey had had, or that Burnside be allowed to deal with him in a more drastic way, which gave Grant the impression that Burnside wanted to have the man shot. Grant intervened, and Swinton got off with nothing worse than a return ticket to Washington. As things finally worked out, both he and Crapsey eventually returned to the army; the other correspondents adjusted themselves — that is, they went on covering the war just as they had been doing — but neither Meade nor Burnside ever got any favors from the press.[11]

Meanwhile, there was work to be done, and Grant applied himself to it.

From the beginning of the campaign, Grant had been explicit about one thing: he would shatter Lee's army in battle if he could, but whatever happened he would eventually put Meade's and Butler's armies side by side on the southern bank of the James River. There was no especial magic about being south of the James, of course, except that that was where most of the railroads were — and the final object of everything the Federals were doing in Virginia this spring was to cut the railroad lines that tied Lee's army and the city of Richmond to the rest of the Confederacy. General Humphreys expressed this clearly when he wrote his history of the campaign, after the war; he asserted that the reason for crossing the James was "to carry out the plan with which the Army of the Potomac began the campaign, that is, to destroy the lines of supply to the Confederate depot, Richmond, on the south side of the James as close to that city as practicable, after those on the north side of the river had been rendered useless."

This did not resemble plans for previous Federal campaigns in Virginia; instead, it derived unmistakably from what had been done at Vicksburg and Chattanooga. In the west Grant had learned how to

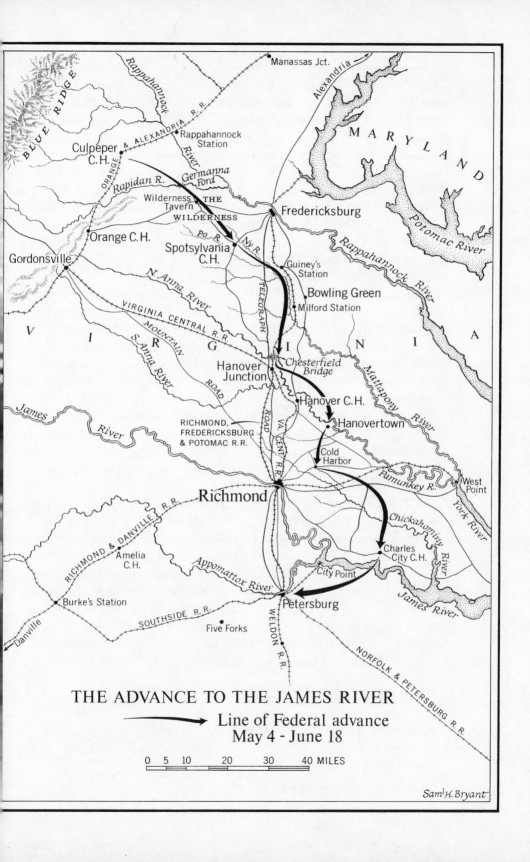

THE ADVANCE TO THE JAMES RIVER

→ Line of Federal advance
May 4 - June 18

0 5 10   20   30   40 MILES

Sam.ᴸH.Bryant

isolate an enemy army and citadel, and he had seen what happened once that was done; which is another way of saying that he had learned about the supreme importance of railroads in wartime. Once he had snipped Vicksburg's railroad to the outer world, at Jackson, Pemberton was helpless. Grant himself had been able to do nothing at Chattanooga until he put his own railroad in shape, and after he had done that he had the game in his hand. Cavalry's young Captain Adams got the point, and two days after the battle at Cold Harbor Adams told Richard Henry Dana, Jr.: "I think Grant will be forced to adopt his Vicksburg tactics — he will have to uncover Washington, cross the James, move up the south bank and then throw himself on the Confederate line of communications and supplies." [12]

This would disturb General Halleck, who believed in making war without taking any risks, and who had urged Grant to stay north of the James, rely on the Fredericksburg Railroad for his own supplies, and stay always between Lee and Washington, approaching Richmond by slow, methodical stages. Grant never had any intention of doing this. On June 3, almost before the noise of the great battle at Cold Harbor had died away, he told Meade not to bother about rehabilitating the York River Railroad, which ran back to the base at White House; inside of ten days that base would be closed and the army would get its supplies from the James.[13] On June 5 Grant sent Halleck a dispatch which shows what he proposed to do and why he proposed to do it.

"A full survey of the ground satisfies me that it would not be practicable to hold a line northeast of Richmond that would protect the Fredericksburg railroad, to enable us to use it for supplying the army," he wrote. "To do so would give us a long vulnerable line of road to protect, exhausting much of our strength in guarding it, and would leave open to the enemy all of his lines of communication on the south side of the James. My idea from the start has been to beat Lee's army, if possible, north of Richmond, then, after destroying his lines of communication north of the James river, to transfer the army to the south side and besiege Lee in Richmond, or follow him south if he should retreat."

Then Grant summed up the moral drawn from a month of combat:

I now find, after more than thirty days of trial, that the enemy deems it of the first importance to run no risks with the armies they now have.

They act purely on the defensive, behind breast-works, or feebly on the offensive immediately in front of them and where in case of repulse they can instantly retire behind them. Without a greater sacrifice of human life than I am willing to make, all cannot be accomplished that I had designed outside of the city.

If all Grant wanted was a war of attrition he was in the right place for it, here at Cold Harbor, and it was not necessary to move another foot. Yet he really wanted something quite different, and in these thirty days of trial he had made steady progress toward his goal. If his foe was gaining a series of technical successes, Grant was getting step by step nearer to a powerful strategic advantage. Now he outlined what the next step was going to be:

I have, therefore, resolved upon the following plan; I will continue to hold substantially the ground now occupied by the Army of the Potomac, taking advantage of any favorable circumstance that may present itself, until the cavalry can be sent west to destroy the Virginia Central Railroad from about Beaver Dam for some 25 or 30 miles west. When this is effected I will move the army to the south side of James river. . . . Once on the south side of the James river I can cut off all sources of supply to the enemy, except what is furnished by the canal.[14]

The sources of supply were the ultimate goal: and here the case was somewhat intricate.

Lee's army and Richmond drew supplies from various places, but what chiefly kept them both alive were the rich granary of the Shenandoah Valley and the enormous supply depot at Lynchburg, a hundred miles west of Richmond, east of the Blue Ridge. Goods from these places got to Richmond in several ways. There was the Virginia Central Railroad, which ran northwest from Richmond, touched the Orange & Alexandria at Gordonsville, and went on to Staunton in the valley; and from Gordonsville a branch line ran southwest through Charlottesville to Lynchburg. There was also the Southside Railroad, which met the Virginia & Tennessee at Lynchburg and, as its name implied, ran east from Lynchburg south of the James; it cut the Richmond & Danville line at Burkeville and then went on to the bigger junction point at Petersburg. Finally, there was the James River canal, coming down from Lynchburg to Richmond in the James River valley.[15]

Grant believed that by going south of the James he could sooner or later break the Southside Railroad, along with all the roads that came up to Richmond and Petersburg from other parts of the south; but he would not really isolate Lee's army and Richmond, even if he did this, unless the Gordonsville connection had also been broken, and he wanted to have that attended to before the Federal army crossed the river. Accordingly, after sending his dispatch to Halleck Grant wrote a directive for Meade:

The object of the cavalry expedition to Charlottesville and Gordonsville is to effectually break up the railroad connection between Richmond and the Shenandoah Valley and Lynchburg. To secure this end they should go as far as Charlottesville and work upon the Lynchburg branch and main line to Staunton for several miles beyond the junction. This done, they could work back this way to where the road is already destroyed, or until driven off by a superior force. It is desirable that every rail on the road destroyed should be so bent or twisted as to make it impossible to repair the road without supplying new rails. After the work is accomplished, herein directed, the cavalry will rejoin the main army.

There was one other important angle to this expedition. General Hunter was moving up the valley with the reorganized army that Sigel had so unerringly led to defeat. Hunter was supposed to pick up General Crook's force from western Virginia at Staunton; once this union was made he would have between 17,000 and 18,000 men, more than enough to take care of himself, and so a junction of Sheridan's cavalry with Hunter's infantry became an added objective of the cavalry raid. Grant's directive to Meade continued:

Instructions will be sent to General Hunter by the cavalry expedition. He will be required to join his force to General Sheridan's and return with him to the Army of the Potomac. If it is found practicable, whilst the cavalry is at the most westerly point reached by it, to detach a brigade or more to go over to the James river and destroy the canal, it will be a service well repaying for three or four days detention.[16]

Hunter at the moment was out of touch. When he relieved the unfortunate Sigel, late in May, and started up the valley (he had about 8,500 men of all arms), he got from Grant the kind of instructions that would naturally be given to an officer on detached service — that is, Grant explained in general terms what he wanted and left the details to the man on the spot. As transmitted through Halleck, Grant's original orders told Hunter to get to Staunton and then move to Charlottesville and Lynchburg if he could, destroying the railroads and, if possible, the canal; after which he might either return to his starting point at the upper end of the valley or move east from Gordonsville to join Meade's army. Now, as Sheridan prepared to take two of his three cavalry divisions off to Gordonsville, Grant gave him a letter to send on to Hunter, who was believed to be at Staunton:

"I see in looking over the letter sent to General Halleck on the subject of your instructions that it rather indicates your route should be from Staunton to Charlottesville. If you have so understood it you will be doing just what I want. The direction I would now give is that if this letter reaches you in the Valley, between Staunton and Lynchburg, you immediately move east by the most practicable route until you strike the Lynchburg branch of the Virginia Central road. From there, move eastward along the line of the road, destroying it completely and thoroughly, until you join General Sheridan." After this union had been made, Hunter and Sheridan together were to come east to the Army of the Potomac.[17]

This letter was clear enough, and the only trouble was that Hunter never got it. He had been moving dutifully up the valley, and on June 5 — the day Grant wrote the directive — he struck a Confederate force of 5,600 men near the town of Piedmont and routed it, killing its commander, General William E. "Grumble" Jones. A few days later, moving on to Staunton, he picked up Crook's column, and although Grant got only vague reports of his progress he knew that Hunter was excellently placed to carry out the plan Grant outlined. However, by the time Hunter learned that Sheridan was moving toward him the picture had changed substantially. Richmond heard about the battle at Piedmont promptly and took alarm: to hold the valley was essential. Hunter must be checked at once, and the only way to do this was to send troops from Lee's army. Lee understood the importance of the valley perfectly, but he also understood the dire threat posed by the presence of Grant's army ten miles from Richmond, and on June 6 he sent a dispatch to Confederate Secretary of War Seddon:

If we can defeat Grant here, the Valley can easily be recovered, but if we cannot defeat Grant I am afraid we will be unable to hold the Valley. I

[279]

am therefore unwilling to weaken my present force, but should the President and yourself decide it best I have Breckinridge's command ready to send there, either by rail or by the common highway, as may be found most expeditious. The matter should be decided at once.[18]

The decision was quickly made, and on June 7 Breckinridge and his little division — probably about 2,500 effectives — started for the valley. On the same day Sheridan got his cavalry on the road, moving north to cross the Pamunkey and then riding northwest along the North Anna, planning to destroy the Virginia Central in the vicinity of Louisa Courthouse and then move on to meet Hunter at Charlottesville. Getting wind of this, Lee on June 8 sent General Wade Hampton with two divisions of cavalry to head him off. The immediate effect of this — it was the only real gain Grant derived from the entire operation, but it was a substantial one — was that Lee was unable to retain enough cavalry to discover and delay any movements that the Army of the Potomac might make. Planning for such movements had begun immediately after the battle of Cold Harbor, because (to repeat) more than he wanted anything else Grant wanted to swing out past the Confederate flank and cross the James.

The logistics were highly involved — to uproot an army of 100,000 men from immediate contact with an alert foe, perform a forty-mile flank march, cross a tidal river and arrive unmolested at a spot far behind the enemy's rear was exceedingly difficult — but the headquarters staffs handled the details with smooth competence.

First, there had to be a reserve line of entrenchments to cover the Chickahominy crossings in rear of the Federal left while the army was moving out, and Meade put his engineers at work building such a line on June 9. On the same day Butler was ordered to send a force across the Appomattox from Bermuda Hundred and see whether Petersburg might not be seized by a sudden blow before the Army of the Potomac even started to move — with all that had been going on, the Confederates might have thinned their Petersburg lines beyond the point of safety. In addition, there was the crossing of the James itself to be arranged. A site was chosen near Wilcox Landing, ten miles downstream from Malvern Hill, and to Wilcox Landing went engineer troops, a vast number of pontoon boats and the planks, beams, cordage and hardware that had to be used with them, not to mention a fleet of tugboats and ferry boats and schooners and storeships, convoyed by monitors and gunboats. It was necessary to work out detailed schedules for the movements of the various army corps. Smith was to return to White House and move by water down around Fort Monroe and up the James to rejoin Butler at Bermuda Hundred, Warren was appointed to cover the flank of the moving army, more pontoon trains had to be assembled to bridge the Chickahominy at various places downstream from Cold Harbor, and everything had to be planned so that once the army marched everybody could go promptly along routes properly mapped and prepared. And, finally, it was above all necessary to deceive General Lee.

At this point Sheridan's expedition paid off simply because it had pulled away most of Lee's cavalry.

The army began to move on the night of June 12, and the one cavalry division remaining with the Army of the Potomac, Wilson's, crossed the Chickahominy and moved forward toward Richmond, driving Confederate patrols away from the old battlefields around White Oak Swamp and Riddell's Shop. It was followed by Warren's army corps, and the next morning, when Lee learned that the Federals had disappeared from the steaming trenches around Cold Harbor, he also learned that Federal cavalry and infantry were present in considerable strength along the roads that led toward Richmond between the Chickahominy and the James. This looked like the start of one of Grant's patented flanking maneuvers, and the logical deduction was that Grant was about to drive for the capital along those war-worn highways of the McClellan campaign, the Charles City and Long Bridge roads. In Hampton's absence, Lee's cavalry was not strong enough to break through the Federal screen and see where the rest of Grant's army was. Confederate intelligence did learn that Smith's corps was embarking at White House, presumably to return to Butler, but beyond that it could learn very little.

Lee was in the dark. He was of course aware that Grant might well be preparing to cross the James and attack Petersburg, but until he was sure he could not take his own army down there to meet him; Petersburg was two days' march away, and if he went there while Grant remained north of the James the Federals could march straight into Richmond. Lee had lost touch with the opposing army, and although he was sure that it was about to strike a new blow he could not tell where the blow was going to land or what he ought to do to counter it. For the moment he could only move his own troops south of the Chickahominy to guard against a Federal advance in that area, and wait for more light.[19]

More light did not come to him until several days had passed. Far out of Lee's sight and reach, the Army of the Potomac was on the move. For the first time in a month Meade's weary infantrymen found themselves marching across country where there were no Confederate cavalry columns or infantry patrols to worry about, the hideous Cold Harbor battlefield was far behind them, and there was a growing realization that something big was under way. Hancock's corps reached the bank of the James on the night of June 13, Burnside and Wright had their men across the Chickahominy, and only the men commanded by Warren and Wilson — maintaining a sporadic and generally harmless fire with Confederate skirmishers between Malvern Hill and White Oak Swamp — were in any sort of contact with Lee's army.

Grant had been a little tense, because if this operation should be bungled anywhere the result might be disastrous; and the night of June 12, when the ticklish job of getting the army out of the Cold Harbor lines began, was one of the few times in the war when he seemed to be nervous. He showed it in small ways — lighting a cigar, laying it down and letting it go out, picking it up a moment later to relight it, and interrupting staff officers' reports with an impatient "Yes, yes" or "Go on — go on" in a most uncharacteristic way. To Horace Porter it seemed that Grant "was wrought up to an intensity of thought and action which he seldom displayed." Next day the tension was gone. A newspaperman at headquarters on the night of June 13 saw Grant lounging on a blanket near a camp fire. Assistant Secretary of War Dana was pacing up and down, angrily complaining that some baggage wagons had mired down and capsized while crossing a little stream and declaring that this was "evidently a piece of damn folly." Grant got up, took a burning brand from the fire, lighted his pipe, and said: "If we have nothing worse than this . . ." He left the sentence unfinished, and returned to his blanket. Rawlins that night wrote to Mrs. Rawlins, assuring her: "From the commencement of this campaign General Grant has not deviated at all from his written plan, but has steadily pursued the line he then marked out." [20]

On the following morning, June 14, Grant rode down to the James. The engineer troops were hard at work, building a causeway across low ground to the water's edge, putting more than a hundred pontoon boats in the river, anchoring schooners upstream to hold the pontoons in position — building a floating bridge nearly two thousand feet long, with a removable section in the middle so that warships and transports could pass. Grant saw that the work was going rapidly, and then he took a steamer to Bermuda Hundred to talk to General Butler.

As ordered, Butler on June 9 had sent General Gillmore across to Appomattox to see if Petersburg could not be seized by a sudden thrust. Gillmore, whose force came to no more than 4,500 men, concluded that the Confederate works were too strong, and came back with nothing accomplished; whereupon Butler, who had disliked him from the start, relieved him of his command. Now Baldy Smith's corps was arriving from White House; and Grant told Butler to reinforce Smith as strongly as possible and send him over the Appomattox early the next morning to strike a blow with real weight behind it. Smith's force was built up to something like 16,000 men, and Hancock's corps, which was now beginning to cross the James, was to march up in support. Petersburg was defended by General Beauregard, who at that moment could muster no more than 9,000 infantry, most of which was holding the Bermuda Hundred line facing Butler. By the evening of June 15, accordingly, the Federals with more than 35,000 men should be able to strike the Petersburg fortifications with overwhelming power. Grant's spirits rose, and before going back to the north side of the James to explain the plan to Meade he sent a dispatch to Halleck:

Our forces will commence crossing the James today. The enemy shows no signs yet of having brought troops to the south side of Richmond. I will have Petersburg secured, if possible, before they get there in much force. Our movement from Cold Harbor to the James River has been made with great celerity and so far without loss or accident.

Next morning, from Washington, came a telegram to Grant from President Lincoln:

HAVE JUST READ YOUR DISPATCH OF 1 P.M. YESTERDAY. I BEGIN TO SEE IT. YOU WILL SUCCEED. GOD BLESS YOU ALL.[21]

CHAPTER FIFTEEN

A Question of Time

Once in a great while it happened. The terrible beauty of an army with banners became visible, the murderous part of the business was deceitfully hidden — by flags in the wind, by guns bright in the sunlight, by endless moving columns of marching men — and to look at the massed might of an army was to see something that was not really there. It happened so with General Grant on the morning of June 15, when he stood on the north bank of the James and watched the Army of the Potomac go across to the southern shore.

It had been like this with him at least once before, when he was on a hill near Chattanooga and watched the Army of the Cumberland go out across the plain toward the grim height of Missionary Ridge. Now he was seeing a bigger army trying a greater thing, and it seems to have moved him deeply. He stood alone — this once, the cigar was not in evidence — with his hands clasped behind him, looking down at the sparkling river with the 2,000-foot bridge, a long column going across, spreading out on the lowland beyond, bunched up on the causeways behind; transports carrying men for whom the bridge had no room, warships cruising upstream alert for enemies, bands on the northern shore blaring out marching tunes (although the men who were on the bridge were not allowed to keep in step) and here and there a plume of white steam when some vessel sounded its whistle. Far away to the northwest there was a dull uneven rumble of artillery fire, as the men commanded by Warren and Wilson sparred at long range with Lee's advance guard, the noise indicating that the Army of Northern Virginia was a long way off. Grant's army was on its way to strike at Petersburg, the city the Confederacy dared not lose, and sometime this evening it could launch its blow with a ten-to-one advantage in numbers. The victory that would justify everything that

had happened in fire and mud and dust, the Wilderness and Spotsylvania and Cold Harbor, might very well be less than twenty-four
hours away. What strategy could do had been done. Now it would be
up to the combat commanders. To them, and to the men they commanded.[1]

The men in the ranks had been ground down unmercifully in the
past six weeks. They were mortally tired, some of the best of them
had been shot, thousands more were simply waiting for their enlistments to expire, the replacements in the ranks were mostly heavy artillerists who had not really enlisted to fight, sullen dismounted cavalrymen who had never imagined themselves as foot soldiers, or bounty
men not worth the limited price of their rations. All in all, taking the
good ones with the bad ones, these men probably had one more hard
fight in their systems. If they won, fine; if they did not there would be
a long delay. Meanwhile, they were on their way to Petersburg.

What they would do there would depend pretty largely on their
leaders, and here as far as Grant could see the chances were good. The
two leaders with important parts to play today were General William
F. Smith, who had charge of the army corps that would get into action first, and General Winfield S. Hancock, whose corps was moving
up in support; and on June 15 Grant would unquestionably have said
that these were the two best men the army could have given him.

The testing ground — for these generals, the men they led and the
strategic design that had brought them there — lay about two miles
east of Petersburg. Here were the Confederate fortifications. They
began in low ground just south of the Appomattox River, went up a
hill that climbed out of a maze of eroded ravines, and then ran south
along a ridge, and the part that would concern Federal soldiers today
was about two miles in length. The Confederates had had a long time
to work on these fortifications, and everything that could be done to
make them strong had been done. There were solid parapets two-
dozen-feet thick, deep ditches in front, tangled abatis and chevaux-de-
frise in front of the ditches, enclosed forts studded with guns at suitable intervals. When he saw the line, Smith said it was more powerful
than Missionary Ridge itself. (He was one of many Federal officers
who still did not quite see how that position had ever been taken.)
Grant, who saw the line after its capture, said it was the most formidable obstacle the army had struck since crossing the Rapidan.[2]

Obviously, if Lee's army had been inside of these works the Army of the Potomac could have done nothing but camp at a respectful distance and wait for a miracle, the sounding of the trumpets of Jericho for choice. But on this fated day, June 15, Lee's army was not there. There were not 8,000 Confederate soldiers within a full day's march, and most of these were north of the Appomattox facing Butler's lines across the neck of Bermuda Hundred. In the Petersburg works today, and immediately available to help out, there were probably fewer than 2,500 men of all arms; hardly 1,500 of them were in the sector the Federals were going to attack. Never had a stronger position been entrusted to a weaker force.

Smith had between 15,000 and 18,000 soldiers, of whom at least 10,000 could be counted first-line infantry, the divisions of General W. T. H. Brooks and General John H. Martindale. He had temporarily left one division behind, at White House, but on Bermuda Hundred he had picked up General Edward W. Hincks's division of colored troops and Kautz's division of cavalry; and he brought all of these men up to the works by noon or a little earlier, spread the cavalry out to his left to protect his flank, overran the advanced picket lines, came under fire of the Confederate artillery, and formed his battle lines a quarter of a mile away from the powerful fortifications. No Federal general with recent memories of Cold Harbor was going to attack a place like this without first taking a long, careful look at it, and Smith was properly cautious. He spent the better part of the afternoon reconnoitering, going forward under fire at considerable risk; he was weary from an all-night march, he was suffering "from the effects of bad water, and malaria brought from Cold Harbor," he had no proper engineer officer to help him, and it was after three when he finished his reconnaissance.

There was a good deal of open ground in front of the works, and Confederate artillery seemed to cover most of it with an effective cross fire. On the Federal right, in the lowland near the Appomattox, prospects for a successful assault looked bad; but it seemed to Smith that opposite his center and left, where the high ground lined with forts jutted forward in a salient, something might be done if heavy skirmish lines could charge with a rush after a sharp bombardment, and this attack he finally ordered. Then he discovered that there had been a blunder. Nobody had told his chief of artillery that there was about to be a fight, and that officer had sent all of the artillery horses away for water, so it would be early evening before the guns could be brought into action.

While he waited, Smith learned that Hancock with the Second Corps had crossed the James and was coming up to join him, and Grant authorized him to call on Hancock to take part in the attack. So at four o'clock Smith sent a note to Hancock, describing the situation and saying: "If the Second Corps can come up in time to make an assault tonight after dark in vicinity of Norfolk and Petersburg railroad" (that is, on the Federal left) "I think we may be successful." He warned Hancock this would be the last chance, because Lee was reportedly crossing troops farther up the James to reinforce the Petersburg garrison.[3]

Hancock was coming up at a moderate pace. There had been a mix-up in his orders — first he was told to wait by the riverside for rations, then after a couple of hours had been lost he was ordered to go on without them — and his directive was so vague that it required him to go to a point that he could not quite identify and that finally turned out to be inside the Confederate lines; on top of which he had been given a map that was quite worthless and he could find no reliable guides. In his report Hancock complained that he "spent the best hours of the day on the 15th in marching by an incorrect map in search of a designated position which, as described, was not in existence or could not be found." Worst of all, as far as he knew he was simply making a routine movement in which no especial haste was called for. During the afternoon he heard artillery fire, far ahead, but he assumed that this came from Kautz's cavalry, which he understood was going to be tapping along the Confederate front; nobody had told Hancock that Petersburg was to be attacked that day. The staff work that got the army out of the Cold Harbor lines and down to the James had been flawless, but on this day — of all days! — it seems almost to have collapsed.

Finally, after five o'clock, a courier from Grant's headquarters reached Hancock with a dispatch saying that Smith was assaulting the Petersburg fortifications and that Hancock must hurry forward to help him; on the heels of which came Smith's dispatch talking about a large-scale attack that night. So at last, for the first time, Hancock knew where he was supposed to go and what was supposed to happen when he got there, and for the first time he understood that he was supposed to hurry. He stepped up the pace, and his two leading divisions went plowing forward — dog-tired, like everybody else in both armies, and plagued by the heat and the dust, but suddenly full of enthusiasm as the word spread along the column that they were about to strike Lee's almost undefended rear.[4]

Time was passing, the sun was going down, the great day of June 15 was ending — and at last, up by Petersburg, seven o'clock or near to it, Baldy Smith got his guns into position, began his bombardment, and then ordered his infantry forward. He discovered almost at once that he was pushing against an open door. This was Chattanooga all over again. The line that was too strong to break collapsed at a touch.

In the low ground near the river Martindale's division did little more than fire at long range — the Rebel line here did not need to be attacked, because it was the high ground farther south that really mattered. But presently the long lines of Brooks's division ran through the fading light up to the big salient on the hill, while the Rebel artillery made a prodigious noise and banked ragged smoke clouds against the sunset but did little real harm because these Federals, spread out skirmish-line style, offered no massed target. Brooks's men took the salient and its guns, and looked over empty country to Petersburg; and off to the left General Hincks's colored infantrymen, the men to whom little had ever been given and from whom nothing in particular was expected, marched up to the dominating ridge, fought their way over the massive trenches and went storming on into the forts.

In half an hour or a little more it was over. The salient was gone, the ridge to the south was crowned with black men in blue uniforms yelling and brandishing their weapons and climbing all over the captured guns, and when the sun went down Smith's troops had taken a mile and a half of trenches, five forts, sixteen pieces of artillery and several hundred prisoners. Between them and Petersburg there was nothing they needed to be afraid of; and now, up through the twilight came General Hancock to tell Smith that his two leading divisions were only a mile behind him. When General Beauregard summed up the situation, after the war, he wrote: "Petersburg at that hour was clearly at the mercy of the Federal commander, who had all but captured it."[5] The difficulty was that the Federal commander did not know it.

He did know it, but it slipped out of his mind, and so the war lasted much longer. In his note to Hancock, Smith had spoken of making "an assault tonight, after dark," but when the twilight gave way to full darkness Smith began to have second thoughts. General Hincks urged him to drive on ahead, saying that Petersburg could be had now, tonight, at once — the darkness would be no great problem because a moon was rising and anyway the Confederates were terribly disorganized and there were not very many of them. But Smith, who had just won what could have been the decisive battle of the war, had grown wary. He told Hincks that Beauregard was being reinforced and by now probably had more men than Smith had; to attack at night would be to risk all that had been won, the most that could be hoped for was to hold on, and this was no time to be rash. When Hancock arrived Smith had gone over entirely to the defensive, and what could have been won vanished under the vision of what might have been lost.

Hancock of course knew nothing about the situation. He could not see much of the ground in front, this was Smith's battle and Hancock had been ordered to support him, and so Hancock simply placed himself and his troops at Smith's disposal and asked for orders. When Smith told him to relieve Smith's men from the captured works and stand by to repel a probable Confederate counterattack, Hancock felt that he could do nothing but follow instructions. Between eleven o'clock and midnight he got Gibbon's and Birney's divisions in the trenches Brooks and Hincks had seized, under orders to prowl forward at daylight and fight if they saw any enemies; the battle was over, and the door that had been wide open began to swing shut.[6]

By evil chance, neither Smith nor Hancock was physically fit. Smith, as stated, felt very unwell; and the wound Hancock had received at Gettysburg, never really healed, had broken open again, so that Hancock was hardly able to stay in the saddle. Within forty-eight hours he would have to go on the sick list, turning over corps command temporarily to General Birney, who was a good man but, unhappily, was not Hancock. If both Smith and Hancock had been normally robust that night, things might have gone differently. Smith might have subdued his caution a few hours longer, Hancock might have ridden forward for a reconnaissance of his own and, having done so, might have insisted on positive action — and, altogether, Petersburg and all of its railroads and everything that depended on them might have been in Federal possession by the morning of June 16.
. . . *Might* have.

General Beauregard was reinforced that night, but not nearly as heavily as Smith believed. Just before the fight at Cold Harbor he had sent Hoke's division, 4,000 men or thereabouts, to General Lee, and on June 15 this division was on its way back to him. The leading elements began to reach him about the time Smith and Hancock were conferring, the rest came in during the night, and by morning Petersburg was held by nearly 7,000 men. Engineer details had been busy all night, improvising a new defensive line behind Harrison's Creek, a few hundred yards west of the works the Federals had taken, but the outlook was grim; 35,000 Federals were present, ideally placed for a new onslaught — at midnight Smith notified Butler that unless he was greatly mistaken he held "the key to Petersburg," and Beauregard undoubtedly would have agreed with him — and on the morning of June 16 Beauregard took the kind of risk that is forced upon the desperate. He ordered Bushrod Johnson's division to evacuate the trenches that sealed off the Federal position on Bermuda Hundred neck, and had it march to Petersburg, leaving only pickets and skirmishers to hold the old line. This gave Butler a chance to lunge forward and break the communications between Petersburg and Richmond — that is, between Beauregard and Lee — but that danger could be met when it developed. The most pressing emergency was at Petersburg, and Beauregard was praying for more men and more time. In the end he got just enough of both.[7]

Grant's headquarters at City Point were on a bluff that was high enough to offer a good view of the James and Appomattox rivers and to promise a chance for an occasional cooling breeze. Here a railroad that came east from Petersburg, seven miles away, reached the tidewater wharves; and to Grant, here, came all the reports, accurate or otherwise, about the huge operation that was in progress. This was the critical day: the Federal army was operating in two separated pieces, and if some danger had been overlooked one of the two halves might come to disaster. There were a good many things for the commanding general to do, but his chief task today was simply to stand the pressure. The tension was great; and yet, characteristically, Grant reflected that the strain on his opponent must be much worse. That night he found time to write a note to Julia:

Since Sunday we have been engaged in one of the most perilous movements ever executed by a large Army, that of withdrawing from the front of an enemy and moving past his flank crossing two rivers over which the enemy has bridges and railroads whilst we have bridges to improvise. So far it has been eminently successful and I hope will prove so to the end. About one half of my troops are now on the south side of James River. A few days now will enable me to form a judgment of the work before me. It will be hard and may be tedious, however I am in excellent health and feel no doubt about holding the enemy in much greater alarm than I ever felt in my life. They are now on a strain that no people ever endured for any great length of time.[8]

Burnside was ordered to bring his corps across the river and to march all night, if necessary, in order to reach the Petersburg front promptly on June 16. Warren was to follow Burnside, Wright was to bring up the rear, and Meade was specifically ordered to go to Petersburg as soon as he could and take overall charge of the battle there. Grant himself rode forward early on June 16 to see things for himself. What struck him most forcibly was the great strength of the fortifications that had been stormed. Not for weeks to come would Grant realize that the real story of the June 15 battle was the story of opportunity missed. His final conclusion, after the war, was a terse "I believed then, and still believe, that Petersburg could have been easily captured at that time," but he did not yet realize that the brightest chance had already been lost. He was in good spirits, and when at noon, riding back to City Point, he met Meade riding to the front, he told him: "Smith has taken a line of works there stronger than we have seen this campaign! If it is a possible thing I want an assault made at 6 o'clock this evening." [9]

It was possible, and at six that evening Meade ordered the attack. Hancock's corps struck hard, with help from Smith and Burnside on the flanks; it took some more ground, gave the Federals a better position for a new attack next day, caused two or three thousand casualties, and hinted that real victory was only a few hours off. Meanwhile, back at City Point, Grant kept getting bright reports from Butler: the Confederates had abandoned their line on Bermuda Hundred neck, Butler's men had occupied the abandoned trenches, details had even reached the Petersburg-Richmond Railroad and were beginning to dismantle it, and if Butler could be reinforced he could interpose between Lee and Beauregard and the whole campaign would end in triumph. Grant reflected on this: with the big push coming up at Petersburg he could hardly mount a second major attack on the Confederate center, and since Lee was at last moving down below the James the Confederates could easily drop off enough men to regain any ground lost on Butler's front. Still, Wright and two divisions of his Sixth Corps would reach City Point that night, and Grant told Butler that if things still looked promising next morning he would send Wright over to Bermuda Hundred.[10]

This was the high week of opportunity, and somehow it was the time when nothing quite worked; because these armies, of the James and of the Potomac, had been built, trained and used so that they would always be just a little out of control. The generals' reflexes were sluggish. Between the will and the act there was always a gap. Orders received were executed late, sometimes at half-stroke; now and then they were reinterpreted on the spot so that what was ordered was not done at all; and nothing could be done about it on June 17 because it was impossible to go back to the beginning now and create a new system. Thus —

The Federals at Bermuda Hundred had twenty-four hours of freedom and they could not use it. On the night of June 16 Lee got troops in front of Butler's lines, drove the Federal advance guard away from the railroad, regained the abandoned trenches, and sent in enough reinforcements to make the situation secure by the time Wright's veterans came up next day; the Confederates being helped by the fact that Butler did not quite know what he wanted Wright to do. And so Butler's people were sealed off again, out of the battle, just as if nothing had happened.

And over at Petersburg Meade ordered Hancock and Burnside forward at dawn on June 17, and one of Burnside's divisions seized a fortified hill near the line of the Norfolk & Petersburg Railroad — the spot Smith had chosen for the after-dark assault that he had at last decided not to make on June 15 — capturing four guns and six hundred prisoners and achieving what could have been a real breakthrough. But the division Burnside ordered up in support failed to get its orders and did not appear until afternoon, and Hancock's attack was long delayed, perhaps because the ailing Hancock lacked his usual driving energy. Warren was supposed to advance into almost empty country below the Confederate right, on the far side of a highway known as the Jerusalem Plank Road, but he was annoyed by active Confederate skirmishes and long-range artillery fire, he concluded that this puzzling emptiness in his front was held in great strength, and he did nothing of any consequence. (Beauregard said afterward that if this Federal advance had been made, "I would have been compelled to evacuate Petersburg without much resistance"; but Warren thought he had better stay where he was.) Even with all of this fumbling, however, by the end of the day the Federals had taken most of the Confederate line, and Beauregard once more was desperately stitching together a new one, a whole mile nearer Petersburg. He could go back no farther than this, and that evening he revealed the extent of the emergency by notifying Lee that he would hold on here while he could but that if reinforcements did not speedily reach him he would have to get out of Petersburg. If he had to retreat, he said, he would cross the Appomattox, try to hold the river crossings, and if worse came to worst would retire to the fortifications below Richmond at Drewry's Bluff.[11]

For the Federals a few hours of opportunity remained, but they were not seized. Meade's soldiers moved forward cautiously at daybreak on June 18 and got into the trenches their enemies had left the night before. Meade learned that Lee's troops had not yet reached Beauregard, and he ordered an attack all along the line at noon. Noon came, each corps commander waited for his neighbor to get into position, no concerted assault was made — and then Lee's hard-marching columns crossed the Appomattox and began to file into the trenches in front of Petersburg. The odds against Beauregard shrank to manageable proportions, and Méade stormed helplessly because of his army's inability to strike. At last, apparently almost beside himself, he angrily told his corps commanders that he found it useless to try to coordinate their movements and so each general must attack when and as he could, without reference to what his neighbors were doing. Paralysis of the army's central nervous system could go no farther.

Disjointed attacks were made that afternoon, costly in Federal lives, completely ineffective, and by night it was all over. The Confederate trenches were held in full strength and a successful frontal assault was out of the question. Meade called the offensive off, and Grant confirmed his decision, remarking that it was time to put the men under cover and give them rest. In four days of fighting the Federals had lost 10,000 men, or more — proof enough that the men in the ranks had fought as bravely as ever. Their valor simply had not been enough to offset the shortcomings of the men who put them into action.[12]

It would be a different war from now on. As far as the main armies in Virginia were concerned, the time of long marches and massive pitched battles was over. The Army of Northern Virginia would never again see northern Virginia, nor would the Army of the Potomac see the Potomac again. They were fixed in position, almost totally immobilized, and henceforth for month after dreary month they would see little more than the desolate trenches, the heavy forts that were built at every weak point, setting the pattern of trench warfare with its eternal round of shelling and sharpshooting and day-by-day discomfort of heat and dust and thirst, with its occasional furious small fights for small advantages. Richmond was a good many miles away, and yet in reality the entire layout of works was the defense of Richmond — a twenty-five-mile set of trenches and forts that began up near White Oak Swamp, east of Richmond, came down across the James, crossed Bermuda Hundred neck, crossed the Appomattox, and then swung south in a long arc just east of Petersburg, the lower end of the arc curving toward the west.

Grant's first task was to make his own line secure so that Lee could not dislodge him, and the long Federal line became a chain of defensive works as powerful as the Confederate works that faced them. Siege artillery was brought in, and heavy guns were mounted in the big forts. Both sides brought up Coehorn mortars — trench mortars, they would be called now, portable affairs that could be mounted in or just behind the trenches and that could drop shells beyond the opposing parapet — and in each army the soldiers tried to escape from the daily toll of wounds and death by building bombproofs, uncomfortable dugouts in which men could huddle when the shelling became too costly. East of Petersburg the opposing lines were close together, and here there was more or less firing every day, with a steady wastage of life. Farther south the Confederate line was withdrawn so that there was half a mile or more of unoccupied country between the trenches, and here there was less activity; the pickets watched each other carefully, of course, but they got along without much fighting, and much of the time they met in wary comradeship, exchanging newspapers and coffee and tobacco and gossip. They got along so well, in fact, that Meade told his wife "I believe these two armies would fraternize and make peace in an hour, if the matter rested with them." [13]

The Federal army, in fact, was beginning to show war weariness, and so were the people back home. The long casualty lists this spring had been heavier than anything anyone had ever heard of; the Federal war effort seemed almost to be stalled — Grant had not taken Richmond, Sherman had not taken Atlanta, Banks's march toward Texas had been a most dismal failure — and it was conceivable that the war might end with nothing settled just because soldiers and civilians alike were bone-weary of fighting. But there were two ways to think about peace. Buried far beneath what Meade grimly referred to as "the pleasant task of sending people to eternity" [14] it was possible that something of consequence was at stake. As the Petersburg deadlock developed Abraham Lincoln addressed himself to this idea.

On June 16 Lincoln had to make a little talk at a Sanitary Commission fair in Philadelphia. He was talking to civilians who were tired and confused, but he spoke of a determination to go beyond the present tragedy in order to win something that could give the tragedy meaning.

"We accepted this war for an object, a worthy object, and the war will end when that object is attained," he said. "Under God, I hope it never will until that time. Speaking of the present campaign, General Grant is reported to have said, 'I am going through on this line if it takes all summer.' I say we are going through on this line if it takes three years more." [15]

Lincoln had a presidential election campaign to win, having been nominated for a second term less than a fortnight earlier. He was a working politician with a politician's ingrained belief that it is fatal to displease the electorate, and he usually acted on that belief. He had shaped policy with a canny eye on what the voters were ready to accept, he had appointed some highly incompetent generals because the men so named had political influence, and he knew very well that the people who had been unreasonably hopeful early in May were deeply depressed because the speedy victory then imagined was nowhere in sight. Clearly, it was time for a soft President to utter soft words; yet Lincoln was saying bluntly that while he was President (and the voters must presently say how much longer this would be the case) there would be no end short of victory. He was as grim as this grimmest of his generals; he would support him all the way no matter how much it cost; he was living up to his part of the bargain, making his partnership with Grant unbreakable. Remaining unbroken, it would be the dominant fact of the war henceforward. . . .

Unable to seize Petersburg by surprise or to take it by storm, Grant had nevertheless come appreciably nearer his goal because he had anchored his army almost within striking distance of those railway lines that had been on his mind from the beginning. Four of these came into Petersburg, and two of them — of very minor importance, as far as Confederate supplies were concerned — the Federals already held: the short line that went east to City Point, and a longer one that angled off southeast to Norfolk. The two that were still in operation were the vital ones. They were the Petersburg & Weldon Railroad, that went south all the way to the great blockade runners' port of Wilmington, and the Southside Railroad that went to Lynchburg, intersecting the Richmond & Danville road at Burkeville, fifty miles west of Petersburg. To break these roads even temporarily would hurt Lee badly; to break them permanently would almost certainly compel Lee to retreat into final disaster.

Before the immobility of siege warfare was accepted Grant wanted to see if those railroads could be struck. On June 22, Meade sent Birney and Wright out past the Federal left flank, a spot on the Jerusalem Plank Road four or five miles south of Petersburg, where Meade's engineers were building a huge strong point known as Fort Sedgwick. It was hoped that this force could plant itself across the Weldon Railroad and reach far enough beyond it to threaten the Southside line; and under cover of this advance General Wilson took his own and Kautz's cavalry divisions, 6,000 troopers, and marched west on a long swing aimed at the railroads much farther behind Lee's position.

The infantry move was one that could have been made almost without effort on June 17, as Beauregard himself testified, but by June 22 it was impossible. Lee was on the alert, and he promptly sent the pugnacious General Hill with three divisions out to meet it. Hill's men got in between the two Federal army corps, which seem to have been inexpertly handled, flanked Birney's force and routed it, captured 1,700 prisoners and compelled Wright to halt in his tracks. The huge number of Federal prisoners taken was a dismaying sign that at least some of the Federal infantry had had about all the combat it could digest, and Grant curtly told Halleck that "the affair was a stampede." All he got out of it was an extension of his line some distance to the southwest of Fort Sedgwick — a minor gain, since it compelled Lee with a smaller army to make a corresponding extension of his own line — but the Federal flank was still nearly two miles short of the

Weldon Railroad. Grant summed up the operation by referring to it simply as "extending our left." [16]

The cavalry thrust got off to a better start. Wilson reached the railroad junction at Burkeville, did a good deal of damage to the railroads there, and then swung on down to the Staunton River, a hundred miles below Petersburg; but the bridge over that river was held too firmly for him to break, Wade Hampton's cavalry came in on him with superior force, and in the end Wilson had to come back to the Federal lines with only a moderate success to show for his efforts. Actually, he came back looking like a man who had been badly defeated. He had done a good deal of harm to Lee's communications, and for a few weeks Lee was seriously handicapped by the break Wilson had made, but Wilson's entire force narrowly escaped destruction and when he returned he had lost 1,500 troopers, a dozen guns and all of his wagons. The final effect of his bold dash had been nothing much more than a nuisance raid.

Meade had wanted to postpone this offensive, arguing that it would be better to wait and send out Sheridan with the entire cavalry corps, but Grant wanted quick action and overruled him. Meade may have been right. Too late to help Wilson, Sheridan got back from his attempt to break the Virginia Central Railroad and help Hunter take Lynchburg, and his actual achievements did not add up to a great deal. He had had a hard fight and a hard march, when he returned his horses were badly run-down, he needed to reequip his whole force, and it was going to be a little time before the cavalry was ready for another major operation.[17]

Sheridan's return brought the unhappy news (confirmed by Richmond newspapers that came in across the picket lines) that one more Federal expedition had come to grief. The Virginia Central Railroad, to be sure, had been damaged, and Sheridan had had the better of Wade Hampton's cavalry in a hard fight at Trevilian Station, a few miles east of Gordonsville; but the damage to the railroad could soon be repaired, Sheridan and Hunter had failed to make connections, Hampton got back to Lee in time to set out after Wilson, Lynchburg had not been taken, Hunter's army was in full retreat to the West Virginia mountains, and the blow at the important Confederate supply system running by way of Gordonsville to Charlottesville and Lynchburg had ended in flat failure.

Potentially, this offensive had been as big a threat to Lee's communications as the blow at Petersburg itself, the proof of this lying in what Lee unhesitatingly did when he learned about it. He had sent Breckinridge's division away early in June, when Hunter approached Staunton, and as soon as Sheridan set out for Gordonsville Lee sent Hampton pell-mell after him. On June 12, when he learned that Hunter had picked up Crook and had gone on to occupy Lexington, Lee ordered Jubal Early to take his army corps and go to Lynchburg with all speed. This was not a time when Lee could afford to reduce his own strength — with Grant beginning his new flanking maneuver Lee needed every soldier he had — but the prospect of losing Lynchburg, and the railroad network that centered there was unendurable, and on June 13, while Grant's army was marching for the James, Early and his 8,000 infantry were going far away to the west.[18]

Lee's boldness paid off handsomely. Hunter had been given discretion about the course to follow after Staunton had been taken, and he guessed wrong. Instead of coming east through Rockfish Gap to Gordonsville he elected to move on up the valley on the far side of the Blue Ridge so as to approach Lynchburg from the west; every step took him farther away from Sheridan — of whose approach Hunter at that moment knew nothing — and made a meeting of the two forces impossible. Sheridan had his fight with Hampton on June 11, learned next day that Hunter was hopelessly beyond his reach and that Confederate infantry in unknown strength lay between them, and in his report he summed it up: "I therefore made up my mind that it was best to give up the attempt to join Hunter, as he was going from me instead of coming toward me, and concluded to return." Return he did, and Hunter was on his own.

On his own, Hunter did not do well. He moved slowly, on the wrong road, ravaging the countryside as he went, and it was June 17 before he passed the Peaks of Otter, turned east via Buford's Gap and the town of Liberty and came up to the hills just west of Lynchburg; and Lee's Confederates, who had been moving fast, were there ahead of him. Breckinridge had got to Lynchburg, and with his own division and the odds and ends of other forces he picked up there Breckinridge had 9,000 men, 5,000 of them reliable veterans, the rest casuals and strays who would do well enough behind earthworks. Hunter poked gently at the Confederate lines, planned to attack next day, and next day moved in harder — only to learn that Early had reached the

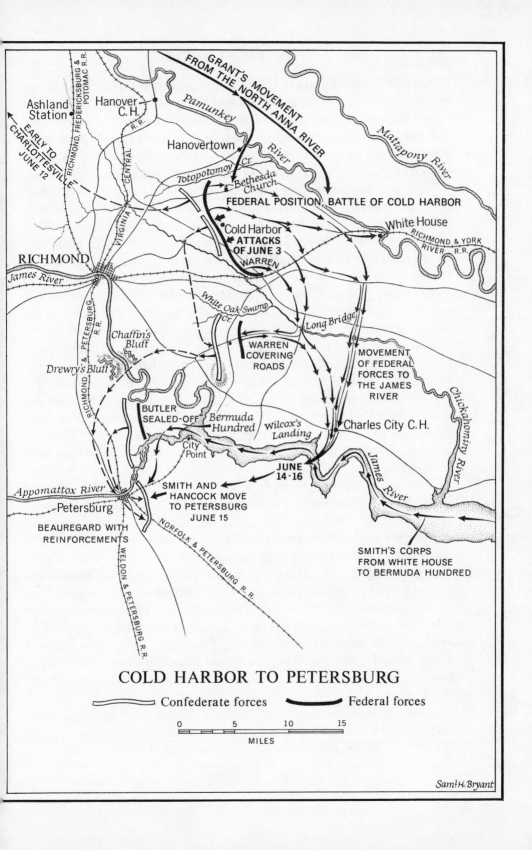

GRANT'S MOVEMENT FROM THE NORTH ANNA RIVER

Ashland Station

Hanover C.H.

EARLY TO CHARLOTTESVILLE JUNE 12

RICHMOND, FREDERICKSBURG & POTOMAC R.R.

Hanovertown

Pamunkey River

Mattapony River

Totopotomoy Cr.

Bethesda Church

VIRGINIA CENTRAL

FEDERAL POSITION, BATTLE OF COLD HARBOR

Cold Harbor

White House

ATTACKS OF JUNE 3

RICHMOND & YORK RIVER R.R.

WARREN

RICHMOND

James River

White Oak Swamp Cr.

Long Bridge

RICHMOND & PETERSBURG R.R.

Chaffin's Bluff

WARREN COVERING ROADS

MOVEMENT OF FEDERAL FORCES TO THE JAMES RIVER

Drewry's Bluff

BUTLER SEALED-OFF

Bermuda Hundred

Wilcox's Landing

Charles City C.H.

Chickahominy River

City Point

James River

Appomattox River

JUNE 14-16

SMITH AND HANCOCK MOVE TO PETERSBURG JUNE 15

Petersburg

BEAUREGARD WITH REINFORCEMENTS

NORFOLK & PETERSBURG R.R.

WELDON & PETERSBURG R.R.

SMITH'S CORPS FROM WHITE HOUSE TO BERMUDA HUNDRED

COLD HARBOR TO PETERSBURG

———— Confederate forces   ⌣ Federal forces

0   5   10   15
MILES

Saml H. Bryant

scene, so that by now there were more Confederates than Federals on hand. The chance to seize Lynchburg was gone, lost somewhere between choosing the wrong road, stopping to burn houses, and the belief that it was time to be cautious, and there was only one thing Hunter could do — retreat. This he immediately did, and now his choice of the wrong approach to Lynchburg became a cruel handicap.

Early and his Confederates were at this moment nearer to Staunton, the road down the valley, the Potomac crossings and Washington itself than Hunter was, and Early was not the man to overlook such an advantage. When Hunter began to retreat Early pressed hard against his rear guard and sent his cavalry over the Blue Ridge to get across Hunter's route to the northeastern end of the valley. Hunter was short of supplies and ammunition and concluded that he could not afford to fight his way through and regain the direct road back to the place he had started from, the area which above everything else he was supposed to protect. When he retreated from Lynchburg his hand was forced, and he could do no better than go west into the mountains, heading for the Gauley River valley and Charleston, saving his army but taking it entirely out of action for three mortal weeks. Early watched his rear guard disappear beyond the western mountain passes and then swung down the Shenandoah Valley toward the Potomac along the old Stonewall Jackson road, looking for a Stonewall Jackson adventure.[19]

That sort of adventure might be hard to get, times having changed since 1862, but Lee had very little choice. He had sent Early west to save Lynchburg and the valley, and he shared the view Grant had expounded to Lincoln some months earlier — that a soldier who is supposed to defend something can often do it better by advancing than by standing still. As long as Early was operating on or near the Potomac no Federal army was going to interfere with the supply lines in the Staunton-Charlottesville-Lynchburg area. This question of supplies was becoming a heavy weight on Lee's mind, and on June 26 he explained his thinking in a letter to President Davis, saying that if Early moved down the valley he would probably draw Hunter after him:

If circumstances favor, I should also recommend his crossing the Potomac. I think I can maintain our lines here against General Grant. . . .

I am less uneasy about holding our position than about our ability to procure supplies for the army. I fear the latter difficulty may oblige me to attack General Grant in his entrenchments, which I should not hesitate to do but for the loss it will inevitably entail. A want of success would in my opinion be almost fatal, and this causes me to hesitate in the hope that some relief may be procured without running such great hazard.[20]

What Lee was saying was that Grant's basic strategy — to constrict the lifelines until the Confederates had to come out from behind earthworks and attack him — was beginning to work. Lee had seen this danger all along. Jubal Early said that some time before this Lee told him: "We must destroy this army of Grant's before he gets to James river. If he gets there it will become a siege, and then it will be a mere question of time." In the same way Lee had warned Hill that unless Grant's approach could be stopped "we shall at last be obliged to take refuge behind the works of Richmond and stand a siege, which would be but a question of time." Now Grant was across the James, and if Lee was not exactly "behind the works of Richmond" he was perilously close to it. Early's march down the valley might bring relief, but in fact it represented Lee's last chance. When Grant got Butler's and Meade's armies solidly entrenched south of the river he had reached the first goal he set for himself when the campaign began. General Porter Alexander, Longstreet's chief of artillery, wrote after the war that Grant's achievement was the beginning of the end.

"The position which he had secured was full of great possibilities, as yet not fully comprehended," wrote Alexander. "But already the character of the operations contemplated removed all risk of serious future catastrophe. However bold we might be, however desperately we might fight, we were sure in the end to be worn out. It was only a question of a few months, more or less. We were unable to see it at once. But there soon began to spring up a chain of permanent works, the first of which were built upon our original lines captured by the skirmishers the first afternoon, and these works, impregnable to assault, finally decided our fate when, on the next March 25, we put them to the test."[21]

Grant saw it the same way, and privately he used the expression Lee had used. Adam Badeau remembered that the day after Cold Harbor Grant told him that "success was only a question of time," and a few days later Grant assured Congressman Washburne that "everything is progressing favorably . . . unless my next move brings on a battle the balance of the campaign will settle down to a siege." [22] He understood very well, however, that it was not going to be automatic. He held a winning position, but his opponent was in the highest degree dangerous, and although the Petersburg railroads were very near the fumbled advance of June 22 proved that Grant would have to move carefully to get at them.

The first step was to make the Petersburg lines so strong that they could be held with a fraction of the army, leaving a large force free to move boldly into Lee's rear, and the next step was to find some way to get more troops. To do this it was necessary to make certain that the Petersburg operation was precisely fitted into the grand strategy of the rest of the war, because what happened here interlocked with what happened elsewhere and Grant was responsible for all of it.

On the lower Mississippi there was a substantial army under General E. R. S. Canby, who had been sent there to pick up the pieces after Banks came to grief on the Red River. Originally, Grant had hoped that Canby's army could advance on Mobile while Sherman was moving toward Atlanta, and he clung to this idea all the time his own force was coming from the Rapidan down to the James. On June 3, just as the battle at Cold Harbor was tapering off, he reverted to it. Butler had suggested that the Nineteenth Corps from Canby's army be brought to the James and added to Butler's command, but Grant told Halleck that this was hardly advisable: it would take a long time to get orders to New Orleans and to bring an army corps back from there, Canby's troops might all be needed where they were, and if they were not "they could be advantageously used against Mobile." But after he got into the lines at Petersburg he began to see that the Federal effort had to be concentrated in two places, Virginia and Georgia, and on June 23 he sent Halleck a dispatch outlining his reasoning:

The siege of Richmond bids fair to be tedious, and in consequence of the very extended lines we must have, a much larger force will be necessary than would be required in ordinary sieges against the same force that now opposes us. With my present force I feel perfectly safe against Lee's army, and, acting defensively, would still feel so against Lee and Johnston combined; but we want to act offensively. In my opinion, to do this effectively, we should concentrate our whole energy against the two principal armies of the enemy.

In other words, nothing should be attempted, except in Georgia and here, that is not directly in cooperation with these moves. West of the Mississippi I would not attempt anything until the rebellion east of it is entirely subdued. I would then direct Canby to leave Smith [General E. Kirby Smith, Confederate commander in the trans-Mississippi] unmolested where he is; to make no move except such as is necessary to protect what he now holds. All the troops he can spare should be sent here at once. In my opinion the white troops of the Nineteenth Corps can all come, together with many of the colored troops. I wish you would place this matter before the Secretary of War and urge that no offensive operations west of the Mississippi be allowed to commence until matters here are settled. Send the Nineteenth Corps and such other troops as you can from the Department of the Gulf to me.[23]

The matter of the number of fighting men in the Army of the Potomac was not well understood at that time, and remains misunderstood today. In the middle of June Halleck had written to his friend Franz Lieber saying that he had sent 40,000 men to Meade's army and that it was stronger than when the campaign began. But as General Humphreys pointed out, Halleck and the War Department counted the paper strength of the reinforcements forwarded, and this bore little relation to the number of combat soldiers who actually reached the army. Meade's own troop returns tell a very different story. On April 30, in the three corps of the Army of the Potomac, in Sheridan's cavalry, and in Burnside's corps, there were 124,000 men listed as present for duty. On June 30, the returns showed that the same units had a present for duty total of slightly more than 86,000 men. The losses between those dates had of course been prodigious — slightly more than 64,000 men killed, wounded and missing — but replacements were far below that figure. Instead of being, as Halleck said, stronger than ever, Meade's army was 38,000 men under the strength it had had when it crossed the Rapidan. The fact that Butler's army was in the trenches beside it did not make up for this loss, because Butler's army had been in action against Lee's rear ever since the campaign began. To make matters worse, the army was continuing to shrink even though costly battles were not being fought, because a steady stream of time-expired troops was flowing away from it. General Lee, who kept himself well informed about the numbers opposing him, estimated that sixty-eight Federal regiments would leave during July. If

Grant was to exploit his advantage he had to have more troops than Washington was sending him and he had to look for them in the less active theaters of war.[24]

Sherman's advance through Georgia had been a good deal like Grant's advance through Virginia; it had been steady and methodical (although it did not create nearly as large a casualty list) but it had not yet reached its goal. Joe Johnston was skillful on the defense. He always chose a strong position and entrenched it thoroughly, holding it until Sherman flanked him out of it and then quickly moving to a new one, equally strong, across his opponent's path. When the Federals did get on Johnston's flank Sherman did not try to go slashing through, Cold Harbor style; instead he advanced by building successive lines of entrenchments of his own, inviting Johnston to attack him — invitations Johnston never accepted because, as he explained, "defeat would have been our ruin." Only once did Sherman try a direct breakthrough of the kind Grant tried at Spotsylvania: at Kenesaw Mountain on June 27, when he made a costly frontal assault that gained nothing whatever. Most of the time the two armies sparred, side-slipped, tapped for soft spots without finding them. Johnston believed that he was playing the game about the way Lee played it, and after the war he asserted that "my course was as like his as the dissimilarity of the two Federal commanders permitted." [25]

By the end of June, Johnston had had to retire to a strong defensive line covering the crossings of the Chattahoochee River, a few miles west and northwest of Atlanta; a position not entirely unlike the one Lee held in respect to Grant. In Georgia as in Virginia, the Federal advance was close to its chosen goal, but a powerful enemy in a powerful position still barred the way, and unhappy folk in the North began to feel that neither campaign was really succeeding. Stalemate at Petersburg seemed to be balanced by stalemate in front of Atlanta, each army seemed to be fighting a continuous battle with nothing much to show for it; it was beginning to be hard to take.

While Grant was arranging his position around Petersburg President Lincoln dropped in on him, coming unannounced and apparently wanting nothing much more than a little chat with the general on whom he was relying so heavily. As Horace Porter described it at the time the visit was almost painfully devoid of formality. To Mrs. Porter, Porter wrote:

A few days ago we were sitting in front of the General's tent when there appeared very suddenly before us a long, lank-looking personage, dressed all in black, and looking very much like a boss undertaker. It was the President. He said, after shaking hands with us all, 'I just thought I would jump aboard a boat and come down and see you. I don't expect I can do any good, and in fact I'm afraid I may do harm, but I'll put myself under your orders and if you find me doing anything wrong just send me right away.' Gen. Grant informed him bluntly that he would certainly do that. The old fellow remained with us till the next day, and told stories all the time. He did not ask and said he did not want to know Grant's plans. On the whole he behaved very well. The black troops received him most enthusiastically, grinning from ear to ear and displaying an amount of ivory terrible to behold.[26]

Early in July Grant wrote a letter to his Chicago friend, Russell Jones, emphasizing that the military situation was much brighter than it seemed to be. Each of the two Confederate generals, Lee and Johnston, desperately needed to break out of the coil that was beginning to bind so tightly, and neither man could strike a blow because the odds against success were so long and the price of failure so prohibitive. To Jones Grant wrote:

You people up North must be of good cheer. Recollect that we have the bulk of the Rebel army, in two grand armies, both besieged and both conscious that they cannot stand a single battle outside their fortifications with the armies confronting them. . . . If the Rebellion is not perfectly and thoroughly crushed it will be the fault and through the weakness of the people North. Be of good cheer and rest assured that all will come out right.[27]

CHAPTER SIXTEEN

So Fair an Opportunity

THERE had been no rain for a month, the air was almost unendurably hot and heavy, and when the soldiers marched from here to there they kicked up so much dust that nobody in the moving column could see anything but the backs of the men in the next rank ahead. Grant said that he did not want to "give the troops any violent exercise" until the weather moderated, and no matter what the weather did it would be a week or more before Sheridan's weary cavalry was fully ready for field service. But even if nothing could be done at once it was time to start planning, and on July 3 Grant told Meade to examine the possibilities for a new offensive.

To begin with: "Do you think it possible, by a bold and decisive attack, to break through the enemy's center, say in General Warren's front somewhere?" Grant made it clear that this time he was not talking about a simple order for another head-on assault, the order sent forward in the evening and the assault coming next morning; this time "we would want full preparations made in advance so there should be no balk," and the major strength of the army would be concentrated in one hard blow on a relatively narrow front. This meant building roads so that troops could be brought forward rapidly, placing heavy artillery to flatten opposing fortifications, and strengthening the Federal works on either side of the place chosen for the attack so that they could be held with the smallest possible force.

Grant was thinking about siege warfare, which he had foreseen immediately after the failure of the final assault at Cold Harbor. He was prepared to make a siege if he had to but he wanted to avoid it if he could, and his proposal for an attack on the Confederate center was in fact an attempt to make a siege unnecessary.

The routine of siege warfare had been developed over many centuries. It involved a ritualized procedure with a formal, eighteenth-century flavor, in which nothing whatever was either hurried or left to chance; and all professional soldiers knew it, from the textbooks if not from actual experience. (It was a business the engineers, especially, were required to be familiar with.) In siege warfare the besieging army advanced by "regular approaches," as military jargon had it; which is to say that it inched its line forward step by step, making each new position secure before seeking a new one, building "covered ways" or approach trenches so that troops could be brought to the firing line safely, laying out massive gun emplacements after each forward move, trying to create a succession of fortified places from which overwhelming fire could be laid on a selected part of the defensive line.

In this way, given plenty of time, men and equipment, the attacking force could in the end break almost any defensive line. Under proper conditions, the process was slow but sure. Right now, however, proper conditions did not exist and there was scant prospect that they ever would.

In a real siege, as at Vicksburg, the enemy's stronghold was surrounded, cut off from supplies and reinforcements, and if nothing else worked the enemy at last was starved into defeat. But Petersburg was by no means surrounded. To the north and west and southwest it was wide open, its major railroad lines were still in use, and until they were permanently broken the place could not really be besieged. It was the railroads rather than Petersburg itself that were Grant's real objective anyway; if he could once surround this city he would not have to besiege it because the mere act of surrounding it would give him what he wanted. To rely on siege warfare now, accordingly, would be both risky and absurd; if there was still a chance to break the line, Grant wanted the chance examined. If the line could not be broken, Grant told Meade what the alternative would be: "If it is not attempted we will have to give you an army sufficient to meet most of Lee's forces and march around Petersburg and come in from above. This probably could not be done before the arrival of the Nineteenth Corps." [1]

Meade looked into matters and reported that an immediate assault on the enemy's works seemed out of the question. He did not care much for a move around the Rebel flank, either, because it would divide the army and leave Lee between the separated columns, the flanking force would run into strong entrenchments before it got to its goal, and the campaign to date had shown "the facility with which the enemy can interpose to check an onward movement." The only hope Meade saw was to send the cavalry out against Lee's communications, and meanwhile to rely on the regular approaches of siege warfare. He conceded, however, that the kind of attack Grant wanted might be helped by an idea General Burnside had just suggested.

Burnside was digging a mine, thinking to destroy a Confederate fort that blocked his progress, and although Meade was skeptical about it he asked his chiefs of artillery and engineering to look into it; it might be that it would fit into Grant's program well enough. The technicians investigated, and in a few days they reported that the outlook was bleak. Siege warfare was the only thing. The Confederate works were powerful, the operation would be slow because "as soon as one line of works is carried another equally strong will be found behind it," the mine might be helpful but the fort it was supposed to destroy would eventually have to be taken by regular approaches, with covering trenches and a lavish use of heavy artillery — and, all in all, "the advantages of position on the part of the enemy . . . will make the success of our operations difficult and probably costly both in time and men." [2]

So Burnside's mine was downgraded almost to the point of invisibility; which was a pity, because it could have won the war. Everything was against it — stuffy professionalism, bitter antagonism between generals, Burnside's own deficiencies as a tactician, and the army's fatal, ineradicable tendency to let details look after themselves. In the end the thing was a dismal failure, providing the perfect case history of the way things went wrong in the Army of the Potomac.

It began with a remark by a private soldier. Part of Burnside's line was held by the 48th Pennsylvania, which contained many coal miners from the anthracite fields; and one of these, looking over the parapet one day at a Rebel fort directly opposite, reflected that if there was one thing this regiment knew all about it was working underground. Why not, he asked, dig a long tunnel, plant a few tons of gunpowder under the fort, and blow the whole thing to glory? This soldier presented the idea to his regimental commander, Lieutenant Colonel Henry Pleasants, a mining engineer who had dug tunnels not only for mines but also for railroads, and Pleasants was impressed and went to see the division commander, General Robert Potter. Potter promptly took Pleasants to Burnside, who approved the scheme and told Pleasants to get to work at once. Burnside talked about it to

Meade a few days before Meade got Grant's order to study the chances for a new offensive.

Meade gave Burnside grudging approval; he would permit this operation but he had little faith in it, and any work Colonel Pleasants and his mine gangs did must be done on their own. The army engineers said that the tunnel would have to be more than 500 feet long, and they remarked that no military tunnel of that length ever had been or ever could be dug; the shaft could not be ventilated and the soldiers would be suffocated if they were not first buried by falling earth, the enemy would find out what was up and would dig countermines to stop it, and in sum "it was all clap-trap and nonsense." Pleasants had to devise his own tools, take over an old sawmill to cut the lumber he needed, and ask Burnside to send to Washington for a theodolite (which the army engineers could have provided) so that the exact distance to the enemy fort could be measured; and although the regiment began work on June 25 it took a month to finish the job. Afterward the miners said the work could have been done in a week or ten days if the army had really supported it. . . . Probably the venture would have died on the vine if Grant had not demanded a new offensive. Even then, Pleasants got no real help; his only gain was that the job became part of the official program.[3]

A small part: a bit of military byplay, tolerated because it would keep the soldiers busy, becoming great at last only because it exerted its own logic. To go on with the offensive Grant needed more men, and he now learned that instead of getting more he was going to have fewer; General Jubal Early was taking full advantage of the open road down the Shenandoah, and Grant had to send troops north to meet him. To strike at Lee Grant had to use the means immediately available, and these narrowed down until at last they included the mine and very little more. Meade's army finally put its hopes on the mine because there was no other place to put them.

Early's move to the Potomac put heavy pressure on Grant, even though it did not quite work out as Lee had planned. Lee wanted to make Grant strike at him head-on, all along the line, for a repetition of Cold Harbor. When he learned that Federal troops were being sent north Lee wrote to President Davis: "It is so repugnant to Grant's principles and practice to send troops from him that I had hoped before resorting to it he would have preferred attacking me." A few days later, confirming the report about troop movements, Lee repeated the complaint: "I had hoped that General Grant, rather than weaken his army, would have attempted to drive us from our position. I fear I shall not be able to attack him to advantage." At this time, of course, Lee knew nothing about the mine, but his notes to Davis indicate that when he sent Early north ,he wanted to compel Grant to make the kind of attack that would wreck the Federal army.[4] This did not happen; even so, Lee's use of Early accomplished a great deal and materially prolonged the war.

It took Grant and Meade a little time to learn just what Early was doing. As late as July 3 they thought Early had come back to Petersburg and that no Confederates were going down the valley except for a handful under Breckinridge. Then they began to get the picture into focus and suspected that Early was moving north with real strength, and Grant told Halleck that if the Confederates crossed the Potomac "I can send an army corps from here to meet them or cut off their return south." Once Early was north of the river Washington itself would be in danger, and Halleck warned that the Federal defenses were in bad shape. Sigel, who still commanded troops along the upper Potomac, had been collecting the units at his disposal and had them on Maryland Heights, across the Potomac from Harper's Ferry. Washington and Baltimore contained nothing but militia and not much of that. Nobody knew where Hunter was. Rumor said that the advancing Confederates had from 20,000 to 30,000 men, and although this was a wild exaggeration the Federals would be in trouble if Early crossed the Potomac with even half that many men.

Later that day Halleck reported that if Hunter was not yet on hand he was at least in sight — far-off but identifiable, coming toward the Potomac after a slow steamboat voyage down the Kanawha and up the Ohio — and Halleck did not think Grant needed to send anybody to Washington except perhaps for his dismounted cavalry. At midnight, however, Grant concluded that the situation was serious, and he told Meade to send a good infantry division and all the dismounted cavalry up to Washington without delay. Meade acted at once, and on July 6 the troops embarked — Ricketts's division from Wright's corps, nearly 5,000 infantry, and 4,000 of Sheridan's unhorsed cavalrymen, of whom 1,500 lacked arms. Grant told Halleck the troops were on the way, adding: "We now want to crush out and destroy any force the enemy have sent north. Force enough can be spared from here to do it. I think now there is no doubt but Ewell's corps is away from here." (Early commanded the troops once led by Ewell, and at this time the Federals usually referred to his force as Ewell's corps.)[5]

Grant believed that Early's advance actually gave the Federals an opportunity. With Hunter's army, Ricketts's division and the odds and ends that were otherwise available, he thought that the Confederate invading force could be destroyed. He did not know it, but he saw this situation just as Lincoln had seen a much more serious one nearly a year earlier, when Lee moved into Pennsylvania. At that time Lincoln argued that the invasion offered the Federals a strategic opening: they could get south of Lee and compel him to fight his way back to Virginia — which, because the Federals had much the bigger army, should lead to Lee's destruction. Grant had the same idea now, and he was already thinking about what would happen afterward. He was beginning to insist, in messages to Halleck and to Meade, that once Early was destroyed Hunter could again move up the valley, destroying the railroads around Charlottesville and depriving Lee of supplies from the valley and Lynchburg. Then the basic operation against Lee's southern communications could be resumed.[6]

However, it was beginning to be obvious that to defeat Early was going to take a two-handed effort. Halleck was growing deeply pessimistic. He warned Grant that Hunter was not going to arrive in time, and said that the Federal force in Maryland was desperately shorthanded and badly organized to boot. General Canby in New Orleans had started to send the Nineteenth Corps north, and the first division, 6,000 men, was due to reach Fort Monroe soon; could not these men be sent on to Washington? Grant's response shows his rising concern. On July 9 he telegraphed Halleck:

"If you think it necessary order the Nineteenth Corps as it arrives at Fortress Monroe to Washington. About the 18th or 20th is the time I should like to have a large force here; but if the rebel force now north can be captured or destroyed I would willingly postpone aggressive operations to destroy them, and could send in addition to the Nineteenth Corps the balance of the Sixth Corps." A few hours later, without waiting for a reply, he ordered Wright and the rest of his corps to Washington, and that evening he sent Halleck an additional message:

Forces enough to defeat all that Early has with him should get in his rear south of him and follow him up sharply, leaving him to go north, defending depots, towns, etc., with small garrisons and militia. If the President thinks it advisable that I should go to Washington in person I can start in an hour after receiving notice, leaving everything here on the defensive.[7]

On July 10 Grant heard from President Lincoln, who said the situation had grown worse. General Lew Wallace, an officer in whom Grant had had scant confidence ever since he missed an assignment at Shiloh, had fought with Early on the Monocacy River near Frederick, Maryland, using Ricketts's division and a scattering of other troops; he had been badly beaten and could hope to do no more now than protect Baltimore, to which city he had retreated. With some 100-day troops and casuals from hospitals and headquarters details it might be possible to defend Washington, whose outskirts Early had reached. For the rest:

Now what I think is that you should provide to retain your hold where you are certainly, and bring the rest with you personally and make a vigorous effort to destroy the enemy's force in this vicinity. I think there is really a fair chance to do this if the movement is prompt. This is what I think, upon your suggestion, and it is not an order.[8]

Having a general-in-chief whom he implicitly trusted, President Lincoln had come of age as a war president. He was no longer using his authority as President to issue a binding command to his principal strategist; on request he was telling what he thought, but the final statement — *it is not an order* — made it clear that what Grant did now was entirely up to Grant.

Grant studied the matter carefully, and on the night of July 10 he telegraphed to President Lincoln:

I have sent from here a whole corps commanded by an excellent officer, besides over three thousand other troops. One division of the Nineteenth Corps, six thousand strong, is now on its way to Washington. One steamer loaded with these troops having passed Ft. Monroe today. They will probably reach Washington tomorrow night. This force under Wright will be able to compete with the whole force under Ewell.

Before more troops can be sent from here Hunter will be able to join Wright in rear of the enemy, with at least ten thousand men, besides a force sufficient to hold Maryland Heights.

I think on reflection it would have a bad effect for me to leave here, and with Gen. Ord at Baltimore and Hunter and Wright with their forces following the enemy up, could do no good.

I have great faith that the enemy will never be able to get back with much of his force.[9]

One thing that influenced Grant was the belief that if he himself went to Washington to direct the operations against Early both friend and foe would assume, with much reason, that the whole Petersburg campaign had been a flat failure. He had an instinctive reluctance to let his opponent impose a plan of action on him, and he told his staff that he was not going to Washington because "this is probably just what Lee wants me to do." In Grant's absence the Federals obviously would not resume the offensive against the Petersburg railroad network, and in this case Grant feared that Lee might send troops to Georgia to help Joe Johnston defeat Sherman. Adam Badeau wrote that Grant "never dreamed of relaxing his grasp on Lee, or abandoning his position threatening the southern railroads," and here Badeau undoubtedly read Grant's mind correctly.[10]

In addition, Grant had given Washington all the troops it needed. Wright got his divisions into the Washington fortifications on the evening of July 11, and Early canceled an assault he had planned to make on July 12 — assuming that the assault must fail if the lines were held by veterans — and withdrew across upper Maryland, crossing the Potomac and getting back into Virginia near Leesburg on July 14. The immediate threat had been met, and there were enough Federal soldiers present to prevent a repetition. At the same time, the hope that Early's total defeat would quickly follow turned out to be wrong. What Grant had been unable to appraise correctly was the utter disorganization of command in Washington.

There were plenty of generals there. Wright was a first-class soldier; Ord, given temporary command at Baltimore, was another; the Washington garrison was capably commanded by General C. C. Augur; Sigel had been relieved, and Hunter, who was at last bringing his army to the scene, still had Grant's confidence even though the War Department had lost all faith in him. But nobody was really in charge.

Grant tried to fix this on July 12 when he ordered Halleck to put Wright in supreme command of all the troops that moved out against Early, regardless of the rank of other commanders, and specifying:

"He should get outside the trenches with all the force he possibly can, and should push Early to the last moment." Wright moved promptly enough, but his problems were great. He had to operate in and across four military departments, making a compact force out of elements drawn from all of them, and this called for an overriding authority Wright simply did not have. He could do no more than the War Department allowed him to do, and the department crippled him. Looking back after the war, Grant commented: "It seemed to be the policy of General Halleck and Secretary Stanton to keep any force sent there, in pursuit of the invading army, moving right and left so as to keep between the enemy and our capital; and generally speaking they pursued this policy until all knowledge of the whereabouts of the enemy was lost."

On top of this, communications between City Point and Washington were bad. The telegraph line was subject to failure, and a telegram often had to go part of the way by steamboat; at times it took twenty-four hours or longer for a message from Grant to reach the War Department, or for news from the department to reach Grant, the situation in the valley was extremely fluid, and Grant warned the department that he could hardly issue "positive orders or directions" about troop movements. He tried to rely on Halleck; Badeau asserted that Grant repeatedly "directed Halleck to give orders on his own responsibility, he being the senior officer near the field of operations, but again and again Halleck declined." Halleck blandly declared that he would not exercise any discretion in the control of troops but would just "carry out such orders as you may give." Washington kept Wright from exercising real control and left everything up to Grant, who found that coordination by remote control was impossible.[11]

On July 15 Grant sent Colonel Comstock to Washington to see Halleck, bearing a letter in which Grant explained what he wanted.

He understood, Grant said, that Early had left Maryland and was withdrawing up the valley. If so, Hunter ought to follow him, and Wright with the Sixth and Nineteenth Corps should return to City Point so that they could be used before Early's men could rejoin Lee. Pressing against Early's force, Hunter would either compel that officer to stay in the valley or would be able himself to reach Gordonsville and Charlottesville, and "the utter destruction of the road at and between those two points will be of immense value to me." It was not possible, on the basis of what Grant knew, to issue a hard and fast order, however: "I do not intend this as an order to bring Wright back whilst he is in pursuit of the enemy with any prospect of punishing him, but to secure his return at the earliest possible moment after he ceases to be absolutely necessary where he is." [12]

This was clear enough, but Halleck was in a difficult mood. Halleck had disapproved of Grant's move across the James from the beginning, holding that the Army of the Potomac ought always to stay between Lee and Washington, and Early's presence along the Potomac evoked a strong "I told you so" response. Comstock said that when he saw Halleck the general laughed at him, and that "his first question, in a rather sneering way, was when were we going to do something." Comstock said Halleck wanted the Army of the Potomac withdrawn to the north side of the James, and he noted in his diary: "Said it was useless to talk about elements of strategy — that Lee was in a central position in reference to A. of P. and troops at Washn and could act on either at pleasure. That if Wright & 19 Corps were withdrawn Early would at once come back & play the same game over. Asked him what he supposed we could do with a siege of Richmond on North side — he said that was not for him to say — that he might return by asking what we could do by a siege on S. side." Comstock apparently sent the gist of this on to Grant, who on July 16 sent a new message to Halleck:

I want if possible to get the 6th & 19th corps here to use them before the enemy can get Early back. With Hunter in the Shenandoah Valley and always between the enemy and Washington force enough can always be had to check an invasion until reinforcements can go from here. This does not prevent Hunter from following the enemy even to Gordonsville and Charlottesville if he can do it with his own force and such other improvised troops as he can get. But he should be cautious.

This accomplished nothing whatever. Given discretion, Halleck continued to do just what he had been doing. Wright and the two army corps were not sent back to Petersburg. On the day he got this message Halleck wrote a chatty, revealing letter to Sherman:

Entre nous, I fear Grant has made a fatal mistake in putting himself south of James river. He cannot now reach Richmond without taking Petersburg, which is strongly fortified, crossing the Appomattox and recrossing the James. Moreover, by placing his army south of Richmond he opens the capital and the whole North to Rebel raids. Lee can at any time detach 30,000 or 40,000 men without our knowing it till we are actually threatened. I hope we may yet have full success, but I find that many of Grant's general officers think the campaign already a failure.[13]

With the Army's chief of staff in this frame of mind Grant had little chance to get vigorous on-the-spot direction of the effort to defeat Early; and Halleck's lack of touch with military reality is shown by his assumption that Lee in this summer of 1864 could if he chose send 40,000 men to reinforce Early. Grant of course knew that Lee had no such number to spare; but at the same time he did not know what Early was going to do, and he believed that if he relaxed the pressure in Virginia Lee might recall Early and dispatch him to Georgia to help Johnston. On July 15, Grant told Meade to have Sheridan and the cavalry go out to cut both the Weldon and the Richmond & Danville railroads; this would make it impossible for Lee to send troops south from Richmond, and anyway "to cut both roads will be a great help to us." However, both Sheridan and Meade reported that this would fail unless the cavalry could be supported by a strong force of infantry, so Grant suspended the move until the Sixth and the Nineteenth Corps came down from Washington.

He did not know when this would happen. Any plan he made had to be flexible, and he could never forget that everything he did in Virginia rested finally on the need to destroy the railroads that kept Lee and Richmond connected with the rest of the Confederacy. Part of that job had to be done in and near the valley no matter what happened at Petersburg, and on July 22 Grant sent Halleck a modification of his earlier orders:

"You need not send any force back until the main force of the enemy are known to have left the Valley. Is Wright still where he can make connections with Hunter? If the two can push the enemy back, and destroy railroads from Charlottesville to Gordonsville, I would prefer that service to having him here." Two days later Grant repeated the substance of this: "I would prefer a complete smash-up of the enemy's roads about Gordonsville and Charlottesville to having the same force here. If Wright and Hunter can do the job, let them do it." [14] Far from trying to mass superior strength against the main force of the enemy, Grant wanted to use whatever manpower was available to reach out and strike his opponent's soft spots.

Unified command around Washington was essential, and on July 18 Grant told Halleck that "to prevent a recurrence of what has just taken place in Maryland" he wanted the separate military departments there merged into one, with one man in command of the whole. To run this new department he suggested his old friend, General William B. Franklin, who was in the east just now on sick leave from his assignment in Louisiana. Two days passed and nothing happened, so Grant telegraphed again to ask what was being done. Halleck replied on July 21 that nothing was being done; the matter was in Secretary Stanton's hands, but Halleck felt Grant ought to know that "General Franklin would not give satisfaction."

Franklin was an odd case. He had been a favorite of McClellan (which did not add to his popularity in the War Department) and he was held at least partly responsible for the failure of Burnside's Fredricksburg offensive and the abortive mud march, at the end of 1862; the administration simply was not going to promote him. A confirmed gossip, he was an intimate of Baldy Smith, who was now conducting a campaign to get Franklin put in Meade's place, and the atmosphere around City Point and Bermuda Hundred was growing murky with intrigues and rumors of intrigues. Meanwhile, Washington refused to act, and on July 25 Grant appealed directly to Lincoln. In a letter he told the President about the request he had made and went on:

I do not insist that the departments should be broken up, nor do I insist upon General Franklin commanding. All I ask is that one general officer, in whom I and yourself have confidence, should command the whole. General Franklin was named because he was available and I know him to be capable and believe him to be trustworthy. It would suit me equally as well to call the four departments referred to a "military division" and to have placed in command of it General Meade. In this case I would suggest General Hancock for command of the Army of the Potomac and General Gibbon for command of the Second Army Corps. With General Meade in command of such a division I would have every confidence that all the troops within the military division would be used to the very best advantage from a personal examination of the ground, and he would adopt means of getting the earliest information of any advance of the enemy and would prepare to meet it . . . Many reasons might be assigned for the changes here suggested, some of which I would not care to commit to paper, but would not hesitate to give verbally. I send this by Brigadier General Rawlins, chief of staff, who will be able to give more information of the situation here than I could give you in a letter.[15]

Obviously it was going to take time to get all of this straightened out, and some sort of stopgap arrangement had to be made for command of the troops that were trying to cope with General Early. On Grant's insistence, Secretary Stanton at last, on July 27, notified Halleck that since orders must be issued directly from Washington for proper use of the troops there, control of the departments and the men in them was lodged in Halleck's hands and that Halleck was "to take all military measures necessary for defense against any attack of the enemy and for his capture and destruction." At the same time Stanton telegraphed Grant to ask when he could meet the President at Fort Monroe for a discussion of the entire problem. Grant was obliged to reply that he could not go to such a meeting at once because pressing matters on the Petersburg front were going to demand his personal attention.[16]

A few days earlier Meade had given Grant a report on Burnside's mine, which was at last finished, ready to load and use. Meade felt that the success of this venture would depend largely on whether the Confederates had built a second line of defense on the high ground half a mile behind the fort that was to be destroyed. His engineers believed that such a line did exist, and if they were right the whole area between the fort and Petersburg would be swept by fire and an assault would be impossible. Meade thought the chance was very poor — one of Burnside's staff officers was privately complaining about "the cold apathy with which it [the mine] had been regarded by most of the army" — but he would try it if Grant thought it necessary.[17]

Grant now devised a new plan. Clearly, he was not going to get any infantry from Washington for a long time to come.— Early was moving up toward the Potomac again, the War Department was running a temperature and calling for more troops, and it was necessary to send on the balance of the Nineteenth Corps, which had just arrived from New Orleans — but it was time to strike a blow on the Petersburg front with the means at hand. He told Meade, as a result, to make a powerful demonstration north of the James, "having for its real object the destruction of the railroad on that side." Let Hancock and his Second Corps cross the river at Deep Bottom, on the north side of Bermuda Hundred Neck, accompanied by Sheridan and all available cavalry. While the infantry made menacing motions toward Richmond Sheridan could move out behind this screen, swing north and west in a wide arc, and strike at the Virginia Central Railroad as close to Richmond as possible. (The Quartermaster's department could send two hundred railroad workers along with Sheridan to help take the railroad apart.) Once the road was thoroughly broken, all hands could return; at the very least, Lee's ability to get supplies from the valley and to exchange troops with Early would be crippled.

There were other possibilities, as well. Grant remarked that this move might just possibly catch the Rebels by surprise so that Hancock and Sheridan between them could drive right on into Richmond. This seemed unlikely, to be sure, and Grant did not want a regular attack on the Richmond trenches; he just wanted the commanding officers to look for an opening and make a quick stab if they saw one. Meanwhile, it was also possible that to meet this move Lee might bring troops up from the Petersburg front, in which case Burnside's mine should be exploded and an attack made there.

Meade ordered Hancock to start the move on the night of July 26. He also told Grant that a new study of the ground on Burnside's front indicated that the entrenched line on the high ground beyond the fort did not, after all, exist, so that Burnside's chances looked better than had been expected. Grant replied that he believed the Federals now were relatively stronger in front of Petersburg than they had been since the middle of June. An assault by Burnside, therefore, should be planned, "to be made if further developments justify." [18]

So far the plan was tentative, based actually on the knowledge that if the Federals were pressed for manpower along the James Lee was pressed even more desperately; if he had to shuffle troops about to meet a new threat there was a good chance that he would make himself vulnerable in one place or another, and the task now was to find the vulnerable spot and hit it. Meade's headquarters continued to doubt that Burnside could do very much, and on July 26 Burnside got from General Humphreys some lukewarm instructions. If he thought that the enemy had discovered his mine and was countermining to destroy it, he must be prepared to spring it at once; still, "it is not intended by the commanding general to follow up the explosion of the mine by an assault or other operation." Grant's problem here was to keep the army from exploding the mine to no good purpose, just to get it off the agenda. [19]

Then things began to develop. Hancock crossed the river and found the Confederates reinforcing heavily in front of Richmond. Sheridan moved out as directed and found more of the same; ran into a solid force of Rebel infantry, had a bruising four-hour fight, and realized that he could not now go on and strike the railroad. On the night of July 28 Grant summed it up in a wire to Halleck:

WE HAVE FAILED IN WHAT I HOPED TO ACCOMPLISH —THAT IS, TO SURPRISE THE ENEMY AND GET ON TO THEIR ROADS WITH THE CAVALRY NEAR TO RICHMOND AND DESTROY THEM OUT TO THE SOUTH ANNA. I AM YET IN HOPES OF TURNING THIS DIVERSION TO ACCOUNT, SO AS TO YIELD GREATER RESULTS THAN IF THE FIRST OBJECT HAD BEEN ACCOMPLISHED.

It was time, in short, to use the other string to the bow, and suddenly the coal miners' long tunnel was all-important, and the despised mine became the most vital item on the horizon. Grant notified Meade that nothing could be done north of the James and said that it was time to strike directly at the Petersburg lines; could Burnside's assault be made tomorrow morning? Meade replied that this would be too soon, but said that the attack could be made at or before dawn on July 30, and it was so ordered. Meade told Burnside to explode the mine at three-thirty on that morning and then to send assault columns forward to seize the high ground beyond. Plenty of artillery would be posted to provide supporting fire, and Burnside would be aided on his right and left by the Eighteenth Corps and the Fifth Corps.[20]

This offensive had been a long time aborning, and it had grown out of many things: the overriding need to strike at Lee's communications and the impossibility of doing it either by sending cavalry past his flanks or by moving infantry up the valley; the collapse of command around Washington, which limited the resources available at Petersburg and yet at the same time made it imperative to strike a blow there; the unorthodox idea brought forward by amateurs and adopted most unwillingly by professionals; and, finally, the maneuver north of the James that failed utterly but suddenly shifted the odds so profoundly that it gave this army the brightest chance for victory it had had since it first crossed the Rapidan.

For Lee had risen to the bait. Moving to block the thrust by Hancock and Sheridan, he had put five-eighths of his army north of the James, leaving only three divisions to hold five miles of fortifications in front of Petersburg. His engineers knew about the mine, but they seem to have had no more faith in it than Meade's engineers had, and gossip about the project had filtered down to become a subject for wisecracks by the very soldiers who were about to be blown up. The "second line" that worried Meade so much had never been built; in front of Burnside there was a first line of Rebel works, with the fort for an anchor, and beyond there was nothing much but open country. From the Federal point of view conditions were ideal. All that had to be done was explode the mine and then send a storming column forward through the gap.

Before the Federals could rush through the gap, however, they must first rush through their own line — a log-and-dirt trench eight feet deep, with a heavy barrier of abatis out in front. Meade told Burnside to prepare the way: that is, to level the trench and remove the abatis, under cover of night, so that his four divisions could charge in proper formation. Incredibly, Burnside did not do it.

Perhaps the mere effort of bringing his idea to adoption had used all of his imagination and energy; or perhaps he was thrown out of gear by a last-minute switch Meade told him to make in his battle plan. Burnside had a division of colored troops led by General Edward Ferrero, and he proposed to put this division in the first wave because it had seen little fighting and so was fresher than the others. Meade had little faith in Negro troops, and he also felt that if this assault failed he would be accused of wantonly sacrificing the colored soldiers in a doomed offensive, so he told Burnside to lead with someone else. Burnside could think of nothing better than to call in his other three division commanders and tell them to draw straws to see which should lead the way. The honor went to the First Division, commanded by General James H. Ledlie.

If the Army of the Potomac had tried it could not have made a more unfortunate choice. Ledlie was a cipher. A brigadier who served under him said that Ledlie "was a drunkard and an arrant coward . . . It was wicked to risk the lives of men in such a man's hands"; and apparently everybody knew it except the corps and army commanders.[21] It was that kind of an army. Elementary preparations for the big assault simply were not made, and the key job was given to a man who should long since have been removed from command but whose incapacity had never been discovered by the authorities.

Anyway, the mine was sprung at twenty minutes before five o'clock on the morning of July 30. It went off with a nerve-shattering crash. A Confederate gunner posted not far off remembered it: "A slight tremor of the earth for a second, then the rocking as of an earthquake, and, with a tremendous blast which rent the sleeping hills beyond, a vast column of earth and smoke shoots upward to a great height, its dark sides flashing out sparks of fire, hangs poised for a moment in mid-air, and then hurtling downward with a roaring sound showers of stones, broken timbers and blackened human limbs, sub-sides — the gloomy pall of darkening smoke flushing to an angry crimson as it floats away to meet the morning sun." [22] The Confederate fort and the men in it disappeared forever; where they had been there was a vast hole in the ground, a hundred and seventy feet wide, fifty feet across and thirty feet deep, the jagged bottom littered with torn bodies and half-buried weapons, great hunks of clay half the size of a house poised on its sloping sides. The tidal wave of reddened dust and smoke went drifting off toward the rising sun, bearing heaven knows what message, and the stout Confederate trenches for two or three hundred yards on each side were deserted as dazed men stumbled off for safety. At last the dust settled — and here, in front of General Burnside, there was a completely empty space a quarter of a mile wide.

There was a heavy silence, touched by thin cries and shouts, lasting for thirty seconds or five minutes — nobody ever knew, because nobody just then was keeping track of such things — and then the Federal guns, a hundred and sixty of them, siege pieces and field artillery and mortars, went off with a rolling explosion louder than the sound of the mine itself, blasting at all of the places from which the Confederates might open fire on a column of assault. Now it was time for the charge.

Burnside had 15,000 infantry, and Meade's plan was to have these men charge in four successive waves, each division advancing on a brigade front, the first one fanning out on both sides of the crater to hold the empty Confederate trenches, the others going past the crater and the First Division to sweep on to the crest that overlooked Petersburg. Fifteen minutes would have done it. Nowhere on the field was there a Confederate battery or infantry firing line in condition to make any opposition. Burnside's front line was on the top of a small ridge, with room behind it for the assaulting divisions to form line of battle in perfect security. Meade may have come to this late, but his plan was flawless; afterward, Grant testified that "I think now it was all we could have done; I think he could not have done better." [23]

If the plan was flawless the execution of it was in the highest degree wretched. Advancing to make the charge, Ledlie's men found that the only way they could get out of the Federal trench was through an improvised opening ten feet wide. Instead of forming a broad line of battle, a whole brigade in front with a second close behind, they ran forward in a thin, straggling column of men who went along by twos and threes. Straight ahead of them was that awesome hole in the ground. Nobody had told them to swing out around it; nobody, in fact, had told them anything at all; and they kept on going, got down into the crater, goggled at the wounded Confederates who were trying to disentomb themselves, and reflected that they had occupied the enemy's first line of works. They were a little too battle wise for their own good, and they had learned during the last month or two that in any fight it was wise to get into a secure rifle pit so as to avoid enemy bullets. Nobody was firing at them just now but here was the great-grandfather of all rifle pits, and they flocked into it, by hundreds and hundreds, and stayed there.

This, of course, was the time for the division commander to take charge, moving the men out of the crater, forming a battle line on the far side, and taking them on to the empty crest beyond, but the division commander was far away. General Ledlie had gone into a safe dugout many yards behind the Union line and there he stayed, drinking rum, now and then receiving a written order sent along by Burnside and giving it to a runner to carry forward to brigade commanders. From first to last he never saw this battle. Needing good leadership more desperately than ever before, his division today got no leadership at all.

Behind this division there was a traffic jam. Meade's expectation that the other divisions would be massed in line of battle ready to go forward quickly was totally mistaken. A covered way — in effect, a six-foot-deep lane three or four feet wide — led up to the Federal firing line from the rear, and most of the supporting divisions in Burnside's corps came up this congested path. After a scramble that took a good deal of time they got into the open and went forward, some of them crowding into the crater (so packed, by now, that the men in it could not have moved if they had wanted to) and others swinging out to get into the abandoned trenches on either side; hardly anyone trying, or even being urged by anyone in authority, to go on through and make for the final goal. Grant learned afterward that not one of the four division commanders in this corps was up in front trying to lead his men.

It is hard to believe that it all really happened so. For half an hour the Confederates could make no resistance at all, and for another half hour they could make very little, and the door was wide open with nothing behind it and nobody moving through it. To have an advantage like that is the most any army can hope for; this army had sixty minutes of it and could not use it. The hour passed, and the Confederates brought up reinforcements. Guns were put where they could drop shells into the crater (where they did fearful execution in the dense mass), tough infantry got into line along the crest, more artillery opened from the right and the left, and now there was a killing fire that stopped the assault with deadly finality. At about this time, with the bright chance utterly gone, Ferrero's colored division somehow was ordered forward. It ran into the confused mass of huddled Federals, did its pathetic best to no avail, and made a large contribution to the casualty list. Before ten o'clock Grant and Meade realized that the whole attack had been a disastrous failure and told Burnside to call his men back. It took Burnside (who thought the attack ought to be continued) the rest of the day to get them back, and when the accounts were squared it developed that more men had been lost in the retreat than in the advance, because by now the whole place was alive with Confederate bullets.[24]

One of the men responsible for the repulse was the Confederate General William Mahone, who commanded a division opposite General Warren, just to the left of Burnside's sector, and who took two brigades over to help drive Burnside back. (This left only a skeleton force to oppose Warren, who had been told to attack if the Confederates drew troops away from his front; Warren failed to detect the move, reported that he saw no opening, and did nothing. On a day marked by more spectacular errors, this oversight went virtually unnoticed.) Mahone's postwar comment on the narrow escape Lee's army had had was scathing:

If the mine — itself a success, making an immense breach in General Lee's works, unsupported by any reserve force, and consternation all around the breach rampant — had been followed up by a vigorous attacking column, and the force was there, it may not be too much to say that the retreat to which he was compelled nine months later would then have been unavoidable and most likely in the order of the d——l take the hindmost. After the explosion there was nothing on the Confederate side to prevent the orderly projection of any column through the breach which had been effected, cutting the Confederate army in twain . . . opening wide the gates to the rear of the Confederate capital.[25]

The Federal high command saw things just as Mahone did, but with more bitterness. Meade and Burnside had a furious argument that afternoon, and Horace Porter, who was present, wrote that the row "went far toward confirming one's belief in the wealth and flexibility of the English language as a medium of personal dispute." Grant told Halleck that the bungled attack "was the saddest affair I have witnessed in this war," adding: "Such an opportunity for carrying fortifications I have never seen and do not expect again to have." In the same vein he sent Meade a note on August 1: "Have you any estimate of our losses in the miserable failure of Saturday? I think there will have to be an investigation. So fair an opportunity will probably never occur again for carrying fortifications." [26]

Federal losses added up to about 4,000 men; not a staggering total, as battle casualties went in that campaign, except that they were so unmistakably the price paid for the incompetence that had prevented final victory. There was a formal Court of Inquiry a bit later. It blamed Burnside and Ledlie for the disaster, and had sharp words for some of their subordinates; Burnside went on leave and was never recalled to duty, Ledlie was quietly released from the service, and the spilled milk was more or less wiped up. Still later the Committee on the Conduct of the War held extensive hearings, doing its ineffective best to show that Meade rather than Burnside had been chiefly at fault. Grant testified at some length. Asked why the Federal trenches and abatis had not been opened to permit the proper formation of a coherent column of assault, he replied:

I think if I had been a corps commander, and had had that in charge, I would have been down there and would have seen that it was done right; or, if I had been the commander of the division that had to take the lead, I think I would have gone in with my division . . . I think the cause of the disaster was simply the leaving the passage of orders from one to another down to an inefficient man. I blame his seniors also for not seeing that he did his duty, all the way up to myself.[27]

And there it rested. On the whole Petersburg front the situation was just as it had been before, except that there was that huge scar in the ground in front of the trenches of the Ninth Army Corps.

CHAPTER SEVENTEEN

Roughshod or On Tiptoe

H E HAD promised to fight it out on this line if it took all summer, and now he was being put to the test. All summer was here with a vengeance, he was still on this line, and whether he could stay on it depended entirely on the firmness of his own resolution. The supreme command that had been given to him meant no more than he himself could make it mean. During July it had been impossible for him to enforce his will either in Washington or on the Petersburg battlefront. In Washington there was the War Department, managing to be both inert and officious at the same time; in front of Petersburg there was a crippling knot of jealousy, suspicion and self-seeking, removable apparently by nothing short of the sword of Alexander. The crisis of the war was here, and in the midst of it Grant had to spend an extraordinary amount of time and energy simply trying to get the machinery in shape so that he could run it.

He began, or tried to, with General Benjamin Butler.

One reason why Grant did not want to leave Petersburg was the fact that if he went away the ranking officer in Virginia would be General Butler, and the thought of letting this man direct all of the operations against Robert E. Lee was enough to make a soldier shudder. Grant got along with Butler well enough, and had a high opinion of the man's ability as an administrator, yet Butler unquestionably did not belong anywhere near a battlefield. Grant had hoped to meet this problem by giving Butler Smith as a corps commander, but this had not worked well because Butler and Smith detested each other so much; Colonel Comstock, who disliked both men, wrote that "neither could get on well with anyone, much less with each other." On July 1, therefore, Grant wrote a carefully phrased letter to Halleck, speaking of "the necessity of sending General Butler to another field of duty" and hoping that a suitable command might be created for him in Kentucky or Missouri. He emphasized that Butler "has always been prompt in his obedience to orders from me and clear in his understanding of them," and said that he "would not be willing to recommend his retirement"; still, the man was a handicap where he was, and if he could be got out of there without too much pain the general-in-chief would find life easier.[1]

Grant had Halleck's sympathy; as one who did not like to take any action at all, Halleck was bound to feel for a man who was trying to do the utterly impossible. He wrote that he had foreseen all along that Grant would want to get rid of Butler, "on account of his total unfitness to command in the field and his generally quarrelsome character," but he pointed out that this case was tough. To send Butler to Kentucky "would probably cause an insurrection in that state," and to send him to Missouri would be worse. Halleck would await further word from Grant before submitting any proposal to the President and the Secretary of War; meanwhile, he suggested the ancient expedient of gently kicking the irremovable man upstairs. They might leave Butler in "local command" of his department and set up his field troops under General Smith.

Grant understood very well that Butler could not just be fired, out of hand; the presidential election was drawing near, the administration's prospects were gloomy, and this definitely was not the time to arouse a storm. Halleck's proposal sounded like a good way out, and on July 6 Grant telegraphed Halleck: "PLEASE OBTAIN AN ORDER ASSIGNING THE TROOPS OF THE DEPARTMENT OF VIRGINIA AND NORTH CAROLINA SERVING IN THE FIELD TO THE COMMAND OF MAJ. GEN. W. F. SMITH AND ORDER MAJOR-GENERAL BUTLER, COMMANDING DEPARTMENT, TO HIS HEADQUARTERS, FORTRESS MONROE." [2]

What Grant was trying to do here was put into effect the course recommended by General Meigs and General Barnard, whom Halleck at Grant's request had sent to Bermuda Hundred in May to see what was wrong with Butler's army. Realizing that Butler was never going to win anything on his own but that he was an untouchable whose desire to look like a victorious soldier had to be gratified somehow, these generals had proposed a scheme by which Smith would run the show while Butler signed papers and posed happily as a great strategist. In his July 6 telegram, Grant had accepted this program; so Secretary Stanton took the papers to President Lincoln, and on July 7 the Adjutant General's office drafted General Order No. 225, with the President's approval, and sent a copy to Grant. This order read:

The troops of the Department of North Carolina and Virginia serving with the Army of the Potomac in the field, under Major General Smith, will constitute the Eighteenth Army Corps, and Maj. Gen. William F. Smith is assigned to the command of the corps. Maj. Gen. B. F. Butler will command the remainder of the troops in that department, having his headquarters at Fort Monroe.[3]

The War Department had tried to give Grant what he wanted, but it had been extremely clumsy, as Grant immediately realized. As the order stood there would now be three armies in the lower part of Virginia — Meade's Army of the Potomac, the troops that Butler continued to control at Norfolk and Fort Monroe, and the enlarged Eighteenth Corps which was no longer on anybody's chain of command. What Grant wanted was precisely what Meigs and Barnard had recommended — a field commander who would take charge of the actual fighting without disturbing Butler's position as department head. Instead, the order simply created an administrative nightmare, setting up a new command without defining it or tracing the new lines of authority, and on July 10 Grant wired Halleck:

"I would not desire this change made, but simply want General Smith assigned to the command of the Eighteenth Corps, and if there is no objection to a brigadier general holding such a position, General W. T. H. Brooks to the command of the Tenth Corps, leaving both of these corps in the Department as before, the headquarters of which is at Fortress Monroe. When the Nineteenth Corps arrives I will add it to the same Department." Grant said he would suspend the order until he got further word from Washington; meanwhile, he wanted one man to lead those troops of Butler which served with the Army of the Potomac, and he asked that Franklin be given that assignment. (This of course was several days before he nominated Franklin for command along the upper Potomac; while this set-to about Butler's position was going on, Grant believed he had settled the Potomac question by giving full powers to Wright.)[4]

The real trouble with Order 225 was that it tried to put into words something that could not be said bluntly and so created enormous misunderstandings.

The essence of the whole proposal was the idea that Butler confine himself to administrative tasks at Fort Monroe. If Butler did that, some man up at the fighting front would obviously direct Butler's troops in battle. Grant was not trying to make Smith that man; he wanted Smith confirmed in his present command, but he wanted some such person as Franklin put in between the two men to exercise the field authority that Butler could not himself wield and would not permit Smith to exercise. In its effort to put into clear English something that had to be quietly agreed upon rather than flatly stated, the War Department had muddied the waters.

Smith and the little coterie that surrounded him misread the order from the beginning. General Wilson congratulated Smith because "General Butler has at last been relieved." Newspaperman Sylvanus Cadwallader, who believed himself much closer to the inside of things than was really the case, wrote after the war about Grant's "promise to make Smith the department commander in Butler's stead." Smith himself saw it in the same light. He asked for a brief leave of absence, got it, and went off to New York — and complained, long afterward, that it had been "a cowardly thing in Grant" to let him go away without confessing that he was not going to put him in Butler's place. Actually, Order 225 said nothing at all about giving Smith Butler's command, and it was not long before the whole deal collapsed.

Butler went to see Grant on July 10, the day Grant told Halleck that he was rescinding the order. Grant told Butler that Smith was to retain command of his own corps — which of course was obvious, since neither the issuance nor the cancellation of the order affected Smith's status at all — and he explained what he wanted done with Franklin. Butler made no objection, and wrote jubilantly to Mrs. Butler that he was better off than he would have been if the matter had never come up. "From Grant's suspension of the order," Butler wrote, "and saying that he proposed to have the 19th corps added to my command, he has vindicated me and my military operations." As far as Grant could see, Butler was happy even after he was told that Franklin was to have field command of Butler's two army corps. Butler's dignity apparently had been preserved.[5]

The next move was up to Grant. Halleck notified him that Order No. 225 had been drafted to carry out Grant's views, and suggested: "If not satisfactory, please make for the Adjutant General a draft of one that will embrace exactly what you want." Before Grant attempted a new draft, however, the whole scene changed. He had a conversation with Smith which showed him that Smith was not, after all, a man he wanted in corps command along the James; and on the heels of this he discovered that he was not going to be able to use General Franklin in high command.

The conversation with Smith came immediately after Grant had had his talk with Butler on Order 225. Smith and Butler confronted each other in Grant's anteroom, but apparently did not pause to chat. Smith went in to see Grant, talked too much and too loosely — and, in the end, talked himself all the way out of the army.

In his letter of July 2 asking for a brief leave, Smith had opened up on Butler, asking Grant "how you can place a man in command of two army corps who is as helpless as a child on the field of battle and as visionary as an opium eater in council." Now Smith told Grant what he thought about Meade, as well, and it developed that he thought little more of Meade than he thought of Butler. Smith explained to one of his cronies a little later that in this conversation with Grant he "tried to show him the blunders of the late campaign with the Army of the Potomac," and spoke of the terrible loss of life due to "a want of generalship in its present commander." Colonel Comstock, who probably got the story from Grant himself, said that Smith "finally asked the general in the most offensive way if he expected he was ever going to do anything with that man [Meade] in command." Having discharged all of this from his system, Smith went north on leave.[6]

He could not have chosen a worse approach if he had tried. A year earlier Grant had turned down command of the Army of the Potomac because he foresaw jealousy and furious backbiting, and now he was getting just what he had tried to avoid. Furthermore, Grant liked Meade and had confidence in him, and if there was one thing he disliked more than anything else it was a soldier who carried personal criticism of a brother officer to his commanding general. On top of everything else Smith had been sniping at Grant himself. Marsena Patrick's diary contained a note that Smith had been "making an attempt to thrash Grant over Meade's shoulders," and said flatly that Smith had been "plotting against Grant." At Butler's headquarters, of all places, Smith complained of Meade to Colonel J. W. Shaffer, Butler's chief of staff, and Grant learned that this complaint included Grant as well. Asked about this, after the war, Smith made one of those odd disclaimers that amount to a confession: "Gen. Grant's name was not mentioned except incidentally and as responsible for Meade's blunders." [7]

It came at a bad time. The Army of the Potomac was beset by strong political currents. A rumor that Meade was on the way out was circulating vigorously. On July 7 Dana either started it or gave it new impetus by telling Stanton that "a change in the commander of the Army of the Potomac now seems probable." Dana said Meade's temper was so bad that "I do not think he has a friend in the whole army," adding that no subordinate could approach him without being insulted and that Meade's own staff officers did not dare speak without being asked, "for fear of either sneers or curses." Dana may have echoed Smith's campaign plus general camp gossip — on the day he wrote to Stanton, Comstock noted that there was "talk about Meade's quarrelling with all his subordinates, and Rawlins talks wildly" — or he may have picked up something more subterranean, but he certainly was not speaking for Grant. (This took place more than two weeks before Grant suggested Meade for the command on the upper Potomac.) Five days after Dana wrote to Stanton, Hancock went to Meade and said that the grapevine had it that Meade was to be removed and Hancock put in his place. Hancock refused to give his source, but said the story seemed to be reliable; he added that Grant opposed the move but was going to be overruled. This of course implied that Grant had lost standing in Washington, and it was clear that someone, somewhere, was trying to shake up the whole system of command. Nobody knew what might happen next.

Meade promptly went to Grant with the story. Grant told him that he had not heard this yarn and did not believe there was anything to it; he would certainly have been consulted, he said, if a serious move to replace Meade was under consideration. Meade remarked that the story might have arisen from a belief that Grant was going to send him off to command the troops around Washington, but Grant did not think so; he had not even thought of this, although he went on to say that if he had to detach one more army corps he would probably send Meade along with it. Meade was assuaged, and he seems to have felt no enmity toward Hancock: to Mrs. Meade he wrote, "I am perfectly willing at any time to turn over to him the Army of the Potomac and wish him joy of his promotion."

Dana undoubtedly overstated the discontent among the generals. Comstock said that while all of the commanders had grievances against Meade they nevertheless respected him, and "he would be the first choice for Cmdg. Genl. both among his staff officers and the Maj. Gens." Meade was secure enough . . . and this was a poor time for Smith to demand that Meade be dismissed. To Badeau, Grant said that he "could not afford to dispense with all his other generals for the sake of retaining a single officer." Smith simply ruined his own standing, and Grant did not go ahead with the task of redrafting Order No. 225.[8]

One reason why he did not was that just at this time he realized that the most pressing command emergency lay in Washington and concluded that that was where he wanted to use Franklin — only to discover, in a matter of days, that he was not going to be allowed to use him anywhere. Another reason for inaction was a good deal simpler. General Butler refused to be pushed upstairs.

From the start this project depended on Butler's willingness to remain at Fort Monroe. His outright removal had never been asked; what Grant wanted to do (unquestionably with Lincoln's blessing) was to clip his wings but save his face, and Grant understood that such an operation required the delicate touch because he himself had once been in a position almost exactly like the one that was being planned for Butler now. In the spring of 1862, just after his victory at Fort Donelson, Grant had got into Halleck's black book and had received a brusque order confining him to headquarters and directing him to turn field command over to a subordinate. Intensely humiliated — he wrote later that he had been virtually under arrest, without a command — Grant had protested so vigorously that the White House intervened and the order was withdrawn. If Butler reacted now as Grant had done two years earlier Butler could shake the entire national administration.

As his letter to Mrs. Butler shows, Butler at first had been agreeable; but he had had second thoughts, all of them negative. Noting that Order No. 225 bore the signature of E. D. Townsend, the Assistant Adjutant General, Butler scornfully told a visiting Congressman that he was not going to be ordered about by any staff officer. In addition, as a good lawyer he perceived that this order contained an enormous loophole. Colonel Lyman of Meade's staff probably got the straight of it when he wrote that Butler had taken a position unassailable under military law. As long as he commanded the department he commanded all the troops that were in it and his headquarters were where he said they were. Now Butler said that headquarters were at Bermuda Hundred; he commanded the troops there, and the only way to get him out was to fire him or subject him to the rough, public downgrading Grant himself had been given along the Tennessee River.

Butler's pride was as great as his political influence — both were simply inordinate — and this was more than Grant could handle. If the administration wanted this done it must do it on its own and not pass the chore down to a subordinate. Politically, Butler was up where he could be reached by nobody but the President, and if the President did not choose to reach him Grant certainly could not. Besides, Smith had made himself impossible. So . . .

So Grant took a few days to reach a final decision — as late as July 16 he sent Meade a note showing that he did not then consider command of the Eighteenth Corps vacant — but he soon made up his mind, and on July 19 he formally issued orders relieving Smith of his command and sending him to New York to await orders. To take Smith's place he selected General Ord. Returning to City Point when his leave expired, Smith got the news from Grant himself.[9]

Smith was outraged. He considered that he had been betrayed and foully dealt with, and he wanted revenge. To get it he set off for Washington, going to see the Senator from his state, Vermont, an eminent Republican named Solomon Foot. Smith gave Foot a letter, almost certainly meant for the eye of Abraham Lincoln, in which he reduced the whole complicated business to a simple charge that Grant had got drunk.

On July 1, said Smith, Grant and Butler visited Smith's headquarters. Butler had given Grant drink, and Grant said this had done him a lot of good and that he would like some more; Smith's servant gave him one drink and then gave him two, and Smith said that Grant's voice "showed plainly that the liquor had affected him." When Grant left, Smith told a staff officer (as he recited it to Senator Foot): "General Grant has gone away drunk. General Butler has seen it, and will never fail to use the weapon which has been put in his hands."

After he himself was dismissed, Smith went on, he learned that Butler had gone to Grant and threatened to expose him if Order No. 225 were not revoked. Smith added that he knew much more about this and that he would be glad to talk about it if anybody wanted to listen, and he assured Senator Foot: "I have not referred to the state of things existing at headquarters when I left, and to the fact that General Grant was then in the habit of getting liquor in a surreptitious manner, because it was not relevant to my case; but if you think, at any time, the matter may be of importance to the country, I will give it to you."

Long afterward, Smith wrote a book giving the text of this letter. He also published what he considered confirmatory evidence, a letter from General I. J. Wistar, who until the middle of May commanded a brigade in Smith's corps, and who gave Smith a tale which he said he had from Assistant Secretary of War John Tucker. According to this tale, when Butler heard about the plan to remove him from his command — Smith and his friends clung to this reading of Order 225 all the way through — he took Grant on a roving tour of different corps headquarters, seeing to it that Grant was given whiskey at each one. "The result," as Wistar's letter ran, "was that the commander in chief became so much and so obviously under the influence of these various samples that he not only exposed his condition to many persons but on his return to headquarters required aid to dismount. To crown all, while he was being assisted from his horse, Rawlins, having come out to see what was the matter, impulsively exclaimed: 'My God, there's the General drunk again after all the promises I have got from the corps commanders.' " [10]

This got Smith nowhere at all; that is, he had been dismissed and he stayed dismissed, and the orders he was told to await at New York never came. But he did succeed in one thing. To this day, the heart of the legend that Grant was a periodic alcoholic in wartime is the story Smith told. He created an enduring myth: the President removed Butler, Grant reinstated him, and the reason was that Butler got him drunk and then threatened to tell: obviously, Butler had a hold on Grant and the hold must have come out of the whiskey bottle.

The story presents difficulties. As even Smith's friend General Wilson pointed out, by this time nobody was going to make a sensation by charging that Grant had taken to drink. The charge had been made too many times, without result; if there was anything Grant had no reason to be afraid of, this was it. Besides, six months later Grant did relieve Butler and sent him home to Massachusetts, and if Butler could have blackmailed Grant in July of 1864 he could have done so in January of 1865. He never did it, but went off duty as meekly as a lamb; in the end it was Smith, not Butler, who tried to apply blackmail. Finally, there is the testimony of John A. Rawlins, who of all living mortals was the first to look for evidence that Grant had been drunk and the first to put his findings on record. Rawlins took no stock in Smith's story for the obvious reason that there was nothing in it, despite the allegation that he had seen a helpless Grant lifted down from his horse and had cried out in dismay that the general was drunk again.

As always, Rawlins was most watchful. On June 29 — several days before the business Smith was talking about — he lamented that Grant, having gone to the front, had taken "a glass of liquor," and he swore that he would not again remain behind when Grant went visiting. But on July 19, the day Grant told Smith to go back to New York, Rawlins sent a letter to Mrs. Rawlins:

General Grant today relieved Major General William F. Smith from command and duty in this army, because of his spirit of criticism of all military movements and men, and his failure to get along with anyone he is placed under, and his disposition to scatter the seeds of discontent throughout the army. I have never been deceived in the man since his promotion, but because of acknowledged ability have done all I could to sustain him. The action of the General is justifiable.[11]

So Butler stayed, Smith departed, a good deal of subsurface ill will was brought out into the open, and if the whole business was a trial for the general-in-chief there is nothing in what he said and wrote to show that it was getting him down. On July 12, when the whole steaming mess was coming to a boil, Grant wrote to Julia casually remarking that most of his staff officers were sick. Joe Bowers and William Rowley, one of Grant's military secretaries, had had to go on leave, Badeau was "laying quite unwell," three others had fallen ill, and "the fact is I am the only one at Head Quarters who has not had a day's sickness since the campaign commenced." Meanwhile, he wanted the children to go to good schools, and Julia must see to it that Fred studied his French. The problems of high command were nothing to bother Julia with, and a week later he assured her that "Richmond will fall before we quit here, but cannot say how soon. Until Richmond does fall I do not expect to go home." [12]

The fall of Richmond was a long way off, and although Grant as always was confident he was learning that the problems of high command were exceedingly intricate. To end the intolerable deadlock along the Potomac he had proposed Franklin for the top command. Finding that this was impossible, he proposed Meade, which brought no response except a summons to talk to the President at the first opportunity. On July 31, the day after the wretched fiasco of the crater, Grant went to Fort Monroe, saw President Lincoln, and learned many things, none of them very helpful.

Neither Lincoln nor Grant ever said much about their July 31 meeting, but what took place is fairly clear. On July 30 Grant had telegraphed to the President, promising to meet him at Fort Monroe the next day, and on the back of this telegram Lincoln scribbled a few words that could only be a listing of the points to be discussed. These words were:

Meade & Franklin / McClellan / Md & Penna

The "Meade & Franklin" bit came first. Lincoln apparently told Grant what Grant already knew: he could not have Franklin. Then he went on to Meade, asking Grant whether Meade would accept the appointment. Grant had mentioned it to Meade a few days earlier, and had received no reply except the remark that Meade was "ready to obey any order that might be given me." Actually, Meade rather liked the idea; he told his wife that "so far as having an independent command, which the Army of the Potomac is not, I would like this change very well," although he confessed that the notion of taking charge of all the different generals who held forth in the Washington area and dealing directly with Stanton and Halleck was somewhat sobering. In any case, the President pointed out that in recent months there had been a good deal of agitation for Meade's dismissal, and if the transfer were made now it would look as if the President had given way under pressure. Butler seems to have had a part in this agitation. When the row between him and Smith was at its height he wrote to Mrs. Butler: "Meade fears for his place — I do not want it, but I will have him out." However all of this may have been, Grant after his chat with Lincoln gave no more thought to the plan for sending Meade to the Potomac.[13]

That Lincoln included a "Md & Penna" item is not surprising. He understood the need for a unified command and was ready to go along with it, the only question being the choice of the man to hold that command. It is here that his jotted "McClellan" becomes of interest. A note in Marsena Patrick's catchall diary of headquarters understandings provides a clue. Shortly after this meeting, Patrick wrote:

"The same proposition of consolidation was urged in behalf of McClellan by very strong Republicans for two reasons. One, that by giving him military position it would dispose of him politically — the other, that his name would bring forward a host of volunteers." Patrick added that "the plan was rejected at Washington," but either the rejection had not yet been made final, or some of Lincoln's official family had not got the word. More was going on here than Patrick realized.

The Democrats were to hold their convention at the end of August in Chicago, and it was generally assumed that McClellan was going to be the nominee. Various Republican leaders wanted to head this off; and in May Postmaster General Montgomery Blair had begun writing letters to the New York financier and Democratic party notable, S. L. M. Barlow, who was close to McClellan. In these letters Blair had suggested a clever deal: let the Democrats and moderate Republicans make common cause against the Republican radicals, uniting behind Lincoln, with McClellan removing himself from the political race and for recompense accepting a high command in the army. This would ensure Lincoln's reelection, and would also be good for McClellan: "He is young, and there is a great future opening to one of his genius and antecedents" — and, in fine, he could run for the presidency after the war was over and Lincoln had finished his second term.

Barlow said that Thurlow Weed, Republican leader in New York, had made the same suggestion to him, and later in the summer he told McClellan that reliable sources said Lincoln was looking for Democratic support, offering to put McClellan back in high command in return. On July 20 — less than two weeks before Lincoln and Grant had their meeting — one of Barlow's informants reported that Francis P. Blair, Senior, was in New York, trying to get an appointment with McClellan. This appointment Blair presently got, and he urged McClellan to apply for a military assignment, remarking that if Lincoln refused to give it to him "he would then be responsible for the consequences." McClellan gave him a noncommittal answer, and if the plan interested him he never did anything about it. Presumably he thought it best to go ahead with the political race, especially since the war was going badly and a useful political issue was the fact that McClellan was not being used. (Barlow had wondered if anyone "will forgive Mr. Lincoln for the monstrous crime of permitting the great fight of the war to take place without the benefit of his personality?" [14])

This bears all the earmarks of a deal that is a little too clever. The Blairs often promised more than they could deliver, and Weed was not the only high Republican to fall into a panic this summer. That Lincoln himself took much stock in this gambit is doubtful. But he knew about it, and he would not have put McClellan's name on the agenda if he had not intended to discuss the matter with Grant.

And there it was. Grant could not make a routine military appointment without reflecting on the presidential election; indeed, the political tide was so strong and so confusing that routine military acts all became extraordinary, as if something great had to be fought out in men's minds before anyone could act on the battlefield.

A peace movement was going on, and General Meade remarked that "the camp is full of rumors and reports of many kinds" as a result. The movement was largely the creation of Horace Greeley, the hard-war abolitionist editor of the New York *Tribune*, who occasionally carried a pundit's eccentricity to excess and who now had gone off on a tangent. Greeley somehow had got in touch with Confederate agents in Canada and had absorbed the idea that Lincoln could end the war if he would just sit down and talk reasonably with reasonable Confederates about a peace that would be honorable and satisfying to both sides. Greeley wrote despairingly to Lincoln about "our bleeding, bankrupt, almost dying country," he failed to realize that the only peace Richmond wanted was one that saved both Southern independence and Southern slavery . . . and unfortunately he did not know that the Confederates in Canada had no authorization to talk to Lincoln about anything. Lincoln called his bluff, giving Greeley full power to bring the supposed Confederate emissaries to the White House; Greeley finally learned that he had been talking to the wrong people and went away sorrowing, aware that he had been had and feeling that the President had been too stiff-necked. It all came to nothing, but it was one of the things that had to be thought about when the military campaign was up for discussion.[15]

Another was the state of mind of the Republican radicals — the real radicals, harder and less eccentric than Greeley: the people the Blairs wanted to beat. Lincoln had just applied a pocket veto to the Wade-Davis bill, in which Senator Ben Wade of Ohio and Congressman

Henry Winter Davis of Maryland, radicals who burned with an undying flame, had persuaded Congress to lay down stern terms for the eventual restoration of the Union. (It would never be restored on anybody's terms until somebody got Jubal Early away from the Potomac, but the point was not raised.) Lincoln announced that the measure would never become law with his consent, but remarked that any repentant Southern state that wanted to come back into the Union on the Wade-Davis terms could do so, and all of this put the bill's authors into a great fury. On August 5 they issued a formal manifesto, attacking Lincoln with unmeasured venom. What they and their followers would have said if McClellan had been restored to a high military command just then goes beyond the reach of any normal imagination. Anyway, here was another point to consider.

Which brought to mind, inevitably, General Butler. Nobody really knew what Butler was up to — to this day, nobody really knows — but he was both a hard-war man, a Democrat, and a politician who appealed powerfully to the radicals, and the situation offered possibilities. General Patrick noted that Butler visited Meade on July 20, and wrote: "He has been offered the Chicago nomination and is playing everyone to get some power over each individual." Nobody had actually "offered" Butler anything, but anything could happen, and if he went off the reservation he could almost certainly keep Lincoln from being reelected. His chief of staff, Colonel Shaffer, went to New York to take soundings, and on August 17 he wrote to Butler assuring him that "the country has gone to hell unless Mr. Lincoln can be beat by a good loyal man."

Shaffer's analysis offers a picture of the frenzy that had come upon the political scene. If the Democrats nominated a peace man, said Shaffer, the Republican leaders felt that the Republicans ought to have a new convention and name a candidate other than Lincoln, who was both too warlike for the peace-minded and too lacking in grimness for the warlike. Shaffer said that Thurlow Weed, Seward's political guardian and the Republican boss in New York, "thinks Lincoln can be prevailed upon to draw off," and he added that the same feeling had been expressed by Leonard Swett of Illinois, one of the group that had rammed Lincoln's nomination through the 1860 convention. The leading Republicans, as Shaffer sized things up, agreed that Lincoln must withdraw as soon as the Democratic convention was over: "Nearly all speak of you as the man" — remember, this letter was addressed to Butler — "but I studiously avoid bringing your name in." The most that could be expected of Lincoln, Shaffer concluded, was that he would help keep other men from running, thereby preserving a clear path for Butler . . . and if someone, somewhere, had quietly dangled a carrot in front of General Butler's nose, it can only be said that this was that kind of summer; to which might be added the reminder that Grant did rescind Order No. 225.[16]

It was that kind of summer. Everything interlocked; the Army of the Potomac, having been built to a political pattern, reflected the doubt and suspicion politics had created, so that failure was fated. Four days before the battle of the crater, General Patrick had a long talk with Meade and foresaw disaster because of "the jealousy on the part of Corps Commanders against each other & against Meade — especially the bad blood that exists between Meade & Burnside — preventing unanimity of counsels, or concert of action, even among the troops belonging to the Army of the Potomac." Patrick went on to say: "The same spirit alluded to . . . so hostile to Burnside will prevent Meade, probably, from taking hold with any vim to carry out Burnside's idea of an assault following the explosion of his mine; which if a successful 'Blow up' as it seems to me can be followed up by an assault which will carry everything before it." Patrick believed after this chat that both Grant and his advisers recognized "the feeling in the North & East that Grant has failed in this campaign" and said that the administration was looking for a scapegoat.

Patrick to be sure was a gossipmonger, but the feeling he detected was caught by others. An army surgeon, Dr. John H. Brinton, who had known Grant from the old days at Cairo and now was on duty around Washington, wrote at this time that Grant "had not many friends amongst the Army of the Potomac men. They were all McClellan men, and insisted that Grant was only treading the same path followed by McClellan and that his bloody victories were fruitless. They did not like him and had no confidence in him. The Northern people as a mass believed in him; the Eastern, especially the troops of the Army of the Potomac, did not." Congressman James Ashley of Ohio warned Rawlins in mid-July that having visited the army he found "a good deal of discontent and mutinous spirit among staff officers of the Army of the Potomac," and said that "a good deal of McClellanism . . . was manifested." General Warren was writing angrily that "the popular idea of Grant is, I believe, very wrong . . .

To sit unconcerned on a log, away from the battlefield whittling — to be a man on horseback or smoking a cigar — seems to exhaust the admiration of the country; and if this is really just, then Nero fiddling over burning Rome is sublime."

The feeling of a certain part of the officer corps was summed up by Lieutenant Colonel Carswell McClellan, who had served on General Humphrey's staff up to the opening of this campaign. Grant, said Colonel McClellan, just did not understand the Army of the Potomac:

"The army was composed of citizens of our entire Union — men of the North and South, and East and West, stood side by side in its ranks and led its columns. The conquering of 'sectional feeling' was the very duty that had called out and created, from an untrained mass of patriots, an army of loyal veterans — 'the grandest army gathered on this continent, at all times true to its commander-in-chief, whoever it might be.' There was no vain boasting in the grim story written all along the way from the James river up to Gettysburg" — that is, in the army's story in the days before Grant — and although the soldiers did have prejudices they were solidly loyal to the Union, "however blind they may have been to the personal identity of 'that Western man' with the cause for which they fought." [17]

Grant and Lincoln shared something, here. They were westerners, lacking in polish, unable to impress the cultivated easterners. Early in the war Lincoln's minister to Great Britain, Charles Francis Adams, had shuddered visibly when he went to the White House and actually saw the ungainly man who had appointed him and who had so little in common with the Adamses who had lived in the White House. This spring Richard Henry Dana, Jr., also of Massachusetts, had had a similar seizure when he first looked upon General Grant. The East had trouble adjusting itself to the fact that the rude West was dominant. Lincoln and Grant fitted each other perfectly, but to easterners they looked like a gawky ill-chosen team.

Grant's people returned this antagonism, with interest added. Early in August one of Grant's assistant adjutants general, Captain George K. Leet, wrote to the absent Colonel William R. Rowley: "My faith in the Army of the Potomac is gone, gone. Parker says, 'I have had the biggest kind of disgust and dare not express myself on the Potomac Army.' Hudson thinks the Army of the Potomac won't do to tie to." A little later this summer Grenville Dodge spent some time at headquarters, recovering from a wound received in the fighting in front of

Atlanta, and when he visited various corps and division commanders'
tents "discovered a feeling that was a stranger to us in the West — a
feeling, the existence of which seemed to me to bode no good." Everybody was criticizing either the commanding general or some fellow officer, and Dodge said that although he had never heard this sort
of talk in the western army "I must say I heard it in the Army of the
Potomac, and anything but kindly comments by one commander
upon another, and as this was in the dark days of the war I had many
misgivings about what I had heard." He talked about it with Rawlins,
he said, and Rawlins laughed and replied: "General, this is not the old
Army of the Tennessee." [18]

It was not; which was one reason why some of the things Grant
could do in the west could not quite be done here in the east. As he
had guessed a year earlier, this army was too close to Washington,
physically and spiritually, victimized by politics and at the same time
contributing to the force that victimized it. Never for an instant could
anyone forget — as it could be forgotten, now and then, in the west
— that the army had been forged for use in a *civil* war and hence was
as much subject to political pressure as the Post Office or the Treasury
Department. This fact governed everything a commanding general
did.

Except that once in a great while he could ignore it. In a way his
chief responsibility was to recognize and use that once-in-a-while moment when it came.

When Grant had his talk with Lincoln at Fort Monroe, the command situation along the upper Potomac had become intolerable, and
if a solution was not found at this meeting it had to be found immediately afterward. Grant no sooner got back to City Point on July 31
than he got a wire from Halleck saying that Jubal Early had gone
north of the Potomac again and was on his way to Pennsylvania.

This was not entirely unexpected. Early had been edging forward
into the lower part of the Shenandoah Valley for a week, occupying
Martinsburg, sending cavalry squadrons across at Williamsport, Falling Waters and Shepherdstown, and driving Yankee cavalry out of
Hagerstown. Grant believed that although the Federal commanders
— Halleck, Hunter, Wright or whoever — had plenty of troops
they were short of good cavalry, and on the day of the crater battle he
ordered Meade to send a division of Sheridan's cavalry north at once.

Far from taking his main force over the river, Early was just sending cavalry north on a raid, but because this raid touched sensitive political nerves the result might be as harmful to the Union cause as a major battle lost. Early's men believed they had a score to settle with the Yankees because Hunter's troops had burned so many Virginia homes, and on July 30 a Rebel cavalry brigade led by General John McCausland cantered into Chambersburg, Pennsylvania, set fire to the place, and rode off to the west and south, leaving half of the town in ashes. This was in good Republican Pennsylvania with the presidential election only three months away, and if General Grant could not find someone to wage successful war along the Potomac none of his other achievements was likely to mean very much.[19]

On the night of the victory at Chattanooga there had been one general who wanted to press on until the last of the enemy's forces had been broken down and stamped on, and now Grant thought of him. On August 1 Grant told Meade he was going to send Phil Sheridan north, and he got off this telegram to Halleck:

I am sending General Sheridan for temporary duty whilst the enemy is being expelled from the border. Unless General Hunter is in the field in person, I want Sheridan put in command of all the troops in the field, with instructions to put himself south of the enemy and follow him to the death. Wherever the enemy goes let our troops go also. Once started up the Valley they ought to be followed until we get possession of the Virginia Central railroad. If General Hunter is in the field give Sheridan direct command of the Sixth Corps and cavalry division.

On the heels of this Grant had Meade order the second of the army's three cavalry divisions to go north.

Neither Stanton nor Halleck approved of this appointment. Stanton thought Sheridan was altogether too young for such an important assignment, and when Sheridan got to Washington his reception at the War Department was frosty. Halleck warned Grant that if Sheridan were placed in general command Hunter would ask to be relieved, and he added that if this did not happen it would be bad practice to make the Sixth Corps and the cavalry a separate command . . . and altogether there was a good deal of clucking. Abraham Lincoln heard the clucking, and agreed that Sheridan was rather young; but under everything Lincoln also heard the hard ring of trumpets in Grant's order regarding Sheridan, and on August 3 he sent Grant a telegram:

I have seen your dispatch in which you say "I want Sheridan put in command of all the troops in the field, with instructions to put himself south of the enemy and follow him to the death. Wherever the enemy goes let our troops go also." This, I think, is exactly right as to how our forces should move, but please look over the dispatches you may have received from here even since you made that order, and discover, if you can, that there is any idea in the head of anyone here of "putting our army south of the enemy" or of "following him to the death" in any direction. I repeat to you it will neither be done nor attempted unless you watch it every day and hour and force it.[20]

And now suddenly the great crisis of indecision and divided counsels was ended, and the fact that it had ended was as good as a victory. What Grant did that evening illustrated the oddly contradictory aspects of the role he had to play as general-in-chief.

First of all, he ordered a dispatch boat to get up steam for a quick voyage up the bay; he would be on his way to the upper Potomac in less than two hours from the moment he got Lincoln's telegram, not to leave until the situation there had been arranged the way he wanted it. Yet if he was riding through this crisis roughshod in response to a blunt warning from the President, he was at the same moment moving through another crisis on tiptoe, neither shod nor mounted, going as softly as any cat; for he had been unable to remove Ben Butler, and in his absence Butler was going to be in sole command against General Lee. Before boarding his dispatch boat Grant bowed to the necessities of this situation by composing a delicate note for Butler's guidance:

"I find it necessary for me to go to Washington for a day or two to give direction to affairs there. In my absence remain on the defensive, notifying General Meade that if attacked he is authorized to call on such of your troops as are south of the Appomattox. Only expecting to be gone three days I will not relinquish command. But being senior you necessarily would command in any emergency. Please communicate with me by telegraph if anything occurs where you wish my orders." To make such communication easier, Grant pointed out that he was leaving his adjutant general and most of his headquarters staff on duty at City Point.[21]

He had had to compromise, clearly enough, and if Sheridan was going to the Potomac Butler was remaining at Bermuda Hundred; and it would be a few days before all hands realized just what had happened. Among those who were slow to get the word was bumbling

General Franklin, who wrote to his crony Baldy Smith on August 2 in the innocent belief that he and Smith were both still alive. Franklin suspected that Lee would soon invade the north with a considerable force, he reflected that command of Federal troops along the Potomac would be an interesting assignment, and on the whole he was willing to take that assignment, and he told Smith: "If we had a decent force I would not object to taking the command Grant mentions, and if you will take the Shenandoah Valley in charge I think we could make a good thing of it, though there may be hard fighting." [22]

CHAPTER EIGHTEEN

The Hundred-Gun Salutes

G RANT reached the Federal camp on the Monocacy River, forty miles northwest of Washington, on the evening of August 5. Awaiting him there, expecting nothing from him or from anyone else, were between 25,000 and 30,000 Federal soldiers — frustrated men drawn from three armies, sullenly awaiting the touch that would make a new army of them. Right now their only unity was a common knowledge that for the past month they had marched far and hard to no especial purpose. In command of them, and sharing to the full their awareness of wasted effort, was Major General David Hunter, and when Grant that evening asked him where the enemy might be General Hunter confessed that he had no idea. He said that he had received so many orders from the War Department recently, telling him to go from this place to that place and then on to some other place, that he had lost all track of the people he was supposed to fight.

The one thing he knew was that Jubal Early's Confederates had not gone south. A little more than a week earlier they had driven Hunter's advance out of the lower Shenandoah Valley, and now they were believed to be arrayed somewhere near the Potomac, tying up the main line of the Baltimore & Ohio Railroad, sending cavalry raiders off into Pennsylvania, retaining command of the river crossings; full of evil intentions. The Federals on the Monocacy were protecting Washington faithfully enough, but they were not doing much of anything else.

Grant remarked that he would quickly find out where the Confederates were, and he ordered a general advance of the entire force to the hamlet of Halltown, south of the Potomac, four miles southwest of Harpers Ferry. Whatever General Early was doing, he was certain to respond to a Federal advance; Grant suspected correctly that as soon as Early heard of this move he would concentrate his own force some-where near Martinsburg. If he tried to invade the North again, the army at Halltown would be ideally posted to get south of him (as Grant had prescribed) and follow him to the death. Having put the troops in motion — some of them took to the road that evening — Grant sat down to write out instructions governing their use.

Basically, these instructions were simple: find out where the enemy is and then go and get him. The Shenandoah Valley was to be taken away from Confederate use permanently, so that it could never again be an avenue for raiders nor a granary for Lee's army, and the orders were grim:

In pushing up the Shenandoah Valley, as it is expected you will have to do first or last, it is desirable that nothing should be left to invite the enemy to return. Take all provisions, forage and stock wanted for the use of your command. Such as cannot be consumed, destroy. It is not desir-able that the buildings should be destroyed — they should, rather, be pro-tected; but the people should be informed that so long as an army can subsist among them recurrences of these raids must be expected, and we are determined to stop them at all hazards.

Bear in mind, the object is to drive the enemy south; and to do this you want to keep him always in sight. [In short — no more of this business of moving from one defensive position to another until you do not know where the enemy is.] Be guided in your course by the course he takes.

Make your own arrangements for supplies of all kinds, giving regular vouchers for such as may be taken from loyal citizens in the country through which you march.

The idea of laying waste the rich farming region of the valley so that it could no longer support Confederate armies or the Confederate capital had been formulated earlier. On July 14 Grant had written Halleck that when Early left Maryland he should be pursued up the valley by all available troops, who should be instructed to "eat out Virginia clear and clean as far as they go, so that crows flying over it for the balance of the season will have to carry their provender with them." This drew added point now from the fact that for a fortnight Early's troops had been actively helping to harvest crops in the lower valley, with details crossing the Potomac now and then to seize grain the Maryland farmers had already harvested. All along, Early's expe-dition had been partly controlled by the needs of the Confederate commissary.

Having written out the orders, Grant went on to a more delicate matter. Hunter commanded the Department of West Virginia, and so all troops in that part of the country would be under him. But Sheridan was going to be the field commander, answerable to no one but Grant, and Grant now suggested that Hunter make his own headquarters at Cumberland, or at Baltimore, or somewhere else, and let the field commander operate without his direction. This of course was the approach that had been tried so unsuccessfully with Ben Butler; the difference now was that Hunter was not disposed to fight about it. Hunter had grown so discouraged by War Department interference that he told Grant he would like to be relieved altogether; that way he would be spared embarrassment, and the War Department would not have to use an officer it distrusted. Grant agreed with him, and in his *Memoirs* noted that Hunter had shown "a patriotism that was none too common in the army" by surrendering an important command simply because someone else could fill it better.

Having attended to this, Grant wrote out a new order putting the four military departments in the Washington and Potomac area into the hands of a sort of holding company known as the Middle Military Division, and naming Sheridan as its temporary commander; then he telegraphed Sheridan, in Washington, to come to the Monocacy camp at once.[1]

Sheridan got to the camp on August 6, and his interview with Grant was brief. Grant gave him the letter of instructions which he had written the day before for Hunter, telling him that this was to guide his conduct of operations. He explained the concentration at Halltown — by the time Sheridan arrived, hardly any troops remained on the Monocacy — and inside of two hours Sheridan was on his way to the front and Grant was heading back to City Point.

He had met and passed a crisis; that is, he had reasserted his own control of military affairs, which is exactly what Lincoln had wanted him to do. Joe Bowers, who went to the Monocacy with Grant, wrote a letter to Rawlins explaining what Grant had accomplished: "He has settled Halleck down to a mere staff officer for Stanton. Halleck has no control over troops except as Grant delegates it. He can give no orders and exercise no discretion. Grant now runs the whole machine independently of the Washington directory. I am glad to say he is fully himself, works vigorously, and will soon devise another plan for discomfiting all the enemies of the country." Even more significantly,

Bowers wrote to his friend Rowley that Grant had told Sheridan "to drive Early out of the Valley and to receive orders from no live man but Grant himself." [2]

Writing to Julia, Grant was quite matter-of-fact about the whole affair: "I went out to Monocacy, Md., set our troops all in motion, placing in command an officer, Gen. Sheridan, in whom I have great confidence." He almost seemed to be giving more thought just then to the matter of finding a good place in the east where Julia and the children might live within visiting distance of City Point, and while he was dealing with Hunter he sent Colonel Porter off to Princeton, N.J., to see whether a good house might not be rented there. He assured Julia that if nothing could be found in Princeton they might settle in Philadelphia, which struck him as a pleasant place to live; meanwhile, he would try to find time to see the paymaster and draw a month's pay, and if he did this he would send her a thousand dollars: "I have enough on hand to last me a month yet." [3] Musing thus on domestic affairs as the dispatch boat carried him down the river and the bay, Grant was back at City Point on August 9 — and before that morning ended he had as narrow an escape from violent death as he had at any time during the war.

Shortly before noon Grant was sitting in front of his tent on the high ground overlooking the army wharves, talking with General George H. Sharpe, Assistant Provost Marshal General; and Sharpe had just finished saying that he was convinced that Rebel spies were doing nefarious things in and around the City Point camp when an ammunition barge moored just below the bluff exploded with a gigantic crash that reminded people of the Petersburg mine, throwing live shells, fragments of timber, boxes of rifle ammunition and other bits of military hardware all over the space where the headquarters tents were pitched. A mounted orderly at headquarters was killed, three more were wounded, Lieutenant Colonel O. E. Babcock of Grant's staff was struck in the hand by a shell splinter, and down on the docks there was a shambles, with 43 men dead and 126 injured. Joe Bowers wrote that fragments of human bodies were found a quarter of a mile from the scene of the explosion, and added: "Such a rain of shot, shell, bullets, pieces of wood, iron bars and bolts, chains and missiles of every kind was never before witnessed. It was terrible — awful — terrific." Horace Porter remarked that at least one hundred shells exploded in the camp.

Porter was still on his Princeton mission at this time, but he returned a day or so later and was named head of a board to investigate the disaster. Inasmuch as everyone on the barge that exploded had been killed, along with almost everybody else in the immediate vicinity, the board could find no witnesses who had any direct knowledge of the disaster, and although the officers strongly suspected that enemy agents had had a hand in the matter they never could prove it. After the war, however, the mystery was dispelled, when the authorities came upon a report written at the time by one John Maxwell, an agent of the Confederate secret service, who told just what had happened.

Maxwell said that early that morning he and another agent had crept through the Union picket lines carrying a box containing twelve pounds of powder and a clockwork mechanism to set it off. Watching the wharf from a distance, they waited until they saw the skipper of the ordnance barge go ashore; then, as soon as he was out of sight, Maxwell told his companion to wait for him, picked up the box, and as matter-of-fact as any express messenger sauntered up and told the sentry on the wharf that the captain had ordered him to deliver this package aboard the barge. The soldier accepted the story and Maxwell walked to the gangplank, unobtrusively set the time-bomb mechanism, gave the box to a deckhand and said the captain wanted it stowed below, and then walked briskly away from there. He was just nicely out of range when the explosion occurred, and he and his partner were back within their own lines before anyone started looking for them. Attached to Maxwell's report was an endorsement by the Confederacy's expert on mine warfare, General G. J. Rains: "John Maxwell is a bold operator and well calculated for such exploits, and also his coadjutor, R. K. Dillard." [4] Bold operator, indeed!

Army intelligence had learned something but not quite enough about the activities of Rebel saboteurs; in the same way it brought back inexact information about Lee's response to the news that Grant had sent troops to the valley. During the first week in August, Lee sent a division of infantry and a division of cavalry to Culpeper, east of the Blue Ridge, with instructions to watch the Yankees and help Early if he needed help. Federal intelligence got a twisted version of this and reported that three infantry divisions had gone north; and it was obvious that Lee could not send that much infantry away without seriously weakening himself. Partly to take advantage of this supposed weakness and partly to keep Lee from strengthening Early to the point where Sheridan could not handle him, Grant ordered a new offensive on the north side of the James River.

This was virtually a rerun of the movement Hancock had made just before the explosion of the Petersburg mine; once again, Hancock was in charge, moving up toward Lee's extreme left with infantry poised to make a breakthrough if it found an opening and cavalry ready to swing out past the flank and cut the Virginia Central Railroad. Hancock got his force north of the James on August 14 and went to work, only to learn that the Confederates had three divisions where Federal intelligence had said there would be only one. The movement was a flat failure, neither cavalry nor infantry could carry out its assignments, there was hard fighting in which the Federals lost 2,700 men, and Hancock had to report that some of his troops had not behaved well. They had been put into action clumsily against heavier numbers than they had been expected to meet, their ranks contained a great many untrained recruits, by this time Hancock's corps was pathetically short of veteran officers — and altogether the attempt to find a quick way into Richmond went no better than earlier ones had gone.[5]

Nevertheless, the offensive paid off. Like Hancock's similar move three weeks earlier, this thrust forced Lee to weaken his right, south of Petersburg, and on the morning of August 18 Grant took advantage of this by having Meade send Warren with four divisions out past Fort Sedgwick and west to the Weldon Railroad, duplicating the thrust that had been tried without success on June 22. This time it worked. Warren took possession of the road near Globe Tavern, four miles south of Petersburg. That afternoon and all of the next day the Confederates counterattacked violently, catching one of Warren's divisions off-balance and capturing nearly the whole of two brigades of troops, but in the end the Federals held their ground. Warren's new trenches were connected with the Federal lines east of Petersburg and Grant at last had permanent possession of a segment of one of Lee's vital railroads.

This did not mean quite as much as it might have meant, because the break was a short one and the Confederates quickly set up a line of wagon transport to carry goods to Petersburg from a railhead just south of the point of Federal occupation. To interfere with this, Grant on August 22 sent Hancock, with two infantry divisions and some cavalry, out to destroy the Weldon Railroad as far south as Rowanty Creek, some thirteen miles below Warren's position. If this move succeeded, Lee's wagon trains would have to come up roundabout over a thirty-mile pull by way of Dinwiddie Courthouse, and Lee moved vigorously to meet the threat. On August 25 Hill's corps struck Hancock's divisions at Ream's Station, five miles south of Warren's position, and after a hard fight drove the Federals away from the railroad. Once again Hancock had to report that some of his troops — John Gibbon's division, once one of the best in the army — had fought poorly, and Hancock finally had to retreat after more than 1,700 of his men had been captured. Significantly, it was the untrained replacement troops that had failed so dismally. Veterans who were present fought as well as ever; the trouble was that by this time a dismayingly high proportion of the Second Corps was recruits.[6]

The Ream's Station move, in short, had failed, and it was clear that the Second Corps could not be used for offensive work for some time to come. Yet if there had been repulse and heavy loss on two of these three offensives the Federals nevertheless had made a net gain; tactically unsuccessful, they had won a strategic success. The Weldon road after all had been broken, Warren's corps held the ground it had taken, and the flow of supplies to Confederate army and capital had been permanently reduced. At the very time when Lee was being taxed to the utmost to hold too long a line with too small an army, he was compelled to make the line even longer. By striking north and south of the James at the same time, Grant was developing a technique that tried his opponent to the utmost. Moreover, he was achieving all of this at a time when his own numbers were surprisingly low. At the end of August, Meade's three infantry corps contained an effective strength of only 28,900 officers and men, while the infantry effectives in Butler's army numbered hardly more than 17,000. Never had the margin over Lee been so small — and never had there been less substance to the charge that Grant was fighting a war of attrition based on his possession of unlimited numbers.[7]

That the increasing Federal pressure was having its effect is clear from the letters Lee wrote during August. On August 22 he told President Davis:

As I informed your Excellency when we first reached Petersburg, I was doubtful of our ability to hold the Weldon road so as to use it. The proximity of the enemy and his superiority of numbers rendered it possible for him to break the road at any time, and even if we could drive him from the position he now holds we could not prevent him from returning to it or to some other point, as our strength is inadequate to guard the whole road. These considerations induced me to abandon the prosecution of the effort to dislodge the enemy.

I think it is his purpose to endeavor to compel the evacuation of our present position by cutting off our supplies, and that he will not renew the attempt to drive us away by force . . . It behooves us to do everything in our power to thwart his new plan of reducing us by starvation.

The day after he wrote this, Lee warned Secretary of War Seddon that his need for reinforcements was most pressing: "Unless some measures can be devised to replace our losses, the consequences may be disastrous . . . Without some increase of our strength I cannot see how we are to escape the natural military consequence of the enemy's numerical superiority." And to Davis, on September 2, Lee sent firsthand testimony about the effectiveness of Grant's recent activities:

The enemy's position enables him to move his troops to right or left without our knowledge, until he has reached the point at which he aims, and we are then compelled to hurry our men to meet him, incurring the risk of being too late to check his progress and the additional risk of the advantage he may derive from their absence. This was fully illustrated in the late demonstration north of the James river, which called troops from our lines here who if present might have prevented the occupation of the Weldon railroad.[8]

What all of this meant was that the Federals held a winning advantage if they continued to apply the pressure. Lee understood this and so did Grant, but there were many in the North who did not and the war might yet be lost if those who did not understand got panicky. In the middle of August General Halleck, for example, wrote to Grant to say that the term of service of many regiments of hundred-day soldiers was about to expire. These troops had been used extensively to guard supply depots, railway lines, prison camps and other points that could not be left unguarded, and now it might be necessary to withdraw troops from the main armies to take their places. Worse yet, a sinister combination was forming to resist the draft — in New York, Pennsylvania, Indiana, Kentucky and elsewhere — and it seemed likely that the projected draft of 300,000 men could not be held unless combat troops were sent to the rear to suppress disorder and overawe the copperheads. Consequently, asked Halleck: "Are not the appearances such that we ought to take in sail and prepare the ship for a storm?"

As far as Grant could see that storm was already at its height, and his reply was uncompromising:

"If there is any danger of an uprising in the North to resist the draft or for any other purpose our loyal Governors ought to organize the militia at once to resist it. If we are to draw troops from the field to keep the loyal states in harness it will prove difficult to suppress the rebellion in the disloyal states. My withdrawal now from the James River would insure the defeat of Sherman." This threat, in short, must be met by the individual states.

This drew an immediate response from President Lincoln, who telegraphed Grant: "I HAVE SEEN YOUR DESPATCH EXPRESSING YOUR UNWILLINGNESS TO BREAK YOUR HOLD WHERE YOU ARE. NEITHER AM I WILLING. HOLD ON WITH A BULLDOG GRIP, AND CHEW AND CHOKE AS MUCH AS POSSIBLE." Something about the President's wording tickled Grant, and when he finished reading it he broke into laughter — a rare thing, for although he smiled and chuckled a good deal he hardly ever laughed aloud. Staff officers came over to see what had struck him so, and he handed them the telegram and remarked: "The President has more nerve than any of his advisers." [9]

Grant set forth his understanding of the situation in a revealing letter to Congressman Washburne, written the day after he sent the stiff note to Halleck. After remarking that the weather was so hot that "marching troops is nearly death," Grant got down to it:

I state to all Citizens who visit me that all we want now to insure an early restoration of the Union is a determined unity of sentiment North. The rebels have now in their ranks their last man. The little boys and old men are guarding prisoners, rail-road bridges and forming a good part of their garrisons for intrenched positions. A man lost by them cannot be replaced. They have robbed the Cradle and the grave equally to get their present force. Besides what they lose in frequent skirmishes and battles they are now loosing from desertions and other causes at least one regiment per day. With this drain upon them the end is visible if we will be true to ourselves. Their only hope now is in a divided North. This might give them reinforcements from Tenn. Ky. Maryland and Mo. whilst it would weaken us. With the draft quietly enforced the enemy would become dispondent and would make but little resistance.

I have no doubt but the enemy are exceedingly anxious to hold out until after the Presidential election. They have many hopes from its effects. They hope for a counter revolution. They hope for the election of the peace Candidate. In fact, like McCawber, they hope *something* to turn up.

Our peace friends, if they expect peace from separation, are much mistaken. It would be but the beginning of war with thousands of Northern men joining the South because of our disgrace allowing separation. To have peace "on any terms" the South would demand the restoration of their slaves already freed. They would demand indemnity for losses sustained, and they would demand a treaty which would make the North slave hunters for the South. They would demand pay or the restoration of every slave escaping to the North.

Two days later Grant put the same thoughts into briefer compass in a letter to his boyhood friend, the naval officer Dan Ammen. After giving Ammen a sketch of the unsuccessful attempts to take Petersburg, Grant continued:

We will peg away, however, and end this matter if our people at home will be but true to themselves. If they would but reflect, everything looks favorable. The South now have every man in the ranks, including old men and little boys. They have no longer means to replace a man lost; whilst by enforcing the draft, we have abundance of men. Give us half the men called for by the draft and there will hardly be any resistance made. The rebellion is now fed by the bickering and differences North. The hope of a counter-revolution over the draft, or the Presidential election, keeps them together. Then, too, they hope for the election of a "peace candidate" who would let them go. "A peace at any price" is fearful to contemplate. It would be but the beginning of the war. The demands of the South would know no limits. They would demand indemnity for expenses incurred in carrying on the war. They would demand the return of all their slaves set free in consequence of war. They would demand a treaty looking to the rendition of all fugitive slaves escaping into the Northern states, and they would keep on demanding until it would be better dead than to submit longer.[10]

Although Grant had no party ties whatever he was defining strategy precisely as such Republicans as Lincoln defined it. In this completely political war there were political versions of strategy; inevitably, because the war after all was an attempt to settle a purely political problem. Grant had never been an antislavery man, but he had said long ago that the war for reunion must destroy slavery. Now he was saying that the war must be carried through to complete victory; there could never be a compromise peace, no matter how ardently people wanted one, because neither the union nor human slavery could stay just partly alive. Grant was saying almost exactly what Lincoln himself was saying on the eve of the Democratic convention. Lincoln assured two visitors from Wisconsin that "there is no program intended by the Democratic party but what will result in the dismemberment of the Union," and he continued in words that Grant might have used:

The slightest acquaintance with arithmetic will prove to any man that the Rebel armies cannot be destroyed with Democratic strategy. It would sacrifice all the white men of the North to do it . . . You cannot conciliate the South, when the mastery and control of millions of blacks makes them sure of ultimate success. You cannot conciliate the South when you place yourself in such a position that they see they can achieve their independence. The War Democrat depends upon conciliation. He must confine himself to that policy entirely.

Whether Grant and Lincoln were right or wrong in the belief that the war would be lost if a Democratic administration now took control of it, they obviously did believe it, and they were quite right in arguing that the war had to be won politically as well as on the battlefield. That was what made it necessary to put up with incompetence in command at Bermuda Hundred at the same time that it was necessary to get rid of incompetence in command on the upper Potomac — and that, in the end, was why there could not be a general in high command who was genuinely nonpartisan. McClellan like Grant was a soldier who had lost his political innocence, and this fall he was accepting the fact that there was a Republican strategy and a Democratic strategy bearing profoundly different connotations. To his friend Barlow, a little after this, McClellan wrote that "Grant has gone clean over to the enemy." McClellan had his sources of information about army politics, and he saw that a good many leading soldiers were going to keep quiet until things came to a head: "Hancock is on the fence, waiting to see which is the winning side. So will many genls, including Meade. Gibbon, Hunt, Bartlett and Patrick are perfectly sound."

As he faced all of this Grant was matter-of-fact, and he probably neither knew nor cared how the other generals felt about the election or about the terms on which peace could be made. Lincoln was in Washington, getting a different view of things, and at times what he saw was darkened by the haunted shadow which his own realism cast across his belief in democracy. On August 23 he wrote that strange, secret message predicting his own defeat and quietly put it away for future reference: "This morning, as for some days past, it seems exceedingly probable that this administration will not be re-elected. Then it will be my duty to so co-operate with the President-elect as to save the Union between the election and the inauguration; as he will have secured his election on such ground that he cannot possibly save it afterwards." [11]

What Grant could see more clearly than anyone in Washington could see was that from the military point of view the war was actually going well. Since the Virginia and Georgia campaigns opened on May 4 the Confederacy had been put under the kind of continuing strain it had never before had to endure. Something was bound to give — and now, in Georgia, the collapse was beginning to take place and the soundness of Federal strategy was being emphasized by its results.

Over and over, during two months and more, Grant had told correspondents that the Confederate armies could no longer afford to make a stand-up fight in the open field; that they dared not take risks and would fight only on the defensive, behind breastworks, because if they fought in the open they must eventually be defeated. He had said this many times, often when the outlook on his immediate front was not good, and sometimes it sounded like the empty brag a nervous man makes when he wants to keep up his own courage. Yet it had been a literal statement of the truth, and for proof of it there was the record of recent events in front of Atlanta.

Because General Joe Johnston had not been able to keep Sherman from crossing the Chattahoochee River and coming up to the very edge of the city, President Davis had removed him in mid-July and put General John B. Hood in his place. Hood's one big virtue was that he could be relied on to force the fighting, and he forced it now, valiantly and disastrously. First he attacked Sherman along the line of Peachtree Creek, and two days later he attacked him on the east side of Atlanta, over in the direction of Decatur; and on July 28, a week plus one day after the first battle, he attacked a third time west of Atlanta, at Ezra Church. Hood was beaten in each fight; worse yet, he lost something like 20,000 men, many more than he could afford to lose, and when the dead had been buried and the wounded had been hauled off to hospital it could be seen that Sherman's grip on Atlanta had not been shaken in the least; on the contrary he now had a stranglehold, and Hood was too weak to break it. Day after day Sherman extended his lines west and south of Atlanta, reaching out to cut the railroad lines (once again, it was a railroad war!) that kept city and army supplied.

Federal losses in all of this had been less than half of the Confederate loss, the costliest single item being the death of the commander of the Army of the Tennessee, General James B. McPherson, for whom both Grant and Sherman had great admiration and deep personal affection. McPherson was killed in action during the second of Hood's battles, and for temporary command Sherman called on John A. Logan, head of the Fifteenth Corps, a good soldier and a prime favorite with the enlisted men. Grant would have liked to see Logan get the assignment permanently, but Sherman wanted a professional for the top job and gave the position to Oliver O. Howard, and Grant refused to interfere. This was putting an outsider in a place held by a homegrown hero, and it was also putting a West Pointer over a political general to command soldiers who strongly preferred amateurs, and if this army had had one-half of the proud touchiness of the Army of the Potomac there would have been a fearful storm. As it was, after a few sputters everybody accepted the situation and Logan quietly returned to corps command. One unexpected result of the appointment was the resignation of Joe Hooker, who had a poor opinion of Howard and considered himself insulted when Howard was promoted to a place Hooker wanted. Sherman did not care much for Hooker and accepted his resignation without the least delay; then, just to rub Hooker's nose in it, he gave Hooker's Twentieth Corps to Henry Slocum, the one man in the United States army whom Hooker hated most. And then they all got on with the war.[12]

They did this with a good deal of vigor. Early in August Sherman assured Grant: "One thing is certain, whether we get inside of Atlanta or not it will be a used-up community when we are done with it." He brought the city under continuous fire of siege guns to implement his prediction, and sent cavalry and infantry swinging out to west and south with orders to "make a circle of desolation around Atlanta"; and at last, while the Democrats in Chicago were nominating McClellan and composing a platform based on the assumption that the war was a failure, General Hood realized that it was time to go if he wanted to get his army out alive. He had a last stiff, unsuccessful fight with Howard's troops at Jonesboro, fifteen miles south of the city, and then he marched away, setting fire to the munitions and rations he could not carry with him. Slocum's corps held the line immediately opposite Atlanta, and during the night the soldiers saw great lights flashing as repeated explosions rocked the sky: and on the morning of September 2 Slocum marched his men in past abandoned fortifications and the wreckage left by fire and bombardment, and he sent the War Department a laconic, self-effacing telegram: "GENERAL SHERMAN HAS TAKEN ATLANTA." Later in the day Sherman got off his own dispatch, with the jubilant assertion "So Atlanta is ours, and fairly won," and there was a frenzied celebration in Washington.[13]

Grant got the news on the evening of September 4, while he was sitting in a camp chair in front of his headquarters tent, smoking a cigar and chatting with members of his staff. He had that day been informed that Early's army was leaving the valley in order to help drive the Federals away from the Weldon Railroad, and although this was unconfirmed and later proved untrue it did seem likely that Lee would make another effort to break the grip on the Globe Tavern position. (Theodore Lyman had aptly remarked that "it is touching a tiger's cubs to get on that road!") Grant had alerted everybody, pointing out that if Lee did attack he would certainly weaken his defensive strength elsewhere, and he had told Federal commanders to be prepared to attack all along the line from Globe Tavern to the James River if the Confederate offensive developed. Now he got his telegram announcing Sherman's victory. He read it aloud to the officers who were within listening distance and he ordered Meade's and Butler's headquarters to have a one hundred-gun salute fired, with shotted guns, from every battery that bore on the Rebel works. While the racket from this firing rolled up and down the long front he wrote a hasty telegram of congratulations to Sherman, telling him about the salute, and a few days later he sent a slightly more extended note: "I feel you have accomplished the most gigantic undertaking given to any general in this war, and with a skill and ability that will be acknowledged in history as not surpassed, if not unequalled. It gives me as much pleasure to record this in your favor as it would in favor of any living man, myself included." [14]

The lieutenant general commanding, supposedly so taciturn, was obviously bubbling over, and there was good reason for it. The capture of Atlanta put everything done since May 4 in a new light, and suddenly it was clear that the war was not at a stalemate, after all; it was being *won*. There had been a clear breakthrough in Georgia and now there would be another in Virginia, and General Grant began to focus his attention on General Sheridan and the campaign in the Shenandoah Valley.

Sheridan had got off to a slow start. He commanded three infantry corps — Wright's, from the Army of the Potomac; William H. Emory's, from Louisiana, and George Crook's, from Hunter's old Army of West Virginia — and they were of uneven quality, far below proper strength and new to each other and to their commanding general. Because he was responsible for protecting all manner of places behind the fighting lines and beyond the mountains in West Virginia Sheridan's combat force was never anywhere near the total reported in his command in the regular monthly returns. Secretary Stanton had warned him to be cautious, because a military reverse just now would be too costly politically; and Grant himself had told him to be careful because the reinforcements Lee had sent to Early "will put him nearer on an equality with you in numbers than I want to see." The size of the force Lee forwarded was exaggerated, first by the reports from Grant's headquarters and later by Sheridan's own intelligence service, and from the very beginning Early's strength had been somewhat overestimated; and all in all more than a month passed after Sheridan's appointment with nothing much accomplished.

Sheridan began by advancing and maneuvering Early into a retreat to Fisher's Hill, twenty miles or more south of Winchester. It seemed to Sheridan that this position was too strong to be carried by assault with the force he had available, and he put his cavalry to work on the job of devastation Grant had called for in the orders originally drawn up for Hunter. As Grant saw it, this was part of the vital task of cutting off supplies for Lee's army. On August 26 he told Sheridan that Lee would probably recall troops from the valley before long because of Federal seizure of the Weldon Railroad, and he added: "Watch closely, and if you find this theory correct push with all vigor. Give the enemy no rest, and if it is possible to follow to the Virginia Central railroad, follow that far. Do all the damage to railroads and crops you can. Carry off stock of all descriptions, and Negroes so as to prevent further planting. If the war is to last another year we want the Shenandoah Valley to remain a barren waste." [15]

The destructive part of the job Sheridan carried out with energy, but push the enemy back he could not do. He learned that the reinforcements Lee had posted at Culpeper were crossing the Blue Ridge to join Early's army; his own position had no defensive strength, the reinforced Early seemed likely to go over to the offensive, and the young general sent Grant a plaintive, un-Sheridan-like message: "I should like very much to have your advice." Step by step, he withdrew along the road by which he had come, going back past Winchester to Berryville, finding that there did not seem to be a good defensive position for a Federal army anywhere south of the Potomac, and coming to rest at last near Halltown, his original starting point. His people and Early's people skirmished intermittently all along the western slope of the Blue Ridge and on the open floor of the great valley; Early took up a strong position near Winchester, behind the difficult crossings of Opequon Creek, and he sent detachments on to Martinsburg to harry the long-suffering Baltimore & Ohio Railroad once more and to threaten a new march into Maryland.

The situation apparently was about as it had been before Sheridan had been appointed. The War Department's liking for a static defensive might be satisfied — although the vigorous complaints of the B. & O. people were beginning to make even Halleck feel that Early ought to be driven away — but this was not at all what Grant had been looking for . . . and now he got a dispatch from Sheridan saying that although the Confederates could do no particular harm in their present position it would be impossible for him to resume the offensive unless Early sent troops back to Lee.

As a matter of fact this was about to happen. The extension of line forced on Lee by Federal operations in the middle of August left Lee badly pressed for manpower, and now he called for the return of General J. B. Kershaw's infantry division — the same which had taken position at Culpeper and whose appearance in the valley, the size of it grossly magnified by inexact reporting, had induced Sheridan to retreat from in front of Fisher's Hill. Grant did not know that this was happening but he knew that Lee had to hold his Petersburg-Richmond lines and that he could not be strong there and in the Shenandoah as well; and anyway it was time to break things up, wherever the strength lay, and on September 14 Grant set off to see Sheridan face-to-face, "to have him attack Early or drive him out of the Valley and destroy that source of supplies for Lee's army." In his *Memoirs* Grant remarked that he had to do this by personal interview because he had to avoid War Department interference: "I knew it was impossible for me to get orders through Washington to Sheridan to make a move, because they would be stopped there and such orders as Halleck's caution (and that of the Secretary of War) would suggest would be given instead and would, no doubt, be contradictory to mine." To an extent, this remark may have reflected the distaste which Grant developed after the war for both Halleck and Stanton; yet it had some substance, because Stanton at all times kept firm personal control over the military telegraph lines, messages from Grant to commanders in the field passed through his hands, and delays and alterations of text were not unheard-of.

In any case, Grant curtly notified Halleck that he was not going to stop in Washington on this trip unless the President or the Secretary of War insisted on it, and he added: "Everything is very quiet here and all indications are that it will remain so until I take the offensive." His mind was at rest on one point — he did not have to leave Butler in command. Butler was off on leave at the moment, and Grant could turn things over to Meade. So he went up to the Shenandoah Valley, where on September 16 he had a talk with Sheridan.[16]

The visit was brief enough. Grant had taken with him a plan for a campaign by which Sheridan could drive Early away from Winchester, but Sheridan had at last learned that Kershaw's division was going back to Petersburg and he had a plan of his own drawn up; he outlined it to Grant, tracing troop positions and lines of march on a map, while the two men paced back and forth in an open field near Sheridan's headquarters. Grant liked Sheridan's plan, kept his own in his pocket, and asked Sheridan how soon he could make his move; by the following Tuesday, perhaps? (This day happened to be Friday.) Sheridan said he could do better than that; his army could be on the march before daylight on Monday. Grant told him to go ahead, and immediately started off on his return journey.

There are two little sidelights on this visit . . .

For one: while Grant and Sheridan talked together, a sergeant in Wright's corps lounged against a rail fence not far away, watching them, and when a comrade came up the sergeant jerked a thumb at the pair and remarked: "That's Grant." Then, meditatively, he continued: "I hate to see that old cuss around. When that old cuss is around there's sure to be a big fight on hand."

For the other: on his way to the valley Grant met John W. Garrett, President of the B. & O., who asked when he could count on putting men to work on the railroad so as to restore it to service. Grant promised to let him know as soon as he had a good answer, and when Garrett met him again on the return trip Grant told him that he could send the repair gangs out by the following Wednesday — four days away. This, to be sure, was putting himself out on a limb, because Sheridan's army had not yet left its camp, but Grant had no doubt that it would move when Sheridan had said it would move or that it would win the victory Sheridan had promised.

His confidence is also shown by the fact that he took a day off after his talk to Sheridan. Julia had come east, and after looking in vain for a house in Philadelphia (the Princeton project having faded out earlier) she had found one in nearby Burlington, N.J., and so Grant went back to City Point by way of Burlington. With the all-important battle for control of the valley due to take place within twenty-four hours, what he wanted most was to see Julia, inspect the new house, and discuss the schooling the children could get in Burlington. As usually happened when he got away from the army he was surrounded by crowds of people, and this made it hard to get much privacy; after he got back to camp he wrote to Julia: "The scene at the house on Sunday morning was what I had to go through the whole way. It is but little pleasure now for me to travel." [17]

Grant reached his headquarters on the night of Monday, September 19. As he had assumed, all had been quiet during his absence, and Lee had shown no sign of taking the offensive. Casually, Grant remarked that he had ordered Sheridan to move out and whip Early, and some officer in the campfire group, somewhat struck by this informality, suggested: "I presume the actual form of the order was to move out and attack him." Grant refused to be corrected. "No, I mean just what I say," he replied. "I gave the order to whip him."

This order Sheridan carried out to the letter, and by the time Grant had his chat at headquarters the battle was over. News came a day later in the form of an exultant telegram from Sheridan:

I have the honor to report that I attacked the forces of General Early on the Berryville pike at the crossing of Opequon Creek, and after a most stubborn and sanguinary engagement, which lasted from early in the morning until 5 o'clock in the evening, completely defeated him, and, driving him through Winchester, captured about 2,500 prisoners, 5 pieces of artillery, 9 army flags and most of their wounded. . . . The conduct of the officers and men was most superb. They charged and carried every position taken up by the rebels from the Opequon creek to Winchester. The enemy were strong in number and very obstinate in their fighting.

It mattered not at all that Sheridan had bungled the opening of this battle, crowding troops and wagons into a narrow approach road in such a way that the first contingents to go into action lacked support and were almost driven from the field. By midday he had recovered himself, getting all of his men into action at last and by dashing front-line leadership atoning for the morning's tactical errors. All that really mattered was that one of the most significant battles of the war had been won decisively, and the country took to its heart a jaunty message in which Sheridan asserted: "We have just sent them whirling through Winchester, and we are after them tomorrow. This army behaved splendidly." He followed this by making a vigorous pursuit of his beaten foe; three days later he found Early making a stand on his old position at Fisher's Hill, attacked him there, routed him, and sent him off in full-speed retreat far up the valley. Once again Grant ordered the armies at Petersburg to fire hundred-gun salutes, and when he urged the War Department to have Sheridan made brigadier general in the regular army and given permanent tenure of his position as commander of the Middle Military Division the request was immediately granted. After a few days Grant caught a chance to send Julia a little note, reminding her that he had not forgotten his little call at Burlington: "My visit was a very pleasant one, and General Sheridan by his brilliant victories has added much to it. In a few days more I shall make another stir here and shall hope before many weeks to so wind up matters that I will be able to spend at least a portion of my time at home." [18]

After the gloomiest of summers, Grant could see sunlight and blue sky again.

CHAPTER NINETEEN

I Will Work This Thing Out Yet

THE good news from the valley picked everybody up. The most confirmed pessimist in the army, probably, was Colonel Charles Wainwright, Warren's chief of artillery, who had been steeped in gloom ever since McClellan left, and who complained at the end of June that "Grant has used the army up" and ruined its morale. Now, on September 25, Wainwright was writing in his diary: "At times I cannot help thinking that these victories are the beginning of the end, the death-blows to the rebellion." The depression that began after Cold Harbor and grew bottomless after the tragedy of the crater was undeniably lifting, and Wainwright went on with the air of one surprised by his own optimism: "I have never seen the time when the army thought the war was so near its close. The men are in good spirits, and I think will behave well should anything be attempted." [1]

To hope that the army would behave well in its next fight was to admit that it had behaved badly in its last one, and gloomy Wainwright was not alone in this confession. Grant himself never spoke a word in criticism of these soldiers, yet after the fighting along the Weldon Railroad Joe Bowers sensed that battlefield failures were making the general uncommonly anxious.

"His plans are good," wrote Bowers, "but the great difficulty is that *our troops cannot be relied on.* The failure to take advantage of opportunities pains and chafes him beyond anything that I have ever before known him to manifest." The best Bowers could say was that the soldiers "may yet accidentally *blunder* into Richmond," and he drew such hope as he could from the belief that the spirit of Lee's army was no better than that on the Union side. A fellow staff officer lamented: "If we only had some of our old Western troops, with their own Generals to command them, down here just now, we could smash Lee most effectually. Joe has not much confidence in the Army of the Potomac, either soldiers or officers. He says there appears to be no vim or snap." [2]

What the men needed most was a glimpse of daylight ahead, and this at last they got from the distant victories that touched off the great hundred-gun salutes. At the end of September Grant called on them for another of those two-handed offensives, one blow struck north of the James balancing a blow struck to the south, with always a gambler's chance that Lee would not be able to meet both; and this time the troops won a smart success and displayed enough vim and snap to satisfy anybody. If they did not make the decisive breakthrough Grant always hoped for they did not actually miss it by very much, and the spirit they displayed looked like a throwback to the days when the war was young.

This time instead of sending Hancock north of the river Grant used Butler, who drew up the battle plan that was used and, truth to tell, drew it up with complete competence; its actual execution not being harmed by the fact that Grant himself was on hand when the fighting took place. Butler sent 14,000 men across the James at night, on pontoon bridges, and on the morning of September 29, under cover of a wispy fog, General Ord took 4,000 of them and marched for Fort Harrison, which lay a mile and a quarter inland from the great Confederate river fortification at Chaffin's Bluff. Fort Harrison was a big oblong on a hill, with stout ramparts and heavy guns, good trenches on either side anchoring it firmly to the rest of the Confederate defense system, and in order to reach it Ord's men had to cross a mile of open ground under rifle and artillery fire; and just as the fog lifted Ord's skirmish line strode out into the clearing, line of battle coming along behind it, and here was a smash at the strongest part of the line just as if the lessons of the last three months had been forgotten.

Perhaps these lessons did not apply here. Fort Harrison was held by a small force — Lee had most of his men south of the river, because of the continuing threat to the railroads, and he kept a skeleton force in the lines to the north — and although reinforcements were hurried to the fort the Federals came on irresistibly. Ord's soldiers crossed the open fields, halted close to the fort to re-form, then went down into the ditch and up over the ramparts, storming into the fort and driving out the last of its defenders. Ord was with them, organizing columns to sweep along the trench lines to right and left; on the left his men carried the line almost to Chaffin's Bluff, but the attack on the right failed, Ord himself was badly wounded, and at last the offensive died down. A mile farther north Butler's other column, 10,000 men under General Birney, struck at Fort Gilmer, and if this place had fallen Richmond would have fallen too; but the Confederates held it after a hard fight, Birney was driven back with substantial losses, and Ord's men worked all night to build a parapet across the open throat of Fort Harrison to guard against the counterattack that Lee was sure to make.

He made it next day, September 30, and he failed: two divisions of Confederate troops tried three attacks and were repulsed each time. Late in the day the firing died down, and the Federals in Fort Harrison climbed up on the ramparts in gleeful triumph, waved all their flags, and sang "The Battle Cry of Freedom." Song on a battlefield! Nothing like this had happened since the innocent days of 1862.[3]

The position finally was stabilized, and if the Federals had the fort the Confederates had the rest of the line, or most of it, and the Yankees had not taken Richmond. It had been a near thing, though, and there had been some tense hours in the Confederate capital. When Fort Harrison fell the tocsin was sounded, and the city guard went through the streets like a press-gang, seizing every adult male for emergency defense service — sweeping up, in regrettable fact, two indignant cabinet members, releasing them later, presumably with adequate apology.

Meanwhile Meade had taken advantage of the Confederate preoccupation with the fighting north of the James and had sent a column westward beyond Warren's position at Globe Tavern, striking toward the Boydton Plank Road and the Southside Railroad. His advance could not reach these objectives, but it did drive Lee's troops away from a big swatch of territory around the Peebles Farm and the Poplar Springs Church, and here in the next few weeks the Federals built one of the biggest earthworks known to the Civil War — Fort Fisher, a massive anchor for entrenchments that compelled Lee to extend his own lines by three miles. When the fighting ceased, on the evening of October 2, Lee still held his ground north and south of the river — but once more he was being forced to live beyond his means, occupying a line that kept growing longer with an army that continued to grow smaller. Also, the Federals were a long step closer to the vital supply lines.[4]

The performance of Ord's troops was unquestionably the bright spot in all of this; and yet it would be possible to make too much of it. Morale was reviving, to be sure, but there was still some distance to go, largely because so many of the troops nowadays had never had any morale to begin with. Replacements this year tended to be of deplorable quality; the army contained too many men who did not particularly want to fight and never had wanted to, human refuse sent to camp by the substitute broker and the high bounty system. General John G. Parke, who had replaced Burnside in command of the Ninth Corps, pointed out that to make soldiers of these recruits "requires time for drilling and disciplining . . . we have to contend against the demoralizing influence of the bounty jumper, whose sole ambition is to shirk and desert." Grant wrote bitterly of soldiers "who have never done any fighting and never intended to when enlisted," and said that "of this class of recruits we do not get one for every eight bounties paid to do good service." [5]

The Civil War armies had been built on the volunteer system and this system had long since collapsed because it had been asked to carry too much. Once it brought in the country's best men and now it brought in its worst, and army commanders who used to prefer volunteers to conscripts now wanted conscripts if they could get them. The trouble was that they could not always get them, because the draft was so often used simply as a stimulus for recruiting. When the President issued a call for men each Congressional district was required to raise its quota, and if it could meet that quota with volunteers nobody in the district would be drafted. Since the draft was unpopular there was always pressure to give the districts time to bring in recruits via the high bounty system, and if this put arrant shirkers into uniform nobody noticed it except the men up front who had to do the fighting. Lincoln this summer had called for 300,000 men but there were rumors that the conscription would be postponed, and on September 11 Grant sent Stanton an anxious telegram:

I hope it is not the intention to postpone the draft to allow time to fill up with recruiting. The men we have been getting in this way nearly all desert, and out of five reported North as having enlisted we don't get more than one effective soldier.

Stanton promptly replied that the draft would not be postponed one day, and he suggested that it would be helpful if Grant would send him a letter that he might publish to show the necessity for the draft. Grant returned this message:

My despatch to you on the subject of enforcing the draft was suggested by reading Secretary Seward's Auburn speech, where he intimates that volunteers were coming in so rapidly that there would be no necessity for a draft, and your despatch stating that volunteers were coming in at the rate of 5,000 per day. We ought to have the whole number of men called for by the President in the shortest possible time. A draft is soon over, and ceases to hurt after it is made. The agony of suspense is worse upon the public than the measure itself. Prompt action in filling our armies will have more effect upon the enemy than a victory over them. They profess to believe, and make their men believe, that there is such a party North in favor of recognizing Southern independence that the draft cannot be enforced. Let them be undeceived. Deserters come into our lines daily who tell us that the men are nearly universally tired of war, and that desertions would be much more frequent but they believe peace will be negotiated after the fall elections. The enforcement of the draft and prompt filling up of our armies will save the shedding of blood to an immense degree.[6]

Grant's preoccupation with numbers was constant. Although he of course outnumbered his opponent, as always, he did not this fall have the kind of margin with which legend then and thereafter credited him, and his ability to act was sharply limited by the available means. The general situation was described in a letter written to a fellow staff officer late in October by Joe Bowers:

We are busy doing nothing, positively nothing, and I confess to you that I see no prospect of our doing anything for some time to come. Everything is at a dead lock. We have men enough to make our present positions safe, but none with which to get up "side shows" or inaugurate new movements. We are not receiving reinforcements to any considerable extent. The accessions are barely sufficient to make up for losses in battle and by expiration of enlistments. . . . We hear of many men in rendezvous, but they don't come and it is evidently not the intention of the Government to send them until after the election. Everything now hinges on the elections.

The army's strength was coming up slowly, and Grant was not nearly as strong as people back home imagined. The lowest point had been reached at the end of August, when the Army of the Potomac and the Army of the James put together could muster no more than

44,000 bayonets. Then the strength began to rise. By the end of September Meade and Butler between them had just over 64,000 infantry (enlisted men, present for duty equipped) and in October Meade got 8,000 more, with Butler's infantry strength rising slightly. On the eve of the election the two armies had an aggregate strength — counting cavalry, artillery, provost guard, garrisons for fixed posts, and so on — of approximately 90,000 men. This was a sharply inflated figure as far as battle action was concerned, because the army's method of counting listed thousands upon thousands of supernumeraries who were never seen in combat.

In view of the fact that the government did its level best all year long to keep these armies adequately reinforced it is clear that a terrible wastage had been taking place; but although the campaign from the Wilderness on had been fearfully expensive the greater part of this wastage had not been due to enemy action. At the end of 1864, Meade's medical director issued a report which showed that the Army of the Potomac during the year had at one time or another put 228,076 men on sick report. Some 23 percent of these went to hospital with gunshot wounds; the rest were victims of disease, of which fevers and diarrhea were the commonest. Although 186,505 of the hospital patients had, by the end of the year, returned to duty, more than 10,000 had died, 23,000 were still on sick report, and the rest had been invalided out of the army, had deserted, had been given extensive furloughs, or had in other ways vanished from the army's service. Merely to keep an army in the field, in short, was a fearful drain on the nation's resources regardless of combat losses.[7]

In the mysterious economy of all-out war it paid to endure this drain if the Confederates, with smaller resources, had to stand an equal drain; and because this was so there was one rich manpower resource which Grant and Stanton resolutely refused to touch even when the pressure was at its worst. They would not reach out to reclaim the thousands of good veteran soldiers who were in Confederate prison camps, even though these men could be brought back to duty quickly enough if the general and the secretary would agree to resume the abandoned practice of prisoner exchanges.

Early in the war the Union and Confederate governments had devised a system to relieve each side of the burden of housing and feeding large numbers of prisoners for extended times. There were rules under which prisoners taken would be swapped, on a man-for-man basis, and if there were captures in unequal numbers the side which held a surplus would release the extra men on parole, with an understanding that these men would not be restored to duty until formal notice of exchange had been sent across the lines. Under this system a soldier captured by the enemy could count on getting back to his own army in a comparatively short time, and although the business was cumbersome and involved a great deal of figure juggling it worked tolerably well. However, in 1863 it broke down, and by the summer and fall of 1864 it was almost completely inoperative.

The breakdown came for a number of reasons. One was the fact that the Confederacy refused to recognize escaped slaves in Federal uniform as soldiers but insisted on returning them to servitude, and announced that white officers commanding them were liable to prosecution under state laws designed to keep people from fomenting slave insurrections. This of course was more than the Federal authorities would stand for, and Stanton announced (with Lincoln's full support) that no Confederate prisoners would be released until the Confederacy agreed to treat all Union prisoners alike. In addition, it was charged that most of the Confederates paroled when Vicksburg and Port Hudson fell had been put back into service illegally, without benefit of proper exchange. Other irregularities were alleged . . . and as a matter of fact the whole parole and exchange system rested on a gentlemen's agreement that was bound to collapse once the rigors of a civil war got past the bounds of gentlemanly conduct, which had long since happened to this one.

So soldiers who were captured now went to prison camps and stayed there, for month upon weary month, and a fantastic number of them died there. (Considering the amount of sickness in the Army of the Potomac, where men got the best care their own government could provide, the mortality rate in a place like Andersonville is not really surprising.) Northern publicists made weighty propaganda out of the prison camp horrors, as a means of keeping anti-Confederate sentiment at a proper wartime pitch, but the effort backfired; Northerners horrified by the way their men fared in Southern camps came to feel that these men ought to be brought back north even at the price of sending Confederate prisoners south, and the no-exchange policy became highly unpopular back home. Like every other development in this overheated year, this had a direct bearing on the forthcoming presidential election.

[371]

The no-exchange policy was Stanton's and he never tried to hide the fact. He explained the policy to Grant shortly after Grant became lieutenant general. To make exchanges on Southern terms, he said, was simply to abandon the Negro troops and their officers to punishment and to countenance cheating on the matter of paroles; furthermore, since the Confederacy was being drained of manpower the South stood to gain much more than the North could gain by exchanges and paroles. Grant agreed with him wholeheartedly, and was so firm on the policy that in the South it came to be looked on as his rather than Stanton's. Explaining the reason for it in a letter to Secretary Seward, Grant flatly asserted: "We ought not to make a single exchange nor release a prisoner on any pretext whatever until the war closes. We have got to fight until the Military Power of the South is exhausted, and if we release or exchange prisoners captured it simply becomes a war of extermination."

Officially, exchanges in the eastern theater of war were handled by Ben Butler. By this time the rare exchanges that took place were arranged on a personal basis, with one side or the other asking for the release of certain favored individuals and offering equivalent releases in return. This meant that the Confederates now and then had to ask favors of Beast Butler, of all people: outrageous, but one of the hardships of war. (As a matter of fact Butler was not a hard man to do business with, government by special favor being a thing he understood very well.)

In a letter to Butler written at about the time he discussed the manpower problem with Seward, Grant made his own position clear:

It is hard on our men held in southern prisons not to exchange them, but it is humanity to those left in the ranks to fight our battles. Every man we hold, when released on parole or otherwise, becomes an active soldier against us at once, either directly or indirectly. If we commence a system of exchange which liberates all prisoners taken, we will have to fight on until the whole South is exterminated. If we hold those caught they amount to no more than dead men. At this particular time to release all Rebel prisoners North would insure Sherman's defeat and would compromise our safety here.[8]

Officially, it was the Confederate policy in regard to Negro troops that was the sticking point. On October 1 General Lee wrote to

Grant proposing that the armies in Virginia exchange prisoners on a straight man-for-man basis. In reply, Grant pointed out: "Among those lost by the armies operating against Richmond were a number of colored troops. Before further negotiations are had upon the subject I would ask if you propose delivering these men the same as white soldiers?" When Lee replied that "deserters from our service and Negroes belonging to our citizens are not considered subjects of exchange and were not included in my proposition," Grant notified him that the deal was off: the Northern government "is bound to secure to all soldiers received into her armies the rights due to soldiers." [9]

Grant unquestionably would have wanted to rule out prisoner exchanges no matter what the South did with captured Negroes, but it must be said that Southern stubbornness on this point gave the Northern officials all the pretext they needed. As a matter of fact the treatment given ex-slaves who had been captured after entering the United States army was a real and pressing issue, and desperately as they wanted their own men sent back to them the Confederate authorities could not admit that a fugitive slave was anything but a fugitive slave no matter what uniform he wore. Additional correspondence between Grant and Lee on this point developed a little later in this month of October, when Ben Butler discovered that Lee's army was employing Negroes to rebuild and extend the fortifications at Fort Gilmer and that among these Negroes were black soldiers recently captured from the Union army. Butler promptly took a hundred Confederate prisoners of war and put them to work on a canal he was digging across a neck of land at Dutch Gap, on the James — a strictly military project which, like the work at Fort Gilmer, required labor parties to toil within range of enemy guns — and he sent word across the lines that he was doing this in retaliation for the treatment that was being given Union prisoners.

At the request of his government, then, Lee wrote to Grant: explaining, first, that runaway Negroes who owed service or labor to Confederate citizens still owed it, that the Confederate government would see to it that they paid what they owed, and that Confederate policy in this matter had abundant historical and constitutional justification. He then went on to say that the reclaimed slaves in whose behalf Butler was committing retaliations had been put to work at Fort Gilmer against Lee's instructions, and said they had been sent behind the lines to proper civilian employment once he found out about them. Recaptured slaves, in fine, were still slaves, but they would not again be used on frontline spade work.

Reading this, Grant told Butler to take the Southern prisoners out of the lines and send them back to a regular prison camp. He notified Lee that he had done this, and went on somewhat tartly:

I shall always regret the necessity of retaliating for wrongs done our soldiers, but regard it my duty to protect all persons received into the Army of the United States, regardless of color or nationality. When acknowledged soldiers of the Government are captured they must be treated as prisoners of war, or such treatment as they receive inflicted upon an equal number of prisoners held by us. I have nothing to do with the discussion of the slavery question, therefore decline answering the arguments adduced to show the right to return to former owners such Negroes as are captured from our Army. . . . All prisoners of war falling into my hands shall receive the kindest possible treatment consistent with securing them, unless I have good authority for believing any number of our men are being treated otherwise. Then, painful as it may be to me, I shall inflict like treatment on an equal number of Confederate prisoners.[10]

In their refusal to treat ex-slaves as soldiers the Confederates were acting partly on high principle — once admit that a slave could cease to be a slave by anything but his lawful owner's consent, and the floodgates were loosed — and partly on considerations of practical politics. It seemed likely that the refusal of Grant and Stanton to strike a bargain for the return of Northern prisoners would cause many people to vote against Lincoln in the November election. Undeniably the pressure was heavy, from civilians and from men in the army. The Federal War Department had even received petitions drawn up by men in Andersonville, begging that exchanges be made . . . and moving documents they were. The Georgia statesman Howell Cobb recently had gone to the length of urging the Confederate War Department to comb the prison camps for anti-Lincoln men, paroling these forthwith and sending them north in time to vote. All of this effort to turn resentment over the no-exchange policy into anti-administration votes, to be sure, would have affected Grant only indirectly — Stanton was the target most of the discontented were shooting at, and the stray shots and overs were hitting the President rather than the general-in-chief — except that this election was going to be held in the army as well as out of it.[11]

This most violent of civil wars was about to come to its climax in the orderly formalities of a quadrennial election, because after all it was that kind of war: testing whether any nation so conceived and so dedicated could long endure. The strangest part about it was that the soldiers themselves were going to vote — those who were old enough, anyway — even though it was clear that a soldier who wanted to fight no more, disliked his generals or had lost track of what he was fighting for would assuredly vote for the opposition, which if it won would be under strong compulsion to call the war off altogether. To give soldiers that much control over their own destiny was unprecedented, and it might well be very risky, but it was unavoidable; and now Grant had to determine how much electioneering could take place in the ranks of an army which every day in every month was engaging the enemy on the battlefield.

Grant took a long look at the matter, and he put his thoughts on paper in a manner showing that the head of the democracy's armies understood democracy to the full; understood that the democratic process need not be feared as long as the men who used it acted with boldness and good sense. Writing thus, Sam Grant at last came of age, and turned a routine document into a triumphant affirmation of the faith America fought for. On September 27 he sent Mr. Stanton this letter:

The exercise of the right of suffrage by the officers and soldiers of armies in the field is a novel thing. It has, I believe, generally been considered dangerous to constitutional liberty and subversive of military discipline. But our circumstances are novel and exceptional. A very large proportion of legal voters of the United States are now either under arms in the field, or in hospitals, or otherwise engaged in the military service of the United States.

Most of these men are not regular soldiers in the strict sense of that term; still less are they mercenaries, who give their services to the Government simply for its pay, having little understanding of the political questions or feeling little or no interest in them. On the contrary they are American citizens, having still their homes and social and political ties binding them to the States and districts from which they come and to which they expect to return.

They have left their homes temporarily to sustain the cause of their country in the hour of its trial. In performing this sacred duty they should not be deprived of a most precious privilege. They have as much right to demand that their votes shall be counted in the choice of their rulers as those citizens who remain at home. Nay, more, for they have sacrificed more for their country.

I state these reasons in full, for the unusual thing of allowing armies in the field to vote, that I may urge on the other hand that nothing more than the fullest exercise of this right should be allowed, for anything not absolutely necessary to this exercise cannot but be dangerous to the liberties of the country. The officers and soldiers have every means of understanding the questions before the country. The newspapers are freely circulated, and so, I believe, are the documents prepared by both parties to set forth the merits and claims of their candidates.

Beyond this nothing whatever should be allowed. No political meetings, no harangues from soldiers or citizens, and no canvassing of camps or regiments for votes. I see not why a single individual not belonging to the armies should be admitted into their lines to deliver tickets. In my opinion the tickets should be furnished by the chief provost-marshal of each army, by them to the provost-marshal (or some other appointed officer) of each brigade or regiment, who shall on the day of election deliver tickets irrespective of party to whoever may call for them. If, however, it shall be deemed expedient to admit citizens to deliver tickets, then it should be most positively prohibited that such citizens should electioneer, harangue or canvass the regiments in any way. Their business should be, and only be, to distribute on a certain fixed day tickets to whoever may call for them.

In the case of those States whose soldiers vote by proxy, proper State authority could be given to officers belonging to regiments so voting to receive and forward votes. As it is intended that all soldiers entitled to vote shall exercise that privilege according to their own convictions of right, unmolested and unrestricted, there will be no objection to each party sending to armies, easy of access, a number of respectable gentlemen to see that these views are fully carried out.[12]

In the end: no problem. The soldiers talked things over among themselves, soldier fashion, but there was no general electioneering to disturb army morale or discipline, and the men showed they could take a national election in their stride. As election day drew nearer it became quite obvious that these soldiers were not in any significant numbers going to try to vote themselves out of the war. They had affectionate admiration for McClellan, but he lost many votes in the army he once commanded because the men felt that he had been made the victim of a stop-the-war faction that had dominated the Democratic convention; men who were using great batteries of siege guns to salute immense victories were not ready to embrace a party whose platform called the war a failure. Elated Republicans in the election districts back home were boasting that they needed no campaign speeches except the dispatches from Sherman and Sheridan (although just to be on the safe side they sent out every orator they had); and the soldier vote began to look so safe that in states which had no absentee-voter laws Republican party leaders pulled wires to get the men furloughed by regiments, confident that nearly all of them would vote for Lincoln.[13] And now, near the end of the third week in October, Sheridan sent in another dispatch which told the North that it need never again worry about Jubal Early or Confederate operations in the Shenandoah Valley. Sheridan had won a third victory, and this time it was conclusive.

When Sheridan defeated Early at Winchester and Fisher's Hill late in September Grant wrote to him: "Keep on, and your good work will cause the fall of Richmond," but thereafter things had not gone according to plan.

What Grant wanted most was what he had wanted ever since May: to get a strong Federal army up the valley and across the Blue Ridge so that it could break the Charlottesville-Lynchburg railroad, the James River canal and the Virginia Central line east to Richmond, thus making Lee's army and the Confederate capital wholly dependent on the Southside and the Richmond & Danville roads, toward which the Army of the Potomac was inexorably extending its lines. Sheridan began well enough, sending cavalry ahead to break the Virginia Central near Staunton, and Grant tried to spur him along by sending fresh encouragement: "Your victories have caused the greatest consternation. If you can possibly subsist your army to the front for a few days more, do it, and make a great effort to destroy the railroads about Charlottesville and the canal whenever your cavalry can reach it."

Sheridan pointed out that he could not do this just now: "The difficulty of transporting this army through the mountain passes on to the railroad at Charlottesville is such that I regard it as impracticable with my present means of transportation. . . . I think that the best policy will be to let the burning of the crops in the Valley be the end of this campaign, and let some of this army go elsewhere."

If Grant's plan could not be carried out — and Grant was usually willing to go along with the judgment of the man on the spot — to get

Wright's hard-hitting Sixth Corps back would be a fine second best. There was an especially strong reason for accepting Sheridan's recommendation; he was urging a reduction in the size and importance of his own command, and no general who ever lived would do that lightly. Grant approved, but he had not entirely given up on his original design, and while Sheridan was moving back toward the lower valley and sending Wright's corps away Grant forwarded new instructions to Halleck: "After sending the Sixth Corps and one division of cavalry here, I think Sheridan should keep up as advanced a position as possible towards the Virginia Central railroad and be prepared with supplies to advance on that road at Gordonsville and Charlottesville at any time the enemy weakens himself sufficiently to admit of it. The cutting of that road and the canal would be of vast importance to us."

Now misunderstandings began. Sending Grant's order on to Sheridan, Halleck modified it to meet his own ideas; so Sheridan gathered that Grant wanted him to provision and fortify a new base at Manassas Junction, and to move from there on an offensive toward the railroad lines. Sheridan immediately recalled Wright, notifying Halleck: "If any advance is to be made on Gordonsville and Charlottesville it is not best to send troops away from my command."

Meanwhile, General Lee played his last card as far as the Shenandoah Valley was concerned; he reinforced Early once more, sending him Kershaw's infantry division (which had been withdrawn just before the battle of Winchester) and a brigade of cavalry — if the Federals were giving up the valley, that once again was a vulnerable flank for Grant, and Lee would strike it no matter how straitened he might be in front of Petersburg and Richmond. Thus strengthened, Early began to move back down the valley, and soon he approached the position to which Sheridan had retired at Cedar Creek, twenty miles south of Winchester.

Early hoped to induce Sheridan to retire farther — like Sheridan, he knew that a Northern invader could find no good defensive position between this point and the Potomac — and so Early resorted to a ruse. He caused his signal station on Massanutten Mountain, which operated in plain view of the Federal outposts, to send a message addressed to Early and signed by James Longstreet, who had just returned to duty in Lee's lines north of the James; and this message, craftily written by Early himself and innocently copied by the deluded Yankees, said that Longstreet's famous army corps was coming up to the valley so that Longstreet and Early together could destroy Sheridan.

Sheridan had gone to Washington to confer with Halleck, leaving Wright in command of the troops at Cedar Creek; and because he believed that Early was passive and would remain so, Sheridan had ordered two cavalry divisions to start through the Blue Ridge to operate to the eastward. Now he got this message, and to his own good fortune he swallowed it whole: ordered the cavalry back to Cedar Creek at top speed, put Wright on the alert, and cut short his own trip to Washington. Sheridan reached Winchester on his return journey on the afternoon of October 18. The next morning, as he mounted there to ride on to camp he heard the muted flutter of gunfire, far off to the southward. Puzzled and vaguely disturbed, he quickened his pace, heard the noise getting heavier and nearer, found the Valley Turnpike getting clogged with fugitive Union soldiers, and rode up to his lines at a thundering gallop to learn that his army had been whipped and that it now held a somewhat insecure position several miles north of the camp it had slept in the night before.[14]

Early had struck hard in the concealing mists of dawn, hitting the flank and rear of the Union left, smashing Crook's corps and forcing it into a headlong retreat that involved a good part of Emory's corps as well. Wright, who had been wounded but was still on duty, his beard all clotted with blood, had got things stabilized, and when Sheridan came up the situation undoubtedly looked worse than it really was. Sheridan's army had been roughly handled but it had a good three-to-two advantage in numbers, and Early's Confederates, with a rich camp to loot, were almost as disorganized by victory as Wright's Federals were by defeat. The Confederate offensive had in fact spent its force, and it is quite possible that Early had simply tried to win a battle that would have been too big for him in any case. There was bound to be a powerful Federal counterattack whether Sheridan returned or not.[15]

But he did return, and when the counterattack came it was all his, flaming across the field under the autumn sunset at the bidding of a man who was a storybook genius at battlefield leadership. Cedar Creek was like Chattanooga, a battle that passed into legend while it was still being fought, a spectacle that caught the nation's attention and made a badly needed victory look miraculous, something to be remembered forever. Early's army was shattered, and neither he nor any other Confederate would ever again make anything bigger than nuisance warfare in the Shenandoah. There was a finality to this victory and no one could fail to see it.

Grant got the news next day, while he sat in his headquarters tent writing letters. The telegraph operator came up past the staff officers who sat in a loose semicircle outside the tent, and went inside to hand Grant a telegram. After a few minutes Grant came out, telegram in hand, and announced that he was going to read a message from Sheridan. As Horace Porter remembered it Grant made quite an act out of it, looking grave and somehow giving the impression that bad things had happened. In a tense hush the officers listened while he read:

I have the honor to report that my army at Cedar Creek was attacked this morning before daylight, and my left was turned and driven in confusion; in fact, most of the line was driven in confusion, with the loss of twenty pieces of artillery. I hastened from Winchester, where I was on my return from Washington, and joined the army between Middletown and Newtown, having been driven back about four miles.

Grant paused, here, shook his head solemnly, and murmured: "That's pretty bad, isn't it?" Heads were wagged solemnly, although some of the officers may have noticed a gleam in the general's eye. Grant went on reading:

I here took the affair in hand, and quickly united the corps, formed a compact line of battle just in time to repulse an attack of the enemy's, which was handsomely done at about 1 P.M. At 3 P.M., after some changes of the cavalry from the left to the right flank, I attacked with great vigor, driving and routing the enemy, capturing according to last reports 43 pieces of artillery and very many prisoners. I do not yet know the number of my casualties or the losses of the enemy. Wagon-trains, ambulances and caissons in large numbers are in our possession. . . . Affairs at times looked badly, but by the gallantry of our brave officers and men disaster has been converted into a splendid victory. Darkness again intervened to shut off greater results.[16]

The headquarters group broke up in cheers and delighted caperings. Grant sent Stanton a wire saying that to turn defeat into victory the way it was done at Cedar Creek marked Sheridan "one of the ablest of generals," and Meade, who had never been exactly enthusiastic about the tough little man who still, technically, commanded Meade's cavalry corps, told Grant that Sheridan had achieved "one of the most brilliant feats of the war" and sent his congratulations. That evening Grant wrote Julia a letter dealing mostly with the behavior of sons Fred and Jesse (behavior good enough, apparently, but admonition needed) and concluded: "I have no special news to write you this evening. I have just had a salute of one hundred guns fired for Sheridan's last victory in the Valley. I hope we will have one here before a great while to celebrate." [17]

He made the effort a week later, moving 30,000 infantry out beyond the left to strike Lee's flank at Burgess's Mill, where an important traffic artery known as the Boydton Plank Road coming southwest from the Confederate camp crossed a winding stream called Hatcher's Run. Once more, Butler was ordered to make a feint and look menacing north of the James, and while he made this attempt to distract Lee's attention Hancock and Warren moved for the river crossing at the other end of the line. They drove off Lee's outposts easily enough and then ran into trouble; the Rebels had dammed the stream and slashed the timber all along its banks, fords were obstructed by fallen trees, riflemen in good trenches were posted to lay down an effective fire, Hancock and Warren seemed unable to coordinate their movements — and presently Grant accepted the fact that Lee was too well prepared and called the troops back to their lines. He described the move, in a telegram to Stanton, as "this reconnaissance, which I had intended for more," and he was obviously disappointed at the failure to gain anything; the thrust had been aimed at the Southside railroad, which was now only six miles away. Apparently it was based on the belief that Lee's entrenched right did not reach as far as Hatcher's Run, and it was given up as soon as it was clear that the Confederates were ready and waiting. When he wrote to Julia, Grant was philosophical: "I will work this thing out all right yet." [18]

Success was elusive . . . yet matters were not really going badly. Once again a tactical failure had left the Federal position a little stronger than it had been before. Lee now held a thirty-five-mile front, his left on the Williamsburg road east of Richmond, his right on Hatcher's Run far to the southwest of Petersburg, and with the threat in the valley eliminated it was certain that the strength of the Federal armies that pressed against this front would continue to in-

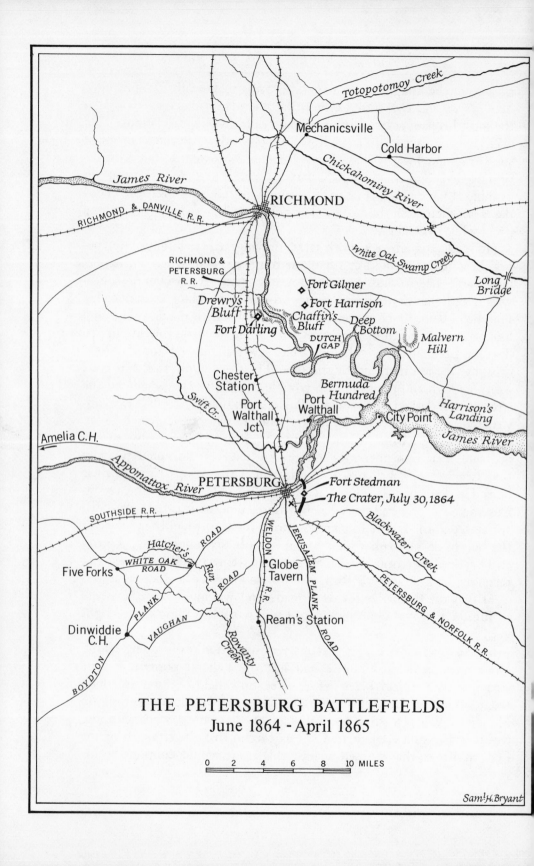

THE PETERSBURG BATTLEFIELDS
June 1864 - April 1865

Totopotomoy Creek

Mechanicsville

Cold Harbor

Chickahominy River

James River

RICHMOND

RICHMOND & DANVILLE R.R.

White Oak Swamp Creek

Long Bridge

RICHMOND & PETERSBURG R.R.

Fort Gilmer

Fort Harrison

Drewry's Bluff

Chaffin's Bluff

Deep Bottom

Malvern Hill

Fort Darling

DUTCH GAP

Chester Station

Bermuda Hundred

Port Walthall Jct.

Port Walthall

City Point

Harrison's Landing

Swift Cr.

James River

Amelia C.H.

Appomattox River

PETERSBURG

Fort Stedman

The Crater, July 30, 1864

SOUTHSIDE R.R.

Blackwater Creek

Hatcher's Run

WHITE OAK ROAD

WELDON R.R.

JERUSALEM PLANK ROAD

PETERSBURG & NORFOLK R.R.

Five Forks

Globe Tavern

PLANK ROAD

VAUGHAN

Dinwiddie C.H.

Ream's Station

Rowanty Creek

BOYDTON

0   2   4   6   8   10 MILES

Sam¹ H. Bryant

crease. On November 2 Lee sent a gloomy letter to Davis: "Grant will get every man he can, and 150,000 men is the number generally assumed by Northern papers and reports. Unless we can obtain a reasonable approximation to his force I fear a great calamity will befall us." Grenville Dodge, who visited Grant at this time, agreed that "Lee is not filling up his army, and is evidently prepared to evacuate any day or night." All that worried Dodge was the behavior of some of the generals Grant had to command. To Governor Richard Oglesby of Illinois, Dodge sent a chatty report on what he saw and felt at Grant's headquarters.

The Army of the Potomac, he said, contained fine troops, but Dodge did not see "that *heartiness* among the leading officers that we see in the west." So many of Grant's plans had been ruined by his subordinates that "I sometimes wish he had different men under him." Dodge specified: "Three different times has Richmond and Petersburg been virtually in his hands and by some *unexcusable neglect* or *slowness* each time his plans were ruined and the *opportunity lost.* How Grant stands it I do not see." It seemed to Dodge that too many officers carried out their assignments without vigor, solely from a sense of duty, "and this in my opinion is one great cause of the mistakes." Things would be better, once the election was over; "the men are right in sentiment, though many leading officers are McClellanized." [19]

If Grant had any doubts about how the election was going to go he kept them to himself. On election night he and his staff sat up late around the campfire in front of the commanding general's tent, waiting for election returns, and Grant was so little worried about the outcome that he indulged in a slightly heavy-handed practical joke. According to Brigadier General M. R. Morgan, commissary general at headquarters, Grant received reports from the headquarters telegraph operator and read them out for everyone to hear; and all evening long he read telegram after telegram that showed McClellan far ahead. Most of the officers who listened to him were good Lincoln men, and some of them went off to bed dejected, convinced that Lincoln had lost. Before he himself retired, after midnight, Grant confessed (to those who had stayed up long enough to hear him) that it had all been a hoax; every report that came in, throughout the evening, had showed Lincoln in the lead.

What pleased Grant most was not merely that Lincoln had won but that this election in the middle of a civil war had gone so quietly, so much like any peacetime election, as if the country knew that it was going to go on and on electing Presidents and accepting the electoral verdicts for all time to come. He expressed himself in a telegram to Secretary Stanton:

"Enough now seems to be known to say who is to hold the reins of government for the next four years. Congratulate the President for me for the double victory. The election having passed off quietly, no bloodshed or riot throughout the land, is a victory worth more to the country than a battle won. Rebeldom and Europe will so construe it." To his friend J. Russell Jones he wrote in the same vein: "The overwhelming majority received by Mr. Lincoln and the quiet with which the election went off will prove a terrible damper to the Rebels. It will be worth more than a victory in the field both in its effect on the Rebels and in its influence abroad." He wrote to Julia saying that he hoped the verdict of the people would be accepted everywhere: "If there was less clamor and dissention in the North the rebellion would be much sooner put down. The hopes of the South are constantly fed by the sayings of our Northern people."

Then he got down to the practical business at hand, and sent a wire to Halleck:

"I suppose, without my saying anything about it, all the troops now in the North will be hurried to the field, but I wish to urge this as of the utmost importance. Sherman's movement may compel Lee to send troops from Richmond, and if he goes I want to be prepared to annoy him." [20]

What Grant was saying was that the war was entering its final phase. General Sherman and 60,000 soldiers had left Atlanta and were beginning to march to the sea.

CHAPTER TWENTY

Much Is Now Expected

THE march to the sea was conclusive, and the fact that it hit nothing at all was precisely the point. This thrust that went clear to the heart was made with what the Federal power had left over after all other demands were met. It was an expenditure from surplus funds, and the Confederacy did not have the resources to meet it. Nine months earlier Grant had remarked that "the enemy have not got enough army," and here was the proof of it. If the Southern nation could not oppose this offensive it obviously was not going to remain a nation much longer.

This triumphal parade across Georgia was a logical consequence of the capture of Atlanta. In all of the rejoicing that followed Sherman's occupation of the city Grant had been unable to forget that Hood's Confederate army was still very much alive, and that Sherman's victorious force after all depended on a single-track railroad that ran all the way back to Chattanooga, every foot of it exposed to Hood's interference. Clearly, the situation was not static; either Sherman had never really finished his old campaign or he was obliged to begin a new one without delay. About a week after he learned of the fall of Atlanta, Grant sent Sherman a telegram stressing the need for continued action: "We want to keep the enemy constantly pressed to the end of the war. If we give him no peace whilst the war lasts, the end cannot be distant." He went on to make a concrete suggestion: "Now that we have all of Mobile Bay that is valuable, I do not know but it will be the best move to transfer Canby's troops to act upon Savannah, whilst you move on Augusta. I should like to hear from you, however, in this matter."

Ever since he talked with General Banks in New Orleans a year ago, Grant had wanted to see Mobile occupied and made the base for a strong Federal column that could move north to work with a Fed-

eral army in the interior of Georgia. He had had to modify this notion: General Canby, commanding along the Gulf, could not invest
Mobile because he was compelled to send troops up the Mississippi to
cope with an invasion attempted by the Confederate General Sterling
Price, and although Farragut's fleet had closed the port of Mobile, and
some of Canby's troops had occupied the forts at the entrance to Mobile Bay, it was not yet possible to capture the city itself. Now Grant
was beginning to think of something else, and Sherman's reply to his
telegram invited reflection on a different approach.

"If I could be sure of finding provisions and ammunition at Augusta
or Columbus, Georgia," Sherman wrote, "I can march to Milledgeville
and compel Hood to give up Augusta or Macon, and then turn on the
other . . . If you can manage to take the Savannah river as high up as
Augusta, or the Chattahoochee as far up as Columbus, I can sweep the
whole state of Georgia."

Making plans by telegraph was not good enough, and on September
12 Grant sent Horace Porter down to Atlanta to talk with Sherman,
bearing a letter and an unwritten synopsis of headquarters planning.
In this letter Grant was, in effect, thinking out loud and inviting Sherman to do the same. He explained that the army in Virginia would
take the offensive as soon as it was strong enough, and said that when
it moved it would continue to strike for the railroads. Then came a
new note: "At the same time this move is made, I want to send a force
of from six to ten thousand men against Wilmington."

With Mobile Bay closed to traffic, Wilmington was the last Confederate port of any consequence open to the blockade runners, and it
was the flow of goods that entered here that made the Weldon Railroad such a vital line for Lee and the people in Richmond. Once again,
Grant was hoping to strike beyond his immediate front. To cut the
Weldon Railroad was good, but to stop the source of the freight this
road carried would be much better, and so an offensive against Wilmington was in the cards:

The way I propose to do this is to land the men north of Fort Fisher
and hold that point. At the same time a large naval fleet will be assembled
there, and the iron-clads will run the batteries as they did at Mobile. This
will give us the same control of the harbor of Wilmington that we now
have of the harbor of Mobile.

What you are to do with the forces at your command I do not see. The difficulties of supplying your army, except when you are constantly moving, beyond where you are, I plainly see. If it had not been for Price's movements Canby would have sent twelve thousand more men to Mobile. From your command in Mississippi an equal number could have been taken. With these forces my idea would have been to divide them, sending one half to Mobile and the other half to Savannah. You could then move as proposed in your telegram, so as to threaten Macon and Augusta equally. Whichever was abandoned by the enemy you could take and open up a new base of supplies.

My object now in sending a staff officer is not so much to suggest operations for you as to get your views and have plans matured by the time everything can be got ready. It will probably be the 5th of October before any of the plans herein indicated will be executed.[1]

For nearly a year Grant had had a vague but persistent notion of a march across the Deep South to the seacoast. In the spring he had sent Sherman a map, with a blue line jagging down from Atlanta to Milledgeville and on to Savannah; earlier, from Tennessee he had written to Halleck about the great things an army could do if it got far into the Confederate interior and then cut loose. Right after the victory at Chattanooga he had given Sherman the picture of a devastating cavalry raid cutting down from the Great Smokies to the Atlantic, soldiers having no base and no fixed line of march because "they go not to fight but to avoid fighting if possible" — a destructive column whose mere existence would undermine every Confederate fixed position, contributing to the enemy's defeat simply by showing how easily an invader could move across the enemy's most vital territory. Yet all of this was no more than a sketchy reminder of a possibility that ought to be explored some day, and as the exploration at last began everything Grant and Sherman proposed was still highly conditional.[2]

Sherman told Porter that if, after Wilmington fell, Grant's amphibious expedition could go on to capture Savannah and open the Savannah River up as far as Augusta, "I would feel pretty safe in picking up the bulk of this army and moving east, subsisting off the country." It seemed to Sherman that if this happened Hood would probably march north, into Tennessee, and on the whole this would be good; "I would be willing to give him a free ticket and pay his expenses," because Sherman could detach enough troops to keep Hood from doing any real harm and "with the bulk of my army I could cut a swath through to the sea, divide the Confederacy in two, and be able to move up in the rear of Lee or do almost anything else that Grant might require of me." [3]

The thing could be done, *if:* the big condition being the seizure of a seacoast base toward which Sherman's army could march. And while the ins and outs of this were being explored, it became more and more clear that an advance to some part of the coast was sooner or later going to be necessary simply because Sherman could not hope to remain in Atlanta indefinitely. For a full month after the capture of the city Sherman moved in vain up and across his railroad supply line, trying without success to bring Hood to battle and crush him so that this line could be safe, growing more and more exasperated as Hood eluded him. Grant conceded that if Sherman protected this railway properly he would not have enough troops left to do anything else; and Sherman, to whom this had become obvious, began to argue that he ought to cut his communications entirely, vanishing from sight and sound and slashing his way through to the coast, taking along some iron rations and collecting most of his supplies from the fat Georgia countryside.

It no longer seemed necessary for the Federals to seize a seaport in advance. It would be enough, said Sherman, if the Navy could have a convoy of provision ships ready to bring in as soon as Sherman's army broke through the crust and showed itself beside the Atlantic. With rising enthusiasm, Sherman wrote a letter for Colonel Porter to give to Grant, closing with this: "I admire your dogged perseverance and pluck more than ever. If you can whip Lee and I can march to the Atlantic, I think Uncle Abe will give us a twenty days leave of absence to see the young folks."

When Porter brought this message back to City Point, Grant's whole staff joined in a debate that went on night after night. Rawlins was stoutly against the whole idea, arguing that the march to the sea would make sense only if Hood's army were first disposed of: it seemed most unlikely that this could be done, because Hood had concentrated far over in northern Alabama and President Davis had incautiously announced that Hood would invade Tennessee and perhaps Kentucky, operating against Sherman's base. Grant at first had strong reservations about marching away from an army as good as Hood's without first crippling it, and he warned Sherman that he himself could no longer plan on seizing a seaport for Sherman's use — if Sherman wanted to come out at Savannah, for instance, he would have to capture Savannah by himself.

As he thought more about it, however, Grant came to feel that the decision had best be left to the man on the spot. He wrote to Sherman that if Sherman moved southeast while his Confederate opponent lay northwest of him, "I do not believe you would meet Hood's army but would be bush-whacked by all the old men, little boys, and such railroad guards as are still left at home." He concluded: "If there is any way of getting at Hood's army I would prefer that, but I must trust to your own judgment."

Sherman was making preparations. Back to Tennessee went George Thomas to hold the line there. Thomas had only part of his own Army of the Cumberland, but he would be able to draw troops from other areas — A. J. Smith's corps, which had gone up the Red River with Banks and had unhappily toiled in the Mississippi Valley since then, was under orders to join him — and it seemed likely that Thomas would be strong enough to meet any threat. In Atlanta Sherman had more than 60,000 men — veterans, all the invalids sent back to Tennessee, the best men kept for the job ahead — and on October 12 Grant approved his plan and sent along his own ideas on the things these veterans ought to do when they took to the road:

On reflection I think better of your proposition. It will be much better to go South than to be forced to come North. You will no doubt clean the country where you go of railroad tracks and supplies. I would also move every wagon, horse, mule and hoof of stock as well as the Negroes. As far as arms can be supplied either from surplus on hand or by capture I would put them in the hands of Negro men. Give them such organization as you can. They will be of some use.

Grant was a hard-war man, and the proof of it was not the number of men killed in his battles — other generals were fully as grim, courtly Lee among them. What was really hard about Grant was his uncompromising approach to the act of making war at all. He had told Sheridan to ravage the Shenandoah Valley until a foraging crow would starve there, because in the end that would weaken the Rebel armies, and now he was telling Sherman to do the same thing to Georgia, for the same reason. There was nothing in his spirit to make him use the kind of exultantly brutal talk Sherman used about making this kind of war; his orders were flat and unemotional, but they were specific . . . every horse, every mule, every cow, every wagon, every slave — and while you are about it, arm the Negroes as you remove them from restraint, because they may be of some help to you. In the upshot, to be sure, Sherman armed no Negroes, and he went to great lengths to persuade the slaves to stay quietly on the plantation until Washington could work out some program for the transition from bondage to freedom. The terrible Sherman dreaded the chaos that might come from arming the field hands quite as much as Old Massa himself did, and it was the quiet, soft-spoken Grant who was proposing that the South's worst nightmare be brought in from the far edge of night. Grant was not trying to create terror; he simply wanted his lieutenant to make full use of every possible advantage his army might win in a collapsing nation.

If Sherman got credit for devising the plan for a march to the sea, Grant was the man who had to take the responsibility for it with the President and the Secretary of War, and eventually of course with the country as a whole. Lincoln and Stanton had serious reservations, which were not made any lighter by the fact that dedicated Rawlins himself quietly but earnestly appealed to Stanton to quash this dangerous expedition. Grant, to be sure, did not at this time know of Rawlins's intervention, but he did find out about it later and was made bitter by the discovery; his autobiography contains an icy reference to the fact that "my chief of staff . . . appealed to the authorities at Washington to stop it." [4] Meanwhile, on October 13 Grant sent his reasoned assurances to the Secretary of War:

> On mature reflection I believe Sherman's proposition is the best that can be adopted. With the long line of railroad in rear of Atlanta, Sherman cannot maintain his position. If he cuts loose, destroying the road from Chattanooga forward, he leaves a wide and destitute country for the rebels to pass over before reaching territory now held by us. Thomas could retain force enough to meet Hood by giving up the road from Nashville to Decatur and thence to Stevenson and leave Sherman still force enough to meet Hood's Army if it took the other and most likely course. Such an army as Sherman has (and with such a commander) is hard to corner or capture.

At this moment Grant was expressing a little more confidence than he actually had, and he wrote to Sherman stressing the desirability of crushing Hood before beginning the march. But as he continued to think about this Grant finally concluded that for Sherman to run Hood to earth and destroy him would cost much more in time and energy than it would be worth, and at last he wrote: "I really do not see that you can withdraw from where you are to follow Hood without giving up all we have gained in territory. I say, then, go as you propose." He followed this with more formal approval, telegraphed on November 7:

I see no present reason for changing your plan; should any arise, you will see it; or if I do I will inform you. I think everything here favorable now. Great good fortune attend you. I believe you will be eminently successful, and at worst can only make a march less fruitful of results than is hoped for.[5]

Sherman left Atlanta on November 16, cutting the telegraph wires and burning most of the city, and he marched straight off the map, so that no one in the North knew anything about him at all — not where he was, or where he was going to appear next, or what might be happening to him. The President and the Secretary of War, who had such grave doubts, knew nothing, and neither did the general-in-chief, who had sent Sherman off with his blessing and who now remarked that Sherman's army was like a mole under a lawn — you'd never know where it was until at last it came to the surface. President Lincoln took what comfort he could from the reflection that the war must be going very well, because Grant's apparent willingness to risk the loss of Sherman's whole army must rest upon the conviction that the Union cause could survive without it . . . The President deleted from his December message to Congress a sentence containing this reflection, concluding that this was not quite the thing to say in public; and the fact that the President was even thinking it indicates the weight of the responsibility Grant was carrying.[6]

It occurred to Grant that among the people deeply concerned with Sherman's movement was Robert E. Lee, who might send troops to Georgia to meet him, and Grant warned Meade that if that happened he would leave Butler's army to watch the Richmond-Petersburg trenches and take the Army of the Potomac off southward in hot pursuit. Meade was to be prepared to make such a move, taking all of his infantry and cavalry, providing the men with twelve days' rations and forty extra rounds of ammunition, and selecting his best batteries at the rate of one gun for every thousand foot soldiers. Grant was careful to explain the degree of readiness that was called for:

It is not intended that these preparations shall be made to start at a moment's notice, but that the articles shall be where they can be reached and loaded, and all preparation made for starting by the time your troops can be relieved by the troops of General Butler after such movement on the part of the enemy is discovered.[7]

Facing no foes of any consequence, because Hood was marching into Tennessee and Georgia contained nothing but home guards, scatterings of cavalry, and unhappy farmers waiting to be despoiled, Sherman's army moved out of sight, an army that marched not to fight but to avoid fighting; and the tension in the North rose, as if the war now went by a faster drumbeat. Yet this faster beat brought a sluggish response, here and there, and Grant was driven by an increasing impatience. It was impossible, for instance, to get the expedition against Wilmington mounted quickly, although speed was important because Grant suspected that as Sherman approached the coast the Confederates would reduce their force at Wilmington in order to meet him, and powerful Fort Fisher might be weakly held.

The delay here was surprising because the preparations were Butler's job, and he was at least a good organizer; and it appeared presently that he was beset by a curiosity half scientific and half idle, a bemused desire to know what would happen if a shipload of black powder exploded near the seaward ramparts of Fort Fisher. He would find out, before he got through, but his preparations to find out took more time than could properly be spared.

By Grant's order, Butler was preparing a force of two infantry divisions, 6,500 effectives, to be commanded by General Godfrey Weitzel, who had served with Butler in New Orleans, a soldier in whom Butler had confidence. Weitzel was to put his men ashore, with the help and protection of the navy, on the long finger of land that ran down between the ocean and the Cape Fear River, and he was to entrench them from ocean to river a mile or more north of the fort, cutting the place off from Wilmington, which lay twenty miles upstream. The navy, using the most powerful fleet it could muster, would bombard the fort heavily, and if the army could then take it by storm that would be excellent; but if the army merely stayed in its trenches that would be just about as good, because the port would be sealed and Wilmington could receive no more blockade-runners. The army would be able to reach the desired position without great trouble if it got there while the disposable Confederate troops at Wilmington were down in Georgia waiting for Sherman.

So ran Grant's plan; but there was this matter of a powder ship. When he learned that Butler wanted to try to subdue the fort in this way Grant raised no objection: there were down-at-the-heel steamboats to spare, the army had plenty of condemned powder that was not fit for regular issue but was no doubt good enough for a project like this, the stunt could do no harm and of course if it worked the army would gain a great victory on the cheap. Grant may have been influenced a little by the fact that the officer who was to have charge of the navy's half of the expedition, Admiral David Dixon Porter, a man whom Grant held in high regard, was almost as much fascinated by the powder ship idea as Butler himself. Anyhow, the army engineers got a small propeller, the *Louisiana*, removed its masts and armament, added a dummy smokestack and a new paint job in order to disguise the craft as a blockade-runner, and then built a false deck in the hold just below the waterline. All of this done, 215 tons of powder were put aboard, in open-ended barrels and in canvas bags, and an intricate network of fuses was arranged so that all of the separate containers could be reached by flame at the same instant.

The engineers were skeptical. Butler apparently had been impressed by accounts of the accidental explosion, that autumn, of two British powder barges on the lower Thames, and by the flattening effect the blast had on the landscape in the immediate vicinity. The engineers were less impressed; they noted that the explosion had done no great harm at any distance, it seemed probable that the open air would absorb most of the force of Butler's blast, the massive earthworks at Fort Fisher were extremely solid, not likely to be harmed much by an explosion out beyond the surf . . . but Butler was in command, orders were orders, and so the *Louisiana* was turned into an infernal machine. This may not have been the whole cause of the delay. Butler complained that the navy was not ready on time, although Grant seems to have taken no stock in this complaint. In any case the expedition was more than a fortnight late when it moved.

On November 30 Grant read Southern newspaper stories saying that Braxton Bragg was taking most of the troops at Wilmington down to Georgia, and so Grant warned Butler to get Weitzel off as soon as possible. He repeated this warning on December 4, saying that Sherman would reach the coast any day now and that Bragg would then be free to return to Wilmington; Bragg's mission, to protect Augusta, would end as soon as Sherman struck at Savannah, and so Butler must get his people started at once, "with or without your powder boat." Two days later Grant made another call for speed, he repeated it on December 7, and on December 11 he told Butler that Sherman now was reported within twenty-five miles of Savannah, so "if you do not get off immediately you will lose the chance of surprise and weak garrison." Three days later he applied the spur, remarking: "It is a great pity we were not 10 or 12 days earlier." And at last, that evening, Weitzel and his two divisions sailed from Hampton Roads, reaching the point of rendezvous with the navy, New Inlet, not far from Fort Fisher, twenty-four hours later.[8]

Yet even when the amphibious expedition finally sailed the tension did not end, because there were two great handicaps. For one, a week of bad weather intervened, making any kind of active operations impossible; for another, Ben Butler went along in active command, making successful operations highly improbable no matter how the weather went. This was a last minute switch. It had been clearly understood all along that Butler would organize the expedition but that Weitzel would sail in command of it; but after all the whole thing was taking place in Butler's department, and if Butler wanted to go along he had a clear legal right to do so. Grant learned at the last minute that Butler was going to sail, but he was not greatly disturbed, partly because he supposed the man simply wanted to go as a spectator and partly because Grant's written orders so definitely named Weitzel as the commanding officer. Grant assumed as matter of course that Butler had passed these orders along properly, and he said later that it never entered his head that Butler was going to assume operational control: "I rather formed the idea that General Butler was actuated by a desire to witness the effect of the explosion of the powder boat."[9]

Grant probably worried about all of this with only part of his mind, because what was really bothering him was the situation in Tennessee.

Hood had moved north, as he had threatened to do, while Thomas, at Nashville, was organizing an army out of the rejects and the bits and pieces he had been given from all over the western theater of war. Thomas had an advance guard of 25,000 men under General Schofield at Franklin, Tennessee, and Hood made a savage attack on this force on November 30. The battle was one of the most desperate and tragically needless of the whole war; Hood lost 6,000 men in one afternoon's fighting, gaining nothing that he would not have gained if he had simply waited. Schofield retreated that night to Nashville, just as he would have done if he had not been attacked at all; he had halted at Franklin only to give his wagon trains time to get away, and in the battle his losses were far below Hood's. Hood followed him, took position on the hills just south of Nashville, and somewhat aimlessly waited for Thomas to make the next move.

Hood was not strong enough to attack, to retreat would be to lose face, he did not feel able to sidestep and move on into Kentucky, and in sober fact he was altogether at a dead end; and his army, standing-to in the bleak December sunlight, was doing little more than wait for the executioner. But from afar this doomed army looked like the certified shadow of death, and Washington took alarm and felt mortal anguish, which it passed on to the general-in-chief who had been appointed to bear such burdens. What made this burden so intolerable, in the White House and in the War Department, was the awful suspicion that the victory which at last was beginning to look so near might disappear forever if anything went seriously wrong in Tennessee.

Final triumph was in sight. It was coming down to the sea with Sherman, moving under fire and smoke across the rice fields toward Savannah, destined to come on up the coast across the Carolinas until the Army of the Potomac would have to do no more than reach out its hand in order to grasp it firmly, and it seemed that nothing could stop it except some inexplicable disaster far off to the west. The disaster, to be sure, was most improbable, and yet it was impossible to keep from thinking about it because it would be so terrible if it did happen. Although he did not share the deep gloom that leaked down from Washington, Grant realized that much more was at stake than he could afford to lose, and during this first fortnight in December he was beset by a total inability to get anyone to move *fast*. It was bad to see Butler so late when Fort Fisher (as it was thought) could be had for the taking, and it was worse to see Thomas equally tardy when Hood was so vulnerable; and it was altogether maddening to realize that as Sherman approached the climax of his great adventure it was impossible to get speedy action either in his front or in his rear. Probably Colonel Porter did not miss it by much when he wrote that this was "the most anxious period of Grant's entire military career."

V.'hat was feared both at Washington and at City Point was not that Hood would overpower Thomas and capture Nashville but that he would slip past him, get into Kentucky, perhaps all the way to the Ohio River, and rampage about there so destructively that the underpinning for all of the Federal operations in the east and southeast would be destroyed. During the summer General Early had shown how much harm a comparatively small force could do once it got behind an invading army, and if Hood got loose it would be much worse because Hood was accompanied by Bedford Forrest and Forrest's hand-raised, hard-fighting cavalry. Over the long run, of course, anything Hood and Forrest might do could probably be neutralized, but Grant was afraid that if Hood got north of the Cumberland it might be necessary to send troops from the east to head him off; all of which would be very bad for the Federal campaigns in Virginia and in Georgia.

General Thomas, to be sure, was a defensive genius, but he had genius's legendary capacity for taking infinite pains, and while he was taking them there was no rushing him. Until he got his military house in order he was not going to bring Hood to battle no matter what anybody said. He was carefully building an army out of many separate elements, most of which were late in reaching him, and he had brought General James Wilson from the east to reorganize and refit his cavalry, which was numerous but lacked horses, and it all took a good deal of time. Unfortunately, Grant underestimated the weight of the obstacles Thomas had to move . . . but by this time Grant had seen too many bright chances lost because some general was unable to hurry or saw good reason for letting orders from above go unexecuted, and he was out of patience altogether. He wrote later that Thomas's delay was unaccountable — "sitting there and permitting himself to be invested, so that, in the end, to raise the siege he would have to fight the enemy strongly posted behind fortifications" — and he was not disposed to accept excuses. Even if he had felt more tolerant of delay, Washington was breathing down his neck, and on December 2, the day Hood pulled his battered army up in front of the Federal lines at Nashville, Secretary Stanton sent Grant a sharp reminder:

The President feels solicitous about the disposition of General Thomas to lay in fortifications for an indefinite period "until Wilson gets equipments." This looks like the McClellan and Rosecrans strategy of do nothing and let the Rebels raid the country. The President wishes you to consider the matter.[10]

Grant was considering it, and he did not like it at all. He had already warned Thomas that to let Hood sit facing him, unmolested, was to risk the loss of all of central Tennessee, and after he got Stanton's telegram he sent Thomas another message urging him to take the offensive: "You will now suffer incalculable injury upon your railroads if Hood is not speedily disposed of. Put forth therefore every possible exertion to attain this end. Should you get him to retreating, give him no peace." A few days later Stanton sent word that "Thomas seems unwilling to attack, because it is hazardous — as if all war was anything but hazardous," and Grant, replying that there was no better man than Thomas to repel an attack, felt obliged to add that "I fear he is too cautious to take the initiative." He warned Thomas that delay probably strengthened the Confederates as much as the Federals, and then curtly ordered him: "Attack Hood at once and wait no longer for a remnant of your cavalry. There is great danger of delay resulting in a campaign back to the Ohio river." Thomas, who was methodically getting ready but who was not going to cut any corners even though the skies fell, replied that things were not quite in hand yet, and Grant sent an appeal that almost begged Thomas to move:

Why not attack at once? By all means avoid the contingency of a foot race to see which, you or Hood, can beat to the Ohio. . . . Now is one of the finest opportunities ever presented of destroying one of the three armies of the enemy. If destroyed he can never replace it. Use the means at your command, and you can do this and cause a rejoicing that will resound from one end of the land to the other.

All of these demands for action were sandwiched in with similar demands to Ben Butler, who was waiting for his powder ship to be remodeled, and Grant's feelings were not greatly improved when Thomas replied that he had been on the verge of ordering a general attack but that "a terrible storm of freezing rain has come on today, which will make it impossible for our men to fight to any advantage." The projected offensive, therefore, was postponed. It would be executed as soon as the ice melted.

From all accounts the sleet storm was a once-in-a-lifetime affair, covering roads and fields with glare ice and making it quite impossible to move horses or guns and almost impossible to move people, and nobody who was in Nashville at the time doubted that Thomas was justified in calling off his attack. But a commanding general who is told that an offensive already a week overdue has been indefinitely postponed because of bad weather is not likely to take it very well, and Grant told Halleck to draft an order relieving Thomas of his command and putting General Schofield in his place. Halleck gave him a blunt reply:

"If you wish General Thomas relieved, give the order. No one here will, I think, interfere. The responsibility, however, will be yours, as no one here, as far as I am informed, wishes General Thomas's removal."

Grant notified Halleck that he would not call for a removal order until he got further word from Thomas, and it seemed to Colonel Porter that the administration was carefully building a record — it would be Grant's fault if Hood broke loose and went to the Ohio, but it would also be Grant's fault if the country concluded that the great Rock of Chickamauga had been unfairly relieved just when he was about to win another victory. This did not bother Grant, because that is the sort of heat generals-in-chief are supposed to endure, but he did want action; and Halleck quietly warned Thomas that Grant was exceedingly dissatisfied. Stoutly enough, Thomas told Grant that if he were relieved from his command he would submit without a whimper; but meanwhile the ice was still on the ground and there would be no battle until it melted.[11]

By now this telegraphic exchange was doubtless a trial to everybody, but when a soldier of Thomas's stature is threatened with removal he is entitled to an explanation, and Grant sent one: "I have as much confidence in your conducting a battle rightly as I have in any other officer; but it has seemed to me that you have been slow, and I have had no explanation of affairs to convince me otherwise." An order removing Thomas (Grant went on) had been drafted, but it had been suspended pending further word. Meanwhile: "I hope most sincerely that there will be no necessity of repeating the order, and that the facts will show that you have been right all the time." Completely subordinate, but also completely immovable, Thomas replied that the storm continued and he would fight when the weather moderated. Grant sent back word that he hoped Thomas's next telegram would say the battle had begun, and he closed with the order: "Delay no longer for weather or reinforcements." The best Thomas could say to this was that the ice was still there, and that an immediate attack would be costly and unwise.

By now it was December 14, and Grant had had enough. He could not see what was so easily seen at Nashville — that Hood was at the end of the passage, unable to strike or to go away, waiting for the finishing blow to fall on him. All Grant knew was that a battle essential to his whole strategic program was not being fought because a sleet storm had immobilized a notoriously deliberate general; and John A. Logan, on leave from Sherman's army, was at City Point just now, and to him Grant gave an order relieving Thomas from command and putting Logan in his place. With the written order Grant gave Logan oral instructions: He was to start for Nashville at once, and if when he reached Louisville Thomas had made his move Logan was to keep the order in his pocket and get in touch with Grant by telegraph. If not, he was to go through with it.

Logan was the soldier who took command of the Army of the Tennessee in the middle of the battle of Atlanta, the day McPherson was killed, and he had had spectacular success on the field, riding along hard-pressed battle lines with his long mustache astream, shouting encouragement in a great barrelhouse voice, while the enlisted men chanted his nickname: "Black Jack! Black Jack!" He was one of the greatest of the political generals — brilliant, outspoken, sometimes hard for a regular army officer to get along with — and much to his disappointment after the battle Sherman refused to retain him as army commander, and put Howard in his place. By the oddest chance it had been Thomas who talked Sherman into rejecting Logan; Thomas found Logan contentious and dreaded the prospect of working beside him, Thomas in command of one army, Logan in command of another. Sherman as a matter of fact had planned to keep Logan in command, but he valued harmony in the chain of command as much as Grant did, and he let Thomas have his way. As it happened, neither Grant nor Logan knew of this; and now Logan was on his way west carrying Grant's order that would empower him to take Thomas's command.

Meanwhile Grant did some more thinking and concluded that he himself had to go west. Whether Thomas was to be sustained or removed, Grant ought to do it in person and on the spot, and above all it was time for the general-in-chief to make certain that Hood was beaten and his army removed from the board. So Grant packed a bag and took the night boat for Washington, sending a hasty note to Meade saying "I am unexpectedly called away" and explaining that Rawlins would handle or forward any messages. And that evening in Nashville the Tennessee weather finally moderated and it was warm, all the ice melting; and Thomas wrote orders for an attack on Hood's lines first thing the next morning.[12]

Grant got to Washington on the morning of December 15, and the first thing he saw was a note from Halleck giving the text of Thomas's order for a battle that day. If there was going to be a fight Grant would wait; and after he had waited awhile he learned that Thomas had attacked all along the line and was everywhere successful, and so Grant's plan to go to Nashville dissolved forever and he sent Thomas a message urging: "Push the enemy and give him no rest until he is entirely destroyed. Your army will cheerfully suffer many privations to break up Hood's army and render it useless for future operations. Do not stop for trains or supplies, but take them from the country as the enemy has done. Much is now expected."

Here, after many delays and frustrations, was the old note again, the demand that each victory be made absolute: what has been won is great but *much is now expected*, and this was the everlasting essence of General Grant . . . That night Thomas reported he had driven the enemy for miles and would drive him some more next day, and Grant replied: "I congratulate you and the army under your command for today's operations, and feel a conviction that tomorrow will add more fruits to your victory." In Louisville John Logan realized that he was never going to be an army commander after all, and he telegraphed Grant: "People here jubilant over Thomas's success . . . It would seem best that I return to join my command with Sherman." Grant agreed, telling him: "The news from Thomas so far is in the highest degree gratifying. You need not go farther." [13]

And suddenly the tension was gone, and to the end of the war it was never again as bad as it had been during the first fortnight in December. Thomas drove Hood down past the Tennessee River and on out of Tennessee forever, and although Hood saved most of his army it had been wrecked and it never again carried any appreciable amount of weight for the Confederacy. On December 17 the Army of the Potomac — the luckless army that did the drudgery while the other armies had the fun and won the headlines — fired another of those hundred gun salutes, celebrating the great battle of Nashville. A week later, Meade ordered still another one; Sherman had brought his swinging, loose-jointed army down to the coast and had captured Savannah. The victory was slightly ragged, because the 10,000 Confederates who defended Savannah should have been captured and were not, but that made very little difference; the march to the sea had ended in triumph, and the Confederacy now amounted to little more than the men, the land and the frozen hopes that lay between Savannah and Richmond. Sherman sent Lincoln an inspired telegram offering Savannah as a Christmas gift; Meade's gunners dutifully hammered out their interminable salute; and the long journey Grant began in April, when he left Tennessee to go to Washington, was by the year's end fairly close to completion.[14]

Fairly close: with a note of failure to be fitted somewhere into the triumphal harmony, because Ben Butler, consistent to the end, failed to take Fort Fisher. He finally got there, waited for better weather, learned that his famous powder ship had been blown up without having the least effect, watched the navy make a prolonged bombardment of the massive sandhill stronghold, and on Christmas day got his troops ashore just where they were supposed to go. Once the men were in line facing the fort, Butler's high hopes left him; neither the powder vessel nor the bombardment seemed to have done the fort very much harm, Godfrey Weitzel reported that he did not think the fort could be carried by storm, Grant's orders to dig in and wait it out were forgotten — and, after a short time, Butler reembarked his troops and sailed back to Hampton Roads, comforting himself with the thought that he had extracted his troops from a situation of great peril without incurring a useless loss of life. (His casualties: one man drowned, two killed, one officer captured through error, and ten men wounded by fragments from the navy's shells.)

After repeated efforts, Butler had at last tried his luck too far. The failure here was spectacular and unrelieved, and there was no possible way to blame it on anybody else. Grant had sent Colonel Comstock along as an observer, and Comstock reported that the same number of troops under the same conditions could take the fort if the attempt were made again. Admiral Porter told the Navy Department the same thing, and when Lincoln asked what had gone wrong Grant wrote an indignant reply:

The Wilmington expedition has proven a gross and culpable failure. Many of the troops are now back here. Delays and free talk of the object of the expedition enabled the enemy to move troops to Wilmington to defeat it. After the expedition sailed from Fort Monroe three days of fine weather was squandered, during which the enemy was without a force to protect himself. Who is to blame I hope will be known.

Grant had no trouble satisfying himself on the last point. He talked to Butler immediately after he sent that message to Lincoln, and Colonel Porter reported that the session was heated. Grant learned that Weitzel, who was supposed to be commanding the operation, had never been shown the orders Grant had written, and Butler had clearly been flatly disobedient in withdrawing his troops without a fight. Secretary of the Navy Gideon Welles notified Grant that Admiral Porter would hold the fleet together, in case Grant wanted to try Fort Fisher again, and Grant sent a quick word to the admiral: "Please hold on where you are for a few days and I will endeavor to be back again with an increased force and without the former commander." [15]

Then — on January 4, 1865 — Grant settled the business once and for all, sending the following letter to Secretary Stanton:

I am constrained to request the removal of Maj. Gen. B. F. Butler from the command of the Department of Virginia and North Carolina. I do this with reluctance, but the good of the service requires it. In my absence General Butler necessarily commands, and there is a lack of confidence felt in his military ability, making him an unsafe commander for a large army. His administration of the affairs of his department is also objectionable.

As it happened, Secretary Stanton was not in Washington at this time. As soon as he found out about this Grant sent a wire to President Lincoln:

"I wrote a letter to the Secretary of War, which was mailed yesterday, asking to have General Butler removed from command. Learning that the Secretary left Washington yesterday, I telegraph you asking that prompt action may be taken in the matter." [16]

White House and War Department moved promptly — possibly responding, like the lieutenant general commanding, to the fact that a presidential election no longer lay just ahead — and on January 8 Butler was formally served with the papers that ended his military career. General Ord was named to replace him, and General A. H. Terry was given the command unlucky Weitzel had had, with orders to get back to Fort Fisher as soon as might be.

The only thing out of the ordinary about Grant's message to Secretary Stanton was the fact that in it, for the first time, Grant criticized Butler as an administrator. Odd things had been taking place in Butler's department. Contraband goods seemed to be moving through the lines in considerable volume — a good deal of stuff, it was said, went direct to Lee's army, which Grant was trying so hard to choke to death — and Butler had arbitrarily arrested various persons who were thought to know too much about what was going on. After the Fort Fisher expedition had sailed Grant sent a slightly cryptic note to Halleck:

"I wish you would order one of the inspectors-general to report to me for special duty. I want to get in an official form some facts that I have learned in regard to arbitrary arrests and punishment by the commander of the Department of North Carolina and Virginia."

Nothing much ever came of this. Nobody ever found a very clear trail where Butler had been; it occurs to one, occasionally, that Butler was the favored child of fortune of the principal investigating agency of those days, the Joint Congressional Committee on the Conduct of the War. About all that is clear about Butler's removal is that Grant had a completely free hand and used it without hesitation. After he had reflected on the matter for a few weeks, Grant wrote to his old friend, Captain Dan Ammen of the navy:

"You have no doubt seen by the papers that the very thing you so strongly hoped had already taken place. I mean, Butler had been removed at my request. The failure at Fort Fisher was not without important and valuable results." [17]

CHAPTER TWENTY-ONE

A Letter from General Lee

O N THE first day of January, 1865, there was a fragile quiet along the Petersburg and Bermuda Hundred trenches. A few days earlier the picket-line grapevine, that unofficial means of communication which the enlisted men had devised for their own purposes, brought to the Federals the word that Lee's army was going to have a New Year's Day feast. Friends back home had sent packages of food, local citizens had given what they could, the hungry Confederates were going to make a holiday of it — and across the picket line came a reminder that when the Yankees celebrated Thanksgiving Day in this manner, a few weeks earlier, the Southerners had refrained from firing on them. Informed of this, Grant sent out orders that there should be no firing on New Year's Day except in reply to shots from the Confederate side. Writing to his wife, John Rawlins declared: "We are not to be outdone, either in fighting or magnanimity." [1]

To Grant himself the new year brought restored health. Just before Christmas he had been assailed by one of the devastating bilious attacks that struck him now and then, and it was not a good time for him to be laid up. He took a whole handful of pills and several Seidlitz powders without effect, spent a day in his cot eating no meals and even abstaining from cigars, and he unhappily wrote to Julia: "I have felt more like a spell of sickness than at any time since the beginning of the war . . . It would not do for me to get sick at this time when there is so much to do and when we have it in our hands to do so much towards the suppression of the rebellion." A couple of days later he was more hopeful, less because of the medicines than because he had simply made up his mind not to be sick, and he wrote: "Today is the first time I have been out to dinner for three days. I know how much there is dependent on me and will prove myself equal to the task. I believe determination can do a good deal to sustain one, and I have that quality certainly to the fullest extent." On January 1 he was quite well again, although he thought he would begin to take quinine regularly.

Grant was careless about what he ate, and there were those who felt that this caused his periodic headaches. Years later Hamlin Garland talked to a good many of the headquarters people and put down his verdict: "He was a very injudicious eater, and his stomach was his weak point. He ate very little — too little, in fact — but he was quite as apt to eat pickles and cake, mingled with cream and vinegar and lettuce, as he was to take more wholesome foods. . . . Such lack of care had often brought about indigestion."

Grant himself probably would have replied that it was army cooking that laid him low. Early in October Julia suggested that she bring east a girl from Galena who had cooked for them sometime earlier, and Grant wrote an enthusiastic reply: "The twenty-five or thirty dollars that it will cost to get her east is nothing to the comfort of having a good cook. I want of all things good cooking when I get back home. It makes the greatest difference to my feeling well." [2]

In any case Grant was back in shape when the new year began, and he had plenty to do. Late in December he had been studying the way to bring Sherman's army up from Savannah to the Petersburg area. He had intended to move it by sea, but he found that to get the ships together would take at least two months, and to waste two months at this stage of the war was inadmissible. Sherman, who was beginning to believe that his men could do anything, coolly proposed that the army march north across the Carolinas, although the unpaved roads in tidewater lowlands were supposed to be impassable in the rainy winter months. Grant quickly agreed, and began arranging to have reinforcements and supplies on hand to meet Sherman at some point halfway up the coast.

The projected seizure of Fort Fisher would mesh with this nicely — Wilmington would make an ideal Federal base — and even before Butler had been removed Grant had the expeditionary force afloat again, with a new commander, General Alfred H. Terry, who had a division in Ord's corps. Terry was a quiet man who had never gone soldiering before the war. A lawyer, he was clerk of the Superior Court at New Haven when the war broke out, and he had led a regiment down to Bull Run along with all the other political colonels.

Since then he had gone on various coastal expeditions and had learned a good deal about amphibious warfare, and he sailed now bearing sealed orders and Grant's firm warning that he was expected to get along harmoniously with Admiral Porter. On January 8 Terry's transports met Porter's fleet at Beaufort, North Carolina. Five days later, while Porter's fleet pounded Fort Fisher with the heaviest naval bombardment the world had yet seen, Terry got his men ashore; and Ben Butler, who had put the same men ashore in the same place a few weeks earlier, but had failed to keep them there, and who more recently had composed and issued to his troops a windy, overblown message of farewell, was preparing to tell his story in Washington to the sympathetic members of the Committee on the Conduct of the War.[3]

What was done in the Carolinas was just part of the complicated task that engaged Grant as the new year opened. The Confederacy was visibly shaky, and the power to bring it down forever was at hand if it could be used quickly, all the efforts coordinated under an intelligent plan; the point being that the quickness, the coordination and the plan itself had to come from General Grant. In the west there were idle troops, and on the coast and in the Deep South there were vulnerable points to be struck; and in many places, too, there was inertia to overcome, a leisurely habit of mind to which empty weeks that drifted away unused seemed like nothing lost. In Washington there was President Lincoln, who saw things as Grant saw them and who wrote to Secretary Stanton: "*Time*, now that the enemy is wavering, is more important than ever before. Being on the downhill, and somewhat confused, keep him going."[4]

Grant looked first at Tennessee, where Thomas had the army that had given Hood such a decisive beating. As things stood this army could go just about anywhere in the South it was told to go, but Grant did not think Pap Thomas was the man to take it there; rightly or wrongly, he was convinced that Thomas was simply unable to move fast, and he told Sherman that he feared now it would be impossible to get any action out of Thomas before spring. So as a first step Grant ordered Thomas to send Schofield east at once with his Twenty-third Corps, 21,000 men. By the time Schofield reached the seaboard, Grant believed, Fort Fisher would have been taken; Schofield and Terry together could then occupy Wilmington, and after that they could move inland to Goldsboro, fifty miles southeast of Raleigh, picking up a Federal garrison of 4,000 from New Berne as they went. At Goldsboro they could either await Sherman's army or attack the rear of any force that might be opposing it.

While this was happening, Thomas was to send A. J. Smith and 16,000 men to Canby, who was then to take Mobile and come ranging northward across Alabama. Blending Smith's force with his own, and leaving troops on the coast to garrison Mobile and other points, Canby would be able to form a marching column of at least 20,000 men; and they would not be operating alone. To cooperate with them, Thomas would send Wilson and his cavalry corps into Alabama from Eastport, Mississippi, probably toward Selma and Montgomery. Wilson would have to meet the terrible Bedford Forrest, but Forrest's strength was not what it had been; and besides, Wilson's force was one of the most formidable roving columns put together during the war. One reason Thomas had risked his career postponing his attack on Hood had been to give Wilson time to reorganize the cavalry, and now the work was beginning to pay off. When Wilson finished re-equipping and reorganizing he would have 12,000 superbly mounted men, all of them armed with repeating rifles and trained to fight on foot; they had more firepower than an infantry corps, they could move much faster than any infantry, and there was nothing in the South that could stop them.

All of these operations were keyed to the move Sherman was going to make, and Grant notified Sherman that their commanders would be subject to Sherman's orders. Thomas would have an infantry reserve in Tennessee that could be used wherever it was needed: if Lee, under final pressure, tried to escape westward by way of Lynchburg, these men could stand in his path until help came. Meanwhile, Thomas had 4,000 cavalry in east Tennessee under General George Stoneman, who had commanded Joe Hooker's cavalry back in the Chancellorsville era; and Stoneman now was directed to ride down through the mountains into South Carolina, jarring things loose ahead of Sherman and returning to his own lines by way of Salisbury, North Carolina, where there was a big prisoner-of-war camp to be taken. Finally, if anything unexpected went wrong on Sherman's march northward, Grant could send at least 30,000 men to the rescue from the troops in front of Petersburg.[5]

This program had a continental sweep. Its scope and terms implied that the Confederacy had already been defeated and that it was time now to cut up the fragments and put them away for keeps; unless

Federal commanders missed their cues through gross inattention or delay there was not really very much the Southern leaders could do to prevent it. The separate acts in a long drama were at last coming into perspective. The Federals were applying an inexorable pressure that did not come from the sheer weight of numbers; after all, they had had that weight at their disposal from the day the war began. Strategic advantages gained far apart in time and space — May to December, Tennessee and Virginia to Alabama and Georgia — had a cumulative effect, and the weight of them now was irresistible. People who cried out against stupid reliance on brute strength had failed to see that things had been moving to a broad pattern with consistent speed. In spring the Southern nation had still been a unit, westward to the sunset and southward to the Gulf, and it had been reasonable to think that Europe might someday recognize it as a permanent creation; now it was mere fragments strewn across the twilight in the winter rains, and only the dedicated few could dream that it would live much beyond the spring.

What clouded the prospect was the fact that so many people, in the North and also in the South, could see nothing but Lee's army when they looked at the war. That army seemed to be about where it had been all along, defiant and undefeated, and when people stared at it fixedly they were apt to conclude that the Federals were not getting anywhere. In the middle of January Mrs. Meade wrote to her husband that she heard a good deal of harsh criticism of General Grant, and Meade replied: "Grant undoubtedly has lost prestige, owing to his failure to accomplish more, but as I know it has not been in his power to do more I cannot approve of unmerited censure, any more than I approved of the fulsome praise showered on him before the campaign commenced." Meade believed the Committee on the Conduct of the War would uphold Butler's part in the Fort Fisher fiasco, and he predicted: "This is the beginning of a war on Grant." [6]

In Congress there were indeed members who were growing restive, and as they came to like Grant's looks less some of them liked Sherman's more; it was rumored that a bill to create another lieutenant general might be passed this winter. In Savannah Sherman heard about it, and as he prepared for his march into South Carolina he wrote Grant that he had asked his brother, Senator John Sherman, to stop it, adding: "It would be mischievous, for there are enough rascals who would try to sow differences between us, whereas you and I now are in perfect understanding. I would rather have you in command than anybody else; for you are fair, honest, and have at heart the same purpose that should animate all. I should emphatically decline any commission calculated to bring us into rivalry."

Grant was not worried, and he wrote Sherman a warm reply which shows the depth of the attachment he felt for him:

"No one would be more pleased at your advancement than I, and if you should be placed in my position and I put subordinate it would not change our relations in the least. I would make the same exertions to support you that you have ever done to support me, and I would do all in my power to make our cause win." [7]

Grant had occasion this winter to write to his friends on Capitol Hill regarding promotion in the army, but this had nothing to do with the Sherman business (of which, incidentally, nothing more was heard); instead, Grant was trying to get justice for General Meade, who beneath his furious temper was a highly sensitive person, grieved now because his promotion to major general of regulars, sent to the Senate weeks earlier, was not being acted on. Grant wrote to Congressman Washburne, asking him to put in a word with influential Senators in Meade's favor, and he repeated a strong endorsement of his own: "Gen. Meade is one of our truest men and ablest officers. He has been constantly with that Army confronting the strongest, best appointed and most confident army in the South. He therefore has not had the same opportunity of winning laurels so distinctly marked as have fallen to the lot of other Generals. But I defy any man to name a commander who would do more than he has done with the same chances." Grant also wrote to Senator Henry Wilson, chairman of the Committee on Military Affairs, and before the fortnight was out the Senate confirmed the promotion and Meade got the reward he was entitled to.

For his part, Meade had been thinking about Grant's abilities. He was concluding, at last, that these abilities were substantial, although like Sherman Meade was never quite ready to say that Grant was really *great*. Sherman, rising to his peroration, had said that Grant was fair, honest and devoted, definitely to be preferred to anyone else. Meade said much the same thing, in a letter sent during late autumn to Henry A. Cram of New York, brother-in-law of Mrs. Meade.

"Grant is not a mighty genius," wrote Meade, "but he is a good soldier of great force of character, honest and upright, of pure purposes, I think, without political aspirations . . . His prominent quality is unflinching tenacity of purpose, which blinds him to opposition and obstacles — certainly a great quality in a commander, when controlled by judgment, but a dangerous one otherwise.

"Grant is not without his faults and weaknesses. Among these is a want of sensibility, an almost too confident and sanguine disposition, and particularly a simple and guileless disposition, which is apt to put him, unknown to himself, under the influence of those who should not influence him and desire to do so only for their own purposes. Take him all in all, he is in my judgment the best man the war has yet produced." [8]

Not long after this Grant wrote letters about still another promotion — this time, a brigadier generalship in the regular army, which he asked and got for General Terry, former clerk of courts. Terry's troops stormed and took Fort Fisher on January 15 after a two-day naval bombardment, closing the Confederacy's last seaport and neatly completing the job Butler had considered impossible. Terry and Porter had worked together smoothly — the navy even sent 2,000 sailors and marines ashore to make a diversionary attack while Terry's men stormed the fort's landward face; the navy got severe casualties out of this while the army got most of the glory, but interservice harmony was unbroken. Terry got promotion, and the formal thanks of Congress to boot, and he became a career soldier and stayed in the army as a general officer after the war, commanding the Yellowstone River expedition of 1876 in which George Custer slipped the leash and rode off to death and stained glory; and because fame is most freakish Terry is remembered today largely as Custer's last commander, his excellent Civil War record almost forgotten.

Anyway, Fort Fisher was gone, Federal warships were at anchor inside the Cape Fear River, and the era of the blockade-runner was over. Schofield and his troops came east fast, and before January ended they were at the head of navigation on the Potomac, waiting for an ice jam to melt so that they could go south and make the attack on Wilmington. (The first step in getting Sherman north from Savannah, thus, was to uproot 21,000 men from the middle of Tennessee and take them on a journey 1,400 miles long; all to the end that hardtack, bacon and shoes could be laid down in eastern North Carolina, at a proper date in the spring.) Schofield's men would be able to start down the Potomac about February 1, on which day Sherman's army would move into South Carolina, with secession's birthplace Charleston lying helpless beside its path. As he supervised these moves, Grant also busied himself with the more routine chores that were attached to his job.

The Army of the James of course had a new commander, E. O. C. Ord, and its old corps had been broken up. In their place were two new groups — Twenty-fourth Corps, under John Gibbon, who was brought over from the Army of the Potomac, and Twenty-fifth Corps under Godfrey Weitzel, whose standing had suffered no harm from his inability to evade Butler's crippling hand during the first thrust at Fort Fisher. All of the colored troops in the Army of the James were put in Weitzel's corps, along with the colored division from the Ninth Corps of Meade's army, and fame (to repeat) comes in around unexpected corners; two years earlier in New Orleans, Weitzel had protested that he did not believe in colored troops and did not want to command them, and now he sat at the gates of Richmond in command of many thousands of them, and when the citadel fell he would lead them in and share with them the glory of occupying the Rebel capital.[9]

Grant this winter was getting a closer look at the trade with the enemy that had gone on so vigorously under Butler around Norfolk, and it was exactly like what he had seen earlier in the Mississippi valley. There the rapacity of the cotton traders had led him to send his own father ignominiously back to Ohio, and after this he had exploded with an ill-judged, quickly withdrawn attack on Jews as the authors of infamy. What was going on in Virginia, as elsewhere, was a steady southward movement of Northern sugar, bacon, salt, coffee and other military necessities in return for bales of Southern cotton. To a man the traders who kept this movement going had Treasury Department permits, and some of them had letters from Abraham Lincoln himself — letters that usually said no more than that the President was willing for these men to carry on their trade provided the army authorities immediately concerned saw no harm in it: meaningless enough, yet weighty when flourished before some dazed outpost officer far down the chain of command. Lincoln had assured Grant that "I wish you to be judge and master on these points," and on February 7 he told Grant that a man named Laws was pestering him about a steamboat load of contraband which Grant had refused to let him take south. "Tonight Mr. Laws calls on me," wrote the President, "and I have told him, and now tell you, that the matter as to his passing the lines is under your control absolutely; and that he can have any relaxation you choose to give him and none other."

Grant did not in the least mind saying no to cotton traders, but he did want to be sure that when he said it he was not going to be reversed by the President, and Lincoln's letter to him crossed a bristling telegram Grant had just sent to Secretary Stanton:

A Mr. Laws is here with a steamer partially loaded with sugar and coffee, and a permit from the Treasury Department to go through into Virginia and North Carolina and bring out 10,000 bales of cotton. I have positively refused to adopt this mode of feeding the Southern army unless it is the direct order of the President. It is a humiliating fact that speculators have represented the location of cotton at different points in the South, and obtained permits to bring it out, covering more than the entire amount of the staple in all the cotton-growing states.

When Grant talked in that tone, people in Washington listened, and Stanton immediately replied:

The President directs that you will regard all trade permits, licenses or privileges of every kind, by whomsoever signed . . . as subject to your authority and approval . . . and such permits as you deem prejudicial to the military service by feeding or supporting the Rebel armies . . . you may disregard and annul, and if necessary to the public safety seize the property of the traders.

That was that, and Grant passed the word on to Canby at New Orleans, where the pressure for trade with the enemy was worst of all. Grant said that Canby should restrict the movement of Southern produce with a sole eye to military necessities. He himself (he went on) had always believed that entire nonintercourse with the people in rebellion was the best way to bring about a lasting peace, but a good many people back home thought this sort of trade useful because it helped to meet the expense of the war, and "speculators who have trade permits, universally a worse class of people with an army than the worst rebels falling within our lines, do all they can to stimulate this opinion." [10]

In the end-of-the-year reorganization the Army of the Potomac lost Winfield Scott Hancock, and it did not look quite the same without him. In the spring of 1862, during the first fighting on the Virginia peninsula, McClellan called Hancock "the superb," and the name stuck, largely because Hancock often *was* superb. Ever since then he had been one of the country's most famous soldiers. Hancock had never quite recovered from his Gettysburg wound, and as his proud Second Corps (thinned way down and then bloated with bounty men) fell far below its old fighting form he had an unhappy summer. Early in November he said privately that he was tired of serving with this army, remarking testily that "we do not get any of the credit, considering the fighting we do." He heard that Meade was going to be relieved and that he himself would get Meade's job, but he said that he did not want it, adding that the place would probably go to Sheridan anyway. It seems probable that Hancock had been listening to some out-of-date gossip; in July Grant had considered putting him in Meade's place but he dropped that idea when Sheridan took over in the Shenandoah, and now Meade's standing was firm enough. Anyway, Hancock was morose, and Grant told him about a plan to give him a new field of service.

The War Department, Grant told Hancock, was going to enlist a corps of veterans — time-expired men in good physical condition who had served at least two years and were of course no longer subject to the draft — and when some 20,000 of these men had been enrolled they would form a separate group for special service under a commander responsible to the general-in-chief. Grant offered this command to Hancock, who promptly accepted, and by the end of November Hancock had been ordered to Washington to look after the enrolling and organization of this corps, and his old Corps in the Army of the Potomac was given to General Humphreys. Of the four corps commanders in this army, only Warren held the position he had held when the army crossed the Rapidan last May.[11]

Early in January there was a pleasant interlude. From Philadelphia came word that the people had noted with regret that Mrs. Grant had looked in vain for a house there. A citizens committee had been formed and had acted, and now came a letter, signed by local notables, saying that "it affords us great pleasure to present to yourself and family a house furnished and ready in our City of Homes," the same being given "in gratitude for eminent services." Grant lost no time in making formal reply:

[413]

It is with feelings of gratitude and pride that I accept this substantial testimonial of esteem of your loyal citizens — gratitude, because it is evidence of a deep-set determination on the part of a large number of citizens that this war shall go on until the Union is restored — pride that my humble efforts in so great a cause should attract such a token from a city of strangers to me.

I will not predict a day when we shall have peace again with a Union restored. But that that day will come is as sure as the rising of tomorrow's sun. I have never doubted this in the darkest days of this dark and terrible rebellion. Until this happy day of peace does come, my family will occupy and enjoy your magnificent present. But until then I do not expect nor desire to see much of the enjoyments of a home fireside.

To Julia he wrote less formally and with quite obvious enthusiasm: "I think you had as well arrange to move into your new house at once. . . . It may be that going into a new house you will want many things the house is not provided with. If so write to me about how much you will want and I will get the money. The house being furnished it is likely $1,000.00 will fit you up elegantly. I can get that for you easily. Recollect now that you want to save out of your $500.00 per month to buy you a carriage. I will then give you Egypt and another good horse to go with him." [12]

Three months earlier people in Chicago had prepared to give the Grants a home in that city, and Grant wrote to his friend and financial adviser, Russ Jones, to head it off. He would be general-in-chief of the army for the rest of his career, once peace came his headquarters would be in Washington, and if his home were in Chicago he would see little of his wife and children. Philadelphia was different. As trains ran then it was five and one-half hours from Philadelphia to Washington, and he assured Julia that as soon as the war ended headquarters could do without him for days at a time: "In time of peace it would not be necessary for me to be there more than once each week, and not always that." Philadelphia, then, was an ideal location, and the fact that the new house would be fully furnished was an important item; when Julia had been trying to find a place to rent Grant had urged her to take one that was furnished, because "at present rates it would take five or six thousand to furnish a house."

The commanding general of the armies of the United States would necessarily have a different living standard than the retired army captain who ran a harness shop in Galena; simply to furnish his house would take more money than the ordinary citizen spent on house and lot together, the general's wife must have a carriage and proper horses, and all in all there had been a coming-up in the world. Yet Grant, who had known grinding poverty for so long, was thinking of security rather than ostentation when he planned his financial future. He had been sending as much as he could to Russ Jones to invest for him, and late in October he wrote Julia summing up the state of his investments:

What I am anxious to do and what I am trying to do is to save and invest enough to give us an income of $6,000 per year and a home. You would then be independent if anything should happen to me. With that income I would not care a cent to increase, and would be perfectly willing that you should spend and give to friends every dollar as it would come in.

When he thought of a home Grant of course thought first of Julia, but hand in hand with this went his concern over the schooling his children would get. This always worried him — when he was in Chattanooga, planning his next strike at the Confederacy, when he was in Washington getting ready for the 1864 campaign, and when he was at City Point, coping with Lee's army. He liked having the older children in St. Louis, with Cousin Harry and Cousin Louisa, but he kept wondering: are the schools in St. Louis good enough for them? Early in July, when affairs in front of Petersburg were taking so much of his thought and energy, he insisted that the children must have the best education possible, and he told Julia: "I want the children to prosecute their studies, and especially in languages. Speaking languages is a much greater accomplishment than the little parapharnalias of society such as music, dancing, etc. I would have no objection to music being added to Nellie's studies, but with the boys I would never have it occupy one day of their time or thought." (Here spoke the tone-deaf Grant, who could not for the life of him tell one tune from another.)

He once thought the move to Princeton would be good, because "I find they have as fine schools as there are to be found in the country," and a little earlier he had written: "I want the children to be at good schools and without loss of time. If you cannot make suitable arrangements in St. Louis you may go where you think best, East or West." He did not especially care where they finally established themselves, but "I want the children to be at a good school." He liked the idea of making a home in Philadelphia because he believed that was "a place where my children could have the benefit of good schools." When he heard that his oldest son Fred had been getting into fistfights he asked for particulars, and added a fighting man's word of advice: "I do not want him to feel afraid to *pitch in* when boys impose on him, but he had better avoid boys who are inclined to quarrel." [13]

. . . When Schofield came east Grant took him down to Fort Fisher, to discuss the move on Wilmington and Goldsboro with Terry and Admiral Porter. Aside from this, he spent almost all of his time at City Point, and through most of the winter he was able to have Julia with him there. The tent city that had been headquarters all summer was replaced during the fall by a great array of wooden huts, and Grant had a fairly substantial one with office space in front and living quarters behind. All of the staff, of course, knew Mrs. Grant from her earlier visits, and they liked her and enjoyed having her around. She was thoughtful. If anyone at headquarters fell ill, Julia Grant was sure to call on him to see that he was getting along all right, and she would make certain that the cook prepared some special sick-room dish or other. She took her meals with Grant's mess, and Colonel Porter felt that there was a much more cheerful atmosphere at table when she was present. He also noticed that "she and the General were a perfect Darby and Joan," and said that on quiet evenings as they sat together in the headquarters building they would hold hands, looking shy and mildly fussed if anyone noticed that they were doing it.

Julia's presence was slightly embarrassing once, through no fault of hers. The Confederates had six ironclad gunboats in their part of the James, and on the night of January 23 these came down the river bent on mischief. The Federal navy had a powerful ironclad on patrol, obstructions had been planted in the river some distance upstream from City Point, and headquarters did not look for any serious trouble; after the first reports seemed to show that everything was under proper control the Grants went off to bed. Then, suddenly, the news became more serious; some way or another the Confederate warships had got past the obstructions and were coming on down, and if they ever came close enough to bombard the immense supply base at City Point they could do serious harm. Somebody knocked on Grant's door and gave him the news, and he threw on some clothes and came out, and there was so much commotion that after a little while Julia Grant got dressed and went into his office to see what was going on.

She found everybody a little edgy, with Grant at his desk writing orders and puffing vigorously at a cigar, and in a lull she asked him if the Rebel gunboats were likely to shell the bluff where the general's quarters were. Grant said that he did not think so, largely because the big Federal ironclad, *Onondaga*, would keep them thoroughly occupied; and then word came that the skipper of this warship had lost his head and had steamed off down the river out of range, and Grant sent couriers to warn commanders of riverside batteries that they would have to make a fight of it.

Calmest person present seemed to be Mrs. Grant, but she wanted guidance, and so she hitched her chair forward and asked her husband: "Ulyss, what had I better do?" Grant could give her nothing much better than a half-humorous "Well, the fact is, Julia, you oughtn't to be here." A staff officer volunteered to get an ambulance and take Mrs. Grant back out of range, but Grant said that after all the Rebel fleet had not actually appeared yet, and that for the time being everyone would concentrate on stopping it. In the end all was well. It developed that only four of the Confederate gunboats had actually started out, two had run aground, only one had passed the obstructions, one boat had been destroyed by Federal fire, *Onondaga* had got back into action after all . . . and the Grants finished their night's sleep undisturbed.[14]

Small tasks as well as big ones came to the general's desk this winter. Just before the end of the old year Grant wrote to Halleck a note bearing odd echoes from the past — from the recent election all the way back to the first springtime of the war, when Captain Sam Grant cooled his heels at department headquarters in Ohio, waiting in vain for a spruce young commanding general to see him:

I am just in receipt of a letter from Gen. G. B. McClellan saying that he purposes visiting Europe soon, with his family, and that Mrs. McClellan desires to see her father before starting and requests a leave of absence for Col. Marcy that this desire may be gratified. I do not know the special duty that Col. Marcy may be on at this time and do not therefore wish to order the leave granted lest it may interfere with important duties. If not inconsistent with public service, however, I wish this leave to be granted from Washington. Col. Marcy I believe is in Memphis, Tenn., at this time.[15]

There was a melancholy overtone to a note received in January from President Lincoln:

Please read and answer this letter as though I was not President, but only a friend. My son, now in his twenty-second year, having graduated at Harvard, wishes to see something of the war before it ends. I do not wish to put him in the ranks, nor yet to give him a commission to which those who have already served long are better entitled, and better qualified to hold. Could he, without embarrassment to you, or detriment to the service, go into your Military family with some nominal rank, I, and not the public, furnishing his necessary means? If no, say so without the least hesitation, because I am as anxious, and as deeply interested, that you shall not be encumbered as you yourself can be.

Grant immediately sent back a letter saying that he would be happy to have young Robert Todd Lincoln in his military family, and he proposed the rank of captain for him: in fairness to Robert, this should be a real commission and not just "nominal rank." It was so arranged, and the two men chiefly responsible for great armies and terrible fighting dealt delicately with a young man who "wanted to see something of the war" before it was too late. Young Robert, apparently, could not help himself. Adam Badeau set forth the staff's reaction in a letter to his friend General Wilson: "Capt. Lincoln is here; he is a nice fellow; bright, manly, gentlemanly. He's young, but I like him. He says he wanted to be in the service long ago, but his father would not allow it." That the person who was really being protected was almost certainly the emotionally unstable Mary Lincoln was mentioned by nobody, and the young captain doubtless would have been glad to see more of the war than might be visible to an assistant adjutant general of volunteers on the staff of the lieutenant general commanding the armies of the United States.[16]

From Galena, southern Ohio and St. Louis that winter came a number of plain folk who had known Grant before the war, anxious now to have a look at him, pass the time of day and see how things were at City Point. Provided they could get through the lines below Washington and reach the Hampton Roads area (which was usually hard to do) they found it easy enough to get in to see Grant; considering the fact that he was a three-star general he was not hard to get at, he remembered everybody and enjoyed chatting about the old days, and although nobody could pry any military news out of him his callers who remembered Hardscrabble Farm and the small-town store were impressed mostly by the fact that he did not seem to have changed very much. Hamlin Garland talked with a good many of them, in the years after the war, and he wrote that Grant was "so plain and neigh-borly" that his visitors mostly went away baffled, almost disap-pointed:

He was altogether too simple and transparent. They would have better enjoyed the deep thunder of a martial voice, the imperative clap of bells, the swift spring of saluting aides. They were troubled in some cases with the conviction that "Ulyss Grant was not so much of a general, after all." . . . They told the folks at home that Ulyss was mighty glad to see them and talk things over with them, and they didn't see how in the world he ever came to get in that position, anyhow. It was just his darn luck.[17]

There were many sorts of visitors. Grant got back to City Point from his trip to Fort Fisher, on January 31, to find that three Confed-erates were waiting to see him, their mere appearance being an indica-tion that the war was taking a new turn.

Two days before, three eminent Southern civilians had appeared under a flag of truce on the picket lines in front of John Parke's Ninth Corps, bearing a letter addressed to General Grant saying that they wanted to go to Washington to confer with President Lincoln regarding peace. Their mission, the letter said, grew out of a recent visit to Richmond by Francis P. Blair, who if he had not actually come as President Lincoln's spokesman had at least carried a pass signed by President Lincoln, and who had talked with President Davis about peace negotiations. The commissioners assumed that General Grant knew all about this, and said that if he did not they would like to talk to him about it. Anyway, here they were, and everybody in both armies was all excited because they had appeared. There was excite-ment in Washington, too, with the radical Republicans complaining that busybody Old Man Blair was likely to maneuver Lincoln into a compromise peace just as the war was being solidly won. Grant, who had known nothing about the deal, had the commissioners brought to headquarters and asked Washington what he ought to do with them.

The origins of the affair were both simple and irregular. Blair had gone to Richmond at the end of December, not empowered to say very much but nevertheless saying it, Blair-fashion, with an air of au-thority; understanding, to be sure, what the President was not willing to give up. Blair and Davis agreed on the need for peace negotiations. The difficulty was that Blair, on Lincoln's instructions, said that peace should be brought back to "the people of our one common country," while Davis insisted on talking about an effort "to secure peace to the two countries," and in the gap between these two concepts there was all the difference between a war won by the Federal government and a war won by the Confederacy. Now the commissioners were in Grant's headquarters, being introduced.

The one Grant was most interested in was Alexander Stephens, Vice President of the Confederacy, an old-line leader of the Democracy whom Grant (never a Republican until the war drove him that way) had always greatly admired; a tiny frail man who looked twice his natural size out of doors, because he wore an enormous great woolen overcoat that magnified his inconsiderable breadth in a fantastic way. With him were John A. Campbell, the Confederacy's Assistant Secretary of War and a onetime justice of the United States Supreme Court, and R. M. T. Hunter of Virginia, President pro tem of the Confederate Senate. Grant saw to it that they were suitably housed on a headquarters steamer, the *Mary Martin*, which was tied up at the City Point wharf, and waited to see what would happen next.

For a time it seemed that nothing would happen. Mr. Stanton sent down a messenger, Major T. T. Eckert, and told Grant to let Eckert interview the three Southerners to see what sort of negotiations they had in mind. If they were ready to accept a restored Union and the abolition of slavery Eckert was to take them to Fort Monroe, where Secretary of State Seward would be waiting, and if they were not ready to accept that they could talk to nobody. Meanwhile, there was to be no armistice of any kind, and Grant was warned in a wire signed by Lincoln: "LET NOTHING WHICH IS TRANSPIRING CHANGE, HINDER OR DELAY YOUR MILITARY MOVEMENTS OR PLANS." Grant replied that he understood: "THE TROOPS ARE KEPT IN READINESS TO MOVE AT THE SHORTEST NOTICE IF OCCASION SHOULD JUSTIFY IT."

Eckert talked to the commissioners and found that they felt bound by Davis's stipulation about peace for "the two countries," which meant that their mission had failed before it even began. Grant was disturbed. He had got a little acquainted with these men; liking and respecting them, he felt that he understood what they really wanted. He had refused to discuss peace terms with them, because that was none of his business, but he did not want a chance for peace missed through technicalities, and it struck him that the man at the top ought to know how he felt. On February 1 he somewhat diffidently sent a telegram to the Secretary of War:

Now that the interview between Major Eckert, under his written instructions, and Mr. Stephens and party has ended, I will state confidentially, but not officially to become a matter of record, that I am convinced, upon conversation with Messrs. Stephens and Hunter, that their intentions are good and their desire sincere to restore peace and union. I have not felt myself at liberty to express even views of my own or to account for my reticency. This has placed me in an awkward position, which I could have avoided by not seeing them in the first instance. I fear now their going back without any expression from any one in authority will have a bad influence. At the same time I recognize the difficulties in the way of receiving these informal commissioners at this time, and do not know what to recommend. I am sorry, however, that Mr. Lincoln cannot have an interview with the two named in this dispatch, if not all three now within our lines. Their letter to me was all that the President's instructions contemplated, to secure their safe conduct, if they had used the same language to Major Eckert.

Here Grant was referring to a letter the commissioners had addressed to him when they first tried to cross the lines. In this letter they had said that they wanted to go to Washington to talk to President Lincoln, in accordance with the rules originally laid down by Lincoln's instructions to Blair; which hinted that they were willing to talk about peace even if that meant talking about one common country and not two. This hint was strongly reinforced by a new note they gave to Grant's Colonel Orville Babcock to hand on to Eckert, in which they said that they would talk to Lincoln or anyone else on any peace terms "not inconsistent with the essential principles of self government and popular rights upon which our institutions are founded." This could mean anything one chose; obviously the commissioners did not want to return to Richmond without learning for themselves just how Lincoln's mind was working. Back from Washington to Grant came the President's reply: "Say to these gentlemen I will meet them personally at Fortress Monroe as soon as I can get there." [18]

Out of this, in the end, came no agreement, and the war had to go on a while longer. Davis's emissaries made the mistake of thinking they could negotiate their way to the sort of compromise the Confederate armies could no longer win for them, and they were somewhat stunned to learn that Lincoln would not compromise at all. He was ready to be most liberal about the way in which submission might take place, but not about submission itself; flexible about the arrangements for reunion and abolition but totally inflexible about the idea that the union was going to live and slavery was going to die forever. A mere yearning for peace was not enough. Here was the final gateway where the determination to make the war mean something worth its terrible cost met and blended with the determination that had made the war so costly and the victory at last so complete. Out of it could come one more chance for the American people.

Once again, Grant had moved without error through the maze of wartime politics. He had stuck to his role as soldier, not talking peace terms with the Southern commissioners, and not trying to impose his ideas on his own government, never trying to magnify his strictly military role as go-between. Yet he had acted, in a wholly subordinate way, to call an important intangible to the President's attention when the whole operation was about to be crushed to death under rigid formalities. Grant had enabled Lincoln to quiet the complaints of the suspicious radicals almost before they started to voice them: criticism ceased once it was clear that the President had talked to the Southern commissioners only because General Grant had asked him to do so. By going to Fort Monroe on Grant's suggestion, Lincoln had shown that his confidence in the political instincts of this nonpolitical general was unlimited; by their reception of the news that he had gone on Grant's suggestion, the radicals indicated that they felt much the same way.

Out of this affair Grant got a picture of the way Lincoln proposed to make peace. Peace depended on Southern acceptance of reunion and abolition; Lincoln told Grant after the conference that if the Southern commissioners had agreed to accept those points he was almost prepared to give them a blank sheet of paper and let them fill in the terms on which acceptance was to be based. Obviously, the President wanted no reprisals; it was equally obvious that he was not going to get the Southern acceptance he wanted until military victory was absolute. But if the voluntary end of armed resistance became unconditional, almost any conditions the South wanted could be arranged on other points.

Grant's own role in closing out the war was becoming clearer. It was up to him to bring armed resistance to an end, but it was not his job to deal with peace commissioners. It was important for him to know that a peace of reconciliation was intended, but his actual concern was with the armies. A month after the Hampton Roads conference, Lincoln gave Grant in unmistakable terms an outline of the part Grant himself was expected to play.

Toward the end of February General Ord chanced to meet General Longstreet under flag of truce to make some arrangement about the exchange of political prisoners, and the two generals (who had known each other before the war) began to talk about the chance to make peace. It was hard for the Confederate government to work out a deal to end the war because the authorities in Washington refused to admit that a Confederate government even existed, and Washington could make no deals with the nonexistent. Southerners who wanted peace recognized this obstacle, and saw another in the fact that President Davis was not ready to admit that the war was lost. But there might be a way out. A military convention between opposing army commanders was always possible. The device had been used in other wars; when statesmen were too stiff in the neck to make terms they sometimes let the soldiers do it . . . and so, this winter, why should not General Lee have a talk with General Grant? Longstreet took a report of this chat back to Confederate headquarters, and on the evening of March 3, just as he was about to sit down to dinner, Grant got a flag-of-truce letter from General Lee:

Lieutenant General Longstreet has informed me that in a recent conversation between himself and Major General Ord as to the possibility of arriving at a satisfactory adjustment of the present unhappy difficulties by means of a military convention, General Ord stated that if I desired to have an interview with you on the subject you would not decline, provided I had authority to act. Sincerely desiring to leave nothing untried which may put an end to the calamities of war, I propose to meet you at such convenient time and place as you may designate, with the hope that upon an interchange of views it may be found practicable to submit the subjects of controversy between the belligerents to a convention of the kind mentioned. In such an event I am authorized to do whatever the result of the proposed interview may render necessary or advisable.

This was a message of great significance. The Confederacy wanted to make peace. It disliked the stiff terms the Northern government wanted, but perhaps if it sent Lee to talk to Grant, instead of having Stephens talk to Lincoln, there could be some modification; and whatever the chances were, Lee was authorized to go the limit. Now it was up to Grant.

Grant's political instinct did not fail him. He immediately sent the text of this message off to Secretary Stanton, with an explanation of the reason for the meeting between Ord and Longstreet, and a conclusion: "I have not returned any reply but promised to do so at noon tomorrow. I respectfully request instructions."

At noon tomorrow would be the moment Abraham Lincoln was taking the oath of office to begin his second term. The telegram which Grant presently got in reply, signed by Secretary Stanton but written out by Abraham Lincoln personally, was one of the last official documents Abraham Lincoln wrote during his first term. It read:

The President directs me to say to you that he wishes you to have no conference with General Lee unless it be for the capitulation of Gen. Lee's army, or on some minor, and purely military, matter. He instructs me to say that you are not to decide, discuss or confer upon any political question. Such questions the President holds in his own hands; and will submit them to no military conferences or conventions. Meanwhile you are to press to the utmost your military advantages.[19]

Grant sent the word across the lines. The war would go on to a finish, and he and Lee would not have their talk short of Appomattox.

CHAPTER TWENTY-TWO

I Feel Now Like Ending the Matter

THE long mountain ranges that hemmed in the valley of Virginia were still white with snow, but in the low ground the snow was melting and the open fields were patchy, brown and white and faded gray; and except for the worn macadam of the Valley Pike itself all of the roads were deep in villainous mud. Now the 10,000 mounted men in Phil Sheridan's two divisions of cavalry came out of winter quarters and rode southwest from Winchester in a cold heavy rain. It was February 27, and as the long column went splashing past the old battlefields — Kernstown, Cedar Creek, Fisher's Hill — it saw charred farms and spoiled fields, a garden spot that had been ruined to make Lee's army hungry. Infantry had long since left the valley, called to the Petersburg front by the rival commanders at the end of 1864, and these Federals would meet no opposition until they got to Staunton and turned to the left on the road across the Blue Ridge. They would not meet any serious opposition even then, for Jubal Early had no more than 2,000 men in his winter camp at Waynesboro, and he could not hope to do much more than compel this great column to halt long enough to deploy into line. The final campaign had begun, and Sheridan's troopers were riding straight toward the end of the war.

Grant had sent Sheridan his orders in a letter dated February 20, and the letter had spoken less of what this cavalry corps was to do than of the shape the whole war was taking in its closing months.

"As soon as it is possible to travel," Grant had written to Sheridan, "I think you will have no difficulty about reaching Lynchburg with a cavalry force alone. From there you could destroy the railroads and canal in every direction so as to be of no further use to the Rebellion this coming spring, or, I believe, during the existence of the Rebellion. Sufficient cavalry should be left behind to look after Mosby's gang.

From Lynchburg, if information you might get there would justify it, you could strike South, heading the streams in Virginia to get to the westward of Danville and push on and join Sherman."

A long swing, this, for a cavalry general who had spent months just trying to break out of the lower valley; but this was only part of it, because the floodgates had been opened and when he wrote to Sheridan, Grant was simply listing the forces that were moving in to overrun a defeated Confederacy:

". . . this additional raid with one now about starting from East Tennessee under Stoneman, numbering four or five thousand, one from Vicksburg numbering seven or eight thousand cavalry, one from Eastport, Miss., ten thousand cavalry, Canby from Mobile Bay with about thirty-eight thousand mixed troops, the three latter pushing for Tuscaloosa, Selma and Montgomery . . ." Pause for breath, then: "Sherman with a large army eating out the vitals of South Carolina is all that will be wanted to leave nothing for the Rebellion to stand upon." Then came the final admonition:

"I would advise you to overcome great obsticles to accomplish this. Charleston was evacuated on Tuesday last."

Charleston was where it all began, with the pride and the blindness and the palmetto flags when life seemed to be at springtime. It fell easily into Federal hands this winter, taken by a conqueror who did not even bother to go near it. Sherman led his veterans past it with an eye to a broader conquest, and the navy took landing parties up to the historic battery after Confederate Hardee took his defenders off to the interior. Sherman kept going, Schofield got into Wilmington and moved across North Carolina to meet him, and in Richmond Lee warned the new Confederate Secretary of War, General John C. Breckinridge: "I fear it may be necessary to abandon all our cities, and preparation should be made for this contingency." Grant sent his own appraisal of the situation to his friend Elihu Washburne:

"Everything looks like dissolution in the South. A few more days of success with Sherman will put us where we can crow loud." [1]

Sheridan's immediate task was quickly done. He got his mounted column down to Staunton without trouble and then he swung to the left along the road toward the Blue Ridge gap and Charlottesville — the road luckless Hunter might have taken, but did not, nearly ten months earlier. On a ridge just west of the town of Waynesboro General Early had his men in line, waiting; the line was too thin and too short, the unhappy rear guard of a forlorn hope, and a biting wind whipped sleet into the Confederates' faces as George Custer got his division in line and prepared to attack.

Custer's men struck Early's line in front and on the flank, the line broke almost at once, and the Confederate Jed Hotchkiss said that there followed "one of the most terrible panics and stampedes I have ever seen." Victors and vanquished ran through mud and snow, half-hidden in the fog, and Early's Army of the Valley at last went out of existence, artillery all captured, more than 1,500 prisoners taken, hardly anyone escaping but Early himself and his staff and a few mounted followers, who rode eastward in the icy twilight to find a last refuge with Lee's army. Next day Sheridan's cavalry occupied Charlottesville, tearing up the railroad track that Grant had so long hoped to see destroyed, breaking down bridges, going on to strike the James River canal, and then moving southwest toward Lynchburg.

Roads were knee-deep in mud, mounted columns moved at a crawl, Sheridan's supply train was back on the road somewhere, scouts brought word that the Rebels had strengthened the Lynchburg garrison, and Sheridan concluded that he was not strong enough to take the place. His orders said that now he should cross the James and ride southeast in a long arc to join Sherman, somewhere in North Carolina; but the Rebels had destroyed the bridges he needed to use, the unending rains that made the roads so bad had swollen the river so that it could not be forded, and if this cavalry column was going to ride south of the James it was going to have to wait awhile.

There was no especial reason why it should not wait, but Sheridan was impatient; the war in the Shenandoah was over, except for the minor extravagances of guerrilla skirmishing, Lee's army would never again draw supplies from this area that had so long supported it, and now Sheridan wanted to go east and join Grant in front of Richmond. In short, he wanted to go where the action was, and he explained it bluntly enough when he wrote his *Memoirs:* "Feeling that the war was nearing its end, I desired my cavalry to be in at the death." [2]

He was leaving a good part of his orders unexecuted, but he was never chided for it; the one failing Grant could not excuse now was inaction, and a general who was eager to get on with the war would find forgiveness of sin easy to get. Far down on the Gulf Coast, General Canby was preparing to capture Mobile and come north across Alabama, but he was taking his own time getting ready and Halleck warned him: "I hope your expedition will be off before this reaches you, for General Grant is very impatient at delay and too ponderous preparations. He says that nearly all our generals are too late in starting and carry too much with them."

Canby had given a subordinate command to Gordon Granger, although Grant had warned him that the man would not be very helpful, and he would have given one to Baldy Smith if Grant had not heard about it and flatly forbidden it; and at last, when it seemed that the Mobile campaign could not begin before spring, Grant wrote Canby a wrathful letter.

He had learned (Grant wrote) that Canby had made requisitions for a construction corps and material to build seventy miles of railroad line. Canby would be given none of this, because he was not supposed to build railroads. Instead: "I expected your movements to be cooperative with Sherman's last. This has now entirely failed. I wrote to you long ago, urging you to push promptly and to live upon the country, and destroy railroads, machine shops, etc., not to build them. Take Mobile and hold it, and push your forces to the interior — to Montgomery and to Selma. Destroy railroads, rolling stock and everything useful for carrying on war, and when you have done this take such positions as can be supplied by water. By this means alone you can occupy positions from which the enemy's roads in the interior can be kept broken."

Grant wanted men who would get things moving. In the middle of March he told Secretary Stanton that as soon as Sheridan could be spared he would send him down to take Canby's place, unless Canby "does far better in the next few weeks than I now have any reason to hope for." If Grant did this, he would put General Crook in charge of the Army of the Potomac's cavalry. In the end Grant did not send Sheridan to the Gulf because he needed him where he was, but to the end of his life Grant was bothered by the delay. Twenty years after the war was over, looking back on Canby's campaign against Mobile and on the sweeping cavalry raids of Wilson and Stoneman — all ordered for midwinter, all delayed because their leaders wanted to make elaborate preparations and lost weeks doing it — Grant summed it up with these words: "They were all eminently successful, but without any good results. Indeed, much valuable property was destroyed and many lives lost at a time when we would have liked to spare them. The war was practically over before their victories were gained." A great impatience possessed Grant as the spring of 1865 drew near.[3]

His biggest worry this winter, Grant admitted, was the fear that Lee might slip away from him some night, letting the Confederate capital fall with his blessing on it, seeking the open country off to the west or south where he would have to be brought to bay all over again. Richmond of course was doomed, but even after it fell the Confederacy would still retain a convulsive grip on life if its armies lived, even though there was nothing the armies could win. Lee himself understood this very well. In January, appearing at a closed hearing of a joint Congressional committee, Lee pointed out that the defense of the capital was a drag on him because he had to "permit the enemy to make my plans for me" — a statement indicating the soundness of the general strategy Grant had followed in the Richmond campaign. One Senator understood Lee to say that once Richmond fell Lee might be able to prolong the war for two years on Virginia soil. To President Davis early in March Lee gave his sober appraisal: "The greatest calamity that can befall us is the destruction of our armies. If they can be maintained we may recover from our reverses, but if lost we have no recourse." [4]

Determined to prevent the escape of the Army of Northern Virginia, Grant this winter began to reap the advantages gained by the endless, inconclusive battles of late summer and fall. Lee's line ran down from White Oak Swamp, east of Richmond, to the almost equally swampy ground along Hatcher's Run, southwest of Petersburg; holding this line Lee was on the inside of a great crescent, his flanks gripped so that an orderly retreat was impossible. To slip away unseen, as Grant had done at Cold Harbor, was out of the question unless that grip on the flanks could be broken, and the only way to break it was to strike the Federal trenches so hard that Grant would be forced to shorten his own lines: a long shot, but the only shot there was. Lee ordered the offensive for the morning of March 25. . . . Grant did not know it, but he was at last to get what he had been wanting ever since the end of the battle of the Wilderness — Lee's army was going to come out of its trenches and attack him on his own ground.

Sherman this winter had been urging Grant to stay where he was until Sherman's army came up and made a sure thing of it, but Grant believed that as comparative strengths were now any battle that did not require a headlong assault on a prepared Confederate position was a sure thing, or near enough, and he proposed to move out past Lee's right flank as soon as the heavy winter roads dried out enough to carry artillery and wagon trains. His immediate anxiety was to have Sheridan and his cavalry at his side, and he sketched his plans in a dispatch to Sheridan written March 19.

Moving east from Charlottesville, Sheridan was making for White House on the Pamunkey, where he would discard his disabled horses and men, collect remounts and then come on down to Petersburg, where his cavalry force could pick up reinforcements. Grant told him that he himself would move out by his left with at least 50,000 infantry, and Sheridan's assignment would be to destroy the Southside and Danville railroads and then either rejoin Grant's army or go on to Carolina and join Sherman. Which of these two things he did, said Grant, "I care but little about"; what mattered was "the destruction of the only two roads left to the enemy at Richmond." Two days later, Sheridan having reached White House, Grant told him to get his horses well shod and rested, but he remarked that there was a certain urgency: "There is now such a possibility, if not probability, of Lee and Johnston attempting to unite that I feel extremely desirous not only of cutting the lines of communication between them, but of having a large and properly commanded cavalry force ready to act with in case such an attempt is made." Meanwhile, things were moving: "Stoneman started yesterday from Knoxville with a cavalry force of probably 5,000 men to penetrate southwest Virginia as far toward Lynchburg as possible. . . . Wilson started at the same time from Eastport toward Selma with a splendidly equipped cavalry force of 12,000 men. Canby is in motion, and I have reason to believe that Sherman and Schofield have formed a junction at Goldsboro." [5]

Schofield having joined him, Sherman now had an army of better than 80,000 men, and it was only a little more than a hundred and forty miles south of Grant's lines below Petersburg. The distance really was farther than it looked on the map, because Sherman faced his old opponent from the Atlanta campaign, General Joe Johnston, belatedly recalled to duty by a Confederate government made numb by the approach of night. Johnston's force was much smaller than Sherman's, an annoyance rather than a real and present danger, but Johnston was an able strategist and Sherman could not simply brush past him and go on to Petersburg. Johnston had attacked a wing of

Sherman's army a couple of days earlier at Bentonville, N.C., and although finally driven off had handled it roughly. Sherman was in no danger, but when he moved he would move cautiously. Far north in the lower Shenandoah Valley, Hancock's new corps of veterans was coming into being: when Hancock had posted all the troops necessary to guard the trunk line of the Baltimore & Ohio Railroad and other lines of communication he would have a force of 30,000 that could be used wherever Grant chose. For the time being Grant wanted Hancock to sit tight; if Lee fled from Petersburg and went west, Hancock would be well placed to go to Lynchburg to intercept him.

Federal armies, in short, could go just about where they chose, if they used proper care, once the roads got dry; and now, just as they prepared for their final effort, a singular phenomenon was visible in the North. As Washington correspondent Noah Brooks recalled it, there was a strong newspaper campaign, "led by Horace Greeley and others of this stamp" demanding that the administration make peace. Greeley, who had bobbed up in the summer of 1864 when the presidential campaign and the war itself were darkest with an almost hysterical appeal to Lincoln to open negotiations in order to save "our bleeding, bankrupt, almost dying country," could see that the tone of things had improved since midsummer but he still wanted something done. In the middle of March he was writing to leading Democrat S. L. M. Barlow that Lincoln ought to offer the Southern people "terms of accommodation such as a great nation can well afford to offer and as they may honorably accept." If Lincoln approved, Greeley himself was willing to go to Richmond and personally tell Davis and the others what Lincoln would demand and give "with regard to the Union, emancipation, confiscation, amnesty, restoration to political equality in Congress, etc., etc." This, of course, said Greeley with some skepticism, was based on the assumption that Lincoln really wanted an end to "the wholesale carnage and devastation now desolating our country and exciting the amazement of Christendom." [6]

Thus Greeley . . . a man of good will and poor judgment, wanting a compromise with rebellion in collapse. Grant went on planning, and by March 24 he had his spring offensive taped and ready to use. He outlined the plan in identical letters to Meade, Ord and Sheridan.

. . . to Meade, Ord *and Sheridan:* the hard little cavalryman had been upgraded. When Sheridan last saw the Petersburg area he had been commander of the cavalry corps of the Army of the Potomac, strictly one of Meade's subordinates. Now he was commanding general of the Middle Military Division, with great victories behind him, a man on roving assignment, still commanding Meade's cavalry but not entirely under Meade's orders. He was in fact one of the three army commanders to whom Grant confided his military plans, and because he was leading the flanking column on the last great move against Lee the whole army might well be following him before the campaign ended. Without actually ordering any change in command, Grant had in effect made a change of far-reaching consequence.

This was clear from the opening paragraph of the order of March 24, which announced:

"On the 29th instant the armies operating against Richmond will be moved by our left, for the double purpose of turning the enemy out of his present position around Petersburg and to insure the success of the cavalry under General Sheridan, which will start at the same time in its efforts to reach and destroy the South Side and Danville roads."

To do all of this, Meade and Ord were to be ready to give up most of the endless lines of entrenchments that had been won so hard and held so long. Ord was to leave Godfrey Weitzel and three divisions on the line in Bermuda Hundred and in front of Richmond, and Meade was to detail Parke's Ninth Corps to hold the lines east of Petersburg; everything else would be fluid, with troops either moving off to the left or ready to move on order, while Sheridan's 13,000 cavalry swung far out to the east to get clear of Lee's flank and drive north and northwest for the railroads.

Altogether, this would give the flanking infantry force the greater part of three army corps from the Army of the Potomac and one from the Army of the James; a powerful force, but this was tangled country in which any marching column could easily be taken at a disadvantage by an alert foe. Grant warned his generals: "The enemy, knowing this, may as an only chance strip their lines to the merest skeleton, in the hope of advantage not being taken of it, while they hurl everything against the moving column, and return. It cannot be impressed too strongly upon commanders of troops left in the trenches not to allow this to occur without taking advantage of it."

As the weaker party, Lee could not attack the Federals anywhere without weakening his lines in order to collect a striking force, and Grant remarked that "the very fact of the enemy coming out to attack, if he does, might be regarded as almost conclusive proof of such a weakening of his lines." Consequently, every division and corps commander in the army should be ready to attack without orders as soon as the Rebels forced the fighting anywhere on the front. Even Parke's corps, holding the pivot while the others marched, might thus wind up breaking the Confederate line, going without warning from defensive to offensive; so Parke's men must draw marching rations the same as everybody else even though they were not really expected to do any marching.

Grant's plan was wide open. The infantry was to swing to the left, perhaps to help Sheridan break the railroads, perhaps to win a victory on its own hook, and it might make its hardest thrust right where it planned to make none at all. Sheridan might be sent on south to help Sherman beat Johnston, once the railroads were broken — a prospect that made Sheridan sulky, because he did not want to be in North Carolina while Lee's army was being done to death in Virginia. Anything could happen, because the plan was as flexible as the plan at Chattanooga. To Sherman, Grant frankly confessed that what happened next would depend largely on the openings that developed on the battlefield: "When this movement commences I shall move out by my left, with all the force I can, holding present entrenched lines. I shall start with no distinct view, further than holding Lee's forces from following Sheridan. But I will be along myself and will take advantage of anything that turns up."

Another glimpse at Grant's thinking is provided in a letter he sent to his father Jesse Grant a few days before he wrote his overall directive:

We are now having fine weather and I think will be able to wind up matters about Richmond. I am anxious to have Lee hold on where he is a short time longer so that I can get him in a position where he must lose a great portion of his army. The rebellion has lost its vitality, and if I am not much mistaken there will be no Rebel army of any great dimensions a few weeks hence. Any great catastrophe to one of our armies would of course revive the enemy for a short time. But I expect no such thing to happen.[7]

Meanwhile, having laid out his program, Grant did an odd thing: he invited President Lincoln to pay him a visit, sending him this note:

"Can you not visit City Point for a day or two? I would like very much to see you, and I think the rest would do you good."

Long after the war, Grant remarked that a member of his staff had suggested that he invite Lincoln to come down to City Point. "I answered that the President was in command of the army and could come down when he wished," said Grant. "It was then hinted that the reason he did not come was that there had been so much talk about his interference with generals in the field that he felt delicate about appearing at headquarters. I at once telegraphed Mr. Lincoln that it would give me the greatest pleasure to see him."

The suggestion pleased Lincoln, and he promptly replied:

"Your kind invitation received. Had already thought of going immediately after the next rain. Will go sooner if any reason for it. Mrs. L. and a few others will probably accompany me. Will notify you of exact time, once it shall be fixed upon."

With the decisive campaign of the war about to open, the commanding general's headquarters was no place for visitors, and of course Grant knew it. Yet at this time of all times he invited the President — "the browsing President," McClellan had called him, dreading his visits — to descend on him along with the whole White House entourage, and he made the stay so pleasant that Lincoln extended it to a fortnight. (The President as a matter of fact got a longer respite from the White House burden this spring, visiting Grant, than he got at any other time during his presidency.) Grant no doubt wanted to touch base once more before the final battle; he was going to have a delicate line to follow when it came to imposing surrender terms, and it could do no harm to know exactly how the President's mind was working. Yet there probably was more to it than this. Between these two leaders who seemed so unlike but who fitted each other so perfectly and needed each other so deeply, there had in the past year developed much sympathy and understanding. Just as the final curtain went up it was inevitable that they should get together.

In any case, the President and his party reached the landing at City Point around nine o'clock on the evening of March 2, and Grant and his staff went down to the wharf as the President's steamer, *River Queen*, made fast. Mrs. Lincoln was with the President, and so was Tad, and there were various ladies from Washington, and everybody went up to the headquarters huts on the bluff. General and Mrs. Meade were there, and General and Mrs. Ord, and of course Julia Grant was hostess, and there was a short social hour here in this log cabin a few miles east of the long battle lines. Next morning, back on his steamer, President Lincoln sent a telegram to Secretary Stanton, explaining that the party had made a good trip and a safe arrival, and adding: "ROBERT JUST NOW TELLS ME THERE WAS A LITTLE RUMPUS UP THE LINE THIS MORNING, ENDING ABOUT WHERE IT BEGAN." [8]

The President did not know it, but in that casual sentence he had summed up the last offensive battle ever waged by Robert E. Lee.

In the darkness just before daybreak Lee had sent a striking force east from Petersburg, hitting the front of Parke's Ninth Corps in the area where Baldy Smith shrank away from greatness in June of 1864. A surprise attack won Fort Stedman, an enclosed strongpoint a little more than a mile west of Meade's headquarters, along with sections of Federal trench just north and south of the fort. Patrols had gone on through toward the Federal rear areas, about half of Lee's army was held ready to exploit the breakthrough and compel Grant to withdraw the left wing of his encircling army, and all in all big things had been planned. Meade was back at Grant's headquarters when the blow was struck, communications were temporarily interrupted, and for the time being command of the entire front rested with Parke, the senior officer present.

Parke was equal to the test. He brought up reserves, contained the force that had taken Fort Stedman, held the line firmly to north and south, routed the patrols that were working their way toward the rear, and in a couple of hours had things under control. There was no real breakthrough, the Rebels who held Fort Stedman had to retreat, and the great attack Lee planned had failed before it could fairly begin. Lee lost 4,000 men; and that afternoon President Lincoln and the top brass went ahead with a troop review a mile or two from the place where the fighting had taken place, just as if nothing had happened. The massed Federals who had not been needed in this battle marched by to the sound of music, while several thousand Confederate prisoners went on past to the provost marshal's stockades, and here was the end in a long progression: the little rumpus had ended the terrible line of Confederate offensives coming down from Gaines's Mill and Chancellorsville and Gettysburg. Now Grant had the initiative again, and Lee's army had just over a fortnight to live.

There was another review next day, March 26, north of the James, with a steamboat taking the presidential party up the river to see Ord's troops parade. Phil Sheridan went along, in a bad mood because he feared he would have to join Sherman in North Carolina; and it seemed to Sheridan that Lincoln was depressed, making none of his legendary jokes, worrying darkly lest the enemy come down and seize City Point as soon as Grant opened his offensive. Horace Porter, chosen to preside over a carriage that took Julia Grant and Mary Lincoln from the steamer's dock to the place where the review was to be held, reported that there was gloom here, also, with Mrs. Lincoln unhappy because rough roads and spirited horses gave her a bumpy ride. According to a famous account written long afterward by Adam Badeau, Mrs. Lincoln made an unpleasant scene because she felt that Mrs. Ord, accompanying the official party on horseback, rode a little too close to President Lincoln. (Julia didn't remember it that way at all. She said Mary Lincoln displayed no jealousy and made no complaint except to remark quietly: "Mrs. Ord is making the President a little ridiculous. I wish the President wouldn't do that.") [9]

Altogether, the expedition seems not to have been very gay. Things were much brighter on the following day, when a captured blockade-runner turned in from the open reach of the James and slid up to the City Point landing, and General William T. Sherman came ashore.

Grant met him at the foot of the gangplank, and the two men exchanged a long handshake, reminding Colonel Porter of nothing so much as two schoolboy chums coming together after a vacation. They went up the hill to headquarters, and in no time Sherman was perched on a seat by the campfire telling a fascinated semicircle about the fabulous march through Georgia. It was a monologue, and a good one, and it went on for an hour; and at last Grant broke in to say that the President of the United States was waiting on the *River Queen*, and the two generals went off to see Mr. Lincoln. This was no more than a get-acquainted meeting; the important talk would come next day. Presently Grant and Sherman were back at Grant's headquarters, where Julia asked them if they had paid their respects to Mary Lincoln. Grant unblushingly replied that they had not, and Sherman said he had not even known she was present, and Julia broke out: "Well, you are a pretty pair!" and they agreed to present themselves to Mrs. Lincoln next day.

Then the two soldiers started to talk about what the armies would do next, and when Julia suggested that perhaps she ought not to be listening to military secrets Sherman asked Grant: "Do you think we can trust her?" Grant said he was not sure; public documents that began, "Know all men by these presents" might just as well say "Know one woman" (said Grant) because what one woman knew today everybody would know tomorrow. So Sherman said that he would conduct a cross-examination to see whether the lieutenant general's wife knew enough about the war to betray anything to the enemy; and he fixed her with a stern look and began to ask nonsensical questions, to which she returned nonsensical answers, and this went on for a long time, as arch and ponderous and full of friendship and understanding as the clumsy badinage at an alumni luncheon. . . . On the *River Queen*, next morning, Grant made a great point of asking if he and Sherman could see Mrs. Lincoln, only to be told that she did not feel very well and would like to be excused. Presumably Grant's report squared him with his wife.[10]

Among those who came to talk to Sherman and Grant was Sheridan, who was visibly irritated by Sherman's casual assumption that Sheridan's cavalry would be down in North Carolina before long. In the end, Grant quietly took Sheridan aside and explained that all of this talk about sending him down to join Sherman was simply a blind, inserted in the written record largely because of the activity of the negotiate-now peace party in the North. Grant's notion was that if the move against Lee's flank and rear met with a repulse, the peace group would accuse the administration of having blundered into another defeat when it ought to be sitting quietly about a conference table; if the army's move could be presented simply as a move to create close contact with Sherman, this criticism would not arise. Sheridan need not worry, because Grant did not intend to send him off on a tangent: "I mean to end the business here." Sheridan's dark face brightened and he struck his leg with his palm, saying: "That's what I like to hear you say. Let's end the business here." [11]

When President Lincoln sat down with Grant and Sherman he wanted reassurance; Sheridan apparently read him correctly when he saw anxiety in him. The President feared that at the last minute something would go wrong. In Sherman's absence, might not Johnston slip away, join Lee, and spoil the spring campaign before it began? They told him that this could not happen. Sherman's army, with Schofield as second-in-command, was in good hands; it had a lock on Johnston, his escape was impossible, and in any case Sherman would go back to North Carolina as soon as this conference ended. Lincoln was at last convinced, although he kept insisting that Sherman should rejoin his troops as quickly as possible; and he hoped very much (although neither general could give him reassurance on this point) that the whole business could be settled without another big battle. As commander-in-chief of all the armies, Lincoln made no attempt to find out just what Grant and Sherman proposed to do next; he simply wanted to be told that they were sure they could do it.

More important was the talk about the terms that should be given to the Confederates on surrender, and the conviction both soldiers got was that President Lincoln wanted an easy peace. He hoped that Jefferson Davis might somehow escape from the country altogether, he wanted nothing so much as to see the Confederate soldiers back on their farms or in the shops, and he wanted no reprisals. Grant remembered that Lincoln told Sherman what he had tried to indicate to the Confederate commissioners, two months earlier — that "before he could enter into negotiations with them they would have to agree to two points; one being that the Union should be preserved, and the other that slavery should be abolished; and that if they were ready to concede these two points he was almost ready to sign his name to a blank piece of paper and permit them to fill out the balance of the terms on which we would live together." Sherman missed the little word "almost." He remembered this about Lincoln's remarks:

He distinctly authorized me to assure Governor Vance [Governor Zebulon Vance, the slightly lukewarm Confederate governor of North Carolina] that as soon as the Rebel armies laid down their arms and resumed their civil pursuits they would at once be guaranteed all their rights as citizens of a common country; and that to avoid anarchy the State governments then in existence, with their civil functionaries, would be recognized by him as the government *de facto* till Congress could provide others.

In all of this, Grant and Sherman got a good picture of Lincoln's attitude toward the dominant problem of restoration of the Union. What Sherman also got, unfortunately, was a fuzzy notion of what he himself as a soldier was supposed to do about it. Grant had been firmly notified, by Stanton and by Lincoln, that he was not to do anything more than impose terms on Lee for the surrender of Lee's army. Sherman saw it differently. He went away with the feeling, not only that he knew how the President's mind was working, but that he himself was authorized to deal with the civilians once Johnston's army surrendered. One of the most unexpected factors in the whole situation was that it was Sherman, of all people — Sherman, the living breathing image of the hard, pitiless warrior, who had devastated Georgia, burned Columbia and left a smoking path of ruin across the heart of the South — Sherman, the American Attila, who wanted to make a soft peace.[12]

Before the war could be settled it had to be won, and they got at it. Sherman hurried back to his army, Lincoln stayed on his steamer — keeping in touch with Secretary Stanton at Washington and learning that there was nothing in particular to call him back to the capital if he did not want to go there — and Grant's armies began to move.

While the conferences were going on Sheridan had taken his hard, cocky cavalrymen across the James and started moving down below the army lines toward the open country beyond the Union left, and Ord had brought three divisions of his army over the river and had begun to go toward the Union left. It is noteworthy that Grant had Ord accompany his troops. Technically, Ord commanded the army directly in front of Richmond and might be expected to stay there; Grant wanted him with the moving force, and had him leave Weitzel in charge of the holding force. Meade was quietly being downgraded; Grant liked him and trusted him, but on this final move he wanted commanders who thought his way — Sheridan and Ord. The blow at the Confederate flank was not going to be left entirely in Meade's hands.

On March 29, Ord's troops replaced Humphreys and the Second Corps, and Humphreys moved to the left, out to the gloomy wooded flatlands beyond Hatcher's Run; Warren and the Fifth Corps took to the roads and went still farther, coming up on Humphreys's left, driving off Confederate skirmishers and taking position a little beyond the strong position where Lee had positioned his right flank, a country crossroads known from its one distinguishing feature, Burgess's Mill. A little more than a mile ahead of Warren was an east-west highway called the White Oak Road. It was a road Lee had to hold, because it was the only route by which he could send a force westward to stop Sheridan. Sheridan, meanwhile, floundering along muddy roads, was coming up to the hamlet of Dinwiddie Courthouse, which was six or seven miles southwest of Lee's trenches at Burgess's Mill. Sheridan took with him Grant's orders: "It is not the intention to attack the enemy in his entrenched position, but to force him out if possible. Should he come out and attack us, or get himself where he can be attacked, move in with your entire force in your own way, and with the full reliance that the army will engage or follow, as circumstances will dictate."

This involved a great deal of cross-country marching by a large number of troops, and the soldiers were not inspired. In the area beyond Hatcher's Run and approaching Burgess's Mill the men felt that "the infernal country smacked too much of The Wilderness" — it was flat, covered with timber and underbrush, seamed by swampy creeks and rivers, a bad place to march in, a worse place to make a bivouac, and apparently a wholly impossible place for a battle. One veteran remembered that "we went slipping and plunging through the black slimy mud in which pointed rocks were bedded, now stumbling over a rotten tree, now over the stiffening corpse of some poor comrade by whose side we soon might lie," and nobody was very happy. Here was one more move by the left, the kind of move that had been going on ever since the army left the Wilderness, and somebody spoke of "Sheridan the left-hand man of Grant the left-handed"; and just when things were at their worst it began to rain, and it rained in great drenching sheets, the flat country had no proper drainage so that the smallest creek quickly became a deep stream and the meadows turned to heavy swamps, and the roads became mud beds in which artillery and wagon trains could not move. At headquarters Rawlins (with others) began urging Grant to call everything off, order everybody back to the starting point, and wait for the country to dry up before starting over again.[13]

Grant's determination was unshaken. He had said goodbye to President Lincoln on the morning of March 29, leaving the President to wait for news at City Point while he himself moved on to field headquarters far to the west, on the Vaughan Road behind the Union left. He now had an unbroken front extending in a vast semicircle all the way from the Appomattox River just below Petersburg to the gloomy swamps beyond Hatcher's Run, with five infantry corps in line and Sheridan's cavalry free beyond the flank; and although he had said, five days earlier, that he was starting out "with no distinct view" his mind now came to a sharp focus. To Sheridan, on the night of March 29, with the rain coming down harder and harder, he sent a revealing dispatch:

I feel now like ending the matter, if it is possible to do so, before going back. I do not want you, therefore, to cut loose and go after the enemy's roads at present. In the morning, push around the enemy, if you can, and get on to his right rear. The movements of the enemy's cavalry may, of course, modify your action. We will all act together as one army until it is seen what can be done with the enemy.

He was no longer trying to cut the lifelines of Lee's army, although that had been his aim for nine months. Instead he was striking directly at the army itself, looking for a final victory. While Warren and Humphreys moved up to closer contact with the Confederates, both Parke and Wright, farther east, reported that the forces opposing them seemed to be thinned out to the breaking point and said they believed they could assault successfully. But the rain kept coming down, the roads grew worse and the little streams grew broader and deeper, and the army seemed to be bogging down. Getting supplies out to Sheridan looked impossible, and Grant briefly considered telling Sheridan to leave a force to hold Dinwiddie Courthouse and bring the rest of his men back for food and forage. Sheridan did not think this was necessary, and on the evening of March 30 he came back to headquarters to say so. The eternal rain was still falling, and Sheridan's horse went to its knees in the mud with every step, but the cavalryman was full of optimism. He said he could beat the Rebel cavalry that faced him, if he had some infantry he could crush Lee's right, and forage was no problem — he would haul it out if he had to set every man to work corduroying roads — and he told the staff officers who came out to greet him: "I tell you, I'm ready to strike out tomorrow and go to smashing things." The officers told him that was the kind of talk Grant liked to hear, and took him in to tell his story.

Staff was right: this was exactly what Grant wanted to hear, and he immediately gave Sheridan new orders:

If your situation is such as to justify the belief that you can turn the enemy's right with the assistance of a corps of infantry entirely detached from the balance of the army, I will so detach the Fifth corps and place the whole under your command for the operation. Let me know, as early in the morning as you can, your judgment in the matter, and I will make the necessary orders. Orders have been given Ord, Wright and Parke to be ready to assault at daylight tomorrow morning. They will not make the assault, however, without further directions . . . If the assault is not ordered in the morning, then it can be directed at such time as to come in co-operation with you on the left.[14]

Tomorrow morning was a little too early. Lee had sent Pickett with two divisions of infantry to reinforce the cavalry that confronted Sheridan, and Sheridan had a hard fight on his hands just to hold his position at Dinwiddie Courthouse. Several miles to the north, at a road intersection known as Five Forks, where the all-important White Oak Road crossed the road that ran north from Dinwiddie Courthouse, breastworks were built, for Pickett and the cavalry to use if Sheridan drove them back from Dinwiddie, and this point was several miles beyond Lee's extreme flank in the vicinity of Burgess's Mill. The connecting link was the White Oak Road, running west. To break this road would be to isolate the Confederate force facing Sheridan, and this task was given to Warren's corps.

Warren came to grief. The kind of hard, swift movement the situation demanded was beyond him. He was a soldier who had to get ready by slow stages, reflecting on the things that might go wrong; on March 30 he exchanged messages with Meade's headquarters, explaining why the move he was supposed to make that night was not quite possible, and enlarging on the accidents that might befall him, and by the morning of March 31 he had his army corps spread out in depth, ready for anything except immediate action. His first division, under General Ayres, was in front, and one of Ayres's brigades faced the Rebel works on the White Oak Road, another was off on the left looking into vacancy toward the far-off Sheridan, and the third was on the right, looking eastward. The second division was well back to the rear and the third division was still farther back, out of touch with the enemy, waiting further instructions. In time, no doubt, Warren would have managed the advance that was expected of him, but time was lacking. Lee hit him first.

Lee did not have much to hit him with: just four infantry brigades for a total of perhaps 5,000 men, and Warren's corps numbered at least 15,000 effectives. The trouble was that Warren had his units all disconnected, so when Lee made his attack Ayres's men were outnumbered. They went into action one brigade at a time, and were routed one at a time, each of the three leading brigades outnumbered or outflanked. Ayres's luckless division ran to the rear, coming back to the next division, that of General Samuel Crawford, which was unready and out of position. This division collapsed, and two Federal divisions were running, the poorly handled many beaten by the well-handled few; and a little after noon the fugitives fell back on Warren's last division, which was led by a tough character named General Charles Griffin. Griffin made a stand, Meade got a division over from Humphreys's corps to help, the rout was over, and Meade sent a dispatch to Grant telling him what had happened and reporting that the Rebel advance had been stopped. Grant sent a caustic reply:

"If the enemy has been checked in Warren's front, what is to prevent him from pitching in with his whole corps and attacking before giving him time to entrench or return in good order to his old entrenchments? I do not understand why Warren permitted his corps to be fought in detail. When Ayres was pushed forward he should have sent other troops to their support." [15]

Actually, no great harm had been done. The army had had nothing worse than a minor setback, and the damage was soon made good. The real loser was Warren, who moved slowly when the army was supposed to move fast. Grant wanted to crush Lee's right with cavalry and infantry under Sheridan, and the infantry Sheridan used had to be Warren's corps because it was the only infantry within reach. Grant was in a hurry, Sheridan was more so, and here was another of those generals who had to take extra time to get everything ready before making a move. On this day of March 31 Sheridan notified Grant that the Confederates had dug in at Five Forks: "If the ground would permit I could, with the Sixth Corps, turn the enemy's right, or break through his lines; but I would not like the Fifth Corps to make such an attempt."

Grant understood how Sheridan felt, but he could not give him Wright's Sixth Corps; Wright was far over toward the center of the line, there was no time to make the shift, and besides: "Wright thinks he can go through the line where he is, and it is desirable to have troops and a commander there who feel so, to co-operate with you when you get around." [16]

The final campaign was on, the Confederates could be beaten, and *it is desirable to have troops and a commander there who feel so.* Grant had seen victories vanish, in the last ten months, over and over, because of generals who did not feel so, and with the final prize coming up he was going to take no more chances — which is the big reason why he was relying on Sheridan now. That night he sent orders: Warren was to move west and report to Sheridan, who felt that he could smash things; and Warren's men, who had had a hard day and a lot of fighting, made a night march, finding little brooks now too deep to be waded, halting to tear down barns for timber to build bridges, plodding along in the dull hope that the high command knew what it was doing, coming up at last on April 1 to join the fuming, restless Sheridan.

The Confederates in front of Dinwiddie Courthouse, knowing that Federal infantry was coming west, pulled back to Five Forks and waited. There were enough of them, cavalry and infantry together, to keep Yankee cavalry at bay, but there were not enough to hold off Sheridan's cavalry plus a regular Federal army corps, and they were miles away from the main Confederate army with no chance of help. April 1 came in, the rain had stopped, the advance elements of Warren's corps came up to Sheridan, and by midafternoon Sheridan was getting ready to make his big attack. While he was getting everybody lined up he was joined by Grant's Colonel Babcock, who had a message from the lieutenant general commanding: Sheridan had complete control, and if he did not think Warren was up to his job Sheridan was authorized to relieve him of his command and put somebody else in charge of the Fifth Corps.

This was both a broad authorization and a broad hint. Grant had been using the Army of the Potomac since May of 1864, and he had come to know General Warren: a good man, conscientious, careful, and eternally given to waiting just a little longer until he had appraised all of the risks, which had led him to miss certain wide-open opportunities — at the Wilderness, at Spotsylvania, and at Petersburg. Grant had suggested that he be dismissed at Spotsylvania, and Meade had saved the man; a little later Meade wanted to get rid of him, and Grant had saved him; and now, with everything riding on the next pitch, Grant felt that Warren was not quite the man and he put Warren's fate in the hands of Sheridan, who had no use for him. The war at last had got past the point where the old-line Army of the Potomac generals could handle it. Warren sealed his own fate on March 31, when he let his 15,000 be defeated by Lee's 5,000, and now was the time for generals who knew how to smash things. It was too bad, but it was inevitable.[17]

Sheridan struck the Confederates at Five Forks late in the afternoon and almost annihilated them. He sent his dismounted cavalry in, head-on, and he brought Warren's corps in on the flank, and the battle was over before the top Confederate commanders, Cavalry General Fitzhugh Lee and Infantry General George Pickett, quite knew what was happening. Forty-five hundred Confederates were taken prisoner, Lee's flank guard ceased to exist, and when the sun went down the Federal army had won its most decisive victory of the war . . . and General Warren was riding unhappily back to Grant's headquarters, relieved of his command by Sheridan because his corps had come to the scene late, had gone into action by haphazard, and had not been directed by a man with fire in his eye.

Grant got the news of the victory around eight o'clock that night, when Colonel Horace Porter, who had been with Sheridan, came back to headquarters in a spattering gallop, so excited by the good tidings he carried that a fellow officer concluded that he was drunk — most unfair, because Porter was notoriously one of the most abstemious officers on the staff. Porter sang out the news while he was dismounting, the headquarters crowd yelled and tossed their hats in the air, and Grant who had been sitting in a canvas chair by the campfire, listened impassively and then went into his tent to scribble out an order. He came out a moment later to remark quietly: "I have ordered an immediate assault all along the lines."

It was only a slight overstatement. Humphreys was to push ahead, advancing troops so that Lee could not at the last minute concentrate against Sheridan's force. Ord was to watch his front carefully, advance if the enemy weakened force, and be prepared to send help to the troops on his right or left as circumstances might dictate. For the rest, Grant's dispatch to Meade contained these words:

"Wright and Parke should be directed to feel for a chance to get through the enemy's line at once, and if they can get through should push on tonight. All our batteries might be opened at once, without waiting for preparing assaulting columns. Let the corps commanders know the result on the left, and that it is being pushed."

Having got things in motion, Grant went back to write another message — a note to President Lincoln, back at City Point, telling him that a great victory was being won.[18]

CHAPTER TWENTY-THREE

Our Countrymen Again

THE Army of the Potomac had always been a hard-luck outfit, and it had been looking at the Petersburg trenches ever since June, 1864, not liking what it saw. Now the orders were that these trenches were to be taken by storm, and although the staff officers who brought the orders were full of fine talk about a great victory won somewhere off at Five Forks the Federal infantry had its own ideas about what was likely to happen here. It was after midnight, there was a cold mist, nobody could see anything and nobody really knew anything, and the soldiers went by the only light they had and wrote their names on slips of paper and pinned the papers to their uniforms, just to make things simpler for the flag-of-truce burial parties that would go out later. Federal artillery had been banging away for an hour, lighting the sky with great spurts of flame and creating a tremendous racket, which did not always mean as much as the gunners believed; and around four-thirty, when the dawn had begun to thin the darkness, the gunfire stopped. The infantry scrambled out of its rifle pits, groped and stumbled through the tangled abatis, and ran head-on into a blistering semicircle of rifle fire.

Long experience had taught the army that good men could hold good trenches against five times their own numbers, and it seemed that the lesson was about to be repeated. Confederate musketry swept the dim slopes, and it was like Cold Harbor all over again; Wright's corps lost 1,100 men in fifteen minutes, and Parke's men had it about the same. Then, suddenly, it was not like Cold Harbor. Grant's belief that Lee could not fight on the far Confederate right without weakening his entrenched lines past the breaking point turned out to be true.

True enough, in one spot, for victory. Parke's corps got into the first line of Rebel works just east of Petersburg and could go no farther, but Wright's men farther west hit a sector that had been thinned

[446]

down just a little too much and they kept on going. There were wild flurries of hand-to-hand fighting along the parapet, and then the blue infantry went up and over, taking prisoners, seizing cannon and running on into the open country beyond, breaking Lee's line squarely in half. One brigade stayed to hold the captured trenches, and the others wheeled and went to the left, sweeping the Confederate defenders away from everything up to the works along Hatcher's Run; and as they came into these they met Ord's troops, which had made a frontal assault at the same time, and there was wild shouting and also a huge traffic jam, with men from different units all mixed together, everybody capering and tossing his cap in the air. Stray patrols and disorganized celebrants ran on ahead, groping without orders for isolated pockets of Confederate resistance. Some of these hotshots, in an unexpected cornfield encounter, killed one of Lee's most famous lieutenants, the legendary General A. P. Hill.

On the left of Ord's corps Humphreys had advanced, and after clearing out the defenders who had not already taken flight because of what had been happening farther east most of Humphreys's corps went north, to join Sheridan and the cavalry and the Fifth Corps — now commanded by General Griffin — in an attempt to complete the rout of the Confederates who had been beaten yesterday at Five Forks. Lee had sent reinforcements over here, the Confederates were making a stand at Sutherland's Station, on the Southside Railroad, and the victorious Federals prepared to attack them. Farther east, Grant and Meade got Wright's and Ord's men sorted out and wheeled them about to move directly on Petersburg, coming up to this place at last from due west. Lee's army was broken, and the only question now was whether he could hold the city until darkness so that he could unite his own troops and the Richmond garrison in an orderly retreat.[1]

Grant that morning came about as close as he ever came to outright excitement. The state of his emotions shines through a hasty note he scribbled to Julia, some time before noon. He started to head it "City Point," scratched that out, wrote down the date, April 2, and then went at it:

Dear Julia: I am now writing from far inside what was the Rebel fortifications this morning but what are ours now. They are exceedingly strong and I wonder at the success of our troops carrying them by storm.

[447]

But they did do it, and without any great loss. We have captured about 12,000 prisoners and 50 pieces of artillery. As I write this news comes of the capture of 1,000 more prisoners. Altogether this has been one of the greatest victories of the war. Greatest because it is over what the Rebels have always regarded as their most invincable army and the one used for the defence of their Capitol. We may have some more hard work but I hope not. Love and kisses for you and Jess.

Ulyss[2]

It was not possible to finish the job on April 2. Lee still held the lines in front of Parke's corps, and made several hard but fruitless counterattacks there; the Confederate troops at Sutherland's Station held on until nearly dusk, retreating at last to the north side of the Appomattox River; and just west of Petersburg, die-hard Confederates made a stand in a pair of forts built long before the siege of Petersburg began, and were dislodged by John Gibbon's soldiers only after a bitter fight. At four-thirty that afternoon, realizing that no more substantial advance could be made that day, Grant sent a message back to President Lincoln at City Point, telling him about the victory that had been won and suggesting that the President come out and see things for himself next morning. Lincoln sent a quick reply:

"Allow me to tender you, and all with you, the nation's grateful thanks for the additional and magnificent victory. At your kind suggestion I think I will meet you tomorrow."

Tomorrow was April 3, with Lee in full retreat on the far side of the Appomattox. Grant learned that Petersburg had been evacuated and he rode into the city and made temporary headquarters on the porch of a house on Market Street, the home of a man named Thomas Wallace. Up the walk, before long, came President Lincoln, accompanied by Robert, by Tad and by Admiral Porter, who had unexpectedly become the President's unofficial guide and traveling companion. One of the officers present noticed that Lincoln came up the front walk with long strides, and when Grant went down the steps to meet him the President seized his hand for a long, fervent shake. Then the President said:

"Do you know, General, that I have had a sort of sneaking idea for some days that you intended to do something like this?"

It might be borne in mind that as far as Lincoln knew, Grant had not planned anything more than to hold Lee in position and wait for

Sherman to come up and make victory certain. Grant once remarked that of all the headquarters visitors he ever had, Lincoln was the only one (except for Secretary Stanton) who had a right to ask what his plans were, and that Lincoln was the only one who never asked about them. In his *Memoirs*, Grant explained: "I would have let him know what I contemplated doing, only while I felt a strong conviction that the move was going to be successful, yet it might not prove so; and then I would only have added another to the many disappointments he had been suffering for the past three years."

Now he told the President: "I had a feeling that it would be better to let Lee's old antagonists give his army the final blow and finish up the job. I have always felt confident that our troops here were amply able to handle Lee."

Grant and Lincoln sat on the porch, not saying much, waiting to see if word would come that Richmond had fallen. No word came: but suddenly the yard was full of Negroes, who had been slaves up to the moment the blue troops entered Petersburg, and all of them were looking wonderingly at President Lincoln, who was looking intently at them; no one saying a word. At last Grant said his goodbyes and rode off to get his troops in motion.[3]

He was not going to cross the Appomattox River and make a direct pursuit of Lee. Lee presumably was assembling his army somewhere along the upper part of the Richmond & Danville Railroad, and to make his escape he would have to follow the line of this road, which ran southwest. At Burkeville, forty miles from Richmond, this road crossed the Southside Railroad, which came west from Petersburg and went on west to Lynchburg. If Lee got either rations or forage they would come up through Burkeville, either from Lynchburg or from Danville, and if Lee meant to join Joe Johnston — the only move that was left to him, really, if he hoped to go on with the war — he would have to pass through Burkeville and go on down the line of the Richmond & Danville. The all-important fact now was that Grant was nearer to Burkeville than Lee was, and for that matter nearer to Danville, and to Johnston's army down beyond the Roanoke River. Instead of chasing Lee, Grant wanted to head him off, and he ordered Sheridan with his cavalry and Griffin's infantry to march for Burkeville as fast as they could, with cavalry squadrons roving out to the right to keep in touch with Lee. Meade with Humphreys's and

Wright's corps was to follow Sheridan; Ord would march for Burkeville along the line of the Southside Railroad, farther south, and Parke would follow Ord, guarding the railroad.

Leaving the President, Grant rode to Sutherland's Station, where he found General Gibbon and his troops waiting for orders. As Gibbon rode up to greet the commanding general a courier came galloping and gave Grant a dispatch. Grant read it and told Gibbon unemotionally: "Weitzel entered Richmond this morning at half past eight." Staff officers and sundry unattached persons who were near enough to hear this rode off and began to shout the news, and there was a great tumult. Gibbon went to take his place at the head of his column, to march for Burkeville, and he heard a jubilant man in the ranks yelling: "Stack your muskets and go home!" [4]

As the soldiers moved, Grant stopped to send word to Sherman. He told him what had happened — big breakthrough at Petersburg, Lee's army in full retreat, and so on — and said that he was going to try to beat Lee to Burkeville. He added that if Lee got past him, "you will have to take care of him with the force you have for a while," but he went on to say that if he got to Burkeville first and Lee went west toward Lynchburg, "there will be no special use in you going any farther into the interior of North Carolina."

Then Grant's thoughts went back to the thing that had haunted him ever since he came east — the idea that there was something wrong with the Army of the Potomac and that it could not quite be used as effectively as western armies were used. He disposed of that in a final paragraph:

"This army has now won a most decisive victory and followed the enemy. That is all it ever wanted to make it as good an army as ever fought a battle." [5]

Next day, April 4, was a day of hard marching. Sheridan's far-roving cavalry learned that Lee's army was concentrating at Amelia Courthouse — a town south of the Appomattox on the Richmond & Danville, fifteen miles northeast of Burkeville — in a desperate attempt to reach the railroad junction before the Federals did. But for Lee things were not working right. To begin with, it took time to get all of the Confederates assembled, and the last of the troops from Richmond would not reach Amelia Courthouse for twenty-four hours. For another thing, the supplies Lee expected to find at Amelia Courthouse were not there. He had ordered rations sent down from

Richmond just before he left Petersburg, but in the confusion that lay upon his own headquarters and the Confederate War Department at Richmond these orders were never sent, or if sent were not received, or if received were not executed; so Lee's army, totally without food, had to wait while patrols scoured the countryside in an unprofitable effort to find bacon and corn. Finally, Sheridan had got on the railroad. He had a cavalry division across the line at a place called Jetersville, halfway between Amelia Courthouse and Burkeville, and while the cavalry was getting into position Griffin's infantry came up and got in line with it, and Meade was coming on hard with two more army corps; and Grant sent a telegram to Secretary Stanton:

"The army is pushing forward in the hope of overtaking or dispersing the remainder of Lee's army." Lee's army, Grant said, was south of the Appomattox, staggering toward the southwest, shredding off wounded men and stragglers everywhere, and: "I shall continue the pursuit as long as there appears to be any use in it." That night Grant got a message from Sheridan, who described the situation where he was and concluded: "If we press on we will no doubt get the whole army." [6]

So there appeared to be some use in it. . . . On April 5, discovering that Federal troops lay squarely across his path in too great strength to push aside, Lee began to swing far around by his right, in the hope that he could circle past the opposition and continue on — to Danville if possible, to Lynchburg if necessary, to some haven where he could feed and refit his army and get in shape to carry on the fight. On the same day Sheridan had a cavalry division out on his left, and the cavalry captured wagons and guns that Lee had sent on ahead and Sheridan began to see what Lee was up to. Two Federal infantry corps were already across the railroad, and a third one, Humphreys's Second Corps, was coming up, and Meade believed that the thing to do was to dig in, wait for morning, and then advance on Amelia Courthouse and attack Lee there.

This was exactly the right course if Lee meant to stay at Amelia Courthouse; but if he should be trying to slip past the Federal flank this move would take the Army of the Potomac east just when Lee was going west. Sheridan knew that Lee's wagons and some of his guns were already on the road and he sensed that Lee's entire army was going to follow them; actually, Lee began this march that very evening, driving his unfed infantry on an all-night march in a race for survival. Sheridan wanted to stop him. Meade of course ranked Sheridan and commanded all of the Federal troops present, but Sheridan now did not hesitate to go over Meade's head. Late in the afternoon, Sheridan sent Grant a message telling him how things were and saying bluntly: "I wish you were here yourself. I feel confident of capturing the Army of Northern Virginia if we exert ourselves. I see no escape for Lee."

Earlier that afternoon Grant had sent a telegram to Sherman: "Let us see if we cannot finish the job with Lee's and Johnston's armies," closing with the significant statement: "Rebel armies now are the only strategic points to strike at." So now, after darkness came on April 5, he got this note from Sheridan, indicating that this particular Rebel army might get away if the right move were not made. Grant got four of his staff officers, with a squad of fourteen cavalrymen for escort, and set out cross-country, riding from his camp at Nottoway Courthouse on the Southside Railroad to join Sheridan at Jetersville.

This was taking a risk. Grant was riding across no-man's-land, with guides who were not entirely sure that they knew the roads, he had sixteen miles to go, Rebel campfires were flickering in the night, there was a strong risk of meeting Rebel infantry or cavalry at any moment . . . and if the Confederates had captured U. S. Grant that night the war might have taken an unexpected new turn. The little cavalcade kept going, fortune was kind, and shortly after ten o'clock Grant rode up to Sheridan's pickets, who were dumbfounded to see the lieutenant general riding in out of nowhere at this hour of the night.

Meade's tent was some distance away from Sheridan's, and Grant was weary. He sent word to Ord that Lee "will be pursued at 6 A.M. from here if he leaves to go south . . . otherwise an advance will be made upon him where he is." Then he sent a message to Meade, explaining the message that had been sent to Ord, and adding: "I would go over to see you this evening, but it is late and I have rode a long distance today." An hour later he changed his mind, and with Sheridan at his side rode over to Meade's tent, reaching him a little after midnight.[7]

When he talked to Meade, discussing the things that might happen next day, Grant did not countermand Meade's orders for an advance on Amelia Courthouse. He suggested, however, that it would be advisable to make a change if it should be found that Lee was making a flank march, and cautioned Meade to keep a careful watch. Meade discovered the flank march next morning before his infantry had gone more than a few miles from Jetersville, when part of Lee's moving column was clearly visible off to the west, and he immediately wheeled his three corps about and sent them off in the same direction, with Sheridan's cavalry riding in front, stabbing at Lee's flanks. Now the Federals and Confederates were marching west on parallel courses not far apart, the van of Lee's army farther west than the Federal van, the tail of it moving ever more slowly as exhausted soldiers stumbled along after a sleepless night. The movement became even slower when Humphreys's soldiers, marching hard, began to catch up with the Confederate rear and attacked it; the Confederates had to stop to fight them off, and the despairing line of Southern troops grew longer and longer as the head of the column outdistanced the rear.

Lee's immediate goal was the town of Farmville, on the Appomattox River. Lee's chance to get around Grant's flank and move south to Danville had become too small to think twice about, but if he could get to Farmville (where the Appomattox was too deep for a moving army to cross unless it had bridges) he could go to the north side of the river, destroying the bridges behind him, and keep on moving west to Lynchburg, where there was an abundance of rations and where he might have some chance to stop and pull his broken army together. Some of his men were beginning to give way to weariness, hunger and despair, and his line of march now was marked by something that had never marked it before — hundreds of muskets, bayonets attached, stuck in the ground, butt ends upward, where beat-out soldiers had abandoned them. Some of these men vanished and tried to go home; most of them stayed with the army, unarmed and useless but pathetically trying to keep up with the only solid thing their universe still contained. The army was coming apart as it moved, and a great many of the men in it now were unarmed; yet if there could be a couple of free days at Lynchburg, where the men could rest and get a refit and proper food, there might still be a chance.[8]

It was up to Grant to prevent this, and his men were moving hard, marching desperately to get ahead of their foes. On April 6, while Meade was pressing the Confederate rear, Ord sent a detachment of cavalry and infantry on ahead to seize the bridges over the Appomattox a few miles downstream from Farmville. This detachment got there just too late, ran into too many Confederates, and was all but destroyed; but Sheridan and the leading element of Meade's army,

Wright's corps, kept striking at Lee's moving column — and Grant was reminded once more that with final victory so near he must think about the peace that would come afterward. To him, this afternoon, came a message from Lincoln at City Point.

Lincoln had gone up to captured Richmond and there he talked with Justice John A. Campbell, who had been a member of the peace commission that had accomplished nothing, early in the winter. Now Lincoln emphasized that what he wanted immediately was to get the separate Southern states to withdraw their troops from Confederate service — in other words, to give up — and he told Grant:

Judge Campbell thought it not impossible that the Rebel legislature of Virginia would do the latter if permitted, and accordingly I addressed a private letter to General Weitzel, with permission for Judge Campbell to see it, telling him that if they attempt to do this to permit and protect them, unless they attempt something hostile to the United States, in which case to give them notice and time to leave and to arrest any remaining after such time.

I do not think it very probable that anything will come of this, but I have thought best to notify you so that if you should see any signs you may understand them. From our recent dispatches it seems that you are pretty effectually withdrawing the Virginia troops from opposition to the government. Nothing I have done, or probably shall do, is to delay, hinder or interfere with you in your work.[9]

Lincoln's notion that there was not much left for the Virginia legislature to do was justified. Late that afternoon Sheridan sent his cavalry in on a segment of Lee's army at a dismal stream crossing on Sayler's Creek, half-a-dozen miles short of Farmville. Wright's infantry was at hand, and Sheridan got the men into position beside his dismounted horsemen and ordered a charge. The Confederate line collapsed, utterly overwhelmed, some 6,000 prisoners were taken, famous generals surrendering, Lee had received a mortal blow; and late that night Grant sent Lincoln a message he had just received from Sheridan, who said proudly:

I attacked them with two divisions of the Sixth Army Corps and routed them handsomely, making a connection with the cavalry. I am still pressing on with both cavalry and infantry. Up to the present time we have captured Generals Ewell, Kershaw, Barton, Corse, DeBose and Custis Lee, several thousand prisoners, 14 pieces of artillery with caissons and a large number of wagons. If the thing is pressed I think Lee will surrender.

This dispatch got diverse reactions. One of Sheridan's staff officers brought a copy to Meade, and Meade was infuriated because Sheridan was taking all the credit to himself — "I attacked them," "I am still pressing on," and so forth. To the staff officer Meade said angrily: "Oh, so General Wright wasn't there?" Innocently enough, the staff officer replied: "Oh yes. General Wright *was* there." Meade turned on his heel — he had begun to understand how Sheridan would be the hero of this campaign — and stalked off without a word.

Lincoln responded differently. On the following morning he sent a message to Grant:

"Gen. Sheridan says, 'If the thing is pressed I think that Lee will surrender.' Let the thing be pressed." [10]

Despite the pressure, Lee's army won the race to Farmville, where for the first time since the retreat began there were rations to be issued. Lee's plan now was to get north of the Appomattox, delaying pursuit by destroying all of the bridges, and then to strike west for Lynchburg, which was only three days' march away. Trains loaded with food and forage were ordered forward from Lynchburg along the Southside Railroad to a stop called Appomattox Station, a few miles away from the hamlet of Appomattox Courthouse, and if he got here promptly Lee could refresh his worn-out soldiers and pull his frayed-out divisions together. It just might be possible for him to swing south, ahead of the advancing Federals, and march toward Danville; if not, he could at least go on to Lynchburg.

All of this depended on Lee's ability to get away from Farmville quickly and leave the Federals hung up on the unfordable Appomattox River, and now the little luck that remained to the Army of Northern Virginia ran out entirely. (Another way to put it is to say that the unremitting energy Grant had at last infused into the Army of the Potomac was beginning to have its effect.) The bridges at Farmville were destroyed, but during the morning of April 7 the advance of Humphreys's corps, moving along with a drive that would have satisfied even Sheridan, captured a wagon bridge a few miles downstream before the Confederate rear guard could destroy it. Humphreys promptly put two divisions over the river and began to advance, Lee had to spend the day fighting off this threat, and he was unable to continue his retreat until after dark. He had lost twelve hours, most of the rations at Farmville went uneaten, instead of catching its breath his army had to make another night march — and Sheridan's cavalry, moving west south of the river, now had a chance to reach Appomattox Station before Lee could get there.[11]

Grant got to Farmville that afternoon. He had left all of his baggage behind on that night ride to Jetersville and he had nothing with him but the clothing he wore, which was badly spattered with mud. He sat on the porch of the village hotel and waited there, watching the men of Wright's corps marching through town on their way to join Humphreys north of the river. Here, as evening came on, he got a note from Sheridan: Sheridan had learned that rations were waiting for Lee at Appomattox Station and he was hurrying on, convinced that he could get there in time to capture them. Grant also was told that one of the Confederate officers taken the day before — peppery, one-legged Dick Ewell, Stonewall Jackson's right-hand man in the old days — had told his captors that the Confederate cause now was hopeless and that while he did not know what Lee was going to do he hoped he would surrender. While Grant was assaying these items of news, Generals Ord and Gibbon came up, to get the orders that would send their troops hurrying on after Sheridan. Gibbon remembered that Grant presently looked up and, "in his quiet way," unexpectedly said: "I have a great mind to summon Lee to surrender."

No sooner said than done. (Gibbon suspected that Grant's decision was not quite as spur-of-the-moment as it sounded.) Grant got writing materials and wrote this letter for General Lee, dating it at Farmville April 7, 1865:

The results of the last week must convince you of the hopelessness of further resistance on the part of the Army of Northern Virginia in this struggle. I feel that it is so, and regard it as my duty to shift from myself the responsibility of any further effusion of blood by asking of you the surrender of that portion of the Confederate States army known as the Army of Northern Virginia.

An officer spurred off for the north side of the river, to get the letter through the lines by flag of truce, and for a time Grant had nothing to do but wait. He had something to look at. All up and down the little street bonfires had been built, and as the Sixth Corps marched past and darkness came down the men grabbed burning brands, turned the march into a torchlight parade, and began to sing "John Brown's Body," breaking off to cheer mightily as they passed Grant. The general and the soldiers had had reservations about each other for

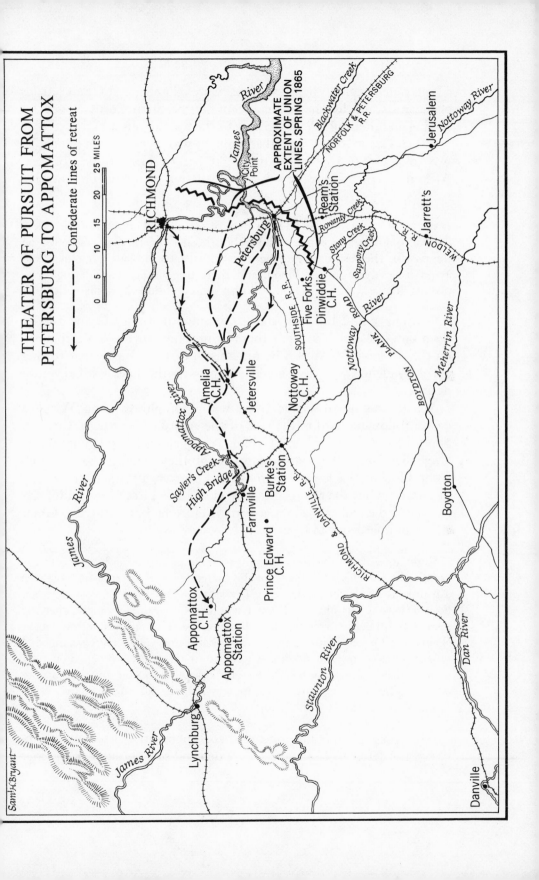

THEATER OF PURSUIT FROM
PETERSBURG TO APPOMATTOX

- - - - Confederate lines of retreat

0   5   10   15   20   25 MILES

Sam'l H. Bryant

a long time but now the reservations were all gone; and Grant left his chair and stood by the railing, silent, as the Sixth Corps moved by singing and shouting under the flare of the waving torches.

When Grant went to bed that night he was given a room which, he was told, Lee had occupied the night before. His rest was broken. After midnight an officer came in with a letter from Lee. This message read:

GENERAL: I have received your note of this date. Though not entertaining the opinion you express of the hopelessness of further resistance on the part of the Army of Northern Virginia, I reciprocate your desire to avoid useless effusion of blood, and therefore, before considering your proposition, ask the terms you will offer on condition of its surrender.[12]

Nothing could be done about this until morning. Grant got his sleep out — whether in Lee's room or in some other — and promptly on the morning of April 8 he rode north of the river so that further correspondence with Lee could go through the lines with the least delay.

Meade was north of the river, with Humphreys's and Wright's corps, following hard in the rear of the Army of Northern Virginia. South of the river Ord and Griffin were making a prodigious march after Sheridan; if they moved fast enough they could get across Lee's front, blocking his last escape route and forever cutting off his supply of rations, while the rest of the army closed in on Lee's rear, and if this happened the end was about at hand. Before he left Farmville, Grant wrote another letter to Lee:

Your note of last evening in reply to mine of the same date, asking the conditions on which I will accept the surrender of the Army of Northern Virginia, is just received. In reply I would say that, peace being my great desire, there is but one condition I would insist upon — namely, that the men and officers surrendered shall be disqualified for taking up arms against the Government of the United States until properly exchanged. I will meet you, or will designate officers to meet any officers you may name for the same purpose, at any point agreeable to you, for the purpose of arranging definitely the terms upon which the surrender of the Army of Northern Virginia will be received.

Note that this was not a demand for unconditional surrender. Between this letter to Lee and the curt demand sent through the lines at

Fort Donelson to General Simon Bolivar Buckner, three years earlier, there was a world of difference; since the earlier note was written there had been a world of change. Grant now was offering the easiest terms that could be offered to a beaten army, and he was stipulating that responsible leaders on both sides would sit down together to work out the details. Far from demanding unconditional surrender, Grant in effect was saying that he would accept almost any conditions as long as the army was definitely surrendered.

There was no fighting to speak of on April 8, and for a few hours what was left of the war was almost pleasant. Lee's army was a few miles in the lead, and although Meade drove his men hard they could not quite get close enough to force any important rear-guard actions on the retreating foe. The sun was bright, the spring weather was mild, this country had not been ravaged by marching armies, and the men's spirits rose, the spirits of general officers rising with them; when Grant overtook Meade he brightly greeted that grizzled soldier as "Old Fellow," which struck Theodore Lyman as highly irregular. Both of these officers, it developed, were in miserable shape physically. Meade for days had had chills and fever and had made a good part of this march lying in an ambulance, and Grant this afternoon came down with a blinding headache and was hardly able to stay in the saddle. When the cavalcade stopped for the night Grant took refuge in a farmer's house and applied quaint remedies, bathing his feet in hot water and mustard and putting mustard plasters on his wrists and the back of his neck, getting no relief thereby. Unfortunately the house he selected contained a piano, and bright staff officers hammered at the piano all evening, leading Colonel Lyman to marvel that Grant (who disliked music even when he did not have a headache) never ordered them to stop. Grant's spirits were not improved when he got a letter from Lee, late that night. The letter read:

GENERAL: I received at a late hour your note of today. In mine of yesterday I did not intend to propose the surrender of the Army of Northern Virginia, but to ask the terms of your proposition. To be frank, I do not think the emergency has arisen to call for the surrender of this army, but, as the restoration of peace should be the sole object of all, I desired to know whether your proposals would lead to that end. I cannot, therefore, meet you with a view to surrender the Army of Northern Virginia; but as far as your proposal may affect the Confederate States forces under my command, and tend to the restoration of peace, I should be pleased to meet you at 10 A.M. tomorrow on the old stage road to Richmond, between the picket lines of the two armies.[13]

This was a switch, and Grant was disturbed; long afterward, he told John Russell Young that "Lee does not appear well in that correspondence — not nearly so well as he did in our subsequent interviews." Lee had suddenly changed the subject, raising it to a field Grant was not allowed to enter. He and Grant had been writing about the surrender of the Army of Northern Virginia, which was the only thing Grant was permitted to discuss with him. Now Lee was saying that he did not want to surrender this army, but that he would like to talk about terms affecting "the Confederate States forces under my command." This could not mean anything except that he wanted to discuss an overall peace settlement, because he commanded all Confederate soldiers everywhere; like Grant, he was general-in-chief. Grant had been most explicitly ordered to get into no such talks with Lee or with anybody else.

As he read Lee's letter Grant shook his head in disappointment, saying: "It looks as if Lee meant to fight. I will reply in the morning." He may have toyed briefly with the notion of meeting Lee anyway, on the theory that he could hold the discussion to the matter of the surrender of the Army of Northern Virginia, but Rawlins was indignant, insisting that Lee had changed his tune only in order to gain time; and in any event Grant by now knew that the game was just about won. He had just received a note from Sheridan, who had got a division of cavalry into Appomattox Station, capturing there a Confederate guard, a park of artillery, and four freight trains loaded with Confederate rations. The head of Lee's army had reached Appomattox Courthouse, a few miles away, but Griffin and Ord were making an all-night march to join Sheridan and Sheridan believed that if they came up promptly "we will perhaps finish the job in the morning." He added a warning: "I do not think Lee means to surrender until compelled to do so."

Grant got little sleep that night. At four in the morning Colonel Porter found him restlessly walking back and forth in the yard, both hands pressed to his head. Porter tried to be a comforter, saying that usually when Grant had one of these migraine headaches it was quickly followed by good news; to which Grant replied that all he wanted just now was to get rid of the pain. At dawn he went over to

Meade's headquarters, had a cup of coffee, felt a little better, and wrote to Lee:

GENERAL: Your note of yesterday is received. I have no authority to treat on the subject of peace; the meeting proposed for 10 A.M. today could lead to no good. I will state, however, General, that I am equally anxious for peace with yourself, and the whole North entertains the same feeling. The terms upon which peace can be had are well understood. By the South laying down their arms they will hasten that most desirable event, save thousands of human lives, and hundreds of millions of property not yet destroyed. Seriously hoping that all our difficulties may be settled without the loss of another life, I subscribe myself, etc., U. S. GRANT, LIEUTENANT GENERAL.[14]

While this letter was on its way through the picket lines Grant rode to Meade's front and saw that Humphreys and Wright were moving forward. From the invisible distance far to the west came the faint rumble of artillery fire: Sheridan had been joined by Griffin and Ord just in time, the Confederate attempt to drive this force out of the way had failed, Lee was boxed in . . . and now Grant wanted to go to Sheridan. With his staff he struck off on a road leading down toward Appomattox Courthouse, swinging south of the place where Meade's corps were preparing to fight. Grant had ridden no more than a few miles when he was overtaken by a staff officer from Meade, bearing a new letter from Lee —who by now had discovered that his road was blocked. Grant dismounted, sat down on a grassy bank, and read this:

GENERAL: I received your note of this morning on the picket line, whither I had come to meet you and ascertain definitely what terms were embraced in your proposal of yesterday with reference to the surrender of this army. I now ask an interview in accordance with the offer contained in your letter of yesterday for that purpose.

R. E. LEE, GENERAL

Grant got his order book out and scribbled a quick reply:

Your note of this date is but this moment (11:50 A.M.) received, in consequence of my having passed from the Richmond and Lynchburg roads to the Farmville and Lynchburg road. I am writing this about four miles west of Walker's Church, and will push forward to the front for the purpose of meeting you. Notice sent to me on this road where you wish the interview to take place will meet me.

Grant gave this to Colonel Orville Babcock, telling him to deliver it to Lee and to escort Lee to whatever meeting place Lee might choose. Babcock delayed just long enough to get a fresh horse from the wagon train; then, accompanied by another staff officer, Captain W. M. Dunne, Jr., he galloped ahead, riding for Sheridan's lines because the quickest way to Lee now lay that way. More leisurely, Grant rode after him.

Babcock found Sheridan pacing back and forth restlessly. A flag of truce had come out from the Confederate lines, saying that Lee and Grant were going to meet and discuss surrender, and there was a temporary cessation of hostilities along this front, but Sheridan was disappointed and he told Babcock: "Damn them, I wish they had held out an hour longer and I would have whipped hell out of them." After Babcock had gone on through the lines Adam Badeau, who for some reason was going on ahead of Grant's party, came up, and Sheridan questioned him in furious suspicion: "What do you think? What do you know? Is it a trick? Is he negotiating with Grant? I've got 'em — I've got 'em like that!" He brandished a tightly clenched fist.[15]

Grant reached Sheridan sometime after this, having made the happy discovery that his headache left him altogether the moment he read Lee's last letter. He found Sheridan discontented, and he said afterward that the cavalryman told him that he was "suspicious about the whole business, feared that there might be a plan to escape, that he had Lee at his feet and wanted to end the business by going in and forcing an absolute surrender by capture." Sheridan's attitude, in fact, had been clearly visible earlier when he rode into the Confederate lines to arrange the cease-fire. The Confederate General John B. Gordon wrote about it thus:

Truth demands that I say of General Sheridan that his style of conversation and general bearing, while never discourteous, were far less agreeable and pleasing than those of any other officer of the Union army whom it was my fortune to meet. I do not recall a word he said that I could regard as in any degree offensive, but there was an absence of that delicacy and consideration which was exhibited by other Union officers.

If any general ever had the killer instinct it was Phil Sheridan; and where he and Grant differed was that Grant could see that this instinct, invaluable up to this moment, was out of place now. Grant explained his own point of view: "My campaign was not Richmond, not the defeat of Lee in actual fight, but to remove him and his army out of the contest and, if possible, to have him use his influence in inducing the surrender of Johnston and the other isolated armies." Lee's army was closed in, front and rear, and it could certainly be broken to bits in a storm of fire and steel, as Sheridan wanted to do; but nothing would quite be settled because remnants of the army would still exist. There would be survivors to take to the hills, rally others to them, and wage a guerrilla warfare that would cost the country more than it could ever pay. Grant wanted a victory that could be turned into lasting peace, and Sheridan did not have the recipe for it.[16]

A few miles to the east Meade had his troops ready to attack Lee's rear. Meade knew nothing about the contents of Lee's final note to Grant, and when a flag came into his lines asking for a cease-fire while the commanding generals conferred Meade flared up. "Hey! What!" he cried. "I have no sort of authority to grant such suspension. General Lee has already refused the terms of General Grant. Advance your skirmishers, Humphreys, and bring up your troops! We will pitch into them at once!" He was persuaded, with difficulty, to hold off for a time, but he was as edgy as Sheridan, and he cooled off only when Colonel Forsyth of Sheridan's staff, escorted by one of Lee's officers, who had led him through the Confederate lines, came up with a note from Colonel Babcock, who at last had met and talked to Lee. Babcock's note read: "I am with Gen'l Lee for the purpose of conducting him to an interview with Gen'l Grant on the matter of his surrender, will you please maintain the truce until you hear from Gen'l Grant." Meade accepted this, the Federal advance (which had actually begun) was halted, and the danger that Lee would be overwhelmed before he could surrender was averted.

So Babcock and Lee rode into Appomattox Courthouse, along with Colonel Charles Marshall of Lee's staff, and they went to the home of a man named Wilmer McLean, made themselves comfortable in the parlor, and waited, while Babcock sent an orderly off to tell General Grant where they were. The three men had a little while to wait, and Colonel Marshall recalled that "we talked in the most friendly and affable way." Then there was a clumping of boots on the steps, and Babcock looked out the window and saw Grant coming up on the porch, followed by Sheridan, Ord, Rawlins and assorted staff officers. Babcock went to the door and brought Grant inside, while the others waited outside; and for the first time during the war the two great commanders met face-to-face.

They were in striking contrast, these two. Lee wore a bright new uniform, with a sash and a jeweled sword, looking every part of the patrician he was; Grant's sword and all of his fresh clothing were back with his lost baggage, his muddy pants were tucked into muddy boots, he was short and slouchy, bearing his eternal air of not looking like anyone of any consequence, and Colonel Marshall thought that "he looked as though he had had a pretty hard time." Colonel Amos Webster of Grant's staff put it more bluntly, recalling that "Grant, covered with mud in an old faded uniform, looked like a fly on a shoulder of beef." Approaching the meeting place, Grant had worried about his appearance — not because he minded going to an important meeting all unpressed and travel-stained but because he was "afraid Lee might think I meant to show him studied discourtesy by so coming." The two men chatted easily for a few moments, recalling the time they had met in Mexico, years before; and either then or a bit later, after finding that Lee had no objection, Grant had a number of the Federal officers brought in and they were formally presented to Lee. (Grant's Colonel Ely Parker said that Lee shook hands with each "in a most courteous, condescending and yet affable manner.") Those who could find chairs sat down, and the rest stood against the walls.

There were three tables in the room: a small round marble-topped table, at which Grant sat, a small table with a square top of marble, where Lee sat, and a larger wooden table by the windows where Grant's Assistant Adjutant General, Joe Bowers, established himself to do whatever paper work might be needed. And at last they got down to business. Colonel Babcock wrote about it as follows:

Gen'l Lee said he had desired to meet Gen'l Grant on the matter of terms of surrender of his army. Gen'l Grant asked in what especial respect. Gen'l Lee said as to enlisted men. Gen'l Grant replied, he proposed to parole the men, the officers signing the parole for the men, the men to go to their own homes and obey the laws at their homes and not to take up arms against the United States again until duly exchanged according to the cartel. These liberal terms seemed to surprise Gen'l Lee, and to lift a weight from his mind. He remarked, how about the officers. Gen'l Grant said, I propose to accept their parole also, and on the same terms. Gen'l

Lee then continued the conversation in general a few moments, when Gen'l Grant interrupted him by asking him the business like question, Gen'l Lee, do I understand you to accept my terms? Gen'l Lee replied, I do, when Gen'l Grant called for writing materials, remarking that he would put it in writing.[17]

Grant got his order book — a bound book of sheets of yellow flimsy paper, with black sheets of carbon between the pages — got his pipe, and for a moment puffed vigorously; he confessed afterward that he had not arranged his thoughts and did not know how to begin. At last he waved the smoke aside, took up his pencil, and began to write. Finishing at last, he handed the book to Lee, who read the terms carefully. When Lee finished reading, Grant asked: "General, is that satisfactory?" As Ely Parker recalled it, Lee replied: "Yes, I am bound to be satisfied with anything you offer. It is more than I expected." There was a brief discussion of a clause or two whose meaning did not seem to be clear, one or two interlineations were made, and at last the document was complete. It read:

GENERAL: In accordance with the substance of my letter to you of the 8th instant, I propose to receive the surrender of the Army of Northern Virginia on the following terms, to wit: Rolls of all the officers and men to be made in duplicate, one copy to be given to an officer to be designated by me, the other to be retained by such officer or officers as you may designate. The officers to give their individual paroles not to take up arms against the Government of the United States until properly exchanged; and each company or regimental commander to sign a like parole for the men of their commands. The arms, artillery and public property to be parked and stacked, and turned over to the officers appointed by me to receive them. This will not embrace the side-arms of the officers, nor their private horses or baggage. This done, each officer and man will be allowed to return to his home, not to be disturbed by U.S. authority so long as they observe their paroles and the laws in force where they may reside.

U. S. GRANT, LIEUTENANT GENERAL

Grant's powers today were limited: he was allowed to do no more than fix the terms on which Lee's army was to be surrendered. Yet in the final sentence of his letter he reached far beyond this limitation, taking everything that Lincoln felt and everything he himself felt about the necessity to make a peace that would include no reprisals, firmly committing the United States government to it for all the years to come. Because of that final sentence, no Confederate soldier, from Lee on down, could ever be prosecuted for treason; in effect, this was a general amnesty. There could never be a proscription list to poison the peace with the spirit of vengeance and hatred. Grant had ruled it out.

Lee had one more point to raise. In the Confederate army, he said, cavalrymen and artillerymen owned the horses they used. Would these men be allowed to keep these animals? Grant replied that they would not; as written, the terms permitted this only to the officers. Lee reread the draft of the letter and said: "No, I see the terms do not allow it; that is clear." His face showed that he was disappointed, and Grant began musing aloud:

"Well, the subject is quite new to me. Of course I did not know that any private soldiers owned their animals, but I think this will be the last battle of the war — I sincerely hope so — and that the surrender of this army will be followed soon by that of all the others, and I take it that most of the men in the ranks are small farmers, and as the country has been so raided by the two armies it is doubtful whether they will be able to put in a crop to carry themselves and their families through the next winter without the aid of the horses they are now riding, and I will arrange it in this way; I will not change the terms as now written, but I will instruct the officers I shall appoint to receive the paroles to let all the men who claim to own a horse or mule take the animals home with them to work their little farms."

Here again, Grant was speaking for Lincoln, who had said that he wanted to see the Confederate soldiers back on the farm as soon as possible. Lee remarked: "This will have the best possible effect upon the men. It will be very gratifying and will do much toward conciliating our people." So Grant handed the order book over to Joe Bowers, to make a fair copy in ink.

Bowers had been left behind at City Point when the army marched away from Petersburg, and he had rejoined the staff just this morning. Now he found himself flustered; he had a historic document to write, and it was too much for him. He spoiled his first sheet of paper, took another and began over, spoiled that, spoiled a third, and at last called Colonel Parker to his side, saying: "Parker, you will have to write this, I can't do it." Parker, a full-blooded Iroquois Indian, was imperturbable, and he sat down, wrote out the final copy, and gave it to

Grant for signature. Grant signed, Parker took the letter, folded it in three folds, and sealed it in a big official envelope, addressing the envelope to General Lee. He gave this to Grant, who in turn handed it to Lee, who broke the seal and read the document.

Meanwhile, Colonel Marshall had been preparing Lee's letter of acceptance. After a brief discussion he finished it to Lee's satisfaction. Colonel Marshall wrote out a fair copy and handed it to Lee, who signed it. This letter was brief. It said:

GENERAL: I have received your letter of this date containing the terms of surrender of the Army of Northern Virginia as proposed by you. As they are substantially the same as those expressed in your letter of the 8th instant, they are accepted. I will proceed to designate the proper officers to carry the stipulations into effect.

R. E. LEE, GENERAL

This was folded and put into a sealed envelope, and Lee gave it to Grant; and when Grant took it the surrender was an accomplished fact — and every soldier in the Confederate army was home free. Grant did not open Lee's envelope. He gave it to Parker and did not bother to look at it until that evening. He explained that Lee's oral assurance that the terms were accepted was good enough. The letter was just a formality.

There were small details to settle. Lee held a number of captured Federals as prisoners, and these were to be sent into the Union lines. Lee's army was entirely out of rations, and Grant agreed to send a supply over — taking it, as a matter of fact, from the Confederate trains Sheridan had captured the night before. While the talk was going on, unrelenting Sheridan unbent and casually remarked to Colonel Marshall, who happened to be next to him: "This is very pretty country." Marshall replied that he had not seen it by daylight — "all my observations have been made by night, and I haven't seen the country at all myself." The two men chuckled; and then it was all over, and Lee and Marshall went out to return to Lee's camp, the Union officers who waited outside snapping to attention and saluting when Lee came on the porch. Colonel Babcock escorted Lee and Marshall back to the Confederate picket lines.[18]

Grant came out, at last, mounted, and rode back to his headquarters tents, which had been pitched not far away. (Apparently the headquarters baggage wagons had come up at last.) On the way, Horace

Porter asked Grant if he did not think that news of the surrender was worth divulging to the War Department. Grant confessed, without embarrassment, that he had forgotten all about it. The cavalcade halted, and Grant sat down on a stone by the roadside, borrowed Badeau's notebook, and wrote a telegram for Secretary Stanton. It read:

General Lee surrendered the Army of Northern Virginia this afternoon on terms proposed by myself. The accompanying additional correspondence will show the conditions fully.

U. S. GRANT, LIEUTENANT-GENERAL

Word of the surrender had got about, the soldiers were jumping up and down with excitement, and Federal artillerists began to fire salutes. The racket disturbed Grant. Neither this army nor Lee's would ever come under fire again, and from now on these guns would be museum pieces . . . and anyway what had just happened struck Grant as too big and deep to go off in a loud noise. He sent staff officers around to stop the firing, saying: "The war is over. The Rebels are our countrymen again." [19]

CHAPTER TWENTY-FOUR

Stranger in a Strange Land

G RANT stopped the firing of salutes in the part of the army that was nearest to him, but his order never got through to the soldiers who were with Meade a few miles farther east. All they got was the simple news that the surrender papers had been signed. When this news arrived everybody lost control, starting with Meade himself. A soldier in Humphreys's corps remembered seeing a wild group of mounted men galloping down the road, Meade in front, staff officers behind, two squadrons of cavalry following, everybody yelling and waving swords and riding like mad. Meade was bareheaded, both arms in the air, shouting: "It's all over, boys! Lee's surrendered! It's all over!" The soldiers responded with "such a shout as none of them will ever hear again," and everybody wanted to throw something high in the air. The veteran did his best to give a picture of it:

The air is black with hats and boots, coats, knapsacks, shirts and cartridge boxes, blankets and shelter tents, canteens and haversacks. They fall on each others' necks and laugh and cry by turns. Huge, lumbering, bearded men embrace and kiss like school-girls, then dance and sing and shout, stand on their heads and play at leapfrog with each other. . . . All the time, from the hills around, the deep-mouthed cannon give their harmless thunders, and at each hollow boom the vast concourse rings out its joy anew that murderous shot and shell no longer follow close the accustomed sound.

Colonel Lyman said that everybody went crazy, shouting, screaming and dancing up and down; "and there was General Meade galloping about and waving his cap with the best of them." One of Wright's officers wrote to his wife to say: "Notwithstanding the privations and hardships I have endured, and the great suffering I have undergone,

[469]

the glory of this day more than compensates me for all." Some of the men simply lay on their backs and cried. Now and again a few would get together to sing a hymn, but most of the time the song could not be heard because every band in camp was playing, no two of them using the same tune. Beyond the simple joy in victory won there was the marvelous assurance that everybody was going to live; the man who tossed his canteen over the treetops did so in the certainty that he was not going to have to go out tomorrow and risk a shell fragment in the stomach or a minie ball in the eye. No one would ever shoot at him again.

The racket died down at last, probably because everybody was exhausted, and Ely Parker remembered that the night was strangely quiet. Here they were, with the other army camped just beyond the picket lines, but there was no rattle of shots from the outer darkness; "the only sounds to be heard were the steady, monotonous tramp of the sentinels and their occasional challenges, either to the vigilant officer of the guard or the belated soldier." Everybody got a good sleep that night.[1]

Grant wanted to talk to Lee again, and at the McLean house they had arranged to meet the next morning. At nine o'clock on April 10 Grant rode out, accompanied by a number of officers, to draw rein on a rise overlooking the Confederate camp, while a Confederate courier rode off to tell the commanding general that Grant had arrived. After a few moments Lee came up, unattended, riding at a gallop. He removed his hat, the officers all saluted, Grant and Lee shook hands; then everybody else withdrew out of earshot while Grant and Lee remained in the saddle side-by-side to have their talk.[2]

Grant had been ordered to discuss nothing with Lee but the surrender of the Army of Northern Virginia, but with Lee's surrender letter in his pocket he was prepared to give his orders a liberal interpretation, and years later he told John Russell Young what happened:

I urged upon Lee the wisdom of ending the war by the surrender of the other armies. I asked him to use his influence with the people of the South — an influence that was supreme — to bring the war to an end. General Lee said that his campaign in Virginia was the last organized resistance which the South was capable of making — that I might have to march a good deal and encounter isolated commands here and there; but there was no longer any army which could make a stand. I told Lee that this fact only made his responsibility greater, and any further war would be a

[470]

crime. I asked him to go among the Southern people and use his influence
to have all men under arms surrender on the same terms given to the
Army of Northern Virginia. He replied he could not do so without consultation with President Davis. I was sorry. I saw that the Confederacy
had gone beyond the reach of President Davis, and that there was nothing
that could be done except what Lee could do to benefit the Southern
people. I was anxious to get them home and have our armies go to their
homes and fields. But Lee would not move without Davis, and as a
matter of fact at that time or soon after Davis was a fugitive in the woods.

Colonel Marshall said that he got a different and far more interesting version from Lee when Lee returned to the Confederate camp.

General Lee told me when he came back [wrote Colonel Marshall] that
General Grant asked him if he would go and meet President Lincoln. . . .
Grant said "I want you to meet him. Whatever you and he agree upon
will be satisfactory to the reasonable people of the North and South." He
said, "If you and Mr. Lincoln will agree upon terms, your influence in the
South will make the Southern people accept what you accept, and Mr.
Lincoln's influence in the North will make reasonable people of the North
accept what he accepts, and my influence will be added to Mr. Lincoln's."
General Lee was very much pleased and would have been delighted to
do anything in the world that he could to bring about a pacification, but
he said: "General Grant, you know that I am a soldier of the Confederate
army, and I cannot meet Mr. Lincoln. I do not know what Mr. Davis is
going to do, and I cannot undertake to make any terms of that kind."
General Grant then said he would go himself at once, and while he
understood the reasons of General Lee's position, he regretted that he
would not go. I think myself, and have always thought, that if General
Lee and Mr. Lincoln could have met as General Grant proposed, we could
have had immediate restoration of peace and brotherhood among the people of these States.[3]

Of all the fascinating might-have-beens of the Civil War, there is
nothing quite as poignant as this might-have-been meeting between
Lincoln and Lee. It never took place, and if it had it might have
brought nothing; yet a generation which is only beginning to grapple
with the problems left by the war is bound to be haunted by it. What
might have happened . . .
Within the limits of his concept of his duty, Lee did what he could.
On April 20, back in Richmond, he sent President Davis a letter re-

porting on the surrender of his army and the reasons for it, and he closed with this paragraph:

From what I have seen and learned, I believe an army cannot be organized or supported in Virginia, and as far as I know the condition of affairs, the country east of the Mississippi is morally and physically unable to maintain the contest unaided with any hope of ultimate success. A partisan war may be continued, and hostilities protracted, causing individual suffering and the devastation of the country, but I see no prospect by that means of achieving separate independence. It is for your Excellency to decide, should you agree with me in opinion, what is proper to be done. To save useless effusion of blood, I would recommend measures be taken for suspension of hostilities and the restoration of peace.[4]

It was too late. Davis was in flight down across the Carolinas; he held his last cabinet meeting on April 24, on May 10 he was captured by Federal troops in Georgia, and as Grant said the Confederacy had gone beyond his reach.

When Lee rode up to Grant, three of the generals who had ridden with Grant — Sheridan, Rufus Ingalls, and Seth Williams, who was Grant's inspector general — asked and were given Lee's permission to go into his camp and look up some old army friends. They returned as the conversation ended, bringing with them Longstreet, Gordon, Heth and others who wanted to pay their respects to Grant. There was a general handshaking and exchange of greetings — friendly, but a little restrained: Adam Badeau remembered that the Confederates, naturally enough, "behaved with more courtesy than cordiality." There was one moment of warmth, when Grant met Longstreet, a longtime friend, whom he had last seen in the hard days back in St. Louis before the war, when Grant came to town on a wood-peddling trip, saw Longstreet, and sat down with him to a game of brag. Now he took Longstreet by the arm and said: "Pete, let's have another game of brag to recall the old days." Longstreet was moved, and when he told about it afterward he could only say: "Why do men fight who were born to be brothers!"[5]

Grant left Appomattox that afternoon, not waiting for the formal surrender ceremonies, which were planned for April 12, and not even bothering to go to Richmond to look at the capital city his armies had captured. He wanted to get back to work and cut the size of the war program, which was costing $4,000,000 a day, and he spent the rest of that day and all the next in the saddle, coming at last to Burkeville, where he took a train on the Southside Railroad for Petersburg. He reached City Point near dawn on April 12, and after greeting Julia — who had waited for him there, instead of following his telegraphed suggestion that she go back North by herself [6] — he went to his old headquarters office and attacked some paper work, while two or three aides sat about in the room waiting for orders. After a few minutes he stopped writing, looked off into space, grinned, and remarked to nobody in particular: "More of Grant's luck."

Stanton hoped Grant would get back to Washington quickly, and sent a telegram that day to say so. Grant replied that he would start at once, and he took a steamer that evening, reaching Washington on the morning of April 13. After he and Stanton had conferred, Stanton made public announcement that all recruiting and drafting were stopped and that the ordering of supplies was being curtailed, which was almost the equivalent of saying that peace had returned. The War Department closed early that afternoon, and in the evening there was a grand "illumination," with people all over Washington putting lighted candles in their windows and with lighted transparencies adorning public buildings. Either that afternoon or next morning Grant received a telegram from General Gibbon at Appomattox Courthouse:

The surrender of General Lee's army was finally completed today. We have paroled from 25,000 to 30,000 men. One hundred and forty-seven pieces artillery have been received, about 10,000 small arms, and 71 flags. . . . I have conversed with many of the surrendered officers and am satisfied that by announcing at once terms and a liberal, merciful policy on the part of the Government we can once more have a happy, united country.[7]

April 14 was Good Friday, and there was a cabinet meeting in the White House at eleven o'clock. Grant was there, very much the lion of the day, and he had to tell everyone about Lee's surrender; the meeting was long but somewhat informal, Lincoln all aglow with the feeling that the war at last was just about over, and there was a good deal of discussion about ways to restore normal commercial intercourse between North and South. When Treasury Secretary Hugh McCulloch suggested that he would be glad to be relieved of the treasury agents who controlled the movement of cotton, Grant remarked that he was against the lot of them and thought their work highly demoralizing; and when Navy Secretary Gideon Welles proposed that the whole Atlantic coast be thrown open to normal trade, Grant said that this might well be extended to include all of the country east of the Mississippi. Stanton presented the draft of a plan for restoring civil government in the Southern states, and it was agreed that everybody would study a copy of the draft and be ready to discuss it at the next meeting.

All in all, the meeting was pleasant and relaxed; and yet the faint shadow of a coming event touched the cabinet room, although nobody recognized it for what it was until later. The talk returned to military matters, and people wanted to know how Sherman was making out against Johnston. Grant could only say that everything looked good and that he was expecting news hourly. And then Lincoln said that he had no doubt good news would come soon, because he had last night had a strange dream that always seemed to foretell some great event. He dreamed, he said, that he was on an indescribable ship of some kind, moving over dark waters toward an indefinite shore, and he had dreamed this way before, on the eve of news of great victories like Antietam, Gettysburg, Stone's River, Vicksburg and so on. According to Welles, Grant spoke up — he still did not like Rosecrans — to say that Stone's River was no victory, but Lincoln was undisturbed. The dream had come, it meant that something prodigious was about to happen, and he believed they would soon hear from Sherman. . . .

After a while the meeting ended, and Grant chatted with the President. Mr. and Mrs. Lincoln had arranged a theater party for that evening, with General and Mrs. Grant as their guests; but while the cabinet met a messenger arrived with a note for Grant from Julia. She wanted to get back to Burlington and see the children, the theater party apparently appealed to her not at all, and as Grant put it, "Some incident of a trifling nature had made her resolve to leave that evening." He confessed, afterward: "I was glad to have the note, as I did not want to go to the theater." So he made his excuses to the President, and after a while he left the White House to join his wife.[8]

The weather turned bad that afternoon, and by evening the air was cold and raw, with sudden gusts of wind. When darkness came, Grant and his wife got into a carriage to go to the railroad station. Mrs. Grant was uneasy. She had lunched that day with friends in a hotel dining room, and one man in a group at a nearby table had watched her closely, apparently trying to overhear her conversation and being so rude that she finally left the table. Now, as they rode along Pennsylvania Avenue, the man appeared again — a lone horseman, who rode past their carriage at a gallop, circled around it, came up close and peered through the window at them, and then dashed away. Later on, Grant came to believe that this horseman was John Wilkes Booth. Whoever he was and whatever his appearance meant, the Grants reached the station safely and got aboard the private car of John W. Garrett, president of the Baltimore & Ohio Railroad, to go to Philadelphia. Grant remembered that as the train started the conductor locked the doors of the car; at Havre de Grace, or somewhere near there, a man apparently tried to force an entrance and was rebuffed by the train crew.

A railroad trip from Washington to Philadelphia was a slow ride in those days, and it was after midnight when the Grants reached Philadelphia, where they were to stay the night. They went to Bloodgood's Hotel, and took a room; and to this room, soon after they had checked in, came a messenger boy with a telegram. Admitted to the room, the boy saw Mrs. Grant sitting on a couch removing her hat. There was food on a table, and Grant was just about to sit down and eat. He remained standing and opened the telegram the boy handed him; as he read it, the boy remembered, "not a muscle of his face quivered." He handed the message to Julia, who started to read it and then buried her face in her hands and began to cry. The telegram was from Major Thomas Eckert, chief of the War Department telegraph office, and it read:

THE PRESIDENT WAS ASSASSINATED AT FORD'S THEATER AT 10:30 TONIGHT AND CANNOT LIVE. THE WOUND IS A PISTOL SHOT THROUGH THE HEAD. SECRETARY SEWARD AND HIS SON FREDERICK WERE ALSO ASSASSINATED AT THEIR RESIDENCE AND ARE IN A DANGEROUS CONDITION. THE SECRETARY OF WAR DESIRES THAT YOU RETURN TO WASHINGTON IMMEDIATELY. PLEASE ANSWER ON RECEIPT OF THIS.

Grant at once prepared for the return trip. Julia would go on to their home in Burlington, and Grant would get in touch with her when he could. Before he could start for Washington he got a telegram from C. A. Dana at the War Department, dispatched at 12:50 A.M.:

PERMIT ME TO SUGGEST TO YOU TO KEEP CLOSE WATCH ON ALL PERSONS
WHO COME NEAR YOU IN THE CARS OR OTHERWISE; ALSO, THAT AN ENGINE BE
SENT IN FRONT OF THE TRAIN TO GUARD AGAINST ANYTHING BEING ON THE
TRACK.[9]

It was a long ride back, and daylight had come by the time Grant
got to Washington, where he learned that Lincoln was dead. With
good reason he remembered this as "the darkest day of my life." Not
only had he lost the man who gave his own life an added dimension; it
seemed to him that the war that was just being won had taken on a
fearful new guise, becoming something that nothing in all his experience fitted him to meet. He told John Russell Young, long afterward:
"I did not know what it meant. Here was the Rebellion put down in
the field, and starting up in the gutters; we had fought it as war, now
we had to fight it as assassination." [10]

This feeling that the war had gone underground — that the murder
and the attempted murders were part of a far-reaching plot tied directly to the defeated Southern nation — was widespread that morning; men have to judge things by the best light they have, and the light
on April 15 was extremely murky and incomplete. Francis Lieber, the
German-born political scientist and educator, who had written schol-
arly treatises for the War Department on the management of armies
and on the relationship of guerrilla warfare to the regular usages of
war, was a man of good will and good balance, sober and self-
contained as a man need be. Yet on this morning he was seized by a
desperate desire for vengeance by violence, and he wrote an almost
hysterical letter to Halleck:

My God! That even this should befall us! It is Slavery, Slavery! Can I
do anything? Dispose, my friend, wholly of me, if there be aught I can
help to do. The draft ought to go on again, or volunteers be called, to
sweep, literally to sweep the South. No coquetting! Drive the fiends from
our soil and let Grant be a stern uncompromising man of the sword, and
the sword alone, until the masses in the States rise against their own fiends,
and hang them or drive them out, and until the masses offer themselves, re-
revolutionized, back to the Union, freed from slavery and assassins and
secret society . . . The murder of poor, good Lincoln is no isolated fact.
It is all, all one fiendish barbarism.[11]

What bookish Lieber could feel men of action could also feel, and
Grant took up his tasks that morning in his War Department office in

a mood of cold fury such as he never displayed at any other time in his life. He received a note from Stanton, calling his attention to "the large number of Rebel officers and privates, prisoners of war, and Rebel refugees and deserters that are among us" and ordering him to see that "adequate force and vigilance" were used. The note closed with the injunction: "I feel it my duty to ask you to consider yourself specially charged with all matters pertaining to the security and defense of this national capital." Presumably, at some time during the day, Grant saw a message that had come in the evening before from Ord in Richmond, addressed to President Lincoln and saying that John A. Campbell and R. M. T. Hunter wanted permission to visit Washington to see the President, "I think with important communications." This message reached Washington after Lincoln had left for the theater, and of course Lincoln never saw it; but this afternoon of April 15 Grant sent to Ord a telegram breathing the exact opposite of the spirit of amnesty and reconciliation that had lighted Mr. McLean's parlor at Appomattox. Grant's message read:

Arrest J .A. Campbell, Mayor Mayo and the members of the old council of Richmond, who have not yet taken the oath of allegiance, and put them in Libby prison. Hold them guarded beyond the possibility of escape until further orders. Also arrest all paroled officers and surgeons until they can be sent beyond our lines, unless they take the oath of allegiance. The oath need not be received from anyone who you have not good reason to believe will observe it, and from none who are excluded by the President's proclamation, without authority of the President to do so. Extreme rigor will have to be observed whilst assassination remains the order of the day with the Rebels.

Ord was appalled. As he saw it this meant starting the war all over. He was far enough from fever-stricken Washington to take a more balanced view, and he promptly replied:

Cipher dispatch directing certain parties to be arrested is received. The two citizens I have seen. They are old, nearly helpless, and I think incapable of harm. Lee and staff are in town among the paroled prisoners. Should I arrest them under the circumstances I think the Rebellion would be reopened. I will risk my life that the present paroles will be kept, and if you will allow me to do so trust the people here who, I believe, are ignorant of the assassination, done I think by some insane Brutus with few accomplices. Mr. Campbell and Hunter pressed me earnestly yesterday to send them to Washington to see the President. Would they have done so, if guilty? Please answer.

Grant became calmer, and that evening he sent this reply to Ord:

On reflection I will withdraw my dispatch of this date directing the arrest of Campbell, Mayo and others so far as it may be regarded as an order, and leave it in the light of a suggestion, to be executed only so far as you may judge the good of the service demands.

Ord had averted a calamity, and Grant never again showed the furious mood that had been on him that day. He remained grim, however. A few days later Hancock sent a message asking for advice; he had summoned the famous guerrilla leader, John S. Mosby, to surrender, and had granted a brief truce while Mosby thought it over. Now Mosby was asking a ten-day extension of the truce so that he could learn what was happening to Johnston's army. Grant's reply was implacable:

"If Mosby does not avail himself of the present truce, end it and hunt him and his men down. Guerrillas, after beating the armies of the enemy, will not be entitled to quarter." [12]

When Grant was talking "no quarter" he was Lieber's man of the sword incarnate. He soon abandoned the notion that the assassination was part of a formal plot blessed at Richmond, however, and one reason may have been a message he received April 16 from the Confederate General Dick Ewell, confined with other general officers in Fort Warren. Ewell's persuasive message read:

You will appreciate, I am sure, the sentiment which prompts me to drop you these lines. Of all the misfortunes which could befall the Southern people, or any Southern man, by far the greatest, in my judgment, would be the prevalence of the idea that they could entertain any other than feelings of unqualified abhorrence and indignation for the assassination of the President of the United States and the attempt to assassinate the Secretary of State. No language can adequately express the shock produced upon myself, in common with all the other general officers confined here with me, by the occurrence of this appalling crime, and by the seeming tendency in the public mind to connect the South and Southern men with it. Need we say that we are not assassins, nor the allies of assassins, be they from the North or from the South, and that coming as we do from most of the states of the South we would be ashamed of our own people were we not assured that they will reprobate this crime. [13]

On April 16 Grant sent a letter to Julia to reassure her about his own safety. He admitted that the assassination plot "contemplated the destruction of more than the President and Sec. of State," but said that it seemed to have blown itself out and that there was nothing more to fear. Meanwhile: "I shall occupy a room in the office which is well guarded and will be occupied by Bowers and probably two or three others. I shall only go to the Hotel twice a day for my meals and will stay indoors of evenings. The change which has come upon the country so suddenly will make it necessary for me to remain in the city for several days yet. Gen. Halleck will go to Richmond to command there and Ord to Charleston. Other changes will have to be made, and the apparent feeling that I should remain here until everything gets into working order under the new regime will probably retain me here until next Saturday." [14]

There was enough to keep him busy. Sherman had not yet forced Joe Johnston to surrender, and Grant warned Sheridan, who had his cavalry down at Nottoway Courthouse, that it might be necessary for him to go on to North Carolina. Johnston, said Grant, might "follow his usual tactics of falling back whenever too hard pressed," and if he did Sherman did not have enough cavalry to head him off and capture his army. Sheridan accordingly must be prepared to push south and lend a hand. Sherman should be in Raleigh any day now (he was there by the time Grant sent this message, as a matter of fact) and if he needed help Sheridan would have to move down and join him.

The funeral service for President Lincoln was held in the White House on April 19. Draped in crape and black cloth, the casket lay in the East Room on a little platform under a domed canopy of black cloth supported by four pillars and lined with fluted white silk. President Andrew Johnson, members of the Supreme Court and the cabinet, the uniformed diplomatic corps, and other dignitaries, were seated in the room. At the foot of the catafalque were chairs for members of Mr. Lincoln's family, represented today only by young Robert Lincoln, Mrs. Lincoln feeling unable to attend. At the head of the catafalque, all through the service, stood General Grant, alone. Correspondent Noah Brooks said that the general "was often moved to tears." Grant reflected that he would always be glad to remember that Lincoln had spent most of his final days in Grant's company, and when he tried to sum up the man he could only say: "He was incontestably the greatest man I have ever known." [15]

Leaving the White House after the services, Grant went back to his office; and there, that afternoon, he at last got news from Sherman — a message sent by steamer from New Berne, North Carolina, two days before and telegraphed on from Fort Monroe. Sherman announced that Joe Johnston was about to surrender.

On Good Friday — while Lincoln was telling the cabinet about his strange prevision of a great event to come, and was happy in the belief that it meant good news from North Carolina — Johnston had written to Sherman to suggest a meeting "to permit the civil authorities to enter into the needful arrangements to terminate the existing war." Sherman immediately replied that he was fully empowered to discuss the surrender of Johnston's army, that he would abide by the terms made between Grant and Lee, and that he was "willing to confer to that end." The two men had a preliminary meeting at Durham Station, not far from Raleigh, on April 17, and it was the news of this meeting that Sherman put into the message Grant got on the day of the funeral.

"Johnston," said Sherman, "evidently seeks to make terms for Jeff Davis and his cabinet," and Sherman and Johnston were to meet again next day; with them would be John Breckinridge, the Confederate Secretary of War. It seemed to Sherman that "there is great danger that the Confederate armies will dissolve and fill the whole land with robbers and assassins, and I think this is one of the difficulties Johnston labors under. The assassination of Mr. Lincoln shows one of the elements in the Rebel army which will be almost as difficult to deal with as the main armies." [16]

For the moment, that was all the news there was. Like Grant, Sherman wanted a formal, final surrender of the army that faced him, and greatly feared that unless this came soon there might be a disastrous lapse into the terrors of guerrilla warfare. If his remarks about terms for the Confederate President and cabinet, and the presence at the next meeting of Secretary Breckinridge, hinted that he was going to talk about more than just Johnston's surrender, there was nothing that could be done about this now. This second meeting would have been held by the time Sherman's wire reached Grant.

Elsewhere in the military field events were moving fast. Canby had at last taken Mobile, Wilson had captured the munitions center of Selma, Alabama, and had gone on to take Montgomery, where the Confederacy had been born; and, as Grant said, these achievements would have been important if they had happened earlier. Now they were just part of the mopping-up process. What Washington wanted now was final word from Sherman.

Next day, April 20, late in the afternoon, Grant was thinking about going to New Jersey to spend the weekend with his family when he got a telegram from Fort Monroe signed by Sherman's Major Henry Hitchcock, who said he had a dispatch for Grant from Sherman containing the text of an agreement signed by Sherman and Johnston. Major Hitchcock was taking a steamer for Washington at once . . . and Grant's hope that he might go home vanished. He stayed in Washington, and on the afternoon of April 21 Major Hitchcock arrived and Grant read Sherman's dispatch.

Sherman was in high spirits. The enclosed copy of his agreement with Johnston, he said, "if approved by the President of the United States, will produce peace from the Potomac to the Rio Grande . . . You will observe that it is an absolute submission of the enemy to the lawful authority of the United States, and disperses his armies absolutely, and the point to which I attach most importance is that the dispersion and disbandment of these armies is done in such a manner as to prevent their breaking up into guerrilla bands." [17]

This was fine news, well worth waiting for, and Grant turned to the surrender document . . . and, as he read it, realized at once that it just would not do.

Sherman had done what Grant himself had been flatly ordered not to do: he had arranged a general treaty of peace, covering not only the surrender of all the Confederate armies but also the terms on which the separate Southern states would be readmitted to the Union. The document he and Johnston had signed was headed "A Memorandum or Basis of Agreement," and although the two generals confessed that they lacked the power to lay down any such terms as these they agreed that they would try to get "the necessary authority" to put them into effect.

All Confederate troops were to march to their state capitals, disband, and deposit their weapons in state arsenals, abstaining thereafter from acts of war and submitting to Federal authority. State officials and members of legislatures would take the oath of allegiance, whereupon the state governments would be recognized as legal despite their secessionist past. Courts would be reopened, all Southerners would regain full political rights and their "rights of person and property, as defined by the Constitution and of the states, respectively" would be guaranteed. There would be universal amnesty, and an armistice pending final ratification in Washington. Sherman's covering letter contained the hopeful remark: "If you can get the President to simply indorse the copy and commission me to carry out the terms, I will follow them to the conclusion." [18]

Grant could see that this demanded attention by someone higher than himself, and he quickly sent a message around to Stanton's house:

I have received and just completed reading the dispatches brought by special messenger from General Sherman. They are of such importance that I think immediate action should be taken on them and that it should be done by the President in council with his whole cabinet. I would respectfully suggest whether the President should not be notified, and all his cabinet, and the meeting take place tonight.

Stanton was at dinner. He hurried back to the War Department, read Sherman's papers, talked to Grant, and then took Grant off to see President Johnson. Messengers were sent hurrying about town, and by eight o'clock the cabinet was assembled. Grant read Sherman's memorandum aloud.

It could not have reached Washington at a worse time or found a more hostile audience. The President and his ministers simply were not ready to think about reconciliation and an easy peace, and to have these presented to them, only two days after Lincoln's funeral, as an accomplished fact engineered by Sherman, who had always seemed a little unsound politically, was more than they could endure. The kind of anger that gripped Francis Lieber had touched all of these men. Moved by it, they felt an enormous, all-embracing suspicion. As far as they could see, under Sherman's terms the Confederate armies could pick up their weapons and start fighting again whenever it seemed good to them; unredeemed state governments would regain their old standing (and doubtless their old thorny arrogance) overnight, and slavery itself might be legalized all over again. It might be that this document even amounted to recognition of the Confederate government. Only a few days before, President Johnson had declared that "treason is a crime and must be punished as a crime"; it could not be written off "as an unsuccessful rebellion, to be overlooked and forgiven," but it must be punished and "the instigators of this monstrous rebellion" must pay the full penalty. When he said that, Johnson spoke for all of his associates. He and they would feel differently a bit later, but that was how they felt tonight. Sherman's document was unanimously disapproved. Johnson and Stanton even said that Sherman's action skirted the edge of treason, and Stanton seemed especially bitter. Grant objected sharply to this, defending Sherman's motives with some heat; but he agreed that the surrender paper Sherman had sent in could not be approved.[19]

When the meeting ended Grant went back to the War Department. His first act was to write an extended letter to Sherman. This letter was for the record, to formalize the rejection of Sherman's treaty; it would not be sent down by courier because Grant was going to deliver it in person. It began:

The basis of agreement entered into between yourself and General J. E. Johnston for the disbandment of the Southern army and the extension of the authority of the General Government over all the territory belonging to it, sent for the approval of the President, is received. I read it carefully myself before submitting it to the President and Secretary of War and felt satisfied that it could not possibly be approved. My reasons for these views I will give you at another time in a more extended letter. Your agreement touches upon questions of such vital importance that as soon as read I addressed a note to the Secretary of War notifying him of their receipt and the importance of immediate action by the President, and suggested in view of their importance that the entire cabinet be called together that all might give an expression of their opinions upon the matter.

The result was a disapproval by the President of the basis laid down, a disapproval of the negotiations altogether, except for the surrender of the army commanded by General Johnston, and directions to me to notify you of this decision. . . . Please notify General Johnston immediately on receipt of this of the termination of the truce and resume hostilities against his army at the earliest moment you can, acting in good faith.

Finishing this, Grant took time to write a letter to Julia:

"It is now nearly 11 o'clock at night and I have received directions from the Sec. of War and President to start at once for Raleigh, North Carolina. I start in an hour. Gen. Meigs, Maj. Leet, Capt. Dunn and Major Hudson go with me. I will write to you from Morehead City or New Berne."

At this point Grant apparently paused to reflect. A special steamer was waiting for him, but he had something on his mind and he was not going to be hurried. Since Lee's surrender everything had changed.

He had been all soldier, the commander of armies, director of a great fight; now victory had been won and he was an executive at a desk in Washington, determining whether more cavalry horses ought to be bought, saying which units would be demobilized first, passing on claims and protests, adding up columns of figures and examining treaties of peace. Somehow a light had gone out. The job he had was not what it had been, and all he had to sustain him was the thought that with him and through him his country had won a great victory. Yet perhaps victory itself was not quite enough; along with great power there had to be moral greatness . . . if one just knew where to find it. He tried to explain, and his letter continued:

I find my duties, anxieties and the necessities for having all my wits about me increasing instead of diminishing. I have a Herculean task to perform and shall endeavor to do it, not to please anyone but for the interest of our great country that is now beginning to loom above all other countries, modern and ancient. What a spectacle it will be, to see a country able to put down a rebellion, able to put half a million soldiers in the field at one time and maintain them! That will be done, and is almost done already. That Nation, united, will have a strength that will enable it to dictate to all others, *conform to justice and right*. Power I think can go no further. The moment conscience leaves, physical strength will avail nothing, in the long run.

Grant had never in any letter given his wife much news about what was going to happen next. With the war ending he could not change now; no military secrets would ever be found in his letters home. He concluded:

I only sat down to write you that I was suddenly required to leave on important duty, and not feeling willing to say what that duty is, you must await my return to know more. Love and kisses for you and the children.

U. S. GRANT[20]

Grant's steamer put him ashore at Fort Monroe next afternoon. He stayed there only long enough to let Stanton know where he was, and to send a telegram to General Halleck, who now commanded the occupation forces in and around Richmond. The message to Halleck said:

"The truce entered into by General Sherman will be ended as soon as I can reach Raleigh. Move Sheridan with his cavalry toward Greensborough as soon as possible. I think it will be well to send one corps of infantry with the cavalry. The infantry need not go farther than Danville unless they receive orders hereafter."

The old fear that Johnston's army might simply break up, with determined men going off to take up the kind of guerrilla warfare that would put the land in turmoil for months to come, was still strong. When Sherman renewed his negotiations with Johnston, Grant wanted enough Federal troops present to make certain that all of Johnston's troops were thoroughly hemmed in. Having sent this dispatch, Grant transferred to an ocean-going steamer for the voyage down the Carolina coast. He got to Beaufort on the evening of April 23, and from that point he sent a brief message to Stanton:

"Have just reached here and will start for Raleigh as soon as a train can be obtained. No news here from Sherman. I shall not telegraph to him that I am on the way."

Grant was trying to keep his mission a secret because he did not want to embarrass Sherman any more than he had to. He knew that he could explain, when he saw that general, how and why the meeting with Johnston had to be done all over again; but if news of the trip became public it would be clear to everyone that Sherman had made a mistake which only the presence of the commanding general could set right.

Actually, Sherman had begun to sense how the wind was blowing. On the day Grant arrived at Beaufort Sherman received a bale of northern newspapers. They had been printed before Sherman's memorandum of agreement with Johnston had reached Washington, but they were full of stories showing the extent of the blind anger that had swept across the North after the tragedy at Ford's Theater, and Sherman immediately sent them along to Joe Johnston with a warning letter:

". . . I fear much the assassination of the President will give such a bias to the popular mind which, in connection with the desire of our politicians, may thwart our purpose of recognizing 'the existing local governments.' . . . I believe this assassination of Mr. Lincoln will do the cause of the South more harm than any event of the war, both at home and abroad, and I doubt if the Confederate military authorities had any more complicity with it than I had." Sherman added the information that Ord had withdrawn the earlier permission for the Virginia legislature to meet. It was clear enough that the memorandum he and Johnston had signed was apt to have rough sledding.[21]

Grant finally got to Raleigh early on the morning of April 24. He went at once to Sherman, who was both surprised and pleased to see him, and he made his entry so unobtrusively and kept himself so much in the background that most of Sherman's soldiers did not know he was present. Grant showed Sherman the letter he had written, told him about the cabinet meeting (leaving out the harsh remarks the President and the Secretary of War had made) and suggested that he notify Johnston that the truce was off and that another meeting was necessary. Sherman did so without delay, showing the messages to Grant before sending them. Sherman also read a letter Stanton had asked Grant to give him, which said that in any dealings with Johnston Sherman must be guided by the order Lincoln had given Grant during the winter — discuss no peace terms whatever but limit yourself strictly to the surrender of the army that is facing you. Sherman remarked dryly that "it would have saved a world of trouble" if he could just have seen this earlier. Grant in turn sent a message back to Stanton, trying to explain that when he made his deal with Johnston Sherman had been guided by the best lights he had:

> I reached here this morning and delivered to Gen. Sherman the reply to his negociations with Johnston. He was not surprised but rather expected this rejection. Word was immediately sent to Johnston terminating the truce and information that civil matters could not be entertained in any convention between army commanders.
>
> Gen. Sherman has been guided in his negociations with Johnston entirely by what he thought was prescedents authorized by the President. He had before him the terms given by me to Lee's army and the call of the Rebel legislature of Va., authorized by Weitzel, as he supposed with the sanction of the President and myself. At the time of the Agreement Sherman did not know of the withdrawal of authority for the meeting of that legislature. The moment he learned through the papers that authority for the meeting of the Va. legislature had been withdrawn he communicated the fact to Johnston as having bearing on the negociations here.[22]

It took a little time to arrange a new conference (at which Grant would not be present) and next day Grant wrote a letter to Julia. Grant had lost all trace of the vengeful spirit that descended on him when he first learned of Lincoln's assassination. He was back now in Lincoln's mood, thinking about reconciliation and an end to punishment; he was once more the soldier, pitiless while the war lasted but capable (like the Sherman whose attitude he defended before the President and the Secretary of War) of becoming a different person the moment the fighting stopped. To Julia he wrote:

We arrived here yesterday and as I expected to return today did not intend to write until I returned. Now however matters have taken such a turn that I suppose Sherman will finish up matters by tomorrow night and I shall wait and see the result. Raleigh is a very beautiful place. The grounds are large and filled with the most beautiful oaks I ever saw. Nothing has been destroyed and the people are anxious to see peace restored so that further devastation need not take place in the country. The suffering that must exist in the South the next year, even with the war ending now, will be beyond conception. People who talk now of further retaliation and punishment, except of the political leaders, do not conceive of the suffering endured already, or they are heartless and unfeeling, and wish to stay at home, out of danger, while the punishment is inflicted.[23]

Matters at Raleigh were soon wound up. Sherman met again with Johnston and they wrote out a surrender paper which duplicated the terms Grant had given Lee. Johnston's army laid down its arms, and Grant quietly went back to Washington as soon as he had read the new agreement and had written "Approved: U. S. Grant" across the bottom of it. The storm broke a few days later, when the papers were full of Stanton's angry denunciation of Sherman, along with a message officious Halleck had broadcast to Union troops all across the South telling them that Sherman's truce had been canceled and that they were to pay no attention to any orders Sherman might issue under it. Halleck had thoughtfully (and quite erroneously) informed Mr. Stanton that Jefferson Davis in his flight was taking an immense amount of gold from the Confederate treasury along with him, and in the newspapers it was made to appear that some of Sherman's troop movements might well have the effect, designed or accidental, of enabling Davis to escape to Europe with this loot. For a few days all of this was the talk of the town in Washington, and it earned for Halleck and Stanton General Sherman's undying hatred. It was a short-lived sensation, however, and in the end it did nothing to reduce the high regard the people of the North had for Sherman — or, for that matter, the bitterness the people of the South felt toward him.

Grant got back to Washington and resumed his chores. Military matters were still to be wound up, and for a while Grant would be unable to get back to Burlington and his family. He explained this to Julia in a letter written early in May, saying that he was now in telegraphic touch with Wilson's cavalry, far down in Macon, Georgia, and that in a few more days every point in the South would be in reach of his telegraphed orders. This was the surest sign that the war was over: "But a short thirty-five days ago we had a defiant enemy holding the South; today we are telegraphing, through their own operators, and over the wires which they controlled so short a time since, regarding dispositions for the capture of their pretended President and Cabinet. Management is all that is now wanted to secure complete peace." [24]

First item on this job of management was to issue new orders to General Sheridan.

Sheridan had taken his cavalry down to the Virginia–North Carolina border, in obedience to Grant's earlier orders, but when Johnston's second surrender agreement was signed he was not needed there and he marched his cavalry back to Washington, looking forward to leading his men in the grand review of the Army of the Potomac, which was scheduled for May 23. Sheridan had as much pride as the next man, probably a little more than most, and he looked forward to this chance to march at the head of his mounted host before the admiring public; now, a week before the parade was to be held, he was dismayed to be told that he must go at once to Texas.

In Texas a Federal army of 50,000 men was being assembled "to restore Texas, and that part of Louisiana held by the enemy, in the shortest practicable time." The cavalry itself was to stay in Washington, but Sheridan had been named to command this new army and there would be no parade for him. The troops were being assembled from Canby's force at Mobile, from Federal troops in Arkansas, and from the men Ord had commanded along the James, and as their commander Sheridan must make certain that the Confederacy's trans-Mississippi army surrendered at once.

This assignment impressed Sheridan as both unwelcome and odd. The Southern Confederacy had gone out of existence. Jefferson Davis had been captured, what was left of the government had been dispersed, the last troops east of the big river had laid down their arms, and the Confederate commander west of the river, General Edmund Kirby Smith, was obviously not disposed to keep the struggle alive to the last ditch. He commanded 40,000 men but he and they were orphans now, and Grant pointedly told Sheridan that if Smith and his men held out "without even an ostensible government to receive orders from or to report to" they would be nothing better than outlaws. Smith understood the situation perfectly, and there was every reason to suppose that his surrender would be just a matter of time. This being so, why put a large army under Phil Sheridan on the Rio Grande?

Grant quickly gave Sheridan enlightenment. He was not thinking about Edmund Kirby Smith as much as he was thinking about Maximilian, the Austrian emperor of Mexico, and about the French army that sustained him there. In Grant's mind Maximilian and this French army represented a bit of unfinished business that had to be attended to; and in feeling this way Grant was responding partly to the imperatives of high politics but even more to an uneasy conscience and to an emotion that came down from his own vanished youth. Like that other taciturn, hardcase soldier, Stonewall Jackson, Grant had been in love with Mexico ever since he fought there. The memory of the people and the atmosphere of that strange land, so little like his own Middle West, tugged at him where he was most sensitive; and furthermore, he had a sense of guilt. To the end of his days he considered the war with Mexico a resounding act of injustice on the part of the United States, and saw the great Civil War itself as the retribution that had been visited upon his country for that act. As he saw it, America was in Mexico's debt, and somehow that debt was profoundly involved in the process of taking the Southern Confederacy apart; things would not quite be settled until Mexico was liberated. So now Grant had these orders for Sheridan.

Sometime afterward Sheridan told Hamlin Garland what Grant had said to him.

"He informed me," said Sheridan, "that there was an additional motive in sending me to the new command, a motive not explained by the instructions themselves, and went on to say that, as a matter of fact, he looked upon the invasion of Mexico by Maximilian as a part of the Rebellion itself, because of the encouragement that invasion had received from the Confederacy, and that our success in putting down secession would never be complete until the French and Austrian invaders were compelled to quit the territory of our sister republic. With regard to this matter he said that it would be necessary for me to act with great circumspection, since the Secretary of State, Mr. Seward, was much opposed to the use of our troops along the border in any active way that would be likely to involve us in a war with European powers.

"Under the circumstances, my disappointment at not being permitted to participate in the review had to be submitted to, and I left Washington without an opportunity of seeing again in a body the grand Army of the Potomac." [25]

Sheridan and his new army did not have to fight anyone. Smith surrendered on May 26, bringing the last of the Civil War to a close. Secretary Seward quietly notified the French government that the presence in Mexico of a French army, maintaining a government not chosen by the people of Mexico themselves, was "a cause of serious concern" to the United States government; and with 50,000 Federal veterans under America's most warlike soldier camped along the Rio Grande this warning was all that was needed. The French eventually withdrew all of their troops, the Maximilian government collapsed — and if this adventure had been, as Grant suspected, "part of the rebellion itself," it was closed out quietly and for keeps. But Sheridan did miss the grand review.

There were two grand reviews, really, but it was all one mighty parade, spreading over two days, bringing down a curtain on something done, raising a curtain on something too incalculable to understand. Never before had there been so many people in Washington. They came from everywhere, and a great many of them slept on park benches — weather in Washington is mild, near the end of May — and there were grandstands all along Pennsylvania Avenue from the Capitol to the White House, filled with people waiting to cry and cheer and wave little flags. The men who marched and those who watched them noticed that the city itself had changed. All of the badges of mourning had disappeared. The White House flag was at the top of the staff for the first time since April 15, the black banners were gone from the public buildings, and as Abraham Lincoln's armies marched the time of mourning for Lincoln ended. This parade was for the men who lived, the indomitable survivors, and there were two days of marching soldiers, seven miles of cavalry clattering along in front, artillery brigades trundling past, rank upon endless rank of marching infantry moving along to the sound of a great crying. On the sidewalks were women with baskets of flowers, tossing the blossoms under the feet of the soldiers.

In front of the White House there was a special grandstand with President Johnson to take the salute, Grant by his side, cabinet all there, foreign diplomats in uniform, and such other notables as could wangle seats. On the second day, when Sherman came down the avenue at the head of his army, it was noted that "there was something almost fierce in the fever of enthusiasm" roused in the crowd. As Sherman's infantry came down toward the Treasury building, people in the stands began to sing "John Brown's Body." The marching soldiers picked it up and came down the street chanting out the chorus, and suddenly the whole endless column was singing the great marching song of the Union army, tramping out the cadence, until "the long vista glittered as a river of fire, with the sunlight reflected from the thousands of bayonets undulating with the lazy swinging stride of the Western troops." Grant could not tell one tune from another — he had last heard this one that night in Farmville, when Wright's Sixth Corps marched past him by torchlight and the soldiers and the general still had a great purpose to serve — and now he stood by a President who was not Lincoln, taking his last look at an army that was tramping off to the everlasting shadows; standing unmoved as Sherman, coming up into the reviewing stand, gave Secretary Stanton a ferocious glare and refused to take the secretary's offered hand.

The marching column went on and on, carrying the battle flags with the terrible names of many battles, the names that meant so many deaths carried by the men who had lived; and finally it was all over, the enormous armies had gone offstage forever, and a newspaperman looking back long afterward wrote thoughtfully: "In a few weeks this army of two or three hundred thousand men melted back into the heart of the people from whence it came, and the great spectacle of the Grand Army of the Republic on review disappeared from sight."

One of Sherman's veterans, going home with all the rest, found that when the armies did melt back into the heart of the people the adjustment was a little difficult. The men had been everywhere and had seen everything, life's greatest experience had ended with most of life still to be lived, to find a common purpose in the quiet days of peace would be hard: "Old avenues are closed to them, old ambitions are dead, and they walk as in a dream — as strangers in a strange land." The war was over, and now everything would be different.[26]

One of these veterans, moving along a shadowed new path after living in a world where he had seen the path so very clearly, was General Grant.

Notes

Chapter 1 POLITICAL INNOCENT

1. Letter of Rawlins to Grant dated July 30, 1863, in the John A. Rawlins Papers, Chicago Historical Society.
2. *O.R.*, Vol. LII, Pt. One, p. 416.
3. Charles A. Dana, *Recollections of the Civil War*, p. 72, quoting his letter to Secretary Stanton dated July 13, 1863; Dr. E. D. Kittoe, surgeon of the 45th Illinois, after Vicksburg medical inspector of hospitals in Grant's department, quoted in a dispatch from Galena, Ill., in the Chicago *Tribune* of January 21, 1877; Howard K. Beale, ed., *The Diary of Gideon Welles*, Vol. I, p. 386.
4. Letters of McClernand to Secretary Stanton, dated June 27, 1863, and to President Lincoln, dated August 26, 1863; from microfilms of the John A. McClernand Papers loaned by the U. S. Grant Association, Carbondale, Ill.
5. Welles's *Diary*, Vol. I, p. 387.
6. About a month after Fredericksburg, Burnside tried to resume the offensive and got into the fiasco of the famous "Mud March." For an examination of the way his plans were sabotaged by such generals as Joe Hooker, William B. Franklin and William F. Smith, see *Never Call Retreat*, pp. 63–67.
7. Letters of Grant to Dana, dated August 5, 1863, in the Charles A. Dana Papers, Library of Congress; Grant to Washburne, dated August 30, in the Illinois State Historical Library; Senator Henry Wilson to Washburne, dated July 25, in the Washburne Papers, Library of Congress. Grant was notably carefree in his spelling; he knew how to spell but he never let his knowledge bother him, and he often got a word right in one sentence and wrong in the next. The editors of the Official Records seem to have corrected his mistakes in all Grant's messages and reports which appear in that compendium. Where the original papers are cited in this volume, Grant's own version has been followed, and it has not seemed necessary to insert a smug (*sic*) after each misspelled word.
8. Grant's August 30 letter to Washburne, cited in n. 7 above.
9. Issue of the New York *World* dated August 8, 1863.
10. Dana, *Recollections of the Civil War*, p. 102; *O.R.*, Vol. XXIV, Pt. Three, p. 492; letter of Grant to Dana dated August 5, microfilm in the U. S. Grant Association, from original in the Library of Congress.
11. *O.R.*, Vol. XXIV, Pt. Two, pp. 528, 529; Pt. Three, pp. 497, 507–508; letter of Grant to Halleck dated July 24, microfilm from the U. S. Grant Association.
12. Grant to Halleck, July 24, as cited in n. 11 above.
13. Roy Basler, ed., *The Collected Works of Abraham Lincoln* (cited hereafter as Basler), Vol. VI, p. 350.
14. For a good study of Sherman's Jackson campaign, see Edwin C. Bearss, four articles in the *Jackson State Times*, July 31 to August 21, 1960.
15. Letter of Grant to Banks dated July 11, from *The History of America in Documents*, catalog of the Rosenbach Company, Philadelphia, Pt. Three, p. 42; Banks to Grant dated July 18, in *O.R.*, Vol. XXIV, Pt. Three, pp. 527–528; Sherman to Grant, dated July 12, *O.R.*, Vol. XXIV, Pt. Two, p. 522. For a brief review of Banks's first experiences in New Orleans, see *Terrible Swift Sword*, pp. 70–79.
16. Grant to Halleck, dated July 18, *O.R.*, Vol. XXIV, Pt. Three, p. 529; letter of

Grant to Halleck, dated July 24, microfilm from the U. S. Grant Association; Davis to Johnston, dated July 18, *O.R.*, Vol. XXIV, Pt. One, p. 208. Grant first mentioned the Mobile plan in his July 18 dispatch, but he certainly wrote this before he got Banks's dispatch of the same date; there was at that time no direct wire from New Orleans to Vicksburg, and it usually took two days to get a message from one city to the other.

17. *O.R.*, Vol. XXIV, Pt. Three, pp. 538, 562, 569; Vol. XXVI, Pt. One, p. 666. Neither Banks's hurried trip to Vicksburg nor the message he sent that evening to Halleck makes any sense except on the premise that he went there to talk to Grant about Mobile. Note that on July 30 Sherman was writing to General John G. Parke of the Ninth Corps: "I trust we may meet again about Atlanta in October; we by way of the Alabama river, and you by Chattanooga." (*O.R.*, Vol. XXIV, Pt. Three, p. 563.)

18. Halleck to Grant, dispatches dated August 6 and August 9, ibid., pp. 578, 584; Lincoln to Grant, dated August 9, *O. R.*, Vol. XXIV, Pt. Three, p. 584. It should be remembered that messages between Washington and Vicksburg had to go by way of Cairo, Ill., with considerable delay. Halleck's order to Grant to send a corps to New Orleans is dated July 30, and on August 7 Grant notified Banks that he had "just received this important despatch." (*O.R.*, Vol. XXIV, Pt. Three, pp. 562, 580.)

19. *Personal Memoirs of U. S. Grant*, Vol. I, pp. 578–584; *Grant Moves South*, pp. 195–197. The assertion that Halleck refused to let him visit New Orleans — Grant wrote bitterly that "so far as my experience with General Halleck went it was very much easier for him to refuse a favor than to grant one" — is in error. Halleck explicitly gave permission, specifying only that Grant leave an officer at Vicksburg "to receive and carry out any orders that are sent from Washington" (*O.R.*, Vol. XXIV, Pt. Three, p. 584). An indignant reference to French activities in Mexico is in Welles's *Diary*, Vol. I, p. 385.

20. John Russell Young, who knew Grant well in the postwar years, remarked in his book *Men and Memories* (p. 475) that although Grant rarely quarreled he "was not prone to reconciliation." He added: "A quarrel with him did not mean the taking off the glove only to put it on again. It was the closing of the book."

21. *O.R.*, Vol. XXIV, Pt. Three, pp. 546–547, 587; Basler, Vol. VI, p. 374; *O.R.*, Vol. XXX, Pt. Three, pp. 225, 277, 402.

22. *O.R.*, Vol. XXIV, Pt. Three, pp. 538, 539; E. M. Coulter, *The Confederate States of America*, p. 286; A. S. Roberts, "The Federal Government and Confederate Cotton," *The American Historical Review*, Vol. XXXII, No. 2, pp. 272–275.

23. *O.R.*, Vol. XXIV, Pt. Three, pp. 468–469; *Report of the Joint Committee on the Conduct of the War*, 37th Congress, Third Session, Part Three, 1863 (cited hereafter as CCW Report), pp. 611–612; Adam Badeau, *Military History of U. S. Grant*, Vol. I, pp. 409–411.

24. Albert D. Richardson, *Personal History of Ulysses S. Grant*, p. 343. The newspaperman Sylvanus Cadwallader wrote an appreciative tribute to Bowers, a typescript of which is in the Lloyd Lewis Papers.

25. *O.R.*, Vol. XXIV, Pt. Three, pp. 538, 562.

26. *O.R.*, Vol. XXX, Pt. Three, pp. 695–697, 732.

27. Richardson, op. cit., p. 347; John Eaton, *Grant, Lincoln and the Freedmen*, p. 98; Henry Coppee, *Life and Services of General U. S. Grant*, pp. 205–206.

Chapter 2: THE ROAD TO CHATTANOOGA

1. Story in the New Orleans *Era* for September 4, 1863, reprinted in the New York *World* for September 12.

2. Richardson, *Personal History of Ulysses S. Grant*, pp. 347–348.

3. Letter of Banks to Mrs. Banks dated September 5, 1863, in the N. P. Banks Papers, Essex Institute Library, Salem, Mass.; James Grant Wilson, *Life and*

Campaigns of General Grant, pp. 58–59; Henry Coppee, *Life and Services of General U. S. Grant*, pp. 206–207.

4. James Grant Wilson, op. cit., p. 105; Lloyd Lewis, *Captain Sam Grant*, pp. 82, 93–94, 264–265; Banks's letter to Mrs. Banks, cited in n. 3.

5. It seems impossible to get a satisfactory account of this accident. The best seems to be that of James Grant Wilson (op. cit., p. 105) who said that he and Grant were riding in the lead, with Grant slightly behind him; Wilson heard Grant's horse fall, rode back, and found the general unconscious. Brigadier General Thomas Kilby Smith, who was on Grant's staff, wrote that Grant was in the lead and that when his horse fell the officer just behind "rode over him and the trampling of the horse bruised him severely." (Undated letter from the general's son, Thomas Kilby Smith, to William E. Brooks, quoting a wartime letter of the general; in the Lloyd Lewis Papers.) Both Richardson (op. cit., p. 348) and Coppee (op. cit., p. 207) said that Grant's horse fell after colliding with a carriage. It may be that the fine *déjeuner* at Mays made everyone incapable of giving a coherent report. General Banks, who was of the party that day, did not describe the accident at all.

6. The book, *Phoenixana; or, Sketches and Burlesques*, was written by George H. Derby, an army officer who used "John Phoenix" as a pen name. It was published in 1856 and contains a series of articles somewhat like Mark Twain's early efforts: a bit heavy-handed, but nevertheless quite readable and amusing even today. Derby was a West Point plebe while Grant was an upperclassman. He served in the Mexican War, winning a brevet for bravery at Cerro Gordo, remained in the army after the war, and died in May, 1861. Grant tells of his injuries in his *Memoirs*, Vol. I, p. 581.

7. James Grant Wilson, op. cit., p. 105; Richardson, op. cit., p. 348; *O.R.*, Vol. XXVI, Pt. One, pp. 290–292; Vol. XXX, Pt. Three, p. 359; James H. Wilson, *The Life of John A. Rawlins*, p. 154. A minor pitfall for students of this period is that two army officers named James Wilson wrote about it — James Grant Wilson, who accompanied Grant to New Orleans and who wrote a biography that has been cited in the notes accompanying this chapter, and James Harrison Wilson, then inspector general on Grant's staff, an intimate of Rawlins, who wrote a laudatory biography of Rawlins and who also collaborated with Charles A. Dana in a biography of Grant. It was James Harrison Wilson who was largely responsible for the theory that Rawlins functioned as Grant's brain and as the keeper of his conscience, and it is advisable to use his books with caution. Banks's message to Halleck, telling of the accident, is in *O.R.*, Vol. XXX, Pt. Three, p. 359.

8. Letter of Banks to Mrs. Banks, as in n. 3 above; letter of Franklin to General William Farrar Smith, dated December 28, 1863, in the William F. Smith Papers, private collection of Walter Wilgus.

9. Letter of General Washburn to Congressman Washburne dated September 5, 1863, in the Washburne Papers, Library of Congress. When he wrote to his brother about Grant, Washburn did not pull his punches. On March 28, 1863, he said flatly that Grant was a dismal failure, adding: "The truth must be told even if it hurts. You cannot make a silk purse out of a sow's ear." To Washburn, Rawlins was "infinitely Grant's superior . . . the only man of any sense he has got around him." (This letter is also in the Washburne Papers.) It seems incredible that so outspoken a critic would have failed to report the behavior Banks and Franklin were alleging.

10. Rawlins's September 15 letter to James H. Wilson is in Wilson's *Life of John A. Rawlins*, p. 154. For a description of the Lum residence and a sketch of Grant's stay there, see "Vicksburg Family Shared their Home with U. S. Grant," in the Vicksburg *Evening Post*, Centennial Edition, July, 1963.

11. Lewis, *Captain Sam Grant*, pp. 380–381; article in the Chicago *Tribune* for September 16, 1869; Wilson, *Rawlins*, p. 25.

12. Letter of Rawlins to Mary Emma Hurlbut dated November 16, 1863, from the John A. Rawlins Papers in the Chicago Historical Society.
13. Letter of Rawlins to Miss Hurlbut dated October 14, 1863, Rawlins Papers, Chicago Historical Society.
14. Grant to Halleck, September 19, *O.R.*, Vol. XXX, Pt. Three, pp. 732, 841; to Banks, September 21, *O.R.*, Vol. XXVI, Pt. Three, p. 730; to Chase, September 28, copy in the David D. Porter Papers, Huntington Library.
15. Adam Badeau, *Military History of U. S. Grant*, Vol. I, p. 418; *O.R.*, Vol. XXX, Pt. Three, pp. 592, 640.
16. William T. Sherman, *Memoirs*, Vol. I, pp. 346-349, 352-355; *O.R.*, Vol. XXX, Pt. Three, p. 923.
17. Henry Villard, *Memoirs*, Vol. II, p. 185; *O.R.*, Vol. XXX, Pt. One, pp. 220-221. One thing that helped tip the scales against Rosecrans was undoubtedly the story told by Brigadier General James A. Garfield, Rosecrans's chief of staff all through the Chickamauga campaign, who went to Washington not long after the battle to resign his commission and take a seat in Congress. After he got to Washington, Garfield wrote to Rosecrans that he was "disgusted and indignant" at the "crazy slanders that have dogged you"; but he himself told Secretary Chase, who had been Rosecrans's strongest supporter in the cabinet, that Rosecrans had fled from the Chickamauga battlefield in a panic, and he told others, apparently including Secretary Stanton, that Rosecrans had suffered a "collapse of nerve and of will." Garfield's duplicity is examined in William M. Lamers's excellent biography of Rosecrans, *The Edge of Glory*, pp. 408-413.
18. Badeau, op. cit., p. 422; *O.R.*, Vol. XXX, Pt. Four, p. 375; U. S. Grant, "Chattanooga," in *Battles and Leaders of the Civil War* (cited hereafter as *B. & L.*), Vol. III, p. 681.
19. So, at least, according to J. H. Wilson, *Rawlins*, p. 163.
20. Grant, *Memoirs*, Vol. II, pp. 17-19. The text of War Department General Orders No. 337, which established the new command set-up, is in *O.R.*, Vol. XXX, Pt. Four, p. 404.
21. New York *Herald* for October 23, 1863, printing a Louisville dispatch dated October 19.
22. Grant, *Memoirs*, Vol. II, pp. 19, 26; *O.R.*, Vol. XXX, Pt. Four, pp. 414-415, 455, 479.
23. General O. O. Howard, "Grant at Chattanooga," in *Personal Recollections of the Rebellion*, Papers of the New York Commandery, Military Order of the Loyal Legion, Vol. I, pp. 245-246.
24. New York *Herald* for November 9, 1863, printing a Chattanooga dispatch by E. D. Westfall dated October 24; Grant, *Memoirs*, Vol. II, p. 28. Rosecrans's farewell message is in *O.R.*, Vol. XXX, Pt. Four, p. 478. For an account of the coolness that developed between the two generals, see *Grant Moves South*, pp. 316-320.
25. Howard, op. cit., pp. 246-248.
26. The Rev. James B. Rogers, *War Pictures*, p. 228.
27. *O.R.*, Vol. XXX, Pt. Four, p. 467; Pt. One, pp. 216-220; Jefferson H. Jennings in *Personal Recollections of the War*, Paper No. 54, War Papers of the District of Columbia Commandery, Military Order of the Loyal Legion of the United States; letters of Rawlins to Mary Emma Hurlbut dated November 16 and 23, 1863, in the Rawlins Papers, Chicago Historical Society.
28. Donn Piatt, *Memories of the Men Who Saved the Union*, p. 190; W. F. G. Shanks, *Personal Recollections of Distinguished Generals*, pp. 71-72; Wilson, *Rawlins*, pp. 165-167; interview with General Joseph J. Reynolds, in the Hamlin Garland Papers, American Literature Collection, University of Southern California Library; Horace Porter, *Campaigning with Grant*, p. 4.

Chapter 3: I HAVE NEVER FELT SUCH RESTLESSNESS BEFORE

1. *O.R.*, Vol. XXX, Pt. One, p. 793; Vol. XXXI, Pt. One, p. 70.
2. *O.R.*, Vol. XXXI, Pt. Two, p. 29. There is a good discussion of these routes in William M. Lamers, *The Edge of Glory*, p. 370.
3. Thomas B. Van Horne, *History of the Army of the Cumberland*, Vol. I, p. 395 ff. General Smith's report on the Brown's Ferry operation is in *O.R.*, Vol. XXXI, Pt. One, p. 77.
4. Letters of Grant to Julia dated October 24 and October 27, 1863, from the collection owned by Major General U. S. Grant III; *O.R.*, Vol. XXXI, Pt. One, p. 712.
5. Burnside's September 27 message to Halleck (*O.R.*, Vol. XXX, Pt. Three, pp. 904–905) tells why he felt unable to go to Rosecrans's aid. One immense dividend the Federals got from Burnside's occupation of east Tennessee is often overlooked. By going to Knoxville Burnside broke the all-important east-west railroad line from Virginia to Chattanooga. When Richmond sent Longstreet west to help Bragg this route could not be used, Longstreet had to go roundabout, via Atlanta, and much time was lost. If his corps had reached Bragg a week earlier, Rosecrans's army might well have been destroyed.
6. *O.R.*, Vol. XXXI, Pt. One, p. 713. Burnside's troop returns for November are in the same volume, p. 267.
7. Ibid., pp. 739–740, 745.
8. *O.R.*, Vol. XXXI, Pt. One, pp. 79, 81–84, 88–89.
9. Lieutenant W. A. Morgan, in *War Talks*, published papers of the Kansas Commandery, Military Order of the Loyal Legion of the United States, pp. 343 ff; Robert L. Kimberley and Ephraim S. Holloway, *The 41st Ohio Veteran Volunteer Infantry in the War of the Rebellion*, pp. 51, 114; *O.R.*, Vol. XXXI, Pt. One, pp. 49, 78.
10. Van Horne, *History of the Army of the Cumberland*, Vol. I, pp. 398–401; Thomas L. Livermore, "The Siege and Relief of Chattanooga," in the *Papers of the Military Historical Society of Massachusetts*, Vol. VIII, pp. 323–324 (the volumes in this series are cited hereafter as *MHSM Papers*); *O.R.*, Vol. XXXI, Pt. One, pp. 56, 101, 219.
11. Lieutenant W. A. Morgan, as in n. 9, above; William G. LeDuc, "The Little Steamboat that Opened the Cracker Line," *B. & L.*, Vol. III, pp. 676–678; *O.R.*, Vol. XXXI, Pt. One, pp. 60, 67.
12. Letter of General Howard to Senator Henry Wilson dated December 27, 1863, in the Department of Lincolniana, Lincoln Memorial University; typescript of Garland's interview with Colonel L. B. Eaton, in the Hamlin Garland Papers, University of Southern California Library. When he dealt with the Brown's Ferry business in his *Memoirs* (Vol. II, p. 32), Grant was led astray by a lapse of memory. He wrote there that "I issued orders for opening the route to Bridgeport"; at the time, however, he made it clear to Halleck that he had simply approved a plan devised by Smith and set in motion by Thomas.
13. *O.R.*, Vol. XXXI, Pt. Two, p. 29; Pt. Three, p. 10.
14. *O.R.*, Vol. XXXI, Pt. One, p. 729; Pt. Three, pp. 15, 23.
15. *O.R.*, Vol. XXXI, Pt. Three, pp. 26, 38–39, 65. Dodge had been engaged in railroad engineering and surveying before the war; in 1866 he became chief engineer for the Union Pacific and was largely responsible for that railroad's construction.
16. On November 5, Bowers notified Grant that the water level in the Cumberland was adequate, and Burnside arranged to send a regiment to the Big South Fork to guard the stores and did what he could to get the mountain road in better shape (*O.R.*, Vol. XXXI, Pt. Three, pp. 34–35, 45, 48–49, 60).
17. *O.R.*, Vol. XXXI, Pt. Three, pp. 634–635; Vol. LII, Pt. Two, pp. 554–555, 559–560.
18. *O.R.*, Vol. XXXI, Pt. Three, pp. 73–74, 76.

19. Ibid., pp. 84, 88.
20. Ibid., p. 216. In his article "Chattanooga" (*B. & L.*, Vol. III, pp. 679–711) Grant implies a criticism of Thomas, but here as in other cases it seems likely that he saw things differently, twenty years after the war, than he saw them while they were happening.
21. Letters of Grant to Julia dated November 2 and 14, 1863, from the collection owned by Major General U. S. Grant III.
22. Badeau, *Military History of Ulysses S. Grant*, Vol. I, pp. 471–475.

Chapter 4: THE MIRACLE ON MISSIONARY RIDGE

1. Howard left two very similar accounts of the conference at Grant's headquarters: "Grant at Chattanooga," in *Personal Recollections of the War of the Rebellion*, Vol. I, pp. 244–257, and a speech delivered before a meeting of the Society of the Army of the Tennessee in 1908, published in the *Proceedings* of that Society. See also Sherman, *Memoirs*, Vol. I, pp. 360–361; W. F. G. Shanks, *Personal Recollections of Distinguished Generals*, p. 53; *O.R.*, Vol. XXXI, Pt. Three, pp. 69–70, 122, 140, 152.
2. Van Horne, *History of the Army of the Cumberland*, Vol. I, p. 409.
3. Letters of Rawlins: to Mary Emma Hurlbut dated November 16, 1863, in the John A. Rawlins Papers, Chicago Historical Society, and to Grant, same date, in the Palmer Collection, Western Reserve Historical Society, Cleveland.
4. Smith's diary is in the Library of Congress, with a copy in the U. S. Grant Association's Papers. For Dana's letters about Lagow, see *O.R.*, Vol. XXXI, Pt. Two, pp. 54, 60. Hunter's letter to Stanton is in the same volume, Pt. Three, p. 402. This record not only clears Grant of the charge Rawlins brought against him. (Rawlins was not merely saying that Grant had taken a few drinks; he accused him of having been so sodden that "two more nights like the last" would put him completely out of action.) It necessitates a revision of the ancient theory that Grant's friends kept alcohol away from him because he had the true drunkard's fatal inability to take one drink and then stop. Hannah Grant was a strongminded woman who knew her son as well as anyone did, and if she casually sent him a bottle of wine it could only be because she knew no harm would come of it. In addition, Hunter's testimony obviously does not describe a man who goes off the board after one taste of whiskey. One can only remark that with a defender like Rawlins, Grant did not need any accusers.
5. *O.R.*, Vol. XXXI, Pt. Two, p. 31; Pt. Three, pp. 154–155, 177, 190; Badeau, *Military History of Ulysses S. Grant*, Vol. I, pp. 479–481. Part of the flexibility of the battle plan lay in the fact that Hooker might or might not — depending on circumstances — be ordered to capture Lookout Mountain. Such a stroke is called for in the plan Grant sent to Halleck on November 15; three days later it is provided that Hooker may simply be required to hold his ground in Lookout Valley and on the slopes of Raccoon Mountain.
6. Letter of Thomas to Rosecrans dated November 19, 1863, in the Rosecrans Papers at the U.C.L.A. Library.
7. H. V. Boynton, "The Battles About Chattanooga, Lookout Mountain and Missionary Ridge," in *MHSM Papers*, Vol. VII, pp. 386–387; *O.R.*, Vol. XXXI, Pt. Two, p. 32; Grant, "Chattanooga," in *B. & L.*, Vol. III, p. 693; diary of William W. Smith, as cited in n. 4, above.
8. Letter of Grant to Elihu Washburne, dated December 2, 1863, in the Illinois State Historical Library, Springfield.
9. Van Horne, *History of the Army of the Cumberland*, Vol. I, pp. 414–416; *Life of General George H. Thomas*, pp. 170–172; *O.R.*, Vol. XXXI, Pt. Two, pp. 24, 90, 93–95, 251; story in the Richmond *Dispatch* for November 30, 1863, dated from Chattanooga November 23, in the Virginia State Library, Richmond.
10. Diary of William W. Smith; Boynton, op. cit., p. 389.

11. There is an excellent account of this spectacular affair in Boynton, op. cit., pp. 390–391; another, graphic but somewhat overwritten, is in Major James A. Connolly, *Three Years in the Army of the Cumberland*, pp. 152–155. Hooker's report, which is also quite flamboyant, is in *O.R.*, Vol. XXXI, Pt. Two, pp. 314–318. Geary's report, less emotional and very detailed, is in the same volume, pp. 390–400. The glimpse of Grant is from William W. Smith's diary.
12. Sergeant Isaac Doan, *Reminiscences of the Chattanooga Campaign*, pp. 13–15; Boynton, p. 391; John Russell Young, *Around the World with General Grant*, Vol. II, p. 306. Total casualties for Hooker's three divisions in the fighting on Lookout Mountain appear to have been below 500. Hooker's losses for the whole period of the Chattanooga affair are given as 1,086. (*O.R.*, Vol. XXXI, Pt. Two, p. 326.) When losses incurred after Lookout Mountain are deducted, the figure for November 24 is 485.
13. *O.R.*, Vol. XXXI, Pt. Two, pp. 33, 43–44; Boynton, p. 391. In view of later developments, it is important to realize that this order contemplated an all-out attack by Thomas on the crest of Missionary Ridge.
14. Dana's messages to Stanton are in *O.R.*, Vol. XXXI, Pt. Two, p. 67; Stevenson's report, saying that the order to start the movement reached him "about midnight," is in the same volume, p. 722; on pp. 734–735 is the report of one of his brigade commanders, General Alfred Cumming, telling about the artillery fire and giving the time of his arrival at Cleburne's position.
15. Boynton, op. cit., pp. 394–395; Captain Irving Buck, *Cleburne and His Command*, pp. 169–170; A. D. Kirwan, ed., *Johnny Green of the Orphan Brigade: The Journal of a Confederate Soldier* by John Williams Green, p. 110; *O.R.*, Vol. XXXI, Pt. Two, 749–750.
16. Francis F. McKinney, *Education in Violence*, p. 292; Van Horne, *History of the Army of the Cumberland*, Vol. I, pp. 425–428; Boynton, p. 402, quoting General Baird's order to Colonel Ferdinand Van Derveer; Buck, *Cleburne and His Command*, p. 167.
17. *O.R.*, Vol. XXXI, Pt. Two, pp. 34, 68; Badeau, Vol. I, pp. 506–507; Lloyd Lewis, *Sherman: Fighting Prophet*, p. 319; diary of William W. Smith, entry for November 25. Wood's account of his talk with Grant is in his "The Battle of Missionary Ridge," in *Sketches of War History*, Vol. IV, pp. 33–35. In his *Memoirs* (Vol. II, p. 78), Grant wrote that Sherman's condition was getting so critical that the assault for his relief could not be delayed any longer.

It is impossible to harmonize all of the tales of what happened that afternoon on Orchard Knob. In his *Memoirs* (Vol. II, pp. 78–79), Grant says that an hour after the assault was ordered Wood still did not know that an attack was contemplated. Charles A. Dana wrote that Granger was so busy directing the fire of a battery that he forgot to transmit orders to his division commanders (*O.R.*, Vol. XXXI, Pt. Two, p. 68; *Recollections of the Civil War*, p. 149). Badeau (Vol. I, p. 507) has Grant repeating his order to the two corps commanders, Granger and John M. Palmer, immediately after giving them to Thomas. The oddest story is the one told by James H. Wilson (*The Life of John A. Rawlins*, pp. 171–173) who shows both Grant and Thomas as being strangely inert. According to Wilson, Wilson, Baldy Smith and Rawlins conceived the idea of the attack, Rawlins urged it on Grant, Grant mildly suggested it to Thomas, and Thomas ignored him. After an hour's delay, says Wilson, Rawlins returned to Grant and heckled him into repeating the order, upon which Thomas finally got into action. Wilson wrote fifty years after the event, and in this as in various other cases his bias and his massive conceit seem to make him a most unreliable witness. Wood's account as given in the text is accepted largely because it harmonizes with the known sequence of events and with the general logic of the situation.
18. Major General Montgomery C. Meigs, *Journal of the Battle of Chattanooga*, in the M. C. Meigs Papers, Library of Congress; E. P. Alexander, *Military Memoirs*

of a Confederate, p. 476; Grant, letter to "Dear Jones," dated December 5, 1863, in the Grant Papers, Chicago Historical Society; Badeau, Vol. I, p. 508.

19. Dana's comment is in a wire to Secretary Stanton, *O.R.*, Vol. XXXI, Pt. Two, p. 69.

20. The reports in *O.R.*, Vol. XXXI, Pt. Two, make the situation clear. Granger's is p. 132, Wood's is pp. 257–258; for Baird, Hazen, Willich and Beatty, see pp. 264, 281 and 301. Johnson's report is p. 459. For reports by Baird's brigadiers, saying that the charge was made under orders, see pp. 512–513, 528.

In earlier descriptions of this battle, this writer must confess that he simply followed the accounts of Granger and Wood, along with the colorful story "The Army of the Cumberland at Chattanooga," written by Granger's chief of staff, General Joseph S. Fullerton, in *B. & L.*, Vol. III, pp. 724–725. Careful examination of the detailed reports by subordinates makes the whole affair look very different. Note that both Granger and Wood remained on Orchard Knob until after the rifle pits had been taken.

21. *O.R.*, Vol. XXXI, Pt. Two, pp. 189–191; Hosmer P. Holland, *History of the Seventy-Fourth Illinois*, pp. 37–38; Sheridan, *Personal Memoirs*, Vol. I, pp. 309–312.

22. Montgomery Meigs, *Journal of the Battle of Chattanooga*, in the Meigs Papers, Library of Congress; General Joseph Fullerton, op. cit., p. 725; Diary of William W. Smith, entry for November 25; General Cleburne's report in *O.R.*, Vol. XXXI, Pt. Two, p. 752.

23. Meigs's *Journal*, as cited in n. 22, above; James A. Connolly, *Three Years in the Army of the Cumberland*, pp. 158–159; *O.R.*, Vol. XXXI, Pt. Two, p. 69; General O. O. Howard, "Grant at Chattanooga," in *Personal Recollections of the War of the Rebellion*, Vol. I, p. 253.

Chapter 5: THE ENEMY HAVE NOT GOT ARMY ENOUGH

1. Bragg's report is in *O.R.*, Vol. XXXI, Pt. Two, pp. 664–667. His letter of December 10, 1863, to President Davis, saying that the defeat "is justly disparaging to me as a commander" and adding that "we both erred in the conclusion for me to retain command here" is in the Palmer Collection, Western Reserve Historical Society.

2. News story dated November 26, printed in the Richmond *Dispatch* for December 4, 1863, in the Virginia State Library; letter of C. I. Walker dated December 1, in the C. I. Walker War Letters at the Eugene C. Barker Texas History Center, University of Texas.

3. William W. Smith gives an artless account of this in his Diary entry for November 26.

4. Grant's report, *O.R.*, Vol. XXXI, Pt. Two, pp. 35–37; letter of Grant to Jones dated December 5, 1863, in the Chicago Historical Society; letter of Grant to Julia dated November 30, from the collection owned by Major General U. S. Grant III.

5. *O.R.*, Vol. XXXI, Pt. Two, p. 25.

6. Henry M. Cist, *The Army of the Cumberland*, pp. 256–257; Grant to Halleck, November 29, *O.R.*, Vol. XXXI, Pt. Three, p. 270; Dana to Stanton, *O.R.*, Vol. XXXI, Pt. One, pp. 264–265; Badeau, Vol. I, pp. 532–533. In His *Memoirs* (Vol. II, p. 92), Grant wrote that Granger was "very reluctant" to go to east Tennessee, "having decided for himself that it was a very bad move to make."

7. Sheridan's version of this is set forth in his *Personal Memoirs*, Vol. I, pp. 314–318. Grant's comment is from J. Russell Young, *Around the World with General Grant*, Vol. II, pp. 626–627.

8. Orlando M. Poe, "The Defense of Knoxville," in *B. & L.*, Vol. III, pp. 731–745.

9. Editorials in the New York *Herald* for November 28 and the New York *World* for November 26, 1863; Sherman to Grant, *O.R.*, Vol. XXXI, Pt. Three, p. 381;

letter of Rawlins to Mary Emma Hurlbut dated December 8, 1863, in the Rawlins Papers at the Chicago Historical Society. (Rawlins obtained leave and on December 23, 1863, was married to Miss Hurlbut at Danbury, Conn.) Casualty figures are in *O.R.*, Vol. XXXI, Pt. Two, p. 88. Van Horne, *Army of the Cumberland*, Vol. I, p. 437, estimates that Grant had 60,000 men in action.

10. Boynton, "The Battles Around Chattanooga," *MHSM Papers*, Vol. VII, p. 396.

11. Confederate reports for Chattanooga are incomplete, but a careful study of the ones that appear in the *Official Records* makes it clear that there was a good deal of movement toward the right on the last day of the battle. Not only did Stevenson's entire division move over from the Lookout Mountain area; Cheatham's division was put in line that morning on the crest to the right of the spot where Thomas later broke the line, and shortly after noon Bates's division — one of the two that later received the shock of the assault — was ordered to move by the right flank (that is, north along the ridge) to connect with the left of Patton Anderson's line. At one P.M., Hardee sent a brigade north along the west face of the ridge to help repulse Sherman's attack. In addition, during the engagement Cleburne shifted at least one brigade over to his own extreme right so as to extend his line to the railroad that led back to Chickamauga Station.

It is of course true that many of these movements had little to do with giving Cleburne additional strength and do not represent detachments from the center. The important point, however, is that the Federals saw these movements, and when they said that Bragg was moving strong bodies of troops toward his right they were neither falsifying the record nor indulging in daydreams.

Long after the war James H. Wilson insisted that there had been no Confederate troop movement to the right on Missionary Ridge. At the time, however, he was one of the many Federal officers who saw such movement taking place. In a letter to Sylvanus Cadwallader dated February 15, 1905, Wilson wrote: "We all thought we could see from our position on Orchard Knob the movement actually going on, but I am persuaded from a personal inspection of the ground at the top of the Ridge while at Camp Thomas with the First Army Corps in 1898 that even if any such movement had been in progress we could not have seen it, as the road runs along back of the crest and never where it can be seen from Orchard Knob. But the Confederate reports are clear on that point and leave no room to doubt." (From the J. H. Wilson Papers, Library of Congress.)

For the student who wishes to follow the confusing sequence of events, the pertinent Confederate reports are in *O.R.*, Vol. XXXI, Pt. Two, pp. 696–697, 680, 701, 703, 722, 729, 734–735, 746–752.

12. James R. Rusling, *Men and Things I Saw in Civil War Days*, p. 147.

13. Dana's letter to Stanton is in *O.R.*, Vol. XXXI, Pt. Two, p. 72.

14. *O.R.*, Vol. XXXI, Pt. Three, pp. 197–198.

15. Ibid., p. 349.

16. *O.R.*, Vol. XXXI, Pt. Three, pp. 226, 233. The "old army" men referred to are of course the regular army officers who had served in the prewar establishment — the "old army," in wartime jargon, in which everyone knew everyone else.

17. Ibid., p. 263.

18. *O.R.*, Vol. XXXI, Pt. Three, pp. 38–39, 230, 237, 444–445; Vol. XXXII, Pt. Two, p. 145; Vol. LII, Pt. One, pp. 618–621; Ser. 3, Vol. IV, pp. 219, 943–944; Ser. 3, Vol. V, p. 934. It might be noted that the army ration allowance was liberal, so that troops not actively campaigning could get along tolerably well (though not without complaint) on half-rations.

19. *O.R.*, Vol. XXXI, Pt. Three, pp. 429–430, 457–458.

20. *O.R.*, Vol. XXXII, Pt. Two, pp. 43, 99–101, 193–194, 251, 359, 373–375; Cox, *Military Reminiscences of the Civil War*, Vol. II, pp. 76–77.

21. *O.R.*, Vol. XXXII, Pt. Two, pp. 40–42.

22. For Grant's letter to Thomas, see ibid., p. 143. Grant's letter to Halleck is in Vol. XXXIII, pp. 394–395.
23. W. F. Smith to Dana dated January 15, 1864; J. H. Wilson to Dana, also January 15; both from the E. M. Stanton Papers, Library of Congress. The suggestion that these men wrote at Grant's request, which seems likely enough on the face of it, is advanced in Ludwell H. Johnson, *The Red River Campaign*, p. 44.
24. Editorial in the New York *Herald* for December 9, 1863.
25. Letter of Grant to Washburne dated December 12, 1863, in the Illinois State Historical Society.

Chapter 6: THE HIGH PLACE

1. James F. Rusling, *Men and Things I Saw in Civil War Days*, pp. 135–136; William Conant Church, *Ulysses S. Grant and the Period of National Preservation and Reconstruction*, p. 219; Grant to Halleck, dated January 15, in *O.R.*, Vol. XXXII, Pt. Two, p. 99. In this dispatch Grant said that his trip north from Knoxville convinced him that the army in east Tennessee could not be supplied by wagons from the base at Camp Nelson in Kentucky.
2. Sherman to Grant dated December 29, 1863, in *O.R.*, Vol. XXXI, Pt. Three, p. 528; New York *World* for December 18, 1863; editorials in the New York *Herald* for December 15 and 18.
3. Letter of Brown to Grant dated December 7, 1863, in the Grant Papers, Illinois State Historical Library.
4. Grant's letter is in the Illinois State Historical Library; that of Rawlins, dated March 3, 1863, is in the J. H. Wilson Papers, Library of Congress.
5. From the Grant Papers, Illinois State Historical Library.
6. Rear Admiral Daniel Ammen, *The Old Navy and the New*, pp. 530–531; letter of Grant to "My dear General," dated February 28, 1864, owned by Mr. Claude K. Rowland of St. Louis. The recipient is identified as Frank Blair by John Simon of the U. S. Grant Association.
7. Jesse Grant Cramer, ed., *Letters of Ulysses S. Grant to His Father and His Youngest Sister*, pp. 100–101; letter of Porter to Fox dated January 13, 1864, in the G. V. Fox Correspondence, New York Historical Society.
8. Ida M. Tarbell, interview with J. Russell Jones, in *The Life of President Lincoln*, Vol. II, p. 188; Richardson, *Personal History of U. S. Grant*, pp. 380–381.
9. Diary of William W. Smith, Library of Congress; letter of Grant to J. Russell Jones dated July 5, 1864, in the Grant Papers, Chicago Historical Society; Grant's letters to Julia Grant, owned by Major General U. S. Grant III.
10. Tarbell, op. cit., pp. 186–188. A similar account of Grant's letter, and of Jones's visit to President Lincoln, is in the typescript of a brief biography of Jones written by James H. Wilson, in the possession of Jones's grandson, George Russell Jones of Chicago.
11. *O.R.*, Vol. XXXII, Pt. One, pp. 173–179; Pt. Two, pp. 99–101.
12. Rusling, op. cit., p. 136; Hamlin Garland, typescript of his "Notes from a Conversation with Mrs. Grant," in the Garland Papers, University of Southern California Library.
13. Garland's interview as in n. 12, above. As early as the fall of 1861, when he was stationed at Cairo, Grant wrote to Julia confessing that he found it as hard to get along with his sister Clara as Julia did (from Grant's letters to Mrs. Grant, in the collection of Major General U. S. Grant III).
14. Badeau, Vol. I, p. 560; Richardson, *Personal History*, pp. 375–376; Henry Coppee, *Life and Services of General U. S. Grant*, pp. 253–254; General W. R. Marshall, "Reminiscences of General U. S. Grant," in *Glimpses of the Nation's Struggle*, Vol. I, p. 96.
15. General John M. Schofield, *Fifty-six Years in the Army*, p. 111.
16. Diary of William W. Smith, entry for November 29, 1863.

17. Rawlins's letters to Emma Rawlins, dated January 31 and February 1, 3 and 4; to Wilson, dated March 3; from Wilson's *Life of Rawlins*, pp. 187, 393–395.
18. Rawlins's concern about his health keeps recurring in his letters to Emma, notably in those dated January 16 and February 6, 7 and 15. Dr. Kittoe's recollection of the incident on the train is from an interview in the Chicago *Tribune* for January 27, 1877. Rawlins's account of the theater party, and his concern about the future, are in his letter to Mrs. Rawlins dated March 5. (The letters cited in this note are from typescripts in the James H. Wilson Papers, Library of Congress. In some passages they differ slightly from the text as printed in Wilson's *Life of Rawlins*.)
19. Grant's postwar letter to Washburne is from Hamlin Garland, *Ulysses S. Grant: His Life and Character*, p. 465. Rawlins's letter, dated January 20, 1864, is in the Eldridge Collection at the Huntington Library.
20. Memo slip in the James M. Comly Collection, Box 2, No. 100, Ohio State Museum, giving what Comly said was "an exact report" of Grant's words during a conversation in March, 1876. Motley's letter to Holmes is in *The Correspondence of John Lothrop Motley*, Vol. II, p. 210.
21. Noah Brooks, "Lincoln, Chase and Grant," in the *Century Magazine*, Vol. XLIX, No. 4, February, 1895, pp. 616–617; Herbert Mitgang, ed., *Washington in Lincoln's Time* by Noah Brooks, pp. 130–131; *O.R.*, Vol. XXXII, Pt. Two, p. 408.
22. Tyler Dennett, *Lincoln and the Civil War in the Diaries and Letters of John Hay*, p. 167; Mitgang, op. cit., p. 131.
23. Mitgang, pp. 132–134.
24. Letters of Grant to Julia dated February 14 and 17, from the collection of Major General U. S. Grant III. *O.R.*, Vol. XXXII, Pt. Three, pp. 13, 26.
25. Halleck to Lieber dated March 7, 1864, letter in the Lieber Collection at the Huntington Library.
26. *O.R.*, Vol. XXXII, Pt. Three, p. 18.

Chapter 7: CONTINUE TO BE YOURSELF

1. Frederick Dent Grant, *Reminiscences of General U. S. Grant*, paper read before the Illinois Commandery, Military Order of the Loyal Legion of the United States, on January 27, 1910, reprinted in the *Journal of the Illinois State Historical Society*, Vol. VII, No. 1, p. 73; L. E. Chittenden, *Recollections of President Lincoln*, pp. 316–322; Helen Nicolay, *Lincoln's Secretary: a Biography of John G. Nicolay*, p. 194.
2. Diary of Cyrus B. Comstock, entries for March 5 and 6, in the Comstock Papers, Library of Congress; letters of Rawlins to Mrs. Rawlins dated March 8 and 9, in Wilson's *Life of Rawlins*, pp. 402–403. In this book (pp. 198–199, 227) Wilson is sharply critical of Grant's tactics in the 1864 Virginia campaign as wasteful of life, and blames Comstock for it, saying that his influence was "paramount at headquarters" and that his "advice and constant refrain was 'Smash 'em up! Smash 'em up!' " Wilson had personal animus against Comstock. Wilson had been Grant's inspector general in the summer and fall of 1863 and said that under his regime "the troops were brought to a high state of discipline, instruction and efficiency" (*Under the Old Flag*, Vol. I, p. 245). Comstock replaced Wilson that fall, and noted in his diary: "Wilson's papers are four months behind hand. I told General Grant that the returns were valueless except as records. That the sub-inspectors must be kept sharp up to their work and whenever a special inspection shows them in fault they must be relieved or dismissed. Our army lacks organization badly. I fear orders will often be waste paper" (diary entry for December 11, 1863, in the Cyrus B. Comstock Papers, Library of Congress).
3. Horace Porter, *Campaigning with Grant*, pp. 18–21; William O. Stoddard, Jr., ed., *William O. Stoddard, Lincoln's Third Secretary*, pp. 196–197; *Diary of*

Gideon Welles, Vol. I, pp. 538–539; Helen Nicolay, op. cit., pp. 195–196; Noah Brooks, *Washington in Lincoln's Time,* p. 135.

4. Frederick Dent Grant, as in n. 1, above; Nicolay's account, in Helen Nicolay, pp. 196–197; R. Gerald McMurtry, "Lincoln Named Grant Lieutenant General March 9, 1864," in *Lincoln Lore,* No. 1513.
5. Wilson, *The Life of John A. Rawlins,* p. 403.
6. See *ante,* p. 109.
7. Letter of Meade to Mrs. Meade dated March 8, 1864, in George Meade, *The Life and Letters of George Gordon Meade,* Vol. II, p. 176; Grant, *Memoirs,* Vol. II, pp. 116–117.
8. John Russell Young, *Around the World with General Grant,* Vol. II, p. 299; Meade's *Life and Letters,* Vol. II, p. 181.
9. Badeau, Vol. II, p. 16; Meade's *Life and Letters,* Vol. II, p. 189.
10. O.R., Vol. XXXII, Pt. Two, pp. 467–468; diary of Cyrus B. Comstock, entry for March 11, 1864, in the Comstock Papers, Library of Congress.
11. Letters of James H. Wilson to William F. Smith dated February 13, 19 and 27, 1864, in the James Harrison Wilson Papers, Library of Congress.
12. Speech of General Grenville Dodge before the Society of the Army of the Potomac in 1898, reprinted in the Society's report of its twenty-ninth reunion; Young, *Around the World with General Grant,* Vol. II, p. 464; letter of General A. A. Humphreys dated March 10, in the Humphreys Papers, Historical Society of Pennsylvania, Philadelphia.
13. Diary of C. B. Comstock, entry for March 11, 1864.
14. O.R., Vol. XXXII, Pt. Three, p. 58.
15. Ibid., p. 49. In his *Personal History of Ulysses S. Grant,* p. 385, Richardson records Grant's original plan to make his headquarters with Thomas's army.
16. Badeau, Vol. II, p. 26; typescript of Hamlin Garland's interview with General Schofield, in the Hamlin Garland Papers.
17. Grant to Senator Wilson dated April 4, 1864, in Richardson, *Personal History of Ulysses S. Grant,* p. 388.
18. Wilson tells about his efforts in *Under the Old Flag,* Vol. I, pp. 345–346. For the Rawlins letters quoted in the text see Wilson's *Life of John A. Rawlins,* pp. 396, 414–415. An account of the decline of Rawlins's influence is in this same book, pp. 194–195.
19. Wilson to Cadwallader, letter dated September 8, 1904, in the Sylvanus Cadwallader Papers, Library of Congress; Sherman to Colonel A. H. Markland, letter dated July 23, 1887, in the Illinois State Historical Library.
20. Richardson, *Personal History of Ulysses S. Grant,* p. 386.
21. Grenville Dodge, as in n. 12, above. Dodge wrote several accounts of the Nashville meeting, the details varying slightly from one account to another, and it is a little hard to feel certain that the theater party and the oyster stew foray took place at this meeting rather than on an earlier date.
22. Typescript, "Personal Biography of Major General Grenville Dodge," p. 175, in the Iowa State Department of History and Archives.
23. William Conant Church, *Ulysses S. Grant and the Period of National Preservation and Reconstruction,* pp. 248–249.
24. Letter of General Sherman to Senator Sherman dated April 11, 1864, in the William T. Sherman Papers, Library of Congress.
25. Letters of Meade to Mrs. Meade dated March 24 and April 4, 1864, in Meade's *Life and Letters,* Vol. II, pp. 183, 187; letter of Grant to Julia dated March 25, from the collection of Major General U. S. Grant III.

Chapter 8: CAMPAIGN PLANS AND POLITICS

1. The figures are from Badeau, Vol. II, pp. 29–32.
2. O.R., Vol. XXXIV, Pt. One, p. 11; Vol. XXXIII, p. 729.

3. Grant's instructions to Sigel are in *O.R.*, Vol. XXXIII, pp. 765–766, 798–799. For President Lincoln's remark, see U. S. Grant, "Preparing for the Campaigns of 1864," in *B. & L.*, Vol. IV, p. 112.
4. Grant, *Memoirs*, Vol. II, pp. 122–123; Porter, *Campaigning with Grant*, pp. 26–27.
5. *O.R.*, Vol. XXXIII, pp. 734–735, 741, 769–770.
6. Halleck to Sherman dated April 29, 1864, in *O.R.*, Vol. XXXIV, Pt. Three, pp. 332–333; Badeau, Vol. II, p. 44.
7. Wilson, *Life of John A. Rawlins*, p. 423; Comstock's diary entry for April 1, 1864, in the Comstock Papers, Library of Congress; Grant's *Memoirs*, Vol. II, pp. 132–133.
8. Richardson, *Personal History of Ulysses S. Grant*, pp. 388–389.
9. Grant's report is in *O.R.*, Vol. XXXVI, Pt. One, p. 17. For his April 2 order to Butler, see Vol. XXXIII, pp. 794–795.
10. Wilson, *Life of John A. Rawlins*, p. 409. Rawlins's complaint about Julia's absence at Chattanooga is in a letter dated November 16, 1863, in the Rawlins Papers, Chicago Historical Society. References to the people present on the trip and to the sight-seeing tour are in the Comstock Diary, entries dated March 31 and April 2.
11. Letter of Smith to Wilson dated March 18, typescript in the James Harrison Wilson Papers, Library of Congress.
12. A typescript of Rawlins's April 13 letter to Emma is in the Wilson Papers, where much of Rawlins's correspondence finally came to rest. There are significant differences between this version and the one printed in Wilson's *Life of John A. Rawlins*, pp. 415–416.
13. Grant to Sigel, *O.R.*, Vol. XXXIII, pp. 799, 812; to Sherman, Vol. XXXII, Pt. Three, 245–46.
14. The orders for Meade, dated April 9, are in *O.R.*, Vol. XXXIII, pp. 827–828.
15. John Russell Young's interview with Grant printed in the New York *Herald* for July 24, 1878.
16. Allan Nevins, ed., *A Diary of Battle: The Personal Journals of Col. Charles S. Wainwright, 1861–65*, pp. 329, 336, 338.
17. *Army and Navy Journal* for March 26, 1864; *The Life and Letters of George Gordon Meade*, Vol. II, pp. 185, 187. For Stanton's outburst, see Charles A. Dana, *Recollections of the Civil War*, p. 5.
18. General A. A. Humphreys, *The Virginia Campaign of '64 and '65*, p. 83n; Meade's *Life and Letters*, Vol. II, pp. 183, 188–90, 192.
19. J. Russell Young, *Around the World with General Grant*, Vol. II, pp. 445–447; letters of Montgomery Blair to S. L. M. Barlow dated May 1 and May 4, 1864, in the S. L. M. Barlow Papers, Huntington Library; *O.R.*, Vol. XXXII, Pt. Three, pp. 268, 292, 304.

Chapter 9: THE FAULT IS NOT WITH YOU

1. Letter of Grant to Halleck dated April 26, 1864, in the Illinois State Historical Library.
2. *A Stillness at Appomattox*, pp. 39 ff, for a sampling of comments by the enlisted men; George R. Agassiz, ed., *Meade's Headquarters, 1863–65: Letters of Colonel Theodore Lyman* (cited hereafter as Lyman, *Meade's Headquarters*), p. 81; Hamlin Garland's interview with Judge J. H. Robinson, in the Hamlin Garland Papers, University of Southern California Library; letter of Selden Connor dated April 16, 1864, in the Brown University Library. For the army's refusal to cheer Meade, see *Glory Road*, p. 354.
3. Letter of Sherman to Mrs. Edwin F. Hall, in "General Sherman's Own Opinion of Grant," *Century Magazine*, Vol. LIII, No. 6, April, 1897; General W. R. Marshall, "Reminiscences of General U. S. Grant," in *Glimpses of the Nation's*

Struggle, Vol. I, p. 103; typescript, "Note by Mrs. Dr. Baker," in the Hamlin Garland Papers; Morris Schaff, *The Battle of the Wilderness*, pp. 47–48.

4. Jacob Cox, *Military Reminiscences of the Civil War*, Vol. II, pp. 102–103; letter of Sherman to Eugene Casserly dated January 23, 1868, in the Andre de Coppett Autograph Collection, Princeton University Library; interview with M. Harrison Strong, apparently in a Kansas City paper in the 1920's, from an undated clipping in the collection of E. B. Long; also Garland's interview with Strong, in the Hamlin Garland Papers.

5. Letters of Richard Henry Dana, Jr., dated April 21 and May 4, 1864, in the Dana Papers, Massachusetts Historical Society.

6. Statement by Sergeant John D. Reed, in John L. Parker and Robert G. Carter, *History of the Twenty-second Massachusetts Infantry*, pp. 408–409.

7. Lyman, *Meade's Headquarters*, p. 81.

8. *O.R.*, Vol. XXXIII, pp. 770, 826; Vol. XXXIV, Pt. Three, pp. 363, 381; letter of Rawlins to Emma dated April 22, in Wilson's *Life of John A. Rawlins*, p. 422; diary entry for May 1 in the Cyrus B. Comstock Papers, Library of Congress.

9. *O.R.*, Vol. XXXIII, pp. 874, 950; Vol. XXXVI, Pt. One, p. 198.

10. *Army and Navy Journal* for March 26, 1864; Slocum interview in "Broadway Notebook," New York *Tribune* for May 27, 1883; Brigadier General Hazard Stevens, "The VI Corps in the Wilderness," *MHSM Papers*, Vol. IV, p. 178.

11. *Personal Memoirs of P. H. Sheridan*, Vol. I, pp. 340–343, 353–356; letters of Grant to Julia dated April 17 and 27, from the collection of Major General U. S. Grant III.

12. *O.R.*, Vol. XXXIII, p. 721; Vol. XXXII, Pt. Three, p. 261; Vol. XXXIV, Pt. One, p. 8. There is a good reproduction of the map in A. L. Conger, *The Rise of U. S. Grant*, p. 342. Sherman's letter dated April 5, 1864, is in the Cyrus B. Comstock Papers, Library of Congress.

13. *O.R.*, Vol. XXXIII, pp. 904, 1017–1018; Vol. XXXVI, Pt. Two, pp. 354–355. Ingalls underestimated. In the end the army took 4,300 wagons and 56,000 animals (*O.R.*, Vol. XXXVI, Pt. One, p. 277).

14. *O.R.*, Vol. XXXII, Pt. Three, p. 409.

15. *O.R.*, Vol. XXXIV, Pt. Three, pp. 153–154, 252–253, 278–279, 293, 316.

16. There is an excellent summary of the Red River campaign and the salvation of the fleet in Col. Richard B. Irwin, "The Red River Campaign," *B. & L.*, Vol. IV, pp. 345–362. For Canby's appointment see *O.R.*, Vol. XXXIV, Pt. Three, pp. 490–491.

17. Letter of Rawlins to Emma dated April 25, in the typescript of Rawlins's letters, the James H. Wilson Papers; letter of Halleck to Grant, marked "confidential," dated May 3, in *O.R.*, Vol. XXXIV, Pt. Three, p. 409.

18. William O. Stoddard, *Lincoln's Third Secretary*, pp. 197–199.

19. The text of these letters is as given in U. S. Grant, "Preparing for the Campaigns of '64," in *B. & L.*, Vol. IV, p. 112.

Chapter 10: IN THE WILDERNESS

1. Humphreys, *The Virginia Campaign of '64 and '65* (cited hereafter as Humphreys), pp. 18–19; Charles A. Page, *Letters of a War Correspondent*, p. 47; Alanson A. Haines, *History of the 15th Regiment New Jersey Volunteers*, p. 140.

2. Letter of Grant to Julia, May 2, from the collection of Major General U. S. Grant III; Horace Porter, *Campaigning with Grant*, pp. 41–44; Badeau, Vol. II, pp. 90, 108; Richardson, *Personal History of U. S. Grant*, p. 393.

3. Humphreys, pp. 19–22; Porter, op. cit., p. 44; Captain Charles H. Porter, "Opening of the Campaign of 1864," in *MHSM Papers*, Vol. IV, pp. 11, 23. For a vigorous argument that the early halt on May 4 was a mistake and that the trains could have been protected even if the army had marched a good deal

farther, see Francis A. Walker, *History of the Second Army Corps*, pp. 409–410.

4. Porter, pp. 45–46; Humphreys, loc. cit.; Badeau, Vol. II, p. 100.

5. Letter of Cadwallader to Frederic Hudson, in a pamphlet reprinted from the *American Historical Review* for January, 1934.

6. *O.R.*, Vol. XXXVI, Pt. Two, pp. 403, 404; Porter, p. 48; Freeman Cleaves, *Meade of Gettysburg*, pp. 237–240.

7. *O.R.*, Vol. XXXVI, Pt. Two, pp. 417–418; Lieutenant Colonel William W. Swan, "The Battle of the Wilderness," in *MHSM Papers*, Vol. IV, pp. 127–128; Humphreys, pp. 23–25.

8. The staff officer who did all of the riding back and forth between army headquarters, Griffin and the front line was Colonel William W. Swan, who describes this odd sequence of events in his "The Battle of the Wilderness," cited in n. 7, pp. 129–130. The military historian John Codman Ropes, well informed about affairs in this army, wrote: "It is no secret that the best officers of the 5th Corps urged that the attack should be deferred at least until the 6th Corps had got up on the right" ("Grant's Campaign in Virginia in 1864," *MHSM Papers*, Vol. IV, p. 379).

9. Jed Hotchkiss, "Virginia," in *Confederate Military History*, Vol. III, p. 435; *O.R.*, Vol. XXXVI, Pt. Two, p. 948; A. L. Long, *Memoirs of Robert E. Lee*, p. 327.

10. Hotchkiss, op. cit., pp. 435–436; Mason Whiting Tyler, *Recollections of the Civil War*, p. 157; Lieutenant Colonel William H. Powell, *The Fifth Army Corps*, pp. 608–610. Writing of similar conditions on another part of the field, General Hancock observed that "only the roar of the musketry disclosed the position of the combatants" (*O.R.*, Vol. XXXVI, Pt. One, p. 325).

11. Lyman, *Meade's Headquarters*, p. 91.

12. Humphreys, pp. 26–28; *O.R.*, Vol. XXXVI, Pt. One, pp. 189, 539, 659–660.

13. There is a little uncertainty about the time element here. Humphreys, p. 25, says Getty got his orders between nine and ten; in his report, Getty says he got them at noon. Hancock gives the time when he received his own orders as eleven A.M. (*O.R.*, Vol. XXXVI, Pt. One, pp. 318, 676).

14. Walker, *History of the Second Army Corps*, pp. 412–417; Brigadier General Hazard Stevens, "The Sixth Corps in the Wilderness," *MHSM Papers*, Vol. IV, pp. 192–193; entry in the diary of Charles Francis Adams, Jr., in the Massachusetts Historical Society; report of Thomas A. McParlin, Medical Director of the Army of the Potomac, in *O.R.*, Vol. XXXVI, Pt. One, p. 219. McParlin added that a Zouave brigade in Griffin's division, wearing uniforms brightly trimmed in red and yellow, suffered especially heavy losses in the fighting on the Turnpike.

15. Humphreys, pp. 32–35; Hyland C. Kirk, *Heavy Guns and Light of the Fourth New York Heavy Artillery*, p. 156; Major General Alexander S. Webb, "Through the Wilderness," *B. & L.*, Vol. IV, p. 157; *O.R.*, Vol. XXXVI, Pt. One, pp. 318–320, 676–677; "Narrative and Scrapbook of the 5th Maine Regt.'s Participation in Spotsylvania, Cold Harbor, etc.," by Fred Sanborn, in the Manuscript Division, Library of Congress; Rufus R. Dawes, *Service with the 6th Wisconsin Volunteers*, p. 261.

16. T. L. Livermore, "Grant's Campaign Against Lee," *MHSM Papers*, Vol. IV, pp. 423 ff; Webb, op. cit. pp. 158–160; *O.R.*, Vol. XXXVI, Pt. Two, pp. 424–425.

17. Lyman, *Meade's Headquarters*, p. 94.

18. Walker, *History of the Second Army Corps*, pp. 421–426; Webb, op. cit., pp. 158–160; Lyman, op. cit., p. 442.

19. *O.R.*, Vol. XXXVI, Pt. Two, pp. 439–441.

20. Walker, *History of the Second Army Corps*, pp. 426 ff; Humphreys, pp. 43–49. Gibbon's account of this confusing business is in his *Personal Recollections of the Civil War*, pp. 387–411.

21. Humphreys, pp. 49–51; Charles A. Page, *Letters of a War Correspondent*, p. 55; Charles Carleton Coffin, "An Incident of the Wilderness," *Century Magazine*, Vol. XXXI, No. 4, February, 1886, p. 582; Comstock's Diary, entry for May 6, in the Cyrus B. Comstock Papers, Library of Congress; Hyland C. Kirk, op. cit., pp. 162–163; Porter, *Campaigning with Grant*, pp. 68–71; O.R., Vol. XXXVI, Pt. One, p. 2; Lieutenant General Jubal Early, *Autobiographical Sketch and Narrative of the War Between the States*, p. 350. Gordon's account is in his *Reminiscences of the Civil War*, pp. 242–258. It should be added that in his *Under the Old Flag*, Vol. I, pp. 390–391, General Wilson has Grant going into his tent and collapsing in an agony of doubt when the word of the Sixth Corps's collapse came in. The reader can take Wilson's word, or Porter's, at his pleasure; Porter was at Grant's headquarters that night and Wilson was not. It should be noted that in his old age, when he wrote his autobiography, Wilson had become very anti-Grant. He was moved, apparently, by the fact that he had been unable to get a cabinet appointment when Grant became President, and also by Grant's failure to show in his *Memoirs* that Wilson had been one of the leading figures in the climactic campaigns of the Union armies. For a succinct study of this, see Paul C. Pehrson, "James Harrison Wilson: a Partial Biography," thesis for the Department of History in the Graduate School, Southern Illinois University, June, 1967, under the guidance of John Y. Simon.

Chapter 11: IF IT TAKES ALL SUMMER

1. Humphreys, pp. 52, 425; Lyman, p. 101.
2. O.R., Vol. XXXVI, Pt. One, p. 2; Porter, pp. 74, 76.
3. Lyman, p. 102, citing Lyman's Journal entry for May 6; Badeau, Vol. II, p. 127; Humphreys, pp. 53–54; B. & L., Vol. III, p. 237. For all of the 1864 campaign, reliable casualty figures for Lee's army simply do not exist because there are serious gaps in the surviving Confederate army records. The most anyone can do is make an estimate, and all of the estimates would be subject to revision if only there were something solid to revise them with.

   Humphreys (p. 54) remarks that when Early took temporary command of A. P. Hill's Corps on May 8, after Hill became sick, he reported that it then contained about 13,000 infantry. Since this corps reported 20,000 men present for duty on April 20, this would indicate a loss in the Wilderness, for this one corps, of around 7,000 men; and if that figure is accepted, Lee's total loss must have been much higher than most students are prepared to admit. The trouble is that Early seems consistently to have understated his numbers, and the 13,000 total he gives for May 8 seems — to this writer, at least — to be unacceptable.
4. Badeau, Vol. II, pp. 108, 119–120, 123; Diary of Charles Francis Adams, Jr., in the Massachusetts Historical Society; Lyman, p. 91; Charles A. Page, *Letters of a War Correspondent*, p. 49; Marsena M. Patrick, Diary, entry for May 6, in the Library of Congress; Elsie Porter, *An American Soldier and Diplomat, Horace Porter*, pp. 54–55.
5. O.R., Vol. XXXVI, Pt. Two, p. 430.
6. A glimpse at Smith's efforts to have a controlling staff officer put in Butler's tent is provided by a letter Orville Babcock of Grant's staff sent Smith on April 29, 1864. Babcock told Smith that a recent letter from Smith — the subject not stated — had been shown to Colonel Comstock, who took the matter up with Grant. Then Babcock continued: "The General is very fixed in letting Butler have his way with all minutiae. He was so firm in the matter that Comstock and I both think he would decline at once to send such a staff officer. The General thinks General Butler has sufficient number of able generals to render him all necessary aid to execute the details, and he has indicated his starting point and objective point. I would send your letter to Wilson, but I am sure Comstock has more influence than he" (O.R., Vol. XXXIII, p. 1019).

7. Meade's orders are in Humphreys, pp. 425–426. For Lee, see *O.R.*, Vol. XXXVI, Pt. Two, pp. 968–969, and Hotchkiss, "Virginia," *Confederate Military History*, Vol. III, p. 445.
8. Porter, pp. 78–79; Grant, *Personal Memoirs*, Vol. II, p. 210; Frank A. Burr, *Life and Achievements of James Adams Beaver*, pp. 148 ff; Judge J. S. Anderson, *Through the Wilderness with Grant*, in the Report of the Proceedings of the 14th Annual Reunion of the 5th Wisconsin Volunteer Infantry, Chicago, 1900.
9. Porter tells about all of this in his *Campaigning with Grant*, pp. 80, 82.
10. *Personal Memoirs of P. H. Sheridan*, Vol. I, pp. 364–366.
11. *O.R.*, Vol. XXXVI, Pt. Two, p. 552. Anderson gives a good account of his movements that night in a letter to Captain Edward B. Robins, secretary of the Military Historical Society of Massachusetts, printed in the *MHSM Papers*, Vol. IV, pp. 227–230.
12. Humphreys, pp. 68–69; General C. W. Field, "Campaign of 1864 and 1865," in the *Papers of the Southern Historical Society* (cited hereafter as *SHSP*), Vol. XIV, p. 547; C. S. Venable, "The Campaign from the Wilderness to Petersburg," in the same volume, p. 527.
13. *O.R.*, Vol. XXXVI, Pt. Two, pp. 539–541; General Charles L. Peirson, "The Operations of the Army of the Potomac, May 7–11, 1864," *MHSM Papers*, Vol. IV, pp. 214–216; General E. P. Alexander, *Military Memoirs of a Confederate*, pp. 511–512.
14. Grant, *Personal Memoirs*, Vol. II, pp. 214–215. In his diary Colonel Comstock observed that Warren's move to Spotsylvania went very slowly, and at the end of the day's fighting he wrote: "Time wasted until dark, when it was too late to produce any result" (diary entry for May 8, 1864; in the Comstock Papers, Library of Congress).
15. *O.R.*, Vol. XXXVI, Pt. One, pp. 2–3.
16. New York *Herald* for July 30, 1885, reporting a speech by Porter at a Union League Club memorial service for Grant.
17. Porter, *Campaigning with Grant*, pp. 78–79, 83–84; Sheridan, *Memoirs*, Vol. I, pp. 368–369; Journal of Theodore Lyman, quoted in his *Meade's Headquarters*, pp. 105–106.
18. Humphreys, p. 66; Sheridan, *Memoirs*, Vol. I, pp. 369–373.
19. Humphreys, pp. 66–67.
20. Badeau, Vol. II, pp. 148–150; Humphreys, pp. 71–72; Porter, p. 90.
21. Badeau, Vol. II, pp. 150–151; *O.R.*, Vol. XXXVI, Pt. Two, p. 561.
22. *O.R.*, Vol. XXXVI, Pt. Two, p. 567; Badeau, Vol. II, pp. 154–156.
23. Lyman, pp. 99–100. For a description of the Spotsylvania country — and a reminder that it did contain a stand of dense timber that greatly handicapped any offensive thrust — see Walker, *History of the Second Army Corps*, p. 456; see also Humphreys, pp. 75–76. At Vicksburg Grant learned the folly of making a headlong attack on an entrenched foe. However, the Confederate works there had been well prepared in advance and amounted to regular fortifications; at the Wilderness and Spotsylvania the works had been improvised by the men on the firing line, and the supposition was that they were not especially formidable. It is also possible that the comparative ease with which Thomas's soldiers carried the entrenched line on Missionary Ridge gave Grant a faulty idea of the power of good troops to sweep over field entrenchments.
24. Upton's account of the fight, and his explanation of the tactics used, is in *O.R.*, Vol. XXXVI, Pt. One, pp. 667–669.
25. *O.R.*, Vol. XXXVI, Pt. Two, pp. 637, 703, 709; Lyman, p. 110; Walker, *History of the Second Army Corps*, p. 481.
26. Grant, *Personal Memoirs*, Vol. II, pp. 224–225; *O.R.*, Vol. XXXVI, Pt. Two, p. 629; Porter, pp. 97–98; Badeau, Vol. II, pp. 573–574. The original of Grant's famous message, now in the New York Historical Society, shows that he first wrote that he would fight it out "if it takes me all summer." Before he gave the letters to Washburne he crossed out the word "me."

Chapter 12: BEYOND THE BLOODY ANGLE

1. Frank A. Burr, *Life and Achievements of James Adams Beaver;* diary of Luther A. Rose, military telegrapher, entry for May 12, in the Library of Congress; Mason W. Tyler, *Recollections of the Civil War*, pp. 170–171.
2. John D. Black, "Reminiscences of the Bloody Angle," in *Glimpses of the Nation's Struggle*, Ser. IV, p. 424; General Francis A. Barlow, "Capture of the Salient, May 12, 1864," in *MHSM Papers*, Vol. IV, pp. 246–248.
3. C. S. Venable, "The Campaign from the Wilderness to Petersburg," *SHSP*, Vol. XIV, January–December 1886, pp. 529–532; Humphreys, pp. 93–100; John D. Black, op. cit., pp. 425–27; Frank A. Burr, as in n. 1, above; report of General Edward Johnson, *O.R.*, Vol. XXXVI, Pt. One, pp. 1079–1080; McHenry Howard, "Notes and Recollections of the Opening of Campaign of 1864," *MHSM Papers*, Vol. IV, pp. 113–116; Walker, *History of the Second Army Corps*, p. 468.
4. Porter, p. 110; report of Thomas A. McParlin, Medical Director of the Army of the Potomac, *O.R.*, Vol. XXXVI, Pt. One, p. 231.
5. Humphreys, pp. 102–103.
6. Fred G. Sanborn, "Narrative & Scrapbook of the 5th Marine Regiment's Participation in Spotsylvania, Cold Harbor, etc.," mss. in the Library of Congress. On May 11 General Wright notified Meade that he would need to use 8,000 of his corps to hold his rifle pits and his picket lines but that he could spare 6,000 for offensive operations to aid Hancock (*O.R.*, Vol. XXXVI, Pt. Two, pp. 640–41).
7. Porter, pp. 102–105. In his diary entry for May 12, Comstock wrote that Burnside was "rather weak and not fit for a corps command." Once Grant wired sharply that he wanted his orders obeyed and Burnside accused Comstock of having told Grant that Burnside was slow. Comstock said he replied: "Gen. Burnside, I told you, Sir! that I had only telegraphed what you were actually doing — that telegram contained no reference to anything I have telegraphed" (from the Comstock Papers, Library of Congress).
8. *O.R.*, Vol. XXXVI, Pt. Two, p. 654.
9. Porter, p. 108; Lyman, p. 108; Charles A. Dana, *Recollections of the Civil War*, p. 192.
10. *Touched with Fire: Civil War Letters and Diary of Oliver Wendell Holmes, Jr.*, p. 116.
11. Hancock's first estimate of his losses is in *O.R.*, Vol. XXXVI, Pt. Two, p. 661.
12. Porter, p. 106; *O.R.*, Vol. XXXVI, Pt. One, p. 4.
13. Hillyer's telegram to Julia Grant is in the Palmer Collection, Western Reserve Historical Society, Cleveland. On May 12 Stanton sent Grant a telegram saying Hillyer had told him that Mrs. Grant had gone to St. Louis and that she was in good health (*O.R.*, Vol. XXXVI, Pt. Two, pp. 651–652). The return showing the number of prisoners taken through May 12 is in *O.R.*, Vol. XXXVI, Pt. One, p. 280.
14. *O.R.*, Vol. XXXVI, Pt. Two, pp. 698, 702–703. Grant's note to Stanton is in the Grant letters at the Chicago Historical Society.
15. Porter, pp. 114–115; Humphreys, p. 83n; Diary of Marsena Patrick, entry for May 10, in the Library of Congress; letter of Meade to Mrs. Meade dated May 19, in Meade, *Life and Letters*, Vol. II, pp. 197–198.
16. Holmes, *Touched with Fire*, pp. 116–117; John D. Black, as in n. 2, above, p. 427; Fred G. Sanborn, *Narrative*, as in n. 6, above; letter from "Frank" in the Mrs. E. K. Atkinson letters, Southern Historical Collection, University of North Carolina Library; Diary of G. P. Ring, entry for May 15, 1864, in the Southern Historical Association collection, Confederate Memorial Hall, New Orleans.
17. Basler, Vol. VII, p. 334; *Army and Navy Journal* for May 14, 1864; Noah Brooks, *Washington in Lincoln's Time*, pp. 137–138.

18. London *Times* for May 25, as reprinted in the *Army and Navy Journal* for June 11, 1864; Chicago *Tribune* for May 15, 1864. Samples of Stanton's messages to the governors can be found in *O.R.*, Ser. 3, Vol. IV, pp. 382–383, 400, 405, 406.
19. *O.R.*, Vol. XXXVI, Pt. Two, p. 176.
20. Humphreys, pp. 107–108; *History of the Corn Exchange Regiment, 118th Pennsylvania Volunteers*, by the Survivors' Association, pp. 424–425; *O.R.*, Vol. XXXVI, Pt. One, p. 5; Porter, p. 118; Letter of Grant to Julia dated May 13, from the collection of Major General U. S. Grant III.
21. *O.R.*, Vol. XXXVI, Pt. Two, pp. 628, 631, 653, 696; Humphreys, pp. 110n, 117.
22. Humphreys, pp. 110, 115; Meade, *Life and Letters*, Vol. II, p. 197.
23. Major William P. Shreve, "The Operations of the Army of the Potomac May 13–June 2, 1864," *MHSM Papers*, Vol. IV, pp. 297–299; *History of the Corn Exchange Regiment*, p. 426; Hyland C. Kirk, *Heavy Guns and Light of the 4th New York Heavy Artillery*, p. 218.

Chapter 13: ROLL ON, LIKE A WAVE

1. Stanton's dispatch of May 15 is in *O.R.*, Ser. 3, Vol. IV, pp. 382–383. Grant's message to Halleck, May 16, is from Badeau, Vol. II, p. 197.
2. *O.R.*, Vol. XXXVI, Pt. One, pp. 19–20; Humphreys, pp. 134–136; Sheridan, *Memoirs*, Vol. I, pp. 390–392; Alexander, *Military Memoirs of a Confederate*, p. 532.
3. Humphreys, pp. 146–156; Lieutenant Colonel George Bruce, "General Butler's Bermuda Campaign," in *MHSM Papers*, Vol. IX, pp. 310 ff; *O.R.*, Vol. XXXVI, Pt. One, pp. 20–21; Pt. Two, pp. 10–11, 651.
4. The estimate of Grant's losses and Lee's accessions is from Humphreys, pp. 117, 124–125. Lee of course had heavy losses in the campaign thus far, but there is no reliable figure for them and about the only certainty is that they were below the total for the Federals.
5. *O.R.*, Vol. XXXVI, Pt. Two, p. 840.
6. Badeau, Vol. II, pp. 218–227; Humphreys, pp. 119–22; Porter, *Campaigning with Grant*, pp. 133–134.
7. *O.R.*, Vol. XXXVI, Pt. Two, pp. 43–44, 68–69. Halleck's order to Meigs and Barnard is headed, after the names of its recipients, with the word "present," which indicates that he conferred with them when he gave them the order. Their report, filed four days later, includes a study of Butler's characteristics as a general and his relations with Smith and Gillmore, which they would hardly have offered if they had not been told to do so.
8. Grant's messages regarding Butler and Hunter are in *O.R.*, Vol. XXXVI, Pt. One, pp. 7, 8, 24.
9. Letter of Colonel Rufus Dawes to Mrs. Dawes dated May 27, 1864, in the Rufus Dawes papers, courtesy of Rufus D. Beach and Ralph G. Newman; Major William P. Shreve, "The Operations of the Army of the Potomac May 13–June 2, 1864," in *MHSM Papers*, Vol. IV, pp. 316–317.
10. Humphreys, pp. 128–133; Shreve, op. cit., pp. 305–310, 317.
11. *O.R.*, Vol. XXXVI, Pt. Three, pp. 206–207.
12. Meade, *Life and Letters*, Vol. II, pp. 198, 199; Dawes, *Service with the 6th Wisconsin Volunteers*, p. 275; Dana, *Recollections of the Civil War*, pp. 203–204; letter of Warren to his brother dated May 20, from the G. K. Warren Papers in the Manuscripts and History Section, New York State Library, Albany.
13. In his *R. E. Lee*, Vol. III, pp. 356–359, Freeman argues that only an unexpected and severe illness kept Lee from taking full advantage of the opening on the North Anna. General Humphreys (*The Virginia Campaign of 1864 and 1865*, p. 132) asserts that Lee's opportunity was illusory. At best, says Humphreys, Lee could have thrown 36,000 men against 24,000; the Federals were well entrenched,

and Humphreys believed that such an attack would have had little chance to succeed.

14. *O.R.*, Vol. XXXVI, Pt. Two, pp. 177–178; letter of Butler to Mrs. Butler, dated, May 25, from *Private and Official Correspondence of General Benjamin F. Butler*, privately issued, Vol. IV, p. 263; Humphreys, pp. 158–159.

15. Badeau, Vol. II, p. 246; letter of Wilson to Badeau dated March 9, 1867, in the James H. Wilson Papers, Library of Congress.

16. For useful summaries of Federal movements from the crossing of the Pamunkey to the first fight at Cold Harbor, see Humphreys, pp. 162–176, and Captain Charles H. Porter, "The Battle of Cold Harbor," in *MHSM Papers*, Vol. IV, pp. 327–333.

17. Grant, *Personal Memoirs*, Vol. II, p. 276; Walker, *History of the Second Army Corps*, p. 506; Humphreys, pp. 176–178, 182; *O.R.*, Vol. XXXVI, Pt. Three, pp. 478–479.

18. *O.R.*, Vol. XXXVI, Pt. Three, pp. 456–458, 462–463, 466, 478, 494; Badeau, Vol. II, p. 281; Porter, *Campaigning with Grant*, pp. 173–174. The order to attack on June 3 was of course Grant's, but the details were up to Meade. Burnside now was part of the Army of the Potomac, and Smith had temporarily been put under Meade's orders. Tactical control of the battle was all Meade's.

19. Porter, *Campaigning with Grant*, p. 174.

Chapter 14: ON THE BANKS OF THE JAMES

1. *O.R.*, Vol. XXXVI, Pt. One, pp. 671, 739, 744; George T. Stevens, *Three Years in the Sixth Corps*, p. 355; Benjamin F. Cook, *History of the 12th Massachusetts Volunteers*, pp. 202–208; Humphreys, pp. 185–187. An excellent sketch of the battle is in Joseph P. Cullen, *Richmond Battlefields*, National Park Service Historical Handbook Series No. 33, pp. 29–34. See also Alexander, *Military Memoirs of a Confederate*, pp. 540–541.

2. *O.R.*, Vol. XXXVI, Pt. One, pp. 336, 344–345; Gen. John S. Jones, "From North Anna to Cold Harbor," in *Sketches of War History*, Vol. IV, p. 154.

3. Meade, *Life and Letters*, Vol. II, p. 200.

4. The fascinating series of reports received and orders sent at Meade's headquarters on the morning of June 3 can be found in *O.R.*, Vol. XXXVI, Pt. One, pp. 525–553.

5. *O.R.*, Vol. XXXVI, Pt. Three, p. 526; Humphreys, pp. 188–189; Freeman, *R. E. Lee*, Vol. III, p. 389; Porter, *Campaigning with Grant*, pp. 176–177.

6. *O.R.*, Vol. XXXVI, Pt. Three, p. 524; Meade, *Life and Letters*, Vol. II, p. 200; letter of Rawlins to Mrs. Rawlins dated June 4, in the J. H. Wilson Papers, Library of Congress. Humphreys (pp. 191–193) estimates that from the crossing of the Pamunkey to the close of the big fight at Cold Harbor the Federals lost 13,000 men, nearly 10,000 of them at Cold Harbor on June 1, 2 and 3. As usual in this campaign, Confederate returns are extremely uncertain. For the entire Cold Harbor period Humphreys estimated Lee's losses as between 4,000 and 5,000. Beyond any question, Lee's losses on June 3 were small as compared to Grant's.

7. Letter of "E. G." in the 20th Indiana, in Mary A. Livermore, *My Story of the War;* Porter to Mrs. Porter dated June 4, in the Horace Porter Papers, Library of Congress; Charles Francis Adams, Jr., to R. H. Dana, Jr., dated June 5, in the Dana Papers, Massachusetts Historical Society; letter of George Murray, 11th U. S. Infantry, dated July 10, in the letters owned by his grandson, John Merryweather, of Chicago and Highland Park, Ill.; letter of James Keleher of the 3rd N. Y., dated June 8, in the Huntington Library.

8. General John S. Jones, op. cit., pp. 156–157.

9. Grant's June 4 letter to Nelly is from the Grant letters in the Chicago Historical Society.

10. This melancholy sequence is set forth in *O.R.*, Vol. XXXVI, Pt. Three, pp. 599, 600, 603, 604, 638, 639, 666, 667. For the length of time involved in getting notes across the lines, see Lyman, *Meade's Headquarters*, pp. 150–153. General Humphreys (p. 192) remarked that during the nights following the battle of June 3 the Federal soldiers had "made extraordinary efforts to get in their wounded comrades" and suggests that very few remained on the field by the time the truce was arranged.

11. Benjamin P. Thomas, ed., *Three Years with Grant* by Sylvanus Cadwallader; Meade, *Life and Letters*, Vol. II, pp. 202–203; copy of Stanton's June 10 telegram to Meade, in the George G. Meade Papers, the Historical Society of Pennsylvania, Philadelphia; diary of Marsena Patrick, entry of June 8, Library of Congress; letter of Grant to W. R. Rowley, dated August 8, 1884, in the Rowley Papers, Illinois State Historical Library; Louis M. Starr, *Bohemian Brigade*, pp. 278–279. Grant's letters to Julia dated June 6 and 7 are from the collection of Major General U. S. Grant III.

12. Humphreys, p. 198; Adams's June 5 letter to Dana, as in n. 7, above.

13. *O.R.*, Vol. XXXVI, Pt. Three, pp. 245–246, 527.

14. Ibid., p. 598.

15. For an account of Lynchburg's vast importance as a suppy depot, see Captain Charles M. Blackford, "The Campaign and Battle of Lynchburg," in *SHSP*, Vol. XXX, p. 279. Says Captain Blackford: "It was the depot for the Army of Northern Virginia for all commissary and quartermaster stores gathered from the productive territory lying between it and Knoxville, Tennessee, and from all the country tributary to, and drained by, the Virginia & Tennessee Railroad. Here, also, were stored many of the scant medical supplies of the Confederacy."

16. *O.R.*, Vol. XXXVI, Pt. Three, p. 599.

17. Captain Charles H. Porter, "Operations of Generals Sigel and Hunter in the Shenandoah Valley," *MHSM Papers*, Vol. VI, pp. 77–78. See also Badeau, Vol. II, p. 335.

18. Lee's letter is taken from the Robert E. Lee Papers in the Chicago Historical Society. On June 7 Butler notified Grant that Richmond papers of that date said that Hunter had defeated Jones and had occupied Staunton. (*O.R.*, Vol. XXXVI, Pt. Three, p. 691.)

19. For a good summary of Federal activities in this period, see Humphreys, pp. 196–204.

20. Grant, *Personal Memoirs*, Vol. II, pp. 289, 292–296; Porter, *Campaigning with Grant*, 189–190; Charles A. Page, *Letters of a War Correspondent*, p. 111; letter of Rawlins dated June 13, in the James H. Wilson Papers.

21. Humphreys, pp. 196–197, 205–206; *O.R.*, Vol. XL, Pt. Two, pp. 18–19; Basler, Vol. VII, p. 393.

Chapter 15: A QUESTION OF TIME

1. There is a good word-picture of Grant watching the crossing in Porter, *Campaigning with Grant*, pp. 199–200.

2. Porter Alexander, *Military Memoirs of a Confederate*, p. 547; Theodore Lyman, "Crossing the James and Advance on Petersburg," *MHSM Papers*, Vol. V, p. 29; Colonel Thomas A. Livermore, "The Failure to Take Petersburg June 15, 1864," in the same volume, p. 68.

3. General William F. Smith, "The Movement Against Petersburg," *MHSM Papers*, Vol. V, pp. 80–84, 96; *O.R.*, Vol. XL, Pt. Two, p. 59.

4. Hancock's report, *O.R.*, Vol. XL, Pt. One, pp. 303–305.

5. Beauregard, "Four Days of Battle at Petersburg," *B. & L.*, Vol. IV, p. 541. In a postwar letter to General Cadmus Wilcox (printed in Vol. V, *MHSM Papers*, p. 119) Beauregard said that Smith "would certainly have taken Petersburg if he had not 'feared to run any risk.'"

6. Colonel Thomas A. Livermore, article cited in n. 2, above, pp. 67–68; letter of General Hancock to General Butler dated January 12, 1882, in the papers of the Massachusetts Commandery, Military Order of the Loyal Legion of the United States, Houghton Library, Harvard; *O.R.*, Vol. XL, Pt. One, pp. 313–314.

7. Livermore, op. cit., p. 71; *O.R.*, Vol. XL, Pt. Two, pp. 656–657; Beauregard's letter to Wilcox, as cited in n. 5, above. In his official report on the June 15 fight, written the next day, Smith says that "having learned some time before that reinforcements were rapidly coming in from Richmond . . . I thought it prudent to make no farther advance, and made my dispositions to hold what I already had" (*O.R.*, Vol. XL, Pt. One, p. 705.) Years after the war, Smith asserted that Butler on the evening of June 15 not only warned him that Beauregard was being reinforced but flatly ordered him to "cease firing and entrench at once," and he said that he suspended operations in obedience to that order. It does not appear in the *Official Records,* but Smith eventually collected letters and affidavits from wartime signalers saying that such an order had been received. All of this material, along with an extensive memorandum by Smith, "The Story of the Suppressed Despatch," is in the private collection of W. F. Smith's papers owned by Walter Wilgus of Arlington, Va. In this memorandum Smith says he simply forgot about Butler's "cease firing" order when he wrote his report, and laments: "This lapse of memory was unusual to me, and I must leave the explanation to some psychologist for it is beyond me." As a matter of fact, Smith's behavior through the 1864 campaign greatly needs a thorough psychological study.

8. Grant's letter to Julia Grant dated June 15, 1864, from the collection owned by Major General U. S. Grant III.

9. Lyman, *Meade's Headquarters*, p. 164; Grant, *Personal Memoirs*, Vol. II, p. 292.

10. For Grant's exchanges with Butler, see *O.R.*, Vol. XL, Pt. Two, pp. 97–98.

11. Humphreys, pp. 218–221; Beauregard, letter to Wilcox, *MHSM Papers*, Vol. V, p. 121; Alexander, *Military Memoirs of a Confederate*, p. 551.

12. Humphreys, p. 224; Beauregard, "Four Days of Battle at Petersburg," *B. & L.*, Vol. IV, pp. 543–544; *O.R.*, Vol. XL, Pt. Two, pp. 167, 179, 205.

13. Letter of Meade to Mrs. Meade dated June 24, in Meade's *Life and Letters*, Vol. II, p. 207.

14. Letter of Meade to John Sergeant Meade dated June 27, *Life and Letters*, Vol. II, p. 209.

15. Basler, Vol. VII, p. 395.

16. Humphreys, pp. 226–229; *O.R.*, Vol. XL, Pt. One, pp. 13, 14.

17. Letter of Meade to Mrs. Meade dated June 20, in Meade, *Life and Letters*, Vol. II, pp. 209–210; Sheridan, *Memoirs*, Vol. I, pp. 430–436; Humphreys, pp. 236–242.

18. Freeman, *R. E. Lee*, Vol. III, p. 401.

19. *O.R.*, Vol. XXXVI, Pt. One, pp. 796–797; Pt. Three, p. 897; George E. Pond, *The Shenandoah Valley in 1864*, pp. 35–40.

20. *O.R.*, Vol. XXXVII, Pt. One, p. 767.

21. Freeman, *R. E. Lee*, Vol. III, p. 398; *O.R.*, Vol. XL, Pt. Two, p. 703; Alexander, *Military Memoirs of a Confederate*, pp. 557–558.

22. Badeau, Vol. II, p. 318; letter to Elihu Washburne dated June 9, in the Illinois State Historical Library.

23. *O.R.*, Vol. XXXVI, Pt. Three, pp. 314, 524; Vol. XXXIV, Pt. Four, pp. 514–515.

24. Army returns for April 30 and June 30 are in *O.R.*, Vol. XXXVI, Pt. One, pp. 198, 915; Vol. XL, Pt. Two, p. 542. Halleck's boast is in his letter to Lieber dated June 10, in the Lieber Papers at the Huntington Library. Lee's letter to Davis giving his estimate of the time-expired Federal regiments that would go home during July is in *O.R.*, Vol. XXXVII, Pt. Two, p. 593.

25. Johnston, "Opposing Sherman's Advance to Atlanta," *B. & L.*, Vol. IV, pp. 273–277.

26. Letter of Horace Porter to Mrs. Porter dated June 24, 1864, in the Horace

Porter Papers, Library of Congress. It is instructive to note that in his book, *Campaigning with Grant*, pp. 217 ff, Porter gives an account of this visit so different from the account in his letter that it would be impossible to believe they referred to the same occasion except for the dates given. In his book, Porter made the affair properly formal, had Grant and his staff meeting Lincoln's steamer at the dock and going up the gangplank to welcome the President, and altogether dressed the affair up beyond recognition. Porter's book is well written and in general makes good source material, but he appears to have had a weakness for sandpapering the rough edges off of the distinguished men who figure in its pages.

27. Letter of Grant to Jones dated July 5, in the Chicago Historical Society.

Chapter 16: SO FAIR AN OPPORTUNITY

1. Grant's note to Meade is in *O.R.*, Vol. XL, Pt. Two, p. 599.
2. *O.R.*, Vol. XL, Pt. One, pp. 285–286; Pt. Two, pp. 600, 619.
3. Oliver Christian Bosbyshell, *The 48th in the War*, pp. 163–165; William H. Powell, "The Battle of the Petersburg Crater," *B. & L.*, Vol. IV, pp. 545–546. There is a good summary of the whole operation in Henry Pleasants, Jr., *The Tragedy of the Crater*.
   To illustrate the touchy relations between Meade and Burnside: on July 3 Burnside wrote Meade that a three-corps attack following explosion of the mine ought to have a fair chance of success, "provided my corps can make the attack and it is left to me to say when and how the other two corps shall come in to my support." In reply Meade wrote: "I shall exercise the prerogative of my position to control and direct the same, receiving gladly at all times such suggestions as you may think proper to make. I consider these remarks necessary in consequence of certain conditions which you have thought proper to attach to your opinion, acceding to which in advance would not in my judgment be consistent with my position as commanding general of the army" (*O.R.*, Vol. XL, Pt. Two, p. 608).
4. Lee's messages to Davis are in *O.R.*, Vol. XXXVII, Pt. Two, pp. 593, 595.
5. *O.R.*, Vol. XL, Pt. Two, pp. 599, 600; Pt. Three, pp. 3, 4, 6, 31, 32.
6. Badeau, Vol. II, p. 435; *O.R.*, Vol. XL, Pt. Three, pp. 31–33. Lincoln's appraisal of the possibilities in June, 1863, is set forth in *Glory Road*, p. 272.
7. *O.R.*, Vol. XL, Pt. Three, pp. 72, 91–92. A day or so earlier Grant had told Meade to postpone the Petersburg offensive until the men Canby was sending up could be used (ibid., p. 94).
8. Basler, Vol. VII, p. 437.
9. Ibid., p. 438
10. Porter, *Campaigning with Grant*, p. 238; Badeau, Vol. II, p. 450
11. *O.R.*, Vol. XL, Pt. Three, p. 176; George E. Pond, *The Shenandoah Valley in 1864*, p. 71; Badeau, Vol. II, pp. 445, 452; Grant, *Personal Memoirs*, Vol. II, p. 317.
12. *O.R.*, Vol. XL, Pt. Three, p. 223.
13. Diary of Colonel Comstock, entry for July 15, from the Comstock Papers, Library of Congress; *O.R.*, Vol. XL, Pt. Three, pp. 275–276; Vol. XXXVIII, Pt. Five, p. 151. Halleck's attitude was no secret. People at Meade's headquarters knew all about it, and General Marsena Patrick wrote that Halleck all along had urged Grant to keep his army between Lee and Washington, adding: "Halleck was over-ruled and now retorts upon Grant that he warned him of invasion" (entry for August 5 in Patrick's diary, Library of Congress).
14. Badeau, Vol. II, pp. 449, 451, 457–458; *O.R.*, Vol. XL, Pt. Three, pp. 255–256.
15. *O.R.*, Vol. XXXVII, Pt. Two, pp. 374, 400, 408; Pt. Three, p. 436.
16. *O.R.*, Vol. XL, Pt. Three, pp. 456–457, 501–502, 551.
17. Ibid., pp. 424–425; diary of Col. William Hamilton Harris, typescript, in the

Virginia State Historical Society, original in the New York Public Library.
18. *O.R.*, Vol. XL, Pt. Three, pp. 424–426, 437–438, 443, 458–459, 484.
19. Ibid., pp. 474–475.
20. Ibid., pp. 504–505, 551, 553, 596.
21. Stephen M. Weld, "The Petersburg Mine," *MHSM Papers*, Vol. V, p. 217. Grant's slightly prim comment (*Personal Memoirs*, Vol. II, p. 313) was that Ledlie, "besides being otherwise inefficient, proved also to possess disqualification less common among soldiers."
22. Captain W. Gordon McCabe, "Defense of Petersburg," *SHSP*, December, 1876, Vol. II, No. 6, p. 283.
23. Grant's testimony before the Committee on the Conduct of the War, *Report, 1865*, Vol. I, *Battle of Petersburg*, p. 110 (cited hereafter as *CCW Report*).
24. Humphreys, pp. 251–255; Meade's testimony, *CCW Report*, as cited above, p. 35; Brigadier General Stephen M. Weld, "The Petersburg Mine," *MHSM Papers*, Vol. V, pp. 208 ff; Captain Charles H. Porter, ibid., p. 230.
25. General William Mahone, "The Crater," in J. H. Stine, *History of the Army of the Potomac*, pp. 675–676.
26. Porter, *Campaigning with Grant*, p. 267; Grant to Halleck dated August 1, in the U. S. Grant Papers, Huntington Library; Grant to Meade, same date, in the papers of the U. S. Grant Association.
27. Humphreys (p. 263) estimated Federal losses at 3,500 and thought the Confederates might have lost 1,200; Livermore (*Numbers and Losses*, p. 116) put the Federal loss at 3,798; Richard Wayne Lykes, *Petersburg National Military Park*, pp. 12–29, suggests 4,000 as a proper total. Grant's testimony about the failure to prepare for the assault is in *CCW Report*, Vol. I, p. 111.

Chapter 17: ROUGHSHOD OR ON TIPTOE

1. *O.R.*, Vol. XL, Pt. Two, pp. 558–559; Porter, *Campaigning with Grant*, p. 246; Comstock's diary, entry for July 2, 1864.
2. *O.R.*, Vol. XL, Pt. Two, p. 598; Pt. Three, p. 31.
3. *O.R.*, Vol. XL, Pt. Three, pp. 59, 69.
4. Ibid., pp. 122–123.
5. Letter of Wilson to Smith dated July 9, 1864, and of Cadwallader to Wilson dated August 31, 1904, both in the James H. Wilson Papers, Library of Congress; letter of Smith to Wilson dated May 20 in some postwar year, also in the Wilson Papers; letter of Butler to Mrs. Butler dated July 10, 1864, in Butler, *Private and Official Correspondence*, Vol. IV, pp. 481–482.
6. *O.R.*, Vol. XL, Pt. Three, p. 175; Pt. Two, p. 594; letter of Smith to Senator Solomon Foot of Vermont dated July 30, 1864, in Smith, *From Chattanooga to Petersburg under Generals Grant and Butler*, Appendix One, p. 176; Comstock's diary, entry for July 17, 1864.
7. Diary of Marsena Patrick, entry for July 17, 1864; letter of Smith to Wilson dated April 25, 1890, in the James H. Wilson Papers.
8. *O.R.*, Vol. XL, Pt. One, pp. 35–36; letters of Meade to Mrs. Meade dated July 12, 15 and 20, in Meade, *Life and Letters*, Vol. II, pp. 212–213, 215; Comstock's diary, entry for July 7; Badeau, Vol. II, pp. 464–465.
9. Lyman, *Meade's Headquarters*, pp. 192–193; *O.R.*, Vol. XL, Pt. Three, pp. 276, 334, 335; Vol. XXXVII, Pt. Two, p. 331.
10. Smith's letters to Senator Foot, as cited in n. 6, above, Appendix One, pp. 174–175, and Appendix Eight, pp. 192–193; William B. Hesseltine, *Ulysses S. Grant, Politician*, p. 44.
11. Wilson, *The Life of John A. Rawlins*, p. 239; typescript letter of Rawlins to Mrs. Rawlins in the Wilson Papers. (In his *Life of Rawlins*, Wilson printed this letter but omitted the last two sentences.) In his postwar correspondence, Wilson was equivocal about the matter of Smith's dismissal. The newspaperman Cad-

wallader wrote to him saying that the reason Grant did not put Smith in Butler's place "was because of Butler's brow-beatings and threatening about taking a couple of drinks of whiskey in Butler's presence." Wilson agreed: "There is no doubt in my mind that in the final break-up between Butler and Grant, Grant was 'cowed,' and for the reason that he did not care to face scandal which affected his personal habits." A few weeks later, however, Wilson wrote Cadwallader: "The General's drinking habits were so well known that he might have defied everybody at that period of his life" (letters of Cadwallader to Wilson dated August 31, 1904, and of Wilson to Cadwallader dated September 8 and 24, 1904, in the James H. Wilson Papers). It ought to be added that when "the final break-up between Butler and Grant" actually occurred, Grant was not in the least cowed; he fired Butler, and Butler took it.

There is a great deal of literature on the Grant-Butler relationship. A careful treatment is George W. Wolfson, "Butler's Relations with General Grant and the Army of the James in 1864," in the *South Atlantic Quarterly*, Vol. X, No. 4, October, 1911, pp. 376–393. In his *History of the United States from the Compromise of 1850*, pp. 493–496, James Ford Rhodes accepts the theory that Butler was able to put pressure on Grant; Hesseltine, as cited in n. 10, above, p. 365, takes no stock in it. It does seem that anyone who thinks Butler was able to exert enough personal pressure to keep his job in July of 1864 ought to be able to explain why he could not do the same in January, 1865.

12. Letters of Grant to Julia Dent Grant dated July 12 and 18, 1864; from the collection owned by Major General U. S. Grant III.

13. Basler, Vol. VII, p. 470; letter of Meade to Mrs. Meade dated July 29, in Meade, *Life and Letters*, Vol. II, pp. 216–217; letter of Butler to Mrs. Butler dated July 11, in Butler, *Private and Official Correspondence*, Vol. IV, p. 484; diary of Marsena Patrick, entry for August 5, in the Library of Congress.

14. Patrick's diary, as above; letters of Montgomery Blair to S. L. M. Barlow, dated May 1 and 4, and of Barlow to Blair dated May 3; unsigned memo in Barlow's hand dated May, 1864, giving material "embodied in my letter to Thurlow Weed in answer to his request that McC should write a letter to President Lincoln which would enable Lincoln to restore him to command"; letter of Barlow to McClellan, undated but apparently written in August, 1864; letter of Ethan Allen, assistant U. S. district attorney in New York, to Barlow, dated July 20, 1864; all in the Barlow Papers, Huntington Library. See also Nicolay and Hay, Vol. IX, pp. 247–249.

15. Basler, Vol. VII, pp. 435, 440–442; letter of Meade to Mrs. Meade dated July 26, in Meade, *Life and Letters*, Vol. II, p. 216.

16. Diary of Marsena Patrick, entry for July 20; letter of Colonel Shaffer to Butler dated August 17, in Butler, *Private and Official Correspondence*, Vol. V, pp. 67–68.

17. Diary of Marsena Patrick, entry for July 27; John H. Brinton, *Personal Memoirs*, p. 288; *O.R.*, Vol. XXXVII, Pt. Two, p. 331; E. G. Taylor, *Gouverneur Kemble Warren*, p. 186; Carswell McClellan, *The Personal Memoirs and Military History of U. S. Grant versus the Record of the Army of the Potomac*, pp. 42–43.

18. Letter of Leet to Rowley dated August 9, 1864, in the William R. Rowley Papers, Illinois State Historical Library. (The officers to whom Leet refers were Captain Ely Parker, assistant adjutant general, and Captain P. T. Hudson, aide-de-camp.) Dodge's comments are in his *Personal Recollections*, pp. 76–77.

19. *O.R.*, Vol. XXXVII, Pt. Two, pp. 508–510, 527–528; Badeau, Vol. II, p. 493.

20. *O.R.*, Vol. XXXVII, Pt. Two, pp. 558, 573, 582; Sheridan, *Memoirs*, Vol. I, p. 463.

21. *O.R.*, Vol. XLII, Pt. Two, p. 48.

22. Letter of General Franklin to General Smith dated August 2, 1864; from the W. F. Smith Papers in the private collection of Walter Wilgus.

Chapter 18: THE HUNDRED-GUN SALUTES

1. Grant, *Personal Memoirs*, Vol. II, pp. 319–321; Badeau, Vol. II, pp. 493–495; Sheridan, *Memoirs*, Vol. I, pp. 464–465; *O.R.*, Vol. XLIII, Pt. One, p. 719; Vol. XL, Pt. Three, p. 223.
2. Letter of Bowers to Rawlins dated August 10, 1864, in Wilson's *Life of John A. Rawlins*, p. 257; Bowers to William R. Rowley dated August 9, 1864, in the Rowley Papers, Illinois State Historical Library.
3. Letters of Grant to Julia Grant dated August 5 and 8, from the collection owned by Major General U. S. Grant III.
4. *O.R.*, Vol. XLII, Pt. One, pp. 17, 954–956; Porter, *Campaigning with Grant*, pp. 273–275; letter of Bowers to Rowley, as in n. 2, above; letter of Porter to Mrs. Porter dated August 15, 1864, in the Horace Porter Papers, Library of Congress.
5. Humphreys, pp. 268–272. Hancock's report, in *O.R.*, Vol. XLII, Pt. One, pp. 217–218, makes it clear that he did not like the way General Francis Barlow handled the assault. He added that Barlow did set a good example to his troops "by his well-known gallantry and devotion to duty."
6. Humphreys, pp. 278–283; General F. A. Walker, "Reams Station," *MHSM Papers*, Vol. V, pp. 269–305.
7. *O.R.*, Vol. XLII, Pt. One, p. 39.
8. *Wartime Papers of R. E. Lee*, pp. 841–844, 847–848.
9. *O.R.*, Vol. XLII, Pt. Two, pp. 111–112, 193–194; Basler, Vol. VII, p. 499; Porter, *Campaigning with Grant*, p. 279.
10. Letter of Grant to Washburne dated August 16, 1864, in the Illinois State Historical Library; letter to Ammen dated August 18, in Daniel Ammen, *The Old Navy and the New*, pp. 397–399.
11. Basler, Vol. VII, pp. 506–508, 514; letters of McClellan to Barlow dated September 21 and October 13, 1864, in the Barlow Papers.
12. Oliver Otis Howard, "The Struggle for Atlanta," in *B. & L.*, Vol. IV, pp. 314–321; Grenville Dodge, *Personal Recollections*, pp. 77–78; Lloyd Lewis, *Sherman, Fighting Prophet*, pp. 388–389.
13. Lewis, op. cit., pp. 407–409; Badeau, Vol. II, pp. 543–546.
14. Porter, *Campaigning with Grant*, p. 285; Lyman, *Meade's Headquarters*, p. 217; *O.R.*, Vol. XLII, Pt. Two, p. 682; Badeau, Vol. II, pp. 552–553.
15. Sheridan, *Memoirs*, Vol. I, pp. 474–475, 484–486; Pond, *The Shenandoah Valley in 1864*, p. 128.
16. Pond, op. cit., pp. 130–132, 150; Grant, *Personal Memoirs*, Vol. II, p. 327; *O.R.*, Vol. XLII, Pt. Two, pp. 815, 816.
17. Grant, *Personal Memoirs*, Vol. II, pp. 327–329; James H. Croushare, ed., *A Volunteer's Adventures* by John W. De Forest, p. 172; letter of Grant to Julia Grant dated September 20, in the collection owned by Major General U. S. Grant III; *O.R.*, Vol. XLIII, Pt. Two, p. 96.
18. Porter, *Campaigning with Grant*, p. 298; Pond, *The Shenandoah Valley in 1864*, pp. 154–167; *O.R.*, Vol. XLIII, Pt. Two, pp. 110, 118; letter of Grant to Julia Grant dated September 25, from the collection of Major General U. S. Grant III.

Chapter 19: I WILL WORK THIS THING OUT YET

1. Wainwright, *A Diary of Battle*, pp. 430, 465–466, giving journal entries for June 30 and September 25, 1864.
2. Letter of Captain George K. Leet to Colonel W. R. Rowley dated August 23, quoting a letter from Bowers; microfilm in the U. S. Grant Association, from original in the Illinois State Historical Library.
3. Humphreys, pp. 284–289; George A. Bruce, "Petersburg, June 15 — Fort Harrison,

September 29: A Comparison," in *MHSM Papers*, Vol. XIV, pp. 89–97; Freeman, Vol. III, pp. 499–504.
4. John B. Jones, *A Rebel War Clerk's Diary*, pp. 427–428; Humphreys, pp. 295–304.
5. *O.R.*, Vol. XLII, Pt. One, p. 545; letter of Grant to Secretary of State Seward dated August 19, 1864, in the William H. Seward Collection, Rush Rhees Library, University of Rochester.
6. *O.R.*, Vol. XLII, Pt. Two, pp. 783, 804.
7. Letter of Bowers to Rowley dated October 22, 1864, in the Rowley Papers, Illinois State Historical Library; *O.R.*, Vol. XLII, Pt. One, pp. 39–41, 198–199.
8. Benjamin P. Thomas and Harold Hyman, *Stanton: the Life and Times of Lincoln's Secretary of War*, pp. 371–374; William B. Hesseltine, *Civil War Prisons*, pp. 222–223; *O.R.*, Ser. 2, Vol. VII, p. 607.
9. *O.R.*, op. cit., pp. 906–907, 909, 914.
10. Ibid., pp. 990–993, 1010–1012, 1015, 1018–1019.
11. Hesseltine, op. cit., p. 225; *O.R.*, Ser. 2, Vol. VII, pp. 616–622, 796.
12. *O.R.*, Vol. XLII, Pt. Two, pp. 1045–1046.
13. A. K. McClure, *Abraham Lincoln and Men of War-Times*, pp. 202–203. McClure was almost certainly wrong in saying that Lincoln, on the eve of the election, had no idea whether Grant preferred him as a candidate over McClellan. Grant had made no public statement about his preference, but his firm belief that Lincoln's reelection was essential can hardly have been a secret from a man as well informed as the President.
14. Pond, *The Shenandoah Valley in 1864*, pp. 188–219, passim; Grant, *Personal Memoirs*, Vol. II, pp. 336–338; General Hazard Stevens, "The Battle of Cedar Creek," in *MHSM Papers*, Vol. VI, pp. 85–98; Sheridan, *Memoirs*, Vol. II, pp. 62–82.
15. The estimate of numbers is Stevens's, op. cit., pp. 89–90. The Federal advantage is often greatly overstated, Sheridan being credited with more men than he actually had and Early with fewer. In preparing his tables, General Stevens points out that of the Federals supposedly involved in this battle, fully eighteen regiments were on duty behind the lines and were not engaged on October 19. His tables—which the reader can accept or reject, at his own option—show Sheridan's effective strength on this date as 31,610 and Early's as 21,102.
16. Porter, *Campaigning with Grant*, pp. 306–308; *O.R.*, Vol. XLIII, Pt. Two, p. 410.
17. *O.R.*, Vol. XLIII, Pt. Three, p. 281; Pt. Two, p. 423; letter of Grant to Julia Grant dated October 20, 1864, from the collection owned by Major General U. S. Grant III.
18. *O.R.*, Vol. XLII, Pt. One, pp. 22–23; Humphreys, pp. 295–304; General Francis A. Walker "The Expedition to the Boydton Plank Road, October, 1864," in *MHSM Papers*, Vol. V., p. 334; letter of Grant to Julia Grant dated October 28, in the collection owned by Major General U. S. Grant III.
19. *Wartime Papers of R. E. Lee*, p. 868; letter of Grenville Dodge to Richard J. Oglesby dated October 29, 1864, in the Oglesby Papers, Illinois State Historical Library.
20. General M. R. Morgan, "From City Point to Appomattox with General Grant," in the *Journal of the Military Service Institution of the United States*, September-October, 1907; letter of Grant to Julia Grant dated November 9, 1864, from the collection owned by Major General U. S. Grant III: *O.R.*, Vol. XLII, Pt. Three, pp. 581, 582; letter of Grant to J. Russell Jones dated November 13, 1864, from the Grant Papers in the Chicago Historical Society.

Chapter 20: MUCH IS NOW EXPECTED

1. Grant, *Personal Memoirs*, Vol. II, pp. 348–350; Porter, *Campaigning with Grant*, pp. 287–290.
2. *Supra.* pp, 94–95, 167–168.

3. Porter, op. cit., pp. 292–293.
4. Ibid., pp. 295–296, 314–318; Grant, *Personal Memoirs*, Vol. II, pp. 375–376, 596–597. Long after the war the newspaper correspondent Cadwallader wrote to General Wilson that Rawlins did not oppose the march to the sea, but that he "did oppose its being put in motion until Hood had been properly disposed of" (letter dated October 12, 1904, in the James H. Wilson Papers). Since the entire point of the project was to make the march without disposing of Hood at all, Cadwallader's disclaimer actually disclaims nothing.
5. Grant to Stanton, dated October 13, 1864, from the U. S. Grant Papers in the Illinois State Historical Library; Porter, op. cit., p. 319.
6. Basler, Vol. VIII, p. 148.
7. *O.R.*, Vol. XLII, Pt. Three, p. 620.
8. *O.R.*, Vol. XLII, Pt. One, pp. 966–974, 988–989. On December 3 Grant wrote a letter which the navy was to give Sherman as soon as Sherman reached the seacoast. In this letter Grant gave details about the Fort Fisher venture, explaining: "Owing to some preparations that Admiral Porter and General Butler are making to blow up Fort Fisher, and which, while I hope for the best, I do not believe a particle in, there is a delay in getting the expedition off" (Porter, *Campaigning with Grant*, pp. 337–338).
9. Grant, *Personal Memoirs*, Vol. II, p. 604. In his endorsement on General Butler's report on the Fort Fisher operation, Grant wrote: "It was never contemplated that General Butler should accompany the expedition. . . . Major General G. Weitzel was specially named as the commander of it" (*O.R.*, Vol. XLII, Pt. One, p. 970).
10. Colonel Henry Stone, "Repelling Hood's Invasion of Tennessee," *B. & L.*, Vol. IV, pp. 440–453; Porter, *Campaigning with Grant*, p. 334; Grant, *Personal Memoirs*, Vol. II, p. 380.
11. Grant, *Personal Memoirs*, pp. 380–384; Porter, *Campaigning with Grant*, pp. 343–348.
12. Lloyd Lewis, *Sherman: Fighting Prophet*, p. 390; *O.R.*, Vol. XLII, Pt. Three, p. 995; Colonel Henry Stone, op. cit., pp. 454–455.
13. Porter, pp. 348–349.
14. Stone, op. cit., pp. 457 ff; James H. Wilson, "The Union Cavalry in the Hood Campaign," *B. & L.*, Vol. IV, pp. 469–471; *O.R.*, Vol. XLII, Pt. Three, pp. 1024, 1073.
15. Butler's report on the Fort Fisher affair is in *O.R.*, Vol. XLII, Pt. One, pp. 966–970. For an engineer's report on the explosion of the powder vessel, see the same volume, pp. 990–991. Comstock's verdict is in a letter to Bowers dated January 1, 1865, in the Comstock papers, Library of Congress. See also *O.R.*, Vol. XLII, Pt. Three, pp. 1087, 1091; Porter, *Campaigning with Grant*, pp. 362–363.
16. *O.R.*, Vol. XLVI, Pt. Two, pp. 29, 52, 60, 61.
17. Ammen, *The Old Navy and the New*, pp. 532–533; *O.R.*, Vol. XLII, Pt. Three, p. 1044; William D. Hallam, "The Grant-Butler Relationship," in *The Mississippi Valley Historical Review*, Vol. XLI, No. 2, September, 1954, pp. 265–266.

Chapter 21: A LETTER FROM GENERAL LEE

1. Wilson, *Life of John A. Rawlins*, pp. 297–298; *O.R.*, Vol. XLII, Pt. Three, p. 1110.
2. Letters of Grant to Julia Grant dated December 20, 22 and 24, 1864, and January 1, 1865, and also his earlier letter of October 2, 1864, from the collection owned by Major General U. S. Grant III; Hamlin Garland, *Ulysses S. Grant: His Life and Character*, p. 307.
3. Grant, *Personal Memoirs*, Vol. II, pp. 395–396, 401–402, 605–606; *O.R.*, Vol. XLVI, Pt. One, pp. 394–395; Pt. Two, pp. 70–71; Porter, *Campaigning with Grant*, p. 369;

Diary of Gideon Welles, Vol. II, pp. 223–224. There is a sketch of Terry in DAB, Vol. XVIII, pp. 378-379.

4. Basler, Vol. VIII, p. 201.
5. Grant, *Personal Memoirs*, Vol. II, pp. 403–405, 610–611.
6. Meade, *Life and Letters*, Vol. II, p. 256.
7. Porter, *Campaigning with Grant*, pp. 374–375.
8. Letters of Grant to Congressman Washburne and Senator Wilson, both dated January 23, 1865, in the Meade Papers, Historical Society of Pennsylvania, Philadelphia; Meade, *Life and Letters*, Vol. II, pp. 245–246.
9. Thomas O. Selfridge, "The Navy at Fort Fisher," *B. & L.*, Vol. IV, pp. 657–661; Jacob D. Cox, *The March to the Sea, Franklin and Nashville*, pp. 147–149; *O.R.*, Vol. XLII, Pt. Three, pp. 761, 791; Vol. XLVI, Pt. One, pp. 395–402. For Weitzel in New Orleans, see *Never Call Retreat*, p. 73.
10. Basler, Vol. VIII, pp. 267–268; also pp. 20–22, 73, 200, 209–210, 221. Grant's letter to Canby, dated February 13, 1865, is from a copy in the files of E. B. Long of Oak Park, Ill.
11. Letter of Hancock to General Barlow dated November 3, 1864, in the Francis Channing Barlow Papers at the Massachusetts Historical Society, Boston; *O.R.*, Vol. XLII, Pt. Three, p. 728.
12. Dated January 2, 1865, the letter from the Philadelphia citizens' committee is taken from the *Army and Navy Journal* for January 28, 1865. Grant's letter to Julia Grant, dated January 4, is from the collection of Major General U. S. Grant III.
13. Grant's letters to Julia Grant, dated July 7, 12, and 21; August 1, 23, and 25; October 12, 20, 24 and 26, 1864, from the collection of Major General U. S. Grant III.
14. Porter, *Campaigning with Grant*, pp. 284, 329, 377–380; Grant to Halleck dated January 24, 1865, in *The History of America in Documents*, catalogue, The Rosenbach Company, Philadelphia, 1951, Pt. Three, p. 61.
15. Letter of Grant to Halleck dated December 26, 1864, photostat from the U. S. Grant Commission, Springfield, Ill. Colonel Randolph P. Marcy, McClellan's father-in-law, was a regular army officer who served as McClellan's chief of staff when McClellan commanded the Army of the Potomac.
16. Basler, Vol. VIII, pp. 223–224; letter of Adam Badeau to General James H. Wilson, dated February 25, 1865, in the Princeton University Library.
17. Hamlin Garland, *Ulysses S. Grant, His Life and Character*, pp. 291–292.
18. Grant, *Personal Memoirs*, Vol. II, pp. 420–423; Porter, *Campaigning with Grant*, pp. 382–385; Basler, Vol. VIII, pp. 274–285. The stronghold at Hampton Roads was then, as today, properly Fort Monroe, but it was often styled Fortress Monroe even in official government correspondence.
19. Basler, Vol. VIII, pp. 330–331; Porter, *Campaigning with Grant*, pp. 389–391.

Chapter 22: I FEEL NOW LIKE ENDING THE MATTER

1. Grant to Sheridan, February 20, letter printed in *The History of America in Documents*, catalogue, The Rosenbach Company, p. 64; letter of Lee to Breckinridge dated February 19, in *The Wartime Papers of R. E. Lee*, p. 904; letter of Grant to Washburne dated February 23, in the Illinois State Historical Library. The letter to Sheridan is given in a slightly different form in Grant, *Personal Memoirs*, Vol. II, p. 409.
2. Sanford C. Kellogg, *The Shenandoah Valley and Virginia, 1861 to 1865*, pp. 241–245; typescript, "Extracts from the War Diary of Jed Hotchkiss," pp. 11–12, Library of Congress; Sheridan, *Memoirs*, Vol. II, pp. 118–119.
3. Letter of Halleck to Canby dated February 26, 1865, in *B. & L.*, extra-illustrated, Vol. III, at the Huntington Library; Grant, *Personal Memoirs*, Vol. II, pp. 411, 518; Badeau, Vol. III, p. 408; *O.R.*, Vol. XLVI, Pt. Three, p. 28.

4. Interview with Senator Ben Hill, reprinted from the Philadelphia *Press* in the New Orleans *Democrat* for July 5, 1881, clipping in the Alfred Roman Papers, Library of Congress; letter of Lee to Davis dated March 14, 1865, in *The Wartime Papers of Robert E. Lee*, pp. 914–915.
5. Grant, *Personal Memoirs*, Vol. II, pp. 427, 430; *O.R.*, Vol. XLVI, Pt. Three, pp. 46–47, 67.
6. Noah Brooks, *Washington in Lincoln's Time*, p. 218; letter of Greeley to S. L. M. Barlow dated March 15, 1865, in the Barlow Papers, Huntington Library.
7. Grant's letter of March 22 to Meade, Ord and Sheridan is in his *Personal Memoirs*, Vol. II, pp. 616-618. His letter to Sherman, dated March 22, is in the *Memoirs of General W. T. Sherman*, Vol. II, p. 323; his letter to Jesse Grant, dated March 19, is from *The History of America in Documents*, catalogue, 1951, The Rosenbach Company, Pt. One, p. 68.
8. *O.R.*, Vol. XLVI, Pt. Three, pp. 50, 109; Sheridan's *Memoirs*, Vol. II, p. 128; Porter, *Campaigning with Grant*, pp. 402–403; John Russell Young, *Around the World with General Grant*, Vol. II, p. 358.
9. Sheridan's *Memoirs*, Vol. II, pp. 129–130; Porter, op. cit., pp. 413–414; Julia Grant's comment is in a note by Lloyd Lewis covering his interview in 1945 with Mrs. Charles L. Webster.
10. The above is based on Horace Porter's account in his *Campaigning with Grant*, pp. 417–421. See also the *Memoirs* of General Sherman, Vol. II, p. 325.
11. Badeau, Vol. III, p. 451; Grant, *Personal Memoirs*, Vol. II, pp. 437–438; Sheridan, *Memoirs*, Vol. II, pp. 128–129.
12. Grant, *Personal Memoirs*, Vol. II, pp. 514–515; Sherman, *Memoirs*, Vol. II, p. 327; Admiral D. D. Porter, *Incidents and Anecdotes of the Civil War*, pp. 313–317. A good study of Sherman's impressions of Lincoln's talk is in Lloyd Lewis, *Sherman: Fighting Prophet*, pp. 522–523.
13. Major Henry Lee, "The Last Campaign of the Army of the Potomac from a 'Mud-Crusher's' Point of View," *War Papers of the California Commandery*, Military Order of the Loyal Legion, pp. 3–5; Captain Charles H. Porter, "Operations of the Fifth Corps on the Left, March 29 to Nightfall, March 31, 1865," in *MHSM Papers*, Vol. VI, p. 217; Badeau, Vol. III, pp. 451, 455; Lieutenant Colonel William Swan, "The Five Forks Campaign," in *MHSM Papers*, Vol. V, p. 279; Grant, *Personal Memoirs*, Vol. II, p. 438.
14. Porter, *Campaigning with Grant*, pp. 424–426; Badeau, Vol. III, pp. 452–453, 457–458.
15. Swan, op. cit., pp. 320–323; Humphreys, p. 330; *O.R.*, Vol. XLVI, Pt. Three, pp. 305, 337, 362. For a glimpse of the messages Warren exchanged with Meade's headquarters see Badeau, Vol. III, pp. 465–466.
16. Badeau, Vol. III, p. 459.
17. Badeau, Vol. III, p. 498. For a detailed study of the march of the Fifth Corps and the way Sheridan used it, see Humphreys, pp. 338 ff. As an indication of Sheridan's enhanced status at this time, it might be noted that Warren was one of Meade's corps commanders, but that it was Sheridan — technically Meade's subordinate — who was given authority to dismiss him.

There is an extensive literature on Warren's removal, most of it designed to show that the man was not really at fault in the Five Forks operation, and it must be said that the battle was an overwhelming Union victory regardless of the way Warren handled his troops. Some years after the war a Court of Inquiry held Warren blameless. (See the articles in *MHSM Papers*, Vol. VI, pp. 209–408; also Humphreys, pp. 356–362.)

Perhaps the best comments on the affair come from two officers who liked Warren. Morris Schaff (*The Battle of the Wilderness*, p. 98) remarked: "Sheridan's harsh dealing with him was not wholly unstudied; for Warren's relations with Grant, which felt their first strain in the Wilderness and at Spotsylvania, had been at the breaking point and Sheridan knew it." Colonel Theodore Lyman of

Meade's staff said that Warren had had many difficulties with Meade "from his tendency to substitute his own judgment for that of his commanding officer," adding: "It seemed that Grant was much moved against him by this" (*Meade's Headquarters*, pp. 333–334).

18. Badeau, Vol. III, pp. 500–503; Porter, *Campaigning with Grant*, pp. 442–443.

Chapter 23: OUR COUNTRYMEN AGAIN

1. Humphreys, pp. 363–369; General Hazard Stevens, "The Storming of the Lines at Petersburg," *MHSM Papers*, Vol. VI, pp. 412–413, 418, 422–423; Penrose G. Clark, *Red, White and Blue Badge*, p. 321; General Thomas W. Hyde, *Following the Greek Cross*, p. 252.
2. Letter of Grant to Julia Grant dated April 2, 1865, from the collection of Major General U. S. Grant III.
3. Porter, *Campaigning with Grant*, pp. 448–452; Grant, *Personal Memoirs*, Vol. II, pp. 458–459; General M. R. Morgan, "From City Point to Appomattox with General Grant," in the *Journal of the Military Service Institution of the United States*, September and October, 1907.
4. General John Gibbon, "Personal Recollections of Appomattox," in the April, 1902, *Century Magazine*, p. 936; Humphreys, pp. 373–374; Porter, op. cit., p. 452.
5. *O.R.*, Vol. XLVI, Pt. Three, p. 510.
6. Ibid., pp. 545, 556; Colonel Thomas L. Livermore, "The Generalship of the Appomattox Campaign," *MHSM Papers*, Vol. VI, pp. 490–493. For an extended discussion of Lee's inability to get supplies at Amelia Courthouse, see Freeman, *R. E. Lee*, Vol. IV, pp. 66–73.
7. *O.R.*, Vol. XLVI, Pt. Three, pp. 577, 582, 583; Porter, *Campaigning with Grant*, pp. 455–456; Grant, *Personal Memoirs*, Vol. II, p. 469; Sheridan, *Memoirs*, Vol. II, pp. 177–178.
8. Livermore, op. cit., pp. 496–497; Dr. John Herbert Claiborne, "Last Days of Lee and His Paladins," in George S. Bernard, *War Talks of Confederate Veterans*, pp. 255–256.
9. Lincoln's message to Grant is in *O.R.*, Vol. XLVI, Pt. Three, p. 593. Note that in his letter to Weitzel (same volume, p. 612) Lincoln was careful not to refer to the Virginia legislature as such but spoke of "the gentlemen who have acted as the legislature of Virginia in support of the Rebellion."
10. *O.R.*, Vol. XLVI, Pt. Three, pp. 594–595; Lyman, *Meade's Headquarters*, pp. 350–351; Basler, Vol. VIII, p. 392.
11. Humphreys, pp. 386–388, 391.
12. Horace Porter, "The Surrender at Appomattox Court House," *B. & L.*, Vol. IV, pp. 729–730; Gibbon, as in n. 4, above, p. 937; Badeau, Vol. III, pp. 588–589; General M. R. Morgan, as in n. 3 above.
13. Porter, op. cit., pp. 731–732; Lyman, *Meade's Headquarters*, p. 354; Meade, *Life and Letters*, Vol. II, pp. 269–270.
14. *O.R.*, Vol. XLVI, Pt. One, pp. 56–57; Porter, *Campaigning with Grant*, pp. 463–464; Sylvanus Cadwallader in the St. Louis *Globe-Democrat* for February 11, 1887; Badeau, Vol. III, pp. 593–594.
15. Badeau, Vol. III, pp. 599–601; Porter, *Campaigning with Grant*, pp. 466–467; ms., "Lee's Surrender," written by Colonel Orville Babcock and endorsed on February 10, 1877, in Grant's hand: "I have heard the foregoing read and can say that it conforms to my recollection of the events referred to." The manuscript is in the Orville E. Babcock Papers at the Chicago Historical Society.
16. John Russell Young, interview with Grant in the New York *Herald* for July 24, 1878; General John B. Gordon, *Reminiscences of the Civil War*, pp. 441–442; Porter, *Campaigning with Grant*, p. 468; Humphreys, p. 398.
17. Lyman, *Meade's Headquarters*, p. 357; Babcock's manuscript, "Lee's Surrender"; Colonel Charles Marshall, *An Aide-de-Camp of Lee*, pp. 268–269; pamphlet, Ely

S. Parker's *Narrative*, in the Benjamin Harrison Papers, Library of Congress; typescript, "Amos Webster on Grant," in the Hamlin Garland Papers, University of Southern California Library.

18. There are several versions of the surrender ceremony, differing here and there in minor details — the participants could not seem to agree on the exact moment when Grant's officers were brought into the room — but agreeing on the major points. This account has followed those of Marshall, Parker and Babcock, cited above, and has also made use of Horace Porter's well-known version in *B. & L.*, Vol. IV, pp. 735-742. The text of the letters Grant and Lee exchanged is in *O.R.*, Vol. XLVI, Pt. One, pp. 57-58.

19. Letter of Adam Badeau to the Editors, *Century Magazine*, dated September 2, 1885, in the Palmer Collection, Western Reserve Historical Society, Cleveland; Horace Porter, in *B. & L.*, Vol. IV, p. 744, and in *Campaigning with Grant*, p. 486.

Chapter 24: STRANGER IN A STRANGE LAND

1. Major Henry Lee, "The Last Campaign of the Army of the Potomac from a 'Mud-Crusher's' Point of View," pp. 8-9, in *War Papers of the California Commandery*, Military Order of the Loyal Legion of the United States; Lyman, *Meade's Headquarters*, p. 358; letter of Joseph Warren Keifer to Mrs. Keifer dated April 9, 1865, in the Library of Congress; Ely Parker's *Narrative*, pamphlet in the Benjamin Harrison papers, Library of Congress.

2. Ely Parker's *Narrative* gives a brief account of this meeting.

3. John Russell Young, interview with General Grant, in the New York *Herald* for July 24, 1878; Colonel Charles Marshall, *An Aide-de-Camp of Lee*, p. 275. In talking to Young, Grant did not mention having urged Lee to see Lincoln, and Horace Porter ("The Surrender at Appomattox Courthouse," *B. & L.*, Vol. IV, p. 746) says that Grant on his death bed could not remember making such a suggestion. Porter suggests that the story grew out of Grant's proposal that Lee talk to "the President" — meaning Davis, not Lincoln. However, Marshall is accepted as a reliable reporter on other aspects of the events at Appomattox, Lee would have been most unlikely to misunderstand Grant on a point like this, and this writer is inclined to accept Marshall's account of what Lee told him.

4. *Wartime Papers of R. E. Lee*, p. 939.

5. Letter of Adam Badeau to General James H. Wilson, in the Wilson Papers, Library of Congress; interview with Longstreet published in the New York *Times* for July 25, 1885.

6. On April 7 Grant had telegraphed Julia: "I think you had better return home as it may be 10 or 12 days before I return. I shall probably go to Danville before returning and will try in conjunction with Sherman to break up the only thing remaining to be done with Johnston." On the back of this telegram, in Julia's handwriting, is the note: 'I did not obey I waited and returned with the Victorious Genl. J.D.G."

7. General M. R. Morgan, "From City Point to Appomattox with General Grant," in the *Journal of the Military Service Institution of the United States*, September and October, 1907; Hamlin Garland, *Ulysses S. Grant: His Life and Character*, p. 314; *O.R.*, Vol. XLVI, Pt. Three, pp. 718, 726, 734; Porter, *Campaigning with Grant*, pp. 496-497.

8. Letter of Secretary of the Interior John P. Usher to Mrs. Usher, dated April 16, 1865, in Personal Papers, Miscellaneous, Box U, Library of Congress; Gideon Welles, *Diary*, Vol. II, pp. 280-282; John Russell Young, *Around the World with President Grant*, Vol. II, p. 356.

9. Noah Brooks, *Washington in Lincoln's Time*, p. 229; Porter, *Campaigning with Grant*, pp. 496-497; John Russell Young, op. cit., p. 356; Charles E. Bolles,

"General Grant and the News of Mr. Lincoln's Death," in *The Century*, June, 1890; *O.R.*, Vol. XLVI, Pt. Three, pp. 744–745, 756.

10. Young, op. cit., p. 354.

11. Letter of Francis Lieber to Halleck dated April 15, 1865, in the Lieber Collection, Huntington Library.

12. *O.R.*, Vol. XLVI, Pt. Three, pp. 757, 760, 762, 839.

13. Ibid., p. 787. Generations later it became the fashion to express amazement at the size of the shock wave that struck Washington when Lincoln was murdered. Men like Secretary Stanton have been extravagantly condemned because they did not immediately take a calm, rational, balanced view of the situation. These men suspected (for reasons that seemed perfectly good, at the time) a plot that never existed, they acted on their suspicions, and they have been denounced as monsters of hatred and prejudice. A more recent event in Dallas should provide a better understanding of the way men's minds and emotions can react when a wholly irrational act of violence kills a President.

14. Letter of Grant to Julia dated April 16, from the collection owned by Major General U. S. Grant III.

15. *O.R.*, Vol. XLVI, Pt. Three, p. 760; Noah Brooks, op. cit., pp. 233–234; Young, op. cit., pp. 354, 357.

16. *O.R.*, Vol. XLVII, Pt. Three, p. 237. The correspondence between Sherman and Johnston is in the same volume, pp. 206–207, 231.

17. Letter of Grant to Julia dated April 20, from the collection owned by Major General U. S. Grant III; *O.R.*, Vol. XLVII, Pt. Three, pp. 237, 243.

18. *O.R.*, Vol. XLVII, Pt. Three, pp. 243–244.

19. Ibid., p. 263; Benjamin T. Thomas and Harold Hyman, *Stanton: The Life and Times of Lincoln's Secretary of War*, pp. 405–407; Porter, *Campaigning with Grant*, p. 504; Appleton's *Annual Cyclopaedia for 1865*, pp. 800–801.

20. *O.R.*, Vol. XLVII, Pt. Three, p. 263; Grant's letter to Julia dated April 21, from the collection owned by Major General U. S. Grant III.

21. *O.R.*, Vol. XLVI, Pt. Three, p. 888; Vol. XLVII, Pt. Three, pp. 276, 286, 287.

22. Sherman, *Memoirs*, Vol. II, pp. 358–363; letter of Grant to Stanton dated April 24, from the Abraham Lincoln Bookshop, Chicago.

23. Letter of Grant to Julia dated April 25, from the *History of America in Documents*, catalogue, The Rosenbach Company, Pt. One, 1951.

24. Letter of Grant to Julia dated May 9, 1865, microfilm in the U. S. Grant Association from typescript in the Library of Congress.

25. Sheridan, *Memoirs*, Vol. II, pp. 206–208; typescript of Hamlin Garland's interview with Sheridan in the Garland Papers, Library of the University of Southern California.

26. Noah Brooks, *Washington in Lincoln's Time*, p. 284; F. Y. Hedley, *Marching Through Georgia*, p. 488; Augustus Gaylord, "The Wisconsin Adjutant General's Office," in Vol. II, *War Papers* of the Wisconsin Commandery, Military Order of the Loyal Legion of the United States.

Bibliography

MANUSCRIPT SOURCES

Adams, Charles Francis, Jr. Diary, Massachusetts Historical Society.
Atkinson, Mrs. E. K. Letters, Southern Historical Collection, University of North Carolina Library.
Babcock, Orville E. Papers, Chicago Historical Society.
Badeau, Adam. Letter to James H. Wilson, Princeton University Library.
Banks, N. P. Papers, Essex Institute Library, Salem, Mass.
Barlow, Francis Channing, Papers, Massachusetts Historical Society.
Barlow, S. L. M. Papers, Huntington Library.
Blair Family Papers, Library of Congress.
Cadwallader, Sylvanus. Papers, Library of Congress.
Comly, James H. Papers in the Collection, Ohio State Museum.
Comstock, Cyrus B. Papers, Library of Congress.
Connor, Selden. Letter, Brown University Library.
Coppett, Andre de. Collection, Princeton University Library.
Dana, Charles A. Papers, Library of Congress.
Dana, Richard Henry, Jr. Papers, Massachusetts Historical Society.
Dawes, Rufus. Papers, from Rufus D. Beach and Ralph G. Newman.
Dodge, General Grenville M. Typescript biography, Iowa State Department of History and Archives.
The Eldridge Collection. Papers, Huntington Library.
Fox, Gustavus V. Correspondence, New York Historical Society.
Garland, Hamlin. Papers, American Literature Collection, University of Southern California Library.
Grant, U. S. Letters, Microfilms in the U. S. Grant Association, Carbondale, Ill.
Grant, U. S. Letter to Frank Blair, owned by Claude K. Rowland of St. Louis.
Grant, U. S. Letters to Julia Grant, collection owned by Major General U. S. Grant III.
Grant, U. S. Letter to E. M. Stanton, from the Abraham Lincoln Bookshop, Chicago, Ill.
Grant, U. S. Papers, Huntington Library.
Grant, U. S. Papers, Illinois State Historical Library.
Grant, U. S. Papers, Missouri Historical Society.
Harris, Colonel William Hamilton. Diary, Virginia State Historical Society; original in the New York Public Library.
Harrison, Benjamin. Papers, Library of Congress.
Hitchcock, Ethan Allen. Diaries, Gilcrease Museum, Tulsa, Okla.
Howard, General O. O. Letter to Senator Henry Wilson, Department of Lincolniana, Lincoln Memorial University.
Humphreys, General A. A. Papers, Historical Society of Pennsylvania.
Jones, J. Russell. Typescript biography, owned by George Russell Jones of Chicago.
Keifer, Joseph Warren. Letter, Library of Congress.
Keleher, James. Letter, Huntington Library.
Lee, Robert E. Papers, Chicago Historical Society.

Lewis, Lloyd. Various letters and papers in the collection owned by Mrs. Kathryn Lewis, Chicago.

Lieber, Francis. Collection, Huntington Library.

Lincoln, R. T. Collection, Library of Congress.

Massachusetts Commandery, Military Order of the Loyal Legion of the United States. Papers, Houghton Library, Harvard University.

McClernand, John A. Papers, microfilms in the U. S. Grant Association.

Meade, General George G. Papers, Historical Society of Pennsylvania.

Meigs, Montgomery C. Papers, Library of Congress.

Murray, George. Letter from John Merryweather of Chicago and Highland Park, Ill.

Oglesby, Richard. Papers, Illinois State Historical Library.

The Palmer Collection, in the Western Reserve Historical Society.

Patrick, General Marsena M. Diary, Library of Congress.

Pehrson, Paul C. Thesis: "James Harrison Wilson: a Partial Biography," Southern Illinois University.

Porter, David D. Papers, Huntington Library.

Porter, Horace, Papers, Library of Congress.

Rawlins, John A. Papers, Chicago Historical Society.

Ring, G. P. Diary, Southern Historical Collection, Confederate Memorial Hall, New Orleans, La.

Roman, Alfred. Papers, Library of Congress.

Rose, Luther A. Diary, Library of Congress.

Rosecrans, William S. Papers, Library of the University of California at Los Angeles.

Rowley, W. R. Papers, Illinois State Historical Library.

Sanborn, Fred. Mss. "Narrative and Scrapbook," Library of Congress.

Seward, William H. Collection, Rush Rhees Library, University of Rochester.

Sherman, William T. Papers, Huntington Library.

Sherman, William T. Papers, Library of Congress.

Smith, William F. Papers, in the collection of Walter Wilgus, Arlington, Va.

Smith, William W. Diary, Library of Congress.

Stanton, Edwin M. Papers, Library of Congress.

Usher, John P. Personal Papers, Library of Congress.

Walker, C. I. War Letters, Eugene C. Barker Texas History Center, University of Texas.

Warren, G. K. Papers, Manuscripts and History Section, New York State Library, Albany, N.Y.

Washburne, Elihu B. Papers, Library of Congress.

Wilson, James H. Papers, Library of Congress.

NEWSPAPERS AND MAGAZINES

Use was made of numerous newspaper and magazine files. Some of these were in the immense set of clippings collected by Lloyd Lewis; others were consulted in various libraries. Newspapers and magazines quoted in the text include:

Chicago *Times,* Chicago *Tribune,* Cincinnati *Commercial,* Jackson (Miss.) *State Times,* New York *Herald,* New York *Times,* New York *Tribune,* New York *World,* Richmond *Dispatch,* St. Louis *Globe-Democrat,* Vicksburg *Evening Post,* Washington *Post.*

Also *The American Historical Review, Army and Navy Journal, Century Magazine, Iowa Historical Record, Journal of the Illinois State Historical Society, Journal of the Military Service Institution of the United States, Journal of Southern History, Lincoln Lore, The Mississippi Valley Historical Review, North American Review, Proceedings of the Massachusetts Historical Society, The South Atlantic Quarterly.*

Also various issues of the *Papers* of the Southern Historical Society, and the fourteen volume edition of the *Papers* of the Military Historical Society of Massachusetts. In addition, use has been made of the various volumes published by the State Commanderies of the Military Order of the Loyal Legion of the United States. Also, the several issues of *History of America in Documents*, catalogue of the Rosenbach Company, Philadelphia.

BOOKS

A principal reliance in any study of the Civil War is of course the massive War Department compendium, *The War of the Rebellion: A Compilation of the Official Records of the Union and Confederate Armies*. This is cited in the notes simply as *O.R.;* unless otherwise indicated, the volumes are from Series 1. Use also has been made of the companion *Official Records of the Union and Confederate Navies during the War of the Rebellion*.

Other books consulted include these:

BOOKS RELATING DIRECTLY TO U. S. GRANT

Badeau, Adam. *Military History of Ulysses S. Grant.* 3 vols. New York, 1868.

Cadwallader, Sylvanus. *Three Years with Grant.* Edited by Benjamin P. Thomas. New York, 1955.

Church, William Conant. *Ulysses S. Grant and the Period of National Preservation and Reconstruction.* New York, 1897.

Conger, A. L. *The Rise of U. S. Grant.* New York, 1931.

Coolidge, Louis A. *Ulysses S. Grant.* Boston and New York, 1917.

Coppee, Henry. *Life and Services of General U. S. Grant.* Chicago, 1868.

Cramer, Jesse Grant, ed. *Letters of Ulysses S. Grant to His Father and His Youngest Sister.* New York, 1912.

Dana, Charles A. and James H. Wilson. *The Life of Ulysses S. Grant.* Springfield, 1868.

Eaton, John. *Grant, Lincoln and the Freedmen.* New York, 1907.

Fuller, J. F. C. *The Generalship of Ulysses S. Grant.* London, 1929.

Garland, Hamlin. *Ulysses S. Grant: His Life and Character.* New York, 1898.

Grant, U. S. *Personal Memoirs of U. S. Grant.* 2 vols. New York, 1885.

Hesseltine, William B. *Ulysses S. Grant, Politician.* New York, 1935.

Lewis, Lloyd. *Captain Sam Grant.* Boston, 1950.

McMaster, John B. *The Life, Memoirs, Military Career and Death of General Grant.* Philadelphia, 1885.

Porter, General Horace. *Campaigning with Grant.* New York, 1897.

Richardson, Albert D. *A Personal History of Ulysses S. Grant.* Hartford, 1868.

Ringwalt, J. L. *Anecdotes of General Grant.* Philadelphia, 1886.

Wilson, James Grant. *The Life and Campaigns of General Grant.* New York, 1897.

———, ed. *General Grant's Letters to a Friend, 1861–1880.* New York, 1897.

Young, John Russell. *Around the World with General Grant.* 2 vols. New York, 1879.

GENERAL WORKS

Agassiz, George A., ed. *Meade's Headquarters, 1863–65; Letters of Colonel Theodore Lyman.* Boston, 1922.

Alexander, E. P. *Military Memoirs of a Confederate.* New York, 1907.

The American Annual Cyclopaedia and Register of Important Events (Appleton's Cyclopaedia). New York, 1866.

Ammen, Rear Admiral Daniel. *The Old Navy and the New.* Philadelphia, 1891.

Basler, Roy, ed. *The Collected Works of Abraham Lincoln.* 8 vols. Rutgers, N.J., 1953.

Brinton, John H. *Personal Memoirs of John H. Brinton, Major and Surgeon, U.S.V.* New York, 1914.

Buck, Irving. *Cleburne and His Command.* Jackson, Tenn., 1951.

Burr, Frank A. *Life and Achievements of James Adams Beaver.* Philadelphia, 1882.

Beale, Howard K., ed. *The Diary of Gideon Welles.* 3 vols. New York, 1960.

Private and Official Correspondence of Benjamin F. Butler. 5 vols. Norwood, Mass., 1917.

Chetlain, Augustus L. *Recollections of Seventy Years.* Galena, Ill., 1899.

Chittenden, L. E. *Recollections of President Lincoln and His Administration.* New York, 1891.

Cist, Henry M. *The Army of the Cumberland.* New York, 1890.

Cleaves, Freeman. *Meade of Gettysburg.* Norman, Okla., 1960.

Confederate Military History. 12 vols. Atlanta, 1899.

Connolly, James A. *Three Years in the Army of the Cumberland.* Bloomington, Ind., 1959.

Coulter, E. M. *The Confederate States of America.* Baton Rouge, 1950.

Cox, Jacob D. *Military Reminiscences of the Civil War.* 2 vols. New York, 1900.

———. *The March to the Sea, Franklin and Nashville.* New York, 1913.

Croushare, James H., ed. *A Volunteer's Adventures* by John W. De Forest. New Haven, 1946.

Dana, Charles A. *Recollections of the Civil War.* New York, 1902.

Dawes, Rufus. *Service with the 6th Wisconsin Volunteers.* Marietta, Ohio, 1890.

Doan, Isaac. *Reminiscences of the Chattanooga Campaign.* Richmond, Ind., 1894.

Dodge, Major General Grenville. *Personal Recollections.* Council Bluffs, Ia., 1914.

Dowdey, Clifford and Louis H. Manarin, eds. *The Wartime Papers of Robert E. Lee.* Boston, 1961.

Early, Lieutenant General Jubal. *Autobiographical Sketch and Narrative of the War Between the States.* Philadelphia, 1912.

Eaton, Clement. *A History of the Southern Confederacy.* New York, 1954.

Fox, Gustavus V. *Confidential Correspondence of G. V. Fox, 1861–65.* New York, 1920.

Freeman, Douglas Southall. *R. E. Lee.* 4 vols. New York, 1935.

——— and Grady McWhiney, eds. *Lee's Dispatches.* New York, 1957.

Gordon, General John B. *Reminiscences of the Civil War.* New York, 1904.

Govan, Gilbert and James W. Livingood. *A Different Valor: The Story of General Joseph E. Johnston.* Indianapolis, 1956.

Greene, Francis Vinton. *The Mississippi.* New York, 1884.

Heitman, Francis B. *Historical Register and Dictionary of the United States Army.* 2 vols. Washington, 1903.

Henry, Robert Selph. *First with the Most: Forrest.* Indianapolis, 1944.

Hesseltine, William B. *Civil War Prisons.* Columbus, Ohio, 1930.

———. *Ulysses S. Grant, Politician.* New York, 1935.

Horn, Stanley. *The Army of Tennessee.* Indianapolis, 1941.

Howe, Mark DeWolfe, ed. *Home Letters of General Sherman.* New York, 1909.

———, ed. *Touched with Fire: Civil War Letters and Diary of Oliver Wendell Holmes, Jr.* Cambridge, Mass., 1946.

Humphreys, General A. A. *The Virginia Campaign of '64 and '65.* New York, 1883.

Hunt, Gaillard. *Israel, Elihu and Cadwallader Washburne: A Chapter in American Biography.* New York, 1925.

Hyde, General Thomas W. *Following the Greek Cross; or, Memories of the Sixth Army Corps.* Boston, 1894.

Johnson, Ludwell H. *The Red River Campaign.* Baltimore, 1958.

Johnson, R. U. and C. C. Buel, eds. *Battles and Leaders of the Civil War.* 4 vols. New York, 1884–1887.

Joint Committee on the Conduct of the War. *Report.* 3 vols. Washington, 1863; and 3 vols. plus supplements, Washington, 1865.

Kellogg, Sanford C. *The Shenandoah Valley and Virginia, 1861 to 1865.* New York, 1903.

Kirwan, A. D., ed. *Johnny Green of the Orphan Brigade: The Journal of a Confederate Soldier* by John Williams Green. Lexington, 1956.

Lamers, William M. *The Edge of Glory: A Biography of General William S. Rosecrans.* New York, 1961.

Lewis, Lloyd. *Sherman: Fighting Prophet.* New York, 1932.

Livermore, Mary A. *My Story of the War.* Hartford, 1888.

Livermore, T. L. *Numbers and Losses in the Civil War.* Boston and New York, 1900.

Long, A. L. *Memoirs of Robert E. Lee.* New York, 1886.

Mahan, A. T. *The Gulf and Inland Waters.* New York, 1883.

Maurice, Sir Frederick, ed. *An Aide-de-Camp of Lee,* by Charles Marshall. Boston, 1927.

McClellan, Carswell. *The Personal Memoirs and Military History of U. S. Grant versus the Record of the Army of the Potomac.* Boston, 1887.

McClure, Alexander K. *Recollections of Half a Century.* Philadelphia, 1892.

———. *Abraham Lincoln and Men of War Times.* Philadelphia, 1892.

McKinney, Francis F. *Education in Violence: The Life of George H. Thomas.* Detroit, 1961.

Meade, George. *The Life and Letters of George Gordon Meade.* 2 vols. New York, 1913.

Mitgang, Herbert, ed. *Washington in Lincoln's Time* by Noah Brooks. New York, 1958.

The Correspondence of John Lothrop Motley. 2 vols. 1889.

Nevins, Allan, ed. *A Diary of Battle: The Personal Journals of Colonel Charles S. Wainwright, 1861–65.* New York, 1962.

Nicolay, Helen. *Lincoln's Secretary: A Biography of John G. Nicolay.* New York, 1949.

Nicolay, John G. and John Hay. *Abraham Lincoln: A History.* 10 vols. New York, 1886–1890.

Page, Charles A. *Letters of a War Correspondent.* Boston, 1899.

Piatt, Donn. *Memories of the Men Who Saved the Union.* New York, 1887.

Pleasants, Henry, Jr. *The Tragedy of the Crater.* Boston, 1938.

Pond, George E. *The Shenandoah Valley in 1864.* New York, 1885.

Powell, Lieutenant Colonel William H. *The Fifth Army Corps.* New York, 1896.

Porter, Admiral David. *Incidents and Anecdotes of the Civil War.* New York, 1885.

Porter, Elsie. *An American Soldier and Diplomat, Horace Porter.* New York, 1927.

Rhodes, James Ford. *History of the United States from the Compromise of 1850.* New York, 1906.

Rusling, James R. *Men and Things I Saw in Civil War Days.* New York, 1899.

Sandburg, Carl. *Abraham Lincoln: The War Years.* 4 vols. New York, 1939.

Schaff, Morris. *The Battle of the Wilderness.* Boston, 1910.

Schofield, Lieutenant General John M. *Forty-six Years in the Army.* New York, 1897.

Shanks, William F. G. *Personal Recollections of Distinguished Generals.* New York, 1866.

Shannon, Fred A. *The Organization and Administration of the Union Army, 1861–1865.* 2 vols. Cleveland, 1928.

Sheridan, General Philip. *Personal Memoirs of P. H. Sheridan.* 2 vols. New York, 1891.

Sherman, General W. T. *The Memoirs of General William T. Sherman.* 2 vols. New York, 1893.

Stevens, George T. *Three Years in the Sixth Corps.* New York, 1870.

Smith, General W. F. *From Chattanooga to Petersburg Under Generals Grant and Butler.* Boston and New York, 1893.
Starr, Louis M. *Bohemian Brigade.* New York, 1954.
Stoddard, William O., Jr. *William O. Stoddard, Lincoln's Third Secretary.* New York, 1955.
Swiggett, Howard, ed. *John B. Jones: A Rebel War Clerk's Diary.* 2 vols. New York, 1935.
Tarbell, Ida M. *The Life of President Lincoln.* 2 vols. New York, 1900.
Taylor, E. G. *Gouverneur Kemble Warren: The Life and Letters of an American Soldier.* Boston and New York, 1932.
Thomas, Benjamin P. *Abraham Lincoln.* New York, 1952.
—— and Harold Hyman. *Stanton: The Life and Times of Lincoln's Secretary of War.* New York, 1962.
Tyler, Mason Whiting. *Recollections of the Civil War.* New York, 1912.
Van Horne, Thomas B. *Life of General George H. Thomas.* New York, 1882.
——. *History of the Army of the Cumberland.* 2 vols. Cincinnati, 1875.
Villard, Henry. *Memoirs of Henry Villard, Journalist and Financier.* 2 vols. Boston, 1904.
Walker, Francis A. *History of the Second Army Corps.* New York, 1886.
Wallace, Lew. *An Autobiography.* 2 vols. New York and London, 1906.
Williams, T. Harry. *P. G. T. Beauregard: Napoleon in Gray.* Baton Rouge, 1954.
Wilson, James H. *Under the Old Flag.* 2 vols. New York, 1912.
——. *The Life of John A. Rawlins.* New York, 1916.
Young, John Russell. *Men and Memories.* 2 vols. New York, 1901.

At various places in the footnotes this writer has cited his own books to indicate where a reader may find more detailed treatment of matters referred to in this text only briefly. It hardly seemed proper to list these as part of the source materials drawn on, but it may be as well to identify them for the record. They are *Glory Road* (New York, 1952); *A Stillness at Appomattox* (New York, 1953); *Grant Moves South* (Boston, 1960), and *Terrible Swift Sword* (New York, 1963).

REGIMENTAL HISTORIES, SOLDIERS' MEMOIRS, REMINISCENCES, ETC.

To simplify the reader's search for the account of a given unit, entries are listed by title rather than by the name of the author.

The Annals of the War, written by Leading Participants. Philadelphia, 1879.
Army Life: from a Soldier's Journal, by A. O. Marshall. Joliet, Ill., 1884.
Army Life of an Illinois Soldier; Letters and Diaries of the late Charles H. Wills, compiled and published by his sister. Washington, 1906.
Army Memoirs of Lucius W. Barber, Company D, 15th Illinois Infantry. Chicago, 1894.
An Artilleryman's Diary, by Jenkin Lloyd Jones. Madison, Wis., 1914.
Civil War Papers read before the Commandery of the State of Massachusetts, Military Order of the Loyal Legion of the United States. 2 vols. Boston, 1900.
Downing's War Diary, by Sergeant Alexander Downing, edited by Olynthus B. Clark. Des Moines, 1916.
Events of the Civil War, by General Edward Bouton. Los Angeles, 1906.
Experiences in the War of the Great Rebellion, by Edmund Newsome. Carbondale, Ill., 1876.
Fifteen Years Ago; or, the Patriotism of Will County, by George H. Woodruff. Joliet, Ill., 1876.

The 41st Ohio Veteran Volunteer Infantry, by R. L. Kimberly and Ephraim S. Holloway. Cleveland, 1897.

The 44th Indiana Volunteers in the Rebellion, by J. H. Rerick. Lagrange, Ind., 1880.

The 48th in the War, by Oliver Christian Bosbyshell. Philadelphia, 1895.

Glimpses of the Nation's Struggle; papers read before the Minnesota Commandery, Military Order of the Loyal Legion of the United States. 6 vols. St. Paul and Minneapolis, 1887–1909.

Heavy Guns and Light of the Fourth New York Heavy Artillery, by Hyland C. Kirk. New York, 1890.

History of the Corn Exchange Regiment, 118th Pennsylvania Volunteers, by the Survivors' Association. Philadelphia, 1888.

History of Fuller's Ohio Brigade, by Charles H. Smith. Cleveland, 1909.

A History of the Ninth Regiment Illinois Volunteer Infantry, by Marion Morrison. Monmouth, Ill., 1864.

History of the 2nd Iowa Cavalry, by Lyman B. Pierce. Burlington, Ia., 1864.

History of the 6th Iowa Infantry, by Henry H. Wright. Iowa City, 1923.

History of the 6th Regiment Indiana Veteran Volunteer Infantry, by C. C. Briant. Indianapolis, 1891.

History of the 7th Regiment Illinois Volunteer Infantry, by D. Lieb Ambrose. Springfield, 1868.

History of the 12th Massachusetts Volunteers, by Benjamin F. Cook. Boston, 1882.

History of the 15th Regiment Iowa Veteran Volunteer Infantry, by William W. Belknap. Keokuk, Ia., 1887.

History of the 15th Regiment New Jersey Volunteers, by Alanson A. Haines. New York, 1883.

History of the 16th Battery of Ohio Volunteer Light Artillery, compiled by a committee. n.p., 1906.

History of the 21st Regiment Ohio Volunteer Infantry, by Captain S. S. Canfield. Toledo, 1893.

History of the 22nd Massachusetts Infantry, by John L. Parker and Robert G. Carter. Boston, 1887.

History of the 33rd Regiment Illinois Veteran Volunteer Infantry, by Isaac H. Elliott and Virgil G. Way. Gibson City, Ill., 1902.

History of the 50th Regiment Illinois Volunteer Infantry, by Charles F. Hubert. Kansas City, 1894.

History of the 51st Indiana Veteran Volunteer Infantry, by William R. Hartpence. Cincinnati, 1894.

History of the 53rd Regiment Ohio Volunteer Infantry, by John K. Duke. Portsmouth, Ohio, 1900.

History of the 68th Regiment Indiana Volunteer Infantry, by Edwin W. High. Metamora, 1902.

History of the 74th Illinois, by Hosmer P. Holland. Rockford, Ill., 1903.

History of the 77th Illinois Volunteer Infantry, by Lieutenant W. H. Bentley. Peoria, 1883.

History of the 78th Regiment Ohio Veteran Volunteer Infantry, by the Reverend Thomas M. Stevenson. Zanesville, Ohio, 1865.

History of the 83rd Regiment Indiana Volunteer Infantry, by Joseph Grecian. Cincinnati, 1865.

Marching Through Georgia, by F. Y. Hedley. Chicago, 1890.

Memoirs of a Volunteer by John Beatty, ed. by Henry S. Ford. New York, 1946.

Memoirs of the War, by Captain Ephraim A. Wilson. Cleveland, 1893.

Military Essays and Recollections; papers read before the Commandery of the State of Illinois, Military Order of the Loyal Legion of the United States. 4 vols. Chicago, 1894–1907.

Pen and Powder, by Franc B. Wilkie. Boston, 1888.

Personal Memoirs of John H. Brinton, Major and Surgeon, U.S.V., 1861–1865. New York, 1914.
Personal Recollections of the War; war papers of the District of Columbia Commandery, Military Order of the Loyal Legion of the United States. Washington, 1895–1905.
Personal Recollections of the War and the Rebellion; addresses delivered before the New York Commandery, Military Order of the Loyal Legion of the United States. New York, 1891.
Printed Proceedings of the Society of the Army of the Tennessee; pamphlets covering meetings in the years 1866, 1885, 1897, 1906, 1907, 1908.
Recollections of the Civil War, by Oran Perry. Pamphlet in the Lloyd Lewis Papers.
Recollections with the Third Iowa Regiment, by S. W. Thompson. Cincinnati, 1864.
Red, White and Blue Badge; Pennsylvania Veteran Volunteers, by Penrose G. Clark. Harrisburg, 1911.
Report of the 29th Reunion, Society of the Army of the Potomac. n.p., 1898.
The Secret Service, the Field, the Dungeon and the Escape, by Albert D. Richardson. Hartford, Conn., 1865.
Sketches of War History, 1861–1865; papers read before the Ohio Commandery, Military Order of the Loyal Legion of the United States. 5 vols. Cincinnati, 1888–1903.
A Soldier of the Cumberland, by Mead Holmes, Jr., Boston, c. 1864.
The Story of the 55th Regiment Illinois Volunteer Infantry, by a Committee. Clinton, Mass., 1897.
The Story of the Sherman Brigade, by Wilbur F. Hinman. Alliance, Ohio, 1897.
The Story of a Thousand; being a History of the Service of the 105th Ohio Volunteer Infantry, by Albion W. Tourgee. Buffalo, 1896.
The 35th Ohio Regiment; a Narrative of Service, by F. W. Keil. Fort Wayne, 1894.
War Memoranda, by Colonel Charles Whittlesey. Cleveland, 1884.
War Papers read before the Indiana Commandery, Military Order of the Loyal Legion of the United States. Indianapolis, 1898.
War Papers read before the Commandery of the State of Maine, Military Order of the Loyal Legion of the United States. Portland, 1898.
War Papers read before the Commandery of the State of Wisconsin, Military Order of the Loyal Legion of the United States. Milwaukee, 1891.
War Papers of the California Commandery, Military Order of the Loyal Legion of the United States.
War Papers and Personal Reminiscences, 1861–1865, papers read before the Commandery of the State of Missouri, Military Order of the Loyal Legion of the United States. St. Louis, 1892.
War Pictures, by the Reverend J. B. Rogers. Chicago, 1863.
War Sketches and Incidents; papers of the Iowa Commandery, Military Order of the Loyal Legion of the United States. 2 vols. Des Moines, 1898.
War Talks; papers of the Kansas Commandery, Military Order of the Loyal Legion of the United States. Leavenworth, 1894.
War Talks of Confederate Veterans, by George S. Bernard. Petersburg, Va. 1892.

Acknowledgments

I is not possible to write a book of this kind without becoming deeply indebted to a great many people — manuscript collectors, librarians and curators, historians, research assistants, experts of high and low degree, and so on through the almost endless list of people who enable a biographer to get his job done. To list by name all of those who have been helpful in connection with the preparation of this book would take more space than is available here; about the best that can be done is to make this general acknowledgment of invaluable help graciously given.

In a few cases the weight of my indebtedness requires a more specific word of thanks.

First of all, there is Mrs. Kathryn Lewis of Chicago, who permitted me to use the extensive file of notes on U. S. Grant and the Civil War period collected over many years by her husband, the late Lloyd Lewis. To a great extent, this book has used that collection as its foundation, and it has been an honest attempt to complete the work so ably begun by Lloyd Lewis in *Captain Sam Grant*. For letting me have a part in that project and work with those papers I shall always be grateful to Mrs. Lewis.

I am almost equally indebted to E. B. Long, of Oak Park, Illinois, one of the most industrious and well informed of all Civil War scholars. His tireless research work and his vast knowledge of the period under study have been invaluable to me. In mentioning his help I must also include the work done by his charming wife Barbara.

Major General U. S. Grant III, U. S. Army retired, grandson of the Civil War general, permitted me to read and to use wartime letters written by his grandfather to Julia Dent Grant.

Dr. John Simon, of the U. S. Grant Association, Carbondale, Illinois, was of help on occasions and in ways too numerous to mention.

Special thanks are also due to Clyde Walton, Margaret Flint and Paul Spence, of the Illinois State Historical Library; and to Ralph Newman, proprietor of the Abraham Lincoln Bookshop, Chicago, and to his assistants, Margaret April and Richard Clark.

Dr. Allan Nevins permitted me to examine some of his notes. Lloyd A. Dunlap of the Library of Congress deserves my thanks for special search among the papers of John A. Rawlins. To Edwin C. Bearss and Elden Billings, of Washington; to Paul C. Pehrson, former graduate student at Southern Illinois University; to Harvey Snitiker, who examined much Grant material for me; to staff members of the manuscript division of the Library of Congress, of the Newberry Library and the Library of the Chicago Historical Society, and of the Huntington Library at San Marino, California; and, finally, to Caroline Evans, Mary Dawn Earley and Patricia Grellier for highly competent help in preparing the final draft of this manuscript — to all of these must go my sincere thanks.

Index

Index

Raleigh, North Carolina, 101, 168, 406, 483
Rankin's Ferry, 50
Rapidan River, 153–155, 179, 182, 184, 200, 206–208, 256; Grant crosses at Germanna Ford, 181
Rappahannock River, 208
Rappahannock Station, 183
Rawlins, Emily, daughter of John, 28
Rawlins, Emily Smith, 28–29
Rawlins, James, son of John, 28
Rawlins, James D., 28
Rawlins, Jennie, 28
Rawlins, Lieut. Col. (later Brig. Gen.) John A., 25–27, 37, 114, 115, 150, 180, 256, 317, 342, 440; Grant's emissary to Washington, 3–7; described, 4; as brigadier general of volunteers, 6; and Mary Emma Hurlbut, 28–29, 65, 91, 115–117, 128, 136, 147, 150, 151, 163, 174, 282, 335, 404; his fear of alcohol, 28, 128; describes Bridgeport-Chattanooga supply road, 38; arrives in Chattanooga, 40; on army transportation problems, 56; and Grant's drinking, 65–67, 117, 136, 334–335; praises Grant's victory at Chattanooga, 91; expresses Grant's political views to Wilson, 108; and official report of Chattanooga, 116; his health, 116–117, 125, 136; his anxiety to protect Grant, 116–118, 133, 136; in Washington with Grant, 125, 128, 132; as army chief of staff, 135–137; confers with Grant at Nashville, 137; impression of Butler, 147; appraisal of W. F. Smith's plans, 151–152; describes political limitations on Grant's moves, 174; at Wilderness, 189; at Cold Harbor, 267–268; and march to the sea, 388, 390; and Lee's surrender terms, 460, 464
Rawlins, Mrs. John A. See Hurlbut, Mary Emma
Ream's Station, Virginia, 352
Red River campaign, 100, 101, 112, 141–142, 152, 302; and Banks's political ambitions, 110; supersedes Sabine Pass operation, 168; handicaps Grant's western plan, 172–175
Republican Party, 157, 338–339; and election of 1864, 355–356, 377
restoration. See Civil government, restoration of
reunion, 339, 419–422, 438
Reynolds, Gen. Joseph J., 40, 69
Richardson, Albert D., 147–148

Richmond, Virginia, 101–102, 104, 151, 168, 335; and Butler's force, 148–149, 153, 169, 205–206, 217–218, 274; time schedule for, 152–153; supply problems, 169, 206, 276–278; defense of, 294, 367, 429; Negro regiments in capture of, 411; destruction of roads to, 430; fall of, 449, 450
Richmond & Danville Railroad, 277, 296, 316, 377, 430, 432, 449, 450
Richmond Dispatch, 72, 87
Richmond, Fredericksburg & Potomac Railroad, 248, 251
Richmond–Petersburg Railroad. See Petersburg–Richmond Railroad
Ricketts, Gen. James B.: at Wilderness, 182, 185, 200; and defense of Washington, 310–312
Riddell's Shop, 281
Rio Grande River, 100, 152
River Queen, presidential steamer, 434, 436, 437
Roanoke River, 151, 449
Robinson, Gen. John, 190; at Spotsylvania, 213
Rockfish Gap, 298
Rosecrans, Gen. William S., 29–31, 47–48, 62, 68, 71, 114, 142, 152, 474; described, 30; and Chickamauga, 31–33, 196; relieved of command, 34–35, 91; meets with Grant in Stevenson, 36; warns Hooker about Bridgeport-Chattanooga supply road, 38; delays sending troops to front, 164
Rossville Gap, Georgia, 78
Rowanty Creek, 352
Rowley, Col. William R., 335, 341, 349
Rusling, James F., 104–105, 113

Sabine Crossroads, Louisiana, 173
Sabine Pass, Texas, 25, 168
sabotage, 350
St. Charles Hotel, New Orleans, 22
St. Louis, Missouri, 49, 269–270
Salisbury, North Carolina, 407
Sanitary Commission Fair: at St. Louis, 269–270; at Philadelphia, 295
Savannah, Georgia, 168, 385, 387, 389, 394, 395, 405; Sherman captures, 401
Savannah River, 386, 387
Sayler's Creek, Virginia, 454
Schaff, Lieut. Morris, 160
Schofield, Maj. Gen. John M., 11, 100, 115, 398; on Grant's self-confidence, 135, 136; at Franklin, Tennessee, 395;

and crossing of the James, 281, 282, 284; and Petersburg, 291–293, 324, 351–352, 367; on Grant's popularity, 340–341; and Hatcher's Run, 381; in war's final offensive, 439, 441–444; relieved of command, 445

Washburn, Maj. Gen. Cadwallader C., 26–27

Washburne, Elihu, Congressman from Illinois, 3, 8, 26–27, 180, 274; Grant's correspondence with, 7, 71, 103, 354–355; and Grant's lieutenant generalcy, 103, 118, 120–121; Lincoln consults, 110–111; accompanies Grant to Old Point Comfort, 150; reports victory at Spotsylvania, 222–223, 236; Grant assures of favorable balance in Virginia campaign, 301–302; and Meade's promotion, 409; Grant's appraisal of Southern dissolution to, 426

Washington, D.C., 132; Grant inspects defenses of, 127; and Army of Potomac, 148, 163; and Early's march to Potomac, 310–316, 318, 346; disorganization of command in, 313, 317–318, 320, 332; final troop review in, 490–492. *See also* White House

Wauhatchie, 46, 50, 53, 73

Wautauga River, 48

Waynesboro, Virginia, 425–427

Webster, Col. Amos, 464

Weed, Thurlow, 337–339

Weitzel, Gen. Godfrey, 392–394, 401–403, 432, 439; and Twenty-fifth Corps, 411; enters Richmond, 450, 454

Weldon, North Carolina, 151

Weldon Railroad, 296, 297, 316, 351–352, 359, 361, 365; and Wilmington offensive, 386

Welles, Gideon, 4–6, 126, 247; and Fort Fisher offensive, 402; proposes resumption of North-South trade, 474

West Virginia, 58–59, 142, 153, 248

Western Atlantic Railroad, Bragg's supply source, 59

Whaley, K. V., Congressman of West Virginia, 144

White House (Washington), 139; Grant commissioned general-in-chief at, 124–128, 132; Lincoln's funeral at, 479

White House, Virginia, 253, 255, 257, 269, 273, 281, 286; reached by Sheridan, 430

White Oak Road, 439, 442

White Oak Swamp, 281, 282, 294, 429

Wilcox Landing, 280–281

Wilderness, battle of the, 179–201, 242, 245, 254, 256, 285, 440; Grant joins march, 180; geography of, 181, 186, 196; strategy for, 182, 188, 193–194, 199; Federal position, 183–184; Confederate position, 184–185; time lag, 187; battle begins, 188; Federal losses, 189–190, 192 (officers), 193, 203, 204, 207; Longstreet's counteroffensive, 196–197, 222; Confederate losses (estimated), 204; Federals consider as victory, 207–208, 215

Wilderness Tavern, 181–185, 190, 194; Sixth Corps division near, 190

Willard's Hotel, Washington, 124, 161

Willcox, Maj. Gen. Orlando B., 96; at Wilderness, 194–196, 199; at Spotsylvania, 229

Williams, Gen. Seth, 472

Williamsburg, Virginia, 205

Williamsport, Pennsylvania, 342

Willich, Gen. August, 82

Wilmington, North Carolina, 101, 296, 386, 387, 392–393, 405–406; failure of expedition, 401–402; and Schofield, 410, 416, 426

Wilson, Senator Henry, 8, 55–56; and Rawlins's appointment to chief of staff, 135; and confirmation of Meade's promotion, 409

Wilson, Col. (later Brig. Gen.) James Harrison, 27, 28, 33, 94, 108, 115, 116, 256, 284, 396, 418, 430, 488; describes Grant's reception in Chattanooga, 40; and Mobile offensive, 101, 102, 407, 428; and Meade, 130–131, 150; and Rawlins's promotion, 135–136; and Smith's "three propositions," 151–152; and Army of Potomac's cavalry, 166; at Wilderness, 186; and Spotsylvania, 211–213; at Cold Harbor, 268; crosses Chickahominy, 281; and the railroads, 296–297; congratulates Smith on Butler's relief, 329; and stories of Grant's drinking, 334; takes Selma, 480

Winchester, Virginia, 360–362, 364, 377–379; Sheridan's winter quarters at, 425

Wistar, Gen. I. J., 334

Wood, Gen. Thomas J., 79–80, 82

Wright, Gen. Horatio, 328; at Wilderness, 188–191, 201; replaces Sedgwick, 217; at Spotsylvania, 218–220, 222, 226, 230–231, 239, 241; crosses North Anna River, 251–252; at Cold Harbor, 258–260, 264–266; crosses Chickahominy, 282; at Petersburg, 291, 292, 296; and defense of Washington, 310–316; in